BOOKS rule 15

DEBORAH L. RHODE, JUSTICI

CHARLES DICKENS, BLEAK H
Penguin Books 1971) (185:

21 CHARLES ALAN WRIGHT
AND PROCEDURE § 1006 (2

D1557732

pamphlets **rule 15**	WOMEN'S BUREAU, U.S. DEⱯ ᵢ ᵤ. ᵤ. WOMAN'S GUIDE TO HER JOB RIGHTS 4 (1978).
works in collection **rule 15.5**	Kay Deaux & Brenda Major, *A Social-Psychological Model of Gender, in* THEORETICAL PERSPECTIVES ON SEXUAL DIFFERENCE 89, 89 (Deborah L. Rhode ed., 1990).
	OLIVER WENDELL HOLMES, *Law in Science and Science in Law, in* COLLECTED LEGAL PAPERS 210, 210 (1920).
	John Adams, Argument and Report, *in* 2 LEGAL PAPERS OF JOHN ADAMS 285, 322–35 (L. Kinvin Wroth & Hiller B. Zobel eds., 1965).

PERIODICAL MATERIALS rule 16

consecutively paginated journals **rule 16.4**	David Rudovsky, *Police Abuse: Can the Violence Be Contained?*, 27 HARV. C.R.-C.L. L. REV.465, 500 (1992).
	Thomas R. McCoy & Barry Friedman, *Conditional Spending: Federalism's Trojan Horse*, 1988 SUP. CT. REV. 85, 100.
nonconsecutively paginated journals **rule 16.5**	Barbara Ward, *Progress for a Small Planet,* HARV. BUS. REV., Sept.–Oct. 1979, at 89, 90.
student-written work **rule 16.7.1**	Ellen London, Comment, *A Critique of the Strict Liability Standard for Determining Child Support in Cases of Male Victims of Sexual Assault and Statutory Rape,* 152 U. PA. L. REV. 1957, 1959–63 (2004).
	Note, *The Death of a Lawyer,* 56 COLUM. L. REV. 606 (1956).
book review **rule 16.7.2**	Bruce Ackerman, *Robert Bork's Grand Inquisition*, 99 YALE L.J. 1419, 1422–25 (1990) (book review).
newspapers **rule 16.6**	Andrew Rosenthal, *White House Tutors Kremlin in How a Presidency Works*, N.Y. TIMES, June 15, 1990, at A1.
	Cop Shoots Tire, Halts Stolen Car, S.F. CHRON., Oct. 10, 1975, at 43.
INTERVIEWS **rule 17.2.5**	Telephone Interviews with Michael Leiter, President, Harvard Law Review (Oct. 22, 1999).
FORTHCOMING **PUBLICATIONS** **rule 17.3**	Sarah Greenberger, Comment, *Enforceable Rights, No Child Left Behind, and Political Patriotism: A Case for Open-Minded Section 1983 Jurisprudence,* 153 U. PA. L. REV. (forthcoming in Jan 2005).
THE INTERNET **rule 18.2**	Eric Posner, *More on Section 7 of the Torture Convention,* VOLOKH CONSPIRACY (Jan. 29, 2009, 10:04 AM), http://www.volokh.com /2009/01/29/more-on-section-7-of-the-torture-convention/.
TREATIES **rule 21.4**	Treaty of Friendship, Commerce and Navigation, Japan-U.S., art. X, Apr. 2, 1953, 4 U.S.T. 2063.
UNITED NATIONS OFFICIAL RECORDS **rule 21.7.1**	U.N. GAOR, 56th Sess., 1st plen. mtg. at 3, U.N. Doc. A/56/PV.1 (Sept. 12, 2001).

Published and Distributed by
The Harvard Law Review Association
Gannett House
1511 Massachusetts Avenue
Cambridge, Massachusetts 02138
U.S.A.

First Printing 2020
Second Printing 2021
Third Printing 2022
Fourth Printing 2022
Printings are updated as appropriate.

Coordinating Editor:
Mary Miles Prince, Associate Director for Library Services
(ret.)
Vanderbilt University Law School Library

Type composition by Mayerchak + Company, LLC

ISBN 978-0-578-66615-0

THE BLUEBOOK®

A Uniform System of Citation®
Twenty-First Edition

www.legalbluebook.com

Compiled by the editors of
the Columbia Law Review,
the Harvard Law Review,
the University of Pennsylvania Law Review,
and The Yale Law Journal.

FREE TRIAL
BLUEBOOK ONLIN

Register a FREE trial account at WWW.LEGALBLUEBOOK.COM and redeem the key below for an additional 30 days' access to the Bluebook Online

BLUEBOOK ONLINE ACCESS KEY:
a86f52d6-37fa-4bf9-b896-2f4ff7a93604

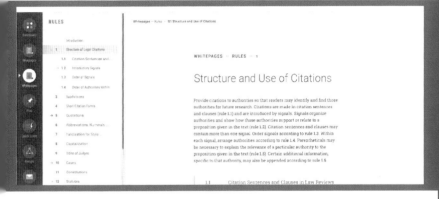

The Bluebook provides the comprehensive, standardized citation system for the legal profession in the United States.

Counterfeit Bluebooks have been sold in online marketplaces. Many of these books contain significant errors and inconsistencies as compared to the authentic Bluebook purchased through www.legalbluebook.com and retail bookstores.

If you believe you have purchased a counterfeit book, please contact us at orders@legalbluebook.com.

Preface to the Twenty-First Edition

This edition of *The Bluebook* retains the same basic approach to legal citation established by its predecessors. Some citation forms have been expanded, reduced, or modified from previous editions. *The Bluebook* strives to be responsive to suggestions from the legal community. In this edition, we have focused on making *The Bluebook* more practical for modern legal practice. We made hundreds of edits, large and small. Here are some of the most noteworthy changes, in order of appearance:

To address word limit constraints in court documents, **B6** now provides practitioners with the option of closing up abbreviations in reporter names. **Bluetable BT2** has been heavily revised to reflect the current local citation rules in the federal and state courts.

Rule 1.4 no longer dictates an order of authorities within a signal. Instead, authorities should be ordered in a logical manner, with more authoritative sources preceding less authoritative ones. **Rule 1.5(b)** has been revised to clarify the placement of "hereinafter" and "last visited" parentheticals in citations to internet sources. **Rule 3.3(d)** has been added to illustrate citations to flush language and examples, such as in Treasury Regulations. **Rule 9(a)** has been revised to clarify the use of first names for judges. **Rule 10.6.2** was added to bring *The Bluebook* into conformity with current U.S. Supreme Court practice regarding citations to stay or bail applications ruled on by a single Justice. **Rule 10.8.1(a)** provides clearer guidance on citing to case docket numbers. **Rule 12** has been modified in several places to simplify citations to statutory sources. **Rule 12.3** has been changed to require citation to the official federal code "if available," rather than "whenever possible." This change is intended to facilitate citation to unofficial codes in online databases. **Rule 12.3.2** no longer requires a date in citations to the federal code, whether official or unofficial. For state sources of law, **rule 12.5(b)** now allows citation to online sources for official state and municipal statutes and ordinances *whenever* available online, rather than when *only* available online. The citation formats for dissertations and theses were updated in **rule 17.2.2**. **Rule 18** has been updated throughout to provide a consistent format for indicating a time marker in an audio or video recording. **Rule 18.8** has been added to provide guidance on citing photographs and illustrations. **Rule 21** has been updated to reflect the growing availability of online sources of international law.

The tables have also been updated. **Table T1** has been revised to reflect the most current titles for the various statutory compilations, session laws, and administrative compilations and registers. **Table T2** has been removed from the print version of *The Bluebook* and now resides exclusively online at www.legalbluebook.com, free of charge. It is the compilers' hope that the move online will enable more frequent updates to the content of this table. For the Twenty-First Edition, eleven jurisdictions in Table T2 have been comprehensively updated and one new jurisdiction has been added. The compilers are indebted to the legal scholars from these jurisdictions who dedicated their time to improving *The Bluebook*. Abbreviations for case names in citations, abbreviations for institutional authors in citations, and abbreviations for periodical titles in citations have been combined into **table T6**. Accordingly, table T13.1 from the Twentieth Edition, containing abbreviations for common institutional names, has become **table T13** in the Twenty-First Edition. Terms have been added to or modified in **tables T6, T7, T10, T13**, and **T15** as appropriate.

The compilers wish to thank our Coordinating Editor Mary Miles Prince for working with us in updating and improving *The Bluebook*. The compilers would also like to acknowledge outside commentators who contributed their expertise to the Twenty-First Edition of *The Bluebook*. The compilers are grateful to the many law review editors, law librarians, and practitioners who responded to our calls for feedback with helpful comments and advice.

Finally, the compilers request that any errors, omissions, or suggestions for revisions be reported to the Harvard Law Review, Gannett House, 1511 Massachusetts Ave., Cambridge, Massachusetts 02138 or to editor@legalbluebook.com. Errors may be corrected in the Bluebook Online, at www.legalbluebook.com, prior to their correction in the next printing of *The Bluebook*. Online subscribers are encouraged to look there for the most up-to-date version of *The Bluebook*.

Acknowledgments

The Bluebook: A Uniform System of Citation is compiled by the editors of the *Columbia Law Review*, the *Harvard Law Review*, the *University of Pennsylvania Law Review*, and *The Yale Law Journal*. *The Bluebook* is published and distributed by the Harvard Law Review Association. The Coordinating Editor of *The Bluebook* is Mary Miles Prince, Associate Director for Library Services (ret.), Vanderbilt Law School Library.

May 2020

Contents

Preface VII
Introduction 1
    Structure of The Bluebook 1
    General Principles of Citation 1
    Getting Started 2

The Bluepages: An Introduction to Basic Legal Citation

Introduction 3
  B1 Structure of Legal Citations 3
  B2 Typeface for Court Documents 6
  B3 Subdivisions 7
  B4 Short Citation Forms 8
  B5 Quotations 8
  B6 Abbreviations, Numerals, and Symbols 9
  B7 Italicization for Style and in Unique Circumstances 9
  B8 Capitalization 10
  B9 Titles of Judges 10
  B10 Cases 11
  B11 Constitutions 18
  B12 Statutes, Rules, and Restatements 18
  B13 Legislative Materials 21
  B14 Administrative and Executive Materials 22
  B15 Books and Other Nonperiodic Materials 22
  B16 Periodical Materials 23
  B17 Court and Litigation Documents 24
  B18 The Internet 26
  B19 Services 27
  B20 Foreign Materials 28
  B21 International Materials 28

The Bluepages Tables

  BT1 Court Documents 29
  BT2 Jurisdiction-Specific Citation Rules and Style Guides 30
      BT2.1 Federal Courts 30
      BT2.2 State Courts 46
      BT2.3 Territories 59

Rules

  Rule 1 Structure and Use of Citations 61
    1.1 Citation Sentences and Clauses in Law Reviews 61
    1.2 Introductory Signals 62
    1.3 Order of Signals 64
    1.4 Order of Authorities Within Each Signal 65
    1.5 Parenthetical Information 65
    1.6 Related Authority 67
  Rule 2 Typefaces for Law Reviews 68
    2.1 Typeface Conventions for Citations 69
    2.2 Typeface Conventions for Textual Material 70

Rule 3 Subdivisions **72**
   3.1 Volumes, Parts, and Supplements 72
   3.2 Pages, Footnotes, Endnotes, and Graphical Materials 73
   3.3 Sections and Paragraphs 76
   3.4 Appended Material 77
   3.5 Internal Cross-References 78

Rule 4 Short Citation Forms **79**
   4.1 "Id." 79
   4.2 "Supra" and "Hereinafter" 81

Rule 5 Quotations **83**
   5.1 Formatting of Quotations 83
   5.2 Alterations and Quotations Within Quotations 84
   5.3 Omissions 86

Rule 6 Abbreviations, Numerals, and Symbols **87**
   6.1 Abbreviations 87
   6.2 Numerals and Symbols 89

Rule 7 Italicization for Style and in Unique Circumstances **90**

Rule 8 Capitalization **91**

Rule 9 Titles of Judges, Officials, and Terms of Court **94**

Rule 10 Cases **95**
   10.1 Basic Citation Forms 96
   10.2 Case Names 96
      10.2.1 General Rules for Case Names 97
      10.2.2 Additional Rules for Case Names in Citations 102
   10.3 Reporters and Other Sources 103
      10.3.1 Parallel Citations and Which Source(s) to Cite 103
      10.3.2 Reporters 104
      10.3.3 Public Domain Format 104
   10.4 Court and Jurisdiction 105
   10.5 Date or Year 107
   10.6 Parenthetical Information Regarding Cases 108
      10.6.1 Weight of Authority 108
      10.6.2 In-Chambers Opinions 108
      10.6.3 Quoting/Citing Parentheticals in Case Citations 109
      10.6.4 Order of Parentheticals 109
   10.7 Prior and Subsequent History 109
      10.7.1 Explanatory Phrases and Weight of Authority 110
      10.7.2 Different Case Name on Appeal 112
   10.8 Special Citation Forms 112
      10.8.1 Pending and Unreported Cases 112
      10.8.2 Fifth Circuit Split 114
      10.8.3 Briefs, Court Filings, and Transcripts 114
      10.8.4 Court Administrative Orders 116
   10.9 Short Forms for Cases 116

Rule 11 Constitutions **119**

Rule 12 Statutes **120**
   12.1 Basic Citation Forms 120
   12.2 Choosing the Proper Citation Form 121
      12.2.1 General Rule 121

      12.2.2 Exceptions 122
  12.3 Current Official and Unofficial Codes 123
      12.3.1 Additional Information 123
      12.3.2 Year of Code 125
  12.4 Session Laws 125
  12.5 Electronic Databases and Online Sources 127
  12.6 Other Secondary Sources 127
  12.7 Invalidation, Repeal, Amendment, and Prior History 128
      12.7.1 Invalidation 128
      12.7.2 Repeal 128
      12.7.3 Amendment 129
      12.7.4 Prior History 129
  12.8 Explanatory Parenthetical Phrases 129
  12.9 Special Citation Forms 130
      12.9.1 Internal Revenue Code 130
      12.9.2 Ordinances 130
      12.9.3 Rules of Evidence and Procedure 130
      12.9.4 Model Codes, Principles, Restatements, Standards,
             Sentencing Guidelines, and Uniform Acts 131
      12.9.5 ABA Code of Professional Responsibility and
             Opinions on Ethics 133
  12.10 Short Forms for Statutes 133

Rule 13 Legislative Materials **135**
  13.1 Basic Citation Forms 135
  13.2 Bills and Resolutions 136
  13.3 Hearings 137
  13.4 Reports, Documents, and Committee Prints 138
  13.5 Debates 140
  13.6 Separately Bound Legislative Histories 140
  13.7 Electronic Databases and Online Sources 140
  13.8 Short Forms for Legislative Materials 141

Rule 14 Administrative and Executive Materials **142**
  14.1 Basic Citation Forms 142
  14.2 Rules, Regulations, and Other Publications 142
  14.3 Administrative Adjudications and Arbitrations 144
      14.3.1 Names 145
      14.3.2 Which Source(s) to Cite 145
      14.3.3 Issuing Agency 146
  14.4 Commercial Electronic Databases 146
  14.5 Short Forms for Regulations 146

Rule 15 Books, Reports, and Other Nonperiodic Materials **147**
  15.1 Author 148
  15.2 Editor or Translator 149
  15.3 Title 150
  15.4 Edition, Publisher, and Date 150
  15.5 Shorter Works in Collection 151
      15.5.1 Works in Collection Generally 152
      15.5.2 Collected Documents 152
  15.6 Prefaces, Forewords, Introductions, and Epilogues 153
  15.7 Serial Number 153

15.8 Special Citation Forms. 153
15.9 Electronic Databases and Online Sources. 154
15.10 Short Citation Forms 155
    15.10.1 Short Forms for Works in Collection 155

Rule 16 Periodical Materials **157**
16.1 Basic Citation Forms 157
16.2 Author 159
16.3 Title 159
16.4 Consecutively Paginated Journals 160
16.5 Nonconsecutively Paginated Journals and Magazines. 160
16.6 Newspapers. 161
16.7 Special Citation Forms. 163
    16.7.1 Student-Written Law Review Materials 163
    16.7.2 Non-Student-Written Book Reviews 164
    16.7.3 Symposia, Colloquia, and Surveys. 165
    16.7.4 Commentaries and Other Special Designations. 165
    16.7.5 Multipart Articles 165
    16.7.6 Annotations. 166
    16.7.7 Proceedings, Regular Publications by Institutes,
        and ABA Section Reports. 166
    16.7.8 Newsletters and Other Noncommercially Distributed
        Periodicals 167
16.8 Electronic Databases and Online Sources. 167
16.9 Short Citation Forms 167

Rule 17 Unpublished and Forthcoming Sources **169**
17.1 Basic Citation Forms 169
17.2 Unpublished Materials 169
    17.2.1 Manuscripts 169
    17.2.2 Dissertations and Theses. 170
    17.2.3 Letters, Memoranda, and Press Releases 170
    17.2.4 E-mail Correspondence and Listserv Postings 171
    17.2.5 Interviews. 171
    17.2.6 Speeches and Addresses. 171
17.3 Forthcoming Publications. 172
17.4 Working Papers 172
17.5 Electronic Databases and Online Sources. 173
17.6 Short Citation Forms 173

Rule 18 The Internet, Electronic Media, and
Other Nonprint Resources **174**
18.1 Basic Citation Forms 174
18.2 The Internet. 176
    18.2.1 General Internet Citation Principles. 176
    18.2.2 Citations to Internet Sources 177
18.3 Commercial Electronic Databases 182
18.4 CD-ROM and Other Electronic Storage Media. 182
18.5 Microform 182
    18.5.1 Microform Collections Reproducing Preexisting
        Materials 182
    18.5.2 Microform Collections Containing Original Materials . . 183
18.6 Films, Broadcasts, and Noncommercial Video Materials 183

18.7 Audio Recordings 184
    18.7.1 Commercial Recordings 184
    18.7.2 Noncommercial Recordings 184
    18.7.3 Podcasts and Recordings Available Online 184
18.8 Photographs and Illustrations 184
18.9 Short Citation Forms 185

Rule 19 Services **186**
19.1 Citation Form for Services 186
19.2 Short Citation Forms 188

Rule 20 Foreign Materials **188**
20.1 Jurisdiction 188
20.2 Non-English-Language Documents 189
    20.2.1 Documents Appearing in More than One Language . . . 189
    20.2.2 Titles and Names of Documents in Languages
         Other than English 189
    20.2.3 Abbreviations in Languages Other than English 189
    20.2.4 Languages That Do Not Use the Roman Alphabet 190
    20.2.5 Citations to Translations of Non-English-
         Language Documents 191
20.3 Cases 191
    20.3.1 Common Law Cases 191
    20.3.2 Civil Law and Other Non-Common Law Cases 192
20.4 Constitutions 192
20.5 Statutes 192
    20.5.1 Statutes in Common Law Systems 192
    20.5.2 Statutes in Civil Law and Other Non-Common Law
         Jurisdictions 193
20.6 Non-English-Language and Foreign Periodicals 193
20.7 Short Citation Forms 194

Rule 21 International Materials **195**
21.1 Basic Citation Forms 195
21.2 Non-English-Language Documents 197
21.3 Jurisdiction Not Evident from Context 197
21.4 Treaties and Other International Agreements 197
    21.4.1 Name of the Agreement 198
    21.4.2 Parties to the Agreement 198
    21.4.3 Subdivisions 199
    21.4.4 Date of Signing 199
    21.4.5 Treaty Sources 199
21.5 International Law Cases 201
    21.5.1 The International Court of Justice and the
         Permanent Court of International Justice 201
    21.5.2 European Union Courts 204
    21.5.3 European Court of Human Rights 205
    21.5.4 Inter-American Commission on Human Rights 206
    21.5.5 Inter-American Court of Human Rights 207
    21.5.6 International Tribunal for the Law of the Sea 208
    21.5.7 International Criminal Court and Other Tribunals 208
    21.5.8 Other International Courts 209
    21.5.9 International Cases in National Courts 209

21.6   International Arbitrations and Claims Commissions 209
21.7   United Nations Sources 210
    21.7.1   Verbatim and Summary Records 211
    21.7.2   Resolutions and Decisions 211
    21.7.3   U.N. Reports 212
    21.7.4   Masthead Documents 213
    21.7.5   U.N. Press Releases and Memoranda 214
    21.7.6   Adjudicatory Bodies Established by the United Nations 214
    21.7.7   Sales Publications 215
    21.7.8   Yearbooks and Periodicals 215
    21.7.9   Regional Organization Documents 216
    21.7.10 U.N. Charter 216
    21.7.11 U.N. Internet Materials 216
21.8   League of Nations 216
21.9   European Union 217
21.10 Council of Europe 220
21.11 World Trade Organization 220
21.12 International Monetary Fund 222
21.13 Other Intergovernmental Organizations 223
21.14 International Non-Governmental Organizations (NGOs) 224
21.15 Yearbooks 225
21.16 Digests 225
21.17 Short Citation Forms 226

Tables

Table T1   **United States Jurisdictions** **227**
  T1.1   Federal Judicial and Legislative Materials 227
  T1.2   Federal Administrative and Executive Materials 230
  T1.3   States and the District of Columbia 242
    Alabama (Ala.) 242
    Alaska (Alaska) 243
    Arizona (Ariz.) 244
    Arkansas (Ark.) 245
    California (Cal.) 246
    Colorado (Colo.) 247
    Connecticut (Conn.) 248
    Delaware (Del.) 249
    District of Columbia (D.C.) 251
    Florida (Fla.) 252
    Georgia (Ga.) 253
    Hawaii (Haw.) 253
    Idaho (Idaho) 254
    Illinois (Ill.) 255
    Indiana (Ind.) 256
    Iowa (Iowa) 257
    Kansas (Kan.) 258
    Kentucky (Ky.) 258
    Louisiana (La.) 259
    Maine (Me.) 261
    Maryland (Md.) 261

Massachusetts (Mass.) 263
Michigan (Mich.) 264
Minnesota (Minn.) 265
Mississippi (Miss.) 265
Missouri (Mo.) 266
Montana (Mont.) 267
Nebraska (Neb.) 268
Nevada (Nev.) 268
New Hampshire (N.H.) 269
New Jersey (N.J.) 269
New Mexico (N.M.) 270
New York (N.Y.) 271
North Carolina (N.C.) 276
North Dakota (N.D.) 277
Ohio (Ohio) 278
Oklahoma (Okla.) 279
Oregon (Or.) 280
Pennsylvania (Pa.) 281
Rhode Island (R.I.) 282
South Carolina (S.C.) 283
South Dakota (S.D.) 284
Tennessee (Tenn.) 285
Texas (Tex.) 286
Utah (Utah) 289
Vermont (Vt.) 290
Virginia (Va.) 291
Washington (Wash.) 292
West Virginia (W. Va.) 292
Wisconsin (Wis.) 293
Wyoming (Wyo.) 294
T1.4 Other United States Jurisdictions 295
American Samoa 295
Canal Zone 295
Guam 295
Navajo Nation 296
Northern Mariana Islands 296
Oklahoma Native Americans 297
Puerto Rico 297
Virgin Islands 298
Table T2   Foreign Jurisdictions (Online Only) 299
Table T3   Intergovernmental Organizations 299
T3.1 United Nations 299
T3.2 League of Nations 299
T3.3 European Union 300
T3.4 European Commission of Human Rights 300
T3.5 European Court of Human Rights 300
T3.6 Inter-American Commission on Human Rights 301
T3.7 Inter-American Court of Human Rights 301
T3.8 International Tribunal for the Law of the Sea 301
T3.9 Intergovernmental Organizations 301

Table T4 **Treaty Sources** **302**
    T4.1 Official U.S Sources 302
    T4.2 Intergovernmental Treaty Sources 303
    T4.3 Unofficial Treaty Sources 303
Table T5 **Arbitral Reporters** **303**
Table T6 **Common Words in Case Names, Institutional Author
    Names, and Periodical Titles** **304**
Table T7 **Court Names** **307**
Table T8 **Explanatory Phrases** **310**
Table T9 **Legislative Documents** **311**
Table T10 **Geographical Terms** **312**
    T10.1 U.S. States, Cities, and Territories 312
    T10.2 Australian States and Canadian Provinces and Territories 313
    T10.3 Countries and Regions 313
Table T11 **Judges and Officials** **319**
Table T12 **Months** **319**
Table T13 **Institutional Names in Periodical Titles** **320**
Table T14 **Publishing Terms** **323**
Table T15 **Services** **323**
Table T16 **Subdivisions** **327**

Index

Index 329

THE
BLUEBOOK®

A Uniform System of Citation®

Twenty-First Edition

Introduction

Welcome to *The Bluebook*, the definitive style guide for legal citation in the United States. For generations, law students, lawyers, scholars, judges, and other legal professionals have relied on *The Bluebook*'s uniform system of citation. In a diverse and rapidly changing legal profession, *The Bluebook* continues to provide a systematic method by which members of the profession communicate important information about the sources and legal authorities upon which they rely in their work.

The Bluebook can often be intimidating for new users. This introduction is meant to assist you as you begin what will likely become a lifelong relationship with the *Bluebook* system of legal citation.

Structure of The Bluebook

The Bluebook contains three major parts. The first part contains the Bluepages, a how-to guide for basic legal citation. Unlike the remainder of *The Bluebook*, which is designed in a style and at a level of complexity commensurate with the needs of the law journal publication process, the Bluepages provide easy-to-comprehend guidance for the everyday citation needs of law students, summer associates, law clerks, practicing lawyers, and other legal professionals. The examples used throughout the Bluepages are printed using simple typeface conventions common in the legal profession.

The second part, printed on white paper, is the heart of the *Bluebook* system of citation: the rules of citation and style. This part is subdivided into two main sections: the first section, consisting of rules 1 through 9, establishes general standards of citation and style for use in all forms of legal writing. The second section, consisting of rules 10 through 21, presents rules for citation of specific kinds of authority such as cases, statutes, books, periodicals, and foreign and international materials. The examples used throughout this part are printed using typeface conventions standard in law journal footnotes.

The third part consists of a series of tables to be used in conjunction with the rules. The tables show, among other things, which authority to cite and how to abbreviate properly. Individual tables are referenced throughout the book. Finally, there is a comprehensive index.

General Principles of Citation

The central function of a legal citation is to allow the reader to efficiently locate the cited source. Thus, the citation forms in *The Bluebook* are designed to provide the information necessary to lead the reader directly to the specific items cited. Because of the ever-increasing range of authorities cited in legal writing, no system of citation can be complete. Therefore, when citing material of a type not explicitly discussed in this book, try to locate an analogous type of authority that is discussed and use that citation form as a model. Always be sure to provide sufficient information to allow the reader to find the cited material quickly and easily.

Getting Started

The Bluepages provide the best place to begin your study of *The Bluebook* system of legal citation. Indeed, first-year legal writing professors may wish to rely on the Bluepages as a teaching aid. The Bluepages provide only an abbreviated introduction to *The Bluebook* system, however, and do not contain answers to more difficult citation questions. For this reason, the Bluepages contain references to related rules and tables found in other parts of *The Bluebook*.

INTRODUCTION

The Bluepages are a guide for practitioners and law clerks to use when citing authority in non-academic legal documents. Please keep the following in mind:

Local Rules. Many courts have their own rules of citation that differ in some respects from The Bluebook. Make sure to abide by any citation requirements of the court to which you are submitting your documents. An index of jurisdiction-specific citation rules is contained in **Bluepages table BT2**.

Typeface. The Bluepages keep the tradition of underscoring certain text. So long as you are consistent, however, you may substitute *italics* wherever underscoring is used in the Bluepages. The remainder of The Bluebook employs a more complex array of typeface conventions, including ordinary roman type, *italics*, and LARGE AND SMALL CAPS. These differences are explained in **Bluepages B2**.

The Whitepages. Where the Bluepages and local court rules are silent regarding the citation of a particular document, you may use the other rules in The Bluebook, referred to as the "Whitepages," to supplement the Bluepages. Keep in mind the typeface differences between academic documents and non-academic legal documents as explained in **Bluepages B2**.

The Elements of a Citation. Generally, a legal citation is composed of three elements: (1) a signal; (2) the source or authority; and (3) parenthetical information. The Bluepages explore each of these elements in detail.

Special Note for Law Students: The Bluebook is primarily written for two types of users: academics and practitioners. The Whitepages provide rules for academic publications such as law review articles and research papers. The Bluepages set forth permissible deviations from the Whitepages that are designed to accommodate the needs of lawyers and law clerks. The Bluepages are used primarily for briefs, motions, memoranda, and opinions. For the most part, the Bluepages only provide examples of how a citation should look. For comprehensive discussions of the elements of a citation, you should refer to the corresponding Whitepages as cross-referenced in the Bluepages.

- **Bluepages Tip:** The Bluepages parallel the Whitepages in numbering and content. You may use a Whitepage rule to supplement a corresponding Bluepage rule.

Structure of Legal Citations   B1

. . . .

Citation Sentences and Clauses   B1.1

In non-academic legal documents, such as briefs and opinions, citations generally appear within the text of the document immediately following the propositions they support. Footnotes should only be used in non-academic legal documents when permitted or required by local court rules.

A citation may be inserted into the text of a document in one of two ways: as a stand-alone citation sentence or as a citation clause.

Citation sentences begin with a capital letter and end with a period. One citation sentence may contain multiple citations separated by semicolons. Use citation sentences to cite sources and authorities that relate to the <u>entire</u> preceding sentence:

> The U.S. Supreme Court has the power to invalidate statutes that are repugnant to the U.S. Constitution. <u>Marbury v. Madison</u>, 5 U.S. (1 Cranch) 137, 177–79 (1803) (federal laws); <u>Fletcher v. Peck</u>, 10 U.S. (6 Cranch) 87, 139 (1810) (state laws); <u>Dred Scott v. Sandford</u>, 60 U.S. (19 How.) 393, 449 (1856), <u>superseded by constitutional amendment</u>, U.S. Const. amend. XIII. The U.S. Supreme Court also has the power to review state court decisions. <u>Martin v. Hunter's Lessee</u>, 14 U.S. (1 Wheat.) 304, 377–78 (1816) (civil cases); <u>Cohens v. Virginia</u>, 19 U.S. (6 Wheat.) 264, 350 (1821) (criminal cases).

Citation clauses are set off from the text by commas and immediately follow the proposition to which they relate. Do not begin a citation clause with a capital letter unless the citation clause begins with a source that would otherwise be capitalized. Do not end a citation clause with a period, unless it is the last clause in the sentence. Use citation clauses to cite sources and authorities that relate to only <u>part</u> of a sentence:

> The Supreme Court adopted a broad reading of the Commerce Clause during the New Deal, <u>see</u> <u>Wickard v. Filburn</u>, 317 U.S. 111, 128–29 (1942), though in recent years the Supreme Court has reined in its broad reading somewhat, <u>see</u> <u>United States v. Lopez</u>, 514 U.S. 549, 624 (1995); <u>United States v. Morrison</u>, 529 U.S. 598, 612–13 (2000); <u>Nat'l Fed'n of Indep. Bus. v. Sebelius</u>, 132 S. Ct. 2566, 2587 (2012); <u>but see</u> <u>Gonzales v. Raich</u>, 545 U.S. 1, 39 (2005).

B1.2   Introductory Signals

A **signal** is a shorthand message to the reader about the relationship between a **proposition** and the source or authority cited for that proposition. Refer to **rule 1.2** for more information on how to use these signals.

- **Bluepages Tip:** Signals are capitalized when used to begin a citation sentence but are lowercase when used to begin a citation clause.

Signal	Use
[no signal]	The authority directly states a proposition, is the source of a quotation, or was mentioned in the proposition
<u>E.g.</u>,	The authority is one of multiple authorities directly stating the same proposition
<u>Accord</u>	The authority is one of multiple authorities directly stating or supporting the proposition, and one of the other authorities was mentioned in the proposition
<u>See</u>	The authority supports, but does not directly state, the proposition

See also	The authority provides additional material supporting the proposition
Cf.	The authority is different from the main proposition but sufficiently analogous to lend support
Compare ... [and] ... with ... [and] ...	The authorities are similar or different in important respects
Contra	The authority directly states a proposition contrary to the main proposition
But see	The authority clearly supports a proposition contrary to the main proposition
But cf.	The authority supports a proposition analogous to the contrary of the main proposition
See generally	The authority is helpful background material related to the proposition

- **Bluepages Tip:** You may combine "<u>e.g.</u>," with "<u>see</u>" and "<u>but see</u>" to form "<u>see, e.g.</u>," and "<u>but see, e.g.</u>," respectively.

When using more than one type of signal in a citation sentence, the signals (together with the authorities they introduce) should appear in the order in which they appear in the table above. For more information about the grouping and ordering of signals, see **rule 1.3**.

Separate authorities within each signal with semicolons. If certain authorities are considerably more helpful or authoritative than the other authorities, you may list the more helpful authorities first.

For further guidance on the order of authorities, see **rule 1.4**.

⋯⋯⋯

Explanatory Parentheticals   B1.3

Regardless of the type of authority you cite, it may be helpful to include additional information to explain the relevance of the cited authority. Append this information parenthetically at the end of your citation (but before any subsequent history).

Explanatory parentheticals should begin with a present participle unless the parenthetical contains a quoted sentence or a short statement. You may omit extraneous words such as "the" unless doing so would cause confusion. Do not begin with a capital letter or end with a period <u>unless</u> the parenthetical consists of a quotation that reads as a full sentence:

> <u>See</u> <u>Flanagan v. United States</u>, 465 U.S. 259, 264 (1984) (explaining that the final judgment rule reduces potential for parties to "clog the courts" with time-consuming appeals).

> <u>Atl. Richfield Co. v. Fed. Energy Admin.</u>, 429 F. Supp. 1052, 1061–62 (N.D. Cal. 1976) ("Not every person aggrieved by administrative action is necessarily entitled to the protections of due process.").

> 5 U.S.C. § 553(b) (2000) (requiring agencies to publish notice of proposed rulemaking in the <u>Federal Register</u>).

> Such standards have been adopted to address a variety of environmental problems. <u>See, e.g.</u>, H.B. Jacobini, <u>The New International Sanitary Regulations</u>, 46 Am. J. Int'l L. 727, 727–28 (1952) (health-related water quality); Robert L. Meyer, <u>Travaux Preparatoires for the UNESCO World Heritage Convention</u>, 2 Earth L.J. 45, 45–81 (1976) (conservation of protected areas).

For further guidance on explanatory parentheticals, see **rule 1.5**.

B2 Typeface for Court Documents

Court documents and legal memoranda use two typefaces: ordinary type and *italics* (or <u>underscoring</u>).

While the Bluepages use underscoring rather than italics, keep in mind that underscoring is the equivalent of italics. For citations appearing in non-academic legal documents, follow these general rules:

Italicize (or underscore) the following information in a citation clause:

> Case names, including procedural phrases introducing case names;
>
> Titles of books and articles;
>
> Titles of some legislative materials;
>
> Introductory signals;
>
> Explanatory phrases introducing subsequent case history;
>
> Cross references, such as <u>id.</u> and <u>supra</u>; and
>
> Words and phrases introducing related authority, such as "<u>quoted in</u>."

Italicize (or underscore) the following information in the text of a legal document:

> Titles of publications, such as *The New York Times*;
>
> Words italicized in the original source of a quotation; and
>
> Any other word that would otherwise be italicized, such as an uncommon foreign word.

Key differences between academic citations (the Whitepages) and non-academic citations (the Bluepages):

	Academic Citations (Whitepages)	Non-Academic Citations (Bluepages)
Typeface: Italics	The following are *italicized*:	The following are *italicized* or <u>underscored</u>:
	Introductory signals	Introductory signals
	Short form case names	Full and short form case names
	Procedural and explanatory phrases in case citations	Procedural and explanatory phrases in case citations
	"*Id.*"	"*Id.*" or "<u>Id.</u>"
	Titles of articles in periodicals	Titles of books, articles, and essays
	Titles of congressional committee hearings	Titles of some legislative materials
	Punctuation that falls within italicized material	Punctuation that falls within italicized or underscored material
	Introductory phrases for related authority	Introductory phrases for related authority
	Internal cross-references	Internal cross-references
Typeface: Caps	The following are in Large and Small Caps:	Large and Small Caps are not required (but may be used for stylistic purposes)
	Authors and titles of books, including institutional authors	
	Titles of periodicals	

Subdivisions   B3

Give page numbers before date parentheticals, without any introductory abbreviation such as "p." or "at." Cite nonconsecutive pages by giving the individual page numbers separated by commas (e.g., "101, 103").

To cite a footnote or endnote, give the page on which the note appears, "n.," and the footnote number:

> <u>United States v. Carolene Prods. Co.</u>, 304 U.S. 144, 152 n.4 (1938).

When the volumes are numbered, cite the volume number in Arabic numerals. If the author of the entire work is cited, the volume number precedes the author's name:

> 3 Ronald E. Mallen, Jeffrey M. Smith & Allison D. Rhodes, <u>Legal Malpractice</u> 101–02 (2014).

If an authority is organized by section (§) or paragraph (¶), you may cite to these subdivisions.

Most subdivisions (such as columns or sections) in citations are abbreviated. See **table T16** for a list of subdivision abbreviations.

B4 Short Citation Forms

You may use "<u>id.</u>" when citing the immediately preceding authority, but <u>only</u> when the immediately preceding citation contains only one authority. Always indicate when a subsequent citation refers to a different page number in the same source (e.g., "<u>id.</u> at 5").

You may use "<u>supra</u>" and "hereinafter" to refer to legislative hearings; court filings; books; pamphlets; reports; unpublished materials; non-print resources; periodicals; services; treaties and international agreements; regulations, directives, and decisions of intergovernmental organizations; and internal cross-references. You should not use "<u>supra</u>" and "hereinafter" to refer to cases, statutes, constitutions, legislative materials (other than hearings), restatements, model codes, or regulations, except in extraordinary circumstances, such as when the name of the authority is extremely long.

B5 Quotations

B5.1 Generally

Enclose all quotations, except block quotations, with quotation marks. Place commas or periods inside the quotation marks, but place all other punctuation outside the quotation marks unless such punctuation is part of the quoted text:

> "When, as here, the plaintiff is a public figure, he cannot recover unless he proves by clear and convincing evidence that the defendant published the defamatory statement with actual malice, i.e., with 'knowledge that it was false or with reckless disregard of whether it was false or not.'" <u>Masson v. New Yorker Mag., Inc.</u>, 501 U.S. 496, 510 (1991) (quoting <u>N.Y. Times Co. v. Sullivan</u>, 376 U.S. 254, 279–80 (1964)).

> "We refused to permit recovery for choice of language which, though perhaps reflecting a misconception, represented 'the sort of inaccuracy that is commonplace in the forum of robust debate to which the <u>New York Times</u> rule applies.'" <u>Masson v. New Yorker Mag., Inc.</u>, 501 U.S. 496, 519 (1991) (citation omitted).

- **Bluepages Tip:** A quotation appearing within another quotation can either be parenthetically attributed to its original source or otherwise acknowledged by indicating that a citation has been omitted.

For further guidance on quotations, including omissions and alterations of quoted material, see **rule 5**.

B5.2 Block Quotations

Quotations of <u>fifty</u> or more words should be single spaced, indented on both sides, justified, and without quotation marks. This is known as a **block quotation**. Quotation marks <u>within</u> a block quotation should appear as they do in the quoted material. The citation following a block quotation should not be indented but should begin at the left margin on the line following the quotation:

▶ [T]his presumptive privilege must be considered in light of our historic commitment to the rule of law. This is nowhere more profoundly manifest than in our view that "the twofold aim [of criminal justice] is that guilt shall not escape or innocence suffer." We have elected to employ an adversary system of criminal justice in which the parties contest all issues before a court of law. . . . To ensure that justice is done, it is imperative to the function of courts that compulsory process be available for the production of evidence needed either by the prosecution or by the defense.

United States v. Nixon, 418 U.S. 683, 708–09 (1974) (citation omitted). The Court then balanced this interest against the evils of forced disclosure. Id. at 710.

Abbreviations, Numerals, and Symbols   B6

Tables at the end of this book contain lists of specific abbreviations for arbitral reporters (**T5**), case names, institutional author names, and common words in periodical titles (**T6**), court names (**T7**), explanatory phrases (**T8**), legislative documents (**T9**), geographical terms (**T10**), judges and officials (**T11**), months (**T12**), institutional names in periodical titles (**T13**), publishing terms (**T14**), services (**T15**), and subdivisions (**T16**).

Close up adjacent single capitals (U.S.), but do not close up single capitals with longer abbreviations (S. Ct.). Every abbreviation should be followed by a period (Univ.), except those in which the last letter is set off by an apostrophe (Soc'y).

Because many court systems impose word limits on briefs and other documents submitted to the court, abbreviations in reporter names may optionally be closed to conserve space, even if they would normally be separated under this rule. For example, "S. Ct." would become "S.Ct." and "F. Supp. 2d" would become "F.Supp.2d."

Spell out the numbers zero to ninety-nine. Use numerals for larger numbers (unless they begin a sentence).

For more information about abbreviations, numerals, and symbols, see **rule 6**.

Italicization for Style and in Unique Circumstances   B7

Words and phrases may be italicized (or underscored) for emphasis.

You may italicize (or underscore) non-English words and phrases unless they have been incorporated into common English usage. Most Latin words and phrases that are used in legal writing are in common English usage. Obsolete or uncommon Latin words and phrases, however, should be italicized (or underscored).

"Id." is always italicized (or underscored).

For more information about italicizing for style, see **rule 7**.

B8   Capitalization

In addition to capitalizing "Court" when naming any court in full or when referring to the U.S. Supreme Court, also capitalize "Court" in documents when referring to the court that will receive your documents.

While court documents can be abbreviated in accordance with **Bluepages B17.1.1** and **Bluepages table BT1** in citations, do not abbreviate the titles of court documents in textual sentences:

> This Court has already ruled on Defendants' Motion to Dismiss.

> **But:** The court in <u>Watkins</u> was attempting to distinguish earlier precedent pointing in the other direction.

Only capitalize party designations such as "Plaintiff," "Defendant," "Appellant," and "Appellee" when referring to parties in the matter that is the subject of your document:

> Plaintiff denies Defendant's baseless allegations of misconduct.

> **But:** In <u>Smith</u>, the plaintiffs alleged that the defendant acted in bad faith.

Capitalize the title of a court document only when: (1) the document has been filed in the matter that is the subject of your document; and (2) the reference is to the document's actual title or a shortened form thereof. Do not capitalize references to the generic name of a court document:

> In their Memorandum of Points and Authorities in Opposition to Defendants' Motion to Dismiss, Plaintiffs argue that Defendants are strictly liable for Plaintiffs' injuries.

> The Court's Order of May 7, 2004, directed Plaintiffs to cease production immediately.

> **But:** There is no doubt that the initial temporary restraining order was within the bounds of this Court's discretion.

- **Bluepages Tip:** Do not abbreviate the titles of court documents in textual sentences:

> For all of the above reasons, Appellant's Petition for Rehearing ought to be granted.

> **Not:** For all of the above reasons, Appellant's Pet. Reh'g ought to be granted.

B9   Titles of Judges

Justices are referred to as "Justice Story" and "Chief Justice Jay." Parenthetical references are to "Holmes, J.," "Cardozo, J.," and "Black & White, JJ." Judges are referred to as "Judge Wisdom," "Judge Hand," and "Chief Judge Friendly."

For more information on how to refer to judges and other officials, see **rule 9**.

Cases **B10**

. . . .

Full Citation **B10.1**

A full case citation includes five components: (1) the name of the case; (2) the published or unpublished source in which the case can be found; (3) a parenthetical indicating the court and year of decision; (4) other parenthetical information, if any; and (5) the subsequent history of the case, if any:

> Engel v. Vitale, 370 U.S. 421, 430 (1962) ("The Establishment Clause, unlike the Free Exercise Clause, does not depend upon any showing of direct governmental compulsion . . . .").

> Thompson v. Hanson, 174 P.3d 120, 125 (Wash. Ct. App. 2007) (holding that a creditor may obtain a judgment against a transferee even in the absence of intent to defraud), aff'd, 239 P.3d 537 (Wash. 2009) (en banc).

- **Bluepages Tip:** If an opinion is only available through a court's website, the opinion's webpage URL may be included at the end of the citation.

Case Names **B10.1.1**

(i) Omit all parties other than the first party listed on each side of the "v.":

> Dow Jones & Co. v. Harrods, Ltd.

Not: Dow Jones & Company, Inc., Plaintiff, v. Harrods, Limited and Mohamed Al Fayed, Defendants

(ii) For names of individuals, use only last names, omitting first names, middle names, and initials:

> Darwin v. Dawkins

Not: Charles Robert Darwin v. Clinton Richard Dawkins and Edward Osborne "E. O." Wilson

(iii) Omit words indicating multiple parties (such as "et al.") and alternative names (such as "a.k.a."):

> Kant v. Bentham

Not: Immanuel Kant, et al. v. Jeremy Bentham, a.k.a. The Father of Utilitarianism

(iv) Some case names may include a **procedural phrase**. Abbreviate "in the matter of," "petition of," and similar procedural phrases to "In re." Abbreviate "on the relation of," "on behalf of," and similar procedural phrases to "ex rel." When adversary parties are named, omit all procedural phrases except "ex rel.":

> Dombroski ex rel. Dombroski v. Chi. Park Dist.

Not: Michael Dombroski, as Administrator of Estate of His Minor Child, Samuel Dombroski v. Chicago Park District, et al.

> Ex parte Zeidner

Not: Ex parte Richard Zeidner

> In re Fairfax

Not: In the Matter of J. Fairfax

(v) Abbreviate words listed in **table T6**, unless the citation appears in a textual sentence as explained in (vi) below. Abbreviate states, countries, and other geographical units according to **table T10**, unless the geographical unit is a named party. Never abbreviate "United States" when it is a named party. Omit "The" as the first word of a party's name, unless it is part of the name of the object of an in rem action. You may abbreviate any words with eight letters or more if substantial space is saved and the result is unambiguous. You may also abbreviate entities with widely recognized initials, such as NAACP and FCC:

> Seattle Times v. Univ. of Wash.

Not: The Seattle Times v. The University of Washington

> United States v. Haskell

Not: U.S. v. Erin Haskell, et al.

> Indus. Chems., Inc. v. City of Tuscaloosa

Not: Industrial Chemicals, Inc. v. The City of Tuscaloosa

> Laidlaw Corp. v. NLRB

Not: The Laidlaw Corporation v. National Labor Relations Board

For more guidance on abbreviation, see **rule 10.2**.

• **Bluepages Tip:** Underline the entire case name up to but not including the comma that follows the case name.

(vi) When referring to the full name of a case in a textual sentence, as opposed to a citation sentence or clause, underline the case name and only abbreviate widely known acronyms and the following eight words: "&," ("and"), "Ass'n," ("association"), "Bros.," ("brothers"), "Co.," ("company"), "Corp.," ("corporation"), "Inc.," ("incorporated"), "Ltd.," ("limited"), and "No.," ("number"). The first time you mention a case in the text, follow the case name with the remaining elements of a full citation, set off by commas:

> In <u>Penn Central Transportation Co. v. City of New York</u>, 366 N.E.2d 1271 (N.Y. 1977), the court applied a version of the diminution in value rule.

Not: In <u>Penn Cent. Transp. Co. v. City of New York</u>, 366 N.E.2d 1271 (N.Y. 1977), the court applied a version of the diminution in value rule.

In a subsequent reference to the case within the same general discussion, you may simply refer to one party's name (or a readily identifiable shorter version of one party's name) if the reference is unambiguous:

> The Supreme Court's recent takings jurisprudence has gradually moved away from the New York Court of Appeals's formulation in <u>Penn Central</u>.

Not: The Supreme Court's recent takings jurisprudence has gradually moved away from the New York Court of Appeals's formulation in <u>City of New York</u>.

Reporters and Pinpoint Citations   B10.1.2

Cite a **reporter** by listing: (1) the volume number of the reporter in which the case is published; (2) the abbreviated name of the reporter (listed in **table T1**); and (3) the page on which the case report begins. If word limits are a consideration, **Bluepages B6** optionally permits reporter abbreviations in court documents to be closed.

To point your reader to the specific pages that relate to the cited proposition, you must also include a **pinpoint citation**, often called a "**pincite**." Place pincites after the page on which the case report begins, separated by a comma.

A pincite may consist of a **page range**, in which instance you should indicate the first and last page of the range separated by an en dash or hyphen. Where the page numbers consist of three or more digits, drop any repetitious digits other than the final two digits (e.g., 102–06; 1020–30). To cite **multiple pages that are not consecutive**, list each page or page range, separated by commas (e.g., 103, 106–08, 132). If the material you wish to reference appears on more nonconsecutive pages than is convenient to list in one citation, you may use <u>passim</u> in lieu of a pincite. To cite a **footnote**, give the page on which the footnote appears, "n.," and the footnote number, with no space between "n." and the footnote number (e.g., 199 n.4):

> <u>Baker v. Carr</u>, 369 U.S. 186, 195 (1962).

> <u>Newdow v. U.S. Cong.</u>, 328 F.3d 466, 471 n.3 (9th Cir. 2003).

> <u>Garfias-Rodriguez v. Holder</u>, 702 F.3d 504, 514 (9th Cir. 2012) ("This is a permissible reading of the statute.").

- **Bluepages Tip:** If the pincite is the first page of the case, simply repeat the page number:

> <u>United States v. Baxter</u>, 492 F.2d 150, 150 (9th Cir. 1973).

For further guidance on pincites, see **rule 3.2**.

Court and Year of Decision   B10.1.3

Indicate parenthetically the deciding court followed by the year of decision (immediately following the page reference). When citing decisions of the United States Supreme Court, however, do not include the name of the deciding court. **Table T1** lists the correct abbreviations for courts in U.S. jurisdictions.

(i) The United States Supreme Court: Cite <u>United States Reports</u> (U.S.) if the opinion appears therein; otherwise, cite to <u>Supreme Court Reporter</u> (S. Ct.):

> <u>Meritor Sav. Bank v. Vinson</u>, 477 U.S. 57, 60 (1986).

> <u>Weyerhaeuser Co. v. U.S. Fish & Wildlife Serv.</u>, 139 S. Ct. 361, 365 (2018).

(ii) Federal Courts of Appeals: Cite <u>Federal Reporter</u> (F., F.2d, or F.3d) and indicate the name of the court parenthetically:

> <u>Env't Def. Fund v. EPA</u>, 465 F.2d 528, 533 (D.C. Cir. 1972).

> <u>United States v. Jardine</u>, 364 F.3d 1200, 1203 (10th Cir. 2004).

(iii) Federal District Courts: Cite <u>Federal Supplement</u> (F. Supp., F. Supp. 2d, or F. Supp. 3d) and indicate the name of the court parenthetically:

> <u>W. St. Grp. LLC v. Epro</u>, 563 F. Supp. 2d 84, 91 (D. Mass. 2008).

> <u>Harris v. Roderick</u>, 933 F. Supp. 977, 985 (D. Idaho 1996).

- **Bluepages Tip:** The correct abbreviation for each state is listed in **table T10**. Some state names are abbreviated with two capital letters (e.g., **N.Y.**), while others are abbreviated with one capital letter and several lowercase letters (e.g., **Mich.**). Do not include a space between adjacent single capital letters (e.g., **S.D.N.Y.**), but <u>do</u> include a space between a single capital letter and a longer abbreviation (e.g., "**D. Conn.**" for "District of Connecticut" and "**S.D. Cal.**" for "Southern District of California"). For more guidance on abbreviations, see **rule 6.1**.

(iv) State High Courts: Cite the regional reporter for the region in which the court sits, if the opinion appears therein; otherwise, cite the state's official reporter, as listed in **table T1**. Indicate the state parenthetically, unless it is unambiguously conveyed by the reporter title:

> <u>People v. Armour</u>, 590 N.W.2d 61 (Mich. 1999).

> <u>Campbell v. Gen. Motors Corp.</u>, 649 P.2d 224 (Cal. 1982).

> <u>Bates v. Tappan</u>, 99 Mass. 376 (1868).

(v) Other State Courts: Cite the regional reporter for the region in which the court sits, if the opinion appears therein; otherwise, cite the state's official reporter, as listed in **table T1**. Indicate parenthetically the state and court of decision, unless unambiguously conveyed by the reporter title. Do not indicate the department or district of intermediate state courts:

> <u>Lundman v. McKown</u>, 530 N.W.2d 807 (Minn. Ct. App. 1995).

> <u>Rusk v. State</u>, 406 A.2d 624 (Md. Ct. Spec. App. 1979), <u>rev'd</u>, 424 A.2d 720 (Md. 1981).

> <u>Campbell v. Parker-Hannifin Corp.</u>, 82 Cal. Rptr. 2d 202 (Ct. App. 1999).

Parallel Citation in State Court Documents

In documents submitted to state courts, all case citations should be to the reporters required by **local rules**. To find local rules for the court to which you are submitting a document, refer to **Bluepages table BT2**.

Local rules sometimes require citation of both the official state reporter *and* the unofficial regional or state-specific reporter. This is called **parallel citation**. Where a pincite is necessary, include one for each reporter citation. When the state or court is clear from the official reporter title, omit it from the date parenthetical:

> <u>Pledger v. Halvorson</u>, 324 Ark. 302, 921 S.W.2d 576 (1996).

> <u>Kenford Co. v. Cnty. of Erie</u>, 73 N.Y.2d 312, 537 N.E.2d 176, 540 N.Y.S.2d 1 (1989).

B10.1.4 Pending and Unreported Cases

(i) LEXIS and Westlaw cases: Cite to the LEXIS or Westlaw electronic report of the case when one is available.

The proper format is as follows: (1) case name; (2) case docket number; (3) database identifier and electronic report number; (4) star page number; and (5) court and full date parenthetical:

> Albrecht v. Stranczek, No. 87 C 9535, 1991 U.S. Dist. LEXIS 5088, at *1, *3 (N.D. Ill. Apr. 15, 1991).

> Kvaas Constr. Co. v. United States, No. 90-266C, 1991 WL 47632, at *2–3 (Cl. Ct. Apr. 8, 1991).

- **Bluepages Tip:** Different courts and publishers use different formats for case docket numbers (e.g., CIV-A, Civ. A., Civ., No.). Cite the case docket number exactly as it appears. If more than one docket number is assigned to a case, the lead-in language (e.g., CIV-A, Civ. A., Civ., No.) may be omitted after the first reference:

> PKFinans Int'l Corp. v. IBJ Schroder Leasing Corp., Nos. 93 Civ. 5375, 96 Civ. 1816 (SAS) (HBP), 1996 WL 525862 (S.D.N.Y. Sept. 17, 1996).

(ii) Slip opinions: When a case is unreported, but is separately available as a slip opinion, give the docket number, the court, and the full date of the most recent major disposition of the case:

> Groucho Marx Prods. v. Playboy Enters., No. 77 Civ. 1782 (S.D.N.Y. Dec. 30, 1977).

For further guidance on slip opinions, see **rule 10.8.1(b)**.

(iii) Opinions only available online, but not in an electronic database: Some cases, particularly ones that are pending, can only be accessed through a court's website. In this situation, the webpage URL may be included:

> Kaye v. Trump, No. 5128, slip op. at 1 (N.Y. App. Div. Jan. 29, 2009), http://www.nycourts.gov/reporter/3dseries/2009/2009_00452.htm.

Weight of Authority and Explanatory Parentheticals   B10.1.5

To add information indicating the weight of the cited authority to a citation, insert an additional parenthetical following the date parenthetical. Indicate when you are citing a concurring or dissenting opinion:

> Bush v. Gore, 531 U.S. 98, 144 (2000) (5-4 decision) (Breyer, J., dissenting) ("The political implications of this case for the country are momentous.").

> Zuni Pub. Sch. Dist. v. Dep't of Educ., 550 U.S. 81, 113 (2007) (Scalia, J., dissenting) ("The sheer applesauce of this statutory interpretation should be obvious.").

> Webb v. Baxter Healthcare Corp., 57 F.3d 1067 (4th Cir. 1995) (unpublished table decision).

> Wersba v. Seiler, 393 F.2d 937 (3d Cir. 1968) (per curiam).

An **explanatory parenthetical** may also be added to explain briefly the proposition for which the case stands:

> Green v. Georgia, 442 U.S. 95, 97 (1979) (per curiam) (holding that exclusion of relevant evidence at a sentencing hearing constitutes denial of due process).

15

For further guidance on explanatory parentheticals, see **Bluepages B1.3** and **rule 1.5**.

B10.1.6 Prior or Subsequent History

A full citation should include the **prior** or **subsequent history** of the case, subject to several exceptions discussed in **rule 10.7**. Use one of the abbreviated explanatory phrases listed in **table T8** to introduce the prior or subsequent history. Include commonly used explanatory phrases such as "<u>aff'd</u>," "<u>aff'g</u>," "<u>cert. denied</u>" (subject to a two-year limitation per **rule 10.7**), "<u>cert. granted</u>," "<u>rev'd</u>," and "<u>rev'd on other grounds</u>" for every applicable citation. Underscore or italicize the explanatory phrase:

> <u>Gucci Am., Inc. v. Gold Ctr. Jewelry</u>, 997 F. Supp. 399 (S.D.N.Y. 1998), <u>rev'd</u>, 158 F.3d 631 (2d Cir.).

> <u>Cooper v. Dupnik</u>, 924 F.2d 1520, 1530–31 (9th Cir. 1991) (holding that police officers' actions did not rise to level of due process violation), <u>rev'd en banc</u>, 963 F.2d 1220 (9th Cir. 1992).

> <u>Cent. Ill. Pub. Serv. Co. v. Westervelt</u>, 342 N.E.2d 463 (Ill. App. Ct. 1976), <u>aff'd</u>, 367 N.E.2d 661 (Ill. 1977).

- **Bluepages Tip:** Explanatory parenthetical information about a case should immediately precede information about subsequent case history.

When the case has a different name in the subsequent history, provide the new case name, preceded by the phrase "<u>sub nom.</u>" ("under the name of"). There is no need to provide the new case name if the parties' names are merely reversed or if the subsequent history is simply a denial of certiorari or rehearing:

> <u>Great W. United Corp. v. Kidwell</u>, 577 F.2d 1256 (5th Cir. 1978), <u>rev'd sub nom. Leroy v. Great W. United Corp.</u>, 443 U.S. 173 (1979).

B10.2 Short Form Citation

Once you have provided a full citation to an authority, you may use a "short form" in later citations of the same authority, so long as (1) it is clear to the reader which authority is referenced; (2) the full citation falls in the same general discussion; and (3) the reader will have little trouble locating the full citation. There are several acceptable short forms for case citations. All of these forms include "at" followed, if necessary, by a pincite.

The following are all acceptable short form citations of page 100 of <u>Palsgraf v. Long Island R.R. Co.</u>, 162 N.E. 99 (N.Y. 1928):

> <u>Palsgraf</u>, 162 N.E. at 100.

> 162 N.E. at 100.

> <u>Id.</u> at 100.

When using only one party name in a short form citation, use the name of the first party, unless that party is a geographical unit, a governmental entity, or another type of common litigant. You may also shorten a long party name, for example from <u>First Nat'l Trust & Inv. Corp.</u> to <u>First Nat'l</u>, so long as the reference remains unambiguous.

Short citations take a slightly different form for cases with parallel citations. <u>Chalfin v. Specter</u>, 426 Pa. 464, 465, 233 A.2d 562, 563 (1967), becomes one of the following:

> <u>Chalfin</u>, 426 Pa. at 465, 233 A.2d at 563.

> 426 Pa. at 465, 233 A.2d at 563.

<u>Id.</u>

"<u>Id.</u>" is the short form used to refer to the immediately preceding authority.

- **Bluepages Tip:** The "i" in "<u>id.</u>" is only capitalized when it begins a citation sentence. The underline always runs under the period.

(i) When used alone, "<u>id.</u>" refers to the identical pincite referenced in the immediately preceding citation:

> The Supreme Court has stated unequivocally that "apprehension by the use of deadly force is a seizure subject to the reasonableness requirement of the Fourth Amendment." <u>Tennessee v. Garner</u>, 471 U.S. 1, 7 (1985). By contrast, minimal police interference will not always constitute a "seizure" for Fourth Amendment purposes. <u>Id.</u>

(ii) To refer to a different page or footnote within the immediately preceding authority, add "at" and the new pincite:

> To determine whether a particular exercise of non-lethal police force was reasonable, courts engage in a balancing process that weighs the nature of the intrusion against the "governmental interests." <u>Id.</u> at 8.

(iii) "<u>Id.</u>" may only be used when the preceding citation cites only <u>one</u> source:

> This process weighs the nature of the exertion of force against the governmental interests at stake. <u>See</u> <u>Heath</u>, 854 F.2d at 9. This is an "objective reasonableness" test. <u>Id.</u>

In the example above, it is clear that "<u>Id.</u>" refers to <u>Heath</u>. By contrast, the use of "<u>id.</u>" in the following example is improper because it is not clear to which authority "<u>id.</u>" refers:

> **Not:** To determine whether a particular exercise of non-lethal police force was reasonable, courts engage in a balancing process. <u>Tennessee v. Garner</u>, 471 U.S. 1, 8 (1985); <u>see also</u> <u>Heath v. Henning</u>, 854 F.2d 6, 8 (2d Cir. 1988). This process weighs the nature of the exertion of force against the governmental interests at stake. <u>See</u> <u>id.</u> at 9.

- **Bluepages Tip:** Sources identified in explanatory parentheticals, explanatory phrases, and prior or subsequent history are ignored for the purposes of this rule.

(iv) The "<u>id.</u>" form for cases requiring parallel citations is as follows:

> The Pennsylvania Supreme Court grappled with a similarly complicated issue in an election dispute in 1967. <u>See</u> <u>Chalfin v. Specter</u>, 426 Pa. 464, 477, 233 A.2d 562, 568 (1967). In <u>Chalfin</u>, the court was forced to reach a decision under a severely rushed schedule. <u>See</u> <u>id.</u> at 468, 233 A.2d at 564.

(v) "<u>Id.</u>" can be used for various types of authorities—not only for cases. For further guidance on the use of "<u>id.</u>," see **rule 4.1**.

B11 Constitutions

> ▷ U.S. Const. art. I, § 8, cl. 10.
> ▷ U.S. Const. amend. XVIII, § 1.
> ▷ Wash. Const. art. I, § 32.

- **Bluepages Tip:** Do not use a short citation form (other than "<u>id.</u>") for constitutions.

For further guidance on citing constitutions, see **rule 11**.

B12 Statutes, Rules, and Restatements

B12.1 Full Citation

B12.1.1 Federal Statutes

A full citation of a federal statute includes: the official name of the act and the published source in which the act can be found. It may also include a parenthetical indicating either (i) the year the source was published or (ii) the year the statute was passed (used for session laws):

> ▷ Comprehensive Environmental Response, Compensation, and Liability Act, 42 U.S.C. §§ 9601–9675.
> ▷ Department of Transportation Act, Pub. L. No. 89-670, § 9, 80 Stat. 931, 944–47 (1966).

- **Bluepages Tip:** Nothing is underlined in a statute citation. "Section" is indicated by the "§" symbol, the plural of which is "§§." For further guidance concerning citation of individual sections and subsections, see **rule 3.3**.

Codes and Session Laws

For statutes, cite a current official or unofficial **code**, an official or privately published collection of **session laws**, or a **secondary source**. **Rule 12** provides a full explanation of these sources and how to decide which one to include in your citation.

If available, cite the current official code for statutes currently in force. The official code for federal statutes is the <u>United States Code</u>, which is abbreviated "U.S.C."

A citation of an official or unofficial code will tell the reader where a statute can be found by listing: (1) the title number; (2) the abbreviated name of the code; (3) the section numbers in which the act is codified; and (4) the year of the cited code edition (not the year the act was passed). The year of the cited code edition may be omitted when citing the official or unofficial United States Code, but not when citing other collections of law. Citations of an unofficial code, such as an "annotated code," must also include the name of the publisher in a parenthetical, alongside the date, if included:

> 1 U.S.C. § 1.

> 15 U.S.C.A. § 205 (West).

To cite an individual provision of a statute, include the original section number of the provision you wish to cite following the statute name. Note that the "original section number" refers to a particular section of the act, not to the section of the code in which that provision has been codified. Thus, in the first example below, "§ 6" refers to section 6 of the Administrative Procedure Act, while "§ 555" refers to section 555 of Title V of the <u>United States Code</u>:

> Administrative Procedure Act § 6, 5 U.S.C. § 555.

> National Environmental Policy Act of 1969 § 102, 42 U.S.C. § 4332.

> Digital Millennium Copyright Act of 1998 § 103, 17 U.S.C.A. § 1201 (West).

Cite the **session laws** if the official or unofficial code is unavailable or insufficient, for example, when the statute does not yet appear in a code or when you need to refer to the historical fact of the statute's enactment.

The official compilation of federal session laws is the <u>Statutes at Large</u>, abbreviated as "Stat." A citation of the <u>Statutes at Large</u> includes the following elements: (1) the official or popular name of the statute; (2) the public law number, abbreviated "Pub. L. No."; (3) the section number, if any; (4) the volume number, followed by "Stat." and the number of the first page of the act; and (5) the year the statute was passed. Session law citations may also pincite the particular provision of the act cited and the particular page of the session laws on which that provision appears:

> Department of Transportation Act, Pub. L. No. 89-670, § 9, 80 Stat. 931, 944–47 (1966).

> Health Professions Education Extension Amendments of 1992, Pub. L. No. 102-408, 106 Stat. 1992.

• **Bluepages Tip:** Omit the year parenthetical if the name of the statute includes its year of enactment.

For guidance on how to indicate a statute's prior or subsequent history, see **rule 12.7**.

State Statutes   B12.1.2

For state statutes, cite an official code if available. **Table T1.3** lists the official and unofficial statutory compilations of each state, with the preferred official code listed first. Although the citation form for individual state codes varies, a full citation of most state codes includes the following elements: (1) the abbreviated name of the code, as listed in **table T1.3**; (2) the cited section number(s); and (3) the year of the cited code edition (not the year the act was passed). Citations of an unofficial state code must also include the name of the publisher in the date parenthetical:

> Wash. Rev. Code § 28B.20.020 (2014).

> Cal. Penal Code § 181 (West 2011).

> N.Y. Bus. Corp. Law § 717 (McKinney 2000).

For guidance on citing state session laws, see **rule 12.4**.

B12.1.3 Procedural Rules, Restatements, Uniform Acts, and Similar Materials

> Fed. R. Civ. P. 12(b)(6).

> Fed. R. Evid. 401.

> Restatement (Second) of Contracts § 90 (Am. L. Inst. 1981).

> Restatement (Second) of Torts § 90 cmt. a (Am. L. Inst. 1965).

> U.C.C. § 2-202 (Unif. L. Comm'n 1977).

> U.S. Sent'g Guidelines Manual § 2D1.1(c) (U.S. Sent'g Comm'n 2004).

For further guidance on citing procedural rules, restatements, and uniform acts, see **rule 12.9**.

B12.1.4 Federal Tax Materials

Citation of federal tax materials is governed by special rules discussed in **rule 12.9.1** and **table T1.2**. In court documents and legal memoranda discussing only the current version of federal tax laws, you may omit the year and publisher parenthetical from citations of the Internal Revenue Code (I.R.C.) and Treasury regulations.

Internal Revenue Code

In citations of the Internal Revenue Code, you may replace "26 U.S.C." with "I.R.C.":

> 26 U.S.C. § 61.

becomes: I.R.C. § 61.

Treasury Regulations

> Treas. Reg. § 1.72-16(a) (1963).

> Treas. Reg. § 1.72-16(a), Q&A (3)(a) (1963).

Treasury Determinations

When citing Treasury determinations in court documents and legal memoranda, you may use the abbreviations contained in the introductory pages of the <u>Cumulative Bulletin</u>. Thus, you may cite General Counsel Memoranda as "G.C.M." When citing Private Letter Rulings, you may use the abbreviation "P.L.R." and you may omit the dashes from the ruling number:

> Rev. Rul. 83-137, 1983-2 C.B. 41.

> I.R.S. P.L.R. 8601012 (Sept. 30, 1985).

> I.R.S. G.C.M. 39,417 (Sept. 30, 1985).

- **Bluepages Tip:** Tax Court and Board of Tax Appeals decisions are cited as court decisions, not agency decisions. For further guidance, see **table T1.1**.

For guidance on citing materials from other administrative agencies, see **table T1.2**.

Short Form Citation

The first mention of a statute, rule, regulation, or legislative material requires a full citation. Subsequent citations in the same general discussion may employ any short form that clearly identifies the source. **Rules 12.10, 13.8,** and **14.5** include tables illustrating acceptable short forms for statutes, regulations, and legislative materials.

You may use "<u>id.</u>" to refer to a statute or regulation codified within the same title as the statute or regulation cited in the immediately preceding citation:

Full Citation	<u>Id.</u> Citation for Identical Provision	<u>Id.</u> Citation for Different Provision Within Same Title
28 U.S.C. § 1331.	<u>Id.</u>	<u>Id.</u> § 1332.
50 C.F.R. § 10.12 (2019).	<u>Id.</u>	<u>Id.</u> § 10.13(c)(1).

Legislative Materials

A full citation to legislative material includes the following components, though not necessarily in the following order: (1) the title of the material; (2) the abbreviated name of the legislative body; (3) the number assigned to the material; (4) the number of the Congress and/or legislative session; and (5) the year of publication:

> H.R. Rep. No. 99-253, pt. 1, at 54 (1985).

> S. Rep. No. 84-2, at 7 (1955).

Enacted Federal Bill

When citing federal bills, include the name of the bill (if relevant), the abbreviated name of the Congressional chamber, the number of the bill, the number of the Congress, the section (if any), and the year of publication:

> S. 1983, 93d Cong. § 10 (1973).

> H.R. 8638, 95th Cong. § 2 (1977).

> Freedom of Information Act, S. 1160, 88th Cong. § 1 (1965).

> Digital Millennium Copyright Act, H.R. 2281, 105th Cong. § 6 (1997).

Unenacted Federal Bill

> Protection from Personal Intrusion Act, H.R. 2448, 105th Cong. § 2(a) (1997).

Federal Congressional Hearing

> <u>Toxic Substances Control Act: Hearings on S. 776 Before the Subcomm. on the Env't of the S. Comm. on Commerce</u>, 94th Cong. 343 (1975).

Federal Congressional Report

> H.R. Rep. No. 99-253, pt. 1, at 54 (1985).

> S. Rep. No. 84-2, at 7 (1955).

State Bills and Resolutions

When citing state bills and resolutions, include: (1) the name of the legislative body; (2) the number of the bill or resolution; (3) the number of the legislative body; and (4) the number of the legislative session. Parenthetically indicate the name of the state and the year of enactment or publication:

> H.D. 636, 1999 Leg., 413th Sess. (Md. 1999).
>
> H.R. 189, 145th Gen. Assemb., Reg. Sess. (Ga. 1999).

For further guidance on citing legislative materials, see **rule 13**.

B14 Administrative and Executive Materials

Cite federal rules and regulations to the Code of Federal Regulations (C.F.R.) by title, section or part, and year:

> 46 C.F.R. § 166.01 (2009).

Citations to rules or regulations in the Federal Register (Fed. Reg.) should give the commonly used name of the rule or regulation, the volume and page on which the rule or regulation begins, and the date of the rule or regulation:

> Federal Acquisition Regulations for National Aeronautics and Space Administration, 55 Fed. Reg. 52782 (Dec. 21, 1990) (to be codified at 48 C.F.R. pt. 1).

For administrative adjudications, cite by the reported name of the first-listed private party or by the official subject-matter title:

> Trojan Transp., Inc., 249 N.L.R.B. 642 (1980).

For arbitration awards, cite as court cases if adversary parties are named and as administrative adjudications if they are not:

> Kroger Co. v. Amalgamated Meat Cutters, Local 539, 74 Lab. Arb. Rep. (BL) 785, 787 (1980) (Doering, Arb.).
>
> Charles P. Ortmeyer, 23 Indus. Arb. 272 (1980) (Stern, Arb.).

For further guidance on citing administrative rules and regulations, see **rule 14**.

B15 Books and Other Nonperiodic Materials

B15.1 Full Citation

Citations to books, treatises, pamphlets, and other nonperiodic materials should include the following elements: (1) the volume number (for multi-volume sets); (2) the full name(s) of the author(s) as written in the publication; (3) the title of the publication (underscored or italicized); (4) a pincite; and (5) a parenthetical indicating the year of publication, the name of the editor (if any), and the edition (if more than one).

Two authors should appear separated by an ampersand ("&") in the order in which they are listed on the publication. If a work has more than two authors, you may either list all of the authors' names or list the first author's name followed by "et al.":

▸ Matthew Butterick, <u>Typography for Lawyers</u> 54 (2010).

▸ J.R. McNeill & William H. McNeill, <u>The Human Web: A Bird's-Eye View of World History</u> 319 (2003).

▸ David Hunter et al., <u>International Environmental Law and Policy</u> 555 (3d ed. 2006).

▸ <u>A Bentham Reader</u> 101 (Mary Peter Mack ed., 1969).

▸ 21 Charles Alan Wright & Arthur R. Miller, <u>Federal Practice and Procedure</u> § 1006 (3d ed. 1998).

There are special citation forms for a few frequently cited works:

▸ <u>Good-Faith Bargaining</u>, <u>Black's Law Dictionary</u> (10th ed. 2014).

▸ 17 Am. Jur. 2d <u>Contracts</u> § 74 (1964).

▸ 88 C.J.S. <u>Trial</u> § 192 (1955).

For further guidance on citing to books and other nonperiodic materials, see **rule 15**.

....

Short Form Citation   B15.2

Use "<u>id.</u>" to refer to a book or other nonperiodical material cited in the immediately preceding citation. Otherwise, use "<u>supra</u>." The "<u>supra</u>" form consists of: (1) the author's last name; (2) "<u>supra</u>," underlined or italicized up to but not including the comma; and (3) a new pincite:

Full Cite	<u>Id.</u> Cite	<u>Supra</u> Cite
Richard Posner, <u>How Judges Think</u> 269 (2010).	<u>Id.</u> at 204–05.	Posner, <u>supra</u>, at 204–05.
Mary L. Dunnewold et al., <u>Judicial Clerkships: A Practical Guide</u> 77 (2010).	<u>See id.</u> at 80.	<u>See</u> Dunnewold et al., <u>supra</u>, at 80.
Fleming James, Jr. & Geoffrey C. Hazard, Jr., <u>Civil Procedure</u> § 2.35 (5th ed. 2001).	<u>Id.</u> § 1.7.	James & Hazard, <u>supra</u>, § 1.7.

• **Bluepages Tip:** For further guidance on short forms, see **rules 4, 15.10, 16.9, 17.6,** and **18.9**.

_____

Periodical Materials   B16
....

Full Citation   B16.1

A full citation of periodical material includes the following elements: (1) the full name(s) of the author(s) as written in the publication; (2) the title of the article (underlined or italicized); (3) the abbreviated name of the publication; (4) a pincite; and (5) the date of publication. The basic citation may differ depending on the type of periodical cited. For further guidance, see **rule 16**.

Consecutively Paginated Journals   B16.1.1

Most law journals are paginated consecutively throughout an entire volume (i.e., an individual issue within a volume does not begin at page "1," but rather picks up where the previous issue left off). To cite material appearing in a consecutively paginated periodical, follow this format: ‹author(s)›, ‹title of work›, ‹volume number› ‹abbreviated periodical name› ‹first page of article›, ‹pincite› (‹year of publication›).

> Fred R. Shapiro & Michelle Pearse, <u>The Most-Cited Law Review Articles of All Time</u>, 110 Mich. L. Rev. 1483, 1489 (2012).

> R.H. Coase, <u>The Problem of Social Cost</u>, 3 J.L. & Econ. 1, 1 (1960).

For appropriate abbreviations of periodical names, see **tables T6 and T13**.

B16.1.2   Nonconsecutively Paginated Journals and Magazines

> Christopher Hitchens, <u>The New Commandments</u>, Vanity Fair, Apr. 2011, at 1.

B16.1.3   Student-Written Work

> Natalie Cotton, Comment, <u>The Competence of Students as Editors of Law Reviews: A Response to Judge Posner</u>, 154 U. Pa. L. Rev. 951, 982 n.104 (2006).

For guidance on citing student-written work, consult **rule 16.7.1**.

B16.1.4   Newspaper Articles

> Abigail Sullivan Moore, <u>This Is Your Brain on Drugs</u>, N.Y. Times, Oct. 29, 2014, at A1.

> Doug Esser, <u>UW Library Freezes Bedbugs Off Infested Books</u>, Seattle Times, Dec. 7, 2012, at A2.

B16.2   Short Form Citation

After providing a full citation of a periodical, you may use "<u>id.</u>" or "<u>supra</u>" in subsequent citations. Use "<u>id.</u>" to refer to periodical material cited in the immediately preceding citation. Otherwise, use the "<u>supra</u>" form introduced in **Bluepages B15.2**.

- **Bluepages Tip:** When your document includes citations of more than one source by the same author, include an abbreviated reference to the title of the cited source in any <u>supra</u> citation:

> Llewellyn, <u>Remarks</u>, <u>supra</u>, at 401–06.

B17   Court and Litigation Documents

This rule focuses on citations to court documents that have been filed as part of the same case. For citations of court documents filed in a different case, consult **rule 10.8.3**.

B17.1   Full Citation

A full citation of a court document includes the following elements: (1) the name of the document, abbreviated where appropriate; (2) the pinpoint citation; and

(3) the date of the document, if required. The citation should also include the Electronic Case Filing (ECF) number found on PACER, if applicable.

Abbreviation

Abbreviate the titles of court documents according to **Bluepages table BT1**. Where there is an official record, such as the Record on Appeal in appellate litigation, always abbreviate "Record" to "R." Do not abbreviate, however, when doing so will confuse the reader:

> Petitioner admits filing suit more than one year after knowledge of the facts underlying its claim, Pet'r's Br. 6, and further admits the applicability of a one-year statute of limitations, Pet'r's Br. 7.

> In Defendant's Memorandum of Points and Authorities in Support of Defendant's Motion for Summary Judgment, Defendant asserts that the dangerous conditions giving rise to the accident resulted from someone else's negligence, Def.'s Mem. Supp. Summ. J. 6, 9, implying that Defendant was, indeed, aware of the risk. Yet, in his Affidavit filed in support of the Motion, Defendant explicitly states that he had no knowledge of the rising water level. Def.'s Aff. ¶¶ 5–7; <u>see also</u> Jones Aff. Ex. A, at 2.

- **Bluepages Tip:** You may enclose citations of court documents in parentheses:

> (Def.'s Resp. to Pl.'s Interrog. No. 3.)

Pinpoint Citations

Provide a precise reference to the cited document, such as to the page and line on which the material appears in a deposition or trial transcript. Use commas only to avoid confusion. Separate page and line references by a colon. Page references should not be preceded by "p.," but other subdivisions should be identified. You are generally not required to precede pincites with "at," though it is customary to use "at" in references to certain sources such as appellate records (e.g., R. at 5):

> Hawkins Aff. 6.
>
> Trial Tr. vol. 2, 31.
>
> Pet'r's Br. 6.
>
> Clark Dep. 15:21–16:4.
>
> Pls.' Am. Answer to Def.'s Countercl. 3–4.
>
> Travis Decl. Ex. B, at 3.
>
> R. at 9.

Date

Provide the date of the cited document when: (1) more than one document has the same title; (2) the date is relevant to the discussion; or (3) the date is needed to avoid confusion:

> Plaintiff alleged that Defendant was driving at a rate far in excess of the posted speed limit. Compl. ¶ 7. However, her sworn testimony is to

the effect that she never saw the Defendant before the accident and was thus unable to gauge his speed. Perryman Dep. 34:15–18, Aug. 7, 2002; Trial Tr. vol. 2, 51–52, Dec. 12, 2002.

Mr. Svensson attests that Plaintiff's president cared not about the age of the inventory but only about its marketability. Svensson Aff. ¶ 5. In addition, Ms. Beatrice swears that Plaintiff's president had the authority to waive the condition concerning the age of the inventory, Beatrice Aff. ¶ 9, May 10, 2003, and that no other corporate official had such authority, Beatrice Aff. ¶ 2, June 2, 2003.

B17.1.4 Electronic Case Filings (ECF)

Court documents filed with the electronic case management system employed by PACER for federal cases are assigned document numbers. Add this Electronic Case Filing (ECF) number to the citations of electronically filed documents.

Feder Dep. 5:30–12:10, ECF No. 6.

Def.'s Mot. Summ. J. 2, ECF No. 15.

- **Bluepages Tip:** Documents filed on PACER are imprinted with an ECF header. If these page numbers are different from the page numbers of the filed document, use the page numbers of the original document.

B17.2 Short Form Citation

After providing a full citation, you may use a short form if: (1) it will be clear to the reader what you are citing; (2) the full citation falls in the same general discussion; and (3) the reader will have little trouble locating the full citation:

First Reference	Succeeding Reference
App. to Pet. Cert. 137–39, ECF No. 15.	App. 137–39, ECF No. 15, <u>or</u> App. 137–39.

- **Bluepages Tip:** For court documents, <u>id.</u> should only be used if significant space will be saved.

The liquid left on the floor by Defendant caused Plaintiff to lose her balance, slip, and fall. Leach Aff. 33–39. This fall led to numerous hospital visits costing well over $10,000. <u>Id.</u> at 52.

But: The liquid left on the floor by Defendant caused Plaintiff to lose her balance, slip, and fall. R. at 5. This fall led to numerous hospital visits costing well over $10,000. R. at 12.

B18 The Internet

B18.1 Full Citation

B18.1.1 Direct Citations

A full citation of an internet source includes: (1) the name of the author(s) (if applicable); (2) the title of the specific page of the website, such as a posting or comment (underlined or italicized) (if applicable); (3) the title of the main page of the website; (4) the date and time (if applicable); and (5) the URL. For further guidance on citing internet sources, see **rule 18.2**:

> David Lat, <u>Movie Night with Justice Breyer</u>, Above the Law (Oct. 27, 2014, 3:31 PM), http://abovethelaw.com/2014/10/movie-night-with -justice-breyer/.

> Fabrizio di Piazza, <u>SCOTUSblog on Camera: Laurence H. Tribe (Part One)</u>, SCOTUSblog, http://www.scotusblog.com/media/scotusblog -on-camera-laurence-h-tribe-part-one/.

> Eugene Kontorovich, <u>Italy Adopts Supreme Court's View of ICJ Authority</u>, Volokh Conspiracy (Oct. 28, 2014, 10:41 AM), http://www .washingtonpost.com/news/volokh-conspiracy/wp/2014/10/28/italy -adopts-supreme-courts-view-of-icj-authority/.

- **Bluepages Tip:** If a source is available in both HTML and PDF (which preserves the pagination of the print version), then you should only cite to the PDF. Whenever possible, provide a pincite for internet sources:

> Ulrich Cubasch et al., <u>Climate Change 2013: The Physical Science Basis</u>, Intergovernmental Panel on Climate Change 121 (2013), http:// www.ipcc.ch/site/assets/uploads/2018/02/WG1AR5_all_final.pdf.

If there is no date associated with the specific webpage, then the citation should list the date when the website was "last modified" or "last updated" after the URL. If these indicators are unavailable, use the date on which you "last visited" the webpage:

> Yahoo! Home Page, http://www.yahoo.com (last visited Mar. 18, 2020).

Parallel Citations   B18.1.2

For printed material, you may provide a parallel citation to an internet source:

> <u>Am. Mining Cong. v. U.S. Army Corps of Eng'rs</u>, No. CIV. A. 93-1754 SSH (D.D.C. Jan. 23, 1997), http://www.wetlands.com/fed/tulloch1.htm.

Short Form Citation   B18.2

After providing a full citation to an internet source, you may use "<u>id.</u>" or "<u>supra</u>" in subsequent citations per **rules 4** and **18.9(a)**:

> Lat, <u>supra</u>.

Services   B19

Cite services by volume, abbreviated title, publisher, subdivision, and date. If the source is a case, include the abbreviated name of the court in the same parenthetical as the date:

> <u>In re Smithfield Est., Inc.</u>, [1985–1986 Transfer Binder] Bankr. L. Rep. (CCH) ¶ 70,707 (Bankr. D.R.I. Aug. 9, 1985).

> <u>SEC v. Tex. Int'l Airlines</u>, 29 Fed. R. Serv. 2d (West) 408 (D.D.C. 1979).

> <u>Kovacs v. Comm'r</u>, 74 A.F.T.R.2d (RIA) 354 (6th Cir. 1994).

When citing looseleaf material that will eventually be bound, add the name of the bound form in parentheses if it is different from the name of the looseleaf form; include the volume of the bound form if available:

> Marietta Concrete Co., 3 Lab. Rel. Rep. (BL) (84 Lab. Arb. Rep.) 1,158 (May 7, 1985).

For further guidance on citing services, see **rule 19**.

B20 Foreign Materials

When citing to any non-U.S. source, whether in English or in another language, indicate the jurisdiction parenthetically at the end of the citation.

For foreign common law cases, indicate the court parenthetically:

> R v. Lockwood (1782) 99 Eng. Rep. 379 (KB).

Cite foreign statutes from common law countries like statutes of the United Kingdom (**table T2.43 United Kingdom**), noting the jurisdiction parenthetically at the end of the citation:

> Emergency Powers Act (Act No. 3/1976) (Ir.).

For further guidance on citing foreign sources, see **rule 20**.

B21 International Materials

Founding Documents:

> U.N. Charter art. 94, ¶ 1.e.
>
> Statute of the International Tribunal for the Law of the Sea art. 1, ¶ 2, Dec. 10, 1982, 1833 U.N.T.S. 561.

Multilateral Treaties:

> U.N. Convention on the Law of the Sea, Dec. 10, 1982, 1833 U.N.T.S. 397.
>
> Organization of American States, American Convention on Human Rights, Nov. 22, 1969, O.A.S.T.S. No. 36, 1144 U.N.T.S. 123.

Bilateral Treaties:

> Treaty of Friendship, Commerce and Navigation, Japan-U.S., art. X, Apr. 2, 1953, 4 U.S.T. 2,063.
>
> Agreement Concerning Payments for Certain Losses Suffered During World War II, Fr.-U.S., Jan. 18, 2001, Temp. State Dep't No. 01-36, 2001 WL 416465.

International Cases:

The standard citation for an international law case includes: (1) the name of the case; (2) the case number; (3) the reporter (if any); (4) the characterization of the decision (judgment, provisional measures, etc.); (5) a pincite (using paragraph numbers, if available, rather than page numbers); and (6) a parenthetical with the date, prefaced by name of court if not otherwise evident from the citation:

- Delimitation of Maritime Boundary in Gulf of Maine Area (Can./U.S.), Judgment, 1982 I.C.J. Rep. 560, ¶ 22 (Nov. 5).

- Prosecutor v. Katanga, ICC-01/04-01/07-3436-AnxI, Minority Opinion of Judge Wyngaert, ¶ 320 (Mar. 7, 2014).

For more on how to cite international sources, see **rule 21**.

THE BLUEPAGES TABLES

Court Documents   BT1

This table provides suggested abbreviations for words commonly found in the titles of court documents. Use these abbreviations in citations to court documents according to **Bluepages B17.1.1** and **B17.2**. This table also indicates certain words that should not be abbreviated. Unless otherwise indicated, plurals are formed by adding the letter "s."

Words of seven or more letters not appearing in this table may also be abbreviated, so long as the abbreviation is unambiguous.

Omit all articles and prepositions from an abbreviated title, unless the result will confuse the reader. Other extraneous words may also be omitted, so long as the reader can unambiguously identify the cited document.

Admission	Admis.	Deny [ing]	Den.
Affidavit	Aff.	Deposition	Dep.
Affirm	Affirm	Discovery	Disc.
Amended	Am.	Dismiss	Dismiss
Answer	Answer	Docket	Docket
Appeal	Appeal	Document	Doc.
Appellant	Appellant	Evidence	Evid.
Appellee	Appellee	Exhibit	Ex.
Appendix	App.	Grant	Grant
Application	Appl.	Hearing	Hr'g
Argument	Arg.	Injunction	Inj.
Attachment	Attach.	Instruction	Instr.
Attorney	Att'y	Interrogatory	Interrog.
Brief	Br.	Joint Appendix	J.A.
Certiorari	Cert.	Judgment	J.
Compel	Compel	Limine	Lim.
Complaint	Compl.	Memorandum	Mem.
Counterclaim	Countercl.	Minute	Min.
Court	Ct.	Motion	Mot.
Cross-claim	Cross-cl.	Objection	Obj.
Declaration	Decl.	Opinion	Op.
Defendant ['s]	Def. ['s]	Opposition	Opp'n
Defendants [']	Defs. [']	Order	Order
Demurrer	Dem.	Petition	Pet.

Petitioner ['s]	Pet'r ['s]		Reporter	Rep.
Petitioners [']	Pet'rs [']		Request	Req.
Plaintiff ['s]	Pl. ['s]		Respondent	Resp't
Plaintiffs [']	Pls. [']		Response	Resp.
Points and Authorities	P. & A.		Stay	Stay
Preliminary	Prelim.		Subpoena	Subpoena
			Summary	Summ.
Produc [e, tion]	Produc.		Supplement [al]	Suppl.
Quash	Quash		Support	Supp.
Reconsideration	Recons.		Suppress	Suppress
Record	R.		Temporary Restraining Order	TRO
Rehearing	Reh'g			
Reply	Reply		Testimony	Test.
Report and Recommendation	R. & R.		Transcript	Tr.
			Verified Statement	V.S.

BT2 Jurisdiction-Specific Citation Rules and Style Guides

This table lists local court rules and other authorities governing legal citations. While this list is intended to be as accurate and comprehensive as possible, it is important for practitioners to check the most recent version of local rules on official court websites.

BT2.1 Federal Courts

United States Court of Appeals for the First Circuit

1st Cir. R. <u>Notice to Litigants</u> (cite as "Loc. R. __ ")

1st Cir. R. 32.1.0 (citation of unpublished opinions)

1st Cir. R. 32.2 (citation of state decisions and law review articles)

Bankruptcy Appellate Panel for the First Circuit

1st Cir. Bankr. App. Panel R. 8001-1(a) (shall cite as "1st Cir. BAP L.R. __ ")

United States Court of Appeals for the Second Circuit

2d Cir. R. 1.1 (cite as "LR __ ")

2d Cir. R. 32.1.1 (citation of summary orders)

United States Court of Appeals for the Third Circuit

3d Cir. R. 1.2 (shall cite as "3d Cir. L.A.R. __ (2011)")

3d Cir. R. 28.3 (citation of various types of legal authority)

3d Cir. R. 113.13 (citation of internet sources)

United States Court of Appeals for the Fourth Circuit

4th Cir. R. 32.1 (citation of unpublished opinions)

United States Court of Appeals for the Fifth Circuit

5th Cir. R. 28.7, 47.5 (citation of unpublished opinions)

United States Court of Appeals for the Sixth Circuit

> 6th Cir. R. 1 (cite as "6 Cir. R. __ ")
>
> 6th Cir. R. 32.1(a) (citation of unpublished opinions)

Bankruptcy Appellate Panel for the Sixth Circuit

> 6th Cir. Bankr. App. Panel R. 8026 - 1 (shall cite as "6th Cir. BAP LBR __ ")
>
> 6th Cir. Bankr. App. Panel R. 8014 - 1(c) (citation of unpublished opinions)

United States Court of Appeals for the Seventh Circuit

> 7th Cir. R. 32.1 (citation of unpublished opinions)

United States Court of Appeals for the Eighth Circuit

> 8th Cir. R. 32.1A (citation of unpublished opinions)

Bankruptcy Appellate Panel for the Eighth Circuit

> 8th Cir. Bankr. App. Panel R. 8005A(b)(1) (cite as "L.R. BAP 8th Cir. __ ")

United States Court of Appeals for the Ninth Circuit

> 9th Cir. R. 36-3 (citation of unpublished opinions)

Bankruptcy Appellate Panel for the Ninth Circuit

> 9th Cir. Bankr. App. Panel R. 8026-2 (shall cite as "9th Cir. BAP R. __ ")

United States Court of Appeals for the Tenth Circuit

> 10th Cir. R. 1.3 (should cite as "10th Cir. R. __ ")
>
> 10th Cir. R. 32.1 (citation of unpublished opinions)

Bankruptcy Appellate Panel for the Tenth Circuit

> 10th Cir. Bankr. App. Panel R. 8026-6 (citation of unpublished opinions)
>
> 10th Cir. Bankr. App. Panel R. 8026-10(a) (must cite as "10th Cir. BAP L. R. __ ")

United States Court of Appeals for the Eleventh Circuit

> 11th Cir. R. Title Page (cite as "11th Cir. R. __ ")
>
> 11th Cir. R. 28-1(k) (citations shall comply with The Bluebook or the ALWD Citation Manual; cross-references for state cases)
>
> 11th Cir. R. 36-2 (citation of unpublished opinions)

United States Court of Appeals for the District of Columbia

> D.C. Cir. R. 28(a)(1)(B) (citation of rulings under review)
>
> D.C. Cir. R. 28(b) (citation of various types of legal authority)
>
> D.C. Cir. R. 32.1(a) (citation of published opinions and statutes)
>
> D.C. Cir. R. 32.1(b) (citation of unpublished opinions)
>
> D.C. Cir. Handbook of Practice and Internal Procedures I.D (cite local rules as "D.C. Cir. Rule __ ")
>
> D.C. Cir. Handbook of Practice and Internal Procedures IX.A.8 (citation of various types of legal authority)

United States Court of Appeals for the Federal Circuit

Fed. Cir. R. 28(e) (citation of cases)

Fed. Cir. R. 32.1 (citation of nonprecedential opinions or orders)

United States District Court for the Middle District of Alabama

M.D. Ala. Civ. R. 1.1(a) (should cite civil rules as "M.D. Ala. LR __ ") (should cite criminal rules as "M.D. Ala. LCrR __ ")

United States Bankruptcy Court for the Middle District of Alabama

Bankr. M.D. Ala. R. 1000-1(a) (shall cite as "Local Rules of the United States Bankruptcy Court for the Middle District of Alabama __ " or "M.D. Ala., LBR __ ")

United States Bankruptcy Court for the Northern District of Alabama

Bankr. N.D. Ala. R. <u>Title Page</u> (cite as "Bankr. N.D. Ala. R. __ ")

United States District Court for the Southern District of Alabama

S.D. Ala. R. 1(a) (cite as S.D. Ala. GenLR__") (cite as "S.D. Ala. CivLR__") (cite as "S.D. Ala. CrLR__")

S.D. Ala. Civ. R. 7(f) (citation of opinions)

United States District Court for the District of Alaska

D. Alaska Adm. R. (a)-1(c) (may cite as "Local Admiralty Rule __ " or "D.Ak. LAR __ ")

D. Alaska Civ. R. 1.2(d) (may cite as "L.Civ.R.__")

D. Alaska Crim. R. 1.1(d) (may cite as "L.Crim.R.__")

D. Alaska Habeas Corpus R. 1.1(b) (may cite as "D.Ak. HCR __ ")

D. Alaska Mag. R. 1(a) (may cite as "D.Ak.LMR __ ")

United States Bankruptcy Court for the District of Alaska

Bankr. D. Alaska R. 1001-1(e) (may cite as "AK LBR __ ")

United States District Court for the District of Arizona

D. Ariz. R. <u>Foreword</u> (may cite civil rules as "LRCiv __ ") (may cite criminal rules as "LRCrim __ ") (may cite bankruptcy rules as "LRBankr __ ")

United States District Court for the Central District of California

C.D. Cal. R. 11-3.9 (citation of various types of legal authority)

C.D. Cal. R. 85-1 (may cite as "Local Rule __ ")

C.D. Cal. Adm. & Mar. R. A.3 (may cite as "LAR __ ")

C.D. Cal. Bankr. App. R. <u>Footnote</u> 1 (should cite as "C.D. Cal. L. Bankr. R. __ ")

C.D. Cal. Crim. R. 61-1 (may cite as "Local Criminal Rule __ ")

United States Bankruptcy Court for the Central District of California

Bankr. C.D. Cal. R. 1001-1(a) (may cite as "LBR __ ")

Bankr. C.D. Cal. R. 9013-2(b)(4) (citation of unpublished opinions)

Bankr. C.D. Cal. R. 9013-2(c) (citation of various types of legal authority)

United States District Court for the Eastern District of California

E.D. Cal. R. 1-100(a) (may cite as "L.R. __ ")

E.D. Cal. R. 5-133(i) (citation of various types of legal authority)

United States Bankruptcy Court for the Eastern District of California

Bankr. E.D. Cal. R. 1001-1(a) (may cite as "LBR __ ")

United States District Court for the Northern District of California

N.D. Cal. Adm. & Mar. R. 1-1 (should cite as "Admir. L.R. __ ")

N.D. Cal. Civ. R. 1-1 (should cite as "Civil L.R. __ ")

N.D. Cal. Civ. R. 3-4(d) (citation of various types of legal authority)

N.D. Cal. Civ. R. 3-4(e) (citation of uncertified opinions)

N.D. Cal. Crim. R. 1-1 (should cite as "Crim. L.R. __ ")

N.D. Cal. Habeas Corpus R. 2254-1 (should cite as "Habeas L.R. __ ")

N.D. Cal. Pat. R. 1-1 (should cite as "Patent L.R. __ ")

United States Bankruptcy Court for the Northern District of California

Bankr. N.D. Cal. R. 1001-1(b) (cite as "B.L.R. __ ")

United States District Court for the Southern District of California

S.D. Cal. Civ. R. 1.1(a) (may cite as "CivLR __ ")

S.D. Cal. Civ. R. 5.1(l) (citation of federal statutes and regulations)

S.D. Cal. Crim. R. 1.1(a) (may cite as "CrimLR __ ")

S.D. Cal. Pat. R. 1.1 (should cite as "Patent L.R. __ ")

United States Bankruptcy Court for the Southern District of California

Bankr. S.D. Cal. R. 1001-6(b)(17) (shall cite as "LBR __ ")

United States District Court for the District of Colorado

D. Colo. Civ. R. 1.1(a) (shall cite as "D.C.COLO.LCivR __ ")

D. Colo. Civ. R. 7.1(e) (citations in motions)

D. Colo. Crim. R. 1.1(a) (shall cite as "D.C.COLO.LCrR __ ")

United States Bankruptcy Court for the District of Colorado

Bankr. D. Colo. R. 1001-1(d) (shall cite as "L.B.R. __ ")

United States District Court for the District of Connecticut

D. Conn. Civ. R. 1(a) (may cite as "D. Conn. L. Civ. R. __ ")

D. Conn. Crim. R. 1(a) (may cite as "D. Conn. L. Cr. R. __ ")

United States Bankruptcy Court for the District of Connecticut

Bankr. D. Conn. R. 1001-1(a) (shall cite as "D. Conn. Bankr. L. R. __ ")

United States District Court for the District of Delaware

D. Del. R. 1.1(a) (shall cite as "D. Del. LR __ ")

D. Del. R. 7.1.3(a)(5) (citations shall be made in accordance with The Bluebook)

- D. Del. R. 7.1.3(a)(6) (citation of earlier-filed papers)
- D. Del. R. 7.1.3(a)(7) (citation of unpublished opinions)

United States Bankruptcy Court for the District of Delaware

- Bankr. D. Del. R. 1001-1(a) (may cite as "Del. Bankr. L.R. __ ")
- Bankr. D. Del. R. 7007-2(a)(v) (citations acceptable if in accordance with The Bluebook)
- Bankr. D. Del. R. 7007-2(a)(vi) (citation of earlier-filed papers)
- Bankr. D. Del. R. 7007-2(a)(vii) (citation of unpublished opinions)

United States Bankruptcy Court for the District of Columbia

- Bankr. D.C. R. 1001-1(a) (may cite as "LBR __ " or "D.C. LBR __ ")

United States District Court for the Middle District of Florida

- M.D. Fla. R. 7.01(b) (shall cite local rules as "Local Rule __ ") (shall cite local admiralty and maritime rules as "Local Admiralty Rule __ ") (shall cite supplemental rules for certain admiralty and maritime claims as "Supplemental Rule __ ")

United States Bankruptcy Court for the Middle District of Florida

- Bankr. M.D. Fla. R. 1001-1(e) (shall cite as "Local Rule __ ")

United States District Court for the Northern District of Florida

- N.D. Fla. R. 1.1 (may cite as "N.D. Fla. Loc. R. __ ")
- N.D. Fla. Adm. & Mar. R. A(2)(a) (shall cite supplemental rules for certain admiralty and maritime claims as "Supplemental Rule __ ")
- N.D. Fla. Adm. & Mar. R. A(2)(b) (shall cite local rules as "Local Rule __ ")
- N.D. Fla. Adm. & Mar. R. A(2)(c) (shall cite local admiralty and maritime rules as "Local Admiralty Rule __ ")

United States Bankruptcy Court for the Northern District of Florida

- Bankr. N.D. Fla. R. 1001-1(A) (may cite as "N.D. Fla. LBR __ ")

United States District Court for the Southern District of Florida

- S.D. Fla. Adm. & Mar. R. 2(a) (shall cite supplemental rules for certain admiralty and maritime claims as "Supplemental Rule __ ")
- S.D. Fla. Adm. & Mar. R. 2(b) (shall cite local admiralty and maritime rules as "Local Admiralty Rule __ ")

United States Bankruptcy Court for the Middle District of Georgia

- Bankr. M.D. Ga. R. Title Page (shall cite as "M.D. Ga. LBR __ ")

United States District Court for the Northern District of Georgia

- N.D. Ga. Civ. R. 1.1 (may cite as "LR __ , NDGa")
- N.D. Ga. Civ. R. 5.1(F) (citation of acts of Congress and regulations)
- N.D. Ga. Crim. R. 1.1(A) (may cite as "LCrR __ , NDGa")
- N.D. Ga. Patent R. 1.1 (may cite as "Patent L.R. __ ")

United States Bankruptcy Court for the Northern District of Georgia

- Bankr. N.D. Ga. R. 1001-1 (may cite as "BLR __ ")

United States District Court for the District of Hawaii

> D. Haw. R. 1.1 (should cite as "LR __ " or "CrimLR __ ")
>
> D. Haw. R. 7.6 (citation of various types of legal authority)

United States Bankruptcy Court for the District of Hawaii

> Bankr. D. Haw. R. 1001-1(a) (may cite as "LBR __ ")

United States District Court for the District of Idaho

> D. Idaho Civ. R. 1.1(a) (may cite as "Dist. Idaho Loc. Civ. R. __ ")
>
> D. Idaho Crim. R. 1.1(a) (may cite as "Dist. Idaho Loc. Crim. R. __ ")
>
> D. Idaho Pat. R. 1.1 (may cite as "Dist. Idaho Loc. Patent R. __ ")

United States Bankruptcy Court for the District of Idaho

> Bankr. D. Idaho R. 1001.1(a) (shall cite as "LBR __ ")

United States District Court for the Central District of Illinois

> C.D. Ill. R. 1.1 (may cite as "CDIL-LR __ ")

United States Bankruptcy Court for the Central District of Illinois

> C.D. Ill. R. 1.1 (may cite as "CDIL-LR __ ")

United States District Court for the Northern District of Illinois

> N.D. Ill. Crim. R. 1.1 (may cite as "LCrR. __ ")

United States Bankruptcy Court for the Northern District of Illinois

> Bankr. N.D. Ill. R. 1001-2(A) (may cite as "Local Bankruptcy Rule __ ")

United States District Court for the Southern District of Illinois

> S.D. Ill. R. 1.1(a) (encouraged to cite as "SDIL-LR __ ")

United States Bankruptcy Court for the Southern District of Illinois

> Bankr. S.D. Ill. R. 1001(A) (shall cite as "S.D. Ill. LBR __ ")

United States District Court for the Northern District of Indiana

> N.D. Ind. R. 1-1 (may cite local civil rules as "N.D. Ind. L.R. __ ")
>
> N.D. Ind. Cri. R. 1-1 (may cite criminal rules as "N.D. Ind. L. Cr. R. __ ")
>
> N.D. Ind. Pat. R. 1-1 (may cite patent rules as "N.D. Ind. L.P.R. __ ")

United States Bankruptcy Court for the Northern District of Indiana

> Bankr. N.D. Ind. R. 1001-1(a) (may cite as "N.D. Ind. L.B.R. B-__")

United States District Court for the Southern District of Indiana

> S.D. Ind. R. 1-1(a) (may cite as "S.D. Ind. L.R. __ ")

United States Bankruptcy Court for the Southern District of Indiana

> Bankr. S.D. Ind. R. 9029-1(a) (may cite as "S.D. Ind. B- __")

United States District Court for the Northern District of Iowa

> N.D. & S.D. Iowa Civ. R. 1(a) (shall cite as "LR __ ")
>
> N.D. & S.D. Iowa Crim. R. 1(a) (shall cite as "LCrR __ ")

United States Bankruptcy Court for the Northern District of Iowa

> Bankr. N.D. Iowa 9004-1(a) (may cite as "Local Rule ___ " or "L.R. ___ ")

United States District Court for the Southern District of Iowa

> N.D. & S.D. Iowa Civ. R. 1(a) (shall cite as "LR ___ ")
>
> N.D. & S.D. Iowa Crim. R. 1(a) (shall cite as "LCrR ___ ")

United States District Court for the District of Kansas

> D. Kan. R. 1.1(d) (should cite as "D. Kan. Rule ___ ")
>
> D. Kan. R. 7.6(c) (citation of unpublished opinions)
>
> D. Kan. R. 83.1.2(a) (must cite standing orders as "D. Kan. S.O. ___ ")

United States Bankruptcy Court for the District of Kansas

> Bankr. D. Kan. R. 1001.1(b) (should cite as "D. Kan. LBR ___ ")
>
> Bankr. D. Kan. R. 9004.1(b) (citation of unpublished opinions)
>
> Bankr. D. Kan. R. 9029.2(a) (must cite standing orders as "D. Kan. Bk. S.O. ___ ")

United States District Court for the Eastern District of Kentucky

> Joint Ky. Civ. Prac. R. 85.1 (may cite as "LR ___ ")
>
> Joint Ky. Crim. Prac. R. 60.1 (may cite as "LCrR ___ ")

United States Bankruptcy Court for the Eastern District of Kentucky

> Bankr. E.D. Ky. R. 1001-1 (may cite as "KYEB LBR ___ ")

United States District Court for the Western District of Kentucky

> Joint Ky. Civ. Prac. R. 85.1 (may cite as "LR ___ ")
>
> Joint Ky. Crim. Prac. R. 60.1 (may cite as "LCrR ___ ")

United States Bankruptcy Court for the Western District of Kentucky

> Bankr. W.D. Ky. R. 5001-1(b) (shall cite as "W.D. Ky. L.B.R. ___ ")

United States District Court for the Eastern District of Louisiana

> E.D. La. Civ. R. <u>Preamble</u> (may cite admiralty rules as "LAR ___ ") (may cite civil rules as "LR ___ ")
>
> E.D. La. Crim. R. <u>Preamble</u> (may cite as "LCrR ___ ")

United States Bankruptcy Court for the Eastern District of Louisiana

> Bankr. E.D. La. R. 1001-1(B) (may cite as "L.R. ___ " or "Local Rule ___ ")

United States Bankruptcy Court for the District of Maine

> Bankr. D. Me. R. 1001-1 (may cite as "D. Me. LBR ___ ")

United States District Court for the District of Maryland

> D. Md. Adm. R. a(2) (may cite admiralty rules as "LAR ___ ")

United States Bankruptcy Court for the District of Maryland

> Bankr. D. Md. R. 1001-1 (shall cite as "Md. L.B.R. ___ ")

United States District Court for the District of Massachusetts

> D. Mass. R. 1.1 (shall cite as "L.R., D. Mass. __" or "L.R. __")

United States District Court for the Eastern District of Michigan

> E.D. Mich. R. 1.1(a) (may cite civil rules as "E. D. Mich. LR __") (may cite criminal rules as "E. D. Mich. LCrR __")

United States Bankruptcy Court for the Eastern District of Michigan

> Bankr. E.D. Mich. R. 9029-1(b) (shall cite as "E. D. Mich. LBR __")

United States District Court for the Western District of Michigan

> W.D. Mich. Civ. R. 1.2 (may cite as "W.D. Mich. LCivR __")
> W.D. Mich. Crim. R. 1.2 (may cite as "W.D. Mich. LCrR __")
> W.D. Mich. Gen. R. 1.2 (may cite as "W.D. Mich. LGenR __")

United States Bankruptcy Court for the Western District of Michigan

> Bankr. W.D. Mich. R. 1001(b) (may cite as "LBR __")

United States District Court for the District of Minnesota

> D. Minn. R. 1.1(a) (may cite as "LR __" or "D. Minn. LR __")

United States Bankruptcy Court for the District of Minnesota

> Bankr. D. Minn. R. 9029-1(d) (may cite rules as "Local Rule __") (may cite forms as "Local Form __")

United States District Court for the Eastern District of Missouri

> E.D. Mo. R. 1.01 (may cite as "E.D. Mo. L.R. __")
> E.D. Mo. R. 2.16 (citation of internet sources)
> E.D. Mo. Pat. R. 1-1 (should cite as "Local Patent R. __")

United States Bankruptcy Court for the Eastern District of Missouri

> Bankr. E.D. Mo. R. 1001(A) (shall cite as "L.R. __")

United States District Court for the Western District of Missouri

> W.D. Mo. R. Preface (should cite as "Local Rule __" or "L.R. __")

United States District Court for the District of Montana

> D. Mont. R. 1.1(a) (may cite civil rules as "L.R. __") (may cite criminal rules as "L.R. CR __")
> D. Mont. R. 1.5(d) (citations shall comply with The Bluebook or the ALWD Citation Manual) (citation of cases and internet sources)

United States Bankruptcy Court for the District of Montana

> Bankr. D. Mont. R. 1001-1(a) (shall cite rules as "Mont. LBR __") (shall cite forms as "Mont. LBF __")
> Bankr. D. Mont. R. 5005-2(a)(7) (citations shall comply with The Bluebook or the ALWD Citation Manual)

United States District Court for the District of Nebraska

> D. Neb. Gen. R. 1.1(a) (cite as "NEGenR __")

D. Neb. Civ. R. 10.1(a)(4) (citation of internet sources)

D. Neb. Civ. R. 85.1 (may cite as "NECivR __")

D. Neb. Crim. R. 49.2(a)(4) (citation of internet sources)

D. Neb. Crim. R. 61.1 (may cite as "NECrimR __")

United States Bankruptcy Court for the District of Nebraska

Bankr. D. Neb. R. 1001-1(A) (shall formally cite as "Neb. R. Bankr. P. __") (may also cite as "Local Rule __")

United States District Court for the District of Nevada

D. Nev. R. 1A 1-1 (may cite as "LR __") (may cite patent rules as "LPR __") (may cite criminal rules as "LCR __") (may cite special proceedings and appeals rules as "LSR __")

D. Nev. Civ. R. 7-3 (citation of various types of legal authority)

United States Bankruptcy Court for the District of Nevada

Bankr. D. Nev. R. 1001(a) (may cite as "LR __")

United States District Court for the District of New Hampshire

D.N.H. Civ. R. 1.1(a) (shall cite as "LR __")

D.N.H. Civ. R. 5.3 (citation of cases)

D.N.H. Crim. R. 1.1(a) (shall cite as "LCrR __")

D.N.H. Pat. R. 1.1(a) (shall cite as "SPR __")

United States Bankruptcy Court for the District of New Hampshire

Bankr. D.N.H. R. Preface (shall cite as "LBR __")

Bankr. D.N.H. R. 1050-1 (citation of cases)

Bankr. D.N.H. R. 9029-2 (citation of administrative orders)

United States District Court for the District of New Jersey

D.N.J. Civ. R. 9.2(a)(2) (may cite admiralty and maritime rules as "LAMR __")

D.N.J. Civ. R. 9.3 (should cite patent rules as "L. Pat. R. __")

D.N.J. Civ. R. 85.1 (may cite as "L.Civ.R. __")

D.N.J. Crim. R. 60.1 (may cite as "L.Cr.R. __")

United States Bankruptcy Court for the District of New Jersey

Bankr. D.N.J. R. 1001-1 (shall cite as "District of New Jersey Local Bankruptcy Rules, D.N.J. LBR __")

United States District Court for the District of New Mexico

D.N.M. Civ. R. 1.1 (cite as "D.N.M.LR-Civ. __")

D.N.M. Crim. R. 1.1 (cite as "D.N.M.LR-Cr. __")

United States Bankruptcy Court for the District of New Mexico

Bankr. D.N.M. R. 1001-1(a) (cite as "NM LBR __")

United States Bankruptcy Court for the Eastern District of New York

Bankr. E.D.N.Y. R. 1001-1(b)(ii) (shall cite as "E.D.N.Y. LBR __")

United States District Court for the Northern District of New York

- N.D.N.Y. R. 1.1(a) (shall cite as "L.R. __ ")
- N.D.N.Y. Adm. & Mar. R. (a)(3) (may cite as "LAR __ ")
- N.D.N.Y. R. Crim. P. 1.1 (shall cite as "L.R. Cr. P. __ ")
- N.D.N.Y. Pat. R. 1.4 (shall cite as "L. Pat. R. __ ")

United States Bankruptcy Court for the Northern District of New York

- Bankr. N.D.N.Y. R. 1001-1(a) (may cite as "Local Bankruptcy Rule __ " or "LBR __ ")

United States Bankruptcy Court for the Southern District of New York

- Bankr. S.D.N.Y. R. 1001-1 (shall cite as "LBR __ ")

United States District Court for the Western District of New York

- W.D.N.Y. Civ. R. 1.1 (shall cite as "L.R.Civ.P. __ ")
- W.D.N.Y. Civ. R. 56(a)(3) (citation of evidence in motions for summary judgment)
- W.D.N.Y. Crim. R. 1(a) (shall cite as "L.R.Crim.P. __ ")
- W.D.N.Y. Pat. R. 1.4 (shall cite as "L.Pat.R. __ ")

United States District Court for the Eastern District of North Carolina

- E.D.N.C. Adm. & Mar. R. A(1) (shall cite as "Local Admiralty Rule __ ")
- E.D.N.C. Civ. R. 1.1 (shall cite as "Local Civil Rule __ ")
- E.D.N.C. Civ. R. 7.2 (citation of opinions)
- E.D.N.C. Crim. R. 1.1 (shall cite as "Local Criminal Rule __ ")
- E.D.N.C. Crim. R. 47.2 (citation of opinions)
- E.D.N.C. Pat. R. 301.1 (should cite as "Local Civil Rule __ ")

United States Bankruptcy Court for the Eastern District of North Carolina

- Bankr. E.D.N.C. R. Preface (will cite as "E.D.N.C. LBR __ ")

United States District Court for the Middle District of North Carolina

- M.D.N.C. Civ. R. Title Page (cite as "LR __ ")
- M.D.N.C. Civ. R. 7.2 (citation of opinions)
- M.D.N.C. Crim. R. Title Page (cite as "LCrR __ ")
- M.D.N.C. Pat. R. 101.1 (should cite as "LR __ ")

United States District Court for the District of North Dakota

- D.N.D. R. Preface (may cite general rules as "D.N.D. Gen. L. R. __ ") (may cite civil rules as "D.N.D. Civ. L. R. __ ") (may cite criminal rules as "D.N.D. Crim. L. R. __ ")

United States District Court for the Northern District of Ohio

- N.D. Ohio Civ. R. 1.1(b) (shall cite admiralty rules as "Local Supplemental Rule __ " or "LSuppR __ ") (shall cite civil rules as "Local Rule __ " or "LR __ ")

N.D. Ohio Crim. R. 1.1(b) (shall cite as "Local Criminal Rule __" or "LCrR __")

N.D. Ohio Pat. R. 1.1 (should cite as "L. P. R. __")

United States Bankruptcy Court for the Northern District of Ohio

Bankr. N.D. Ohio R. 1001-1(b) (shall cite as "Local Bankruptcy Rule __" or "LBR __")

United States District Court for the Southern District of Ohio

S.D. Ohio Civ. R. 1.1(a) (may cite as "S.D. Ohio Civ. R. __")

S.D. Ohio Civ. R. 7.2(b) (citation of various types of legal authority)

S.D. Ohio Crim. R. 1.1(a) (may cite as "S.D. Ohio Crim. R. __")

United States Bankruptcy Court for the Southern District of Ohio

Bankr. S.D. Ohio R. 9013-2(b) (citation of unpublished opinions)

Bankr. S.D. Ohio R. 9029-1(a) (may cite as "Local Rule __" or "LBR __")

United States District Court for the Eastern District of Oklahoma

E.D. Okla. Civ. R. 1.2(e) (may cite as "LCvR __")

E.D. Okla. Crim. R. 1.1(A) (cite as "LCrR __")

United States Bankruptcy Court for the Eastern District of Oklahoma

Bankr. E.D. Okla. R. 1001-1(B) (may cite as "Bankr. E.D. Okla. LR __" or "LR __" or "Local Rule __")

United States District Court for the Northern District of Oklahoma

N.D. Okla. Civ. R. 1.2(e) (may cite as "LCvR __")

N.D. Okla. Crim. R. 1.1 (may cite as "LCrR __")

United States Bankruptcy Court for the Northern District of Oklahoma

Bankr. N.D. Okla. R. 1001-1(B) (may cite as "Bankr. N.D. Okla. LR __" or "LR __" or "Local Rule __")

United States District Court for the Western District of Oklahoma

W.D. Okla. Civ. R. 1.2(d) (may cite as "LCvR __")

W.D. Okla. Crim. R. 1.2(e) (may cite as "LCrR __")

United States Bankruptcy Court for the Western District of Oklahoma

Bankr. W.D. Okla. R. 1001-1(B) (may cite as "Local Rule __")

United States District Court for the District of Oregon

D. Or. R. 1-3 (will cite as "LR __")

D. Or. Adm. P. R. 1000-1(a) (may cite as "LR __")

United States Bankruptcy Court for the District of Oregon

Bankr. D. Or. R. 1001-1(a) (must cite as "LBR __")

United States District Court for the Eastern District of Pennsylvania

E.D. Pa. Crim. R. 1.1(b) (may cite as "Local Criminal Rule __" or "L.C.R. __")

United States Bankruptcy Court for the Eastern District of Pennsylvania

> Bankr. E.D. Pa. R. 1001-1(b) (shall cite rules as "Local Bankruptcy Rule ___ " or "L.B.R. ___ ") (shall cite forms as "L.B.F. ___ ")

United States Bankruptcy Court for the Middle District of Pennsylvania

> Bankr. M.D. Pa. R. 1001-1(b) (may cite rules as "Local Bankruptcy Rule ___ " or "L.B.R. ___ ") (may cite forms as "L.B.F. ___ ")

United States District Court for the Western District of Pennsylvania

> W.D. Pa. Civ. R. 1.1(A) (may cite as "LCvR ___ ")
>
> W.D. Pa. Civ. R. 5.1(L) (citation of internet sources)
>
> W.D. Pa. Crim. R. 1 (may cite as "LCrR ___ ")
>
> W.D. Pa. Pat. R. 1.2 (should cite as "LPR ___ ")

United States Bankruptcy Court for the Western District of Pennsylvania

> Bankr. W.D. Pa. R. 1001-1 (shall cite as "W.PA.LBR ___ ")

United States District Court for the District of Rhode Island

> D.R.I. R. 101(a) (shall cite as "Local Rules" or "DRI LR ___ ")
>
> D.R.I. Adm. R. A(3) (may cite as "LAR ___ ")

United States Bankruptcy Court for the District of Rhode Island

> Bankr. D.R.I. R. 1001-1(a) (shall cite as "R.I. LBR ___ ")

United States District Court for the District of South Carolina

> D.S.C. Civ. R. 1.01 (shall cite as "Local Civ. Rule ___ (D.S.C.).")
>
> D.S.C. Crim. R. 1.01 (shall cite as "Local Crim. Rule ___ (D.S.C.).")

United States Bankruptcy Court for the District of South Carolina

> Bankr. D.S.C. R. 1001-1(a) (may cite as "SC LBR ___ " or "Bankr. D.S.C. R. ___ ")

United States District Court for the District of South Dakota

> D.S.D. Civ. R. 1.1(A) (shall cite as "D.S.D. Civ. LR ___ ")
>
> D.S.D. Crim. R. 1.1(A) (shall cite as "D.S.D. Crim. LR ___ ")

United States Bankruptcy Court for the District of South Dakota

> Bankr. D.S.D. R. 1001-1 (shall cite as "Bankr. D.S.D. R. ___ ")

United States District Court for the Eastern District of Tennessee

> E.D. Tenn. R. 1.1(a) (may cite as "E.D. Tenn. L.R. ___ ")
>
> E.D. Tenn. R. 7.4 (citation of various types of authority)

United States Bankruptcy Court for the Eastern District of Tennessee

> Bankr. E.D. Tenn. R. 1001-1(a) (may cite as "E.D. Tenn. LBR ___ ")

United States District Court for the Middle District of Tennessee

M.D. Tenn. R. 7.01(d) (citation of various types of legal authority)

United States Bankruptcy Court for the Middle District of Tennessee

Bankr. M.D. Tenn. R. 9013-2(b) (citation to Westlaw or Lexis)

Bankr. M.D. Tenn. R. 9014-1(d)(3)(b) (citation to Westlaw or Lexis for contested matters)

Bankr. M.D. Tenn. R. 9019-2 (may cite Alternative Dispute Resolution Program as "LBR 9019-2")

Bankr. M.D. Tenn. R. 9029-1(b) (shall cite as "LBR __ ")

United States District Court for the Western District of Tennessee

W.D. Tenn. Civ. R. 1.1(a) (shall cite civil rules as "LR __ ") (shall cite criminal rules as "LCrR __ ")

W.D. Tenn. Civ. R. 7.2(h) (citation of various types of legal authority)

W.D. Tenn. Civ. R. 7.2(i) (citation of internet sources)

W.D. Tenn. Pat. R. 1.1 (should cite as "LPR __ ")

United States Bankruptcy Court for the Western District of Tennessee

Bankr. W.D. Tenn. R. 1001-1(a) (may cite as "TNWB LBR __ ")

Bankr. W.D. Tenn. R. 7016-1(b) (citation of opinions)

United States District Court for the Eastern District of Texas

E.D. Tex. Adm. R. (a)(3) (may cite as "LAR __ ")

E.D. Tex. Pat. R. 1-1 (should cite as "P. R. __ ")

United States Bankruptcy Court for the Eastern District of Texas

Bankr. E.D. Tex. R. 1001(a) (may cite rules as "LBR __ ") (may cite forms as "TXEB Local Form __ ")

United States Bankruptcy Court for the Northern District of Texas

Bankr. N.D. Tex. R. 1001-1(a) (shall cite as "N.D. Tex. L.B.R. __ ")

United States District Court for the Southern District of Texas

S.D. Tex. Pat. R. 1.1 (to cite as "P. R. __ ")

United States Bankruptcy Court for the Southern District of Texas

Bankr. S.D. Tex. R. 1001-1(a) (may cite as "Bankruptcy Local Rule __ " or "BLR __ ")

United States District Court for the Western District of Texas

W.D. Tex. Civ. R. 1(c) (may cite as "Local Court Rule __ ")

W.D. Tex. Crim. R. 1(c) (may cite as "Western District of Texas Rule __ ")

United States Bankruptcy Court for the Western District of Texas

Bankr. W.D. Tex. R. 1001(a) (shall cite as "Bankruptcy Local Rule __ " or "L. Rule __ ")

United States District Court for the District of Utah

D. Utah Civ. R. 7-2 (citation of unpublished opinions)

Local Rules of Practice Information (shall cite civil rules as "DUCivR __ ") (shall cite criminal rules as "DUCrimR __ ")

United States Bankruptcy Court for the District of Utah

Bankr. D. Utah R. 1001-1(a) (should cite as "Bankr. D. Ut. LBR __ " or "Local Rule __ ")

Bankr. D. Utah. R. 7056-1(i) (citation of unpublished opinions in motions and memoranda for summary judgment)

Bankr. D. Utah R. 9013-1(i) (citation of unpublished opinions)

United States District Court for the District of Vermont

D. Vt. R. 85 (cite civil rules as "L.R. __ ") (cite criminal rules as "L.Cr. R. __ ")

United States Bankruptcy Court for the District of Vermont

Bankr. D. Vt. R. 9029-1(a)(1) (should cite rules as "Vermont Local Bankruptcy Rule __ " or "Vt. LBR __ ")

Bankr. D. Vt. R. 9029-1(a)(2) (cite appendices as "Vt. LB Appendix __ ") (cite forms as "Vt. LB Form __ ")

United States District Court for the Eastern District of Virginia

E.D. Va. Adm. R. 3 (may cite as "LAR __ ")

United States Bankruptcy Court for the Eastern District of Virginia

Bankr. E.D. Va. R. 1001-1 (may cite as "Local Bankruptcy Rule __ " or "LBR __ ")

United States District Court for the Western District of Virginia

W.D. Va. R. 1(d) (may cite general rules as "W.D. Va. Gen. R. __ ") (may cite civil rules as "W.D. Va. Civ. R. __ ") (may cite criminal rules as "W.D. Va. Crim. R. __ ")

United States District Court for the Eastern District of Washington

E.D. Wash. Civ. R. 7(g) (citation of opinions)

E.D. Wash. Civ. R. 10(c) (citation of previously filed pleadings, exhibits, or documents)

E.D. Wash. Civ. R. 85 (shall cite as "LCivR __ ")

E.D. Wash. Crim. R. 61 (may cite as "LCrR __ ")

E.D. Wash. Mag. R. 5 (shall cite as "LMJR __ ")

E.D. Wash. Pat. R. 100 (may cite as "Local Patent Rule __ " or "LPR __ ")

United States Bankruptcy Court for the Eastern District of Washington

Bankr. E.D. Wash. R. 9013-1(d)(2) (citation of opinions)

Bankr. E.D. Wash. R. 9029-1(a) (shall cite as "LBR-__")

United States District Court for the Western District of Washington

W.D. Wash. Civ. R. 85 (may cite admiralty rules as "Local Admiralty Rule __ ") (should cite civil rules as "Local Rules W.D. Wash. LCR __ ") (should cite criminal rules as "Local Rules W.D. Wash. CrR __ ") (should cite magistrate rules as "Local Rules W.D. Wash. MJR __ ") (may cite patent rules as "Local Patent Rule __ ")

W.D. Wash. Civ. R. 10(e)(6) (citation to the record)

W.D. Wash. Supp. Adm. R. 100 (may cite as "Local Admiralty Rule __ ")

W.D. Wash. Supp. Pat. R. 100 (may cite as "Local Patent Rule __ ")

United States Bankruptcy Court for the Western District of Washington

Bankr. W.D. Wash. R. 9029-1 (shall cite rules as "Local Rules W.D. Wash. Bankr. __ ") (shall cite forms as "Local Forms W.D. Wash. Bankr. __ ")

United States District Court for the Northern District of West Virginia

N.D. W. Va. R. Preface (cite general practice rules as "LR Gen P __ ") (cite civil rules as "LR Civ P __ ") (cite criminal rules as "LR Cr P __ ") (cite prisoner litigation rules as "LR PL P __ ")

United States Bankruptcy Court for the Northern District of West Virginia

Bankr. N.D. W. Va. R. Title Page (cite as "N.D.W.V. LBR __ ")

United States Bankruptcy Court for the Southern District of West Virginia

Bankr. S.D. W. Va. R. Title Page (cite as "Bankr. S.D. W.Va. R. __ ")

United States District Court for the Eastern District of Wisconsin

E.D. Wis. Civ. R. 7(j) (citation of unpublished opinions)

United States District Court for the District of Wyoming

D. Wyo. Civ. R. 1.1(a) (may cite as "U.S.D.C.L.R. __ " or "Local Rule __ ")

D. Wyo. Crim. R. 1.1(a) (may cite as "U.S.D.C.L.Cr.R. __ ")

United States Bankruptcy Court for the District of Wyoming

Bankr. D. Wyo. R. 1001-1(A) (may cite as "Wyoming LBR __ ")

United States District Court for the District of Guam

D. Guam R. 1.1(a) (may cite as "GNLR __ ")

D. Guam R. 4.1(b) (citations shall be in the form found in The Bluebook (most recent edition))

D. Guam Adm. R. 3 (shall cite as "ADLR __ ")

D. Guam Bankr. R. 10001-1(a) (may cite as "BKLR __ ")

D. Guam Civ. R. 1(a) (should cite as "CVLR __ ")

D. Guam Crim R. 1 (should cite as "CRLR __ ")

D. Guam Habeas Corpus R. 1(b) (may cite as "HCLR __ ")

D. Guam Tax R. 1(b) (shall cite as "TXLR __ ")

United States District Court for the Northern Mariana Islands

D. N. Mar. I. R. 1.1(a) (should cite as "LR __ ")

D. N. Mar. I. R. 5.2(b) (citations shall be in a generally recognized form)

D. N. Mar. I. R. 15 (citation of internet sources)

D. N. Mar. I. Adm. R. <u>Table of Contents</u> (shall cite as "LAR __ ")

D. N. Mar. I. Bankr. R. <u>Table of Contents</u> (may cite as "LBR __ ")

D. N. Mar. I. Crim. R. <u>Table of Contents</u> (shall cite as "LCrR __ ")

D. N. Mar. I. Disc. R. <u>Table of Contents</u> (shall cite as "LDR __ ")

United States District Court for the District of Puerto Rico

D.P.R. Civ. R. 1(d) (shall cite civil rules as "Local Civil Rule __ " or "L.Cv.R. __ ") (shall cite admiralty rules as "Local Admiralty Rule __ " or "L.Adm.R. __ ") (citation of other districts' local rules or to previous versions of the local rules)

D.P.R. Crim. R. 101(d) (shall cite as "Local Criminal Rule __ " or "L.Crim.R. __ ") (citation to other districts' local rules or to previous versions of the local rules)

United States Bankruptcy Court for the District of Puerto Rico

Bankr. D.P.R. R. 1001-1(a) (may cite rules as "P.R. LBR __ ") (shall refer to official forms as "P.R. LBF __ ")

Bankr. D.P.R. R. 1001-1(b) (shall cite local civil rules as "L.Cv.R. __ ")

United States District Court for the District of the Virgin Islands

D.V.I. R. App. P. 1(a) (shall cite as "V.I. R. App. P. __ " or "VIRAP __ ")

D.V.I. R. App. P. 15(b) (citation of opinions)

D.V.I. R. App. P. 22(i) (citation of opinions)

D.V.I. Bankr. R. 1001-1 (shall cite as "Local Bankruptcy Rule __ " or "LBR __ ")

D.V.I. Civ. R. 1.1(a) (shall cite as "LRCi __ ")

D.V.I. Crim. R. 1.1(a) (shall cite as "LRCr __ ")

D.V.I. <u>Style Guide</u> (I)(A) (unless otherwise noted, all citations should comply with <u>The Bluebook</u> (most recent edition))

<u>Style Guide for the Appellate Division of the District Court</u> (1998)

United States Court of Appeals for the Armed Forces

C.A.A.F. R. 37(c)(2) (citations shall conform with <u>The Bluebook</u>)

United States Court of Appeals for Veterans Claims

Vet. App. R. 30 (citation of nonprecedential and supplemental authority)

United States Court of Federal Claims

U.S. Ct. Fed. Claims R. 1 (may cite as "RCFC __ ")

U.S. Ct. Fed. Claims R. 85 (may cite as the "Rule of the United States Court of Federal Claims __ ")

U.S. Ct. Fed. Claims Pat. R. 1(a) (shall cite as "PRCFC __ ")

United States Court of International Trade

U.S. Ct. Int'l Trade R. 81(m) (citation of various types of legal authority)

U.S. Ct. Int'l Trade R. 88 (may cite as "Rule of the Court of International Trade __ ")

United States Tax Court

> T.C. R. 23(f) (citation of opinions)

BT2.2 State Courts

Alabama

> Ala. R. App. P. 28(a)(10) (citations shall comply with <u>The Bluebook</u> or the <u>ALWD Citation Manual</u> or the style and form used in opinions of the Alabama Supreme Court)
>
> Ala. R. App. P. 49 (shall cite as "The Alabama Rule of Appellate Procedure __ " or "ARAP __ ")
>
> Ala. R. App. P. 53(d) (citation of no-opinion orders of affirmance issued by the Alabama Supreme Court or the Alabama Court of Civil Appeals)
>
> Ala. R. App. P. 54(d) (citation of no-opinion orders of affirmance issued by the Alabama Court of Criminal Appeals)
>
> Ala. R. Civ. P. 85 (may cite as "Alabama Rule of Civil Procedure __ ")
>
> Ala. R. Evid. 1102 (may cite as "Ala.R.Evid. __ ")
>
> Ala. R. Jud. Admin. <u>Preamble</u> (shall cite as "Alabama Rule of Judicial Administration __ ")

Alaska

> Alaska Adoption R. 1(a) (will cite as "Adoption Rule __ ")
>
> Alaska Child in Need of Aid R. of P. 1(a) (will cite as "Child in Need of Aid Rule __ " or "CINA Rule __ ")
>
> Alaska Delinquency R. 1(a) (will cite as "Delinquency Rule __ ")
>
> Alaska Dist. Ct. R. Civ. P. 33 (shall cite as "District Court Rule of Civil Procedure __ ")
>
> Alaska R. of Admin. 51 (shall cite as "Rule Governing the Administration of All Courts __ ")
>
> Alaska R. App. P. 214(d) (citation of unpublished opinions)
>
> Alaska R. App. P. 523 (shall cite as "Rule of Appellate Procedure __ ")
>
> Alaska R. App. P. Appendix D. (citation of testimony presented by deposition)
>
> Alaska R. Crim. P. 58 (shall cite as "Rule of Criminal Procedure __ ")
>
> Alaska R. Evid. 1101 (may cite as "Alaska Rule of Evidence __ ")
>
> Alaska R. of Prob. P. 1(a) (will cite as "Probate Rule __ ")
>
> Alaska Stat. § 01.05.011 (may cite statutes as "AS __ ")

Arizona

> Ariz. R. Civ. App. P. 13(f) (citation of cases)
>
> Ariz. R. Civ. App. P. 28(f) (citation of memorandum decisions)
>
> Ariz. R. Crim. P. 31.10(g) (citation of cases)
>
> Ariz. R. Sup. Ct. 111(c) (citation of memorandum decisions)
>
> Ariz. Rev. Stat. Ann. § 1-101 (may cite as "A.R.S. __ ")
>
> Ariz. Super. Ct. R. App. P. Civ. 17 (may cite as "Superior Court Rule of Appellate Procedure–Civil __ ")

> Ariz. Super. Ct. R. App. P. Crim. 15 (may cite as "Superior Court Rule of Appellate Procedure–Criminal __ ")

Arkansas

> Ark. R. Civ. P. 85 (may cite as "Arkansas Rule of Civil Procedure __ " or "ARCP __ ")

> Ark. R. Crim. P. 1.1 (may cite as "Arkansas Rule of Criminal Procedure __ ")

> Ark. R. Evid. 1102 (may cite as "A.R.E. Rule __ ")

> Ark. Sup. Ct. R. 4-2(a)(7) (citation of opinions)

> Ark. Sup. Ct. R. 5-2 (citation of opinions)

> Ark. Code Ann. § 1-2-113(c) (may cite as "A.C.A. __ ")

> House Style Guide (2010), https://www.arcourts.gov/sites/default/files/House%20Style%20Guide%20September2010.pdf

California

> Cal. App. R. 8.1115 (citation of opinions)

> Cal. R. Ct. 1.200 (citations must be in the style established by the California Style Manual or The Bluebook)

> Cal. R. Ct. 3.1113(c) (citation of opinions)

> California Style Manual (4th ed. 2000), http://www.sdap.org/downloads/Style-Manual.pdf

Colorado

> Colo. App. R. 58 (shall cite as "C.A.R. __ ")

> Colo. R. Civ. P. 1(c) (shall cite as "Colorado Rule of Civil Procedure __ " or "C.R.C.P. __ ")

> Colo. R. Cnty. Ct. Civ. P. 301(b) (shall cite as "Colorado Rule of Civil Procedure __ " or "C.R.C.P. __ ")

> Colo. R. Prob. P. 1(b) (shall cite as "Colorado Rule of Probate Procedure __ " or "C.R.P.P. __ ")

> Colo. R. Prof'l Conduct 9 (shall cite as "Colorado Rule of Professional Conduct __ " or "Colo. RPC __ ")

> Colo. R.P. Small Cl. Cts. 501(a) (shall cite as "Colorado Rule of Civil Procedure __ " or "C.R.C.P. __ ")

Connecticut

> Conn. R. App. P. § 67-11 (citation of opinions)

> The Manual of Style for the Connecticut Courts (3d ed. 2013), http://www.jud.ct.gov/Publications/Manual_of_style.pdf

Delaware

> Del. Sup. Ct. R. 14(g)(i) (cite reported opinions according to The Bluebook)

> Del. Sup. Ct. R. 14(g)(ii) (citation of unreported opinions)

> Del. Sup. Ct. R. 14(g)(iii) (cite other authority according to The Bluebook)

Del. Ch. Ct. R. 171(g) (citations are appropriate if made in accordance with <u>The Bluebook</u>)

Del. Super. Ct. R. Civ. P. 107(d)(4)(a) (cite reported opinions according to <u>The Bluebook</u>)

Del. Super. Ct. R. Civ. P. 107(d)(4)(b) (citation of unreported opinions)

Del. Super. Ct. R. Civ. P. 107(d)(4)(c) (cite other authority according to <u>The Bluebook</u>)

Del. Super. Ct. Crim. R. P. 60 (may cite as "Super. Ct. Crim. R. __ ")

Del. Ct. C.P. Civ. R. 107(c)(4) (citations are appropriate if made in accordance with <u>The Bluebook</u>)

Del. Ct. C.P. Civ. R. 107(c)(5) (citation of unreported opinions and orders)

Del. Fam. Ct. R. Civ. P. 7(b)(6) (citations are appropriate if made in accordance with <u>The Bluebook</u>)

Del. Fam. Ct. R. Civ. P. 10(d) (citations are appropriate if made in accordance with <u>The Bluebook</u>)

Del. Fam. Ct. R. Civ. P. 107(c)(5) (citations are appropriate if made in accordance with <u>The Bluebook</u>)

Del. Fam. Ct. R. Civ. P. 107(f) (citation of unreported and memorandum opinions)

Del. Fam. Ct. R. Crim. P. 1(b) (may cite as "Family Court Rule of Criminal Procedure __ ")

Del. Code Ann. tit. 1 § 101(b) (may cite as "__ Del. C. __ ")

<u>Delaware Uniform Citation</u> (2008), http://courts.delaware.gov/Superior /pdf/de_uniform_citation_2008.pdf

District of Columbia

D.C. Ct. App. R. 27(d)(4) (citation in motions)

D.C. Ct. App. R. 28(g) (citation of unpublished opinions)

D.C. Ct. App. R. 28(h) (citation of administrative agency materials)

D.C. Super. Ct. R. Civ. P. 85 (may cite as "Superior Court Rule–Civil __ " or "SCR–Civil __ ")

D.C. Super. Ct. R. Crim. P. 61 (may cite as "Superior Court Rule of Criminal Procedure __ " or "Super. Ct. Crim. R. __ ")

D.C. Super. Ct. Dom. Rel. R. 1(a) (may cite as "Rule Governing Domestic Relations Proceedings __ " or "Super. Ct. Dom. Rel. R. __ ")

D.C. Super. Ct. Juv. P.R. 47 (citation of opinions from the D.C. Cir.)

D.C. Super. Ct. Juv. P.R. 60 (may cite as "SCR–Juvenile __ ")

D.C. Super. Ct. Land. & Ten. R. 1 (may cite as "Superior Court Rule–Landlord and Tenant __ " or "SCR–LT __ ")

D.C. Super. Ct. Small Cl. R. 1(b) (may cite as "Super. Ct. Sm. Cl. R. __ ")

D.C. Super. Ct. Dom. Vio. R. 1(c) (may cite as "Super. Ct. Dom. Vio. R. __ ")

D.C. Super. Ct. R. Mental Retardation 1 (may cite as "Superior Court Rule–Mental Retardation __ " or "SCR–M.R. __ ")

D.C. Super. Ct. R. Neglect & Abuse Proceedings 43(a) (citation of opinions from the D.C. Cir.)

D.C. Super. Ct. R. Prob. Div. 1(a) (may cite as "SCR–PD __ ")

Citation and Style Guide (2019), http://www.dccourts.gov/sites
/default/files/matters-docs/DCCACitationGuide.pdf

Florida

Fla. R. App. P. 9.010 (cite as "Florida Rule of Appellate Procedure __ " or
"Fla. R. App. P. __ ")

Fla. R. App. P. 9.800 (citation of various types of legal authority)

Fla. R. App. P. 9.800(o) (citations shall be in the form prescribed by The
Bluebook and the Florida Style Manual)

Fla. R. Civ. P. 1.010 (shall cite as "Florida Rule of Civil Procedure __ " or
"Fla.R.Civ.P. __ ")

Fla. R. Crim. P. 3.010 (may cite as "Fla. R. Crim. P. __ ")

Fla. R. Jud. Admin. 2.110 (cite as "Florida Rule of Judicial Administration
__ " or "Fla. R. Jud. Admin. __ ")

Fla. R. Juv. P. 8.000 (may cite as "Fla. R. Juv. P. __ ")

Fla. R. Traffic Ct. 6.010 (cite as "Florida Rule of Traffic Court __ " or "Fla.
R. Traf. Ct. __ ")

Fla. P.R. 5.010 (may cite as "Fla. Prob. R. __ ")

Fla. Small Cl. R. 7.010(a) (shall cite as "Florida Small Claims Rule __ " or
"Fla. Sm. Cl. R. __ ")

Florida Style Manual (8th ed. 2019), http://www.floridastylemanual.com

Georgia

Ga. Ct. App. R. 24(d) (citation of opinions)

Ga. Code § 1-1-8(e) (may cite as "O.C.G.A. __ ")

Ga. Sup. Ct. R. 22 (citation of various authorities)

Hawaii

Haw. R. App. P. 1(c) (shall cite as "Hawai'i Rule of Appellate Procedure
__ " or "HRAP __ ")

Haw. R. App. P. 28(b)(1) (citation of opinions)

Haw. R. App. P. 35(c) (citation of dispositions)

Haw. R. Evid. 100 (may cite as "Rule __ , Hawai'i Rules of Evidence,
Chapter 626, Hawai'i Revised Statutes")

Haw. R. Penal P. 60 (may cite as "Hawai'i Rule of Penal Procedure __ ")

Haw. Fam. Ct. R. 85 (shall cite as "Hawai'i Family Court Rule __ " or
"HFCR __ ")

Haw. R. Civ. P. 85 (may cite as "Hawai'i Rule of Civil Procedure __ ")

Haw. Civ. Traffic R. 1 (shall cite as "Hawai'i Civil Traffic Rule __ " or "HCTR
__ ")

Haw. Dist. Ct. R. Civ. P. 85 (may cite as "District Court Rule of Civil
Procedure __ ")

A Handbook of Citation Form for Law Clerks at the Appellate Courts of
the State of Hawai'i (2008), https://www.law.hawaii.edu/files/content
/library/HandbookofCitationForm.pdf

Idaho

- Idaho R. Evid. 101(a) (shall cite as "Idaho Rule of Evidence __ " or "I.R.E. __ ")
- Idaho Crim. R. 2(b) (shall cite as "Idaho Criminal Rule __ " or "I.C.R. __ ")
- Idaho App. R. 1 (shall cite as "Idaho Appellate Rule __ " or "I.A.R. __ ")
- Idaho R. Civ. P. 87 (may cite as "Idaho Rule of Civil Procedure __ " or "I.R.C.P. __ ")
- Idaho Juv. R. 60 (shall cite as "The Idaho Juvenile Rule __ " or "I.J.R. __ ")

Illinois

- Ill. Sup. Ct. R. 6 (citation of various types of legal authority)
- <u>Style Manual for the Supreme and Appellate Courts of Illinois</u> (5th ed. 2017), https://courts.illinois.gov/StyleManual/SupCrt_StyleManual.pdf

Indiana

- Ind. R. App. P. 22 (citation of various types of legal authority)
- Ind. Small Cl. R. 1(B) (may cite as "S.C. __ ")
- Ind. Code § 1-1-1-1 (may cite as "IC __ ")

Iowa

- Iowa R. App. P. 6.904(2) (citation of various types of legal authority)
- Iowa R. Evid. 5.1103 (shall cite as "Iowa R. Evid. __ ")
- Iowa R. <u>Preface</u> (shall cite rules of civil procedure as "Iowa R. Civ. P. __ ") (shall cite rules of criminal procedure as "Iowa R. Crim. P. __ ") (shall cite rules of evidence as "Iowa R. Evid. __ ") (shall cite rules of appellate procedure as "Iowa R. App. P. __ ") (shall cite rules of electronic procedure as "Iowa R. Elec. P. __ ") (shall cite rules of professional conduct as "Iowa R. of Prof'l Conduct __ ") (shall cite code of judicial conduct as "Iowa Code of Judicial Conduct __ ") (shall cite all other rules as "Iowa Ct. R. __ ")

Kansas

- Kan. Sup. Ct. R. 6.08 (citation of opinions)
- Kan. R. Prof'l Conduct <u>Prefatory Rule</u> (may cite as "KRPC __ ")

Kentucky

- Ky. R. Civ. P. 1(1) (may cite as "Civil Rule __ " or "CR __ ")
- Ky. R. Civ. P. 76.12(4)(g) (citation of statutes and opinions)
- Ky. R. Civ. P. 76.28(4)(c) (citation of unpublished opinions)
- Ky. R. Crim. P. 1.02(1) (may cite as "Criminal Rule __ " or "RCr __ ")
- Ky. R. Evid. 101 (should cite as "KRE __ ")
- Ky. Fam. R.P. & Prac. 1(1) (may cite as "Kentucky Family Court Rule of Procedure and Practice __ " or "FCRPP __ ")
- Ky. Juv. R.P. & Prac. 1(A) (may cite as "JCRPP __ ")
- Ky. Sup. Ct. R. 1.000 (may cite as "Rule of the Supreme Court __ " or "SCR __ ")

Louisiana

- La. Code Civ. P. 2168 (citation of unpublished opinions)
- La. Code Crim. P. 1 (may cite as "C.Cr.P. __ ")
- La. Sup. Ct. Gen. Admin. R. Pt. G. § 8 (citation of opinions) (mandatory use of a uniform public domain citation)
- La. Ct. App. Unif. R. 2-12.4(B)(2) (citation of opinions)

Maine

- Me. R. Civ. P. 85 (may cite as "Maine Rule of Civil Procedure __ ")
- Me. R. Evid. 101(d) (may cite as "Maine Rule of Evidence __ ")
- Me. R. Prob. P. 85 (may cite as "Maine Rule of Probate Procedure __ ")
- Me. R. Small Cl. P. 17 (may cite as "Maine Rule of Small Claims Procedure __ ")
- Me. R. Unified Crim. P. 1(a) (may cite as "Maine Rule of Unified Criminal Procedure __ ")
- Me. Code Jud. Conduct Title Page (may cite as "Maine Code of Judicial Conduct __ ")
- Uniform Maine Citations (2019–20), https://digitalcommons.mainelaw .maine.edu/uniform-maine-citations/15

Maryland

- Md. R. 1-103 (may cite general rules as "Rule __ ")
- Md. R. 1-104(b) (citation of unreported opinions)
- Md. R. 1-105 (citation of various legal authorities)
- Md. R. 6-103 (cite settlement of estates rules as "Rule __ ")
- Md. R. 8-504(a)(1) (citation of opinions)

Massachusetts

- Mass. R. App. P. 16(g) (citation of statutes and opinions)
- Mass. R. App. P. 32 (may cite as "Massachusetts Rule of Appellate Procedure __ " or "Mass.R.A.P. __ ")
- Mass. R. Civ. P. 85 (may cite as "Massachusetts Rule of Civil Procedure __ ")
- Mass. R. Crim. P. 1(a) (may cite as "Massachusetts Rule of Criminal Procedure __ " or "Mass. R. Crim. P. __ ")
- Mass. R. Prof'l Conduct 1(r) (shall cite as "Massachusetts Rule of Professional Conduct __ " or "Mass. R. Prof. C. __ ")
- Mass. Dist. & Mun. App. Div. R. 16(g) (citation of statutes and opinions)
- Mass. Dist. & Mun. App. Div. R. 32 (may cite as "District/Municipal Courts Rule for Appellate Division Appeal __ " or "Dist./Mun. Cts. R.A.D.A. __ ")
- Massachusetts Reports Style Manual (2019–20), https://www.mass .gov/doc/sjc-style-manual/download

Michigan

Mich. Ct. R. 1.101 (may cite as "MCR __ ")

Mich. Ct. R. 7.215(C)(1) (citation of unpublished opinions)

Mich. R. Evid. 1102 (may cite as "MRE __ ")

Mich. Prof'l Conduct R. 1.0(a) (cite as "MRPC __ ")

<u>Michigan Appellate Opinion Manual</u> (2017), https://courts.michigan .gov/Courts/MichiganSupremeCourt/Documents/MiAppOpManual.pdf

Minnesota

Minn. R. Civ. P. 85 (cite as "Rule of Civil Procedure __ ")

Minn. R. Civ. App. P. 136.01(1)(b) (citation of unpublished and order opinions)

Minn. R. Civ. App. P. 146 (may cite as "Rule of Civil Appellate Procedure __ ")

Minn. Gen. R. Prac. 1.01 (may cite as "Minn. Gen. R. Prac. __ ")

<u>Citing Minnesota Legal Sources</u>, https://www.leg.state.mn.us/leg /history/citations

Mississippi

Miss. R. App. P. 28(f)(2) (citation of opinions)

Miss. R. App. P. 35-A (citation of unpublished opinions from the Mississippi Supreme Court)

Miss. R. App. P. 35-B (citation of unpublished opinions from the Mississippi Court of Appeals)

Miss. R. App. P. 49 (may cite as "M.R.A.P. __ ")

Miss. R. Civ. P. 85 (may cite as "M.R.C.P. __ ")

Miss. R. Crim. P. 1.1 (may cite as "MRCrP __ ")

Miss. R. Evid. 1102 (may cite as "MRE __ ")

Miss. Uniform Civ. R. Cir. & Cnty. Ct. P. 1.01 (may cite as "UCRCCC __ ")

Missouri

Mo. Sup. Ct. R. 1.01 (may cite as "Rule __ ")

Montana

Mont. R. App. P. 1 (shall cite as "M. R. App. P. __ ")

Mont. R. Civ. P. 85 (may cite as "M. R. Civ. P. __ ")

AF 06-0632 (02-25-10), <u>In re</u> the Matter of Opinion Forms and Citation Standards of the Supreme Court of Montana

Mont. Code Ann. <u>Preface</u> (cite as "MCA __ ") http://leg.mt.gov/bills /mca/help.htm

Nebraska

Neb. Sup. Ct. R. Ch. 1 <u>Title Page</u> (cite as "Neb. Ct. R. § __ " unless otherwise noted)

Neb. Sup. Ct. R. Ch. 2 <u>Title Page</u> (cite as "Neb. Ct. R. App. P. § __ ")

Neb. Sup. Ct. R. Ch. 3 Art. 5 (cite as "Neb. Ct. R. of Prof. Cond. § __ ")

- Neb. Sup. Ct. R. Ch. 5 Art. 3 (cite as "Neb. Rev. Code of Judicial Conduct § __ ")
- Neb. Sup. Ct. R. Ch. 6 Art. 3 (cite as "Neb. Ct. R. Disc. § __ ")
- Neb. Sup. Ct. R. Ch. 6 Art. 11 (cite as "Neb. Ct. R. Pldg. § __ ")
- Neb. Sup. Ct. R. § 2-102(E) (citation of opinions)
- Neb. Sup. Ct. R. § 2-109(C) (citation of various types of legal authority)
- Neb. Sup. Ct. R. § 6-1505(C) (citation of various types of legal authority)

Nevada

- Nev. R. Alt. Disp. Resol. (B)(2)(D) (may cite as "Nevada Arbitration Rule __ " or "N.A.R. __ ")
- Nev. R. Alt. Disp. Resol. (C)(1)(B) (may cite as "Nevada Mediation Rule __ " or "N.M.R. __ ")
- Nev. R. App. P. 36(c)(3) (citation of unpublished opinions)
- Nev. R. App. P. 48 (shall cite as "Nevada Rule of Appellate Procedure __ " or "NRAP __ ")
- Nev. R. Civ. P. 85 (may cite as "Nevada Rule of Civil Procedure __ " or "NRCP __ ")
- Nev. Short Trial R. 35 (may cite as "Nevada Short Trial Rule __ " or "N.S.T.R. __ ")
- Nev. Sup. Ct. R. 1 (may cite as "Supreme Court Rule __ " or "S.C.R. __ ")
- Nev. Justice Ct. R. Civ. P. 85 (may cite as "Justice Court Rule of Civil Procedure __ " or "JCRCP __ ")
- Nev. Rev. Stat. 220.170(4) (may cite as "Nevada Revised Statutes __ " or "NRS __ ")

New Hampshire

- N.H. R. Evid. 1103 (may cite as "New Hampshire Rules of Evidence __ ")
- N.H. Sup. Ct. R. 12-D(3) (citation of orders)
- N.H. Sup. Ct. R. 16(3)(c) (citation of various types of legal authority)
- N.H. Sup. Ct. R. 20 (citation of orders and opinions)
- N.H. Sup. Ct. R. 25(5) (citation of summary dispositions)
- N.H. Supplemental R. Sup. Ct. 1 (shall cite as "Sup. Ct. 2018 Supp. R. __ ")

New Jersey

- N.J. Ct. R. 1:1-3 (may cite as "R. __ ")
- N.J. Ct. R. 1:36-3 (citation of unpublished opinions)
- N.J. R. App. Prac. 2:6-2(a)(6) (citation of opinions)
- N.J. Stat. 1:1-5.1 (may cite Revised Statutes as "R.S. __ ") (may cite New Jersey Statutes as "N.J.S. __ ")
- New Jersey Manual on Style for Judicial Opinions (2017), https://www.njcourts.gov/attorneys/assets/attyresources/manualonstyle.pdf

New Mexico

- N.M. R. App. P. 12-101(B) (may cite as "Rule 12- __ NMRA")
- N.M. R. App. P. 12-318(E) (follow N.M. Sup. Ct. R. 23-112)
- N.M. R. App. P. 12-405(D) (citation of unpublished or non-precedential opinions)
- N.M. Child. Ct. R. 10-101(E) (may cite as "Rule 10-__ NMRA")
- N.M. Dist. Ct. R. Civ. P. 1-001(D) (shall cite as "Rule 1-__ NMRA")
- N.M. Dist. Ct. R. Crim. P. 5-101(D) (shall cite as "NMRA, Rule 5-__")
- N.M. Magis. Ct. R. Civ. P. 6-101(D) (cite as "NMRA, Rule 6-__")
- N.M. Magis. Ct. R. Crim. P. 6-101(D) (shall cite as "NMRA, Rule 6-__")
- N.M. Metro. Ct. R. Civ. P. 3-101(D) (shall cite as "NMRA, Rule 3-__")
- N.M. Metro. Ct. R. Crim. P. 7-101(D) (shall cite as "NMRA, Rule 7-__")
- N.M. Mun. Ct. R.P. 8-101(D) (shall cite as "NMRA, Rule 8-__")
- N.M. Prob. Ct. R. 1B-101(D) (shall cite as "Rule 1B- __ NMRA")
- N.M. Prob. Ct. R. 1B-301 (may cite forms as "Form 4B- __ NMRA")
- N.M. Sup. Ct. R. 23-112 (citation of various types of legal authority)
- N.M. Sup. Ct. R. 23-112(F) (shall follow the form of citations set forth in The Bluebook)

New York

- N.Y. C.P.L.R. 5529(e) (McKinney 2003) (citation of opinions)
- N.Y. Ct. App. R. 500.1(g), 510.1(a) (citation of various types of legal authority)
- New York Law Reports Style Manual (2017), https://www.nycourts.gov/reporter/files/2017-SM.pdf
- New York Rules of Citation (6th ed. 2011), published by St. John's L. Rev.

North Carolina

- N.C. R. App. P. 1(a) (may cite as "N.C. R. App. P. __ ")
- N.C. R. App. P. 9(b)(4) (citation of pages of records on appeal)
- N.C. R. App. P. 30(e)(3) (citation of unpublished opinions)
- N.C. R. App. P. App. B (citations should be made according to The Bluebook) (citation of regional reporters) (various formatting rules)
- N.C. Bus. Ct. R. 1.5 (shall cite as "BCR __ ")
- N.C. Bus. Ct. R. 7.5 (citation of various types of legal authority)
- The Guidebook: Citation, Style, and Usage at the Supreme Court of North Carolina (2019), https://www.nccourts.gov/assets/inline-files/TheGuidebook_SupremeCourtofNorthCarolina_062019_0.pdf?1lTTY94loM9lL3LuzuIEZ04IbNaxjiSJ
- A Style Manual for the North Carolina Rules of Appellate Procedure (2017), https://www.ncapb.com/wp-content/uploads/2017/09/Appellate_Style_Manual_2017.pdf

North Dakota

- N.D. R. Ct. 11.6 (use of public domain citation format)
- N.D. R. Ct. 11.7 (may cite as "N.D.R.Ct. __ ")
- N.D. R. App. P. 48 (may cite as "N.D.R.App.P. __ ")
- N.D. R. Civ. P. 85 (may cite as "N.D.R.Civ.P. __ ")
- N.D. R. Crim. P. 60 (may cite as "N.D.R.Crim.P. __ ")
- N.D. R. Evid. 1103 (may cite as "N.D.R.Ev. __ ")
- N.D. R. Prof'l Conduct 9.1 (may cite as "N.D.R. Prof. Conduct __ ")
- N.D. R. Juv. P. 21(c) (may cite as "N.D.R.Juv.P. __ ")
- N.D. Sup. Ct. Admin. R. 10 (may cite orders as "N.D.Sup.Ct.Admin.Order. __ ")
- N.D. Sup. Ct. Admin. R. 42 (may cite as "N.D.Sup.Ct.Admin.R. __ ")
- North Dakota Supreme Court Citation Manual (2000), https://www.ndcourts.gov/Media/Default/SupremeCourt/Citation%20Manual.pdf

Ohio

- Ohio R. App. P. 42 (may cite as "Appellate Rule __ " or "App.R. __ ")
- Ohio R. Civ. P. 85 (may cite as "Civil Rule __ " or "Civ.R. __ ")
- Ohio Crim. R. 60 (may cite as "Criminal Rule __ " or "Crim.R. __ ")
- Ohio R. Evid. 1103 (may cite as "Evidence Rule __ " or "Evid.R. __ ")
- Ohio R. Juv. P. 48 (may cite as "Juvenile Rule __ " or "Juv.R. __ ")
- Ohio R. Prof'l Conduct Form of Citation (shall cite as "Prof. Cond. Rule __ ")
- Ohio Sup. Ct. Prac. R. 1.05 (shall cite as "S.Ct.Prac.R. __ ")
- Writing Manual: A Guide to Citations, Style, and Judicial Opinion Writing (2013), http://www.supremecourt.ohio.gov/ROD/manual.pdf

Oklahoma

- Okla. R. Crim. App. 1.0(D) (shall cite as "Rule __ , Rules of the Oklahoma Court of Criminal Appeals, Title 22, Ch.18, App. (‹year›)")
- Okla. R. Crim. App. 3.5(C) (citation of opinions)
- Okla. Stat. Ann. (cite as "__ Okl. St. Ann. § __ ")
- Okla. Sup. Ct. R. 1.1(a) (may cite as "Okla.Sup.Ct.R. __ ")
- Okla. Sup. Ct. R. 1.11(l) (citation of opinions)
- Okla. Sup. Ct. R. 1.200(c) (citation of opinions)
- Okla. Sup. Ct. R. 1.200(f) (opinions shall be cited by reference to a public domain citation system)

Oregon

- Or. R. App. P. 1.10(1) (shall cite as "ORAP __ ")
- Or. R. App. P. 5.20(5) (citation of memorandum opinions)
- Or. R. App. P. 5.35(3) (citations are to be in the form prescribed by the Oregon Appellate Courts Style Manual)
- Or. R. App. P. 16.50(1) (citation of internet sources)
- Or. R. Civ. P. 1(G) (may cite as "ORCP __ ")

Or. Rev. Stat. <u>Preface</u> (should cite as "Oregon Revised Statutes __ " or "ORS __ ")

Or. Tax Ct. Reg. Div. R. <u>Preface</u> (should cite as "Tax Court Rule __ " or "TCR __ ")

Or. Tax Ct. Reg. Div. R. 61(A)(3) (citation of cases)

Or. Tax Ct. Magis. Div. R. <u>Preface</u> (should cite as "Tax Court Rule-Magistrate Division __ " or "TCR-MD __ ")

Or. Unif. Trial Ct. R. 1.070(1) (shall cite rules as "UTCR __ ")

Or. Unif. Trial Ct. R. 1.070(2) (shall cite supplementary local rules as "SLR __ ")

Or. Unif. Trial Ct. R. 2.010(13) (citation of opinions)

<u>Oregon Appellate Courts Style Manual</u> (2018), https://www.courts.oregon.gov/publications/Documents/UpdatedStyleManual2002.pdf

Pennsylvania

Pa. R. App. P. 101 (may cite as "Pa. R.A.P. __ ")

Pa. R. App. P. 126 (citation of opinions)

Pa. R. App. P. 2133 (citation of opinions referenced in below court or government decisions)

Pa. R. Civ. P. 51 (may cite as "Pa. R.C.P. No. __ ")

Pa. R. Ev. 101(b) (shall cite as "Pa.R.E. __ ")

Pa. Orphans' Ct. R. 1.1 (shall cite as "Pa.O.C. Rule __ ")

<u>PAstyle: A Pennsylvania Stylebook and Citation Guide for Legal Writing</u> (5th ed. 2014)

Rhode Island

R.I. Dist. Ct. Civ. R. 1(a) (may cite as "D.C.R. __ ")

R.I. Dist. Ct. R. Crim. P. 60 (may cite as "Dist. R. Crim. P. __ ")

R.I. Dist. Ct. R. Small Cl. P. R. 1.01 (may cite as "D.C.R.S.C.P. __ ")

R.I. Fam. Ct. R. P. 1.1 (may cite as "Family Court R.P. __ ")

R.I. R. Dom. Rel. P. 1(a)(2) (may cite as "R. Dom. Rel. P. __ ")

R.I. R. Evid. R. 100 (may cite as "Rhode Island Rule of Evidence __ ")

R.I. R. Juv. P. 36 (may cite as "R. Juv. P. __ ")

R.I. Super. Ct. R. Prac. 1.1 (may cite as "Superior Court R.P. __ ")

R.I. Super. Ct. R. 16(j) (citation of unpublished orders)

R.I. Super. Ct. R. Crim. P. 1(a)(2) (may cite as "Super. R. Crim. P. __ ")

R.I. Traffic Trib. R. P. R. 1(a) (may cite as "Traffic Trib. R. P. __ ")

South Carolina

S.C. App. Ct. R. 101(b) (may cite as "Rule __ , SCACR")

S.C. App. Ct. R. 220(a) (citation of memorandum opinions)

S.C. App. Ct. R. 268 (citation of various types of legal authority)

S.C. R. Civ. P. 85(a) (may cite as "Rule __ , SCRCP")

S.C. R. Crim. P. 38 (shall cite as "Rule __ , SCRCrimP")

S.C. R. Evid. 1103(a) (may cite as "Rule __ , SCRE")

S.C. Fam. Ct. R. 1 (may cite as "Rule __ , SCRFC")

<u>A Guide to South Carolina Legal Research and Citation</u> (3d ed. 2014)

South Dakota

S.D. R. App. P. § 15-26A-69.1 (citation of opinions)

S.D. R. App. P. § 15-26A-69.2 (shall follow a public domain citation system)

S.D. R. App. P. § 15-26A-93 (may cite as "S.D.R.C. App.P. Rule __ ")

S.D. R. Civ. P. § 15-6-85 (shall cite as "RCP __ ")

Tennessee

Tenn. Code Ann. § 1-2-101(a) (cite as "Tenn. Code Ann. __ " or "T.C.A. __ ")

Tenn. Ct. App. R. 12 (citation of unpublished opinions)

Tenn. Ct. Crim. App. R. 19(4) (citation of unpublished opinions)

Tenn. R. App. P. 27(h) (citation of various types of legal authority)

Tenn. R. App. P. 47 (shall cite as "Tennessee Rule of Appellate Procedure __ ")

Tenn. R. Crim. P. 60 (shall cite as "Tenn. R. Crim. P. __ ")

Tenn. R. Juv. Prac. P. 101(a) (shall cite as "Tennessee Rule of Juvenile Practice and Procedure __ ")

Tenn. Sup. Ct. R. 1 (shall cite Supreme Court Rules as "T.R.A.P. __ " or "Tenn. R. App. P. __ ")

Tenn. Sup. Ct. R. 4(G) (citation of unpublished opinions)

Tenn. Sup. Ct. R. 8 (shall cite Rules of Professional Conduct as "Tenn. Sup. Ct. R. 8, RPC __ ")

Tenn. Sup. Ct. R. 28 § 12 (cite Tennessee Rules of Post-Conviction Procedure as "Tenn. Sup. Ct. R. 28, § __ ")

Texas

Tex. R. App. P. 47.7 (citation of unpublished opinions)

Tex. R. Civ. P. 822 (may cite as "Texas Rule of Civil Procedure __ ")

Tex. R. Ev. 101(a) (may cite as "Texas Rule of Evidence __ ")

<u>The Greenbook: Texas Rules of Form</u> (14th ed. 2018)

Utah

Utah Code Jud. Admin. R. 1-101(1)(E) (may cite as "CJA __ ")

Utah R. App. P. 30(f) (citation of opinions)

Utah R. Civ. P. 85 (may cite as "U.R.C.P. __ ")

Utah R. Crim. P. 37 (citation of opinions)

Utah R. Juv. P. 1(c) (may cite as "Utah R. Juv. P. __ ")

Vermont

Vt. Env't Ct. Proc. R. 7 (may cite as "Vermont Rule for Environmental Court Proceedings __ ")

> Vt. R. App. P. 1(d) (may cite as "Vermont Rule of Appellate Procedure __ " or "V.R.A.P. __ ")
>
> Vt. R. App. P. 28.2 (citation of opinions)
>
> Vt. R. Civ. P. 85 (may cite as "Vermont Rule of Civil Procedure __ ")
>
> Vt. R. Crim. P. 60 (may cite as "Vermont Rule of Criminal Procedure __ ")
>
> Vt. R. Evid. 1103 (may cite as "Vermont Rule of Evidence __ ")
>
> Vt. R. Prob. P. 85 (may cite as "Vermont Rule of Probate Procedure __ ")
>
> Vt. R. Small Cl. P. 14 (may cite as "Vermont Rule of Small Claims Procedure __ ")
>
> Vt. Stat. Ann. § 51 (cite as "__ V.S.A. § __ ")

Virginia

> Va. Sup. Ct. R. 5:1(b) (may cite generally as "Rules of the Supreme Court of Virginia" and specifically as "Rule 5: __ ")
>
> Va. Sup. Ct. R. 5:1(f) (citation of unpublished opinions)
>
> Va. Sup. Ct. R. 5A:1(b) (may cite generally as "Rules of the Court of Appeals of Virginia" and specifically as "Rule 5A: __ ")
>
> Va. Sup. Ct. R. 5A:1(f) (citation of unpublished opinions)

Washington

> Wash. Civ. R. Ct. Ltd. J. 85 (may cite as "Civil Rule for Courts of Limited Jurisdiction __ " or "CRLJ __ ")
>
> Wash. Crim. R. Ct. Ltd. J. 1.8 (may cite as "Criminal Rule for Courts of Limited Jurisdiction __ " or "CrRLJ __ ")
>
> Wash. Infraction R. Ct. Ltd. J. 6.3 (may cite as "Infraction Rule for Courts of Limited Jurisdiction __ " or "IRLJ __ ")
>
> Wash. R. App. P. 10.4(g) (citations shall conform with General Rule 14(d))
>
> Wash. R. App. P. 18.21 (may cite as "RAP __ ")
>
> Wash. R. App. Dec. Cts. Ltd. J. 11.9 (shall cite as "Rule for Appeal of Decisions of Courts of Limited Jurisdiction __ " or "RALJ __ ")
>
> Wash. R. Evid. 1103 (may cite as "Washington Rule of Evidence __ " or "ER __ ")
>
> Wash. R. Gen. Application 14 App. 1 (citations generally must follow The Bluebook, except various abbreviations listed in this rule)
>
> Wash. R. Gen. Application 14.1 (citation of unpublished opinions)
>
> Wash. Super. Ct. Civ. R. 85 (shall cite as "Superior Court Civil Rule __ " or "CR __ ")
>
> Wash. Super. Ct. Mandatory Arb. R. 8.4 (shall cite as "Superior Court Mandatory Arbitration Rule __ " or "MAR __ ")
>
> Wash. Super. Ct. Spec. P. R. Explanation (may cite as "SPR __ ")
>
> Wash. Juv. Ct. R. 11.21 (may cite as "JuCR __ ")
>
> Wash. Rev. Code Ann. § 1.04.040 (cite as "RCW __ ")
>
> Washington Courts Style Sheet (2018), https://www.courts.wa.gov /appellate_trial_courts/supreme/?fa=atc_supreme.style

West Virginia

- W. Va. R. App. P. 21(e) (citation of memorandum decisions)
- W. Va. R. App. P. 38(d) (citation of various types of legal authority)
- W. Va. R. Civ. P. 85 (may cite as "W. Va. R. Civ. P. __")
- W. Va. R. Crim. P. 60 (may cite as "W. Va. R. Crim. P. __")
- W. Va. R. Evid. 1102 (may cite as "West Virginia Rule of Evidence __" or "WVRE __")
- W. Va. Trial Ct. R. 6.04 (citation of various types of legal authority)

Wisconsin

- Wis. Stat. 809.19(1)(e) (cite authorities and the record as set forth in The Bluebook)
- Wis. Stat. 809.23(3) (citation of unpublished opinions)
- Wis. Stat. 911.02 (may cite chapters 901 to 911 as "Wisconsin Rule of Evidence __")
- Wis. Sup. Ct. R. 80.02 (citation of opinions)
- Wis. Sup. Ct. R. 99.03 (shall cite as "SCR __ (‹volume date›)")
- Wisconsin Guide to Citation (9th ed. 2018)

Wyoming

- Wyo. R. App. P. 28 (may cite as "W.R.A.P. __")
- Wyo. R. Civ. P. 85 (may cite as "W.R.C.P. __")
- Wyo. R. Civ. P. Cir. Ct. 11 (may cite as "W.R.C.P.C.C. __")
- Wyo. R. Crim. P. 60 (shall cite as "Wyoming Rule of Criminal Procedure __" or "W.R. Cr. P. __")
- Wyo. R. Evid. 1103 (may cite as "Wyoming Rule of Evidence __" or "W.R.E. __")
- Wyo. R.P. Juv. Ct. 1(a) (cite as "Rules of Procedure for Juvenile Courts __")
- Wyo. Unif. R. Cir. Ct. 1.01 (may cite as "U.R.C.C. __")
- Wyo. Unif. R. Dist. Ct. 100 (may cite as "Uniform Rule for District Courts of the State of Wyoming __" or "U.R.D.C. __")

....

Territories   BT2.3

Guam

- Guam Code Ann. tit. 1, § 101(b) (may cite as "__ GCA __")
- Guam R. App. P. 1 (may cite as "Guam Rule of Appellate Procedure __" or "GRAP __")
- Guam R. App. P. 27 (citation of unpublished opinions)
- Guam Super. Ct. Fam. Ct. R. (may cite as "Family Court Rule __")
- Guam Super. Ct. Gen. R. 1.1 (may cite as "GR __")
- Guam Super. Ct. Gen. R. 4.1 (citation shall be in the form found in the most recent version of The Bluebook)
- Guam Super. Ct. Traffic R. 1 (shall cite as "Superior Court of Guam Traffic Court Rule __")

Northern Mariana Islands

- N. Mar. I. R. Civ. P. <u>Table of Contents</u> (cite as "NMI R. Civ. P. __ ")
- N. Mar. I. R. Civ. P. 82.2 (citation of various types of legal authority)
- N. Mar. I. R. Crim. P. 59 (may cite as "Commonwealth Rule of Criminal Procedure __ " or "Com.R.Cr.P. __ ")
- N. Mar. I. R. Evid. 1103 (cite as "NMI R. Evid. __ ")
- N. Mar. I. R. Prac. (citation of slip opinions must include the designation "slip opinion" and the date filed)
- N. Mar. I. R. Prob. P. 28 (may cite as "The Commonwealth Rules of Probate Procedures __ " or "Com. R. Pro. __ ")
- N. Mar. I. R. Traffic P. 13 (may cite as "Commonwealth Rules of Traffic Procedure __ " or "Com. R. Traf. P. __ ")
- N. Mar. I. Sup. Ct. R. <u>Table of Contents</u> (cite as "NMI Sup. Ct. R. __ ")
- N. Mar. I. Sup. Ct. R. 13(c)(4) (citation to the record)
- N. Mar. I. Sup. Ct. R. 32.1 (citation of unpublished opinions)
- N. Mar. I. Tax R. Prac. P. 152 (citation of oral opinions)
- <u>Northern Mariana Islands Supreme Court Style Manual</u> (2017), http://cnmilaw.org/pdf/courtrules/R27.pdf

Puerto Rico

- P.R. Sup. Ct. R. 44(d) (citation of unpublished opinions)

Virgin Islands

- V.I. Code Ann. tit. 1, § 1(b) (may cite as "__ V.I.C. __ ")
- V.I. R. App. P. 1(a) (may cite as "V.I. R. App. P. __ ")
- V.I. R. App. P. 22(i) (citation of opinions)
- V.I. R. App. P. 15(b) (citations shall be according to <u>The Bluebook</u> and citation to the Supreme Court of the Virgin Islands must indicate it is a Supreme Court case)

STRUCTURE AND USE OF CITATIONS   1

Provide citations to authorities so that readers may identify and find those authorities for future research. Citations are made in citation sentences and clauses (**rule 1.1**) and are introduced by signals. Signals organize authorities and show how those authorities support or relate to a proposition given in the text (**rule 1.2**). Citation sentences and clauses may contain more than one signal. Order signals according to **rule 1.3**. Within each signal, arrange authorities according to **rule 1.4**. Parentheticals may be necessary to explain the relevance of a particular authority to the proposition given in the text (**rule 1.5**). Certain additional information, specific to that authority, may also be appended according to **rule 1.6**.

Citation Sentences and Clauses in Law Reviews   1.1

Citations may be made in one of two ways: in citation sentences or in citation clauses. In law review pieces, all citations appear in footnotes appended to the portions of the text to which they refer. For an explanation of citation sentences and clauses in practitioners' documents, see **Bluepages B1**.

(a) Text. Citations to authorities that support (or contradict) a proposition made in the main text (as opposed to footnote text) are placed in footnotes. A footnote call number should appear at the end of a textual sentence if the cited authority supports (or contradicts) the entire sentence. In contrast, a call number should appear within the sentence next to the portion it supports if the cited authority supports (or contradicts) only that part of the sentence. The call number comes after any punctuation mark—such as a comma, semicolon, or period—with the exception of a dash or a colon. In addition to citation to authorities, a footnote may include textual sentences that are related to the main text to which the footnote is appended.

> ▶ This is sentence one.[1] Sentence two contains two call numbers;[2] however, only one of these—this one[3]—is surprising. Recall one thing[4]: call numbers precede dashes and colons.

(b) Footnotes. If a footnote itself contains an assertion requiring support, a citation to the relevant authority should appear directly after the assertion as either a citation sentence or a citation clause.

(i) **Citation sentences.** Authorities that support (or contradict) an entire footnote sentence are cited in a separate citation sentence immediately after the sentence they support (or contradict). The citation sentence starts with a capital letter and ends with a period.

(ii) **Citation clauses.** Authorities that support (or contradict) only part of a sentence within a footnote are cited in clauses, set off by commas, that immediately follow the proposition they support (or contradict).

(c) Example. The following excerpt illustrates the use of citation sentences and clauses in a law review piece:

> ▶ Some American jurisdictions place the burden of sustaining criminal defenses on the accused.[1] States have required defendants to prove

both insanity[2] and self-defense.[3] In several jurisdictions the defendant must even establish that a homicide was accidental.[4]

▶ [1] *See* John Calvin Jeffries, Jr. & Paul B. Stephan III, *Defenses, Presumptions, and Burden of Proof in the Criminal Law*, 88 YALE L.J. 1325, 1329–30 (1979). The authors point out that the use of affirmative defenses may relieve the state of its duty to prove a sufficient factual basis for punishment, *id.* at 1357, and argue that the reasonable doubt standard should not be limited to those facts formally identified as elements of the offense charged, *id.* at 1327.

▶ [2] *E.g.*, State v. Caryl, 543 P.2d 389, 390 (Mont. 1975); State v. Hinson, 172 S.E.2d 548, 551 (S.C. 1970).

▶ [3] *See, e.g.*, Quillen v. State, 110 A.2d 445, 449 (Del. 1955); State v. Skinner, 104 P. 223, 224 (Nev. 1909). *See generally* WAYNE R. LAFAVE & AUSTIN W. SCOTT, JR., HANDBOOK ON CRIMINAL LAW § 8.1, at 704–06 (2d ed. 1986) (discussing the origin of embezzlement and false pretense).

▶ [4] *See, e.g.*, Chandle v. State, 198 S.E.2d 289, 290 (Ga. 1973); State v. Enlow, 536 S.W.2d 533, 541 (Mo. Ct. App. 1976).

1.2 Introductory Signals

(a) Signals that indicate support.

[no signal] Cited authority (i) directly states the proposition, (ii) identifies the source of a quotation, or (iii) identifies an authority referred to in the text. Use no signal, for example, when directly quoting an authority or when restating numerical data from an authority.

E.g., Cited authority states the proposition; other authorities also state the proposition, but citation to them would not be helpful or is not necessary. "*E.g.*," may be used alone or attached to any other signal (whether supportive or not). When it is attached to another signal, it should be preceded by an italicized comma and followed by a non-italicized comma.

See, e.g.,
But see, e.g.,

Accord "*Accord*" is commonly used when two or more sources state or clearly support the proposition, but the text quotes or refers to only one; the other sources are then introduced by "*accord*." Similarly, the law of one jurisdiction may be cited as being in accord with the law of another.

See Cited authority clearly supports the proposition. "*See*" is used instead of "[no signal]" when the proposition is not directly stated by the cited authority but obviously follows from it; there is an inferential step between the authority cited and the proposition it supports.

See also   Cited authority constitutes additional source material that supports the proposition. "*See also*" is commonly used to cite an authority supporting a proposition when authorities that state or directly support the proposition already have been cited or discussed. The use of a parenthetical explanation of the source's relevance (**rule 1.5**) following a citation introduced by "*see also*" is encouraged.

Cf.   Cited authority supports a proposition different from the main proposition but sufficiently analogous to lend support. Literally, "cf." means "compare." The citation's relevance will usually be clear to the reader only if it is explained. Parenthetical explanations (**rule 1.5**), however brief, are therefore strongly recommended.

(b) Signal that suggests a useful comparison.

Compare . . .
[and] . . .
with . . .
[and] . . .   Comparison of the authorities cited will offer support for or illustrate the proposition. When used as a signal, "*Compare*" must be used in conjunction with "*with*"; the "*with*" is preceded by a comma, as is "*and*" when used. The relevance of the comparison will usually be clear to the reader only if it is explained. Parenthetical explanations (**rule 1.5**) following each authority are therefore strongly recommended.

▶ *Compare* Michael H. v. Gerald D., 491 U.S. 110, 121 (1989) (plurality opinion) (rejecting the claim by a putative natural father of the right to visit his child conceived by a married woman), *and* CATHARINE A. MACKINNON, FEMINISM UNMODIFIED 49 (1987) (contending that what connects all women is their oppression in a sexual hierarchy), *with* Loving v. Virginia, 388 U.S. 1, 12 (1967) (invalidating laws prohibiting interracial marriage), Doe v. McConn, 489 F. Supp. 76, 80 (S.D. Tex. 1980) (holding a cross-dressing ordinance unconstitutional as applied to individuals undergoing therapy for sex-reassignment surgery), *and* Kenneth L. Karst, *The Freedom of Intimate Association*, 89 YALE L.J. 624, 631 (1980) ("The denial of the society of an intimate may be partial, as in the case of a parent who loses a contest over child custody but is allowed visitation rights, or virtually total, as when a noncustodial parent is denied visitation rights.").

(c) Signals that indicate contradiction.

Contra   Cited authority directly states the contrary of the proposition. "*Contra*" is used where "[no signal]" would be used for support.

But see   Cited authority clearly supports a proposition contrary to the main proposition. "*But see*" is used where "*see*" would be used for support.

But cf.   Cited authority supports a proposition analogous to the contrary of the main proposition. The use of a parenthetical explanation of the source's relevance (**rule 1.5**) following a citation introduced by "*but cf.*" is strongly recommended.

"*But*" should be omitted from "*but see*" and "*but cf.*" whenever one of these signals follows another negative signal:

▶ *Contra* Blake v. Kline, 612 F.2d 718, 723–24 (3d Cir. 1979); *see* CHARLES ALAN WRIGHT, LAW OF FEDERAL COURTS (STUDENTS EDITION) § 48 (4th ed. 1983).

(d) Signal that indicates background material.

See generally	Cited authority presents helpful background material related to the proposition. The use of a parenthetical explanation of the source material's relevance (**rule 1.5**) following each authority introduced by "*see generally*" is encouraged.

(e) Signals as verbs. In footnotes, signals may be used as the verbs of textual sentences. When using signals in this way, include material that would otherwise be included in a parenthetical explanation as part of the sentence itself. Signals should not be italicized when used as verbs in textual sentences (**rule 2.1(d)**).

Thus:

▶ *See* Christina L. Anderson, Comment, *Double Jeopardy: The Modern Dilemma for Juvenile Justice*, 152 U. PA. L. REV. 1181, 1204–07 (2004) (discussing four main types of restorative justice programs).

becomes:

▶ See Christina L. Anderson, Comment, *Double Jeopardy: The Modern Dilemma for Juvenile Justice*, 152 U. PA. L. REV. 1181, 1204–07 (2004), for a discussion of restorative justice as a reasonable replacement for retributive sanctions.

"*Cf.*" becomes "compare" and "*e.g.*" becomes "for example" when used in this manner.

1.3   Order of Signals

When more than one signal is used, the signals (along with the authorities they introduce) should appear in the order in which those signals are listed in **rule 1.2**. When "*e.g.*," is used in conjunction with another signal, the other signal's position in **rule 1.2** should be used. Signals of the same basic type—supportive, comparative, contradictory, or background (**rule 1.2(a)–(d)**)—must be strung together within a single citation sentence and separated by semicolons. Signals of different types, however, must be grouped in different citation sentences. For example:

▶ *See* Mass. Bd. of Ret. v. Murgia, 427 U.S. 307 (1976) (per curiam); *cf.* Palmer v. Ticcione, 433 F. Supp. 653 (E.D.N.Y. 1977) (upholding a mandatory retirement age for kindergarten teachers). *But see, e.g.,* Gault v. Garrison, 569 F.2d 993 (7th Cir. 1977) (holding that a classification of public school teachers based on age violated equal protection absent a showing of justifiable and rational state purpose). *See generally* Comment, O'Neil v. Baine: *Application of Middle-Level Scrutiny to Old-Age Classifications*, 127 U. PA. L. REV. 798 (1979) (advocating a new constitutional approach to old-age classifications).

Within a citation clause (**rule 1.1**), however, citation strings may contain signals of more than one type, separated by semicolons.

Order of Authorities Within Each Signal 1.4

Authorities within each signal are separated by semicolons.

Authorities should be ordered in a logical manner. If one authority or several authorities together are considerably more helpful or authoritative than the other authorities cited within a signal, they should precede the others.

Authorities cited in short form are ordered as though cited in full.

Parenthetical Information 1.5

(a) Substantive information. Use parentheticals, as needed, to explain the relevance of a particular authority to the proposition given in the text. Parenthetical information is recommended when the relevance of a cited authority might not otherwise be clear to the reader (see **rule 1.2**). Explanatory information takes the form of a present participial phrase, a quoted sentence, or a short statement that is appropriate in context.

(i) **Phrases not quoting the authority.** Explanatory parenthetical phrases not directly quoting the authority usually begin with a present participle and should never begin with a capital letter:

> ▶ *See generally* Akhil Reed Amar, *Reports of My Death Are Greatly Exaggerated: A Reply*, 138 U. PA. L. REV. 1651 (1990) (arguing that the author and the two-tier theory of federal jurisdiction are still viable).

When a complete participial phrase is unnecessary in context, a shorter parenthetical may be substituted:

> ▶ Such standards have been adopted to address a variety of environmental problems. *See, e.g.*, H.B. Jacobini, *The New International Sanitary Regulations*, 46 AM. J. INT'L L. 727, 727–28 (1952) (health-related water quality); Robert L. Meyer, Travaux Préparatoires *for the UNESCO World Heritage Convention*, 2 EARTH L.J. 45, 45–81 (1976) (conservation of protected areas).

You may omit extraneous words such as "the" unless doing so would cause confusion.

(ii) **Phrases quoting the authority.** If, however, the parenthetical information quotes one or more full sentences or a portion of material that reads as a full sentence, it should begin with a capital letter and include appropriate closing punctuation. Indicate any omissions in the quoted text according to **rule 5.3(b)**.

> ▶ 3 *Consequences of Changing U.S. Population: Hearing Before the H. Select Comm. on Population*, 95th Cong. 11 (1978) (statement of Dr. David Birch) ("[T]here are more mayors of Rockville, Maryland, than there are mayors of Detroit.").

> ▶ Mari J. Matsuda, *Public Response to Racist Speech: Considering the Victim's Story*, 87 MICH. L. REV. 2320, 2381 (1989) ("We are a legalized culture. If law is where racism is, then law is where we must confront it . . . . [L]et us present a competing ideology . . . .").

Not: Mari J. Matsuda, *Public Response to Racist Speech: Considering the Victim's Story*, 87 MICH. L. REV. 2320, 2381 (1989) (explaining that "[w]e are a legalized culture. If law is where racism is, then law is where we must confront it . . . . [L]et us present a competing ideology . . . .").

When directly quoting only a short phrase from an authority, follow **rule 1.5 (a)(i)**:

▶ *But see* Flanagan v. United States, 465 U.S. 259, 264 (1984) (explaining that the final judgment rule reduces the potential for parties to "clog the courts" with a succession of time-consuming appeals).

(b) Order of parentheticals within a citation. When a citation requires multiple parentheticals, place them in the following order:

▶ (date) [hereinafter short name] (en banc) (Lastname, J., concurring) (plurality opinion) (per curiam) (alteration in original) (emphasis added) (footnote omitted) (citations omitted) (quoting another source) (citing another source), http://www.domainname.com (last visited) (explanatory parenthetical), prior or subsequent history.

In citations to online sources that share the characteristics of a print source such that they could be cited according to **rule 18.2.1(b)(ii)**, the URL should immediately precede the explanatory parenthetical.

In citations to online and internet sources that utilize archival tools, the archival link should immediately follow the URL (**rule 18.2.1(d)**).

Note that explanatory parentheticals precede any citation of subsequent history or other related authority (**rule 1.6**):

▶ Atl. Richfield Co. v. Fed. Energy Admin., 429 F. Supp. 1052, 1061–62 (N.D. Cal. 1976) ("[N]ot every person aggrieved by administrative action is necessarily entitled to the protections of due process."), *aff'd*, 556 F.2d 542 (Temp. Emer. Ct. App. 1977).

▶ Louis Loss, *The Conflict of Laws and the Blue Sky Laws*, 71 HARV. L. REV. 209 (1957) (discussing the bewildering array of state laws then governing interstate securities transactions), *reprinted in* LOUIS LOSS & EDWARD M. COWETT, BLUE SKY LAW 180 (1958).

If the material cited quotes or cites two or more different sources, include all sources in the order in which they were cited within one quoting or citing parenthetical. For two sources, use the format "first . . .; and then . . ."; for three or more sources, use "first . . .; then . . .; and then . . ." such that "and then" is always used for the last source.

▶ Duncan v. Louisiana, 391 U.S. 145, 148–49 (1968) (footnote omitted) (first quoting Powell v. Alabama, 287 U.S. 45, 67 (1932); then quoting *In re* Oliver, 333 U.S. 257, 273 (1948); and then quoting Gideon v. Wainwright, 372 U.S. 335, 343–44 (1963)).

Related Authority   1.6

When citing a work, citations to related authorities may be helpful to aid in locating the primary work or to provide relevant information not reflected in the primary citation. Citations to related authority may be appended to the primary citation with the use of an italicized explanatory phrase.

(a) Related authority intended to increase access.

(i) **"In."** When citing a shorter work such as an article, essay, or speech originally published in a volume collecting such works, use "*in*" to introduce the collection as a whole (see **rule 15.5**):

> ▶ Kay Deaux & Brenda Major, *A Social-Psychological Model of Gender*, *in* THEORETICAL PERSPECTIVES ON SEXUAL DIFFERENCES 89, 93 (Deborah L. Rhode ed., 1992).

(ii) **"Reprinted in."** A work that conveniently reprints a source originally published elsewhere may be introduced by "*reprinted in*." As far as possible, provide a complete citation for the original work, followed by "*reprinted in*" and the citation for the volume containing the reprint (see **rule 15.5.2**):

> ▶ Louis Loss, *The Conflict of Laws and the Blue Sky Laws*, 71 HARV. L. REV. 209 (1957), *reprinted in* LOUIS LOSS & EDWARD M. COWETT, BLUE SKY LAW 180 (1958).

> ▶ Thomas Jefferson, Kentucky Resolutions of 1798 and 1799, *reprinted in* 4 THE DEBATES IN THE SEVERAL STATE CONVENTIONS ON THE ADOPTION OF THE FEDERAL CONSTITUTION 540 (Jonathan Elliot ed., 2d ed., Philadelphia, J.B. Lippincott 1888).

To indicate excerpts or partial reprints, add the word "*as*":

> ▶ S. REP. NO. 95-181, at 14 (1977), *as reprinted in* 1977 U.S.C.C.A.N. 3401, 3414.

(iii) **Other phrases.** Other phrases may be used by analogy to **rule 1.6(a)(i)** and **(ii)**, as appropriate (e.g., "*microformed on*" (see **rule 18.5.1**), or "*translated in*" (see **rule 20.2.5**)).

(b) Relevant history. The prior or subsequent history of a case (**rule 10.7**) or of a statute (**rule 12.7**) may be appended to the main citation for that case or statute. See **rules 10.7** and **12.7** for circumstances in which the subsequent history of a case or statute *must* be indicated:

> ▶ Matthews v. Konieczny, 488 A.2d 5 (Pa. Super. Ct. 1985), *rev'd*, 527 A.2d 508 (Pa. 1987).

(c) Commentary. Works that discuss or quote the primary authority may also be appended to the citation without parentheses as related authorities when particularly relevant or when locating the original source may be difficult. Use italicized phrases such as "*noted in*," "*construed in*," "*quoted in*," "*reviewed by*," "*cited with approval in*," and "*questioned in*" to introduce these works. Works that the primary authority discusses, cites, or otherwise mentions, however, should be indicated parenthetically. Thus:

▶ Filled Milk Act § 1, 21 U.S.C. § 61, *construed in* Milnot Co. v. Richardson, 350 F. Supp. 221 (N.D. Ill. 1972).

But: Milnot Co. v. Richardson, 350 F. Supp. 221 (N.D. Ill. 1972) (construing Filled Milk Act § 1, 21 U.S.C. § 61).

2   TYPEFACES FOR LAW REVIEWS

Legal writing uses four typefaces, though choice of font may vary (e.g., Times New Roman, Courier, etc.):

▶ Ordinary Roman (Plain Text)
▶ <u>Underlined</u>
▶ *Italicized*
▶ LARGE AND SMALL CAPITALS

Law reviews use two sets of typeface conventions—one for law review text (either main text or footnote text) (**rule 2.2**) and one for law review citations (**rule 2.1**). Unless otherwise noted, the examples in *The Bluebook* correspond to the convention for law review footnotes.

For an explanation of the typeface conventions commonly used in other forms of legal writing, see **Bluepages B2**. Practitioners can make ready use of the examples in *The Bluebook* by substituting the typeface conventions outlined in the **Bluepages** for those found in the examples throughout the rest of the book.

For example, a practitioner's brief might look like this:

▶ Directors manage the business and affairs of a corporation. <u>See Revlon, Inc. v. MacAndrews & Forbes Holdings, Inc.</u>, 506 A.2d 173, 179 (Del. 1986); <u>see also</u> Del. Code Ann. tit. 8, § 141(a) (2000). In <u>Guth v. Loft</u>, the court held that directors also owe a duty of loyalty to the shareholders. 5 A.2d 503, 510 (Del. 1939) (holding that directors' duty of loyalty demands that "there shall be no conflict between duty and self-interest").

A similar section of a law review article might read:

▶ Directors manage the business and affairs of a corporation.[1] In *Guth v. Loft*, the court held that directors also owe a duty of loyalty to the shareholders.[2]

▶ [1] *See* Revlon, Inc. v. MacAndrews & Forbes Holdings, Inc., 506 A.2d 173, 179 (Del. 1986); *see also* DEL. CODE ANN. tit. 8, § 141(a) (2000).

▶ [2] 5 A.2d 503, 510 (Del. 1939) (holding that directors' duty of loyalty demands that "there shall be no conflict between duty and self-interest").

For additional guidance, see **rule 2.1, rule 2.2**, and **Bluepages B2**.

Typeface Conventions for Citations 2.1

Most law reviews use three different typefaces in citations:

> ► Ordinary Roman (Plain Text), *Italics*, and LARGE AND SMALL CAPITALS

Some replace large and small capitals with ordinary roman type. Thus:

> ► Colin S. Diver, *The Optimal Precision of Administrative Rules*, 93 YALE L.J. 65 (1983).

becomes:

> ► Colin S. Diver, *The Optimal Precision of Administrative Rules*, 93 Yale L.J. 65 (1983).

Other law reviews replace some italics, as well as all large and small capitals, with ordinary roman type:

> ► Colin S. Diver, The Optimal Precision of Administrative Rules, 93 Yale L.J. 65 (1983).

The examples in this book follow the first convention, using all three typefaces. The following list explains the more important typeface conventions used in law review citations:

(a) Case names (rules 10.2, 14.3.1, 20.3, 21.5, and 21.6). Use ordinary roman type for case names in full citations, except for procedural phrases, which are always italicized:

> ► Lochner v. New York, 198 U.S. 45 (1905).

> ► State *ex rel.* Scott v. Zinn, 392 P.2d 417 (N.M. 1964).

When a case name appears within an article title in a citation, do not italicize it:

> ► Thomas J. Madden et al., *Bedtime for* Bivens*: Substituting the United States as Defendant in Constitutional Tort Suits*, 20 HARV. J. ON LEGIS. 469 (1983).

Use italics for the short form of case citations:

> ► *Lochner*, 198 U.S. at 50.

(b) Books (rule 15). Use large and small capitals for both authors and titles:

> ► RICHARD KLUGER, SIMPLE JUSTICE (1976).

(c) Periodicals (rule 16). Italicize article titles and use large and small capitals for periodical names. Authors' names should appear in ordinary roman type:

> ► Katherine K. Baker, *Once a Rapist? Motivational Evidence and Relevancy in Rape Law*, 110 HARV. L. REV. 563 (1997).

> ► Cass R. Sunstein, Lochner*'s Legacy*, 87 COLUM. L. REV. 873 (1987).

> ► David E. Bernstein, Lochner*'s Legacy's Legacy*, 92 TEX. L. REV. 1 (2003).

(d) Introductory signals (rule 1.2). Italicize all introductory signals when they appear within citation sentences or clauses:

▶ *See, e.g.*, Parker Drilling Co. v. Ferguson, 391 F.2d 581 (5th Cir. 1968).

Do not, however, italicize a signal word when it serves as the verb of an ordinary sentence (**rule 1.2(e)**):

▶ For an analysis of risk-allocation rules under the UCC, see Note, *Risk of Loss in Commercial Transactions: Efficiency Thrown into the Breach*, 65 VA. L. REV. 557, 563–72 (1979).

(e) Explanatory phrases (rules 1.6, 10.7, and 12.8). Italicize all explanatory phrases:

▶ Oreck Corp. v. Whirlpool Corp., 579 F.2d 126, 131 (2d Cir.) (en banc), *cert. denied*, 439 U.S. 946 (1978).

Note, however, that phrases in related authority parentheticals, such as "(quoting …)," "(citing …)," and "(translating …)" are not italicized.

(f) Punctuation. Italicize commas, semicolons, and other punctuation marks only when they constitute part of the italicized material, and not when they are merely an element of the sentence or citation in which they appear. For clarity, the italicized items in the examples below appear in blue:

▶ *See, e.g.*, *id.*; Sabine Towing & Transp. Co. v. Zapata Ugland Drilling, Inc. (*In re* M/V Vulcan), 553 F.2d 489 (5th Cir.) (per curiam), *cert. denied*, 434 U.S. 855 (1977).

▶ Nancy Reagan, Editorial, *Just Say "Whoa,"* WALL ST. J., Jan. 23, 1996, at A14.

2.2   Typeface Conventions for Textual Material

(a) Main text. The main text of law review pieces does not contain citations and uses only ordinary roman type and italics. Most material appears in ordinary roman type. Only the following are italicized:

(i) **Case names.** Italicize case names, including the "*v.*" and all procedural phrases such as "*In re*" and "*ex rel.*":

▶ *Missouri ex rel. Gaines v. Canada*

(ii) **Titles of publications, speeches, or articles.** Thus:

▶ The library has a copy of *The Path of the Law*, which was published in the *Harvard Law Review*; a complete set of the *Federal Supplement*; and today's *Wall Street Journal*. It does not have a copy of *Hearings on S. 776* or *Alaska Statutes*.

(iii) **Style.** Italicize words for emphasis or other stylistic purposes (**rule 7**). Also italicize words that are emphasized in quoted matter (**rule 5.2**).

(b) Footnote text. Unlike in the main text, a sentence in footnote text may contain citations, which are placed in citation clauses embedded in the sentence (**rule 1.1(b)**).

(i) **Case names.** When a case name is grammatically part of the sentence in which it appears, it should be italicized:

> ▶ In *Loving v. Virginia*, the Court invalidated Virginia's antimiscegena-
> tion statute.

> ▶ In *Loving v. Virginia*, 388 U.S. 1 (1967), the Court invalidated Virginia's
> antimiscegenation statute.

When the case name is not grammatically part of the sentence, but rather used in a citation clause embedded in the footnote text, use the typeface conventions for citations (**rule 2.1(a)**):

> ▶ The Court has upheld race-specific statutes that disadvantage a racial
> minority, *e.g.*, Korematsu v. United States, 323 U.S. 214 (1944), but
> those decisions have been severely criticized.

> ▶ Justice Harlan quipped that "one man's vulgarity is another's lyric,"
> *Cohen*, 403 U.S. at 25, but failed to provide further explanation.

(ii) **All other authorities.** When referring to any other type of authority, whether or not the reference is grammatically part of the sentence, use the typeface conventions for citations if the full citation or a short form citation (**rule 4**) is given:

> ▶ A different view is expressed in LEARNED HAND, THE BILL OF RIGHTS
> (1958), and HOLMES, *supra* note 2.

If the reference appears without the full or shortened citation information, follow the typeface conventions for the main text of law reviews (**rule 2.2(a) (ii)**):

> ▶ Judge Hand explained his philosophy of judicial review in *The Bill of
> Rights*.

(iii) **Explanatory parentheticals.** In explanatory parentheticals, follow the typeface convention for case names in citation text when a full citation clause is included:

> ▶ Nat'l R.R. Passenger Corp. v. Morgan, 536 U.S. 101, 110 (2002) (citing
> Chevron U.S.A. Inc. v. Nat. Res. Def. Council, Inc., 467 U.S. 837 (1984)).

> ▶ Nat'l R.R. Passenger Corp. v. Morgan, 536 U.S. 101, 110 (2002)
> (addressing an argument based upon Chevron U.S.A. Inc. v. Nat. Res.
> Def. Council, Inc., 467 U.S. 837 (1984)).

> ▶ Nat'l R.R. Passenger Corp. v. Morgan, 536 U.S. 101, 110 (2002)
> (addressing an argument based upon *Chevron*).

(c) Punctuation. Italicize commas, semicolons, etc., only when they constitute part of italicized material, and not when they are merely an element of the citation or sentence in which they appear. For purposes of clarity, the italicized punctuation marks in the examples below appear in blue:

> ▶ When it decided *Sabine Towing*, the Fifth Circuit presented a some-
> what different rationale for its holding.

> ▶ Brannon Denning's article, *Reforming the New Confirmation Process: Replacing "Despise and Resent" with "Advise and Consent,"* suggests amendments to the Senate's procedural rules.

Not: Brannon Denning's article, *Reforming the New Confirmation Process: Replacing "Despise and Resent" with "Advise and Consent,"* suggests amendments to the Senate's procedural rules.

3 SUBDIVISIONS

Most subdivisions (such as columns or sections) in citations are abbreviated. See **table T16** for a list of subdivision abbreviations.

3.1 Volumes, Parts, and Supplements

A single work often appears in separately paginated (or sectioned or paragraphed) volumes, parts, or supplements. A citation to material that appears in one such volume, part, or supplement must identify the separately paginated subdivision in which the material appears.

(a) Volumes. When the volumes are numbered, cite the volume number in Arabic numerals. If the author of the entire work (all volumes) is cited, the volume number precedes the author's name:

> ▶ 2 FREDERICK POLLOCK & FREDERIC WILLIAM MAITLAND, THE HISTORY OF ENGLISH LAW 205–06 (2d ed. 1911).

> ▶ 2 SUBCOMM. ON LAB. OF THE S. COMM. ON LAB. & PUB. WELFARE, 92D CONG., LEGISLATIVE HISTORY OF THE EQUAL EMPLOYMENT OPPORTUNITY ACT OF 1972, at 1007 (1972).

Otherwise, the volume number precedes the volume's title:

> ▶ Donald H. Zeigler, *Young Adults as a Cognizable Group in Jury Selection*, 76 MICH. L. REV. 1045, 1047 (1978).

If no volume number is given but the volume is readily identifiable by year, use the year of the volume as the volume number and omit the year after the pincite:

> ▶ Thomas R. McCoy & Barry Friedman, *Conditional Spending: Federalism's Trojan Horse*, 1988 SUP. CT. REV. 85, 88.

> ▶ Donald A. Dripps, *Delegation and Due Process*, 1988 DUKE L.J. 657.

If the volume designation includes words, use brackets to avoid confusion:

> ▶ [1977–1978 Transfer Binder] Bankr. L. Rep. (CCH) ¶ 66,472

If volumes are numbered in a new series each year, give both the year and volume number, bracketing the year and placing it before the volume number to avoid confusion:

> ▶ [1943] 2 K.B. 154

(b) Separately paginated numbered parts. When a work is divided into separately paginated (or sectioned or paragraphed) series, books, chapters, or other parts, include the relevant subdivisions in the citation:

- ▶ 26 CONG. REC. app. at 156 (1894) (statement of Rep. Hicks).

- ▶ ser. 14, pt. 2, at 150

- ▶ pt. 3, § 4, at 15

(c) Supplements. When citing a separately paginated (or sectioned or paragraphed) supplement, identify the supplement and its date in parentheses:

- ▶ HAW. REV. STAT. § 296-46.1 (Supp. 1984).

- ▶ GEORGE GLEASON BOGERT, THE LAW OF TRUSTS AND TRUSTEES § 496 (rev. 2d ed. Supp. 1985).

To cite both the main volume and the supplement, use an ampersand:

- ▶ 42 U.S.C. § 1397b (1982 & Supp. I 1983).

Pages, Footnotes, Endnotes, and Graphical Materials 3.2

(a) Pages. Give the page number or numbers before the date parenthetical, without any introductory abbreviation ("p." and "pp." are used only in internal cross-references (**rule 3.5**)):

- ▶ ARTHUR E. SUTHERLAND, CONSTITUTIONALISM IN AMERICA 45 (1965).

- ▶ H.R. REP. NO. 82-353, at 4–5 (1951).

Use "at" if the page number may be confused with another part of the citation; use a comma to set off "at." Use this form, for example, when the title of a work ends with an Arabic numeral or when the work uses Roman numerals for pagination:

- ▶ BIOGRAPHICAL DIRECTORY OF THE GOVERNORS OF THE UNITED STATES 1978–1983, at 257 (Robert Sobel & John W. Raimo eds., 1983).

- ▶ Thomas I. Emerson, *Foreword* to CATHARINE A. MACKINNON, SEXUAL HARASSMENT OF WORKING WOMEN, at vii, ix (1979).

If an article, case, or other source within a larger source is not separately paginated, cite the page on which the item begins:

- ▶ Bernard L. Diamond, *The Psychiatric Prediction of Dangerousness*, 123 U. PA. L. REV. 439 (1974).

- ▶ United States v. Bruno, 144 F. Supp. 593 (N.D. Ill. 1955).

- ▶ Government Employees Training Act, Pub. L. No. 85-507, 72 Stat. 327 (1958).

When referring to specific material within such a source, include both the page on which the source begins and the page on which the specific material appears (a pincite), separated by a comma:

▶ Matthew Roskoski, Note, *A Case-by-Case Approach to Pleading Scienter Under the Private Securities Litigation Reform Act of 1995*, 97 MICH. L. REV. 2265, 2271–75 (1999).

▶ CATHARINE A. MACKINNON, *On Exceptionality: Women as Women in Law*, *in* FEMINISM UNMODIFIED 70, 76–77 (1987).

When referring specifically to material on the first page of a source, repeat the page number:

▶ Christina M. Fernández, Note, *Beyond* Marvin: *A Proposal for Quasi-Spousal Support*, 30 STAN. L. REV. 359, 359 (1978).

When citing material within a concurring or dissenting opinion, give only the initial page of the case and the page on which the specific material appears, not the initial page of the concurring or dissenting opinion:

▶ Baker v. Carr, 369 U.S. 186, 297 (1962) (Frankfurter, J., dissenting).

When citing material that spans more than one page, give the inclusive page numbers, separated by an en dash (–) or hyphen (-). Always retain the last two digits, but drop other repetitious digits:

▶ Edward L. Rubin, Note, *Fairness, Flexibility, and the Waiver of Remedial Rights by Contract*, 87 YALE L.J. 1057, 1065–69 (1978).

If a hyphen or dash would be ambiguous because of the page numbering system, use the word "to":

▶ BORIS I. BITTKER & JAMES S. EUSTICE, FEDERAL INCOME TAXATION OF CORPORATIONS AND SHAREHOLDERS ¶ 5.06, at 5-31 to -32 (5th abr. ed. 1987).

Cite nonconsecutive pages by giving the individual page numbers separated by commas:

▶ Kleppe v. New Mexico, 426 U.S. 529, 531, 546 (1976).

If a source uses star paging (such as "*3"), drop the star in the ending page number of a page range, but keep the star in all references to nonconsecutive pages:

▶ 2 WILLIAM BLACKSTONE, COMMENTARIES *152, *155–56.

When a point is often repeated throughout the entire source, use "*passim*" rather than citing specific pages. Do not insert a comma after the initial page number:

▶ Linda S. Mullenix, *The Constitutionality of the Proposed Rule 23 Class Action Amendments*, 39 ARIZ. L. REV. 615 *passim* (1997).

(b) Footnotes. To cite a footnote, give the page on which the footnote appears, "n.," and the footnote number, with no space between "n." and the number:

▶ Akhil Reed Amar, *The Two-Tiered Structure of the Judiciary Act of 1789*, 138 U. PA. L. REV. 1499, 1525 n.80 (1990).

To cite a footnote that spans more than one page, cite only the page on which the footnote begins, "n.," and the footnote number:

> ▶ Akhil Reed Amar, *The Two-Tiered Structure of the Judiciary Act of 1789*, 138 U. Pa. L. Rev. 1499, 1560 n.222 (1990).

When referring only to specific pages of a footnote that spans more than one page, cite only the specific pages, rather than the page on which the footnote begins:

> ▶ Akhil Reed Amar, *The Two-Tiered Structure of the Judiciary Act of 1789*, 138 U. Pa. L. Rev. 1499, 1561–62 n.222 (1990).

To cite both a range of pages and also a single footnote that appears within the page range, cite the page range followed by a comma and then cite the footnote in the typical manner:

> ▶ Akhil Reed Amar, *The Two-Tiered Structure of the Judiciary Act of 1789*, 138 U. Pa. L. Rev 1499, 1523–24, 1524 n.75 (1990).

Cite multiple footnotes (or endnotes) by using "nn.":

> ▶ 141 nn.180–86

Treat nonconsecutive footnotes (or endnotes) like nonconsecutive pages, but (except for internal cross-references) substitute an ampersand for the comma separating two footnotes that appear on the same page or the final comma in a list of three or more footnotes that appear on the same page:

> ▶ 350 n.12, 355 n.18

> ▶ 291 nn.14 & 18, 316 nn.4, 6 & 8–9

To refer to both a page in the text and a footnote that begins on that page, use an ampersand between the page and the note number:

> ▶ Irene Merker Rosenberg, Essay, Winship *Redux: 1970 to 1990*, 69 Tex. L. Rev. 109, 123 & n.90 (1990).

(c) Endnotes. To cite an endnote, give the page on which the endnote appears (not the page on which the call number appears), "n.," and the endnote number, with no space between "n." and the number:

> ▶ John Hart Ely, Democracy and Distrust 215 n.85 (1980).

To refer to both a page in the text and an endnote that has a call appearing on that page, use an ampersand between the text page and the page on which the endnote appears. In the following example, the cited text is on p. 61 and the endnote is on p. 215:

> ▶ John Hart Ely, Democracy and Distrust 61 & 215 n.85 (1980).

Otherwise, cite endnotes in the same manner as footnotes.

(d) Graphical materials. When citing tables, figures, charts, graphs, or other graphical materials, give the page number on which the graphical material appears and the designation, if any, provided in the source, with no space between the abbreviation and the number. Use the abbreviations in **table T16**. For photographs and "art-type" objects, see **rule 18.8**:

> ▶ Kevin M. Clermont & Theodore Eisenberg, Commentary, *Xenophilia in American Courts*, 109 Harv. L. Rev. 1120, 1131 tbl.2 (1996).

To refer to multiple charts, tables, figures, etc., on the same page, pluralize the abbreviated designation according to **table T16**. Use commas and ampersands, not en dashes, to separate:

▶ 9 figs.3 & 4

▶ 1236 tbls.1, 2 & 3

3.3 Sections and Paragraphs

If an authority is organized by section (§) or paragraph (¶), cite to those subdivisions:

▶ 15 U.S.C. § 18 (1982).

▶ 6 JAMES WM. MOORE ET AL., MOORE'S FEDERAL PRACTICE ¶ 56.07 (3d ed. 1997).

A page number may also be provided if useful in locating specific matter within the section or paragraph:

▶ LAURENCE H. TRIBE, AMERICAN CONSTITUTIONAL LAW § 15-4, at 1314, § 15-6, at 1320 (2d ed. 1988).

If an authority is organized in part by indented paragraphs not introduced by paragraph symbols (¶), do not cite such paragraphs with the symbol. Instead use the written abbreviation (para.):

▶ THE DECLARATION OF INDEPENDENCE para. 2 (U.S. 1776).

Do not cite indented paragraphs if the authority is ordinarily cited by page:

▶ *Mandela Trial Scheduled Today*, USA TODAY, Feb. 4, 1991, at A4.

Do not use "at" before a section or paragraph symbol:

▶ *Id.* § 7.

Not: *Id.* at § 7.

▶ MOORE ET AL., *supra* note 5, ¶ 56.07.

Not: MOORE ET AL., *supra* note 5, at ¶ 56.07.

Rule 6.2(c) discusses the use of section and paragraph symbols.

To cite session laws amending prior acts that are divided into sections within sections, see **rule 12.4(d)**.

(a) Subsections. If the source contains punctuation separating sections from subsections, use the original punctuation:

▶ N.M. STAT. ANN. § 4-44-7(G) (1983).

Not: N.M. STAT. ANN. § 4(44)(7)(G) (1983).

If the source contains no such separating punctuation, separate the subsection designations using parentheses, not decimals, hyphens, or other marks. Thus, place "1" and "a" in parentheses ("(1)" and "(a)").

(b) Multiple sections and subsections. When citing multiple sections, use two section symbols (§§). Give inclusive numbers; do not use "*et seq.*" Identical digits or letters preceding a punctuation mark may be omitted, unless doing so would create confusion. Otherwise retain all digits.

▶ WASH. REV. CODE ANN. §§ 18.51.005–.52.900 (West 1989 & Supp. 1991).

▶ DEL. CODE ANN. tit. 9, §§ 817–819 (1989).

Note that letters are sometimes used to designate sections, rather than subsections, and that section designations may contain punctuation within them:

▶ 42 U.S.C. §§ 1396a–1396d.

If an en dash or hyphen would be ambiguous, use the word "to":

▶ 42 U.S.C. §§ 1973aa-2 to -4.
▶ MONT. CODE ANN. §§ 75-1-301 to -324 (1989).

When citing scattered sections, separate the sections with commas:

▶ N.J. STAT. ANN. §§ 18A:54-1, -3, -6 (West 1989).

Repeat digits if necessary to avoid confusion:

▶ N.J. STAT. ANN. §§ 18A:58-17, :58-25, :64A-22.1, :64A-22.6 (West 1989).

When citing multiple subsections within a *single* section, use only one section symbol:

▶ 28 U.S.C. § 105(a)(3)–(b)(1).
▶ 19 U.S.C. § 1485(a)(1)–(3).
▶ DEL. CODE ANN. tit. 9, § 6910(a), (c) (1989).

But when citing multiple subsections within *different* sections, use two section symbols:

▶ 19 U.S.C. §§ 1485(a), 1486(b).

(c) Multiple paragraphs. Multiple paragraphs should be treated like multiple sections, following **rule 3.3(b)**:

▶ 1 BLUE SKY L. REP. (CCH) ¶¶ 4471–4474.
▶ MOORE ET AL., *supra* note 5, ¶¶ 54.32–.35.

(d) Flush language and examples. When the source is organized by section or paragraph, but the text being cited is flush language or an example, indicate this fact in a parenthetical immediately following the section or paragraph identifier, as follows:

▶ I.R.C. § 960(c) (flush language).
▶ Treas. Reg. § 1.704-2(m) (example 1(ii)).

Appended Material 3.4

Indicate an appendix or appended note or comment by placing the appropriate abbreviation (see **table T16**) after the citation to the largest full subdivision to which the item is appended, whether page, section, paragraph, chapter, title, or volume:

▶ James Edwin Kee & Terrence A. Moan, Comment, *The Property Tax and Tenant Equality*, 89 HARV. L. REV. 531 app. (1976).

▶ RESTATEMENT (SECOND) OF TORTS § 623A cmt. a (AM. L. INST. 1977).

Cite a particular page, section, or other subdivision in an appendix as follows:

▶ 50 U.S.C. app. § 454.

▶ Samuel Issacharoff & George Loewenstein, *Second Thoughts About Summary Judgment*, 100 YALE L.J. 73 app. at 124–25 (1990).

Other types of appended material that serve as commentary on the material to which they are appended, or that further discuss a point related to the textual discussion, should be cited as notes or appendices:

▶ FED. R. CIV. P. 60(b) advisory committee's note to 1946 amendment.

▶ RESTATEMENT (SECOND) OF PROP. § 2.1 cmt. c, illus. 2 (AM. L. INST. 1977).

Further information necessary to identify which of several named notes is cited may be added parenthetically:

▶ 42 U.S.C. § 1862 note (Denial of Financial Assistance to Campus Disrupters).

▶ N.Y. BUS. CORP. LAW § 624 note (McKinney 1963) (Legislative Studies and Reports).

Appendices that reprint materials normally cited to another source should be cited according to **rule 1.6(a)**:

▶ An Act for the Prevention of Frauds and Perjuries, 1677, 29 Car. 2, c. 2, § 17 (Eng.), *reprinted in* JOHN P. DAWSON, WILLIAM BURNETT HARVEY & STANLEY D. HENDERSON, CASES AND COMMENTS ON CONTRACTS app. 1, at 942 (5th ed. 1988).

3.5 Internal Cross-References

Portions of text, footnotes, and groups of authorities within the piece may be cited using "*supra*" or "*infra*." Use *supra* to refer to material that has already appeared within the piece. Use *infra* to refer to material that appears later in the piece. Always retain the last two digits, but drop other repetitive digits.

Use a consistent naming convention for subdivisions that are numbered or otherwise designated in the piece (*The Bluebook* suggests using "Part" for main subdivisons and "Section" for all smaller subdivisions); use "note" to refer to footnotes within the same piece; use "p." and "pp." to refer to other pages within the same piece; use "Figure" and "Table" to refer to figures and tables within the same piece. A variety of forms may be used. For example:

▶ *See supra* text accompanying notes 305–07.

▶ *See supra* notes 12–15, 92–97 and accompanying text.

▶ *See* cases cited *supra* note 22.

▶ *But see* sources cited *supra* note 24.

▶ *See* discussion *infra* Sections II.B.2, III.C.1.

- ▶ *See supra* Part IV.
- ▶ *See infra* pp. 106–07.
- ▶ *See infra* p. 50 and note 100.
- ▶ *See supra* Figure 2.
- ▶ *See infra* Table 3.

Note that "*supra*" is also used in short form citations for certain types of sources (see **rule 4.2**).

SHORT CITATION FORMS   4

This rule provides general guidance for all short forms. For guidance as to specific short forms see the following rules:

Cases . . . . **rule 10.9**
Constitutions. . . . . **rule 11**
Statutes . . . . **rule 12.10**
Legislative Materials. . . . . **rule 13.8**
Regulations . . . . **rule 14.5**
Books, Reports, and Other Nonperiodic Materials . . . . **rule 15.10**
Periodical Materials . . . . **rule 16.9**
Unpublished and Forthcoming Sources . . . . **rule 17.6**
Internet, Electronic Media, and Other Nonprint Resources. . . . . . . **rule 18.9**
Services . . . . **rule 19.2**
Foreign Materials . . . . **rule 20.7**
International Materials. . . . . **rule 21.17**

For additional guidance on the use of short forms in court documents and legal memoranda, see **Bluepages B4, B10.2, B12.2, B15.2, B16.2, B17.2,** and **B18.2.**

"*Id.*"   4.1

"*Id.*" may be used in citation sentences and clauses for any kind of authority except internal cross-references (as described in **rule 3.5**). In court documents and legal memoranda, use "*id.*" when citing the immediately preceding authority, *but only when the immediately preceding citation contains only one authority*. In law review footnotes, use "*id.*" when citing the immediately preceding authority within the same footnote or within the immediately preceding footnote *when the preceding footnote contains only one authority*. Note that the period at the end of "*id.*" is always italicized.

Indicate where a subsequent citation varies from the former, such as the specific page number being cited. If the first citation refers only to a shorter work contained within an authority, do not use "*id.*" for a subsequent citation to the entire authority. Instead, use the "*supra*" form (see **rule 4.2(a)**).

The following examples illustrate the use of "*id.*" to refer to a variety of commonly cited materials:

▶ [1] Chalfin v. Specter, 233 A.2d 562, 562 (Pa. 1967).

▶ [2] *Id.* at 563.

▶ [3] 42 U.S.C. § 1983.

▶ [4] *See id.* § 1981.

▶ [5] U.C.C. § 3-302(2) (AM. L. INST. & UNIF. L. COMM'N 1977); *see also id.* § 3-303(a).

▶ [6] Dupuy v. Dupuy, [1977–1978 Transfer Binder] Fed. Sec. L. Rep. (CCH) ¶ 96,048, at 91,701 (5th Cir. May 9, 1977).

▶ [7] *Id.* ¶ 96,052, at 91,705; *see also* U.S. CONST. art. I, § 8, cl. 10 (giving Congress the power to punish "Offences against the Law of Nations").

▶ [8] FLEMING JAMES, JR. & GEOFFREY C. HAZARD, JR., CIVIL PROCEDURE § 1.3–.5 (3d ed. 1985).

▶ [9] *See id.* § 1.7.

▶ [10] 3 WILLIAM S. HOLDSWORTH, A HISTORY OF ENGLISH LAW 255 (3d ed. 1923).

▶ [11] 1 *id.* at 5–17 (2d ed. 1914).

▶ [12] THOMAS C. SCHELLING, A PROCESS OF RESIDENTIAL SEGREGATION: NEIGHBORHOOD TIPPING 2, *reprinted in* ECONOMIC FOUNDATIONS OF PROPERTY LAW 307, 308 (Bruce A. Ackerman ed., 1975).

▶ [13] *Id.* at 3.

▶ [14] JAMES & HAZARD, *supra* note 8, § 1.5.

▶ [15] *See id.*

"*Id.*" may not be used to refer to one authority in a preceding footnote if the preceding footnote cites more than one source:

▶ [16] *See* Robert B. Reich, *Toward a New Consumer Protection*, 128 U. PA. L. REV. 1 (1979); Note, *Direct Loan Financing of Consumer Purchases*, 85 HARV. L. REV. 1409, 1415–17 (1972); *see also* Chalfin v. Specter, 233 A.2d 562 (Pa. 1967).

▶ [17] *See Chalfin*, 233 A.2d at 570.

Not: [17] *See id.* at 570.

Sources identified in explanatory parentheticals, explanatory phrases, or prior/subsequent history, however, are ignored for the purposes of this rule. Thus, the following examples are correct:

▶ [18] Tuten v. United States, 460 U.S. 660, 663 (1983) (quoting Ralston v. Robinson, 454 U.S. 201, 206 (1981)).

▶ [19] *See id.* at 664.

▶ [20] Dillon v. Gloss, 256 U.S. 368, 376 (1921), *quoted in* Nixon v. United States, 506 U.S. 224, 230 (1993).

▶ [21] *See id.* at 374.

▶ [22] Kohler v. Tugwell, 292 F. Supp. 978, 985 (E.D. La. 1968), *aff'd per curiam*, 393 U.S. 531 (1969).

▶ [23] *See id.* at 980.

"*Id.*" may not be used to refer to an internal cross-reference:

▶ [24] *See supra* text accompanying note 2.

▶ [25] *See supra* text accompanying note 2.

Not: [25] *See supra id.*

"*Supra*" and "Hereinafter"   4.2

"*Supra*" and "hereinafter" may be used to refer to legislative hearings; court filings; books; pamphlets; reports; unpublished materials; nonprint resources; periodicals; services; treaties and international agreements; regulations, directives, and decisions of intergovernmental organizations; and internal cross-references. "*Supra*" and "hereinafter" should not be used to refer to cases, statutes, constitutions, legislative materials (other than hearings), restatements, model codes, or regulations, except in extraordinary circumstances, such as when the name of the authority is extremely long:

▶ [26] *In re* Multidistrict Private Civ. Treble Damage Antitrust Litig. Involving Motor Vehicle Air Pollution Control Equip., 52 F.R.D. 398 (C.D. Cal. 1970) [hereinafter *Air Pollution Control Antitrust Case*].

Appropriate short forms for cases, statutes, and legislative materials (other than hearings) are provided in their respective rules.

(a) "*Supra*." When an authority has been fully cited previously, the "*supra*" form may be used (unless "*id.*" is appropriate or "*supra*" is inappropriate for that authority). The "*supra*" form generally consists of the last name of the author of the work, followed by a comma and the word "*supra*." Indicate any particular manner in which the subsequent citation differs from the former.

If the author is an institutional author, use the full institutional name. If no author is cited, use the title of the work; for unsigned student-written law review materials, use the appropriate designation (see **rule 16.7.1(b)**).

Indicate the footnote in which the full citation can be found, unless the full citation is in the same footnote, in which case "*supra*" should be used without any cross-reference. Indicate any particular manner in which the subsequent citation differs from the former. Volume, paragraph, section, or page numbers may be added to refer to specific material:

▶ [27] Reich, *supra* note 16, at 6.

▶ [28] 2 HOLDSWORTH, *supra* note 10, at 6.

▶ [29] JAMES & HAZARD, *supra* note 8, § 7.21; W. PAGE KEETON ET AL., PROSSER AND KEETON ON THE LAW OF TORTS § 1, at 2 (5th ed. 1984); *see also supra* text accompanying note 7.

▶ [30] KEETON ET AL., *supra* note 29, § 2, at 4; Note, *supra* note 16, at 1416.

▶ [31] *Cf.* SCHELLING, *supra* note 12, at 3.

▶ [32] *See* Samuel Issacharoff, *On Political Corruption*, 124 HARV. L. REV. 118, 125 (2010) (describing the *Citizens United* holding as logically consistent); *cf.* Issacharoff, *supra*, at 130–42 (describing other approaches that are also logically consistent, but more regulatory).

Note that citation of a second item or work found within a volume of collected materials already cited takes the form:

▶ [33] CATHARINE A. MACKINNON, *On Exceptionality: Women as Women in Law*, *in* FEMINISM UNMODIFIED 70, 70 (1987).

▶ [34] CATHARINE A. MACKINNON, *Desire and Power*, *in* FEMINISM UNMODIFIED, *supra* note 33, at 46, 47.

(b) "Hereinafter." For authority that would be cumbersome to cite with the usual "*supra*" form or for which the regular shortened form may confuse the reader, the author may establish a specific shortened form. After the first citation of the authority, but before any explanatory parenthetical, place the word "hereinafter" and the shortened form in brackets. The shortened form should appear in the same typeface as in the full citation. In subsequent citations, cite the authority using the shortened form followed by a comma and the appropriate "*supra*" cross-reference (**rule 4.2(a)**):

▶ [35] *Proposed Amendments to the Federal Rules of Criminal Procedure: Hearings Before the Subcomm. on Crim. Just. of the H. Comm. on the Judiciary*, 95th Cong. 92–93 (1977) [hereinafter *Hearings*] (statement of Prof. Wayne LaFave).

▶ [36] RICHARD H. FALLON, JR., ET AL., HART AND WECHSLER'S THE FEDERAL COURTS AND THE FEDERAL SYSTEM 330 (5th ed. 2003).

▶ [37] *Hearings*, *supra* note 35, at 33 (statement of Hon. Edward Becker).

▶ [38] Letter from David Rybicki, Deputy Assistant Att'y Gen., Crim. Div., U.S. Dep't of Just., to Honorable William H. Pryor, Jr., Acting Chair, U.S. Sentencing Comm'n (Aug. 10, 2018) (on file with author) [hereinafter DOJ Letter].

Do not use the "hereinafter" form when a simple "*supra*" form is adequate:

▶ [39] FALLON ET AL., *supra* note 36, at 343.

The "hereinafter" form, however, should be used to distinguish two authorities appearing in the same footnote if the simple "*supra*" form would be confusing:

▶ [40] *See* Edward B. Rock, *Saints and Sinners: How Does Delaware Corporate Law Work?*, 44 UCLA L. REV. 1009, 1016–17 (1997) [hereinafter Rock, *Saints and Sinners*]; Edward B. Rock, *The Logic and (Uncertain) Significance of Institutional Shareholder Activism*, 79 GEO. L.J. 445 (1991) [hereinafter Rock, *Shareholder Activism*].

▶ [41] *See* Rock, *Saints and Sinners*, *supra* note 40, at 1019; Rock, *Shareholder Activism*, *supra* note 40, at 459–63.

QUOTATIONS 5

Formatting of Quotations 5.1

(a) Quotations of fifty or more words.

(i) Indentation and quotation marks. The quotation should be indented on the left and right, fully justified, without quotation marks, and quotation marks within a block quotation should appear as they do in the original:

> ▶ [T]his presumptive privilege must be considered in light of our historic commitment to the rule of law. This is nowhere more profoundly manifest than in our view that "the twofold aim [of criminal justice] is that guilt shall not escape or innocence suffer." We have elected to employ an adversary system of criminal justice in which the parties contest all issues before a court of law . . . . The ends of criminal justice would be defeated if judgments were to be founded on a partial or speculative presentation of the facts. The very integrity of the judicial system and public confidence in the system depend on full disclosure of all the facts, within the framework of the rules of evidence. To ensure that justice is done, it is imperative to the function of courts that compulsory process be available for the production of evidence needed either by the prosecution or by the defense.
>
> United States v. Nixon, 418 U.S. 683, 708–09 (1974) (second alteration in original) (citation omitted). The Court then balanced this interest against the evils of forced disclosure. *Id.* at 710.

(ii) Footnote and citation placement. In law review text (in which citations are not permitted), the footnote number should appear after the final punctuation of the quotation. In law review footnotes, court documents, and legal memoranda (in which citations are permitted), the citation should not be indented but should begin at the left margin on the line immediately following the quotation. In law review footnotes, where the quotation is placed within a parenthetical, it should be enclosed in quotation marks and not otherwise set off from the rest of the text.

(iii) Paragraph structure. The paragraph structure of an indented quotation should be indicated by further indenting the first line of each paragraph. The first sentence of the first quoted paragraph is only indented, however, if the first word of the quoted passage is also the first word of a paragraph in the source being quoted. If language at the beginning of the first paragraph is omitted, do not indent the first line or use an ellipsis. To indicate omission at the beginning of subsequent paragraphs, insert and indent an ellipsis. Indicate the omission of one or more entire paragraphs by inserting and indenting four periods (". . . .") on a new line. The following example illustrates these rules:

> ▶ On appeal to the federal courts via a habeas petition, McCleskey alleged that Georgia's capital sentencing process was administered in a racially discriminatory manner in violation of the Equal Protection Clause of the Fourteenth Amendment. McCleskey based his claims on a study, conducted by respected law and economics Professors Baldus, Pulaski,

and Woodworth . . . . The Baldus study examined roughly 2,500 murder
cases . . . .

. . . .

. . . Professors Baldus, Pulaski, and Woodworth also subjected their
data to an extensive statistical analysis.

(b) Quotations of forty-nine or fewer words.

(i) **Indentation and quotation marks.** The quotation should be enclosed in
quotation marks but not otherwise set off from the rest of the text. Quotation
marks around material quoted inside another quote should appear as single
marks within the quotation in keeping with the standard convention.

(ii) **Footnote and citation placement.** The footnote number or citation should
follow immediately after the closing quotation mark unless it is more accurate
to place it elsewhere shortly before or after the quotation.

(iii) **Paragraph structure.** Do not indicate the original paragraph structure of
quotations of forty-nine or fewer words except when the material quoted would
commonly be set off from the text, such as lines of poetry or dialogue from a
play. In this case, the quotation may appear as a block quote per **rule 5.1(a)(i)**,
regardless of its length.

(iv) **Punctuation.** Always place commas and periods inside the quotation
marks; place other punctuation marks inside the quotation marks only if they
are part of the original text.

5.2   Alterations and Quotations Within Quotations

(a) Substitution of letters or words. When a letter must be changed from
upper to lower case, or vice versa, enclose it in brackets. Substituted words or
letters and other inserted material should also be bracketed:

▶ "[P]ublic confidence in the [adversary] system depend[s upon]
full disclosure of all the facts, within the framework of the rules of
evidence."

(b) Omission of letters. Indicate the omission of letters from a common root
word with empty brackets ("judgment[]").

(c) Mistakes in original. Significant mistakes in the original should be
followed by "[sic]" and otherwise left as they appear in the original:

▶ "This list of statutes are [sic] necessarily incomplete."

(d) Changes to citations.

(i) Use a parenthetical clause after the citation to indicate when the source
quoted contains any addition of emphasis, alteration to the original in the
quoted text, or any omission of citations, emphasis, or footnote call numbers.
When a citation requires multiple parentheticals, place them in the order
indicated in **rule 1.5(b)**:

▶ "The fact that individuals define themselves in a significant way
through their sexual relationships suggests . . . that much of the rich-
ness of a relationship will come from the freedom to *choose* the form

and nature of these *intensely personal bonds*." Bowers v. Hardwick, 478 U.S. 186, 205 (1986) (Blackmun, J., dissenting) (second emphasis added).

▶ The court of appeals recognized the city's substantial interest in limiting the sound emanating from the bandshell. The court concluded, however, that the city's sound-amplification guideline was not narrowly tailored to further this interest, because "it has not [been] shown ... that the requirement of the use of the city's sound system and technician was the *least intrusive means* of regulating the volume."

Ward v. Rock Against Racism, 491 U.S. 781, 797 (1989) (alteration in original) (citation omitted).

(ii) Do not indicate the omission of a citation or footnote call number that follows the last word quoted.

(iii) Do not indicate that emphasis in the quotation appears in the original.

(e) Quotations within quotations. Whenever possible, a quotation within a quotation should be attributed to its original source. Insert a parenthetical following any parenthetical required by **rule 5.2(d)**:

▶ Chief Judge J. Skelly Wright noted Congress's "*firm resolve* to insure that the CIA's 'power that flows from money and stealth' could not be turned loose in domestic investigations of Americans." Marks v. CIA, 590 F.2d 997, 1008 (D.C. Cir. 1978) (Wright, C.J., concurring in part and dissenting in part) (emphasis added) (quoting Weissman v. CIA, 565 F.2d 692, 695 (D.C. Cir. 1977)).

Note that sources included in parentheticals pursuant to this rule should be formatted as though they appear in citation clauses (see **rules 2.1** and **2.2(b) (iii)**).

(f) Internal quotation marks.

(i) Internal quotation marks should be omitted if the opening mark appears at the very beginning of an in-line quotation and the closing mark appears at the very end.

▶ Original: If "the agency's answer is based on a permissible construction of the statute," that is the end of the matter.

▶ The dispositive question is whether "the agency's answer is based on a permissible construction of the statute."

Not: The dispositive question is whether "'the agency's answer is based on a permissible construction of the statute.'"

(ii) Do not omit multiple levels of nested marks except as this rule allows, even though "quoting" parentheticals beyond the first level may be omitted under **rule 10.6.3**. Alternate between double and single quotation marks as appropriate.

▶ Original: In this context, "the distinction between 'jurisdictional' and 'non-jurisdictional' interpretations is a mirage."

▶ The Court noted that, "[i]n this context, 'the distinction between "jurisdictional" and "non-jurisdictional" interpretations is a mirage.'"

Not: The Court noted that, "[i]n this context, 'the distinction between
jurisdictional and non-jurisdictional interpretations is a mirage.'"

(iii) Do not fail to include a "quoting" parenthetical because this rule requires omission of internal quotation marks (rather, omit "quoting" parentheticals only as allowed by **rule 10.6.3**).

(iv) Do not omit internal quotation marks in block quotations.

***

5.3   Omissions

Omission of a word or words is generally indicated by the insertion of an ellipsis, three periods separated by spaces and set off by a space before the first and after the last period ("•.•.•.•"), to take the place of the word or words omitted. Note that "•" indicates a space.

An ellipsis should never be used to begin a quotation, nor should it be used when individual words are merely altered (**rules 5.1(a)(iii)** and **5.2**).

(a) When using quoted language as a phrase or clause. Do not indicate omission of matters before or after a quotation:

▶ Chief Justice Burger wrote that the availability of compulsory process is "imperative to the function of courts" and that "[t]he very integrity of the judicial system and public confidence in the system depend on full disclosure of all the facts."

However, indicate omission of matter within such a phrase or clause with an ellipsis:

▶ Chief Justice Burger wrote that the availability of compulsory process is "imperative to•.•.•.•courts" and that "[t]he•.•.•.•judicial system and public confidence in the system depend on full disclosure of all the facts."

(b) When using quoted language as a full sentence. For example, assume the text of the original language is as follows:

▶ National borders are less of a barrier to economic exchange now than at almost any other time in history. As economic activity continues its relentless drive toward world-wide scope, trademarks become even more important. Why, then, are certain scholars advocating less comprehensive trademark protection? In fact, this seems counterintuitive.

(i) Where the *beginning of* the quoted sentence is being omitted, capitalize the first letter of the quoted language and place it in brackets if it is not already capitalized:

▶ "[B]orders are less of a barrier to economic exchange now than at almost any other time in history."

(ii) Where the *middle* of a quoted sentence is omitted, insert an ellipsis where the language is omitted:

▶ "National borders are less of a barrier•.•.•.•now than at almost any other time in history."

(iii) Where the *end* of a quoted sentence is omitted, insert an ellipsis between the last word being quoted and the final punctuation of the sentence being quoted:

▶ "National borders are less of a barrier to economic exchange now than at almost any other time•.•.•.•."

(iv) Do not indicate the deletion of matter after the period or other final punctuation that concludes the last quoted sentence.

▶ "National borders are less of a barrier to economic exchange now than at almost any other time in history."

(v) Where language *after the end* of a quoted sentence is deleted and is followed by further quotation, retain the punctuation at the end of the quoted sentence and insert an ellipsis before the remainder of the quotation.

▶ "National borders are less of a barrier to economic exchange now than at almost any other time in history.•.•.•.•[E]conomic activity continues its relentless drive toward world-wide scope, [so] trade-marks become even more important."

(vi) If language both *at the end* and *after the end* of a quoted sentence is omitted and followed by further quoted material, use only one ellipsis to indicate both of the omissions:

▶ "National borders are less of a barrier•.•.•.•.•[E]conomic activity continues its relentless drive toward world-wide scope, [so] trade-marks become even more important."

Note that the punctuation at the end of the first sentence should follow the ellipsis:

▶ "Why, then, are certain scholars advocating less•.•.•.•? [T]his seems counterintuitive."

(c) When omitting a footnote or citation. Indicate omission of a footnote or a citation with the parenthetical phrase "(footnote omitted)" or "(citation omitted)" immediately following the citation to the quoted source. Do not insert an ellipsis for an omitted footnote or citation.

ABBREVIATIONS, NUMERALS, AND SYMBOLS 6

Abbreviations 6.1

Tables at the end of this book contain lists of specific abbreviations for arbitral reporters (**T5**), case names, institutional author names, and periodical titles (**T6**), court names (**T7**), explanatory phrases (**T8**), legislative documents (**T9**), geographical terms (**T10**), judges and officials (**T11**), months (**T12**), periodicals (**T13**), publishing terms (**T14**), services (**T15**), and subdivisions (**T16**).

Abbreviations not listed in this book should be avoided unless substantial space will be saved and the resulting abbreviation is unambiguous.

Note that in legal writing the same word may be abbreviated differently for different uses:

▶ F. and Fed.

▶ app. and App'x

(a) Spacing. In general, close up all adjacent single capitals:

▶ N.W.

▶ S.D.N.Y.

But do not close up single capitals with longer abbreviations:

▶ D. Mass.

▶ S. Ct.

In abbreviations of periodical names (see **tables T6** and **T13**), close up all adjacent single capitals except when one or more of the capitals refers to the name of an institutional entity, in which case set the capital or capitals referring to the entity off from other adjacent single capitals with a space. Thus:

▶ Geo. L.J.

▶ B.C. L. Rev.

▶ N.Y.U. L. Rev.

▶ S. Ill. U. L.J.

Individual numbers, including both numerals and ordinals, are treated as single capitals:

▶ F.3d

▶ S.E.2d

▶ A.L.R.4th

But, insert a space adjacent to any abbreviation containing two or more letters:

▶ So. 2d

▶ Cal. App. 3d

▶ F. Supp. 2d

Close up initials in personal names:

▶ W.C. Fields

(b) Periods. Generally, every abbreviation should be followed by a period, except those in which the last letter of the original word is set off from the rest of the abbreviation by an apostrophe. Thus:

▶ Ave.

▶ Bldg.

But:

▶ Ass'n

▶ Dep't

Some entities with widely recognized initials, e.g., AARP, CBS, CIA, EPA, FCC, FDA, FEC, NAACP, and NLRB, are commonly referred to in spoken language by their initials rather than by their full names; such abbreviations may be used without periods in text, in case names, and as institutional authors. Do not, however, omit the periods when the abbreviations are used as reporter names, in names of codes, or as names of courts of decision. Thus:

▶ NLRB v. Baptist Hosp., Inc., 442 U.S. 773 (1979).

But: E. Belden Corp., 239 N.L.R.B. 776 (1978).

United States may be abbreviated to "U.S." only when used as an adjective (do not omit the periods):

▶ U.S. history

But: history of the United States

In addition to the abbreviation "U.S.," always retain periods in abbreviations not commonly referred to in speech as initials (e.g., N.Y., S.D.).

Numerals and Symbols   6.2

(a) Numerals. In general, spell out the numbers zero to ninety-nine in text and in footnotes; for larger numbers, use numerals. This general rule is subject, however, to the following exceptions:

(i) Any number that *begins a sentence* must be spelled out.

(ii) "Hundred," "thousand," and similar *round numbers* may be spelled out, if done consistently.

(iii) When a series includes numbers both less than 100 and greater than or equal to 100, numerals should be used for the entire series:

▶ The plaintiffs gained, respectively, 117, 6, and 28 pounds.

(iv) Numerals should be used if the number includes a decimal point.

(v) Where material repeatedly refers to percentages or dollar amounts, numerals should be used for those percentages or amounts.

(vi) Numerals should be used for section or other subdivision numbers.

(vii) In numbers that appear in text and citations, use commas to separate groups of three digits when those numbers contain four or more uninterrupted digits. Thus:

▶ 1,234,567

Do not employ this convention in citations to pages, statutes, volume numbers, internet database locators, docket numbers, the U.S. Code, or other sources whose classification systems do not themselves include commas:

▶ United States v. Walker, No. 00-40098, 2003 WL 131711 (D. Kan. Jan. 6, 2003).

(b) Ordinals.

(i) Unless part of a citation, ordinal numbers appearing in text and footnotes are controlled by **rule 6.2(a)**. If part of a citation, numerals are used for all ordinal numbers. Do not use superscripts:

▶ 41st Leg.

▶ 4th ed.

(ii) In textual sentences, where **rule 6.2(a)** requires that the numeral be used, use "2nd" or "3rd" for figures representing ordinal numbers ending in two or three. But, in citations, for figures representing ordinal numbers ending in the number two or three, use "2d" or "3d," not "2nd" or "3rd." Do not use superscripts in any case. Thus:

▶ The 102nd Congress could not pass a rule that would bind the 103rd Congress.

But, in citations:

▶ 103d Cong.

▶ 2d ed.

(c) Section (§) and paragraph (¶) symbols. The first word of any sentence must be spelled out. In addition, spell out the words "section" and "paragraph" in the text (whether main text or footnote text) of law review pieces and other documents, except when referring to a provision in the U.S. Code (see **rule 12.10(c)**) or a federal regulation (see **rule 14.5**). In citations, the symbols should be used (except when citing session laws amending prior acts as noted in **rule 12.4(d)**). When the symbols are used, insert a space between "§" or "¶" and the numeral. See **rules 3.3(b)** and **3.3(c)** when citing to multiple sections or paragraphs.

(d) Dollar ($) and percent (%) symbols. These symbols should be used wherever numerals are used, and the words should be spelled out wherever numbers are spelled out, but a symbol should never begin a sentence. There should *not* be a space between "$" or "%" and the numeral.

---

7 ITALICIZATION FOR STYLE AND IN UNIQUE CIRCUMSTANCES

See **rule 2** for a general discussion on the uses of typefaces. The conventions below apply to italicization for emphasis, italicization of foreign words and phrases, and italicization in other unique circumstances.

(a) Emphasis. Words and phrases may be italicized for emphasis.

(b) Foreign words and phrases. Italicize non-English words and phrases unless they have been incorporated into common English usage. Latin words and phrases that are often used in legal writing are considered to be in common English usage and should not be italicized. However, very long Latin phrases and obsolete or uncommon Latin words and phrases should remain italicized. For example:

▶ *expressio unius est exclusio alterius*

▶ *ignorantia legis neminem excusat*

▶ *sero sed serio*

▶ *ex dolo malo non oritur actio*

But:

▶ e.g.	▶ i.e.
▶ res judicata	▶ quid pro quo
▶ amicus curiae	▶ certiorari
▶ corpus juris	▶ ab initio
▶ obiter dictum	▶ de jure
▶ modus operandi	▶ habeas corpus
▶ non obstante veredicto	▶ prima facie
▶ mens rea	▶ en banc

Note, however, that "*id.*" is always italicized. Note also that other typeface rules may control. For example, when "e.g." is used as a signal it should be italicized as per **rule 2.1(d)**. Similarly, always italicize procedural phrases in case names, such as "*In re*" or "*ex rel.*," under **rule 10.2.1(b)**.

(c) Letters representing hypothetical parties, places, or things. Italicize and capitalize individual letters when used to represent the names of hypothetical parties, places, or things:

▶ *A* went to bank *B* in state *X*.

(d) The lowercase letter "l." Italicize the lowercase letter "*l*" when used as a subdivision, as in a statute or rule, to distinguish it from the numeral "1":

▶ § 23(*l*)

▶ cmt. *l*

(e) Mathematical expressions. Italicize mathematical formulas and variables:

▶ $E = mc^2$

▶ $a > 2b$

CAPITALIZATION   8

(a) Headings and titles. Capitalize words in a heading or title, including the initial word and any word that immediately follows a colon. Do not capitalize articles, conjunctions, or prepositions when they are four or fewer letters, unless they begin the heading or title, or immediately follow a colon.

(b) Internet main page titles and URLs. In both text and footnotes, capitalize URLs and words in an internet main page title in accordance with the actual capitalization of the source.

(c) Text. Except for headings, titles, and internet main page titles and URLs, capitalize according to this rule. When this rule does not address a particular question of capitalization, refer to a style manual such as *The Chicago Manual of Style* or the *U.S. Government Publishing Office Style Manual*. Practitioners should also refer to **Bluepages B8** for further advice on capitalization. Additional words that should be capitalized in legal writing include:

(i) **Nouns that identify specific persons, officials, groups, government offices, or government bodies.** These words and phrases should always be capitalized according to the following examples:

▶ the Social Security Administrator

The plaintiff was declared disabled by the Social Security Administrator and was awarded benefits.

▶ the Administrator

For fifty years, the statute has provided that the Administrator make all necessary determinations.

▶ the FDA

The FDA has approved the salts as safe and effective.

▶ the Agency

The Agency reported that all areas of the country met the standard for nitrogen dioxide.

▶ Congress

Members of Congress are immune from false imprisonment claims under certain circumstances.

▶ the President

A sitting President's executive power allows him or her to pardon convicted criminals.

But:

▶ the congressional hearings

The congressional hearings were held on the potential cumulative effects of these three rules.

▶ the presidential veto

The presidential veto does not confer such power upon the President.

(ii) **Exceptions.** Certain words are exceptions to the above rule and should be capitalized according to the following rules:

Act	Capitalize when referring to a specific legislative act:
	▶ A union has a statutory duty of fair representation under the National Labor Relations Act.

▶ The record of the hearing shows that the Act required operators to pay for their own retirees.

Circuit   Capitalize when used with a circuit's name or number:

▶ We have decided to follow the Fifth Circuit and District of Columbia Circuit in that regard, rather than this circuit's unclear precedent.

Code   Capitalize when referring to a specific code:

▶ At least one court considered the significance of the change between the 1939 and 1954 Codes.

Commonwealth   Capitalize if it is a part of the full title of a state, if the word it modifies is capitalized, or when referring to a state as a governmental actor or a party to a litigation:

▶ The Commonwealth of Massachusetts sued several companies.

▶ The Commonwealth may not relitigate the issue in a post-conviction hearing.

Constitution   Capitalize when naming any constitution in full or when referring to the U.S. Constitution, but do not capitalize the adjective form "constitutional." Also, capitalize nouns that identify specific parts of state or the U.S. Constitution when referring to them in textual sentences, but not in citations:

▶ Students in this class have studied the full faith and credit clause of the Pennsylvania Constitution. The students agree that the clause in that constitution is substantially similar to the Full Faith and Credit Clause of the U.S. Constitution.

But: He claims his constitutional rights were violated.

▶ Of all the amendments in the U.S. Constitution, the Fifth Amendment may be the most complex.

▶ Accordingly, there was no violation of Article I, Section 8, Clause 17 of the Constitution.

But: *See* U.S. CONST. art. I, § 8, cl. 17 (granting Congress the power to "exercise exclusive Legislation in all Cases whatsoever . . . over all Places purchased" by the United States).

Court   Capitalize when naming any court in full or when referring to the U.S. Supreme Court (with some exceptions for court documents and legal memoranda, see **Bluepages B8**):

▶ The California Supreme Court found no violation in such a case.

▶ The argument in the state supreme court concerning the lack of prior notice was based solely on state authorities.

▶ When the Court approves the argument, it becomes constitutional doctrine for the entire country.

▶ The court of appeals reversed the trial court.

▶ The Court of Appeals for the Fifth Circuit affirmed.

Federal   Capitalize when the word it modifies is capitalized:

> ▶ The Federal Constitution provides for three branches of government.

> ▶ A higher level of clarity is required in statutes that require federal spending.

Judge, Justice   Capitalize when giving the name of a specific judge or justice or when referring to a Justice of the United States Supreme Court:

> ▶ In one of the first decisions on point, Judge Cedarbaum rejected a group appointment.

> ▶ This era of constitutional non-interference ended when the Justices proclaimed a profound national commitment to the principle that debate on public issues should be uninhibited.

> ▶ The justices of the state's highest court will hear oral arguments on the issue of capital punishment at the end of the month.

State   Capitalize if it is a part of the full title of a state, if the word it modifies is capitalized, or when referring to a state as a governmental actor or as a party to a litigation:

> ▶ The principal issue is whether the State of Kansas may impose its motor fuel tax. The State Commissioner adopted a broad-based policy.

> ▶ The State brought this action two years ago.

Term   Capitalize when referring to a Term of the United States Supreme Court:

> ▶ The United States Supreme Court considered this issue in this Term and in four other Terms since the 1978 Term.

> ▶ The central common law courts sat only four times a year, but customarily the year began with Michaelmas term.

---

9   TITLES OF JUDGES, OFFICIALS, AND TERMS OF COURT

(a) Justices and judges. Justices are referred to as "Justice Ginsburg" and "Chief Justice Roberts." Parenthetical references are to "Breyer, J.," "Kagan, J.," and "Breyer & Kagan, JJ." Judges are referred to as "Judge Surrick" and "Chief Judge Smith." First names are not used for judges, unless a court has two individuals with the same last name, in which case the first name should be included on first reference. Capitalize "justice," "chief justice," and "judge" according to **rule 8(c)(ii)**. For parenthetical references, abbreviate titles of judges and officials as indicated in **table T11**.

(b) Ordering. As a matter of etiquette, lists of judges should be in the order indicated at the beginning of each volume of the official reporter for the court. Justices of the United States Supreme Court are always listed with the Chief Justice first and then in order of seniority.

(c) Term of court. A term of court currently in progress may be referred to as "this term." The immediately preceding term, no longer in progress at the time of publication, should be referred to as "last term." Any term may be indicated by year:

▶ the 1999 term

The Supreme Court Term should be indicated by the year in which the Term began, not the year it ended. Capitalize "term" according to **rule 8(c)(ii)**.

CASES 10

Citation of a U.S. Supreme Court case:

"v." for "versus"   reporter volume no.   first page of case   specific page referred to

Meritor Sav. Bank v. Vinson, 477 U.S. 57, 60 (1986).

first party   second party   reporter abbreviation   date of decision
                                     (U.S. Reports)   (no court is listed because it
                                                          is clear from reporter name)

Citation of a case decided by the U.S. Court of Appeals for the Fourth Circuit, later reversed by the U.S. Supreme Court, with parenthetical information about the Fourth Circuit decision:

reporter abbreviation   span of specific   year of
(Federal Reporter, 2d series)   pages referred to   decision

parties   reporter volume no.   first page of case   deciding court

United States v. MacDonald, 531 F.2d 196, 199–200 (4th Cir. 1976) (resting review of the dispositive issue on the principle of judicial economy),

rev'd, 435 U.S. 850 (1978).

action of higher court   citation of reversal

parenthetical phrase describing decision of Fourth Circuit

Short form for the above case after it has been cited in full:

volume no. and reporter abbreviation   specific page referred to

MacDonald, 531 F.2d at 197.

shortened case name in italics   denotes that page number follows
(do not use governmental party)

Main Elements

Case Names . . . . **rule 10.2**
Reporters and Other Sources . . . . **rule 10.3**
Court and Jurisdiction . . . . **rule 10.4**
Date or Year . . . . **rule 10.5**
Parenthetical Information . . . . **rule 10.6**
Prior and Subsequent History . . . . **rule 10.7**

10.1   Basic Citation Forms

Filed but not decided	Hoshijima v. Jensen, No. 90-345 (D. Mass. filed Sept. 18, 1990).
Unpublished interim order	Sansone v. Sauder, No. 90-346 (D. Mass. Oct. 25, 1990) (order granting preliminary injunction).
Published interim order	Haber v. Scotten, 725 F. Supp. 1395 (D. Mass. 1990) (order granting preliminary injunction).
Unpublished decision	Kitchens v. Grohman, No. 90-347, slip op. at 6 (D. Mass. Dec. 4, 1990).
Decision published in service only	Tice v. Scotten, 1990 Fed. Sec. L. Rep. (CCH) ¶ 102,342 (D. Mass. Dec. 4, 1990).
Decision published in newspaper only	Mishra v. Grohman, N.Y. L.J., Dec. 5, 1990, at 1 (D. Mass. Dec. 4, 1990).
Decision available in electronic database	Yee v. Kitchens, No. 90-348, 1990 U.S. Dist. LEXIS 20837, at *6–8, *10 (D. Mass. Dec. 4, 1990).
Decision available in electronic database after revision	Phibrick v. Haber, No. 90-349, 1990 U.S. Dist. LEXIS 20838, at *4 (D. Mass. Dec. 4, 1990, revised Jan. 3, 1991).
Published decision	Ward v. Reddy, 727 F. Supp. 1407, 1412 (D. Mass. 1990).
Appeal docketed	Yee v. Grohman, 727 F. Supp. 1408 (D. Mass. 1990), *appeal docketed*, No. 90-567 (1st Cir. Dec. 20, 1990).
Brief, record, or appendix	Brief for Appellant at 7, Kitchens v. Scotten, 925 F.2d 314 (1st Cir. 1991) (No. 90-568).
Disposition on appeal	Haber v. Yee, 925 F.2d 314, 335 (1st Cir. 1991).
Disposition in lower court showing subsequent history	Haber v. Yee, 727 F. Supp. 1407, 1412 (D. Mass. 1990), *aff'd*, 925 F.2d 314 (1st Cir. 1991).
Petition for certiorari filed	Grohman v. Tice, 925 F.2d 314 (1st Cir. 1991), *petition for cert. filed*, 60 U.S.L.W. 3422 (U.S. Jan. 14, 1992) (No. 92-212).
Petition for certiorari granted	Scotten v. Kitchens, 925 F.2d 314 (1st Cir. 1991), *cert. granted*, 60 U.S.L.W. 3562 (U.S. Jan. 21, 1992) (No. 92-212).
Disposition in Supreme Court published only in service	Flynn v. Kaplan, 60 U.S.L.W. 4420, 4421 (U.S. Feb. 4, 1992), *vacating as moot* 925 F.2d 314 (1st Cir. 1991).

10.2   Case Names

The only significant differences between case names in textual sentences and case names in citations are the italicization (**rule 2**) and the extent to which the case name is abbreviated. The provisions of **rule 10.2.1** apply to every case name, whether in text or citations, but case names in citations are further abbreviated according to **rule 10.2.2**. Thus:

- ▶ In *Southern Pacific Co. v. Jensen*, 244 U.S. 205 (1917), Justice McReynolds stressed the value of uniform laws.

- ▶ *Southern Pacific* also indicates the breadth of federal lawmaking power under the admiralty jurisdiction.

Not: In *S. Pac. Co. v. Jensen*, 244 U.S. 205 (1917), Justice McReynolds stressed the value of uniform laws.

But: in citations:

- ▶ *See, e.g.*, S. Pac. Co. v. Jensen, 244 U.S. 205, 225–26 (1917) (Pitney, J., dissenting).

Note that the examples throughout **rule 10.2** employ the typeface conventions for law review citations. For an explanation of typeface conventions, see **rule 2**. For typeface conventions in court documents and legal memoranda, see **Bluepages B2**.

. . . .

General Rules for Case Names   10.2.1

Use the case name that appears at the beginning of the opinion in the cited reporter as modified by the paragraphs below. If no name appears in the cited reporter, use a popular name or cite as "Judgment of ‹date›":

- ▶ Shelley's Case

- ▶ Judgment of Oct. 11, 2008

Always retain in full the first word in each party's name (including a relator) except as provided below. In extremely long case names, omit words not necessary for identification; the running head (the short identifier printed at the top of each page of the case) may serve as a guide. Make the following modifications where applicable:

(a) Actions and parties cited. If the case is a consolidation of two or more actions, cite only the first listed:

- ▶ Shelley v. Kraemer

Not: Shelley v. Kraemer, McGhee v. Sipes

Omit all parties other than the first listed on each side. Do not omit the first-listed relator or any portion of a partnership name:

- ▶ Fry v. Mayor of Sierra Vista

Not: Fry v. Mayor & City Council of Sierra Vista

But:

- ▶ Massachusetts *ex rel.* Alison v. Pauly

- ▶ Eisen v. Spradlin, Lincoln & Amorosi

Omit words indicating multiple parties, such as "et al." Also omit alternative names given for the first-listed party on either side:

- ▶ Cheng v. Seinfeld

Not: Cheng et al. v. Seinfeld d/b/a The Man, Inc.

Similarly, for in rem jurisdiction cases, omit all but the first-listed item or group of items:

> ▶ *In re* Three Pink Cadillacs

> **Not:** *In re* Three Pink Cadillacs, Two Turtle Doves, and a Partridge in a Pear Tree

Where real property is a party, use its common street address, if available:

> ▶ United States v. 6109 Grubb Road

> **Not:** United States v. Parcel of Real Property Known as 6109 Grubb Road, Millcreek Township, Erie County, Pennsylvania

In bankruptcy and similar cases, the case name might contain both an adversary and a nonadversary name. If both appear at the beginning of the opinion, cite the adversary name first, followed by the nonadversary name in parentheses. Include a procedural phrase such as "*In re*" or "*ex rel.*" before the nonadversary name, followed by a descriptive or introductory phrase such as "Estate of" or "Interest of," if any. If only an adversary name or only a nonadversary name appears at the beginning of the opinion, cite the name supplied:

> ▶ Wallingford's, Inc. v. Waning (*In re* Waning), 120 B.R. 607, 611 (Bankr. D. Me. 1990).

> ▶ *In re* Drexel Burnham Lambert Grp., Inc., 120 B.R. 724 (Bankr. S.D.N.Y. 1990).

> ▶ *In re* Estate of Benson, No. C7-95-2185, 1996 WL 118367 (Minn. Ct. App. Mar. 19, 1996).

> ▶ State v. Powers (*In re* Interest of Powers), 493 N.W.2d 166 (Neb. 1992).

(b) Procedural phrases. Abbreviate "on the relation of," "for the use of," "on behalf of," "as next friend of," and similar expressions to "*ex rel.*" Abbreviate "in the matter of," "petition of," "application of," and similar expressions to "*In re.*" Omit all procedural phrases except the first. When adversary parties are named, omit all procedural phrases except "*ex rel.*":

> ▶ Gorman v. Bruh

> **Not:** *In re* Gorman v. Bruh

> But:

> ▶ Massachusetts *ex rel.* Kennedy v. Armbruster

> ▶ *Ex parte* Young

Include any introductory or descriptive phrases such as "Accounting of," "Estate of," and "Will of." Thus:

> ▶ *In re* Will of Holt

> ▶ Estate of Haas v. Commissioner

Procedural phrases should always be italicized, regardless of whether the rest of the case name is italicized. Thus, in law review text:

> ▶ *Ex parte Young*

(c) Abbreviations. In textual sentences, whether in main text or in footnote text, abbreviate only widely known acronyms under **rule 6.1(b)** and these eight words: "&," "Ass'n," "Bros.," "Co.," "Corp.," "Inc.," "Ltd.," and "No." If one of these eight begins a party's name, however, do not abbreviate it.

▶ Philadelphia Electric Co. v. Hirsch

Not: PECO v. Hirsch

But: NAACP v. Kaminski

For abbreviations in citations, see **rule 10.2.2**.

(d) "The." Omit "The" as the first word of a party's name, except as part of the name of the object of an in rem action or in cases in which "The King" or "The Queen" is a party. Thus:

▶ Mia. Herald v. Sercus

But:

▶ *In re* The Clinton Bridge

▶ The King v. Broadrup

Do not omit "The" in an established popular name, except when referring to the case textually. Thus:

▶ *See* The Civil Rights Cases, 109 U.S. 3 (1883).

But: Neither of the *Civil Rights Cases* opinions was correct.

Not: Neither of *The Civil Rights Cases* opinions was correct.

(e) Descriptive terms. Omit terms such as "administrator," "appellee," "executor," "licensee," and "trustee" that describe a party already named:

▶ Burns v. McMillen

Not: Burns v. McMillen, Administrator

But: Trustees of Dartmouth College v. Garodnick

(f) Geographical terms. Omit "State of," "Commonwealth of," and "People of," except when citing decisions of the courts of that state, in which case only "State," "Commonwealth," or "People" should be retained:

▶ Blystone v. Pennsylvania, 494 U.S. 299 (1990).

Not: Blystone v. Commonwealth of Pennsylvania, 494 U.S. 299 (1990).

But: Commonwealth v. Ferrone, 448 A.2d 637 (Pa. Super. Ct. 1982).

Omit "City of," "County of," "Village of," "Township of," and like expressions unless the expression begins a party name:

▶ Mayor of New York v. Clinton

Not: Mayor of the City of New York v. Clinton

But: Butts v. City of New York

Omit all prepositional phrases of location not following "City," or like expressions, unless the omission would leave only one word in the name of a party or the location is part of the full name of a business or similar entity:

> ► Surrick v. Board of Wardens

Not: Surrick v. Board of Wardens of the Port of Philadelphia

But: Planned Parenthood of Southeastern Pennsylvania v. Casey

Not: Planned Parenthood v. Casey

> ► Shapiro v. Bank of Harrisburg

> ► Eimers v. Mutual of Omaha

Include designations of national or larger geographical areas except in union names (**rule 10.2.1(i)**). Omit "of America" after "United States":

> ► Flatow v. Islamic Republic of Iran

> ► United States v. Aluminum Co. of America

Retain all geographical designations not introduced by a preposition:

> ► Billman v. Indiana Department of Corrections

Omit all geographical designations that follow a comma:

> ► City of Arlington v. FEC

Not: City of Arlington, Texas v. FEC

(g) Given names or initials. Generally, omit given names or initials of individuals, but not in names of business firms or where a party's surname is abbreviated:

> ► Courtney v. Sandman

Not: Paul Vincent Courtney v. Joseph M. Sandman

But:

> ► Tanya Bartucz, Inc. v. Virginia J. Wise & Co.

> ► Linda R.S. v. Richard D.

Do not omit any part of a surname made up of more than one word:

> ► Van der Velt v. Standing Horse

> ► Abdul Ghani v. Subedar Shoedar Khan

Given names that follow a surname should be retained. Thus, retain the full name where the name is *entirely* in a language in which the surname is given first, such as Chinese, Korean, or Vietnamese:

> ► Yao Zhen Guang v. Yeh Zhi An

> ► Chow v. Ha Quang Jin

Not: Timothy Chow v. Ha Quang Jin

Similarly, if a party's name is of Spanish or Portuguese derivation, cite the surname and all names following:

> ► Ortega y Gasset v. Alcala de Larosa

If in doubt, use the name under which the party appears in the index of the reporter cited.

(h) Business firm designations. Omit "Inc.," "Ltd.," "L.L.C.," "N.A.," "F.S.B.," and similar terms if the name also contains a word such as "Ass'n," "Bros.," "Co.," "Corp.," "Ins.," or "R.R.," clearly indicating that the party is a business firm:

▶ Wisconsin Packing Co. v. Indiana Refrigerator Lines, Inc.

Not: Wisconsin Packing Co., Inc. v. Indiana Refrigerator Lines, Inc.

This rule should be read narrowly. The omission of the business firm designation is appropriate only if the name of the business could not *possibly* be mistaken for the name of some other entity, such as a natural person.

(i) Union and local union names. Cite a union name exactly as given in the official reporter. This general rule is subject, however, to the following exceptions:

(i) Only the smallest unit should be cited:

▶ NLRB v. Radio & Television Broadcast Engineers Local 1212

Not: NLRB v. Radio & Television Broadcast Engineers Local 1212, IBEW, AFL-CIO

(ii) All craft or industry designations, except the first *full* such designation, should be omitted:

▶ Douds v. Local 294, International Brotherhood of Teamsters

Not: Douds v. Local 294, International Brotherhood of Teamsters, Chauffeurs, Warehousemen & Helpers

But: International Union of Doll & Toy Workers v. Local 379

(iii) A widely recognized abbreviation of the union's name (e.g., UAW) may be used in accordance with **rules 6.1(b)** and **10.2.1(c).**

(iv) All prepositional phrases of location, including those of national or larger areas, should be omitted.

(j) Commissioner of Internal Revenue. Cite simply as "Commissioner" or, in citations, "Comm'r."

(k) Common names different from name in reporter. For cases not known by the name that appears in the reporter, but known instead by a common name, the common name must either be substituted for the reporter name in its entirety, or indicated parenthetically in the same typeface as the case name in the reporter:

▶ The Brig Amy Warwick (The Prize Cases), 67 U.S. (2 Black) 635 (1862).

▶ The Prize Cases, 67 U.S. (2 Black) 635 (1862).

Not: The Prize Cases (The Brig Amy Warwick), 67 U.S. (2 Black) 635 (1862).

For cases known by the name in the reporter, but *also* commonly known by a short name different from that appearing in the reporter, the common name may *not* be substituted for the reporter name in its entirety in a full citation, but it may be indicated parenthetically in *italics*:

▶ Youngstown Sheet & Tube Co. v. Sawyer (*Steel Seizure*), 343 U.S. 579 (1952).

Not: *Steel Seizure*, 343 U.S. 579 (1952).

Similarly, for mandamus actions against courts where the case is known by the name of the judge against whom the writ is sought, the name may be indicated parenthetically in *italics*:

▶ United States v. U.S. District Court (*Keith*), 407 U.S. 297 (1972).

And, for cases with multiple dispositions, a helpful identifier of the number of the decision may be indicated parenthetically in *italics*:

▶ Hamdi v. Rumsfeld (*Hamdi III*), 316 F.3d 450 (4th Cir. 2003).

This parenthetical identifier is given only when a case is cited as the primary citation. Once given, the parenthetical identifier alone may be used as the case name when the case is cited again, even in circumstances where a full citation would otherwise be required:

▶ [1] Fox Television Stations, Inc. v. FCC (*Fox I*), 280 F.3d 1027 (D.C. Cir.), *modified on reh'g*, 293 F.3d 537 (D.C. Cir. 2002).

▶ [2] Fox Television Stations, Inc. v. FCC (*Fox II*), 293 F.3d 537, 540 (D.C. Cir. 2002) (quoting *Fox I*, 280 F.3d at 1043).

In conformity with **rule 2.1(f)**, when citing cases according to the above rule, the parentheses themselves should never be italicized in either main text or footnote text.

....

10.2.2 Additional Rules for Case Names in Citations

Cite case names in citations according to the rules given above, but with the following further modifications:

Always abbreviate any word listed in **table T6**, even if the word is the first word in a party's name, unless the word is part of a state, country, or other geographical unit that is the entire name of the party:

▶ S. Consol. R.R. v. Consol. Transp. Co.

▶ *In re* Acad. Answering Serv., Inc.

▶ McGaugh v. Comm'r

But: South Dakota v. Dole

Not: S. Dakota v. Dole

Abbreviate states, countries, and other geographical units as indicated in **table T10** unless the geographical unit is the entire name of the party (as opposed to just a part thereof). This includes "United States." Thus:

▶ *In re* W. Tex. Pepper Co.

▶ LeBeau v. Univ. of Md.

But: Staub v. District of Columbia

▶ Ctr. for Nat'l Sec. Stud. v. U.S. Dep't of Just.

But: Alvarez-Machain v. United States

But: Fritz v. County of Los Angeles

Abbreviate other words of eight letters or more if *substantial* space is thereby saved and the result is unambiguous.

Reporters and Other Sources   10.3

Parallel Citations and Which Source(s) to Cite   10.3.1

The federal and state jurisdictions table (**table T1**) indicates which reporters to cite for the decisions of most courts. Note that many state court decisions are published in two or more sources.

(a) Parallel citations in state court documents. In documents submitted to state courts, all case citations must be to the source(s) required by local rules. Many state rules require that citations to state court decisions include a citation to the official state reporter, *followed* by a parallel citation to a regional reporter. Thus, these local rules, and *not* the citation rules set forth in **table T1**, govern state court filings. See **Bluepages B10.1.3** and **Bluepages table BT2.2** for further guidance concerning jurisdiction-specific citation rules.

(b) Case citations in all other documents. In all other documents, including *ordinary legal memoranda* and *law review pieces*, cite the relevant regional reporter, if the decision is found therein. For example:

▶ Swedloff v. Phila. Transp. Co., 187 A.2d 152 (Pa. 1963).

If the decision is available as an official public domain citation (also referred to as medium-neutral citation), that citation must be provided, as well as a parallel citation to the regional reporter, if available.

If the decision is not found in a regional reporter or available as a public domain citation, cite the other sources indicated in **table T1**. Cite decisions of unlisted courts as you would those of courts listed in the table. If a case is not available in an official or preferred unofficial reporter or as a public domain citation, cite another unofficial reporter, a widely used computer database (**rule 18.3**), a service (**rule 19**), a slip opinion (**rule 10.8.1(b)**), an internet source (**rule 18.2.2**), or a newspaper (**rule 16.6**), in that order of preference:

▶ United States v. Carlisle, No. 90-2465SI, 1991 U.S. App. LEXIS 5863, at *3 (8th Cir. Apr. 10, 1991) (per curiam).

▶ *In re* Smithfield Estates, Inc., [1985–1986 Transfer Binder] Bankr. L. Rep. (CCH) ¶ 70,707 (Bankr. D.R.I. Aug. 9, 1985).

▶ Simmons v. Brothers, No. 90-627 (D. Mass. Dec. 19, 1990).

▶ State v. McArthur, No. C4-99-502 (Minn. Ct. App. Sept. 28, 1999), https://mn.gov/law-library-stat/archive/ctapun/9909/502.htm.

▶ United States v. Palermo, N.Y. TIMES, Aug. 27, 1957, at 24 (S.D.N.Y. Aug. 26, 1957).

For citation to administrative reporters, see **rule 14.3.2**.

10.3.2 Reporters

Bound publications that print only cases (or cases and annotations) are considered reporters and are cited in roman type. A citation to a reporter consists of a volume designation (**rule 3.1**), the abbreviated name of the reporter (as shown in **table T1**), and the page on which the case report begins (**rule 3.2**). For rules on spacing in reporter abbreviations, see **rule 6.1(a)**.

▶ Burt v. Rumsfeld, 322 F. Supp. 2d 189 (D. Conn. 2004).

Early American reporters were often named after their editors rather than after the courts whose cases they reported. Subsequently, official editor-named series have been combined into jurisdiction-named series with continuous volume numbering. Such reporters are now generally cited by the official series name and number only; the name of the reporter's editor is omitted:

▶ Cobb v. Davenport, 32 N.J.L. 369 (Sup. Ct. 1867).

Not: Cobb v. Davenport, 3 Vroom 369 (Sup. Ct. 1867).

However, for United States Supreme Court reporters through 90 U.S. (23 Wall.) and a few early state reporters (see **table T1.3**), give the name of the reporter's editor and the volume of that series. If the pagination of the official jurisdiction-named reprints and the original reporters is the same, use the following form:

▶ Green v. Biddle, 21 U.S. (8 Wheat.) 1 (1823).

▶ Hall v. Bell, 47 Mass. (6 Met.) 431 (1843).

If the pagination differs, give parallel citations to the reprints and the original reporters:

▶ Wadsworth v. Ruggles, 23 Mass. 63, 6 Pick. 63 (1828).

Some very early Pennsylvania federal and state court decisions are reported in the initial volumes of the *United States Reports*. Where such reporting occurs, include the cite to "U.S.," along with a parallel cite to the appropriate lower court reporter:

▶ Barnes's Lessee v. Irwin, 2 U.S. (2 Dall.) 199, 1 Yeates 221 (Pa. 1793).

▶ United States v. Fries, 3 U.S. (3 Dall.) 515, 9 F. Cas. 826 (C.C.D. Pa. 1799) (No. 5126).

10.3.3 Public Domain Format

When citing a decision available in public domain format (also referred to as medium-neutral format), if the jurisdiction's format can be cited in the following form (see **table T1**), provide the case name, the year of decision, the state's two-character postal code, the **table T7** court abbreviation (unless the court is the state's highest court), the sequential number of the decision, and, if the decision is unpublished, a capital "U" after the sequential number of the decision. When referencing specific material within the decision, a pinpoint citation should be made to the paragraph number at which the material appears. If available, a parallel citation to the appropriate regional reporter must be provided.

The following examples are representative of the recommended public domain citation format:

▶ Beck v. Beck, 1999 ME 110, ¶ 6, 733 A.2d 981, 983.

▶ Gregory v. Class, 1998 SD 106, ¶ 3, 584 N.W.2d 873, 875.

▶ Jones v. Fisher, 1998 OK Civ. App. 120U.

If a jurisdiction adopts a public domain format that differs from the above, the requirements of the jurisdiction's format should be observed (**table T1**):

▶ Cannon v. Am. Bowling Cong., 94-0647, p. 1 (La. 4/29/94); 637 So. 2d 463, 463.

▶ Morton v. New Orleans Police Dep't, 96-1799 (La. App. 4 Cir. 2/5/97); 687 So. 2d 699.

▶ Sullivan v. State, 98-KA-00521-SCT (¶ 23) (Miss. 1999).

▶ State v. Brennan, 1998-NMCA-176, ¶ 7, 126 N.M. 389, 970 P.2d 161.

Court and Jurisdiction   10.4

Every case citation must indicate which court decided the case. In American and other common law citations, give the name of the court and its geographical jurisdiction (abbreviated according to **tables T1** or **T2** if included therein and according to **tables T7** and **T10** in all other cases) in the parenthetical phrase that immediately follows the citation and includes the date or year of decision. For court names that include ordinals, format and abbreviate the ordinals in accordance with **rule 6.2(b)**:

▶ Commonwealth v. Virelli, 620 A.2d 543 (Pa. Super. Ct. 1992).

▶ United States v. Andolschek, 142 F.2d 503 (2d Cir. 1944).

For citations to foreign cases, see **rule 20.3** and **table T2**.

A more detailed court designation than those specified by the following paragraphs may be given if necessary.

(a) Federal courts. In citations to *United States Law Week*, the United States Supreme Court is indicated with "U.S." In citations to the *Supreme Court Reporter* and the *United States Reports*, omit the Supreme Court's name. When a Supreme Court Justice sits on a lower court in his or her capacity as a Circuit Justice, cite the decision as:

▶ Redden v. Interstate Com. Comm'n, 956 F.2d 302 (Thomas, Circuit Justice, D.C. Cir. 1992).

United States courts of appeals for numbered circuits, regardless of year, are indicated as:

▶ 2d Cir.

Not: C.C.A.2d

Not: CA2

When citing the United States Court of Appeals for the District of Columbia Circuit and its predecessors, or when citing the Federal Circuit, use the following abbreviations:

▶ D.C. Cir.

▶ Fed. Cir.

For district court cases, give the district but not the division:

▶ D.N.J.

▶ D.D.C.

▶ C.D. Cal.

Not: C.D. Cal. E.D.

Cite the old circuit courts (abolished 1912):

▶ C.C.S.D.N.Y.

▶ C.C.E.D. Mo.

Cite the Judicial Panel on Multidistrict Litigation:

▶ J.P.M.L.

Cite the Foreign Intelligence Surveillance Court and Court of Review:

▶ FISA Ct.

▶ FISA Ct. Rev.

Cite decisions of bankruptcy courts and bankruptcy appellate panels:

▶ Bankr. E.D. Va.

▶ B.A.P. 9th Cir.

(b) State courts. In general, indicate the state and court of decision. However, do not include the name of the court if the court of decision is the highest court of the state:

▶ People v. Armour, 590 N.W.2d 61 (Mich. 1999).

Not: People v. Armour, 590 N.W.2d 61 (Mich. Sup. Ct. 1999).

Omit the jurisdiction and/or the court abbreviation if unambiguously conveyed by the reporter title:

▶ DiLucia v. Mandelker, 493 N.Y.S.2d 769 (App. Div. 1985).

Not: DiLucia v. Mandelker, 493 N.Y.S.2d 769 (N.Y. App. Div. 1985).

▶ Dubreuil v. Witt, 80 Conn. App. 410 (2003).

Not: Dubreuil v. Witt, 80 Conn. App. 410 (App. Ct. 2003).

Thus, when a decision is rendered by the highest court in a particular jurisdiction and the name of the reporter is the same as the name of that jurisdiction, neither the name of the court nor the name of the state need be given:

▶ Bates v. Tappan, 99 Mass. 376 (1868).

Do not indicate the department, district, or county in citing decisions of intermediate state courts unless that information is of particular relevance:

▶ Schiffman v. Corsi, 50 N.Y.S.2d 897 (Sup. Ct. 1944).

When the department, district, or county is of particular relevance, that information should be indicated as follows:

▶ Schiffman v. Corsi, 50 N.Y.S.2d 897 (Sup. Ct. N.Y. Cnty. 1944).

▶ Lee v. Perez, 120 S.W.3d 463 (Tex. App. 14th 2003).

Date or Year   10.5

(a) Decisions published in reporters. If possible, provide the year of decision; use the year of the term of the court only if the year of decision is unavailable. In ambiguous cases, follow the year given in the running head (at the top of each page) in the reporter. Before Volume 108 of the U.S. Reports (1882), opinions do not usually list their date of decision but rather list only the term in which they were decided. For the dates of these opinions, refer to the Librarian of the Supreme Court's list of dates, available at http://www.supremecourt.gov /opinions/datesofdecisions.pdf.

(b) Decisions published in other sources. Give the exact date for all unreported cases and for all cases cited to a looseleaf service, a slip opinion, an electronic database, or a newspaper:

▶ Bedell v. Nessim, No. 90-567, slip op. 3458 (1st Cir. Jan. 19, 1991).

Per **rule 10.5(a)**, the exact date is *not* necessary for cases that are labeled "unpublished" but are nevertheless reported, including cases reported in the *Federal Appendix* and "unpublished" cases reported in the appropriate reporter for the jurisdiction:

▶ United States v. Tando, 68 F. App'x 85 (9th Cir. 2003).

(c) Pending cases and cases dismissed without opinion. Use the date or year of the most recent major disposition. "Major dispositions" include *only*: the initial filing, whether in the trial court or on appeal (e.g., "filed," "*appeal docketed*," "*petition for cert. filed*"), oral argument ("argued"), and, for cases dismissed without opinion, the dismissal ("dismissed"). Indicate the significance of the date within a parenthetical phrase, unless its significance is explained elsewhere:

▶ Bedell v. Nessim, No. 90-567 (1st Cir. argued Jan. 10, 1991).

Otherwise no special notation is necessary:

▶ Bedell v. Nessim, 725 F. Supp. 1407 (D. Mass. 1990), *appeal docketed*, No. 90-567 (1st Cir. Dec. 20, 1990).

(d) Multiple decisions within a single year. When citing a case with several different decisions in the same year, include the year only with the last-cited decision in that year:

▶ United States v. Eller, 114 F. Supp. 284 (M.D.N.C.), *rev'd*, 208 F.2d 716 (4th Cir. 1953).

However, if the exact date of decision is required in either case, include both dates:

▶ DiNapoli v. Ne. Reg'l Parole Comm'n, 764 F.2d 143 (2d Cir. 1985), *petition for cert. filed*, 54 U.S.L.W. 3146 (U.S. Aug. 29, 1985) (No. 85-335).

10.6   Parenthetical Information Regarding Cases

10.6.1   Weight of Authority

(a) Generally. Information regarding the weight of the authority (e.g., en banc; in banc; 2–1 decision; mem.; per curiam; Brandeis, J.; unpublished table decision) may be added in a separate parenthetical phrase following the date of decision:

▶ Webb v. Baxter Healthcare Corp., 57 F.3d 1067 (4th Cir. 1995) (unpublished table decision).

When a case is cited for a proposition that is not the single, clear holding of a majority of the court (e.g., alternative holding; by implication; dictum; dissenting opinion; plurality opinion; holding unclear), indicate that fact parenthetically:

▶ Parker v. Randolph, 442 U.S. 62, 84 (1979) (Stevens, J., dissenting).

▶ Garcia v. San Antonio Metro. Transit Auth., 469 U.S. 528, 570 (1985) (5–4 decision) (Powell, J., dissenting).

Information regarding related authority (**rule 1.6**) or prior or subsequent history (**rule 10.7.1(a)**) that can properly be indicated with an explanatory phrase (**table T8**) should not be given parenthetically. Thus:

▶ Wersba v. Seiler, 393 F.2d 937 (3d Cir. 1968) (per curiam).

But: Wersba v. Seiler, 263 F. Supp. 838, 843 (E.D. Pa. 1967), *aff'd per curiam*, 393 F.2d 937 (3d Cir. 1968).

(b) "Mem." and "per curiam." The abbreviation "mem." stands for the word "memorandum" and should be used in a parenthetical if, and only if, a court disposition was issued without an opinion. District court and other opinions denominated "memorandum decision" are not designated "mem." in citations. The phrase "per curiam" refers to an opinion issued "by the court" as an institution as opposed to a decision issued by a particular judge. "Per curiam" is used in a parenthetical to describe an opinion so denominated by the court.

(c) Seriatim opinions. Prior to the Marshall Court (which began February 4, 1801), the U.S. Supreme Court followed the traditional British practice of each Justice writing his own opinion rather than producing a majority opinion for the Court. To cite such an opinion, include the parenthetical "(opinion of Lastname, J.)."

10.6.2   In-Chambers Opinions

When a Supreme Court Justice rules on a stay, bail, or injunction application, he or she makes that decision "in-chambers" as a "surrogate" of the whole Court. Only a few of those decisions result in written opinions, and they have been published in the U.S. Reports only since Volume 396 in 1969. To cite such an opinion, include the parenthetical "(Lastname, J., in chambers)".

(a) Pre-1969 opinions. These have been gathered by Cynthia Rapp and published in a multi-volume set, *In Chambers Opinions by the Justices of the Supreme Court of the United States*, that also includes the opinions written after 1969. Some of the pre-1969 cases did appear in the U.S. Reports, so that should be consulted first. Use this source and format only for opinions that cannot be found in the U.S. Reports.

▶ Sacco v. Massachusetts, 1 Rapp 16 (1927) (Holmes, J., in chambers).

(b) U.S. Reports. Since 1969, these opinions have been included in the U.S. Reports.

▶ Maryland v. King, 567 U.S. 1301 (2012) (Roberts, C.J., in chambers).

Quoting/Citing Parentheticals in Case Citations 10.6.3

When a case cited as authority itself quotes or cites another case for that point, a "quoting" or "citing" parenthetical is appropriate. Within the parenthetical, the same rules regarding typeface, pincites, and short forms apply to the quoted or cited authority as if it were the direct source:

▶ Zadvydas v. Davis, 533 U.S. 678, 719 (2001) (Kennedy, J., dissenting) (citing Shaughnessy v. United States *ex rel.* Mezei, 345 U.S. 206 (1953)).

Note, however, that only one level of recursion is required. Thus, if a case quotes a case that itself quotes another case, only one level of "quoting" or "citing" parentheticals is necessary. An additional level of parenthetical information may be used if the information conveyed is particularly relevant.

Order of Parentheticals 10.6.4

Parenthetical phrases should be placed in the following order: (i) weight of authority parentheticals; (ii) "quoting" and "citing" parentheticals; (iii) explanatory parentheticals. For more detailed information, see **rule 1.5(b)**. Thus:

▶ Wolf v. Colorado, 338 U.S. 25, 47 (1949) (Rutledge, J., dissenting) (rejecting the Court's conception of the exclusionary rule), *aff'g* 187 P.2d 926 (Colo. 1947), *overruled by* Mapp v. Ohio, 367 U.S. 643 (1961).

If an explanatory parenthetical contains text that *itself* requires a "quoting" or "citing" parenthetical, the two parentheticals should be nested:

▶ Kansas v. Crane, 534 U.S. 407, 409 (2002) ("[T]he statutory criterion for confinement embodied in the statute's words 'mental abnormality or personality disorder' satisfied '"substantive" due process requirements.'" (quoting Kansas v. Hendricks, 521 U.S. 346, 356 (1997))).

▶ Fullilove v. Klutznick, 448 U.S. 448, 519 (1980) (Marshall, J., concurring) (noting that conventional strict scrutiny is "strict in theory, but fatal in fact" (citing Regents of the Univ. of Cal. v. Bakke, 438 U.S. 265, 362 (1978))).

Prior and Subsequent History 10.7

Whenever a decision is cited in full, give the entire *subsequent* history of the case, but omit denials of certiorari or denials of similar discretionary appeals, unless the decision is less than two years old or the denial is particularly relevant. Omit also the history on remand or any denial of a rehearing, unless relevant to the point for which the case is cited. Finally, omit any disposition withdrawn by the deciding authority, such as an affirmance followed by reversal on rehearing. Thus:

> ▶ Cent. Ill. Pub. Serv. Co. v. Westervelt, 342 N.E.2d 463 (Ill. App. Ct. 1976), *aff'd*, 367 N.E.2d 661 (Ill. 1977).

Not: Cent. Ill. Pub. Serv. Co. v. Westervelt, 342 N.E.2d 463 (Ill. App. Ct. 1976), *aff'd*, 367 N.E.2d 661 (Ill. 1977), *cert. denied*, 434 U.S. 1070 (1978).

> ▶ Cheng v. GAF Corp., 631 F.2d 1052 (2d Cir. 1980), *vacated*, 450 U.S. 903 (1981).

Not: Cheng v. GAF Corp., 631 F.2d 1052 (2d Cir. 1980), *vacated*, 450 U.S. 903, *remanded to* 659 F.2d 1058 (2d Cir. 1981).

Give *prior* history only if significant to the point for which the case is cited or if the disposition cited does not intelligibly describe the issues in the case, as in a Supreme Court "mem." Give separate decisions of other issues in the case with their prior and subsequent history only if relevant.

10.7.1 Explanatory Phrases and Weight of Authority

A partial list of explanatory phrases (as abbreviated) appears in **table T8**.

(a) Prior or subsequent history. Append the prior or subsequent history of a case to the primary citation. Introduce and explain each prior or subsequent decision with italicized words between each citation:

> ▶ Cooper v. Dupnik, 924 F.2d 1520, 1530 & n.20 (9th Cir. 1991), *rev'd en banc*, 963 F.2d 1220 (9th Cir. 1992).

If a subsequent disposition occurred in the same year as the primary citation, omit the year from the primary citation's parenthetical.

If subsequent history itself has subsequent history, append the additional subsequent history with another explanatory phrase. For example, in the following case the Supreme Court reversed the Second Circuit, which had reversed the Southern District of New York:

> ▶ Herbert v. Lando, 73 F.R.D. 387 (S.D.N.Y.), *rev'd*, 568 F.2d 974 (2d Cir. 1977), *rev'd*, 441 U.S. 153 (1979).

To show both prior and subsequent history, give the prior history first:

> ▶ Kubrick v. United States, 581 F.2d 1092 (3d Cir. 1978), *aff'g* 435 F. Supp. 166 (E.D. Pa. 1977), *rev'd*, 444 U.S. 111 (1979).

Citations to prior or subsequent history should follow any parenthetical information given for the primary citation (**rule 1.5(b)**).

(b) Significance of disposition. Give the reason for a disposition if the disposition does not carry the normal substantive significance:

> ▶ *vacated as moot*,

> ▶ *appeal dismissed per stipulation*,

(c) Overruled, abrogated, and superseded cases. Also note cases that have been overruled, abrogated, or superseded by statute or constitutional amendment:

(i) **Overruled cases.** Indicate cases where a later decision by the same court (or a court with appellate jurisdiction over the original court) *explicitly* repudiates its earlier decision with the phrase "*overruled by*":

► Nat'l League of Cities v. Usery, 426 U.S. 833 (1976), *overruled by* Garcia v. San Antonio Metro. Transit Auth., 469 U.S. 528 (1985).

Also, when one case is overruled by multiple subsequent decisions by the same court (i.e., separate decisions overrule separate parts of the holding), include "*and*" in italics between the citations to each of the overruling cases:

► Olmstead v. United States, 277 U.S. 438 (1928), *overruled by* Katz v. United States, 389 U.S. 347 (1967), *and* Berger v. New York, 388 U.S. 41 (1967).

(ii) **Abrogated cases.** Cases that are effectively (but not explicitly) overruled or departed from by a later decision of the same court are indicated with the phrase "*abrogated by*":

► Ahrens v. Clark, 335 U.S. 188 (1948), *abrogated by* Braden v. 30th Jud. Cir. Ct., 410 U.S. 484 (1973).

(iii) **Cases superseded by statute or constitutional amendment.** When citing cases where a statute or amendment was enacted with the specific intent of reversing the outcome of the initial case, the statute or amendment *must* always be cited, and a later case recognizing such *may* be cited for support, as long as the later case is decided by the same court (or a court with appellate jurisdiction over the original court) as the superseded case:

► Wards Cove Packing Co. v. Atonio, 490 U.S. 642 (1989), *superseded by statute*, Civil Rights Act of 1991, Pub. L. No. 102-166, 105 Stat. 1071, *as recognized in* Raytheon Co. v. Hernandez, 540 U.S. 44 (2003).

Statutes cited according to this rule should be cited to the session laws (**rule 12.4**) wherever possible and, if appropriate, specific sections of the statute superseding the case may be cited.

(d) Slave Cases. For cases involving an enslaved person as a party, use the parenthetical "(enslaved party)." For cases involving an enslaved person as the subject of a property or other legal dispute but not named as a party to the suit, use the parenthetical "(enslaved person at issue)." For other cases involving enslaved persons, use an *adequately descriptive* parenthetical.

► Dred Scott v. Sandford, 60 U.S. (19 How.) 393 (1857) (enslaved party), *superseded by constitutional amendment*, U.S. Const. amend. XIV.

► Wall v. Wall, 30 Miss. 91 (1855) (enslaved person at issue).

(e) Multiple dispositions. Multiple dispositions by the same court following a primary case citation should be connected with the word "*and*" in italics:

► United States v. Baxter, 492 F.2d 150 (9th Cir.), *cert. dismissed*, 414 U.S. 801 (1973), *and cert. denied*, 416 U.S. 940 (1974).

10.7.2 Different Case Name on Appeal

(a) Name changes in subsequent history. When the name of a case differs in subsequent history, the new name must be given, introduced by the phrase "*sub nom.*":

▶ Great W. United Corp. v. Kidwell, 577 F.2d 1256 (5th Cir. 1978), *rev'd sub nom.* Leroy v. Great W. United Corp., 443 U.S. 173 (1979).

This rule applies even when the difference in the name is slight, such as a change in only the procedural phrases:

▶ Padilla *ex rel.* Newman v. Rumsfeld, 243 F. Supp. 2d 42 (S.D.N.Y.), *aff'd in part, rev'd in part sub nom.* Padilla v. Rumsfeld, 352 F.3d 695 (2d Cir. 2003), *rev'd*, 542 U.S. 426 (2004).

(b) Name changes in prior history. To indicate a different name in prior history, use the following form:

▶ Rederi v. Isbrandtsen Co., 342 U.S. 950 (1952) (per curiam), *aff'g by an equally divided court* Isbrandtsen Co. v. United States, 96 F. Supp. 883 (S.D.N.Y. 1951).

(c) Exceptions. Do not provide a different case name (i) when the parties' names are merely reversed; (ii) when the citation in which the difference occurs is to a denial of certiorari or rehearing; (iii) when, in the appeal of an administrative action, the name of the private party remains the same; or (iv) when the change is simply stylistic (e.g., "State" to "California"):

▶ United Dairy Farmers Coop. Ass'n, 194 N.L.R.B. 1094, *enforced*, 465 F.2d 1401 (3d Cir. 1972).

But: Perma Vinyl Corp., 164 N.L.R.B. 968 (1967), *enforced sub nom.* U.S. Pipe & Foundry Co. v. NLRB, 398 F.2d 544 (5th Cir. 1968).

10.8 Special Citation Forms

10.8.1 Pending and Unreported Cases

(a) Cases available on electronic media. Unreported cases available on a widely available electronic database may be cited to that database. Provide the case name, docket number, database identifier, court name, and full date of the most recent major disposition of the case. Cite to the docket number of a case as it appears on court documents. An initial digit preceding a colon and a judge's initials at the end of the docket number may be omitted. Do not omit any other letters or numbers in the case docket number.

If the database contains codes or numbers that uniquely identify the case (as do LEXIS, Westlaw, and Bloomberg Law), these must be given. Screen or page numbers, if the database assigns them, should be preceded by an asterisk; paragraph numbers, if assigned, should be preceded by a paragraph symbol:

▶ Gibbs v. Frank, No. 02-3924, 2004 U.S. App. LEXIS 21357, at *18–19 (3d Cir. Oct. 14, 2004).

▶ Int'l Snowmobile Mfrs. Ass'n v. Norton, No. 00-CV-229-B, 2004 WL 2337372, at *3, *7 (D. Wyo. Oct. 14, 2004).

If the name of the database is not clear from the database identifier, include it parenthetically at the end of the citation:

▶ Staats v. Brown, No. 65681-9, 2000 WA 0042007, ¶ 25 (Wash. Jan. 6, 2000) (VersusLaw).

Citations to cases that have not been assigned unique database identifiers should include all relevant information, such as the specific collection within the database in which the case can be found:

▶ Lindquist v. Hart, 1 CA-CV 98-0323 (Ariz. Ct. App. July 15, 1999) (Loislaw, Ariz. Case Law).

(b) Cases available in slip opinions. When a case is unreported but available in a separately printed slip opinion, give the docket number, the court, and the full date of the most recent major disposition of the case:

▶ Groucho Marx Prods. v. Playboy Enters., No. 77 Civ. 1782 (S.D.N.Y. Dec. 30, 1977).

Note any renumbering of the docket:

▶ United States v. Johnson, 425 F.2d 630 (9th Cir. 1970), *cert. granted*, 403 U.S. 956 (1971) (No. 577, 1970 Term; renumbered No. 70-8, 1971 Term).

Always give the full docket number:

▶ No. 75-31

Not: No. 31

If the date given does not refer to the date of decision and the significance of the date is not indicated elsewhere, indicate that significance within the parenthetical containing the date:

▶ Ross v. Weissman, No. 90-345 (D. Mass. filed Sept. 18, 1990).

To cite a particular page of a separately paginated slip opinion, use the form:

▶ Ross v. Weissman, No. 90-345, slip op. at 6 (D. Mass. Dec. 4, 1990).

If the case is not separately paginated, cite the page on which the case begins as well as the page on which the particularly cited material appears:

▶ Bedell v. Nessim, No. 90-567, slip op. 3458, 3465 (1st Cir. Jan. 19, 1991).

In pending or unreported adversary proceedings in bankruptcy, supply both the case number of the underlying nonadversary proceeding and the case number of the adversary proceeding:

▶ Brown v. Sachs (*In re* Brown), Ch. 7 Case No. 84-00170-G, Adv. No. 85-1190, slip op. at 5 (E.D. Mich. Jan. 24, 1986).

(c) Other pending and unreported cases. Cases that are not available in slip opinions or on electronic databases may be cited to services (**rule 19**), periodicals (**rule 16**), or the internet (**rule 18.2.2**).

(d) Depublished cases. A number of jurisdictions allow their decisions to be "depublished," usually when review is denied, and generally without a reported order. When there is no reported order depublishing the lower court decision, the fact that the case was depublished should be indicated parenthetically:

▶ Mitchell v. Cal. Fair Plan Ass'n, 260 Cal. Rptr. 3 (Ct. App. 1989) (depublished).

If the order depublishing a case *is* reported, the order should be indicated as subsequent history pursuant to **rule 10.7**, introduced with the explanatory phrase "*depublished by*."

10.8.2 Fifth Circuit Split

On October 1, 1981, the United States Court of Appeals for the Fifth Circuit was divided to create the new Fifth and Eleventh Circuits. Cite cases decided during the transitional period leading to this reorganization according to the following rules: (i) cite decisions rendered in 1981 and labeled "5th Cir." by month; (ii) give unit information whenever available; and (iii) designate as "Former 5th Cir." any nonunit judgment labeled as a Former Fifth judgment and rendered after September 30, 1981:

▶ Birl v. Estelle, 660 F.2d 592 (5th Cir. Nov. 1981).

▶ Haitian Refugee Ctr. v. Smith, 676 F.2d 1023 (5th Cir. Unit B 1982).

▶ Trailways, Inc. v. ICC, 676 F.2d 1019 (5th Cir. Unit A Aug. 1981) (per curiam).

▶ McCormick v. United States, 680 F.2d 345 (Former 5th Cir. 1982).

10.8.3 Briefs, Court Filings, and Transcripts

Citation for a petitioner's brief in a U.S. Supreme Court case:

document name   pincite   case citation

Brief for Petitioner • at • 24, • Scott • v. • Harris, • 550 • U.S. • 372 • (2007) • (No. • 05-1631), • 2006 • WL • 3693418, • at • *17.

docket number   commercial database
                     identifier (optional)

In general, all court filings follow the same general form. The full name of the document, as it appears on the filing, must come first, abbreviated according to **rule 10.2.1(c)**, followed by a pinpoint citation, if any. The full case citation and the docket number should follow the name of the document and the pinpoint citation. If no decision has yet been rendered on the filing cited, cite the case according to **rule 10.5(c)**, but the date in the parenthetical should be the date *on which the filing was made*, regardless of subsequent dispositions (e.g., oral argument). If a decision has been rendered, cite the case as you otherwise would:

▶ Complaint at 17, Kelly v. Wyman, 294 F. Supp. 893 (S.D.N.Y. 1968) (No. 68 Civ. 394).

Always include the docket number, whether parenthetically (when there *is* a reported citation) or *as* the citation (when there is no reported citation):

▶ Brief of Petitioner-Appellant at 48, United States v. Al-Marri, No. 03-3674 (7th Cir. Nov. 12, 2003).

The document number assigned by the court, such as that found on PACER for federal cases, may also be included, but is not necessary unless it is essential to finding the document:

▶ Amended Complaint & Demand for Jury Trial, Viola v. Am. Brands, Inc., No. 85-2496-G (D. Mass. Aug. 1, 1985), ECF No. 14.

With court-produced documents, including oral argument transcripts and transcripts of record, the same general rules apply:

▶ Transcript of Oral Argument at 11, Ayers v. Belmontes, 127 S. Ct. 469 (2006) (No. 05-493).

▶ Transcript of Record at 16–17, Johnson v. Eisentrager, 339 U.S. 763 (1950) (No. 306).

With amicus briefs, the same general rules apply, with the sole exception that if there are more than two signatories to the brief, "et al." may be used:

▶ Brief for Ringling Bros.-Barnum & Bailey Combined Shows, Inc. et al. as Amici Curiae Supporting Respondents, Moseley v. V Secret Catalogue, Inc., 537 U.S. 418 (2003) (No. 01-1015).

Further, though the above information is sufficient, a parallel citation to an electronic database or a website may be provided, if helpful:

▶ Brief for Ringling Bros.-Barnum & Bailey Combined Shows, Inc. et al. as Amici Curiae Supporting Respondents, Moseley v. V Secret Catalogue, Inc., 537 U.S. 418 (2003) (No. 01-1015), 2002 WL 1987618.

Such parallel citations *must* include a pinpoint citation to the electronic database where one is required for the primary document, and vice versa.

With audio recordings of court proceedings, including oral arguments and oral dissents, the same general rules apply, except that the title may be a description of the recording. Time markers should be used for designating pinpoint citations. If the recording is available online, append a URL pursuant to **rule 18.7**:

▶ Oral Argument at 11:38, Roe v. Wade, 410 U.S. 113 (1973) (No. 70-18), http://www.oyez.org/cases/1970-1979/1971/1971_70_18/argument.

▶ Oral Dissent of Justice Ginsburg at 4:25, Ledbetter v. Goodyear Tire & Rubber Co., 550 U.S. 618 (2007) (No. 05-1074), http://www.oyez.org /cases/2000-2009/2006/2006_05_1074/opinion.

For purposes of short forms (**rule 10.9**), a citation to a court document including a case citation suffices as a citation to the case itself. Where the case may be cited in short form per **rule 10.9**, it may be cited in short form in the citation to the court document, but the docket number must still be provided:

▶ [1] Brief for the Petitioner, Demore v. Kim, 538 U.S. 510 (2003) (No. 01-1491).

▶ [2] Petition for Writ of Certiorari, *Demore*, 538 U.S. 510 (No. 01-1491).

Further, the court document itself may be cited using a *supra* form, unlike the case, which may not. A *supra* form for the court document, however, does not count for purposes of the "five footnote rule" (**10.9(a)**). The document title will suffice as a reference so long as it does not create confusion. Hereinafter forms may also be used (**rule 4.2(b)**), if helpful:

▶ [3] Brief for the Petitioner, *supra* note 1, at 12.

10.8.4 Court Administrative Orders

Cite the official reporter, if therein; give the title of the order, if any:

▶ Order Discharging the Advisory Committee, 352 U.S. 803 (1956).

10.9   Short Forms for Cases

(a) Footnotes. In law review footnotes, a short form for a case may be used if it clearly identifies a case that (1) is already cited in the *same footnote* or (2) is cited (in either full or short form, including "*id.*") in *one of the preceding five footnotes*. Otherwise, a full citation is required. Thus in the following example, the use of the short form in footnotes 4 and 7–8 is correct:

▶ [1] United States v. Montoya de Hernandez, 473 U.S. 531 (1985).

▶ [2] *Id.* at 537–38.

▶ [3] *See* United States v. Martinez-Fuerte, 428 U.S. 543, 557 (1976); Cal. Bankers Ass'n v. Shultz, 416 U.S. 21, 62 (1974); Zimmermann v. Jenkins (*In re* GGM, P.C.), 165 F.3d 1026, 1027 (5th Cir. 1999); Cohen v. Drexel Burnham Lambert Grp., Inc. (*In re* Drexel Burnham Lambert Grp., Inc.), 138 B.R. 687, 702 (Bankr. S.D.N.Y. 1992); *In re* Draughon Training Inst., Inc., 119 B.R. 921, 926 (Bankr. W.D. La. 1990).

▶ [4] *See Martinez-Fuerte*, 428 U.S. at 550; *In re Draughon Training*, 119 B.R. at 930.

▶ [5] New York v. Belton, 453 U.S. 454, 457 (1981).

▶ [6] *See id.* at 456.

▶ [7] *See Montoya de Hernandez*, 473 U.S. at 540; *Cohen*, 138 B.R. at 707.

▶ [8] *See Martinez-Fuerte*, 428 U.S. at 550; *Cal. Bankers*, 416 U.S. at 55; *In re GGM, P.C.*, 165 F.3d at 1030.

(i) **Generally**. Use of only one party's name (or a readily identifiable shorter version of one party's name) in a short form citation is permissible only if the reference is unambiguous. When only one party's name (or a short form thereof) is used, it should be italicized. Acceptable short forms include:

▶ Youngstown Sheet & Tube Co. v. Sawyer, 343 U.S. at 585.

▶ *Youngstown Sheet & Tube Co.*, 343 U.S. at 585.

▶ *Youngstown*, 343 U.S. at 585.

▶ 343 U.S. at 585.

▶ *Id.* at 585.

Omit the case name as in the last two examples only if the reader will have no doubt about the case to which the citation refers.

Per **rule 10.2.1(k)**, a case may also be cited in short form by a different name than that which appears in the reporter, so long as the full citation includes both versions:

> ▶ Youngstown Sheet & Tube Co. v. Sawyer (*The Steel Seizure Case*), 343 U.S. 579, 585 (1952).

> becomes: *The Steel Seizure Case*, 343 U.S. at 585.

When citing an entire decision, and not a pinpoint therein, in short form, the citation must include the shorter version of the case name, the volume number, reporter designation, and first page; but do *not* include a jurisdiction/date parenthetical:

> ▶ *The Steel Seizure Case*, 343 U.S. 579.

When using only one party's name in a short form citation, avoid using the name of a geographical or government unit, a government official, or another common litigant. Thus:

> ▶ NAACP v. Alabama *ex rel.* Patterson, 357 U.S. 449, 464 (1958).

> becomes: *Patterson*, 357 U.S. at 464.

> **Not:** *NAACP*, 357 U.S. at 464.

> **Not:** *Alabama*, 357 U.S. at 464.

> ▶ Reno v. Bossier Parish Sch. Bd., 520 U.S. 471, 480 (1997).

> becomes: *Bossier Parish Sch. Bd.*, 520 U.S. at 480.

> **Not:** *Reno*, 520 U.S. at 480.

(ii) **Commercial electronic databases**. For cases that are available on an electronic database (**rule 10.8.1**), use a unique database identifier, if one has been assigned, in constructing a short form:

> ▶ Clark v. Homrighous, No. CIV.A.90-1380-T, 1991 WL 55402, at *3 (D. Kan. Apr. 10, 1991).

> becomes: *Clark*, 1991 WL 55402, at *3.

> ▶ Albrecht v. Stanczek, No. 87-C9535, 1991 U.S. Dist. LEXIS 5088, at *1 (N.D. Ill. Apr. 18, 1991).

> becomes: *Albrecht*, 1991 U.S. Dist. LEXIS 5088, at *1.

> ▶ Lindquist v. Hart, 1 CA-CV 98-0323, at *2 (Ariz. Ct. App. July 15, 1999) (Loislaw, Ariz. Case Law).

> becomes: *Lindquist*, at *2 (Loislaw, Ariz. Case Law).

(iii) **Slip opinions**. For decisions available in only separately printed slip opinions (**rule 10.8.1(b)**), use the following format:

> ▶ Commonwealth v. Sam, No. 4359, slip op. at 12 (Pa. Ct. Com. Pl. Oct. 20, 2005).

> becomes: *Sam*, slip op. at 12.

When citing multiple slip opinions for the same case, either give each decision a unique identifier in its initial citation or include a jurisdiction or date parenthetical in each short form. The following short forms are thus both acceptable:

▶ Doe v. Clenchy (*Clenchy II*), No. CV-09-201, slip op. at 4–6 (Me. Super. Ct. Nov. 20, 2012).

becomes: *Clenchy II*, slip op. at 4–6.

or:

▶ Doe v. Clenchy, No. CV-09-201, slip op. at 4–6 (Me. Super. Ct. Nov. 20, 2012).

becomes: *Clenchy*, slip op. at 4–6 (Me. Super. Ct. Nov. 20, 2012).

(b) Two exceptions when using "*id.*" There are two exceptions when using "*id.*" as a short form for case citations: (i) citation to the same case, but to a different opinion therein; and (ii) citation to the same case where the case citation includes parallel authorities.

(i) "*Id.*" **for different opinions**. When an "*id.*" refers to the same case, and to the same opinion cited in the preceding citation, no parenthetical is necessary. But when an "*id.*" refers to a *different* opinion, that fact *must* be indicated parenthetically, even if the second opinion cited is the majority opinion. Thus, the following examples are all correct:

▶ [1] Youngstown Sheet & Tube Co. v. Sawyer (*The Steel Seizure Case*), 343 U.S. 579 (1952).
▶ [2] *Id.* at 584.
▶ [3] *Id.* at 635 (Jackson, J., concurring).
▶ [4] *Id.* at 638.
▶ [5] *Id.* at 589 (Frankfurter, J., concurring).
▶ [6] *Id.* at 582 (majority opinion).

After an intervening citation to another source, the next time a case is cited, it is presumed to be citing to the majority opinion unless a parenthetical indicates otherwise.

(ii) "*Id.*" **for parallel citations**. For cases in which a parallel citation is required, the "*id.*" form looks slightly different (to avoid confusion). Thus:

▶ Chalfin v. Specter, 426 Pa. 464, 465, 233 A.2d 562, 563 (1967).

becomes: *Id.* at 465, 233 A.2d at 563.

Not: *Id.* at 465.

Not: *Id.* at 465, 563.

(c) Text. A case that has been cited in full in the same general discussion may be referred to (in main text or footnote text) by one of the parties' names without further citation:

▶ The issue presented in *Bakke* has not been fully resolved.

CONSTITUTIONS   11

Citation of Section 2 of the Fourteenth Amendment to the U.S. Constitution:

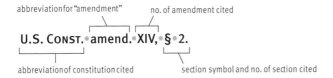

Cite the United States federal and state constitutions by "U.S." or the abbreviated name of the state, respectively (as indicated in **table T10**) and the word "CONST." Abbreviate the subdivisions of constitutions, such as articles and clauses, according to **table T16**:

- ▶ U.S. CONST. art. I, § 9, cl. 2.
- ▶ U.S. CONST. amend. XIV, § 2.
- ▶ U.S. CONST. pmbl.
- ▶ U.S. CONST. art. III, §§ 1–2.
- ▶ LA. CONST. art. X, pt. IV.

Cite constitutional provisions currently in force without a date. If the cited provision has been repealed, either indicate parenthetically the fact and year of repeal or cite the repealing provision in full:

- ▶ U.S. CONST. amend. XVIII (repealed 1933).
- ▶ U.S. CONST. amend. XVIII, *repealed by* U.S. CONST. amend. XXI.

When citing a provision that has been subsequently amended, either indicate parenthetically the fact and year of amendment or cite the amending provision in full:

- ▶ U.S. CONST. art. I, § 3, cl. 1 (amended 1913).
- ▶ U.S. CONST. art. I, § 3, cl. 1, *amended by* U.S. CONST. amend. XVII.

Cite constitutions that have been totally superseded or are otherwise no longer in effect by year of adoption; if the specific provision cited was adopted in a different year, give that year parenthetically:

- ▶ ARTICLES OF CONFEDERATION of 1781, art. IX, para. 1.
- ▶ ARK. CONST. of 1868, art. III, § 2 (1873).

When citing a constitution contained in an electronic database, indicate parenthetically the name of the publisher, editor, or compiler unless the constitution is published, edited, compiled by, or under the supervision of federal or state officials. Also indicate the name of the database and information regarding the currentness of the database as provided by the database itself:

- ▶ WASH. CONST. art. I, § 2 (West, Westlaw through Nov. 2014 amendments).

When referring to multiple amendments, sections within the same article, or clauses within the same section, it is permissible to use a single citation clause.

Otherwise, the second citation should use "*id.*" rather than repeat the name of the constitution:

▶ U.S. CONST. amends. V, XIV.

▶ U.S. CONST. art. I, § 8; *id.* art. II, § 2.

Do not use a short citation form (other than "*id.*") for constitutions.

	Citation	Text
U.S. Constitution	U.S. CONST. art. IV, § 1	Article IV, Section 1 or the Full Faith and Credit Clause
State constitution	S.C. CONST. art. I, § 12	article I, section 12 or the double jeopardy clause

For foreign constitutions, see **rule 20.4**.

12 STATUTES

Citation of an entire statute, the Comprehensive Environmental Response, Compensation, and Liability Act, as codified in the *United States Code*:

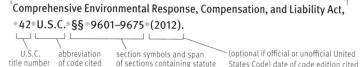

official name of act

Comprehensive Environmental Response, Compensation, and Liability Act, 42 U.S.C. §§ 9601–9675 (2012).

U.S.C. title number — abbreviation of code cited — section symbols and span of sections containing statute — (optional if official or unofficial United States Code) date of code edition cited

Citation of an individual provision of the *United States Code*:

title number — section symbol and specific section cited

28 U.S.C. § 1291 (2012).

abbreviation of code cited — (optional if official or unofficial United States Code) date of code edition cited

12.1 Basic Citation Forms

Official and unofficial codes arrange statutes currently in force by subject matter. Official and privately published session laws report statutes in chronological order of enactment. Citing official codes is preferable, but not required. Cite secondary sources—such as looseleaf services, the CIS microform service, periodicals, newspapers, or electronic databases—only when the above listed sources are not available.

Rule 12.2 explains when to use each of these basic citation forms. The next four rules discuss the citation forms for official and unofficial codes (**rule 12.3**), session laws (**rule 12.4**), electronic media and online sources (**rule 12.5**), and other secondary sources (**rule 12.6**). **Rule 12.7** explains when the prior or subsequent history of a statute may or must be cited, and **rule 12.8** discusses the use of explanatory parenthetical phrases with respect to statute citations. **Rule 12.9** outlines special citation forms for the Internal Revenue Code, ordinances, rules of evidence and procedure, model codes, principles, restatements of the law, standards, sentencing guidelines, uniform acts, and the ABA Code of Professional Responsibility. **Rule 12.10** provides short forms for statutes.

Table T1 lists citation forms for the codes and session laws of the federal and state governments, and other United States jurisdictions.

Cited to current official code	42 U.S.C. § 1983.
	National Environmental Policy Act of 1969 § 102, 42 U.S.C. § 4332.
	Consumer Credit Code, OKLA. STAT. tit. 14A, § 6-203 (1996).
Cited to current unofficial code	12 U.S.C.A. § 1426 (West).
	Parking Authority Law, 53 PA. STAT. AND CONS. STAT. ANN. § 342 (West 2010).
Cited to official session laws	National Environmental Policy Act of 1969, Pub. L. No. 91-190, § 102, 83 Stat. 852, 853 (1970) (prior to 1975 amendment).
Cited to privately published session laws	Uniform Commercial Code—General Provisions, 2004 Minn. Sess. Law Serv., ch. 162, art. 1, § 16 (West) (to be codified at MINN. STAT. ANN. § 336.1-301).
	Uniting and Strengthening America by Providing Appropriate Tools Required to Intercept and Obstruct Terrorism Act, Pub. L. No. 107-56, 2001 U.S.C.C.A.N. (115 Stat.) 272 (2001).
Cited to commercial electronic database	10 U.S.C.A. § 10173 (West, Westlaw through Pub. L. No. 111-4 (excluding Pub. L. No. 111-3)).
Cited to secondary source	Social Security Amendments of 1983, Pub. L. No. 98-21, 51 U.S.L.W. 203 (1983).

Choosing the Proper Citation Form 12.2

General Rule 12.2.1

(a) Statutes currently in force. If available, cite statutes currently in force to the current official code or its supplement. Otherwise, cite a current unofficial code or its supplement, the official session laws, privately published session laws (e.g., *United States Code Congressional and Administrative News*), a commercial electronic database, a looseleaf service, an internet source, or a newspaper—in that order of preference:

▶ National Environmental Policy Act of 1969 § 102, 42 U.S.C. § 4332.

For example, a new main edition of the official *United States Code* is published every six years, and an annual cumulative supplement is published for each intervening year. An exact copy of the *United States Code* in PDF format can be found at https://www.govinfo.gov/app/collection/uscode/; these versions may be cited as if they were the print code. Codified federal statutes enacted subsequent to the latest edition or supplement of the Code should be cited to an unofficial code (e.g., West's *United States Code Annotated*) until published in the *United States Code*.

(b) Statutes no longer in force. Cite statutes no longer in force to the current official or unofficial code if they still appear therein. Otherwise, cite the last edition of the official or unofficial code in which the statute appeared, the session laws, or a secondary source—in that order of preference. In any case, the fact of invalidation, repeal, or amendment must be noted parenthetically according to **rules 12.7.1, 12.7.2,** and **12.7.3**:

▶ Law of June 1, 1895, ch. 4322, § 23, 1895 Fla. Laws 3, 20–21 (repealed 1969).

▶ Clayton Act, ch. 323, § 7, 38 Stat. 730, 731–32 (1914) (current version at 15 U.S.C. § 18).

(c) Private laws. Cite private laws to the session laws if therein; otherwise, cite a secondary source:

▶ Priv. L. No. 94-75, 90 Stat. 2985 (1976).

12.2.2 Exceptions

(a) Scattered statutes. Cite the session laws if a statute appears in so many scattered sections or titles that no useful citation to the code is possible. Indicate parenthetically the general location of the codified sections. Thus:

▶ Tax Reduction Act of 1975, Pub. L. No. 94-12, 89 Stat. 26 (codified as amended in scattered sections of 26 U.S.C.).

But: Robinson-Patman Act, 15 U.S.C. §§ 13–13b, 21a.

If the current version of a statute is split between the main body and the supplement of a code, it should be cited according to **rule 3.1(c)**:

▶ 42 U.S.C. § 1397b (1982 & Supp. I 1983).

If the current version of a statute can be determined only by reference to multiple sources (not just a code and its supplement), it should be cited according to **rule 12.7.3**:

▶ 31 U.S.C. § 3724 (1988), *amended by* Act of Dec. 7, 1989, 31 U.S.C.S. § 3724 (Law. Co-op. Supp. 1990).

(b) Historical fact. The historical fact of enactment, amendment, or repeal should be cited to the session laws. A parenthetical reference to the current version (see **rules 12.7.3** and **12.8**) may be added:

▶ Two years later, Congress passed the Voting Rights Act of 1965, Pub. L. No. 89-110, 79 Stat. 437 (codified as amended at 42 U.S.C. §§ 1971, 1973 to 1973bb-1).

▶ The Sarbanes-Oxley Act of 2002 increased criminal penalties for mail and wire fraud. *See* Pub. L. No. 107-204, § 903(a)–(b), 2002 U.S.C.C.A.N. (116 Stat.) 745, 805 (to be codified at 18 U.S.C. §§ 1341, 1343).

(c) Materially different language. If the language in the current code (including its supplement) differs materially from the language in the session laws and the relevant title has not been enacted into positive law, cite the session laws. A parenthetical reference to the code version, introduced by the phrase "codified with some differences in language at" may be given. If differences in the language merely reflect subsequent amendments, however, cite the current code.

Cite the official code if available. A current list of federal code titles that have been enacted into positive law appears in the preface to the latest edition or supplement of the *United States Code*. Similarly, state codes should indicate whether the titles contained therein have been enacted into positive law.

Current Official and Unofficial Codes 12.3

Cite the *United States Code* (U.S.C.), the official federal code, if available. Unofficial federal codes include the *United States Code Annotated* (U.S.C.A.) and the *United States Code Service* (U.S.C.S.). Official and unofficial codes for each state (where they exist) are listed in **table T1.3**.

As with federal statutes, citing the official state codes is preferred, but not required.

All citations to codes should contain the abbreviated name of the code found in **table T1** printed in large and small capitals; the section, paragraph, or article number(s) of the statute; and the year of the code (determined according to **rule 12.3.2**):

▶ N.C. GEN. STAT. § 1-181 (2003).

Additional Information 12.3.1

Additional information may be required as follows:

(a) Name and original section number. Give the statute's name and original section number (as it appears in the appropriate session laws) only if the statute is commonly cited that way or if the information would otherwise aid in identification. Omit "The" as the first word of a statute's name. Include the year of the statute if it is in the official title. An official name, a popular name, or both may be used:

▶ Labor Management Relations (Taft-Hartley) Act § 301(a), 29 U.S.C. § 185(a).
▶ Family and Medical Leave Act (FMLA) of 1993, 29 U.S.C. § 2601.

(b) Title, chapter, or volume. If a code is divided into separately sectioned or paragraphed titles, chapters, or volumes, the title, chapter, or volume number must be indicated. When citing the federal code, give the title number before the name of the code:

▶ 42 U.S.C. § 1983.
▶ 12 U.S.C.S. § 1710 (LexisNexis 1993 & Supp. 2004).

The form for citation to state codes varies; **table T1.3** indicates whether and in what manner to identify the title, chapter, or volume number of a state code. For example:

▶ DEL. CODE ANN. tit. 13, § 1301 (1999).
▶ NEV. REV. STAT. § 28.501 (1998).

If each title, chapter, or volume of a code contains differently numbered sections or paragraphs, then the volume, chapter, or title number need not be given separately:

▶ GA. CODE ANN. § 21-2-16 (2003).

(c) Subject-matter codes. If a separately sectioned or paragraphed portion of a code is identified by subject matter rather than by a title, volume, or chapter number, give that subject-matter name as part of the code:

▶ CAL. VEH. CODE § 11506 (West 2000).

▶ TEX. FAM. CODE ANN. § 5.01 (Vernon 2002 & Supp. 2004–2005).

Table T1.3 indicates which state codes require this treatment.

(d) Publisher, editor, or compiler. Unless a code is published, edited, compiled by, or under the supervision of federal or state officials, give the name of the publisher, editor, or compiler in the parenthetical phrase containing the year of the code:

▶ 42 U.S.C.A. § 300a-7 (West 2001).

▶ 18 U.S.C.S. § 1307 (LexisNexis 1994 & Supp. 2004).

▶ CAL. VEH. CODE § 11509 (West 2000).

Not: CAL. VEH. CODE § 11509 (Cal. 2000).

Table T1 indicates which federal and state codes require this information.

(e) Supplements. Cite material appearing in supplements (including pocket parts) according to **rule 3.1(c)**:

▶ 18 U.S.C. § 510(b) (Supp. I 1983).

▶ 12 U.S.C. § 1455 (1982 & Supp. I 1983).

(f) Compilations of uncodified laws. If a code contains uncodified laws printed in a separate compilation, cite in this manner:

▶ N.Y. UNCONSOL. LAW § 751 (McKinney 2000).

(g) Appendices. If a statute appears in an appendix to a code, and the statute is numbered and otherwise printed as if it were part of that code, cite according to **rule 3.4**:

▶ 50 U.S.C. app. § 5.

If the statute is not printed as if it were part of a code, cite the session laws and add an explanatory phrase (see **rule 1.6(a)(ii)**) indicating that the statute is reprinted in the code's appendix:

▶ Act of Aug. 31, 1970, ch. 842, 1970 Mass. Acts 732, *reprinted in* MASS. GEN. LAWS ANN. ch. 40 app. at 180 (West 1985).

(h) Notes. If a statute appears in the notes section of a U.S. Code provision, cite according to **rule 3.4**. Information helpful in identifying a specific note should be added parenthetically:

▶ 12 U.S.C. § 1821 note (Continuation of Health Plan Coverage in Cases of Failed Financial Institutions).

Year of Code 12.3.2

Citations to the federal code, whether official or unofficial, do not require a date. When citing a state code, or (if a date is desired), a federal code, when citing a bound volume of the current official or unofficial code, provide parenthetically the year that appears on the spine of the volume, the year that appears on the title page, or the latest copyright year—in that order of preference. If the date on the spine or title page spans more than one year, give all years covered. If the volume is a replacement of an earlier edition, use the year of the replacement volume, not the year of the original:

► NEB. REV. STAT. § 33-114 (1998).

When citing a provision that appears in a supplement or pocket part, give the year that appears on the title page of the supplement or pocket part. If there is none, give the latest copyright year of the supplement or pocket part. In either case, if the date spans more than one year, give all years included:

► IND. CODE ANN. § 29-1-5-3.1 (West Supp. 2003).

To cite material that appears in both the main volume and a supplement or pocket part, give both years according to **rule 3.1(c)**:

► VT. STAT. ANN. tit. 12, § 892 (2002 & Supp. 2004).

If a code is published in looseleaf form, give the year that appears on the page on which the provision is printed or the year that appears on the first page of the subdivision in which the provision appears—in that order of preference—rather than the years indicated above:

► ALASKA STAT. § 28.01.010 (2002).

Other dates (such as the date on which an act becomes effective) may also be given parenthetically according to **rule 12.8**:

► OKLA. STAT. tit. 10, § 7303-1.7 (1998 & Supp. 2005) (effective July 1, 2002).

Session Laws 12.4

(a) Name. When citing session laws, always give the name of the statute and the public law or chapter number. Omit "The" as the first word of a statute's name. An official name, a popular name, or both may be used:

► White-Slave Traffic (Mann) Act, ch. 395, 36 Stat. 825 (1910) (codified as amended at 18 U.S.C. §§ 2421–2424).
► Foreign Assistance Act of 1961, Pub. L. No. 87-195, 75 Stat. 424.

If the statute has no official or popular name, identify the act with a full date. Use the form "Act of ‹date of enactment›," or, if that information is unavailable, "Act effective ‹date of effectiveness›." Other identifying information may be added parenthetically:

▶ Act of Aug. 21, 1974, ch. 85, 1974 N.J. Laws 385 (providing unemployment compensation for jurors).

Not: An Act concerning unemployment compensation for persons serving
on jury duty, and amending R.S. 43:21-4, ch. 85, 1974 N.J. Laws 385.

(b) Volume. Give the volume number (or, if none, the year) of the session
laws, followed by the abbreviated name of the session laws in ordinary roman
type. The official federal session laws, *Statutes at Large*, are abbreviated "Stat."
Abbreviations for official and privately published state session laws appear in
tables T1.3 and **T1.4**. When citing state session laws, begin the abbreviated
title of the session laws with the name of the state abbreviated according to
table T10, even if the state name is not part of the official title; omit words in
the official title not necessary for identification:

▶ 1978 Ark. Acts.

▶ 1935–1936 Ill. Laws 4th Spec. Sess.

▶ 1878 Minn. Laws.

Not: 1878 Laws of Minn.

(c) Pages and sections. When citing an entire act, give the page of the session
laws on which the act begins:

▶ National Environmental Policy Act of 1969, Pub. L. No. 91-190, 83 Stat.
852 (1970).

When citing only part of an act, give the section(s) or subsection(s) cited, the
page on which the act begins, and the page(s) on which the relevant section(s)
or subsection(s) appear(s):

▶ National Environmental Policy Act of 1969, Pub. L. No. 91-190, § 102,
83 Stat. 852, 853–54 (1970).

▶ Act of June 15, 1995, No. 302, § 3602(11), 1995 La. Sess. Law Serv. 344,
344 (West).

(d) Session laws amending prior acts. Session laws amending prior acts are
often divided into sections within sections; that is, the session law is divided
into primary sections, and these sections, in turn, contain sections of the
amended act. Cite the bill's sections by abbreviation (sec.) and the amended
act's sections by symbol (§):

▶ Labor-Management Relations Act, ch. 120, sec. 101, § 8(a)(3), 61 Stat.
136, 140–41 (1947).

(e) Year or date. Give parenthetically the year in which the statute was passed
by the legislature. If no date of enactment is identified, give the date on which
the statute became effective:

▶ McCarran-Ferguson Act, ch. 20, 59 Stat. 33 (1945) (codified as
amended at 15 U.S.C. §§ 1011–1015).

Omit the year of the statute's passage if the same year is part of the name of the
statute or of the session laws:

▶ Securities Act of 1933, ch. 38, 48 Stat. 74 (codified as amended at 15
U.S.C. §§ 77a–77aa).

▶ Act of Apr. 25, 1978, No. 515, § 3, 1978 Ala. Acts 569, 569 (codified as amended at ALA. CODE § 9-3-12 (1987)).

(f) Codification information. If a statute has been or will ultimately be codified and the code location is known, give that information parenthetically:

▶ Act of July 12, 1985, ch. 223, § 3, 1985 Cal. Legis. Serv. 239, 241 (West) (to be codified at CAL. INS. CODE § 11589.5).

Electronic Databases and Online Sources 12.5

(a) Commercial electronic databases. When citing a code contained in an electronic database, give parenthetically the name of the database and information regarding the currency of the database as provided by the database itself (rather than the year of the code according to rule **12.3.2**). In accordance with rule **12.3.1(d)**, also give the name of the publisher, editor, or compiler unless the code is published, edited, or compiled by, or under the supervision of, federal or state officials:

▶ 18 U.S.C.S. § 1956 (LEXIS through Pub. L. No. 113-108).

▶ 18 U.S.C.A. § 1956 (Westlaw through Pub. L. No. 113-93 (excluding Pub. L. No. 113-79)).

▶ CAL. BUS. & PROF. CODE § 1670 (Deering, LEXIS through 1995 Sess.).

▶ CAL. BUS. & PROF. CODE § 1670 (West, Westlaw through 1995 portion of 1995–1996 Legis. Sess.).

▶ WASH. REV. CODE § 13.64.060 (VersusLaw through 1999 legislation).

▶ WIS. STAT. § 19.43 (LEXIS through 1994 legislation).

▶ WIS. STAT. § 19.43 (Loislaw through 1997–1998 Legis. Sess.).

▶ WIS. STAT. ANN. § 19.43 (West, Westlaw through 1995 Act 26).

(b) Internet and online sources. When states and municipalities publish their official statutes or ordinances online, the online source may be directly cited.

▶ BELLINGHAM, WASH., MUN. CODE § 16.60.060 (2015), http://www .codepublishing.com/WA/Bellingham/.

Authentic, official, or exact copies of a source available online can be cited as if they were the original print source (**rule 18.2.1(a)**).

▶ NEV. REV. STAT. § 2-1247 (2007).

Unofficial online sources are cited in accordance with **rule 18.2.2**.

▶ HAW. REV. STAT. § 142-23.5 (2009), http://www.capitol.hawaii.gov /hrscurrent/Vol03_Ch0121-0200D/HRS0142/HRS_0142-0023_0005 .htm.

Other Secondary Sources 12.6

When citing a statute to any source other than a code, session laws, or an electronic database, give the name of the act and public law or chapter number as if citing to session laws (**rule 12.4**). When referring to a particular provision, give the section or subsection number after the public law or chapter number.

If possible, cite federal statutes (particularly those enacted after 1974) to the *United States Code Congressional and Administrative News*, indicating the volume number (and page number, if known) of the *Statutes at Large* where the statute will appear (note that the page numbers in these two sources often differ):

▶ Act of July 19, 1985, Pub. L. No. 99-68, 1985 U.S.C.C.A.N. (99 Stat.) 166.

▶ Act of Aug. 13, 1954, ch. 731, 1954 U.S.C.C.A.N. (68 Stat. 717) 833.

When citing an entire act, give the page on which the act begins. When citing part of an act, give both the page on which the act begins and the pages on which the cited material appears. If the statute has been or will ultimately be codified and the code location is known, give that information parenthetically:

▶ Act of July 9, 1985, Pub. L. No. 99-61, § 110, 1985 U.S.C.C.A.N. (99 Stat.) 113, 115 (to be codified at 31 U.S.C. § 5112).

Cite other secondary sources according to **rule 19** (services) or **16** (periodical materials) in that order of preference. Give the date or year appropriate for the cited source. If the name of a statute cited to a service includes the year, and the service was published in that year, the year of the service may be omitted. If the future location of the act in either a code or session laws is known, give that information parenthetically according to **rule 12.8**:

▶ Presidential and Executive Office Accountability Act of 1996, Pub. L. No. 104-331, [1 Lab. Rel.] Lab. L. Rep. (CCH) ¶ 660 (1997).

If a recent statute has not yet been published in any source, give only the name of the act; the public law or chapter number; the section or subsection number if referring to only part of the statute; the full date of enactment (or, if none, the date of approval by the executive or effective date); and the future location, if known, in a code or session laws:

▶ Alabama Corporate Income Tax Reform Act, No. 85-515 (May 8, 1985).

12.7 Invalidation, Repeal, Amendment, and Prior History

12.7.1 Invalidation

When citing a statute invalidated or declared unconstitutional by a case, indicate this fact by citing the case in full:

▶ Religious Freedom Restoration Act (RFRA) of 1993, Pub. L. No. 103-141, 1993 U.S.C.C.A.N. (107 Stat.) 1488, *invalidated by* City of Boerne v. Flores, 521 U.S. 507 (1997).

12.7.2 Repeal

When citing a statute no longer in force, indicate the fact and date of repeal parenthetically, or include a full citation to the repealing statute when particularly relevant:

▶ Law of June 1, 1895, ch. 4322, § 23, 1895 Fla. Laws ch. 3, 20–21 (repealed 1969).

▶ Act of Jan. 24, 1923, ch. 42, 42 Stat. 1174, 1208, *repealed by* Budget and Accounting Procedures Act of 1950, ch. 946, § 301(97), 64 Stat. 832, 844.

Amendment 12.7.3

When citing a version of a statute that has since been amended, indicate the fact and date of amendment parenthetically, cite the amending statute in full, or cite the current amended version parenthetically:

▶ Supplemental Appropriation Act of 1955, Pub. L. No. 663, § 1311, 68 Stat. 800, 830 (1954) (amended 1959).

▶ 33 U.S.C. § 1232, *amended by* 33 U.S.C. § 1232(f) (Supp. I 1983).

▶ Clayton Act, ch. 323, § 7, 38 Stat. 730, 731–32 (1914) (current version at 15 U.S.C. § 18).

An indication of the amended date is required even if the particular subsection cited was not altered when the statute was amended.

Prior History 12.7.4

When citing the current version of a statute, prior history may be given parenthetically according to **rule 12.8** if relevant:

▶ 33 U.S.C. § 1232(f) (Supp. I 1983) (amending 33 U.S.C. § 1232 (1982)).

▶ 28 U.S.C. § 1652 (originally enacted as Act of June 25, 1948, ch. 646, § 1652, 62 Stat. 869, 944).

▶ 28 U.S.C. § 1652 (corresponds to the Judiciary Act of 1789, ch. 20, § 34, 1 Stat. 73, 92).

▶ Clayton Act § 7, 15 U.S.C. § 18 (original version at ch. 323, § 7, 38 Stat. 730, 731–32 (1914)).

Explanatory Parenthetical Phrases 12.8

Explanatory parenthetical phrases are used to show the code location of statutes cited to session laws (**rules 12.2.2** and **12.4**) or secondary sources (**rule 12.6**); to identify useful dates, such as the effective date of a statute (**rules 12.3.2** and **12.4(e)**); and to indicate the invalidation (**rule 12.7.1**), repeal (**rule 12.7.2**), amendment (**rule 12.7.3**), or prior history (**rule 12.7.4**) of a statute. In addition, explanatory parenthetical phrases may be used to give any other relevant information about a statute:

▶ 5 U.S.C. § 553(b) (requiring agencies to publish notice of proposed rulemaking in the *Federal Register*).

See generally **rule 1.5** (parenthetical information).

12.9   Special Citation Forms

12.9.1   Internal Revenue Code

In citations to the Internal Revenue Code, "26 U.S.C." may be replaced with "I.R.C." Thus:

> ► 26 U.S.C. § 61 .

becomes: I.R.C. § 61.

Citations to the Internal Revenue Code as it appears in an unofficial code should identify the unofficial code by placing the publisher's name in the parenthetical phrase containing, if included, the year of the version cited. Thus, citations to U.S.C.A. should appear:

> ► I.R.C. § 1371 (West Supp. 1991).
> ► I.R.C. § 1247 (West).

See also **rule 12.10** regarding short form citation of statutes. For special citation forms for federal tax materials in court documents and legal memoranda, see **Bluepages B12.1.4**.

12.9.2   Ordinances

Cite ordinances analogously to statutes. Always give the name of the political subdivision (such as a city or county) and the abbreviated state name at the beginning of the citation. Do not abbreviate the name of the political subdivision unless it is abbreviated in **table T10**. If the ordinance is codified, give the name of the code (abbreviated according to **table T1**), the section or other subdivision, and the year of the code (determined according to **rule 12.3.2**). Print the political subdivision, state, and code names in large and small capitals:

> ► MONTGOMERY, ALA., CODE § 3A-11 (1971).
> ► PORTLAND, OR., POLICE CODE art. 30 (1933).
> ► FORT WORTH, TEX., REV. ORDINANCES ch. 34, art. I, § 15 (1950).
> ► S.F., CAL., POLICE CODE art. 16, div. 1, § 1076(a) (2000).

If the ordinance is uncodified, give its number (or, if none, its name) and, in a parenthetical, the exact date of adoption. Print the political subdivision, state, and ordinance name in ordinary roman type:

> ► San Jose, Cal., Ordinance 16,043 (Jan. 17, 1972).
> ► Halifax County, Va., Ordinance to Regulate the Solicitation of Membership in Organizations (Aug. 6, 1956).

12.9.3   Rules of Evidence and Procedure

Citation of a Federal Rule of Civil Procedure:

number of rule cited

FED. R. CIV. P. ● **11.**

abbreviation of set of rules cited

Cite current or uniform rules of evidence or procedure in large and small capitals, without any date. Use abbreviations such as the following or abbreviations suggested by the rules themselves:

▶ FED. R. CIV. P. 12(b)(6).

▶ FED. R. CRIM. P. 42(a).

▶ FED. R. APP. P. 2.

▶ 1ST CIR. R. 6(a).

▶ FED. R. EVID. 410.

▶ UNIF. R. EVID. 404(b).

▶ SUP. CT. R. 17.

When citing rules no longer in force, give the most recent official source in which they appear and indicate the date of repeal parenthetically:

▶ SUP. CT. R. 8, 306 U.S. 690 (1939) (repealed 1954).

Model Codes, Principles, Restatements, Standards, Sentencing Guidelines, and Uniform Acts
12.9.4

Cite model codes, principles, restatements, standards, sentencing guidelines, uniform acts, and similar materials in large and small capitals, by section, rule, or other relevant subdivision. For restatements, give the year in which the restatement was published. For model codes, principles, standards, and sentencing guidelines, give the year in which the code, principles, standards, or guidelines were adopted. In that case, give the year of the last amendment, even when citing a portion not amended at that time. Usually the cover or title page of the source will indicate the date of the most recent amendments incorporated. When naming the code, principles, restatement, standards, or guidelines, use the abbreviations listed in **table T6** (abbreviation of case names and periodicals) or suggested by the source itself. Indicate the author's name parenthetically. Abbreviate the author's name according to **rule 15.1(c)** (institutional authors):

▶ PRINCIPLES OF THE L. OF FAM. DISSOLUTION: ANALYSIS AND RECOMMENDATIONS § 2.07 (AM. L. INST. 2002).

▶ RESTATEMENT (THIRD) OF UNFAIR COMPETITION § 3 (AM. L. INST. 1995).

▶ U.S. SENT'G GUIDELINES MANUAL § 2D1.1(c) (U.S. SENT'G COMM'N 2004).

When citing to a uniform act itself, and not as the law of a particular state, cite it as a separate code. Indicate the author's name parenthetically. Abbreviate the author's name according to **rule 15.1(c)** (institutional authors):

▶ U.C.C. § 2-314 (AM. L. INST. & UNIF. L. COMM'N 1977).

▶ UNIF. TR. CODE § 105 (UNIF. L. COMM'N 2000).

When citing a uniform act to the *Uniform Laws Annotated* (U.L.A.), provide the title of the act using abbreviations in **table T6**, the section number, the year of amendment or repeal (if any), the appropriate volume of the U.L.A., the page number on which the relevant section appears, and the year of publication:

> ▶ UNIF. ADOPTION ACT § 10, 9 U.L.A. 45 (1988).

Give the year in which the uniform act was last amended, even if the section referred to was not amended at that time. If a uniform act or section has been withdrawn, superseded, or amended, indicate that fact parenthetically according to **rule 12.7**:

> ▶ UNIF. PROB. CODE § 2-706 (amended 2020), 8 pt. 1 U.L.A. 291 (2013).

When citing to the law of a particular state, cite as a separate code:

> ▶ OKLA. STAT. tit. 12A, § 2-314 (2004).

If a code, principle, restatement, or set of standards or guidelines is a tentative or proposed draft, indicate that fact parenthetically as it appears on the publication and give the draft number (if available) and the year of the draft:

> ▶ MODEL LAND DEV. CODE § 2-402(2) (AM. L. INST., Proposed Official Draft 1975).

> ▶ RESTATEMENT (SECOND) OF TORTS § 847A (AM. L. INST., Tentative Draft No. 17, 1974).

If a restatement contains a subtitle, retain the subtitle in the citation:

> ▶ RESTATEMENT (THIRD) OF PROP.: WILLS AND DONATIVE TRANSFERS § 2.1 (AM. L. INST. 1999).

When citing a draft of a uniform act, indicate that fact parenthetically and give the date of the draft.

> ▶ ELEC. WILLS ACT (UNIF. L. COMM'N, Draft Jan. 22, 2019).

Cite Generally Accepted Auditing Standards and Generally Accepted Accounting Principles as follows:

> ▶ CODIFICATION OF ACCT. STANDARDS & PROCS., Statement on Auditing Standards No. 1, § 150 (AM. INST. OF CERTIFIED PUB. ACCTS. 1972).

> ▶ RSCH. AND DEV. ARRANGEMENTS, Statement of Fin. Acct. Standards No. 68, § 32 (FIN. ACCT. STANDARDS BD. 1982).

Comments, notes, and other addenda should be cited according to **rule 3.4**:

> ▶ MODEL PENAL CODE § 223.6 note on status of section (AM. L. INST., Proposed Official Draft 1962).

> ▶ RESTATEMENT (SECOND) OF CONFLICT OF LS. § 305 cmt. b, illus. 1 (AM. L. INST. 1977).

> ▶ STANDARDS FOR TRAFFIC JUST. § 4.2 cmt. at 9 (AM. BAR ASS'N 1975).

> ▶ UNIF. PRUDENT INV. ACT § 2 cmt. (UNIF. L. COMM'N 1994).

> ▶ RESTATEMENT (SECOND) OF CONTS. ch. 16, topic 3, intro. note (AM. L. INST. 1981).

Cite application notes, background commentary, introductory commentary, and appendices to sentencing guidelines as follows:

> ▶ U.S. SENT'G GUIDELINES MANUAL § 3D1.4 cmt. n.1 (U.S. SENT'G COMM'N 2004).

▶ U.S. Sᴇɴᴛ'ɢ Gᴜɪᴅᴇʟɪɴᴇs Mᴀɴᴜᴀʟ § 2D1.2 cmt. background (U.S. Sᴇɴᴛ'ɢ Cᴏᴍᴍ'ɴ 2004).

▶ U.S. Sᴇɴᴛ'ɢ Gᴜɪᴅᴇʟɪɴᴇs Mᴀɴᴜᴀʟ ch. 3, pt. D, introductory cmt. (U.S. Sᴇɴᴛ'ɢ Cᴏᴍᴍ'ɴ 2004).

▶ U.S. Sᴇɴᴛ'ɢ Gᴜɪᴅᴇʟɪɴᴇs Mᴀɴᴜᴀʟ app. C (U.S. Sᴇɴᴛ'ɢ Cᴏᴍᴍ'ɴ 2004).

When citing a version of a code, restatement, or set of standards that has been withdrawn or amended, indicate that fact according to **rule 12.7.2 or 12.7.3**:

▶ Mᴏᴅᴇʟ Bᴜs. Cᴏʀᴘ. Aᴄᴛ § 2(f) (1969) (Aᴍ. Bᴀʀ Ass'ɴ, amended 1973).

....

ABA Code of Professional Responsibility and Opinions on Ethics 12.9.5

Cite the old *Model Code of Professional Responsibility* and the new *Model Rules of Professional Conduct* according to **rule 12.9.4**:

▶ Mᴏᴅᴇʟ Cᴏᴅᴇ ᴏғ Pʀᴏ. Rᴇsᴘ. Canon 2 (Aᴍ. Bᴀʀ Ass'ɴ 1980).

▶ Mᴏᴅᴇʟ Rᴜʟᴇs ᴏғ Pʀᴏ. Cᴏɴᴅᴜᴄᴛ r. 3.12 (Aᴍ. Bᴀʀ Ass'ɴ, Discussion Draft 1983).

Cite ethical considerations and disciplinary rules as follows:

▶ Mᴏᴅᴇʟ Cᴏᴅᴇ ᴏғ Pʀᴏ. Rᴇsᴘ. EC 7-36 (Aᴍ. Bᴀʀ Ass'ɴ 1980).

▶ Mᴏᴅᴇʟ Cᴏᴅᴇ ᴏғ Pʀᴏ. Rᴇsᴘ. DR 8-101 (Aᴍ. Bᴀʀ Ass'ɴ 1980).

Cite notes or other commentary according to **rule 3.4**:

▶ Mᴏᴅᴇʟ Rᴜʟᴇs ᴏғ Pʀᴏ. Cᴏɴᴅᴜᴄᴛ r. 1.15 cmt. (Aᴍ. Bᴀʀ Ass'ɴ 1983).

Cite formal and informal opinions of the Committee on Ethics and Professional Responsibility (or the older Committees on Professional Ethics (1958–1971) and on Professional Ethics and Grievances (1919–1958)) by issuing body, opinion number, and year. Abbreviate according to **table T6**; "American Bar Association" may be abbreviated "ABA" for these documents:

▶ ABA Comm. on Pro. Ethics & Grievances, Formal Op. 35 (1931).

▶ ABA Comm. on Ethics & Pro. Resp., Informal Op. 1414 (1978).

The subject of the opinion may be given parenthetically:

▶ ABA Comm. on Ethics & Pro. Resp., Formal Op. 338 (1974) (discussing the use of credit cards for the payment of legal services and expenses).

Short Forms for Statutes 12.10

(a) Text. In law review text and footnote text, use the forms listed in the "Text" column of the table below to refer to statutes. Provide a citation (in full or short form according to **rule 12.10(b)**) in an accompanying footnote when appropriate.

(b) Citations. In law review citations, use any of the forms listed in the "Short Citation" column of the table below that clearly identifies a statute if the statute has already been cited (in either full or short form, including "*id.*") in either the *same footnote* or in a manner such that it can be readily found in *one of the preceding five footnotes*, again including "*id.*" Otherwise, use the "Full Citation" form.

	Full Citation	Text	Short Citation
Named Statutes	Administrative Procedure Act § 1, 5 U.S.C. § 551	section 1 of the Administrative Procedure Act or section 1	§ 1 or 5 U.S.C. § 551 or Administrative Procedure Act § 1
U.S. Code Provisions	42 U.S.C. § 1983	42 U.S.C. § 1983 or § 1983	42 U.S.C. § 1983 or § 1983
State Code Provisions (numbered codes)	DEL. CODE ANN. tit. 28, § 1701 (1999)	title 28, section 1701 of the Delaware Code or section 1701	tit. 28, § 1701 or § 1701
State Code Provisions (named codes)	CAL. EDUC. CODE § 48222 (West 2008)	section 48222 of the California Education Code or section 48222	EDUC. § 48222
Session Laws	National Environmental Policy Act of 1969, Pub. L. No. 91-190, § 102, 83 Stat. 852, 853–54 (1970)	section 102 of the National Environmental Policy Act or section 102	§ 102 or National Environmental Policy Act § 102 or § 102, 83 Stat. at 853–54

(c) "Section." Note that except when referring to *United States Code* provisions, the word "section" should be spelled out in law review text and footnote text, although the symbol "§" may be used in citations. See **rule 6.2(c)**.

(d) Electronic sources. For materials available on an electronic database, use the name of the database in constructing a short form:

► WIS. STAT. ANN. § 19.43 (West, Westlaw through 2007 Act 242).

becomes: § 19.43 (Westlaw).

For materials available online, use the normal short form appropriate for the source. A URL need not be repeated after a full citation.

► UTAH CODE § 4-30-108 (2017), https://le.utah.gov/xcode/Title4/Chapter30/4-30-S108.html.

becomes: § 4-30-108.

LEGISLATIVE MATERIALS 13

Besides statutes (**rule 12**), the legislative process generates bills and resolutions (**rule 13.2**); committee hearings (**rule 13.3**); reports, documents, and committee prints (**rule 13.4**); floor debates (**rule 13.5**); and, sometimes, separately bound legislative histories (**rule 13.6**). When citing any United States legislative material except debates, include the title (if relevant), the abbreviated name of the house, the number of the Congress, the number assigned to the material, and the year of publication. State legislative materials are cited similarly except when indicated otherwise. Abbreviations for commonly used words in legislative materials are listed in **table T9**.

In addition, include parenthetically the session number for House and Senate documents published before the 60th Congress (1907), House Reports published before the 47th Congress (1881), and Senate Reports published before the 40th Congress (1867). For House and Senate materials published after these dates, the session number can be inferred from the year of publication: First sessions always fall in odd-numbered years, while second sessions always fall in even-numbered years. On rare occasions, Congress holds a third session. When citing materials produced during a third session, provide this information parenthetically.

Basic Citation Forms 13.1

Federal bill (unenacted)	Privacy Protection Act of 1998, H.R. 3224, 105th Cong. § 2(a) (1998).
	H.R. 119, 54th Cong. (1st Sess. 1896).
Federal resolution (unenacted)	H.R.J. Res. 79, 106th Cong. (1999).
State bill	H.R. 124, 179th Leg., 1st Spec. Sess. (Pa. 1995).
State resolution	S.J. Res. 836, 118th Leg., 3d Spec. Sess. (Me. 1999).
Committee hearing	*Background and History of Impeachment: Hearing Before the Subcomm. on the Constitution of the H. Comm. on the Judiciary*, 105th Cong. 22–23 (1998) (statement of Rep. Hutchinson, Member, H. Comm. on the Judiciary).
Federal report	H.R. REP. NO. 101-524, at 10 (1990), *reprinted in* 1990 U.S.C.C.A.N. 1448, 1451.
Federal document	H.R. DOC. NO. 102-399, at 3 (1992).
Committee print	STAFF OF H. COMM. ON THE JUDICIARY, 93D CONG., CONSTITUTIONAL GROUNDS FOR PRESIDENTIAL IMPEACHMENT 38 (Comm. Print 1974).
Congressional debate	145 CONG. REC. H1817 (daily ed. Apr. 12, 1999) (statement of Rep. Pease).

Source reprinted in separately bound legislative history	S. COMM. ON LAB. AND PUB. WELFARE, LABOR-MANAGEMENT REPORTING AND DISCLOSURE ACT OF 1959, S. REP. NO. 86-187, at 4 (1959), *reprinted in* 1959 U.S.C.C.A.N. 2318, 2320, *and in* 1 NLRB, LEGISLATIVE HISTORY OF THE LABOR-MANAGEMENT REPORTING AND DISCLOSURE ACT OF 1959, at 397, 400 (1959).

13.2 Bills and Resolutions

(a) Unenacted federal bills and resolutions. When citing federal bills, include the name of the bill (if relevant), the abbreviated name of the house, the number of the bill, the number of the Congress, the section (if any), and the year of publication:

▶ S. 516, 105th Cong. § 2 (1997).

▶ H.R. 422, 106th Cong. (1999).

▶ Clear Skies Act, S. 485, 108th Cong. (2003).

▶ Protection from Personal Intrusion Act, H.R. 2448, 105th Cong. § 2(a) (1997).

A parenthetical indicating the date and stage of the bill may be provided in order to distinguish among multiple versions of the same bill in the same Congress. Subcommittee and committee names may be abbreviated according to **tables T6, T9,** and **T10**:

▶ S. 593, 101st Cong. § 2 (as passed by Senate, May 31, 1989).

▶ S. 593, 101st Cong. § 2 (as reported by S. Comm. on the Judiciary, May 12, 1989).

Cite resolutions analogously, using the following abbreviations:

House Resolution	▶ H.R. Res.
Senate Resolution	▶ S. Res.
House Concurrent Resolution	▶ H.R. Con. Res.
Senate Concurrent Resolution	▶ S. Con. Res.
House Joint Resolution	▶ H.R.J. Res.
Senate Joint Resolution	▶ S.J. Res.
Senate Executive Resolution	▶ S. Exec. Res.

Thus:

▶ H.R.J. Res. 124, 105th Cong. (1998).

A parallel citation to a published committee hearing, a legislative report, or the *Congressional Record* may also be provided if it would assist the reader in locating the bill (**rules 13.3, 13.4,** and **13.5**).

(b) Enacted federal bills and resolutions. Enacted bills and joint resolutions are statutes (**rule 12**). They are cited as statutes except when used to document legislative history, in which case they are cited as unenacted bills.

Enacted simple resolutions, which bind only one house of Congress, and enacted concurrent resolutions, which bind either one or both houses of Congress, should be cited as unenacted bills. Unless otherwise clear in context, the fact of enactment should be noted parenthetically:

▶ S. Res. 141, 106th Cong. (1999) (enacted).

▶ H.R. Con. Res. 196, 106th Cong. (1999) (enacted).

▶ H.R. Res. 811, 108th Cong. (2004) (enacted).

A parallel citation to the *Congressional Record* (for simple resolutions) or to the *Statutes at Large* (for concurrent resolutions) may be provided if it would assist the reader in locating the enacted resolution. Because only enacted resolutions are printed in the *Statutes at Large* ("Stat."), a parenthetical noting enactment is not necessary when a parallel citation to Stat. is given:

▶ S. Res. 218, 83d Cong., 100 CONG. REC. 2972 (1954) (enacted).

▶ S. Con. Res. 97, 94th Cong., 90 Stat. 3024 (1976).

(c) State bills and resolutions. When citing state bills and resolutions, include the name of the legislative body, abbreviated according to **tables T6, T9,** and **T10,** the number of the bill or resolution, the number of the legislative body (or, if not numbered, the year of the body), and the number or designation of the legislative session. Parenthetically indicate the name of the state, abbreviated according to **table T10,** and the year of enactment (for an enacted bill or resolution) or the year of publication (for an unenacted bill or resolution).

▶ H.D. 636, 1999 Leg., 413th Sess. (Md. 1999).

▶ H.R. 189, 145th Gen. Assemb., Reg. Sess. (Ga. 1999).

A parallel citation to state session laws may be provided if it would assist the reader in locating an enacted resolution.

▶ H.R.J. Res. 1, 40th Leg., 2d Spec. Sess., 1974 Utah Laws 7.

Hearings 13.3

(a) Federal committee hearings. When citing federal committee hearings, always include the entire subject matter title as it appears on the cover, the bill number (if any), the subcommittee name (if any), the committee name, the number of the Congress, the page number of the particular material being cited (if any), and the year of publication. Subcommittee and committee names may be abbreviated according to **tables T6, T9,** and **T10.** Cite as follows:

▶ *Protection from Personal Intrusion Act and Privacy Protection Act of 1998: Hearing on H.R. 2448 and H.R. 3224 Before the H. Comm. on the Judiciary*, 105th Cong. 56–57 (1998) (statement of Richard Masur, President, Screen Actors Guild).

▶ *Copyright Protection for Semiconductor Chips: Hearing on H.R. 1028 Before the Subcomm. on Cts., C.L. & the Admin. of Just. of the H. Comm. on the Judiciary*, 98th Cong. 14 (1983) (statement of Jon A. Baumgarten, Copyright Counsel, Association of American Publishers).

Titles of the individuals providing statements may be abbreviated according to **table T11**:

▶ *Tribal Energy Self-Sufficiency Act and the Native American Energy Development and Self-Determination Act: Hearing on S. 424 and S. 522 Before the S. Comm. on Indian Affs.*, 108th Cong. 1 (2003) (statement of Sen. Ben Nighthorse Campbell, Chairman, S. Comm. on Indian Affs.).

▶ *Transforming the Federal Government to Protect America from Terrorism: Hearing Before the H. Select Comm. on Homeland Sec.*, 107th Cong. 23–25 (2002) (statement of John Ashcroft, Att'y Gen. of the United States).

(b) State committee hearings. When citing state committee hearings, follow the same form, but also include the number of the legislative session:

▶ *Tax Credit for Cost of Providing Commuter Benefits to Employees: Hearing on H.D. 636 Before the H. Comm. on Ways & Means*, 1999 Leg., 413th Sess. 5–8 (Md. 1999) (statement of Del. Paul Carlson, Member, H. Comm. on Ways & Means).

13.4 Reports, Documents, and Committee Prints

(a) Numbered federal reports and documents. Citations to numbered federal reports should include the name of the house, the number of the Congress connected by a hyphen to the number of the report, the part and/or page number on which material being cited appears, and the year of publication. Use large and small caps for the house, abbreviation of report, and abbreviation of number:

▶ H.R. REP. NO. 99-253, pt. 1, at 54 (1985).

▶ S. REP. NO. 84-2, at 7 (1955).

Cite conference reports using the following format:

▶ H.R. REP. NO. 98-1037, at 3 (1984) (Conf. Rep.).

▶ S. REP. NO. 95-601, at 5 (1977) (Conf. Rep.).

Cite numbered federal documents analogously, using the following abbreviations:

House Document	▶ H.R. DOC. NO.
Senate Document	▶ S. DOC. NO.
House Miscellaneous Document	▶ H.R. MISC. DOC. NO.

The following citation formats are often used to designate international agreements to which the United States is a party (**rule 21.4.5(a)**):

Senate Executive Document	▶ S. EXEC. DOC. NO.
Senate Treaty Document	▶ S. TREATY DOC. NO.

When possible (and particularly for documents published after 1974), give a parallel citation to the permanent edition of *United States Code Congressional and Administrative News* (**rule 12.6**):

> ▶ S. Rep. No. 95-797, at 4 (1978), *as reprinted in* 1978 U.S.C.C.A.N. 9260, 9263.

(b) Titles and authors. Titles of numbered reports or documents may be indicated; if the title is given, the author should also be named (see **rule 15.1(c)** regarding institutional authors):

> ▶ Carlton Koepge, The Road to Industrial Peace, H.R. Doc. No. 82-563, at 29–30 (1953).

> ▶ U.S. Immigr. Comm'n, Immigration Legislation, S. Doc. No. 61-758, at 613 (3d Sess. 1911).

(c) Unnumbered federal documents and committee prints. Committee prints and unnumbered documents must be cited as works of institutional authors (**rule 15.1(c)**). Note that the number of the Congress is part of the author's name:

> ▶ Staff of S. Comm. on the Judiciary, 81st Cong., Rep. on Antitrust Law 17 (Comm. Print 1950).

If the document or committee print is primarily the work of specific persons, that fact may be noted parenthetically.

(d) Federal legislative agency reports. Legislative reports, like those of the Congressional Research Service (CRS) and the Government Accountability Office (GAO), must be cited as works of institutional authors (**rule 15.1(c)**); include the report number (as given by the agency) as part of the title:

> ▶ Louis Fisher, Cong. Rsch. Serv., RL31340, Military Tribunals: The Quirin Precedent 30 (2002).

> ▶ U.S. Gov't Accountability Off., GAO-08-751, Food and Drug Administration: Approval and Oversight of the Drug Mifeprex 27 (2008).

(e) Federal legislative journals. Cite congressional journals according to the following model:

> ▶ S. Journal, 24th Cong., 2d Sess. 123–24 (1836).

(f) State materials. Citations to state legislative reports, documents, and similar materials must include the name of the legislative body abbreviated according to **tables T6, T9**, and **T10**, the number of the legislative body connected by a hyphen to the number of the report or document, the number of the legislative session, the part or page number on which the material being cited appears, and the year of publication. Unless it is clear from the title or author information appearing in the citation, provide the name of the state abbreviated according to **table T10** parenthetically:

> ▶ S. 178-247, 1st Sess., at 4 (Pa. 1994).

Titles of numbered reports or documents may be indicated; if the title is given, the author should also be named (see **rule 15.1(c)** regarding institutional authors):

> ▶ Commonwealth of Pa. Dep't of Agric., Annual Report of the State Food Purchase Program, S. 178-247, 1st Sess., at 4 (1994).

13.5   Debates

Cite congressional debates after 1873 to the *Congressional Record*; use the daily edition only for matters not yet appearing in the permanent edition. The primary ways in which the *Congressional Record* differs from the daily edition are continuous pagination, altered text, and the dropping of the prefixes H, S, and E before page numbers:

▶ 123 Cong. Rec. 17147 (1977).

▶ 131 Cong. Rec. S11465–66 (daily ed. Sept. 13, 1985) (statement of Sen. Malcolm Wallop).

Cite congressional debates through 1873 according to the following models:

1837–1873	▶ Cong. Globe, 36th Cong., 1st Sess. 1672 (1860).
1824–1837	▶ 10 Reg. Deb. 3472 (1834).
1789–1824	▶ 38 Annals of Cong. 624 (1822).

If the debate occurred in a different year from its publication in the *Congressional Record*, cite the year in which the debate was published.

For volume one of the *Annals* give the name(s) of the editor(s) and year of publication in parentheses:

▶ 1 Annals of Cong. 486 (1789) (Joseph Gales ed., 1834).

13.6   Separately Bound Legislative Histories

The legislative histories of several important acts are published separately (e.g., the Administrative Procedure Act, Titles VII and IX of the Civil Rights Act of 1964, the Clean Air Act Amendments of 1970, the Equal Employment Opportunity Act, the Internal Revenue Acts, the National Labor Relations Act, the Occupational Safety and Health Act of 1970, and the Securities Exchange Act of 1934). If it would aid the reader in locating the source, a parallel citation may be given to such a separate publication. Cite these publications according to **rule 15** (books, reports, and other nonperiodic materials):

▶ H.R. Rep. No. 80-245, at 6 (1947), *reprinted in* 1 NLRB, Legislative History of the Labor-Management Relations Act, 1947, at 292, 297 (1948).

▶ Internal Revenue Amendments, Pub. L. No. 87-834, § 15(a), 76 Stat. 960, 1041–42 (1962) (codified at I.R.C. § 1248(a)), *reprinted in* Joint Comm. on Internal Revenue Tax'n, 90th Cong., Legislative History of the Internal Revenue Code of 1954, at 473–74 (1967).

13.7   Electronic Media and Online Sources

(a) Commercial electronic databases. When citing to materials contained in a commercial electronic database, give the name of the database and any identifying codes or numbers that uniquely identify the material. If the name of the database is not clear from the database identifier, include it parenthetically at the end of the citation:

Federal bill (unenacted)	H.R. 3781, 104th Cong. § 2(b) (1996), 1996 CONG US HR 3781 (Westlaw).
Federal report	H.R. REP. No. 92-98 (1971), *reprinted in* 1971 U.S.C.C.A.N. 1017, 1971 WL 11312.
Congressional debate	142 CONG. REC. H11,460 (daily ed. Sept. 27, 1996) (statement of Rep. Tanner), 142 Cong Rec H 11,452, at *H11,460 (LEXIS).

(b) Internet and online sources. Where a print version is accessible, citation should be made to the print source. Where, however, the print source is difficult or impossible to obtain or the governing authority has designated the electronic source as the official version, citation should be made to the electronic source with consideration of the general principles in **rule 18** regarding authentication and preferred document formats. The URL should be appended to the end of the citation in accordance with **rule 18.2.2(d)**:

> ▶ An Act Prohibiting Writing a Text Message While Driving, H.R. 34, 2009 Sess. (N.H. 2009), http://www.gencourt.state.nh.us/legislation/2009 /HB0034.html.

Short Forms for Legislative Materials 13.8

(a) Main text. In law review text, use the forms listed in the "Text" column of the table below to refer to legislative materials. Provide a citation in full or short form according to **rule 13.8(c)** in an accompanying footnote when appropriate.

(b) Footnote text. Similarly, when referring to legislative materials in law review footnote text, use the forms listed in the "Text" column of the table below. Provide a citation in full or short form according to **rule 13.8(c)** in an accompanying citation clause or sentence when appropriate.

(c) Citations. In law review citations, use any of the forms listed in the "Short Citation" column of the table below that clearly identifies the legislative material if the legislative material is already cited (in either full or short form, including *id.*) in either the *same footnote* or in a manner such that it can be readily found in *one of the preceding five footnotes*. Otherwise, use the "Full Citation" form. See **rule 4.2(a)** regarding the use of "*supra.*"

	Full Citation	Text	Short Citation
Federal Bill (unenacted)	H.R. 3055, 94th Cong. (1976)	House Bill 3055	H.R. 3055
State Resolution	S. Res. 20, 37th Leg., 2d Sess. (Okla. 1979)	Oklahoma Senate Resolution 20	Okla. S. Res. 20
Federal Report	H.R. REP. No. 92-98 (1971)	House Report 98	H.R. REP. No. 92-98
Federal Document	H.R. DOC. No. 94-208 (1975)	House Document 208	H.R. DOC. No. 94-208

(d) Electronic sources. For materials available in an electronic database, use a unique database identifier, if one has been assigned, in constructing a short form:

> ▶ H.R. 3781, 104th Cong. § 1 (1996), 1996 CONG US HR 3781 (Westlaw).

becomes: H.R. 3781 § 1, 1996 CONG US HR 3781 (Westlaw).

For materials available only online, use the normal short form appropriate for the source. A URL need not be repeated after a full citation.

14   ADMINISTRATIVE AND EXECUTIVE MATERIALS

Administrative agencies and other executive institutions produce a tremendous variety of official materials. This rule provides guidance for the most common forms of existing materials. Consult **table T1.2** for information regarding specific federal organizations that use unique citation formats. As with courts, practitioners should comply with an agency's conventions for citation when authoring submissions to that agency, if that convention varies from the rule established herein. Cite state materials by analogy to the federal examples given in this rule.

14.1   Basic Citation Forms

Federal regulation cited to the *Code of Federal Regulations*	FTC Credit Practices Rule, 16 C.F.R. § 444.1 (2019).
Federal regulation cited to the *Federal Register*	Importation of Fruits and Vegetables, 60 Fed. Reg. 50379 (Sept. 29, 1995) (to be codified at 7 C.F.R. pt. 300).
Administrative adjudication	Reichhold Chems., Inc., 91 F.T.C. 246 (1978).
Arbitration	Charles P. Ortmeyer, 23 Indus. Arb. 272 (1980) (Stern, Arb.).

14.2   Rules, Regulations, and Other Publications

Citation of a particular provision of a regulation in the *Code of Federal Regulations*:

C.F.R. title no.   section symbol and specific section cited

7 • C.F.R. • § • 319.76 • (2019).

abbreviation of set of regulations cited   date of code edition cited

(a) Final rules and regulations. Whenever possible, cite federal rules and regulations to the *Code of Federal Regulations* (C.F.R.) by title, section or part, and year:

> ▶ 47 C.F.R. § 73.609 (2019).

Each title of the *Code of Federal Regulations* is revised at least once a year; cite the most recent edition. Give the name of the rule or regulation only if the rule or regulation is commonly cited that way or the information would otherwise aid in identification. The abbreviated name of the issuing body may also be included if helpful:

- ► FCC Broadcast Radio Services, 47 C.F.R. § 73.609 (2019).

- ► FTC Credit Practices Rule, 16 C.F.R. § 444.1 (2019).

- ► Credit Practices Rule, 16 C.F.R. § 444.1 (2019).

Certain titles of the *Code of Federal Regulations* focused on specific subjects have unique citations. For citation to Title 26, *Treasury Regulations*, see **table 1.2**. Title 48, the *Federal Acquisition Regulations*, may be cited as "FAR."

- ► FAR 52.249-2(e) (2019).

The *Federal Register* (Fed. Reg.) publishes rules and regulations before they are entered into the *Code of Federal Regulations*. Citations to rules or regulations in the *Federal Register* should give any commonly used name of the rule or regulation, the volume and page on which the rule or regulation (or any preceding discussion thereof) begins, and the date of the rule or regulation. When citing a part of a rule or regulation, give both the page on which the rule or regulation (or preceding discussion) begins and the page(s) on which the cited material appears. When the *Federal Register* indicates where the rule or regulation will appear in the *Code of Federal Regulations*, give that information parenthetically:

- ► Importation of Fruits and Vegetables, 60 Fed. Reg. 50379, 50381 (Sept. 29, 1995) (to be codified at 7 C.F.R. pts. 300, 319).

- ► Federal Acquisition Regulations for National Aeronautics and Space Administration, 55 Fed. Reg. 52782 (Dec. 21, 1990) (to be codified at 48 C.F.R. pt. 1).

Prohibitively long titles may be shortened as long as the result is unambiguous:

- ► Order Approving NYSE and NASDAQ Proposed Rule Changes Relating to Equity Compensation Plans

Not: Self-Regulatory Organizations; New York Stock Exchange, Inc. and National Association of Securities Dealers, Inc.; Order Approving NYSE and NASDAQ Proposed Rule Changes and NASDAQ Amendment No. 1 and Notice of Filing and Order Granting Accelerated Approval to NYSE Amendments No. 1 and 2 and NASDAQ Amendments No. 2 and 3 Thereto Relating to Equity Compensation Plans

(b) Proposed rules, other notices, and comments. Administrative notices that are not transferred to the *Code of Federal Regulations* should be cited to the *Federal Register*. When citing notices of proposed rules and regulations, follow the form for final rules, but add the status to the date parenthetical:

- ► Control of Air Pollution from New Motor Vehicles and New Motor Vehicle Engines, 56 Fed. Reg. 9754 (proposed Mar. 7, 1991) (to be codified at 40 C.F.R. pt. 86).

Cite notices pertaining to administrative adjudications according to **rule 14.3**. Cite other administrative notices by volume, page, and date. The citation may begin with a description or a commonly used name:

- ► Meeting Notice, 65 Fed. Reg. 3415 (Jan. 21, 2000).

For rules and announcements not appearing in the *Code of Federal Regulations* or the *Federal Register,* cite a service (**rule 19**), the original form of issuance, or an agency or governmental website (**rule 18.2**). When citing comments, provide the name of the commenter and the proposed rule to which the comment pertains. Prohibitively long titles may be shortened as long as the result is unambiguous. Citing to an agency or governmental website is appropriate:

> ► Chamber of Com. of the U.S., Comment Letter on Proposed Rule to Require Registration of Certain Hedge Fund Advisers Under the Investment Advisers Act of 1940 (Sept. 15, 2004), http://www.sec.gov/rules/proposed/s73004/dhirschmann091504.pdf.

(c) Regular reports. Cite in the same manner as periodical materials (**rule 16**). Always give the abbreviated agency name first and then use the abbreviations for periodical names given in **tables T6** and **T13**:

> ► 4 NLRB Ann. Rep. 93 (1939).

> ► 1942 Att'y Gen. Ann. Rep. 22.

> ► 1955–1956 Mich. Att'y Gen. Biennial Rep. pt. 1, at 621.

(d) Other publications. Cite as a work by an institutional author (**rule 15.1(c)**), including a serial number, if any (**rule 15.7**), unless issued as a congressional document (**rule 13.4**):

> ► Off. of Mgmt. & Budget, Exec. Off. of the President, OMB Bull. No. 99-04, Revised Statistical Definitions of Metropolitan Areas (MAs) and Guidance on Uses of MA Definitions (1999).

> ► U.S. Gov't Accountability Off., GAO-01-1163T, Commercial Aviation: A Framework for Considering Federal Financial Assistance (2001).

> ► U.S. Equal Emp. Opportunity Comm'n, EEOC-M1A, A Technical Assistance Manual on the Employment Provisions (Title I) of the Americans with Disabilities Act (1992).

> ► U.S. Food & Drug Admin., Premarket Assessment of Pediatric Medical Devices: Guidance for Industry and Food and Drug Administration Staff (2014).

When citing an opinion letter, cite as a work by an institutional author in ordinary roman type, including the date of its publication and, if available, its subject matter:

> ► U.S. Equal Emp. Opportunity Comm'n, Opinion Letter on Applicability of Age Discrimination in Employment Act to Appointed State Court Judges (Apr. 7, 1987), *as reprinted in* EEOC Compliance Manual (BL), at N:1001 n.2.

> ► U.S. Dep't of Labor, Wage & Hour Div., Opinion Letter (Sept. 14, 1992).

14.3 Administrative Adjudications and Arbitrations

Citations to administrative cases and arbitrations should conform to **rule 10**, except as follows:

Names

(a) Administrative adjudications. Cite by the reported name of the first-listed private party (abbreviated according to **rule 10.2**) or by the official subject-matter title. Omit all procedural phrases:

► Trojan Transp., Inc., 249 N.L.R.B. 642 (1980).

Not: In the Matter of Trojan Transp., Inc., 249 N.L.R.B. 642 (1980).

Not: *In re* Trojan Transp., Inc., 249 N.L.R.B. 642 (1980).

Subject-matter titles may sometimes indicate the nature and stage of an adjudicatory proceeding. It is permissible to shorten such titles, and, if the nature and stage of the proceeding are not clear from the context, such information may be included in a parenthetical phrase at the end of the citation. The parenthetical phrase may consist of terms such as "notice," "initiation," "prelim. neg.," or "determination," or may be more elaborate.

► Bottled Green Olives from Spain, 50 Fed. Reg. 28237 (Dep't of Commerce July 11, 1985) (final admin. review).

Not: Bottled Green Olives from Spain, Final Results of Admin. Review of Countervailing Duty Order, 50 Fed. Reg. 28237 (Dep't of Commerce July 11, 1985).

(b) Arbitrations. Cite as court cases if adversary parties are named and as administrative adjudications if they are not. The arbitrator's name should be indicated parenthetically:

► Kroger Co. v. Amalgamated Meat Cutters, Local 539, 74 Lab. Arb. Rep. (BL) 785, 787 (1980) (Doering, Arb.).

► Charles P. Ortmeyer, 23 Indus. Arb. 272 (1980) (Stern, Arb.).

Which Source(s) to Cite

(a) Official reporters. Cite the official reporter of the agency if the opinion appears therein:

► Tennessee Intrastate Rates & Charges, 286 I.C.C. 41 (1952).

For the official reporters of many federal agencies, see **table T1.2**.

(b) Official releases and slip opinions. If the opinion does not appear in an official reporter, cite the official release or slip opinion. Provide the full date, any helpful publication number, and the number of the case or investigation:

► Iron Construction Castings from Brazil, Canada, India, and the People's Republic of China, Inv. No. 701-TA-249, USITC Pub. 1720 (June 1985) (Preliminary).

If the opinion will later be published in an official bound volume, provide the volume number and the initial page number, if available; if the initial page number is not available, retain the case number:

► Rosenberg Library Ass'n, 269 N.L.R.B. No. 197 (Apr. 24, 1984).

Whenever possible, append a parallel citation to an unofficial reporter, service, or other source, in that order of preference:

▶ Rosenberg Library Ass'n, 269 N.L.R.B. No. 197, 1983–1984 NLRB Dec. (CCH) ¶ 16,238 (Apr. 24, 1984).

Once the official reporter is issued, however, cite only to that reporter:

▶ Rosenberg Library Ass'n, 269 N.L.R.B. 1173 (1984).

(c) Services and electronic databases. Where an agency decision is only available from a service or on the agency's website, cite according to **rule 19** (for services) or **rule 18.2** (for internet sources).

▶ *Carr*, [1990–1992 Transfer Binder] Comm. Fut. L. Rep. (CCH) ¶ 24,933 (Oct. 2, 1990).

▶ MatchNet PLC v. Gordon, Case No. AF-001060 (eResolution Dec. 4, 2001), http://www.disputes.org/decisions/1060.htm.

Many agencies have adopted unique citation formats for opinions not listed in official reporters. Consult **table T1.2** for agency-specific citation formats. For a list of services and service abbreviations, see **table T15**.

14.3.3 Issuing Agency

If the name of the issuing agency is not apparent from the name of the source, include the name of the agency abbreviated according to **rule 15.1(d)** in the parenthetical containing the date:

▶ Gen. Dynamics Corp., 50 Fed. Reg. 45949 (U.S. Dep't of Lab. Nov. 5, 1985).

14.4 Commercial Electronic Databases

When citing to administrative materials contained in a commercial electronic database, give the name of the database and any identifying codes or numbers that uniquely identify the material. If the name of the database is not clear from the database identifier, include it parenthetically at the end of the citation:

▶ FTC Credit Practices Rule, 16 C.F.R. § 444.1 (2000), WL 16 CFR § 444.1.

▶ Reichhold Chems., Inc., 91 F.T.C. 246 (1978), 1978 WL 206094.

▶ 39 Op. Att'y Gen. 484 (1940), 1940 US AG LEXIS 16.

▶ Rev. Rul. 86-71, 1986-1 C.B. 102, 1986 IRB LEXIS 189.

14.5 Short Forms for Regulations

(a) Main text. In law review text, use the forms listed in the "Text" column of the table below to refer to regulations. Provide a citation (in full or short form according to **rule 14.5(c)**) in an accompanying footnote when appropriate.

(b) Footnote text. Similarly, when referring to regulations in law review footnote text, use the forms listed in the "Text" column of the table below. Provide a citation (in full or short form according to **rule 14.5(c)**) in an accompanying citation clause or sentence when appropriate.

(c) Citations. In law review citations, use any of the forms listed in the "Short citation" column of the table below that clearly identifies the regulation if the regulation is already cited (in full or short form) in either the same footnote or in a manner such that it can be readily found (including "*id.*") in one of the preceding five footnotes or the same general textual discussion. Otherwise, use the "Full citation" form.

	Full citation	Text	Short citation
Code of Federal Regulations	FTC Credit Practices Rule, 16 C.F.R. § 444.1 (2014)	16 C.F.R. § 444.1	16 C.F.R. § 444.1 or § 444.1
Federal Register	Importation of Fruits and Vegetables, 60 Fed. Reg. 50379, 50381 (Sept. 29, 1995) (to be codified at 7 C.F.R. pt. 300)	Importation of Fruits and Vegetables	Importation of Fruits and Vegetables, 60 Fed. Reg. at 50381

(d) Electronic sources. See **rule 18.9**.

BOOKS, REPORTS, AND OTHER NONPERIODIC MATERIALS   15

This rule governs the citation of books, treatises, reports, white papers, dictionaries, encyclopedias, and all other nonperiodic materials.

Citation of a particular page within the sixth edition of Francis Carey's *Organic Chemistry*:

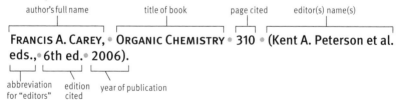

| author's full name | title of book | page cited | editor(s) name(s) |

FRANCIS A. CAREY, • ORGANIC CHEMISTRY • 310 • (Kent A. Peterson et al. eds., • 6th ed. • 2006).

| abbreviation for "editors" | edition cited | year of publication |

Main Elements:

Author . . . .**rule 15.1**

Editor or translator . . . . **rule 15.2**

Title . . . . **rule 15.3**

Page, section, or paragraph
   (if only part of a work is cited) . . . .**rules 3.2 and 3.3**

Edition . . . . **rule 15.4**

Publisher . . . . **rule 15.4**

Date . . . . **rule 15.4**

15.1 Author

The first time a work is cited, always give the author's full name as it appears on the publication, including any designation such as "JR." or "III" (inserting a comma before the designation only if the author does). Do not include a designation such as "Dr." or "Prof." even if it appears on the title page. Use large and small capitals:

> ▶ HAROLD W. FUSON, JR., TELLING IT ALL: A LEGAL GUIDE TO THE EXERCISE OF FREE SPEECH 57–58 (1995).

When citing a single volume of a multivolume work, give only the author(s) of the volume cited. Include the volume number, if any, at the beginning of the citation:

> ▶ 4 CHARLES ALAN WRIGHT & ARTHUR R. MILLER, FEDERAL PRACTICE AND PROCEDURE § 1006 (2d ed. 1987).

(a) Two authors. List the authors' names in the order in which they appear on the title page, separated by an ampersand:

> ▶ CHRIS HEDGES & JOE SACCO, DAYS OF DESTRUCTION, DAYS OF REVOLT 109 (2012).

If the title page establishes an alternative relationship between the two authors, e.g., "WITH" or "AS TOLD TO," use this phrase to separate the authors' names:

> ▶ EARVIN "MAGIC" JOHNSON WITH WILLIAM NOVAK, MY LIFE 39 (1993).

(b) More than two authors. Use the first author's name followed by "ET AL." when saving space is desired and in short form citations. List all of the authors' names when particularly relevant. When listing all of the authors' names, separate the names with commas, except the final name, which should be set off with an ampersand (and without a comma):

> ▶ A. LEO LEVIN ET AL., DISPUTE RESOLUTION DEVICES IN A DEMOCRATIC SOCIETY 77 (1985).
> ▶ 14 CHARLES ALAN WRIGHT, ARTHUR R. MILLER & EDWARD H. COOPER, FEDERAL PRACTICE AND PROCEDURE § 3637 (3d ed. 1998).
> ▶ RICHARD H. FALLON, JR., JOHN F. MANNING, DANIEL J. MELTZER & DAVID L. SHAPIRO, HART AND WECHSLER'S THE FEDERAL COURTS AND THE FEDERAL SYSTEM 330 (6th ed. 2009).
> ▶ RICHARD H. FALLON, JR. ET AL., HART AND WECHSLER'S THE FEDERAL COURTS AND THE FEDERAL SYSTEM 330 (6th ed. 2009).

(c) Institutional authors. Citations to works by institutional authors begin with the author's complete name. Abbreviate according to **rule 15.1(d)**:

> ▶ CITY OF NEW HAVEN, RECYCLE NOW NEW HAVEN (1991).

When an individual author is credited on behalf of an institution, use the individual's name and then the institution's name. Only include subdivisions of the institution if particularly relevant:

> ▶ JUDITH A. LHAMON, NAT'L ASS'N FOR L. PLACEMENT, A FAIR SHAKE: LAWFUL AND EFFECTIVE INTERVIEWING 3 (1987).

▶ S. ELIZABETH GIBSON, FED. JUD. CTR., CASE STUDIES OF MASS TORT LIMITED FUND CLASS ACTION SETTLEMENTS & BANKRUPTCY REORGANIZATIONS 39–45 (2000).

Not: S. ELIZABETH GIBSON, FED. JUD. CTR., WORKING GROUP ON MASS TORTS, CASE STUDIES OF MASS TORT LIMITED FUND CLASS ACTION SETTLEMENTS & BANKRUPTCY REORGANIZATIONS 39–45 (2000).

When no individual author is credited, use the smallest subdivision that prepared the work and then the overall body of which that subdivision is a part:

▶ STATISTICAL ANALYSIS CTR., STATE CRIME COMM'N, CRIME IN GEORGIA 41 (1980).

(d) Abbreviations. Abbreviate the name of an institutional author only if the result will be completely unambiguous. When abbreviating, use the abbreviations found in **tables T6** and **T10**. "United States" should be abbreviated to "U.S." Omit "Inc.," "Ltd.," and similar terms if the name also contains a word such as "Ass'n," "Bros.," "Co.," or "Corp.," clearly indicating that the institution is a business firm:

▶ CONSUMER DEPUTY PROGRAM, U.S. CONSUMER PROD. SAFETY COMM'N, CHILDREN'S SLEEPWEAR 7 (1975).

▶ NAT'L MUN. LEAGUE, A MODEL ELECTION SYSTEM 3 (1973).

Editor or Translator   15.2

(a) Basic format. Always give the full name of an editor and/or translator according to **rule 15.1**, followed by "ed.," or "trans.," in that order if both apply, in the parenthetical containing information about the edition, publisher, and date (see **rule 15.4**). A comma should separate the designation of an editor and/or translator from other publication information:

▶ MICHEL FOUCAULT, DISCIPLINE AND PUNISH 30–31 (Alan Sheridan trans., Vintage Books 2d ed. 1995) (1977).

▶ ETHICS OF CONSUMPTION: THE GOOD LIFE, JUSTICE, AND GLOBAL STEWARDSHIP 118–19 (David A. Crocker & Toby Linden eds., 1998).

▶ AIDS AND THE LAW (Harlon L. Dalton & Scott Burris eds., 1987).

▶ KARL MARX & FREDERICK ENGELS, THE COMMUNIST MANIFESTO (Joseph Katz ed., Samuel Moore trans., Washington Square Press 1964) (1848).

(b) Institutional editors. Follow **rule 15.1(c)**, substituting the name of the institution for the name of the individual editor. Abbreviate the institutional editor's name according to **rule 15.1(d)**:

▶ THE ROLE OF MEDIATION IN DIVORCE PROCEEDINGS 33 (Vt. L. Sch. Dispute Resol. Project ed., 1987).

▶ THE BLUEBOOK: A UNIFORM SYSTEM OF CITATION (Columbia L. Rev. Ass'n et al. eds., 21st ed. 2020).

(c) No named parties. If a work has no named author, editor, or translator, then the work may be designated by the publisher of the edition (**rule 15.4**). Abbreviate the publisher's name according to **rule 15.1(d)**.

15.3   Title

Cite the full main title as it appears on the title page, but capitalize according to **rule 8** (unless the title is not in English, in which case follow **rule 20.2.2(b)**). Give a subtitle only if it is particularly relevant. Do not abbreviate words or omit articles in the title. Use large and small capitals:

▶ CAPITAL FLOWS IN THE APEC REGION (Mohsin S. Khan & Carmen M. Reinhart eds., 1995).

▶ 6 JAMES W. MOORE ET AL., MOORE'S FEDERAL PRACTICE ¶ 56.10 (3d ed. 1999).

When citing a single volume of a multivolume work, give the main title of the volume cited. If the title of a work ends with a numeral, or if distinguishing between the title and page number could otherwise be confusing, the page number should be set off by a comma and the word "at" (see **rule 3.2(a)**):

▶ J.A.S. GRENVILLE, THE MAJOR INTERNATIONAL TREATIES, 1914–1973, at 114–15 (1974).

15.4   Edition, Publisher, and Date

(a) Editions. Always cite the latest edition of a work that supports the point under discussion, unless an earlier edition would be particularly relevant or authoritative.

(i) **Single edition**. When citing a work that has been published in only one edition, indicate the year of publication in parentheses. In general, cite by the date of the edition rather than by the date of a particular printing:

▶ DEBORAH L. RHODE, JUSTICE AND GENDER 56 (1989).

▶ AIDS AND THE LAW (Harlon L. Dalton & Scott Burris eds., 1987).

If a printing differs in a respect relevant to the purposes of the citation, however, give the printing designation and the date of printing instead:

▶ (6th prtg. 1980)

If the title of the work incorporates the date of the work, do not omit the date of publication, even if it is the same date:

▶ HUMAN RIGHTS WATCH, WORLD REPORT 2004: HUMAN RIGHTS AND ARMED CONFLICT 148 (2004).

(ii) **Multiple editions by the same publisher**. When citing a work that has been published by the same publisher in more than one edition, indicate the edition and the year the edition was published. Follow the publisher's terminology when designating an edition (see **table T14** for a list of publishing abbreviations):

▶ FLEMING JAMES, JR. ET AL., CIVIL PROCEDURE § 2.3 (4th ed. 1992).

▶ 1 WILLIAM MEADE FLETCHER ET AL., FLETCHER CYCLOPEDIA OF THE LAW OF PRIVATE CORPORATIONS § 7.05 (perm. ed., rev. vol. 1999).

▶ NYX X. HE, PUBLIC INTEREST LAW: SUPPORTING THE CAUSE (2015–2016 ed. 2000).

► ARISTOTLE, NICOMACHEAN ETHICS bk. IV, at 15–16 (G.P. Goold ed., H. Rackham trans., Harvard Univ. Press rev. ed. 1934) (c. 384 B.C.E.).

(iii) **Editions not by the original publisher.** When citing a work that has been published by someone other than the original publisher, indicate the editor and/or translator, if any (**rule 15.2**), the publisher, the edition cited if not the first, and the date of publication of the edition cited (in that order). Abbreviate the publisher's name according to **rule 15.1(d)**. Unless the work is one that is regularly updated or revised, add a second parenthetical indicating the date of publication of the original edition:

► CHARLES DICKENS, BLEAK HOUSE 49–55 (Norman Page ed., Penguin Books 1971) (1853).

► JOHN C.H. WU, THE GOLDEN AGE OF ZEN 214–15 (Image Books 1996) (1975).

► SIMONE DE BEAUVOIR, THE SECOND SEX, at xvi–xvii (H.M. Parshley ed. & trans., Bantam Books 1961) (1949).

► THE CHICAGO MANUAL OF STYLE ¶ 8.191 (15th ed. 2003).

(b) Photoduplicated reprints. Cite photoduplicated reprints to the original, indicating in parentheses the existence of a reprint and the date of the reprint, followed by the publication date of the original in separate parentheses:

► PAUL W. GATES, HISTORY OF PUBLIC LAND LAW DEVELOPMENT 1 (photo. reprt. 1979) (1968).

(c) Pre-1900 works. Cite works published before 1900 to a scholarly modern edition, according to **rule 15.4(a)**:

► JOHN LOCKE, TWO TREATISES OF GOVERNMENT 137–39 (Peter Laslett ed., Cambridge Univ. Press 1988) (1690).

If there is no modern edition, cite the first edition whenever possible. When citing a pre-1900 edition, indicate the place of publication and the publisher, separated by a comma:

► 1 JAMES FITZJAMES STEPHEN, A HISTORY OF THE CRIMINAL LAW OF ENGLAND 156–57 (London, MacMillan & Co. 1883).

If the place or date of publication is not available, use the abbreviation "n.p." for "no place" or "n.d." for "no date."

(d) Supplements. Cite pocket parts and bound supplements according to **rule 3.1(c)**:

► 4 SYDNEY C. SCHWEITZER & JOSEPH RASCH, CYCLOPEDIA OF TRIAL PRACTICE § 895 (2d ed. Supp. 1984).

► 5 SAMUEL WILLISTON & RICHARD A. LORD, A TREATISE ON THE LAW OF CONTRACTS § 11:8 (4th ed. 1993 & Supp. 1999).

Shorter Works in Collection 15.5

Cite essays and articles in collections according to **rule 15.5.1**. Cite collections of other materials, such as letters, speeches, manuscripts, diaries, debates, newspaper articles, tracts, etc., according to **rule 15.5.2**.

15.5.1 Works in Collection Generally

(a) Works by various authors. To cite an individual shorter work within a volume of collected works by various authors, list the author's full name according to **rule 15.1** in ordinary roman type followed by the title of the shorter work in italics, the word "*in*" in italics, the volume number, if any (**rule 3.1(a)**), and the name of the volume as a whole in large and small capitals. Always note the page on which the shorter work begins as well as any pages on which specific material appears (**rule 3.2(a)**). Editors, translators, edition, publisher, and date should be noted parenthetically according to **rules 15.2** and **15.4**:

- ▶ Andrew G. Ferguson, *Continuing Seizure: Fourth Amendment Seizure in Section 1983 Malicious Prosecution Cases*, *in* 15 NAT'L LAWS. GUILD, CIVIL RIGHTS LITIGATION AND ATTORNEY FEES ANNUAL HANDBOOK 54-1 (Steven Saltzman ed., 1999).
- ▶ Kay Deaux & Brenda Major, *A Social-Psychological Model of Gender*, *in* THEORETICAL PERSPECTIVES ON SEXUAL DIFFERENCE 89, 89 (Deborah L. Rhode ed., 1990).

(b) Works by the same author. If all the shorter works within a volume are by the same author, use the same form as above, but print the author's name in large and small capitals and place the volume number, if any, before the author's name (**rule 3.1(a)**):

- ▶ OLIVER WENDELL HOLMES, *Law in Science and Science in Law*, *in* COLLECTED LEGAL PAPERS 210, 210 (1920).
- ▶ ADRIENNE RICH, *Transcendental Etude*, *in* THE FACT OF A DOORFRAME 264, 267–68 (1984).

15.5.2 Collected Documents

(a) Documents originally published. Use the "*reprinted in*" form (**rule 1.6(a)(ii)**) to cite collected materials that were previously published. As far as possible, provide a complete citation for the original work followed by "*reprinted in*" and the citation of the volume containing the reprint:

- ▶ MARQUIS DE CONDORCET, ESSAY ON THE APPLICATION OF MATHEMATICS TO THE THEORY OF DECISION-MAKING (1785), *reprinted in* CONDORCET: SELECTED WRITINGS 33, 48–49 (Keith M. Baker ed., 1976).

(b) Documents originally unpublished. Cite letters, speeches, manuscripts, diaries, and other similar works that have never been published except in collection as you would any other shorter work in collection (**rule 15.5.1**), but print the name or description of the document in ordinary roman type following **rule 17**. The date of the particular document or other identifying information, if available, may be included in a parenthetical following the document title:

- ▶ Letter from Virginia Woolf to Vita Sackville-West (Dec. 22, 1925), *in* 3 THE LETTERS OF VIRGINIA WOOLF, 1923–1928, 223, 224 (Nigel Nicolson & Joanne Trautmann eds., 1st Am. ed. 1978) (1977).
- ▶ John Adams, Argument and Report, *in* 2 LEGAL PAPERS OF JOHN ADAMS 285, 322–35 (L. Kinvin Wroth & Hiller B. Zobel eds., 1965).

Prefaces, Forewords, Introductions, and Epilogues 15.6

Cite a preface, foreword, introduction, or epilogue by someone other than the author as follows:

▶ L. Maria Child, *Introduction* to HARRIET A. JACOBS, INCIDENTS IN
   THE LIFE OF A SLAVE GIRL 3, 3–4 (L. Maria Child & Jean F. Yellin eds.,
   Harvard Univ. Press 1987) (1861).

▶ Henry M. Hart & Herbert Wechsler, *Preface to the First Edition* of PAUL
   M. BATOR ET AL., HART AND WECHSLER'S THE FEDERAL COURTS AND THE
   FEDERAL SYSTEM, at xxvii, xxx (3d ed. 1988).

Cite to similar material by the author of the work without special designation:

▶ JOHN HART ELY, DEMOCRACY AND DISTRUST, at vii (1980).

Serial Number 15.7

(a) Series issued by the author. When citing a publication that is one of a series issued by the author (other than U.N. documents (**rule 21.7**)), include the serial number as part of the title. The serial number indicator may be abbreviated according to **table T16**:

▶ BUREAU OF INTEL. & RSCH., U.S. DEP'T OF STATE, PUB. NO. 8732,
   WORLD STRENGTH OF THE COMMUNIST PARTY ORGANIZATIONS 65
   (1973).

▶ WOMEN'S BUREAU, U.S. DEP'T OF LAB., LEAFLET NO. 55, A WORKING
   WOMAN'S GUIDE TO HER JOB RIGHTS 4 (1978).

(b) Series issued by one other than the author. To cite a publication that is one of a series issued by someone other than the author, indicate the series and number parenthetically, abbreviating institutional entities according to **rule 15.1(d)**:

▶ Anne C. Vladeck, *Counseling a Plaintiff During Litigation*, *in* EMPLOY-
   MENT LITIGATION 1990, at 77, 80–82 (PLI Litig. & Admin. Prac., Course
   Handbook Ser. No. 386, 1990).

Special Citation Forms 15.8

(a) Frequently cited works. A few frequently cited works require special citation forms:

▶ *Noscitur a sociis*, BALLENTINE'S LAW DICTIONARY (3d ed. 1969).

▶ *Good-Faith Bargaining*, BLACK'S LAW DICTIONARY (9th ed. 2009).

▶ 88 C.J.S. *Trial* § 192 (1955).

▶ 17 AM. JUR. 2D *Contracts* § 74 (1964).

(b) Star edition. In a very few well-known works, the page of the original edition (star page) is indicated, usually by an asterisk (*), in either the margin or the text of all recent editions. In such cases, the date and edition may be omitted and the citation may be made to the star page, unless the material cited was inserted by the editor of the cited edition. There is no space between the asterisk and the page number:

▶ 2 WILLIAM BLACKSTONE, COMMENTARIES *152, *155–56.

(c) Other named works.

(i) **The Federalist**. When citing an entire *Federalist* paper, include the author's name parenthetically and do not indicate a specific edition:

▶ THE FEDERALIST NO. 23 (Alexander Hamilton).

Group together papers written by the same author:

▶ THE FEDERALIST NOS. 23, 78 (Alexander Hamilton), NOS. 10, 51 (James Madison).

When citing particular material within a paper, however, list the usual publication information for the edition cited:

▶ THE FEDERALIST NO. 5, at 53 (John Jay) (Clinton Rossiter ed., 1961).

(ii) **Manual for Complex Litigation**. Citations to the *Manual for Complex Litigation* prepared by the Federal Judicial Center are as follows:

▶ MANUAL FOR COMPLEX LITIGATION (THIRD) § 33.2 (1995).
▶ MANUAL FOR COMPLEX LITIGATION § 2.10 (5th ed. 1982).

However, when citing an edition not prepared by the Federal Judicial Center, identify the source and publication date of the edition cited:

▶ MANUAL FOR COMPLEX LITIGATION § 4.52 (1982) (*supplement* to CHARLES ALAN WRIGHT & ARTHUR R. MILLER, FEDERAL PRACTICE AND PROCEDURE (1969–1985)).

(iii) **The Bible**. Cite the Bible as follows:

▶ 2 *Kings* 12:19.

The version may be indicated parenthetically if relevant:

▶ *Mark* 9:21 (King James).

(iv) **Shakespeare**. A Shakespearean play should be cited in large and small caps and by act, scene, and line number. Do not indicate a date or edition unless particular matter is being quoted:

▶ WILLIAM SHAKESPEARE, HENRY V act 4, sc. 3, l. 65.

(v) **The Bluebook**. *The Bluebook* is cited as follows:

▶ THE BLUEBOOK: A UNIFORM SYSTEM OF CITATION R. 15.8(c)(v), at 154 (Columbia L. Rev. Ass'n et al. eds., 21st ed. 2020).
▶ THE BLUEBOOK: A UNIFORM SYSTEM OF CITATION 293 tbl.T.10 (Columbia L. Rev. Ass'n et al. eds., 16th ed. 9th prtg. 1999).

15.9 Electronic Databases and Online Sources

(a) Commercial electronic databases. When citing secondary materials to a database, provide a complete citation to the document according to **rule 15** as well as a citation to the database. If the database assigns a unique identifier or code to the document, include that identifier or code to assist the reader in locating the document cited.

When a source is available both in print and in a commercial electronic database, a citation to the database may be supplied:

> ▶ ABBEY G. HAIRSTON, LEAVE AND DISABILITY COORDINATION HANDBOOK ¶ 110 (2009), Westlaw LDCHBK.

> ▶ 25 AM. JUR. 2D *Elections* § 100, Westlaw (database updated May 2014).

(b) Internet and online sources. Because books found online may differ in format from the print version, the two sources should not be treated interchangeably unless the online source is an exact copy of the original as dictated by **rule 18.2.1(a)**. If a book or report is only available online, cite to it directly in accordance with **rule 18.2.2**:

> ▶ U.S. DEP'T OF JUST., LEGAL AUTHORITIES SUPPORTING THE ACTIVITIES OF THE NATIONAL SECURITY AGENCY DESCRIBED BY THE PRESIDENT 25 (2006) [hereinafter NSA WHITE PAPER], http://nsarchive.gwu.edu /NSAEBB/NSAEBB178/surv39.pdf.

> ▶ *Lampoon*, DICTIONARY.COM, http://dictionary.reference.com/browse /lampoon (last visited Mar. 19, 2020).

(c) Ebooks. Print versions of books are authoritative; ebooks should be cited only if they are the sole media through which the book is available. Because books published as ebooks may differ in format from the print version, the two sources should not be treated interchangeably. To indicate that an ebook is being cited, place an "ebook" parenthetical after the date:

> ▶ ANNE UMLAND & BLAIR HARTZELL, PICASSO: THE MAKING OF CUBISM 1912–1914, at 25 (2014) (ebook).

If an ebook uses location numbers rather than page numbers, use "loc." to indicate where the cited material can be found:

> ▶ RONALD COLLINS & DAVID SKOVER, WHEN MONEY SPEAKS loc. 2992 (2014) (ebook) ("[T]he *Buckley* wall between contributions and expenditures . . . has been breached.").

Short Citation Forms   15.10

Once a book, report, or other nonperiodic material has been cited in full in a law review footnote, a short form employing either "*id.*" or "*supra*" may be used to refer to the work in subsequent citations. Never use "*infra*" to refer to these materials. In general, follow **rule 4** for short citation forms; however, use **rule 15.10.1** when referring to a shorter work in collection or the collection as a whole.

··

Short Forms for Works in Collection   15.10.1

To cite an essay, article, or document found within a volume of collected shorter works when the shorter work has already been cited in full, you may use "*id.*" to refer to the shorter work if it was cited as the immediately preceding authority within the same footnote or as the sole authority within the immediately preceding footnote. Do not use "*id.*" to refer to the collection as a whole when citing another shorter work within the collection.

Use a "*supra*" form to refer to the collection as a whole. The "*supra*" form for the entire volume should include the title of the collection (rather than an author) regardless of whether the collected pieces have a single author or multiple authors.

Use a "*supra*" form to refer to the shorter work if it was not cited as the immediately preceding authority in the same footnote or as the sole authority in the immediately preceding footnote. The "*supra*" form for the individual work should include the last name of the author or authors, or, if none, the title of the shorter work:

▶ [1] FEMINISM/POSTMODERNISM (Linda J. Nicholson ed., 1990); *see also* THOMAS SCHELLING, A PROCESS OF RESIDENTIAL SEGREGATION: NEIGHBORHOOD TIPPING, *reprinted in* ECONOMIC FOUNDATIONS OF PROPERTY LAW 307, 308 (Bruce A. Ackerman ed., 1975).

▶ [2] Letter from Virginia Woolf to Vita Sackville-West (Dec. 22, 1925), *in* 3 THE LETTERS OF VIRGINIA WOOLF, 1923–1928, at 224 (N. Nicolson & Joanne Trautmann eds., 1st Am. ed. 1978); *cf.* Judith Butler, *Gender Trouble, Feminist Theory, and Psychoanalytic Discourse*, *in* FEMINISM/POSTMODERNISM, *supra* note 1, at 324, 324–25; Andreas Huyssen, *Mapping the Postmodern*, *in* FEMINISM/POSTMODERNISM, *supra* note 1, at 234, 234–35. Butler does not think "woman" can be adequately defined, Butler, *supra*, at 325, but Woolf's observations are especially compelling, Letter from Virginia Woolf to Vita Sackville-West, *supra*.

▶ [3] A wholly different perspective is presented in Ayn Rand, *The Cashing-In: The Student "Rebellion,"* *in* THE NEW LEFT 13, 20–24 (1971). *But see* Huyssen, *supra* note 2, at 234–35 (questioning whether postmodern transformation has generated genuinely new forms).

▶ [4] *E.g.,* SCHELLING, *supra* note 1, at 310.

▶ [5] *Id.*; *see also* THE FEDERALIST NO. 81, at 393 (Alexander Hamilton) (Terrence Ball ed., 2003). *But see* AYN RAND, *The Comprachicos* (arguing that the educational establishment teaches ideas that destroy children's minds), *in* THE NEW LEFT, *supra* note 3, at 152, 203.

▶ [6] *See* Rand, *supra* note 3, at 99; Rand, *supra* note 5, at 201.

▶ [7] 4 RICHARD R. POWELL, POWELL ON REAL PROPERTY ¶ 513[3], at 41–42 (Patrick J. Rohan ed., 1995).

▶ [8] 2 *id.* ¶ 203, at 20–17; *see also* THE FEDERALIST NO. 5, *supra* note 5, at 17 (John Jay).

For materials available only online, use the normal short form appropriate for the source. A URL need not be repeated after a full citation.

PERIODICAL MATERIALS 16

Citation of particular pages within a law review article with parenthetical information about what appears on those pages:

| author's full name | | title of article | journal volume no. | abbreviation of journal | page on which article begins |

Charles A. Reich, *The New Property,* 73 YALE L.J. 733, 737–38 (1964) (discussing the importance of government largess).

span of specific pages cited · date of publication · parenthetical describing content of pages cited

Citation of an entire magazine article:

author's full name · title of article · name of magazine

Robert J. Samuelson, *A Slow Fix for the Banks,* NEWSWEEK, Feb. 18, 1991, at 55.

cover date of issue · separates date from page no. · first page of article

Citation of a signed newspaper article:

author's full name · headline

Seth Mydans, *Los Angeles Police Chief Removed for 60 Days in Inquiry on Beating,* N.Y. TIMES, Apr. 5, 1991, at A1.

abbreviation of newspaper · date of article · separates date from page no. · page on which article appears

Basic Citation Forms 16.1

Article in consecutively paginated journal	Elizabeth F. Emens, *Integrating Accommodation*, 156 U. PA. L. REV. 839, 894 (2008).
Article in nonconsecutively paginated journal or magazine	Benjamin Wittes, *Without Precedent*, ATL. MONTHLY, Sept. 2005, at 39, 40.
Newspaper article	Scott Martelle, *ID Law Keeps Nuns, Students from Polls*, L.A. TIMES, May 7, 2008, at A14.
Online newspaper article	Pamela Mendels, *A Case of Spam and Free Speech at Intel*, N.Y. TIMES (Dec. 11, 1998), http://www.nytimes.com/library/tech/98/12/cyber/cyberlaw/11law.html.
Signed student-written law review note	Bradford R. Clark, Note, *Judicial Review of Congressional Section Five Action: The Fallacy of Reverse Incorporation*, 84 COLUM. L. REV. 1969, 1986 (1984).

Unsigned student-written comment	Case Comment, *Fairness Standards for SEC Approval of Mergers:* Collins v. SEC, 90 HARV. L. REV. 453 (1976).
Student-written book review	Sharon Dolovich, Book Note, *Leaving the Law Behind*, 20 HARV. WOMEN'S L.J. 313, 329 (1997) (reviewing PATRICIA J. WILLIAMS, THE ROOSTER'S EGG: ON THE PERSISTENCE OF PREJUDICE (1995)).
Non-student-written book review	Jane E. Stromseth, *Understanding Constitutional War Powers Today: Why Methodology Matters*, 106 YALE L.J. 845 (1996) (reviewing LOUIS FISHER, PRESIDENTIAL WAR POWER (1995)).
Symposium	Symposium, *The Presidency and Congress: Constitutionally Separated and Shared Powers*, 68 WASH. U. L.Q. 485, 640–51 (1990).
Specially designated article in consecutively paginated journal	John M. Golden, Commentary, *"Patent Trolls" and Patent Remedies*, 85 TEX. L. REV. 2111, 2113 (2007).
Noncommercially distributed newsletter	Douglas Gary Lichtman, *Patent Holdouts in the Standard-Setting Process*, ACAD. ADVISORY COUNCIL BULL. (Progress & Freedom Found., D.C.), May 2006, at 4.

Follow **rule 16.4** or **rule 16.5** to cite articles, essays, commentaries, and all other materials contained within periodicals. Where the periodical is organized by volume, and page numbers continue throughout the volume, it is a consecutively paginated periodical and should be cited according to **rule 16.4**. Where the periodical is paginated separately for each issue and the first page of every issue is 1, it is a nonconsecutively paginated periodical and should be cited according to **rule 16.5**.

Cite newspapers according to **rule 16.6**.

Special citation forms for non-student-written book reviews, student-written law review materials, symposia, colloquia, surveys, commentaries and other special designations, multipart articles, annotations, proceedings, regular publications by institutes, ABA Section Reports, and noncommercially distributed periodicals such as newsletters are given in **rule 16.7**.

Cite sources in electronic media and online sources using **rule 16.8**.

Follow **rule 16.9** for short citation forms.

Capitalize the titles of works cited according to **rule 8(a)**.

The name of the periodical should appear in large and small capitals whether it is a journal, magazine, or newspaper, and should be abbreviated according to **tables T6** (case names, institutional author names, and periodical titles), **T13** (institutional names in periodical titles), and **T10** (geographic abbreviations).

For purposes of this rule, the date of the publication is the cover date of the periodical.

Author 16.2

For signed materials appearing in periodicals (including student-written materials), follow **rule 15.1**, but print in ordinary roman type. Thus:

▶ Kim Lane Scheppele, *Foreword: Telling Stories*, 87 MICH. L. REV. 2073, 2082 (1989).

▶ Robert P. Inman & Michael A. Fitts, *Political Institutions and Fiscal Policy: Evidence from the U.S. Historical Record*, 6 J.L. ECON. & ORG. 79, 79–82 (1990).

▶ Paul Butler et al., *Race, Law and Justice: The Rehnquist Court and the American Dilemma*, 45 AM. U. L. REV. 567, 569 (1996).

▶ Georgette C. Poindexter, LizabethAnn Rogovoy & Susan Wachter, *Selling Municipal Property Tax Receivables: Economics, Privatization, and Public Policy in an Era of Urban Distress*, 30 CONN. L. REV. 157 (1997).

▶ R. Gregory Cochran, Comment, *Is the Shrink's Role Shrinking? The Ambiguity of Federal Rule of Criminal Procedure 12.2 Concerning Government Psychiatric Testimony in Negativing Cases*, 147 U. PA. L. REV. 1403 (1999).

▶ Peter Carlson, *Tales Out of Law School; Repeat After Us: It's Nothing Like 'L.A. Law,'* WASH. POST, July 2, 1989, (Magazine), at W13.

Title 16.3

Cite the full periodical title as it appears on the title page but capitalize according to **rule 8** (unless the title is not in English, as described in **rule 20.2.2(b)**). Do not abbreviate words or omit articles in the title. Use italics:

▶ Edward B. Rock, *The Logic and (Uncertain) Significance of Institutional Shareholder Activism*, 79 GEO. L.J. 445 (1991).

▶ Cecilia Lacey O'Connell, Comment, *The Role of the Objector and the Current Circuit Court Confusion Regarding Federal Rule of Civil Procedure 23.1: Should Non-Named Shareholders Be Permitted to Appeal Adverse Judgments?*, 48 CATH. U. L. REV. 939, 943–46 (1999).

When the title contains a reference to material that would be italicized when appearing in the main text according to **rule 2.2(a)**, such material should appear in ordinary roman type:

▶ Nathaniel A. Vitan, Book Note, *Grounded Paratroopers: On Collins and Skover's* The Death of Discourse, 13 J.L. & POL. 207, 210 (1997).

▶ Seth F. Kreimer, *Does Pro-Choice Mean Pro-Kevorkian? An Essay on* Roe, Casey, *and the Right to Die*, 44 AM. U. L. REV. 803, 812 (1995).

16.4 Consecutively Paginated Journals

Cite works found within periodicals that are consecutively paginated throughout an entire volume by author, title of work, volume number, periodical name, first page of the work, page or pages on which specific material appears (**rule 3.2(a)**), and year enclosed in parentheses at the end of the citation. Consult **tables T6, T10**, and **T13** to abbreviate the names of periodicals:

▶ David Rudovsky, *Police Abuse: Can the Violence Be Contained?*, 27 HARV. C.R.-C.L. L. REV. 465, 500 (1992).

▶ Richard A. Epstein, *The Supreme Court, 1987 Term—Foreword: Unconstitutional Conditions, State Power, and the Limits of Consent*, 102 HARV. L. REV. 4, 44 (1988).

▶ Kenneth W. Tsang et al., *A Cluster of Cases of Severe Acute Respiratory Syndrome in Hong Kong*, 348 NEW ENG. J. MED. 1977, 1977 (2003).

▶ Pauline M. Ippolito & Alan D. Mathios, *New Food Labeling Regulations and the Flow of Nutrition Information to Consumers*, 12 J. PUB. POL'Y & MKTG. 188 (1993).

Some journals maintain separate but consecutive pagination with different page numbering systems. Cite these journals as indicated above, but include the special numbering:

▶ Kenneth R. Feinberg, *Mediation—A Preferred Method of Dispute Resolution*, 16 PEPP. L. REV. S5, S14 n.19 (1989).

Some journals publish special annual issues that do not conform to their consecutive pagination system. Cite these as indicated above but indicate the special issue designation parenthetically and use the numbering from the special issue:

▶ John Ferejohn & Charles Shipan, *Congressional Influence on Bureaucracy*, 6 J.L. ECON. & ORG. (SPECIAL ISSUE) 1 (1990).

▶ George A. Akerlof, *Procrastination and Obedience*, 81 AM. ECON. REV. (PAPERS & PROC.) 1 (1991).

If the periodical has no volume number but is nonetheless consecutively paginated throughout each volume, use the year of publication as the volume number and omit the parenthetical reference to the year:

▶ Thomas R. McCoy & Barry Friedman, *Conditional Spending: Federalism's Trojan Horse*, 1988 SUP. CT. REV. 85, 100.

▶ Stephen D. Sugarman, *Using Private Schools to Promote Public Values*, 1991 U. CHI. LEGAL F. 171.

16.5 Nonconsecutively Paginated Journals and Magazines

Works appearing in periodicals that are separately paginated within each issue should be cited by author, title of work, periodical name, date of issue as it appears on the cover, the word "at" (**rule 3.2(a)**), first page of work, and, if applicable, page or pages on which specific material appears. If there is no author listed, begin the citation with the title of the piece. Consult **tables T6, T10**, and **T13** to abbreviate the names of periodicals:

- Barbara Ward, *Progress for a Small Planet*, HARV. BUS. REV., Sept.–Oct. 1979, at 89, 90.

- Barbara Ehrenreich, *Iranscam: The Real Meaning of Oliver North*, MS., May 1987, at 24, 24.

- Joan B. Kelly, *Mediated and Adversarial Divorce: Respondents' Perceptions of Their Processes and Outcomes*, MEDIATION Q., Summer 1989, at 71.

- *Damages for a Deadly Cloud: The Bhopal Tragedy Will Cost Union Carbide $470 Million*, TIME, Feb. 27, 1989, at 53.

If no date of issue is available, provide the issue number in its place and indicate the volume number before the title of the periodical per **rule 16.4**; also include the year and month of copyright, if available:

- Charles E. Mueller, *The American Who Wants to Give Away His Country but Doesn't Know That's What He's Voting for*, 34 ANTITRUST L. & ECON. REV., no. 1, 2008, at 1, 7.

Newspapers 16.6

(a) In general. Materials appearing in newspapers are generally cited in the same manner as those found in nonconsecutively paginated periodicals (**rule 16.5**) with three exceptions: (i) when appropriate, designate the work as an "Editorial," "Opinion," or "Letter to the Editor," in ordinary roman type, after the author's name but before the title, or at the beginning of the citation if there is no author; (ii) after the date, give the designation of the section in which the piece is found in a parenthetical if necessary to identify the page unambiguously; and (iii) give only the first page of the piece and do not indicate the location of specific material. Substitute "Letter to the Editor" or another designation for the title when no separate title is provided. Citations to signed articles should include the author's full name (**rule 16.2**); citations to unsigned pieces should begin with the title of the piece:

- Ari L. Goldman, *O'Connor Warns Politicians Risk Excommunication over Abortion*, N.Y. TIMES, June 15, 1990, at A1.

- *Cop Shoots Tire, Halts Stolen Car*, S.F. CHRON., Oct. 10, 1975, at 43.

- Jane Gross, *Silent Right: Lawyer Defends Principles from Her Jail Cell*, CHI. TRIB., Mar. 3, 1991 (§ 6), at 6.

- Nancy Reagan, Editorial, *Just Say "Whoa,"* WALL ST. J., Jan. 23, 1996, at A14.

- William J. Clinton, Opinion, *AIDS Is Not a Death Sentence*, N.Y. TIMES, Dec. 1, 2002 (§ 4), at 9.

- Editorial, *Pricing Drugs*, WASH. POST, Feb. 17, 2004, at A18.

▶ Michael Harwood, *The Ordeal: Life as a Medical Resident*, N.Y. TIMES, June 3, 1984 (§ 6), at 38.

(b) Place of publication. Include the place of publication in ordinary roman type in parentheses following the name of the newspaper if not clear from the name:

▶ *Trial Judge Will Not Give Enquiry Evidence*, TIMES (London), June 13, 1990, at 3.

▶ Nancy Johnson, Letter to the Editor, CHRON. HIGHER EDUC. (D.C.), Oct. 8, 2004, at A55.

(c) Consecutively paginated newspapers. Cite an article in a newspaper paginated consecutively by volume according to **rule 16.4**:

▶ *New York County Lawyers Association: Edwin M. Otterbourg to Represent the Association in House of Delegates of American Bar Association*, 124 N.Y. L.J. 1221 (1950).

(d) Wire services. Articles derived from wire services should be cited to a print newspaper in which they are published (**rule 16.6(a)**), a commercial electronic database (**rule 16.6(e)**), or a webpage (**rule 16.6(f)**). Include the name of the wire service (in large and small caps) only if the citation is to the wire service itself:

▶ Richard Carelli, *Judges' Financial Reports Hit Web*, ASSOCIATED PRESS, June 22, 2000, 2000 WL 23358974.

▶ Kevin Drawbaugh, *Obama, Edwards Hit Lobbyists on Private Equity Tax*, REUTERS, Oct. 9, 2007, http://www.reuters.com/article /politicsNews/idUSN0942219020071009.

▶ *Record Labels Sue LimeWire for Enabling Music File-Sharing*, FOXNews.com, Aug. 6, 2007, http://www.foxnews.com/story/record -labels-sue-limewire-for-enabling-music-file-sharing.

(e) Commercial electronic databases. News reports published in electronic databases may be cited according to **rule 16.8**:

▶ *Justice Minister Calls for Solving International Legal Conflicts*, JAPAN ECON. NEWSWIRE PLUS, Apr. 22, 1991, at 1, DIALOG, File No. 612.

▶ *InfoUSA Tells Shareholders to Ignore Hedge Fund*, REUTERS, May 4, 2006, Factiva, Doc. No. LBA000020060504e254001vp.

(f) Internet and online newspapers. Online newspapers may be used in place of print newspapers. Cite to the online source directly in accordance with **rule 18.2.2**. Pagination can be included if available but is not necessary. If the time of posting is available, include it in the parentheses in accordance with **rule 18.2.2**:

▶ John M. Broder, *Geography Is Dividing Democrats over Energy*, N.Y. TIMES, Jan. 26, 2009, at A1.

becomes: John M. Broder, *Geography Is Dividing Democrats over Energy*, N.Y. TIMES (Jan. 26, 2009), http://www.nytimes.com/2009/01/27 /science/earth/27coal.html.

Special Citation Forms   16.7

. . . .

Student-Written Law Review Materials   16.7.1

(a) Signed, student-written materials. Signed and titled notes, comments, projects, etc. are cited in the same manner as any other signed article in a law review (**rule 16.4**), with the author's full name in ordinary roman type at the beginning of the citation (**rule 16.2**), except that the designation of the piece should appear before the title of the work (**rule 16.3**) to indicate that it is student written. Cite student-written book reviews according to **rule 16.7.1(c)**.

A student work is considered signed if a student is credited with writing or contributing to the piece anywhere within the issue in which the work appears—on the first page of the piece, at the end of the piece, or in the table of contents. If a student work is signed only with initials, it is considered unsigned:

> ▶ Ellen London, Comment, *A Critique of the Strict Liability Standard for Determining Child Support in Cases of Male Victims of Sexual Assault and Statutory Rape*, 152 U. Pa. L. Rev. 1957, 1959–63 (2004).

> ▶ B. George Ballman, Jr., Note, *Amended Rule 6.1: Another Move Towards Mandatory Pro Bono? Is That What We Want?*, 7 Geo. J. Legal Ethics 1139, 1162 n.155 (1994).

> ▶ Barry I. Pershkow, Recent Development, Maryland v. Craig: *A Child Witness Need Not View the Defendant During Testimony in Child Abuse Cases*, 65 Tul. L. Rev. 935, 938, 941 (1991).

Signed, student-written commentary that is shorter, that falls under a designation such as "Recent Case," "Recent Statute," "Recent Decision," "Case Note," "Recent Development," or "Abstract," and that carries no title or merely a digest-like heading should be cited by author followed by the designation of the piece as provided in the periodical, both in ordinary roman type. When appearing in the title, a case or statute citation should be formatted according to the typeface conventions in **rule 16.3**. Thus:

> ▶ Sally Anne Moore, Recent Case, H.L. v. Matheson, *101 S. Ct. 1164 (1981)*, 50 U. Cin. L. Rev. 867, 868 (1981).

Not: Sally Anne Moore, Recent Case, *Constitutional Law—Right of Privacy—Abortion—Family Law—Parent and Child—Standing—As Applied to Immature, Unemancipated and Dependent Minors, a State Statute Requiring a Physician To Notify a Pregnant Minor's Parents Prior to the Performing of an Abortion Is Constitutional*—H.L. v. Matheson, *101 S. Ct. 1164 (1981)*, 50 U. Cin. L. Rev. 867, 868 (1981).

(b) Unsigned, student-written materials. Cite unsigned notes, comments, and shorter commentary by the designation given by the periodical, such as "Note," "Comment," "Case Comment," "Project," "Recent Case," "Case Note," etc., in ordinary roman type, followed by the title of the piece, if any, in italics:

> ▶ Note, *A Bad Man Is Hard to Find*, 127 Harv. L. Rev. 2521 (2014).

> ▶ Case Comment, *Evidentiary Use of a Criminal Defendant's Reading Habits and Political Conversations:* United States v. Giese, 93 Harv. L. Rev. 419, 425–27 (1979).

▶ Recent Case, 24 Vand. L. Rev. 148, 151–52 (1970).

▶ Recent Case, American Civil Liberties Union of Illinois v. Alvarez, *679 F.3d 583 (7th Cir. 2012)*, 126 Harv. L. Rev. 1162 (2013).

When there is no separable designation, italicize the entire title:

▶ *Developments in the Law—The Law of Cyberspace*, 112 Harv. L. Rev. 1577, 1624 n.95 (1999).

▶ *The Supreme Court, 1998 Term—Leading Cases*, 113 Harv. L. Rev. 368, 378 n.60 (1999).

(c) Student-written book reviews. If a review is written and signed by a student, include the author's name and the designation "Book Note" (regardless of the journal's designation) to indicate that it is student-written, followed by the title, if any. Add a parenthetical indicating the work under review if relevant to the purpose of the citation and not clear from the surrounding discussion:

▶ William Dubinsky, Book Note, 90 Mich. L. Rev. 1512 (1992) (reviewing Daniel A. Farber & Philip P. Frickey, Law and Public Choice (1991)).

▶ Nathaniel A. Vitan, Book Note, *Irons vs. Rehnquist: A Critical Review of Peter Irons'* Brennan vs. Rehnquist, 12 J.L. & Pol. 141 (1995).

An unsigned, student-written book review should be cited in the same manner as other unsigned student works, with a parenthetical citing the work under review if relevant:

▶ Book Note, *Let Us Reason Together*, 112 Harv. L. Rev. 958 (1999) (reviewing Pierre Schlag, The Enchantment of Reason (1998)).

. . . .

16.7.2 Non-Student-Written Book Reviews

Give the full name of the reviewer according to **rule 16.2**, and the title of the review in italics. Include a second parenthetical after the date parenthetical indicating, if relevant to the purpose of the citation and if not clear from the surrounding discussion, the author, title, and publication date of the book reviewed. If it is unnecessary to identify the book under review, simply include the words "book review" in the second parenthetical:

▶ Colin S. Diver, *Second Governance and Sound Law*, 89 Mich. L. Rev. 1436 (1991) (reviewing Christopher F. Edley, Jr., Administrative Law: Rethinking Judicial Control of Bureaucracy (1990)).

▶ Bruce Ackerman, *Robert Bork's Grand Inquisition*, 99 Yale L.J. 1419, 1422–25 (1990) (book review).

If a non-student-written review is untitled, cite it by the designation "Book Review"; it is unnecessary to include a second parenthetical unless there is a need to identify the book under review:

▶ Howard C. Westwood, Book Review, 45 U. Chi. L. Rev. 255 (1977).

Symposia, Colloquia, and Surveys 16.7.3

When citing a symposium, colloquium, or colloquy as a unit, do not give any author, but include "Symposium," "Colloquium," or "Colloquy" in roman type before the title unless made clear by the title. Cite the first page of the first piece:

▶ Symposium, *Changing Images of the State*, 107 Harv. L. Rev. 1179 (1994).

▶ *The Brennan Center Symposium on Constitutional Law*, 87 Calif. L. Rev. 1059 (1999).

If an article is part of a survey of the law of one jurisdiction, the title of the article should incorporate the title of the survey as follows:

▶ Alain A. Levasseur, *Sales, The Work of the Louisiana Appellate Courts for the 1977–1978 Term*, 39 La. L. Rev. 705 (1979).

Cite an individual article within a symposium, colloquium, colloquy, or survey in the same manner as any other article:

▶ Eric A. Posner, *Law, Economics, and Inefficient Norms*, 144 U. Pa. L. Rev. 1697 (1996).

▶ Kevin R. Vodak, Comment, *A Plainly Obvious Need for New-Fashioned Municipal Liability: The Deliberate Indifference Standard and* Board of County Commissioners of Bryan County v. Brown, 48 DePaul L. Rev. 785 (1999).

Commentaries and Other Special Designations 16.7.4

When citing a "Commentary," "Tribute," "In Memoriam," or other special article designation, the designation should appear in roman type after the author's name but before the title. If the author is unnamed or if the journal's editors are listed as the authors, the designation should appear at the beginning of the citation. "Commentary" should not be confused with "Comment," a term frequently used to describe student-written pieces (**rule 16.7.1**).

▶ Alvin C. Warren, Jr., Commentary, *Financial Contract Innovation and Income Tax Policy*, 107 Harv. L. Rev. 460 (1993).

▶ Sandra Day O'Connor, Dedication, *Lending Light to Countless Lamps: A Tribute to Judge Norma Levy Shapiro*, 152 U. Pa. L. Rev. 1 (2003).

▶ Marguerite A. Driessen, Response, *Not for the Sake of Punishment Alone: Comments on* Viewing the Criminal Sanction Through Latter-day Saint Thought, 2003 BYU L. Rev. 941.

Multipart Articles 16.7.5

To cite an entire article that appears in more than one part, identify the numbers of the parts in parentheses after the article's main title and give the volume number, first page, and publication year for each part:

▶ Harlan F. Stone, *The Equitable Rights and Liabilities of Strangers to a Contract* (pts. 1 & 2), 18 COLUM. L. REV. 291 (1918), 19 COLUM. L. REV. 177 (1919).

If all of the parts appear in one volume, use the shortened form:

▶ L.L. Fuller, *Legal Fictions* (pts. 1–3), 25 ILL. L. REV. 363, 513, 877 (1930–1931).

To cite only some parts of a multipart article, indicate which part or parts are cited and give only the volume number(s), page number(s), and publication year(s) of the part(s) cited:

▶ L.L. Fuller, *Legal Fictions* (pt. 2), 25 ILL. L. REV. 513, 514 (1931).

. . . .

16.7.6 Annotations

Cite discussions in selective case reporters (such as *American Law Reports* and *Lawyers' Reports Annotated*) by the author's full name, followed by the designation "Annotation" in ordinary roman type and the title of the work in italics:

▶ Claudia Catalano, Annotation, *Unlawful Access Under Stored Communications Act, 18 U.S.C.A. § 2701 et seq.*, 1 A.L.R. Fed. 3d Art. 1 (2015).

. . . .

16.7.7 Proceedings, Regular Publications by Institutes, and ABA Section Reports

Cite as periodicals, abbreviating according to **tables T6, T10**, and **T13**:

▶ Herbert F. Goodrich, *Annual Report of Adviser on Professional Relations*, 16 A.L.I. PROC. 48 (1939).

▶ George Vranesh, *Water Planning for Municipalities*, 24 ROCKY MTN. MIN. L. INST. 865 (1978).

If the volumes are unnumbered, use either the number of the institute (or proceedings) or the year of publication as a volume number; in the latter case omit the parenthetical reference to the year:

▶ David J. Beck, *Crude Oil Issues*, 30 INST. ON OIL & GAS L. & TAX'N 1 (1979).

▶ Julius L. Sackman, *Landmark Cases on Landmark Law*, 1979 INST. ON PLAN. ZONING & EMINENT DOMAIN 241.

▶ William J. Curtin, *Reverse Discrimination and Affirmative Action: Practical Considerations for the Utilities Industry*, 1978 A.B.A. SEC. PUB. UTIL. L. REP. 26.

If the publication is organized by paragraph or section numbers, use those numbers in citations:

▶ Max Gutierrez, Jr., *Estate Planning for the Unmarried Cohabitant*, 13 INST. ON EST. PLAN. ¶ 1600 (1979).

To cite part of an article identified by paragraph or section number, cite both the first paragraph or section number of the article and the paragraph or section number(s) where the relevant material appears. Add a page citation if necessary for further identification (see **rule 3.3**):

▶ Walter F. O'Connor, *Taxation of Foreign Investors*, 38 Inst. on Fed. Tax'n § 22.01, § 22.04, at 22-10 (1980).

Newsletters and Other Noncommercially Distributed Periodicals

16.7.8

Materials appearing in newsletters and other similar periodicals not commercially distributed should be cited in the same manner as nonconsecutively paginated journals and magazines (**rule 16.5**), except that a parenthetical should follow the title of the publication indicating the issuing group or organization and its location. Abbreviate the name of the periodical according to **tables T6, T10**, and **T13** and abbreviate the name of the issuing institution according to **rule 15.1(d)**:

▶ *Indictment of Pregnant Woman for Drug Use Dismissed*, Reprod. Rts. Update (ACLU/Reprod. Freedom Project, New York, N.Y.), Oct. 26, 1990, at 5.

▶ *Recent Grants*, FCD Update (Found. for Child Dev., New York, N.Y.), Dec. 1990, at 1, 7.

Electronic Databases and Online Sources

16.8

(a) Commercial electronic databases. When citing periodical materials to a database, provide a complete citation to the document according to **rule 16** and a citation to the database. If the database assigns a unique identifier or code to each document within the database, include that identifier or code to assist the reader in locating the document cited.

Some sources are available in two forms, electronic and paper. To facilitate access to the source, it is permissible to include a direct citation to a commercial electronic database:

▶ T.R. Fehrenbach, *TV's Alamo Tale Fairly Accurate*, San Antonio Express-News, Mar. 17, 1996, at A1, 1996 WL 2824823.

▶ *Justice Minister Calls for Solving International Legal Conflicts*, Japan Econ. Newswire Plus, Apr. 22, 1991, at 1, DIALOG, File No. 612.

(b) Internet and online sources. Where a print version is accessible, citation should be made to the print source. Where, however, the print source is difficult or impossible to obtain, or the governing authority has designated the electronic source as the official version, citation should be made to the electronic source with consideration of **rule 18**'s principles on authentication. If a periodical source is only available online, cite to it directly in accordance with **rule 18.2.2**.

Short Citation Forms

16.9

Once a work in a periodical has been cited in full, use "*id.*" or "*supra*" to refer to it in subsequent citations.

(a) *Id.* If the work cited is the same as the immediately preceding authority within the same footnote or as the sole authority within the immediately preceding footnote, use "*id.*" and indicate any difference in page number:

▶ [1] Lynn Hirschberg, *The Misfit*, VANITY FAIR, Apr. 1991, at 158.

▶ [2] *See id.*; Recent Case, 24 VAND. L. REV. 148, 148 (1970).

▶ [3] *See generally* Abram S. Benenson et al., *Reporting the Results of Human Immunodeficiency Virus Testing*, 262 JAMA 3435 (1989) (stating that actual laboratory results are often obscured by incorrect information).

▶ [4] *Id.* at 3437.

▶ [5] *See, e.g.*, Bruce Ackerman, *Robert Bork's Grand Inquisition*, 99 YALE L.J. 1419 (1990) (book review). *Compare id.* (arguing against constitutional transformation by judicial appointment), *with* Book Note, *Manual Labor, Chicago Style*, 101 HARV. L. REV. 1323 (1988) (arguing against stylistic transformation by self-appointment).

(b) *Supra*. Include the author's last name before "*supra*"; when there is no author, use the title of the piece, or, if listed before or instead of a title, the designation of the piece. However, if the first citation to the work gives a hereinafter form (**rule 4.2(b)**), use the hereinafter form in place of the author's name, the title, or the designation. Give the footnote in which the full citation appears unless the full citation is in the same footnote, in which case "*supra*" may be used without a footnote reference. In using a "*supra*" form, always indicate the page or pages cited except when citing the work in its entirety:

▶ [6] Ackerman, *supra* note 5, at 1425; *see also New York County Lawyers Association: Edwin M. Otterbourg to Represent the Association in House of Delegates of American Bar Association*, 124 N.Y. L.J. 1221 (1950) [hereinafter *Otterbourg to Represent*] (describing internal politics); Note, *The Death of a Lawyer*, 56 COLUM. L. REV. 606, 607 (1956).

▶ [7] Recent Case, *supra* note 2, at 150. *But see* Randy E. Barnett, *A Consent Theory of Contract*, 86 COLUM. L. REV. 269, 275 (1986) (noting circularity of reliance theory of contract); Jennifer Roback, *Southern Labor Law in the Jim Crow Era: Exploitative or Competitive?*, 51 U. CHI. L. REV. 1161, 1164–65 (1984) (describing the importance of interaction between a competitive market and a racially biased government).

▶ [8] *Cf.* David Margolick, *At the Bar: Elitist Yale Breaks Precedent and Invites a Symbol of Populism to Preside at a Legal Rite*, N.Y. TIMES, Apr. 12, 1991, at B16 (describing the reaction to students' decision to invite Judge Wapner to preside over a mock-trial competition at Yale). *See generally* Roback, *supra* note 7, at 1163 (outlining four basic types of legislation that aided enforcement of the labor-market cartel under Jim Crow laws).

▶ [9] *See* Book Note, *supra* note 5, for a cogent analysis of the more significant flaws in the competing theory.

▶ [10] *Otterbourg to Represent*, *supra* note 6; *see also* Note, *supra* note 6 (discussing problems that arise upon the death of a lawyer). *But see*

Cop Shoots Tire, Halts Stolen Car, S.F. CHRON., Oct. 10, 1975, at 43 (discussing the legal ramifications of the officer's action).

For materials available only online, use the normal short form appropriate for the source. A URL need not be repeated after a full citation.

UNPUBLISHED AND FORTHCOMING SOURCES 17

Basic Citation Forms 17.1

Unpublished manuscript	Jennifer Arlen, Public Versus Private Enforcement of Securities Fraud 12–19 (June 22, 2007) (unpublished manuscript) (on file with the Columbia Law Review).
Dissertations and theses	Alexander J. Blenkinsopp, Honesty vs. Expedience: The Deficient Jurisprudence of Punishment and the Legal Labeling Game (Nov. 1, 2005) (A.B. thesis, Harvard University) (on file with the Harvard University Library system).
Letter, memorandum, or press release	Memorandum from President Franklin Roosevelt to Attorney Gen. Robert H. Jackson (July 1, 1939) (on file with the Harvard Law School Library).
E-mail correspondence	E-mail from Laura Bakst, Editor, Harvard Law Review, to author (Feb. 4, 2017, 01:31 EST) (on file with author).
Forthcoming publication	Eduardo Peñalver, *Land Virtues*, 94 CORNELL L. REV. (forthcoming May 2009).
Working paper	Dan Black et al., *Demographics of the Gay and Lesbian Population in the United States: Evidence from Available Systemic Date Sources 9* (Ctr. for Policy Rsch., Working Paper No. 12, 1999).

Unpublished Materials 17.2

In general, cite unpublished materials not scheduled for publication by author; title or description; page or pages, if applicable; the most precise writing date available; and, if possible, information as to where the work can be located. Use ordinary roman type. Refer to **rule 10.8.1** when citing pending and unreported cases and **rule 12.6** when citing statutes too recent to appear in any published source. If unpublished materials are subsequently collected and published, cite according to **rule 15.5.2(b)**.

Manuscripts 17.2.1

Cite unpublished (or not formally published) manuscripts not scheduled for publication in ordinary roman type, beginning with the author's full name (**rule 16.2**). The title of the work as it appears on the title page should follow, capitalized according to **rule 8(a)** (unless the title is not in English, in which case follow **rule 20.2.2(b)**). Provide a subtitle only if it is particularly relevant. Do not abbreviate words or omit articles in the title. The full date of the manuscript should be enclosed in parentheses after the title of the work or the pincite. Append parentheticals indicating that the work is unpublished and describing where it can be found:

> ► Anatoliy Bizhko, Capitalism and Democracy 25 (Feb. 29, 2000) (unpublished manuscript) (on file with author).

Also use this format for student-written comments and notes written under faculty supervision for a law journal, but not selected for publication, with the second parenthetical indicating the type of work:

> ► Victoria E. Anderson, Company Outing: How Consensual Relationship Agreements Adversely Affect Homosexual Employees 12 (Mar. 15, 2004) (unpublished comment) (on file with the University of Pennsylvania Journal of Labor and Employment Law).

17.2.2 Dissertations and Theses

Cite student-written materials, such as dissertations and theses, in the same manner as other unpublished manuscripts (**rule 17.2.1**), but add a parenthetical after the date to indicate the type of work and the institution that awarded the degree:

> ► Barbara G. Ryder, Incremental Data Flow Analysis Based on a Unified Model of Elimination Algorithms (Aug. 15, 1982) (Ph.D. dissertation, Rutgers University) (on file with author).

> ► Alexander Harper, Patronage in the Re-Christianized Landscape of Angevin Apulia: The Rebuilding of Luceria sarracenorum into Civitas Sanctae Mariae (2014) (Ph.D. dissertation, University of Toronto) (ProQuest).

> ► Ambrogino Giusti, The Green Press: Mass Media and the U.S. Environmental Movement 1945–1975 (Aug. 8, 2007) (B.A. thesis, University of Washington) (on file with the Suzzallo and Allen Libraries, University of Washington).

17.2.3 Letters, Memoranda, and Press Releases

When citing unpublished letters, memoranda, and press releases, identify the nature of the document and give the writer and addressee (if any) by name, title, and institutional affiliation. Abbreviate title and institutional affiliation according to **tables T6, T10,** and **T11**:

> ► Letter from Anna Dimitrijevic, Bluebook Ed. Chair, Harvard L. Rev., to Joe Kurtenbach, Bluebook Bus. Chair, Harvard L. Rev. (Feb. 1, 2020) (on file with the Harvard Law School Library).

> ► Memorandum from the Ad Hoc Comm. on Women & Clerkships to the Faculty of Yale Law Sch. 14 (Feb. 13, 1991) (on file with author).

> ► Press Release, Screen Actors Guild, Screen Actors Guild Hails Passage of California Privacy Law (Sept. 30, 1998) (on file with author).

To cite a letter written to the author of the work in which the letter is being cited, omit the addressee's name and use "to author":

▶ Letter from Graham Sternberg, Bluebook Ed. & Strategy Chair, Harvard L. Rev., to author (Feb. 13, 2020) (on file with author).

E-mail Correspondence and Listserv Postings

When citing personal e-mail messages, analogize to unpublished letters (**rule 17.2.3**). The date of the message and the timestamp may be needed for specific identification of the message. Archival information may be included parenthetically and is recommended. The e-mail addresses of the sender and recipient are not required, although they may be included if there is a reason for doing so:

▶ E-mail from Mary Miles Prince, Assoc. Dir., Vanderbilt L. Libr., to Edward C. Brewer, III, Assistant Professor of L., Salmon P. Chase Coll. of L. (Sept. 26, 1999, 06:15 CST) (on file with author).

Postings to listservs should follow a similar format, but should include the author's e-mail address and the address of the listserv:

▶ Posting of Anastasia Pastan, apastan@act.org, to carall-talk@ yahoogroups.com (July 21, 2012) (on file with author).

Interviews

When citing an in-person or telephone interview, include the name, title, and institutional affiliation (if any) of the interviewee and the date of the interview. For an in-person interview, provide the location of the interview before the date. Abbreviate title, institutional affiliation, and location according to **tables T6** and **T10,** and **T11.**

▶ Telephone Interview with John J. Farrell, Senior Partner, Hildebrand, McLeod & Nelson (Nov. 11, 1999).

▶ Interview with Aisha Rich, Managing Ed., Harvard L. Rev., in Cambridge, Mass. (Mar. 2, 2014).

When the author has not personally conducted the interview, provide the name of the interviewer:

▶ Interview by Lauren Brook Eisen with Shane Spradlin, CEO, Nextel Commc'ns, in Potomac, Md. (Mar. 1, 2000).

Speeches and Addresses

When citing speeches and addresses (including those made at panels and conference presentations), identify the speaker by name. Add the speaker's title and institutional affiliation if they are included in the description or transcript of the document, or if they would be particularly helpful to the reader. The title of the speech or address, pincite where available, and date of the speech should follow. Abbreviate the speaker's title and institutional affiliation according to **tables T6** and **T10,** and **T11.**

▶ Bradley Smith, Chairman, Fed. Election Comm'n, Keynote Address at the University of Pennsylvania Law Review Symposium: The Law of Democracy (Feb. 6, 2004).

If the speech or address does not have a formal title, provide a description with identifying information:

▶ Senator Hubert Humphrey, Address at the Harvard Law Review Annual Banquet (Mar. 29, 1958).

If the speech or address has been transcribed but not published, include the location of the transcript in a second parenthetical:

▶ Herbert Wechsler, Remarks at the Meeting of the Bar of the Supreme Court of the United States in Memory of Chief Justice Stone 5 (Nov. 12, 1947) (transcript available in the Columbia Law School Library).

If the speech or address has been published, cite using an "*in*" form according to **rules 1.6(a)(i)** and **15.5.2(b)**:

▶ James A. Baker III, U.S. Sec'y of State, Principles and Pragmatism: American Policy Toward the Arab-Israeli Conflict, Address Before the American Israel Public Affairs Committee (May 22, 1989), *in* DEP'T ST. BULL., July 1989, at 24, 24–25.

17.3 Forthcoming Publications

Cite a book, article, or other work scheduled for publication in the same manner as the published piece would be cited, with the same typefaces, except: (i) do not include a pincite following the title of the journal or book; (ii) add the designation "forthcoming" in the date parenthetical; and (iii) include the month of publication, if available, in addition to the year in the date parenthetical. Omit volume number if not yet available:

▶ Sarah D. Greenberger, Comment, *Enforceable Rights, No Child Left Behind, and Political Patriotism: A Case for Open-Minded Section 1983 Jurisprudence*, 153 U. PA. L. REV. (forthcoming Jan. 2005).

To cite a particular page of a forthcoming publication, add a second parenthetical with the manuscript page cite and a third with the location of the forthcoming document.

▶ F. Brandon Baer & James M. Feldman, *We're Low on Vermouth: The Trials and Tribulations of Two Summer Associates*, 1 J.L. & OPPRESSION (forthcoming 2001) (manuscript at 3) (on file with authors).

17.4 Working Papers

When citing an unpublished work designated as a working paper, provide a parenthetical indicating the name of the sponsoring organization, the working paper designation and number, and the year. Abbreviate institutional entities according to **rule 15.1(d)**:

▶ Alan J. Auerbach & Laurence J. Kotlikoff, *National Savings, Economic Welfare, and the Structure of Taxation* 24–33 (Nat'l Bureau of Econ. Rsch., Working Paper No. 729, 1981).

► Richard Briffault, *The Political Parties and Campaign Finance Reform* 16–17 (Columbia L. Sch. Pub. L. Working Paper, Paper No. 012, 2000), http://papers.ssrn.com/sol3/papers.cfm?abstract_id=223729.73.

When a work is designated as a working paper, but is not numbered, cite according to **rule 17.2.1**.

Electronic Databases and Online Sources   17.5

(a) Commercial electronic databases. When citing unpublished and forthcoming materials to a database, provide a complete citation to the document according to **rule 17**, and a citation to the database. If the database assigns a unique identifier or code to each document within the database, include that identifier or code to assist the reader in locating the document cited.

► Barbara G. Ryder, Incremental Data Flow Analysis Based on a Unified Model of Elimination Algorithms (Aug. 15, 1982) (Ph.D. dissertation, Rutgers University), 23 PQDT 5467.

Some sources are available in two forms, electronic and paper. To facilitate access to the source, it is permissible to include a parallel citation to a commercial electronic database:

► Cass R. Sunstein, *Clear Statement Principles and National Security:* Hamdan *and Beyond*, 2006 SUP. CT. REV. (forthcoming 2007) (manuscript at 17), http://papers.ssrn.com/sol3/papers.cfm?abstract _id=922406.

(b) Internet and online sources. When citing to an electronic source directly, citation should be made according to **rule 18.2.2**.

► *See* Press Release, Nancy Pelosi, Speaker, House of Representatives, Pelosi Statement on Hate Crimes Legislation (Dec. 6, 2007), http:// speaker.gov/newsroom/pelosi-statement-hate-crimes-legislation.

Short Citation Forms   17.6

Use the "*id.*" and "*supra*" forms in the same manner as they are employed for materials appearing in periodicals (**rule 16.9**) and nonperiodicals (**rule 15.10**), substituting the name of the source in place of an author when no author is listed, and enclosing a page citation to the manuscript version of a forthcoming publication in parentheses:

► [1] Interview with Frank Van Dusen, President, Van Dusen Indus., in Rye, N.Y. (Feb. 15, 2000).

► [2] *Id.*; *see also* J. Paul Oetken, Note, *Form and Substance in Critical Legal Studies*, 100 YALE L.J. (forthcoming May 2001) (manuscript at 17) (on file with author). Oetken points out inherent contradictions in CLS rhetoric. *See id.* (manuscript at 10–12); *see also* Adrienne D. Davis, *African American Literature and the Law: Revisi* and Revisiting *Freedom* 3–4 (Dec. 1989) (unpublished manuscript) (on file with The Yale Law Journal) (describing depiction of the law in slave literature).

▶ [3] *See* Oetken, *supra* note 2 (manuscript at 15); Davis, *supra* note 2, at 12; Press Release, Child.'s Def. Fund, 2.8 Million Children of Mexican Heritage Are Among Nearly 4 Million Latino Children Living in Poverty in the United States (May 5, 2004) (on file with author).

▶ [4] Interview with Frank Van Dusen, *supra* note 1; *see* Letter from Asma Hasan to Michael Cannon 2 (Mar. 15, 2000) (on file with author).

▶ [5] *See* Letter from Asma Hasan to Michael Cannon, *supra* note 4, at 3.

▶ [6] *See* Press Release, Child.'s Def. Fund, *supra* note 3.

For materials available only online, use the normal short form appropriate for the source. A URL need not be repeated after a full citation.

---

18 THE INTERNET, ELECTRONIC MEDIA, AND OTHER NONPRINT RESOURCES

This rule covers citation of information found on the internet (**rule 18.2**); widely used commercial databases such as Westlaw and LEXIS (**rule 18.3**); CD-ROMs (**rule 18.4**); microform (**rule 18.5**); films, broadcasts, and noncommercial video materials (**rule 18.6**); audio recordings (**rule 18.7**); and photographs and illustrations (**rule 18.8**).

18.1 Basic Citation Forms

(a) Internet Sources (rule 18.2)

Authenticated or official documents	OFF. OF MGMT. & BUDGET, A NEW ERA OF RESPONSIBILITY: RENEWING AMERICA'S PROMISE (2009).
Unaltered scanned copies of print sources	United States v. Grigg, 498 F.3d 1070, 1072–73 (9th Cir. 2007).
Electronic version improving reader access to source also available in print	SANTA MONICA, CAL., MUN. CODE ch. 3.20 (1976), http://qcode.us/codes/santamonica.
Online-only sources	BEN & JERRY'S, http://www.benjerry.com (last visited Oct. 6, 2008).
Subheadings linked from main page of website	David S. Cloud, *Gates Budget Eyes Next Gen. Warfare*, POLITICO (Apr. 11, 2009, 6:56 AM), http://www.politico.com/news/stories/0409/21123.html.
Dynamic webpages, such as blogs	Asahi Shimbun, *A-Bomb Disease Ruling*, JAPANESE L. BLOG (Mar. 27, 2009, 9:29 PM), http://japaneselaw.blogspot.com/search?q=A-Bomb+Disease+Ruling.

Online sources requiring form, query, or unwieldy URL	Driving Directions from N.Y.C. to New Haven, CT, GOOGLE MAPS, http://maps.google.com (follow "Directions" hyperlink; then search starting point field for "New York, NY" and search destination field for "New Haven, CT").
Online sources that preserve original pagination, such as a PDF	Kenneth W. Simons, *Retributivists Need Not and Should Not Endorse the Subjectivist Account of Punishment,* 109 COLUM. L. REV. SIDEBAR 1, 3 (2009), http://columbialawreview.org/wp-content/uploads/2016/08/Simons.pdf.
Dynamic websites, such as blogs, within larger websites	Vanessa Williams, *'The Cosby Show' and the Black American Dream*, WASH. POST: SHE THE PEOPLE (Oct. 12, 2014, 8:00 AM), http://www.washingtonpost.com/blogs/she-the-people/wp/2014/10/12/the-cosby-show-and-the-black-american-dream.
Social media posts	Ed Markey (@SenMarkey), TWITTER (Oct. 23, 2020, 12:45 PM), https://twitter.com/SenMarkey/status/1319681451277881345.
Archived sources	Rocio Gonzalez, *Puerto Rico's Status Debate Continues as Island Marks 61 Years as a Commonwealth*, HUFFINGTON POST (July 28, 2014, 9:59 AM), http://www.huffpost.com/entry/puerto-rico-status-debate_n_36517557 [http://perma.cc/C6UP-96HN].

(b) Non-Internet Electronic Sources (rules 18.3–.7)

Commercial electronic databases	Bissinger v. City of New York, Nos. 06 Civ. 2325(WHP), 06 Civ. 2326(WHP), 2007 WL 2826756, at *3 (S.D.N.Y. Sept. 24, 2007).
Electronic storage media	46 C.F.R. § 57.105(a) (Westlaw Desk Code of Federal Regulations CD-ROM, current through July 1, 1999).
Microform collections	Petition for Writ of Certiorari for Defendant-Appellant, Cosman v. United States, 471 U.S. 1102 (1985) (No. 84-1585), *microformed on* U.S. Supreme Court Records and Briefs (Microform, Inc.).
Films and broadcasts	THE GODFATHER (Paramount Pictures 1972).
Commercial audio recordings	BEYONCÉ, DANGEROUSLY IN LOVE (Columbia Records 2003).
Noncommercial recordings	Videotape: Andrew Haber Monologue Series (Scarsdale A/V Services 2008) (on file with author).
Podcasts	*This American Life: Mistakes Were Made*, CHI. PUB. RADIO (Apr. 13, 2009) (downloaded using iTunes).

18.2   The Internet

The Bluebook requires the use and citation of traditional printed sources when available, unless there is a digital copy of the source available that is authenticated, official, or an exact copy of the printed source, as described in **rule 18.2.1**.

The rules that follow offer guidance in formatting internet citations. **Rule 18.2.1** lays out general principles applicable to all internet citations. **Rule 18.2.2** sets out rules for direct citations to internet sources. E-mails should be treated as unpublished letters per **rule 17.2.4**.

....

18.2.1   General Internet Citation Principles

(a) Sources that can be cited as if to the original print source. When an authenticated, official, or exact copy of a source is available online, citation can be made as if to the original print source (without any URL information appended). Many states have begun to discontinue printed official legal resources, instead relying on online versions as the official resources for administrative or legislative documents. The federal government is also moving toward increasing access to online versions of legal documents, though it continues to publish official print versions.

(i) Authenticated documents. When citing to such materials, *The Bluebook* encourages citation to "authenticated" sources: those that use an encryption-based authentication method, such as a digital signature or public key infrastructure, to ensure the accuracy of the online source. Generally, an authenticated document will have a certificate or logo indicating that a government entity verified that the document is complete and unaltered.

(ii) Official versions. Some states have designated, either by legislation or other official mechanism, that the online source is the "official" source for a particular legal document. Some online publishers similarly make a distinction as to whether the document has been approved by, contributed by, or harvested from an official source by the content originator, designating such a document "official." Generally, *The Bluebook* prefers citation to an authenticated source, or, if none is available, to the "official" source.

(iii) Exact copies. An exact copy is one that is an unaltered copy of the printed source in a widely used format that preserves pagination and other attributes of the printed work (such as a PDF).

(b) Sources where the URL should be appended.

(i) Obscure sources. If the cited information is available in a traditional source but such source is so obscure as to be practically unavailable, or if a parallel citation to an internet source will substantially improve access to the source cited, citation should be made both to the traditional source and to the internet source by appending the URL directly to the end of the citation.

(ii) Online sources with print characteristics. If an online source shares the characteristics of a print source such that it could be fully cited according to another rule in *The Bluebook,* the citation should be made as if to the print source and the URL appended directly to the end of the citation, even if it is unknown whether the cited information is available in print.

► FED. TRADE COMM'N, CONSUMER FRAUD IN THE UNITED STATES 12 (2007), http://www.ftc.gov/sites/default/files/documents/reports /consumer-fraud-united-states-second-federal-trade-commission -survey-staff-report-federal-trade/fraud.pdf.

► Tim Ganser & Stan Veuger, *Strategic Voting in Proportional Representation Systems* 28–29 (Am. Enter. Inst., Working Paper No. 2014-02, 2014), http://www.aei.org/wp-content/uploads/2014/02/-veuger -strategic-voting-econ-working-paper_085307749177.pdf.

To share the characteristics of a print source, an online source must be a version permanently divided into pages with permanent page numbers, as in a PDF, and have the elements that characterize a given print source, such as a volume number (for law review articles and the like) or publication date (for magazine articles and the like).

If an online source can be formatted in full compliance with another rule in *The Bluebook*, for purposes of citation style it does not matter whether that source has in fact been published in print. As noted above, traditional printed sources or authenticated digital copies are required as a matter of authority; this does not, however, affect the citation rules for print-like online sources.

(c) Order of parentheticals. When such a citation requires multiple parentheticals, place them in the order indicated in **rule 1.5(b)**. Thus, the URL of a source cited in accordance with **rule 18.2.1(b)** should follow format-related parenthetical information (such as "on file with author," "unpublished manuscript," or "emphasis added") and related authority parentheticals (such as "citing" or "quoting"), but precede explanatory parentheticals:

► Polly J. Price, *Precedent and Judicial Power After the Founding*, 42 B.C. L. REV. 81, 84 (2000) (emphasis added) (citing GUIDO CALABRESI, A COMMON LAW FOR THE AGE OF STATUTES 4 (1982)), http://lawdigitalcommons.bc.edu/cgi/viewcontent.cgi?article=2166 &context=bclr (discussing precedent in the context of statutory construction).

(d) Archival. Archiving of internet sources is encouraged, but only when a reliable archival tool is available. For citations to internet sources, append the archive URL to the full citation in brackets:

► Tom Goldstein, *Somewhat Significant Settlement*, SCOTUSBLOG (Feb. 7, 2005, 8:54 PM), http://www.scotusblog.com/2005/02/somewhat -significant-settlement [http://web.archive.org/web/20050208081922 /www.scotusblog.com/movabletype].

► Letter from Rose M. Oswald Poels, President/CEO, Wis. Bankers Ass'n, to Elizabeth M. Murphy, Sec'y, SEC (Sept. 17, 2013), http://www.sec.gov /comments/s7-03-13/s70313-178.pdf [http://perma.cc/B727-D9DJ].

Citations to Internet Sources   18.2.2

An internet source that cannot be cited according to another rule in *The Bluebook* as stated in accordance with **rule 18.2.1(b)(ii)**, should be cited as if to the original print source in accordance with **rule 18.2.1(a)** or according to this rule. All efforts should be made to cite to the most stable electronic location available. The internet citation should include information designed to facilitate the clearest path of access to the cited reference, including the title, pagination, and publication date as they appear on the webpage. The internet URL should be separated by a comma and appended to the end of the citation.

(a) Author. When available, provide author information in ordinary roman type. When no author is clearly announced, omit author information from the citation unless there is a clear institutional owner of the domain. Abbreviate the name of an institutional author according to **rule 15.1(d)**:

▶ Eric Posner, *More on Section 7 of the Torture Convention*, VOLOKH CONSPIRACY (Jan. 29, 2009, 10:04 AM), http://www.volokh.com/2009 /01/29/more-on-section-7-of-the-torture-convention.

▶ *Pavement Planning New Album Release*, GLIDE MAGAZINE (Nov. 6, 2009), http://www.glidemagazine.com/14807/pavement-planning -new-album-release.

If domain ownership is clear from the website's title, omit the name of the institutional author:

▶ DUNKIN', http://www.dunkindonuts.com (last visited Feb. 1, 2020).

▶ *The Butterfly Conservatory*, AM. MUSEUM OF NAT. HIST., https://www .amnh.org/exhibitions/butterflies-moths-exhibition (last visited Feb. 13, 2020).

For postings and comments, cite using the username of the poster. Comments should include the author of the comment when available but need not include the author of the original post:

▶ Martinned, Comment to *More on Section 7 of the Torture Convention*, VOLOKH CONSPIRACY (Jan. 29, 2009, 11:02 AM), http://www.volokh .com/2009/01/29/more-on-section-7-of-the-torture-convention.

For social media feeds, provide the author's name if discernible and verified. If the author uses a username or handle on the social media platform, include the username or handle in parentheses after the name or, if the name is not discernible and verified, use only the username or handle. After author information, include the title of the post if applicable and the name of the social media platform:

▶ November Project, *The Bubble Is GONE!*, FACEBOOK (Mar. 19, 2014), https://www.facebook.com/media/set/?set=a.516646258443810 .1073741983.246449015463537&type=1.

▶ Wendy Davis (@wendydavistexas), INSTAGRAM, http://instagram.com /wendydavistexas (last visited May 20, 2014).

▶ @LegalRebels, TWITTER (Mar. 24, 2014, 10:36 AM), https://twitter.com /LegalRebels/status/448151433222062080.

(b) Titles. Titles should be used to indicate the location of the page being viewed in relation to the rest of the site. Titles should be taken either from the "title bar" at the top of the browser or from any clearly announced heading identifying the page as it appears in the browser. All efforts should be made to include a title that sufficiently identifies the page but that is not unwieldy, long, uninformative, or confusing:

▶ *A Lawsuit in Hartford, Connecticut Seeks to Undermine the State's Landmark Desegregation Case*, Harv. C.R.-C.L. L. Rev. Amicus Blog, https://harvardcrcl.org/a-lawsuit-in-hartford-connecticut-seeks-to -undermine-states-landmark-desegregation-case (Oct. 24, 2018).

Not: *Amicus Blog*, Harv. C.R.-C.L. L. Rev., https://harvardcrcl.org/a -lawsuit-in-hartford-connecticut-seeks-to-undermine-states-landmark -desegregation-case (Oct. 24, 2018).

(i) **Main page titles.** The citation should always include the homepage or domain name of which the particular citation is a part, referred to here as a "main page title." The website's main page title should be cited using large and small caps. Capitalization should conform to the title as it appears on the site. Main page titles should be abbreviated in accordance with **tables T6, T10,** and **T13**:

▶ Daily Kos, http://www.dailykos.com (last visited Jan. 19, 2009).

(ii) **Titles for pages other than the main page.** The title of the specific pages within the domain name and linked from the main page, for example postings or comments to postings, should also be included where relevant. Titles to subheadings should appear in italics. Follow standard rules for capitalizing the titles of sources in accordance with **rule 8**, even if the title bar uses nonstandard capitalization. Where appropriate, subheadings should include language indicating the page's relation to the page to which it responds:

▶ David Waldman, *This Week in Congress*, Daily Kos (Jan. 19, 2009, 9:30:04 AM), https://www.dailykos.com/stories/2009/1/19 /685802/-.

▶ Packerland Progressive, *How Is Sec 115 Constitutional Under* INS v. Chadha?, Comment to *This Week in Congress*, Daily Kos (Jan. 19, 2009, 12:20 PM), http://www.dailykos.com/stories/2009/1/19 /685802/-#comment_26164880.

(iii) **Titles for blogs contained within a larger website**. If the cited source is published under the name of a blog that has its own content and presence within a larger website, both the name of the site and the name of the blog should be included:

▶ Emmarie Huetteman, *2016 Republican Prospects Spar Over Ukraine*, N.Y. Times: The Caucus (Mar. 9, 2014, 2:57 PM), http://thecaucus.blogs.nytimes.com/2014/03/09/2016-republican -prospects-spar-over-ukraine.

▶ Andrew Morse, *Credit Suisse Is Latest Swiss Bank Humbled by U.S. Tax Evasion Crackdown*, Wall St. J.: L. Blog (May 19, 2014, 5:04 PM), http://blogs.wsj.com/law/2014/05/19/credit-suisse-is-latest-swiss -bank-humbled-by-u-s-tax-evasion-crackdown.

(iv) **Descriptive titles**. If the page's headings are not sufficiently clear, a descriptive title can be used. Do not italicize descriptive titles:

▶ Archive of Columns by William Safire, N.Y. Times, https://www.nytimes .com/by/william-safire (last visited Feb. 13, 2020).

▶ Review of *The Hitchhiker's Guide to the Galaxy: Collector's Edition*, ROTTEN TOMATOES, http://www.rottentomatoes.com/m/hitchhikers _guide_to_the_galaxy_the_collectors_edition (last visited Jan. 6, 2004).

(v) **Titles for social media posts**. If the content is contained on a social media website, place titles, if applicable, between the author information and the platform identification. Only include a title if one is clearly intended and conveyed; otherwise omit:

▶ November Project, *The Bubble Is GONE!*, FACEBOOK (Mar. 19, 2014), https://www.facebook.com/media/set/?set=a.516646258443810 .1073741983.246449015463537&type=1.

▶ Ayanna Pressley (@AyannaPressley), TWITTER (Feb. 11, 2020, 11:24 AM), https://twitter.com/AyannaPressley/status/1227267162873778177.

▶ Eugene Volokh, LINKEDIN, http://www.linkedin.com/pub/eugene -volokh-b075bb9a (last visited Mar. 27, 2014).

(c) Date and time. The date should be provided as it appears on the internet site. Use only dates that refer clearly to the material cited. The date should be indicated after the main page title and any pinpoint citation:

▶ Ashby Jones, *Activists, Research Facilities Taking Disclosure Battles to the Courts*, WALL ST. J.: L. BLOG (Feb. 26, 2009, 9:40 AM), http://blogs .wsj.com/law/2009/02/26/activists-research-facilities-taking -disclosure-battles-to-the-courts.

If there is no date associated with the specific subject matter of the citation, "last updated" or "last modified" dates should be supplied in a parenthetical after the URL. If the online resource has been updated or corrected on a date different from the online publication date, use that date in lieu of the original online publication date:

▶ Rowaida Abdelaziz, *Advocacy Groups Renew Calls for Bloomberg to Renounce NYPD's Muslim Surveillance*, HUFFPOST, https://www .huffpost.com/entry/muslim-surveillance-michael-bloomberg-nypd _n_5e5424d5c5b66729cf6067d4 (Feb. 24, 2020, 4:30 PM).

When material is otherwise undated, the date that the website was last visited should be placed in a parenthetical after the URL:

▶ YAHOO!, http://www.yahoo.com (last visited Dec. 15, 2004).

If an archival tool that indicates when a source was archived is utilized, it is not necessary to include a "last visited" parenthetical after the URL.

It is recommended that citations for internet sources include a timestamp whenever possible. Especially when the citation is for a comment to a posting or is otherwise easily identifiable by the time of its posting, the timestamp listed on the subheading should be included with the date:

▶ Donn Zaretsky, *Ruling Is a Setback for Sports Artist*, ART L. BLOG (Aug. 26, 2009, 10:51 AM), http://theartlawblog.blogspot.com/2009/08 /ruling-is-setback-for-sports-artist.html.

(d) The URL. A site's internet address, or URL, should point readers directly to the source cited rather than to an intervening page of links. If there is a shortlink available that clearly indicates the source site (e.g., wapo.st, imdb.to, but not bit.ly), then cite the shortlink. If no shortlink is available, but the full URL is straightforward, then cite the entire URL as it appears in the address bar of the browser:

▶ *Stanley Kubrick Biography*, IMDB, http://www.imdb.com/name/nm0000040/bio?ref_=nm_ql_1 (last visited Feb. 28, 2015).

Not: *Stanley Kubrick Biography*, IMDB, http://imdb.com (search in search bar for "Stanley Kubrick"; then follow "Biography" hyperlink under "Quick Links") (last visited Feb. 28, 2015).

Alternatively, the root URL of the site from which information is accessed may be used if (1) the URL is long, unwieldy, or full of nontextual characters (such as question marks, percentage signs, or ampersands); or (2) the source may be obtained only by submitting a form or query. If the root URL is used and the site's format is not clear from the rest of the citation, a clarifying parenthetical should be added to explain how to access the specific information to which the citation refers:

▶ http://fjsrc.urban.org/noframe/wqs/q_data_1.htm#2001 (choose "2001" from dropdown; then choose "Defendants in Criminal Cases-Administrative Office of the U.S. Courts (AOUSC)"; then click "out" and "submit"; then follow "TTSECMO" hyperlink).

Not: http://fjsrc.urban.org/noframe/wqs/q_e.cfm?cat=3&year=2001&agency=AOUSC&saf=out&var1=TTSECMSO.

Note that some URLs are case sensitive, so cite URLs as they appear in the internet browser.

(e) Multiple URLs. Some popular sites are served by more than one URL. In these cases, a proper citation should use the primary URL rather than a URL that links to an alternate server:

▶ MACY'S, http://www.macys.com (last visited Feb. 28, 2015).

Not: MACY'S, http://www1.macys.com (last visited Feb. 28, 2015).

(f) Document format. If a document is available both in HTML format and in a widely used format that preserves pagination and other attributes of printed work (such as PDF), the latter should always be cited in lieu of an HTML document:

▶ Elizabeth C. McNichol & Iris J. Lav, *State Budgets: On the Edge?*, CTR. ON BUDGET & POL'Y PRIORITIES 1 (Nov. 8, 2006), https://www.cbpp.org/sites/default/files/atoms/files/5-4-06sfp.pdf.

Not: Elizabeth C. McNichol & Iris J. Lav, *State Budgets: On the Edge?*, CTR. ON BUDGET & POL'Y PRIORITIES 1 (Nov. 8, 2006), https://www.cbpp.org/research/state-budgets-on-the-edge.

(g) Pinpoint citations. If the cited document is rendered in a format that preserves the pagination of a print version (such as a PDF file), pinpoint citations should be provided where appropriate. Page numbers should always refer to the numbers that appear on the document itself. Do not use "screen numbers" or other numbers that may appear in a software viewing window or scroll bar. When there is pagination information available, it should be included between the domain name and the date or URL, whichever comes first.

18.3 Commercial Electronic Databases

Because of the reliability and authoritativeness of LEXIS, Westlaw, Bloomberg Law, and other commercial electronic databases such as Dialog, cite such sources, if available, in preference to the other sources covered by **rule 18**. Citations to these electronic databases should be consistent with this present rule regardless of whether the databases are accessed through proprietary software or through a website such as http://www.westlaw.com or http://www.lexisnexis.com. For guidance as to the specific use of commercial electronic databases, see the following rules:

Cases . . . . **rule 10.8.1**
Constitutions. . . . . **rule 11**
Statutes . . . . **rule 12.5**
Legislative Materials. . . . . **rule 13.7**
Regulations . . . . **rule 14.4**
Books, Reports, and Other Nonperiodic Materials . . . . **rule 15.9**
Periodical Materials . . . . **rule 16.8**

18.4 CD-ROM and Other Electronic Storage Media

(a) Print form preferred. Information found on CD-ROM or another medium of electronic distribution (flash drive, etc.) is usually available in print form, and citation to the print form is preferred. If the information is accessed by electronic storage medium, however, it should be cited to that medium.

(b) Citation format. When citing CD-ROM or other similar media, include the title of the material, the publisher of the CD-ROM, the version searched, and the date of the material, if available, or the date of the version searched. The information may be provided in a source-date parenthetical or, if the information is voluminous, as related authority (**rule 1.6**):

> ▶ 7 LAWRENCE P. KING, COLLIER ON BANKRUPTCY ¶ 700.02 (Matthew Bender Authority Bankruptcy Law CD-ROM, rel. 13, Aug. 1999).

18.5 Microform

18.5.1 Microform Collections Reproducing Preexisting Materials

In general, when a document is reproduced in microform, it is not necessary to indicate this fact unless it would otherwise be difficult for a reader to identify and obtain the source. When citing material as "*microformed on*" a service, provide a complete citation to the original document and a citation to the microform in accordance with **rule 1.6** regarding citations to related authority. If the microform service assigns a unique identifier or code to each document reproduced, include that identifier to assist the reader in locating the document cited. Include the name of the publisher of the microform series in parentheses, abbreviated according to **rule 15.1(d)**:

▶ CAL. CODE REGS. tit. 26, § 23-2631(g) (Barclay's 1990), *microformed on* Cal. Code of Reg. 1990 Revised Format, Fiche 143 (Univ. Microforms Int'l).

▶ APPLICATION OF EMPLOYER SANCTIONS TO LONGSHORE WORK, H.R. REP. NO. 101-208 (1989), *microformed on* CIS No. 89-H523-17 (Cong. Info. Serv.).

▶ S. 1237, 99th Cong. § 505 (1985), *microformed on* Sup. Docs. No. Y 1.4/1:99-1237 (U.S. Gov't Publishing Office).

....

Microform Collections Containing Original Materials   18.5.2

When a microform collection contains materials original to that collection, identify the microform set and its publisher, and use the publisher's system for identifying individual forms within the set. Use **rule 18.5.1** as a guide.

Films, Broadcasts, and Noncommercial Video Materials   18.6

Cite films in large and small capitals, and television or radio broadcasts in italics, by title, episode name (if available), and exact date (if available). Include the name of the company or network that produced the film or broadcast. If there is no information as to the producer of the broadcast, include the name of the company or network that aired the broadcast:

▶ AIRPLANE! (Paramount Pictures 1980).

▶ *Law & Order: Tabula Rasa* (NBC television broadcast Apr. 21, 1999).

Cite video materials containing images that have not been commercially displayed or broadcast by the medium of the material, the title of the video or DVD (if any), the name of the person or institution that produced the video, and the year of production. Time markers may be used for designating pinpoint citations, but they are not required:

▶ Videotape: Installing Your CLS-2009 (Emily Weiss Electric Co. 1995) (on file with the Arlington Public Library).

▶ DVD: 2004 Yale Law Revue (Yale Media Services 2004) (on file with author).

When a television broadcast is also available online, a citation to the online source is acceptable in accordance with **rule 18.2.2**.

If the video was originally broadcast online, cite per **rule 18.2.2** for dynamic websites. Consistent with the general principles of that rule, all efforts should be made to cite to the distinct URL for the specific video. Use the creator of the video as the author if available; otherwise treat the person who posted the video as the author. When the site indicates that the video contains contents from another source, use an explanatory parenthetical to indicate that source:

▶ Brown University, *A Conversation with U.S. Supreme Court Justice Sonia Sotomayor*, YOUTUBE (Feb. 26, 2018), https://youtu.be/7 -wOU4kKvnM.

18.7 Audio Recordings

18.7.1 Commercial Recordings

Cite commercial recordings by artist and album title or record title, providing the name of the recording company and the date of release (if available):

- ▶ MC HAMMER, PLEASE HAMMER DON'T HURT 'EM (Capitol Records 1990).

- ▶ THE BEATLES, SGT. PEPPER'S LONELY HEARTS CLUB BAND (EMI 1967).

If a particular song or musical work is referred to, cite it by analogy to shorter works in a collection according to **rule 15.5.1**. Time markers may be used for designating pinpoint citations, using the phrase ", at XX:XX" immediately after the main page title, but they are not required:

- ▶ EARTH, WIND & FIRE, *September, on* THE BEST OF EARTH, WIND & FIRE, VOL. 1 (Am. Recording Co. 1978).

18.7.2 Noncommercial Recordings

If the recording referred to is not commercially available, use ordinary roman type and indicate parenthetically where a copy may be obtained. Time markers may be used for designating pinpoint citations, using the phrase ", at XX:XX" immediately after the main page title, but they are not required:

- ▶ Audiotape: Conference on Business Opportunities in Space, held by the Center for Space Policy, Inc., and the Commonwealth of Massachusetts (Mar. 3–5, 1986) (on file with author).

18.7.3 Podcasts and Recordings Available Online

If the audio recording was accessed online or is available only online, it should be cited using the principles of **rule 18.2.2**. If there is no stable URL available to facilitate access to the source, an explanatory parenthetical should be added explaining how the source should be accessed. Time markers may be used for designating pinpoint citations, using the phrase ", at XX:XX" immediately after the main page title, but they are not required:

- ▶ The New Yorker Radio Hour, *Mass Incarceration, Then and Now*, NEW YORKER, at 01:03 (Jan. 17, 2020), https://www.newyorker.com/podcast/the-new-yorker-radio-hour/mass-incarceration-then-and-now.

- ▶ *Splitting Verbs, Grammar Girl's Quick and Dirty Tips for Better Writing* (Feb. 26, 2009) (downloaded using iTunes).

18.8 Photographs and Illustrations

Cite untitled photographs or illustrations using "‹the artist's name, if significant or relevant›, **Photograph/Illustration of** ‹a description›, *in* ‹full citation of applicable work›."

If the photograph or illustration has a title, the title should be set in italics, followed by a parenthetical noting that it is a photograph or illustration.

When citing a photograph or illustration on an unnumbered page, the pincite should be omitted, and the full citation of the work should be followed by "following p. ‹the numbered page that immediately precedes the photo›."

▶ Photograph of Bill Clinton and President Kennedy, *in* DAVID MARANISS, FIRST IN HIS CLASS (1994), following p.134.

▶ Ansel Adams, *Bridalveil Fall* (photograph), *in* EDWARD WESTON, OMNIBUS (1984), following p.21.

Short Citation Forms   18.9

(a) Internet. When citing to a previously referenced internet site, use a "*supra*" form (**rule 4.2(a)**) with the last name of the author, if any, or the title or description of the document. "*Id.*" may also be used in accordance with **rule 4.1**. If various subsections of a website with no author are cited or if more than one posting by a given author is cited, include the subsection title. A URL need not be repeated after a full citation:

▶ [1] *See* Douglas Gantenbein, *Mad Cows Come Home: Why the Disease Scare May Be Great for the U.S. Food Industry and Consumers*, SLATE (Jan. 2, 2004, 4:29 PM), http://www.slate.com/articles/news_and _politics/the_best_policy/2004/01/mad_cows_come_home.html.

▶ [2] PFIZER, INC., http://www.pfizer.com (last visited Jan. 17, 2020).

▶ [3] Gantenbein, *supra* note 1; PFIZER, INC., *supra* note 2.

(b) Commercial electronic databases. For materials available on an electronic database, use a unique database identifier, if one has been assigned, in constructing a short form:

▶ Int'l Snowmobile Mfrs. Ass'n v. Norton, No. 00-CV-229-B, 2004 WL 2337372, at *3 (D. Wyo. Oct. 14, 2004).

becomes: *Int'l Snowmobile*, 2004 WL 2337372, at *3.

▶ Chavez v. Metro. Dist. Comm'n, No. 02CV458, 2004 U.S. Dist. LEXIS 11266, at *5 n.3 (D. Conn. June 1, 2004).

becomes: *Chavez*, 2004 U.S. Dist. LEXIS 11266, at *5 n.3.

(c) CD-ROM and microform. When citing a separately published document available on CD-ROM or microform, use the short form appropriate for the original document; it is not necessary to indicate the source once it has been given in the first full citation.

(d) Films, broadcasts, and audio recordings. When citing films, broadcasts, audio recordings, photographs, and illustrations "*id.*" and "*supra*" may be used according to **rule 4**:

▶ [4] *Nightline: Microsoft Monopoly* (ABC television broadcast Apr. 3, 2000) (transcript on file with the Columbia Law Review).

▶ [5] *Id.*

▶ [6] *See id.*; MEAT LOAF, *For Crying Out Loud, on* BAT OUT OF HELL (Epic Records 1977).

▶ [7] MEAT LOAF, *supra* note 6; *see also Nightline: Microsoft Monopoly*, *supra* note 4 (describing Microsoft's response to the court ruling).

19 SERVICES

Cases, administrative materials, and brief commentaries are often published unofficially in topical compilations called "services," which appear in looseleaf form initially and are sometimes published later as bound volumes. Consult *Legal Looseleafs in Print*, which is updated annually, for a comprehensive listing of services. **Rule 19.1** provides rules for citing services. Some services are no longer published in print or are otherwise available online.

19.1 Citation Form for Services

Cite services by volume, abbreviated title in ordinary roman type, publisher, subdivision, and date. If the source is a case, include the abbreviated name of the court in the same parenthetical as the date, as you would under **rule 10.4**. Consult **table T15** for service and publisher abbreviations; if a service is not listed, refer to **table T6** to abbreviate the words that make up its title:

▶ *In re* Smithfield Estates, Inc., [1985–1986 Transfer Binder] Bankr. L. Rep. (CCH) ¶ 70,707 (Bankr. D.R.I. Aug. 9, 1985).

▶ SEC v. Tex. Int'l Airlines, 29 Fed. R. Serv. 2d (West) 408 (D.D.C. 1979).

▶ Kovacs v. Comm'r, 74 A.F.T.R.2d (RIA) 354 (6th Cir. 1994).

When citing looseleaf material that will eventually be bound, add the name of the bound form in parentheses if it is different from the name of the looseleaf form; include the volume of the bound form if available:

▶ Marietta Concrete Co., 3 Lab. Rel. Rep. (BL) (84 Lab. Arb. Rep. (BL)) 1158 (May 7, 1985).

When citing to services found on a commercial electronic database, provide a parallel citation to the database, including the database identifier and any codes or numbers that identify the information.

▶ Dynda Thomas, *Conflict Minerals – You Have More to Worry About than Just the SEC*, 38 Chem. Reg. Rep. (BL) 186, 38 CRR 186 (BL) (Feb. 10, 2014).

(a) Volume. The volume designation of a service may be a number, a year, a descriptive subtitle from the volume's spine, or a combination of these. If the volume designation includes words or a year, use brackets to avoid confusion:

▶ 5 Trade Reg. Rep.

▶ 1979-1 Trade Cas.

▶ [Current Developments] Hous. & Dev. Rep.

▶ [1979] 8 Stand. Fed. Tax Rep.

▶ [2 Wages-Hours] Lab. L. Rep.

▶ [1 Estate & Gift] U.S. Tax Rep.

In citing a transfer binder, the volume designation should indicate the years of material included in that binder:

▶ [1994–1995 Transfer Binder] Fed. Sec. L. Rep.

See generally **rule 3.1(a)** (designation of volumes and use of brackets).

(b) Publisher. Every citation to a service, whether looseleaf or bound, must indicate the publisher. Enclose an abbreviation of the publisher's name in parentheses following the service's title. Consult **table T15** for a list of service publisher abbreviations; if a publisher is not listed, abbreviate according to **rule 15.1(d)**.

▶ 4 Lab. L. Rep. (CCH) ¶ 9046.

▶ [1982] 12 Env't L. Rep. (Env't L. Inst.).

(c) Subdivision. Cite services by paragraph or section number if possible, otherwise by page number. See generally **rule 3.2** (pages, footnotes, endnotes, and graphical materials) and **rule 3.3** (sections and paragraphs). Additionally, a report number may be given if it will assist the reader in locating the cited material:

▶ *Rhode Island Insurance Agents Agree Not to Rig Bids*, [Jan.–June] Antitrust & Trade Reg. Rep. (BL) No. 967, at D-11 (June 5, 1980).

▶ *Domination of Markets, AMA Report Finds Consumers Have Few Options*, [Jan.–Feb.] Antitrust & Trade Reg. Rep. (BL) No. 96, at 88 (2008).

(d) Date. When citing a case reported in a service, give the exact date (for looseleaf services) or year (for bound services) of the case (**rule 10.5**):

▶ Defenders of Wildlife, Inc. v. Watt, [1982] 12 Env't L. Rep. (Env't L. Inst.) 20,210 (D.D.C. May 28, 1981).

When citing a statute or regulation, give the exact date of its enactment or promulgation unless the exact date is indicated elsewhere in the citation:

▶ Act of Sept. 26, 1980, Food Drug Cosm. L. Rep. (CCH) ¶ 653.

Citations to other material (such as articles or commentary) should give the exact date, if available. When citing otherwise undated material in a looseleaf service, give the date of the page on which the material is printed or the date of the subsection in which it is printed:

▶ *ERISA Preemption Bills Draw Praise from Labor and Criticism from Business*, [Aug. 1991–June 1993] Pens. Plan Guide (CCH) ¶ 26,263, at 27,037–40 (Aug. 2, 1991).

19.2 Short Citation Forms

(a) Cases. For cases, use short citation forms as provided by **rule 10.9**. Include the complete volume designation for the service binder and substitute paragraph or section numbers for page numbers where appropriate. If a case has page numbers as well as paragraph or section numbers, you may cite individual pages instead of the paragraph or section number in the short form to identify specific material. To cite the entire case in short form, give the paragraph or section number of the case or the first page number of the case, without using "at":

> ▶ [1] *In re* Looney, [1987–1989 Transfer Binder] Bankr. L. Rep. (CCH) ¶ 72,447, at 93,590 (Bankr. W.D. Va. Sept. 9, 1988).

> ▶ [2] *Id.*

> ▶ [3] *Id.* at 93,591.

> ▶ [4] Defs. of Wildlife, Inc. v. Watt, [1982] 12 Env't L. Rep. (Env't L. Inst.) 20,210, 20,211 (D.D.C. May 28, 1981).

> ▶ [5] *In re Looney*, [1987–1989 Transfer Binder] Bankr. L. Rep. (CCH) at 93,591.

> ▶ [6] *Defs. of Wildlife*, [1982] 12 Env't L. Rep. (Env't L. Inst.) at 20,212.

> ▶ [7] This was the approach taken in *Looney*. *See* [1987–1989 Transfer Binder] Bankr. L. Rep. (CCH) ¶ 72,447.

(b) Other materials. Short form citations for other materials found in services, such as statutes, regulations, articles, and commentary, should follow the relevant citation rules as described elsewhere in *The Bluebook*.

20 FOREIGN MATERIALS

Table T2 contains jurisdiction-specific citation examples and is the primary source for the citation of foreign materials. For sources not present in **table T2**, which is now located online, follow the respective country's own citation rules for the sources as modified by these general rules.

20.1 Jurisdiction

When citing any non-U.S. source, whether in English or in another language, indicate parenthetically the jurisdiction issuing the source, abbreviated according to **table T10**, unless the jurisdiction is otherwise clear from the other elements of the citation:

> ▶ Chase v. Campbell, [1962] S.C.R. 425 (Can.).

> ▶ *Berry v Dorsey* (1975) 101 ALR 35 (Austl.).

This parenthetical may be omitted if the jurisdiction is clear from the context:

> ▶ Spain has enacted a separate code governing legal procedure in employment cases.[1]

▶ [1] Labor Procedure Law (R.C.L. 1990, 922).

The parenthetical is located at the end of the citation but before any parallel citations, unless otherwise indicated in **table T2**:

▶ Canada Act, 1982, c. 11 (U.K.), *reprinted in* R.S.C. 1985, app II, no 14 (Can.).

▶ Control of Fishing for Salmon Order 2008 (SI 98/2008) (Ir.), http://www.irishstatutebook.ie/2008/en/si/0098.html.

Non-English-Language Documents   20.2

Documents Appearing in More than One Language   20.2.1

Unless otherwise required by the citation, always cite the most official or authoritative version of the document. The document itself should clarify which version(s) is authoritative. For documents published in multiple languages, use the English-language version whenever it is as authoritative as (or more authoritative than) other versions. If the document is silent on the issue of authority, always cite the English-language version unless the purpose served by the citation requires otherwise.

Titles and Names of Documents in Languages Other than English   20.2.2

(a) Original language and translation. When citing a document in a language other than English, always give the document's full title or name in the original language the first time the document is cited. If desired, the original-language title may be followed by brackets containing its shortened or full-length English title in the same typeface as the original:

▶ Verdrag tot het Vermijden van Dubbele Belasting [Agreement for the Avoidance of Double Taxation]

(b) Capitalization. Capitalize names and titles in languages other than English as they appear on the page. Capitalize translations according to **rule 8**.

Abbreviations in Languages Other than English   20.2.3

The abbreviations of reporters, codes, statutes, statutory collections, constitutions, and periodicals in languages other than English may be unfamiliar to the reader. Therefore, the full form should be given the first time the source is cited, and the abbreviation should be given in brackets. Thereafter for the whole piece, the abbreviated form may be used without cross-reference.

Abbreviations for many legal materials in languages other than English are given in **table T2**; for periodicals, see **rule 20.6**. When abbreviating foreign legal materials for which an abbreviation is not provided, follow the usage of the source.

▶ [1] BÜRGERLICHES GESETZBUCH [BGB] [CIVIL CODE], art. 13 (Ger.).

▶ [2] Bundesgerichtshof [BGH] [Federal Court of Justice] Apr. 16, 2008, 140 ENTSCHEIDUNGEN DES BUNDESGERICHTSHOFES IN ZIVILSACHEN [BGHZ] 245 (Ger.).

▶ [3] BGB art. 12 (Ger.); *see also* BGH Mar. 3, 2009, 141 BGHZ 245 (250) (Ger.).

20.2.4 Languages That Do Not Use the Roman Alphabet

Transliterate all titles, names, or words cited that are not in the Roman alphabet, using a standard transliteration system (for example, the ALA-LC Romanization Tables).

(a) Languages generally. For instructions regarding transliteration that are specific to particular countries, check the relevant entries in **table T2**.

(b) Chinese language.

(i) **Chinese language romanization**. For citations to Chinese language sources, regardless of jurisdiction or place of publication, always provide romanization as instructed here. Whenever possible, also provide Chinese characters for authors, titles, and case names. Do not use Chinese characters without accompanying romanization, as some publishers or databases may drop them from citations. Use simplified or traditional characters to reflect the usage of the source. Generally, add an English translation or shortened form in English as provided in **rule 20.2.2**. Do not cite a Chinese language source in English only.

For romanization of Chinese language citations, use the Pinyin romanization system as set forth in the international standard, *Hanyu Pinyin Fang'an* (1958), and related documents. Do not include tone marks. Do not use "v" to represent "ü." Competing standards exist for word division in Pinyin. Follow commonly accepted guidelines for word division in scholarly publications as summarized in the examples below and in **table T2**. Note that the Pinyin standard used in many libraries differs with regard to word division and separates most syllables, so when searching for sources in library catalogs, it may be necessary to break up compound words into separate syllables.

For capitalization in Pinyin romanization, follow **rule 8** and related guidelines. Do not capitalize the possessive "de" (的).

邓小平	Deng Xiaoping
对外贸易经济合作部	Duiwai Maoyi Jingji Hezuo Bu
行政院	Xingzhengyuan
香港法例	Xianggang Fali
臺北地方法院	Taibei Difang Fayuan

(ii) **Chinese personal names**. When citing a Chinese author or editor's name, regardless of jurisdiction or place of publication, follow **rules 15.1** and **16.2**, giving the full name in the order it appears on the document. Repeat the full name in subsequent short citations to the source. For Chinese personal names in case citations, follow **rule 10.2.1(g)**.

(A) **Chinese language sources**. In Chinese language texts the surname is always given first. Transcribe authors and editors of Chinese texts in Pinyin, joining multiple syllables of surname and/or forename without hyphens or commas.

▶ CHEN HONGYI (陈弘毅), FAZHI QIMENG YU XIANDAI FA DE JINGSHEN (法制启蒙与现代法的精神) (1998).

▶ WANG TAISHENG (王泰升), TAIWAN FALÜ DE DUANLIE YU LIANXU (台灣法律的斷裂與連續) (2002).

▶ Ma Chao (马超), Yu Xiaohong (于晓虹) & He Haibo (何海波), *Dashuju Fenxi: Zhongguo Sifa Caipan Wenshu Shangwang Gongkai Baogao* (大数据分析: 中国司法裁判文书上网公开报告) [Big Data Analytics: A Report on Publishing Court Opinions on China Judgements Online], *Zhongguo Falü Pinglun* (中国法律评论) [CHINA L. REV.], no. 4, 2016, at 195, 207–08, 222.

(B) **English language sources**. Chinese names in English texts may follow either Chinese (surname first) or English (surname last) word order. They also may or may not be spelled according to the Pinyin system and may vary in fullness. Transcribe the full name in the order and in the spelling in which it appears on the document.

▶ ALBERT HUNG-YEE CHEN, AN INTRODUCTION TO THE LEGAL SYSTEM OF THE PEOPLE'S REPUBLIC OF CHINA (3d ed. LexisNexis 2004) (1992).

▶ TAY-SHENG WANG, LEGAL REFORM IN TAIWAN UNDER JAPANESE COLONIAL RULE (2000).

▶ ZHU SANZHU, SECURITIES REGULATION IN CHINA 8–13 (2001).

▶ Guanghua Yu, *Towards a Market Economy: Security Devices in China*, 8 PAC. RIM L. & POL'Y J. 1 (1999).

Citations to Translations of Non-English-Language Documents 20.2.5

If desired, a work that conveniently reprints the primary authority in translation may be cited when referring to a foreign-language source that is not widely available to researchers in the United States. In such cases, provide the citation to the original source in accordance with **rules 20** and **21**, and provide a parallel citation to the translated version, according to **rule 1.6(a)**, introduced by "*translated in*":

▶ Ley Federal de Derechos de Autor [LFDA], Diario Oficial de la Federación [DOF] 21-12-1963 (Mex.), *translated in* COPYRIGHT LAWS AND TREATIES OF THE WORLD 521 (U.N. Educ., Sci. & Cultural Org. et al. eds., 1992).

Cases 20.3

Cite foreign cases according to **rule 10** as modified by the following instructions.

Common Law Cases 20.3.1

If the reporter does not clearly indicate the court deciding the case, indicate the court parenthetically:

▶ R v. Lockwood (1782) 99 Eng. Rep. 379 (KB).

But if the court involved is the highest court in the jurisdiction, only the jurisdiction needs to be identified unless the jurisdiction is otherwise clear from context:

▶ Chase v. Campbell, [1962] S.C.R. 425 (Can.).

20.3.2 Civil Law and Other Non-Common Law Cases

Cite cases from non-common law countries according to **table T2** as modified by the following instructions.

(a) Name of the court. Identify courts as indicated in **rule 20.1**. If not otherwise clear from the context, include an English translation of the court designation:

▶ Bundesgerichtshof [BGH] [Federal Court of Justice] Apr. 7, 2003, 154 Entscheidungen des Bundesgerichtshofes in Zivilsachen [BGHZ] 53 (126) (Ger.).

(b) Source. Cite the sources listed, with their abbreviations, in **table T2**. As required by **rule 20.2.3**, give the full form the first time a source is cited, indicating in brackets the abbreviation that will be used subsequently.

Many civil law decisions do not appear in official reporters. If a case cited does not appear in an official source, cite a journal or periodical, issued within the jurisdiction if possible, or a reprint or translation of the decision according to **rules 1.6(a)** or **20.2.5** respectively.

(c) Jurisdiction. If the national jurisdiction is not evident from the citation or the context, include the jurisdiction, abbreviated according to **table T10**, in parentheses at the end of the citation, as required by **rule 20.1**.

(d) Annotations. Annotations to civil law cases are cited according to **rule 3.4**:

▶ Cour de cassation [Cass.] [supreme court for judicial matters] 1e civ., Dec. 14, 1982, Bull. civ. I, No. 360 note (Fr.) (note of Aynès).

20.4   Constitutions

Cite all foreign constitutions by name. If the nature of the document is not otherwise clear from the context, include "Constitution" in brackets following the document name or abbreviation in the first citation. Successive citations may exclude this note. If the country is unclear from the title of the constitution, include the country abbreviation in a parenthetical at the end of the citation.

▶ Bundesverfassung [BV] [Constitution] Apr. 18, 1999, SR 101, art. 29 (Switz.).

20.5   Statutes

20.5.1 Statutes in Common Law Systems

Cite like U.S. statutes (**rule 12**) if the jurisdiction's statutes appear in a codification or other compilation:

▶ Extradition Law, 5714–1954, 8 LSI 144, (1953–1954) (Isr.).

Otherwise, cite like statutes of the United Kingdom (**table T2.43 United Kingdom**), noting the jurisdiction parenthetically at the end of the citation if not otherwise clear from the context:

▶ Emergency Powers Act, 1976 (Act No. 33/1976) (Ir.).

....

Statutes in Civil Law and Other Non-Common Law Jurisdictions

20.5.2

Cite generally according to rules found in **table T2**. When citing a code, do not indicate the year of the code unless citing a version no longer in force. In accordance with **rule 20.2.3**, use the full publication name the first time the publication is cited, indicating in brackets the abbreviation that will be used subsequently. Thereafter, the abbreviated form may be used:

▶ CODE CIVIL [C. CIV.] [CIVIL CODE] art. 1112 (Fr.).

Give the publisher or editor and date of privately published sources only when citing an annotation rather than the code itself:

▶ CODE CIVIL [C. CIV.] [CIVIL CODE] art. 1098 (64th ed. Petits Codes Dalloz 1965) (Fr.).

Non-English-Language and Foreign Periodicals

20.6

(a) In general. For all foreign periodicals, including both English- and non-English-language sources, abbreviate the periodical name according to **tables T6** and **T13**. Include the country of origin in a parenthetical if not otherwise clear from the context.

▶ Catherine Labrusse-Riou, *La filiation et la médecine moderne*, 38 REVUE INTERNATIONALE DE DROIT COMPARÉ [R.I.D.C.] 419 (1986) (Fr.).

For foreign newspapers, cite according to **rule 16.6**.

▶ Marianne Kearney, *Indonesia Risks Becoming Like Balkans: Mega*, STRAITS TIMES (Sing.), Oct. 29, 2001, at 3.

(b) Foreign-language sources. Cite foreign-language periodicals according to **rule 16**, as modified by **rule 20.2**. Give the author; the title in the original language, followed by a translation or shortened name in English, if desired (**rule 20.2.2**); the volume number of the periodical if appropriate (**rule 16.4**); the full name of the periodical, if it is being cited for the first time, followed by the official abbreviation in brackets (**rule 20.2.3**); the page number(s); the year (**rules 16.4** and **16.5**); and the abbreviation of the country of publication, if not otherwise clear from the context. A hereinafter form, provided in brackets at the end of the citation, may be given if desired:

▶ [1] Marie-Thérèse Meulders-Klein, *Le droit de l'enfant face au droit à l'enfant et les procréations médicalement assistées* [*The Right of a Child Versus the Right to Have a Child and Medically Assisted Procreation*], 87 REVUE TRIMESTRIELLE DE DROIT CIVIL [REV. TRIM. DR. CIV.] 645, 657 (1988) (Fr.).

▶ ² *Aktuelle Fragen der Schutzbereichsbestimmung im deutschen und europäischen Patentrecht* [*Current Issues in Identifying the Scope of Protection in German and European Patent Law*], 2003 GEWERBLICHER RECHTSSCHUTZ UND URHEBERRECHT [GRUR] 905 (Ger.) [hereinafter *Scope of Protection*].

▶ ⁴ *Scope of Protection, supra* note 2, at 906; *see also* Benjamin Taibleson & Rebecca Krauss, *Embracing Convergence: Forty Countries in Comparative Perspective*, 106 REV. TRIM. DR. CIV. 119 (2007) (Fr.).

20.7   Short Citation Forms

(a) Cases. For common law citations, use short forms analogous to those provided in **rule 10.9**, when permitted. For civil law citation forms, the short form should include enough information to uniquely identify the original source and any additional information that would be helpful to the reader:

▶ ¹ Corte Suprema de Justicia de la Nación [CSJN] [National Supreme Court of Justice], 18/7/2001, "Frenquel, Adolfo c. Centro de Ortopedias / recurso extraordinario," La Ley [L.L.] (2001-D-22) (Arg.). *But see* Corte Suprema de Justicia [C.S.J.] [Supreme Court], 15 noviembre 1954, "Suárez, Alfredo c. Perez, Estela," Rol de la causa: 124-2008 s., divorcio, REVISTA GACETA JURÍDICA [R.G.J.] No. 190 p. 145 (Chile).

▶ ² CSJN, 18/7/2001, "Frenquel, Adolfo," L.L. (2001-D-23). *But see* C.S.J., 15 noviembre 1954, "Suárez, Alfredo," R.G.J. No. 190 p. 146.

(b) Constitutions. Do not use a short form, other than "*id.*," for constitutions.

(c) Statutes. Use short forms analogous to those provided in **rule 12.10**, when possible. Otherwise, include enough information to uniquely identify the original source and any additional information that would be helpful to the reader. The jurisdiction parenthetical may be included in the short form if it is not evident from either the elements of the short form citation or the context:

▶ ¹ Loi 85-699 du 11 juillet 1985 tendant à la constitution d'archives audiovisuelles de la justice [Law 85-699 of July 11, 1985 for the Formation of Audiovisual Archives of the Judiciary], JOURNAL OFFICIEL DE LA RÉPUBLIQUE FRANÇAISE [J.O.] [OFFICIAL GAZETTE OF FRANCE], July 12, 1985, p. 7885.

▶ ² Ley No. 217, 2 May 1996, Ley General del Medio Ambiente y los Recursos Naturales [Ley del Medio Ambiente] [Environmental and Natural Resources Law] tit. III, ch. II, sec. I, LA GACETA, DIARIO OFICIAL [L.G.], 6 June 1996 (Nicar.).

▶ ³ Law 85-699 of July 11, 1985, art. 4 (Fr.); Environmental and Natural Resources Law, tit. III, ch. II, sec. II (Nicar.).

(d) Periodicals. Use short forms analogous to those provided in **rule 16.9**.

INTERNATIONAL MATERIALS 21

Basic Citation Forms 21.1

(a) Treaties and other international agreements. (rule 21.4)

Bilateral Treaty	Treaty of Friendship, Commerce and Navigation, Japan-U.S., art. X, Apr. 2, 1953, 4 U.S.T. 2063.
	Agreement Concerning Payments for Certain Losses Suffered During World War II, Fr.-U.S., Jan. 18, 2001, Temp. State Dep't No. 01-36, 2001 WL 416465.
	Treaty of Neutrality, Hung.-Turk., Jan. 5, 1929, 100 L.N.T.S. 137.
Multilateral Treaty	Geneva Convention Relative to the Treatment of Prisoners of War art. 3, Aug. 12, 1949, 6 U.S.T. 3316, 75 U.N.T.S. 135.
	Inter-American Police Convention, Feb. 29, 1920, 127 L.N.T.S. 433.
	North American Free Trade Agreement, Dec. 17, 1992, 32 I.L.M. 289.

(b) International law cases. (rule 21.5)

International Court of Justice	Military and Paramilitary Activities in and Against Nicaragua (Nicar. v. U.S.), Judgment, 1986 I.C.J. 14 (June 27).
	Fisheries Jurisdiction (U.K. v. Ice.), Interim Protection Order, 1972 I.C.J. 12 (Aug. 17).
	Diversion of Water from Meuse (Neth. v. Belg.), Judgment, 1937 P.C.I.J. (ser. A/B) No. 70, at 7 (June 28).
	Reservations to Convention on Prevention and Punishment of Crime of Genocide, Advisory Opinion, 1951 I.C.J. 15 (May 28).
Court of Justice of the European Union	Case C-213/89, The Queen v. Sec'y of State for Transp. *ex parte* Factortame Ltd., 1990 E.C.R. I-2433.
European Court of Human Rights	Kampanis v. Greece, 318 Eur. Ct. H.R. 29, 35 (1995).
	Ireland v. United Kingdom, 23 Eur. Ct. H.R. (ser. B) at 23 (1976).
Inter-American Commission on Human Rights	Tortrino v. Argentina, Case 11.597, Inter-Am. Comm'n H.R., Report No. 7/98, OEA/Ser.L./V/II.98, doc. 7 rev. ¶ 15 (1997).
Inter-American Court of Human Rights	Restrictions to the Death Penalty (Arts. 4(2) and 4(4) American Convention on Human Rights), Advisory Opinion OC-3/83, Inter-Am. Ct. H.R. (ser. A) No. 3, ¶ 70 (Sept. 8, 1983).
International Tribunal for the Law of the Sea	M/V Saiga (No. 2) (St. Vincent v. Guinea), Case No. 2, Order of Jan. 20, 1998, 2 ITLOS Rep. 4, 5.

International Criminal Court	Prosecutor v. Dyilo, ICC-01/04-01/06-2842, Judgment pursuant to Art. 74 of the Statute, ¶ 107 (Mar. 14, 2012), http://www.icc-cpi.int/iccdocs/doc/doc1379838.pdf.
	Prosecutor v. Katanga, ICC-01/04-01/07-3436-AnxII, Concurring opinion of Judges Diarra and Cotte, ¶ 5 (Mar. 3, 2014), http://www.icc-cpi.int/iccdocs/doc/doc1748105.pdf.
International criminal tribunals	Prosecutor v. Tadić, Case No. IT-94-1-I, Decision on Defence Motion for Interlocutory Appeal on Jurisdiction, ¶ 70 (Int'l Crim. Trib. for the Former Yugoslavia Oct. 2, 1995).
	Prosecutor v. Kayishema, Case No. ICTR 95-1-T, Judgment, ¶ 126 (May 21, 1999).

(c) International arbitrations. (rule 21.6)

| | Amoco Int'l Fin. Corp. v. Iran, 15 Iran-U.S. Cl. Trib. Rep. 189 (1987). |
| | Savarkar (Fr. v. Gr. Brit.), Hague Ct. Rep. (Scott) 275 (Perm. Ct. Arb. 1911). |

(d) United Nations sources. (rule 21.7)

Verbatim and summary meeting records	U.N. GAOR, 57th Sess., 42d plen. mtg. at 3, U.N. Doc. A/57/PV.42 (Nov. 1, 2002).
U.N. Charter	U.N. Charter art. 2, ¶ 1.
Resolutions	G.A. Res. 832 (IX), at 19 (Oct. 21, 1954).
	G.A. Res. 47/1, ¶ 2 (Sept. 22, 1992).
Reports	U.N. Secretary-General, *An Agenda for Peace: Preventive Diplomacy, Peacemaking and Peace-Keeping: Rep. of the Secretary-General*, ¶ 14, U.N. Doc. A/47/277-S/24111 (June 17, 1992).

(e) European Union materials. (rule 21.9)

| | Council Directive 2001/18, 2001 O.J. (L 106) 1 (EC). |

(f) World Trade Organization. (rule 21.11)

Panel decisions	Panel Report, *United States—Sections 301–310 of the Trade Act of 1974*, WTO Doc. WT/DS152/R (adopted Jan. 27, 2000).
Appellate Body decisions	Appellate Body Report, *Brazil—Export Financing Programme for Aircraft*, ¶ 19, WTO Doc. WT/DS46/AB/R (adopted Aug. 20, 1999).
Founding agreements	Marrakesh Agreement Establishing the World Trade Organization, Apr. 15, 1994, 1867 U.N.T.S. 154.
Ministerial documents	World Trade Organization, Ministerial Declaration of 14 November 2001, WTO Doc. WT/MIN(01)/DEC/1, 41 I.L.M. 746 (2002).

Non-English-Language Documents   21.2

For non-English-language documents, see **rule 20.2**.

Jurisdiction Not Evident from Context   21.3

When citing a non-U.S. source, whether in English or another language, indicate parenthetically the jurisdiction issuing the source, abbreviated according to **tables T3** and **T10**, unless the jurisdiction is otherwise clear from the context or other elements of the citation:

> ▸ Council Directive 66/45 art. 15, 1965–1966 O.J. SPEC. ED. 265, 268
> (Euratom).

Treaties and Other International Agreements   21.4

Citation of a treaty between two parties:

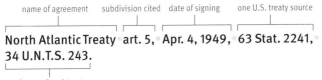

Citation of a treaty among more than two parties:

name of agreement   subdivision cited   date of signing   one U.S. treaty source

North Atlantic Treaty art. 5, Apr. 4, 1949, 63 Stat. 2241,
34 U.N.T.S. 243.

one international treaty source

Citation of a convention published by an international organization:

> ▸ Organization of American States, American Convention on Human
> Rights, Nov. 22, 1969, O.A.S.T.S. No. 36, 1144 U.N.T.S. 123.
> ▸ U.N. Convention on the Law of the Sea, Dec. 10, 1982, 1833 U.N.T.S.
> 397.

Citation of a founding document creating a new international court or organization:

> ▸ U.N. Charter art. 94, ¶ 1.
> ▸ League of Nations Covenant art. 16.

A citation of a treaty or other international agreement—other than the U.N. Charter and the Covenant of the League of Nations—should include the agreement's name (**rule 21.4.1**); the state parties, if applicable (**rule 21.4.2**);

the subdivision referred to, if applicable (**rule 21.4.3**); the date of signing (**rule 21.4.4**); and the source(s) in which the treaty can be found (**rule 21.4.5**):

▶ Statute of the International Tribunal for the Law of the Sea art. 1, ¶ 2, Dec. 10, 1982, 1833 U.N.T.S. 561.

21.4.1 Name of the Agreement

Use the English-language version of a treaty name whenever possible. See **rule 20.2.2** regarding the treatment of treaties whose names are not in English.

(a) First citation. The first citation of a treaty should contain its full name, including both its form (**rule 21.4.1(a)(i)**) and its subject matter (**rule 21.4.1(a)(ii)**):

▶ Convention for the Suppression of Unlawful Seizure of Aircraft, Dec. 16, 1970, 22 U.S.T. 1641, 860 U.N.T.S. 105.

(i) **Form of agreement**. The title of the treaty should indicate the form of the agreement (e.g., Agreement, Convention, Memorandum, Protocol, Treaty, Understanding). Use only the first form designation that appears on the title page, unless doing so would create ambiguity:

▶ Convention

Not: Convention & Supplementary Protocol

Cite lesser-included documents as subdivisions (**rule 21.4.3**).

(ii) **Subject matter**. Use the subject-matter description that appears as part of the title of the agreement:

▶ Kyoto Protocol to the United Nations Framework Convention on Climate Change

(b) Subsequent citations. If a treaty's name is very long, or if the treaty is commonly known by a popular name, the first citation of the treaty should end with a bracketed "hereinafter" short-form citation (**rule 4.2(b)**) to be used in all subsequent citations. The short-form citation must be in the same typeface as the original:

▶ [1] Protocol for the Prohibition of the Use in War of Asphyxiating, Poisonous or Other Gases, and of Bacteriological Methods of Warfare, June 17, 1925, 26 U.S.T. 571 [hereinafter Geneva Protocol].

▶ [3] Geneva Protocol, *supra* note 1, at 572.

21.4.2 Parties to the Agreement

When citing an agreement between two parties, indicate both parties, abbreviating their names according to **table T10**:

▶ Japan-U.S.
▶ Fr.-Ger.

Parties' names should appear in alphabetical order:

▶ Agreement for Financing Certain Educational and Cultural Exchange Programs, Taiwan-U.S., Apr. 23, 1964, 15 U.S.T. 408.

Subdivisions 21.4.3

When citing only part of an agreement, or when citing an appended document, give the subdivision or appended document:

> ▶ Treaty on Commerce and Navigation, Iraq-U.S., art. III, ¶ 2, Dec. 3, 1938, 54 Stat. 1790.

> ▶ Declaration on the Neutrality of Laos, Protocol, July 23, 1962, 14 U.S.T. 1104, 456 U.N.T.S. 301.

When citing a subdivision, it is not necessary to include a pincite for the treaty series because the article, paragraph, or section number is sufficient. For a discussion of citations to subdivisions and appendices, see **rules 3.3** and **3.4**.

Date of Signing 21.4.4

Give the exact date of signing:

> ▶ Protocol to Amend the Convention for the Suppression of the Traffic in Women and Children, Nov. 12, 1947, 53 U.N.T.S. 13.

When multiple dates of signing are given for an agreement or exchange of notes between two parties, give the first and last dates of signing:

> ▶ Agreement on Weather Stations, Colom.-U.S., Apr. 27–May 13, 1964, 15 U.S.T. 1355.

If a treaty was not signed on a single date, use the date on which the treaty was opened for signature, approved, ratified, or adopted, and indicate the significance of the date in italics:

> ▶ Treaty on the Non-Proliferation of Nuclear Weapons, *opened for signature* July 1, 1968, 21 U.S.T. 483, 729 U.N.T.S. 161.

The date on which a treaty entered into force or other such date may be added parenthetically at the end of the citation if it is relevant:

> ▶ U.N. Convention on the Law of the Sea, *opened for signature* Dec. 10, 1982, 1833 U.N.T.S. 397 (entered into force Nov. 16, 1994).

For abbreviations of the months of the year, see **table T12**.

Treaty Sources 21.4.5

See **table T4** for a list of international treaty sources. Treaty sources of some foreign states are listed with the other materials of those states in **table T2**.

(a) Agreements to which the United States is a party.

(i) **Bilateral treaties**. For agreements between the United States and another party, cite one of the following sources, in the following order of preference: U.S.T. (or Stat.); T.I.A.S. (or T.S., or E.A.S.); U.N.T.S.; Senate Treaty Documents or Senate Executive Documents; Department of State Dispatch; Department of State Press Releases. If the agreement has not appeared in one of these official sources, cite an unofficial treaty source (**rule 21.4.5(c)**):

▶ Treaty on the Limitation of Anti-Ballistic Missile Systems, U.S.-U.S.S.R., May 26, 1972, 23 U.S.T. 3435.

▶ Agreement on Defense and Economic Cooperation, Greece-U.S., at 4, Sept. 8, 1983, T.I.A.S. No. 10,814.

▶ Tax Convention, Fin.-U.S., Sept. 21, 1989, S. TREATY DOC. No. 101-11 (1990).

▶ Memorandum of Understanding Regarding Bilateral Verification Experiment and Data Exchange Related to Prohibition of Chemical Weapons, U.S.-U.S.S.R., art. V(1), Sept. 23, 1989, DEP'T ST. BULL., Nov. 1989, at 18 [hereinafter Chemical Weapons MOU].

▶ Cuban-American Treaty, Cuba-U.S., art. I, Feb. 16–23, 1903, T.S. No. 418.

▶ Agreement Regarding Mutual Assistance Between Their Customs Administrations, Ir.-U.S., art. 3, Sept. 16, 1996, 2141 U.N.T.S. 51.

(ii) **Multilateral treaties**. For agreements among three or more parties to which the United States is a party, cite one of the U.S. domestic sources listed in **rule 21.4.5(a)(i)**, if therein. Additionally, a parallel citation may be added from one source published by an international organization (e.g., U.N.T.S., L.N.T.S., O.A.S.T.S., Pan-Am. T.S., O.J., E.T.S., or C.E.T.S.), if therein:

▶ North Atlantic Treaty art. 5, Apr. 4, 1949, 63 Stat. 2241, 34 U.N.T.S. 243.

If none of these official sources can be obtained, cite an unofficial treaty source (**rule 21.4.5(c)**) or another reliable source where the treaty can be found.

(b) Agreements to which the United States is not a party. Cite one source published by an international organization (**rule 21.4.5(a)(ii)**), if therein:

▶ Treaty of Neutrality, Hung.-Turk., Jan. 5, 1929, 100 L.N.T.S. 137.

▶ Agreement for the Avoidance of Double Taxation, Neth.-Swed., art. 4, Apr. 25, 1952, 163 U.N.T.S. 131.

If not, cite the official source of one signatory, if therein, indicating parenthetically the jurisdiction whose source is cited according to **rule 21.3** if it is not clear from the context. If the treaty is not found in a signatory's treaty source, cite an unofficial treaty source (**rule 21.4.5(c)**):

▶ Agreement on Trade, Economic, and Technical Cooperation, Austl.-Oman, Oct. 20, 1981, [1982] A.T.S. 4.

(c) Unofficial treaty sources. When a treaty does not appear in a required source listed in **rule 21.4.5(a)(i)** or **21.4.5(a)(ii)**, cite International Legal Materials (I.L.M.), if therein:

▶ Olivos Protocol for the Settlement of Disputes in Mercosur art. 6, Feb. 18, 2002, 42 I.L.M. 2.

If a treaty is not found in I.L.M., cite another unofficial treaty source. These sources include the websites of governments and intergovernmental organizations, electronic databases, and sources such as the Foreign Relations of the United States series, Parry's Consolidated Treaty Series, Hein's microfiche treaty service, and Martens Nouveau Recueil:

► Agreement Concerning Payments for Certain Losses Suffered During World War II, Fr.-U.S., Jan. 18, 2001, Temp. State Dep't No. 01-36, 2001 WL 416465.

If no other citation is available, you may cite a book (**rule 15**), periodical (**rule 16**), or online source (**rule 18**).

International Law Cases   21.5

Cite according to **rule 10** as modified by the following instructions. If no authoritative English-language source is available, cite foreign-language sources according to **rule 20.2**.

The standard citation for an international law case includes: (1) the name of the case; (2) the case number; (3) the reporter (if any); (4) the characterization of the decision (judgment, provisional measures, etc.); (5) a pincite (using paragraph numbers, if available, rather than page numbers); and (6) a parenthetical with the date, prefaced by name of court if not otherwise evident from the citation.

For online-only decisions, refer readers to the court or tribunal's website (preferably to the specific webpage or PDF that includes the court or tribunal's decision).

· ·

The International Court of Justice and the Permanent Court   21.5.1
of International Justice

The International Court of Justice (I.C.J.), also known as the World Court, replaced the Permanent Court of International Justice (P.C.I.J.) in 1946.

Cite a case before the International Court of Justice or the Permanent Court of International Justice by: (1) the case name (**rule 21.5.1(a)**); (2) the parties' names, if any (**rule 21.5.1(b)**); (3) the characterization of the decision (Preliminary Objection, Provisional Measure, Advisory Opinion, Judgment, etc.), if relevant; (4) the volume and name of the publication in which the decision is found (**rule 21.5.1(c)**); (5) the page or case number (**rule 21.5.1(d)**); (6) the pincite, if any, with preference for paragraph number when available (indicated by the pilcrow symbol "¶"); and (7) the date (**rule 21.5.1(e)**):

► Military and Paramilitary Activities in and Against Nicaragua (Nicar. v. U.S.), Judgment, 1986 I.C.J. 14, ¶ 190 (June 27).

► Reservations to Convention on Prevention and Punishment of Crime of Genocide, Advisory Opinion, 1951 I.C.J. 15 (May 28).

► Diversion of Water from Meuse (Neth. v. Belg.), Judgment, 1937 P.C.I.J. (ser. A/B) No. 70, at 7 (June 28).

► Delimitation of Maritime Boundary in Gulf of Maine Area (Can./U.S.), Judgment, 1982 I.C.J. 560, ¶ 22 (Nov. 5).

When citing a separate opinion of a judgment in a published report, include the first page of the judgment and a pincite for the separate opinion. Include a parenthetical identifying the author of the separate opinion:

▶ Military and Paramilitary Activities in and Against Nicaragua (Nicar. v. U.S.), Judgment, 1986 I.C.J. 14, 181, ¶ 3 (June 27) (separate opinion by Ago, J.).

Do not include the first page of the judgment when short citing:

▶ Nicar. v. U.S., 1986 I.C.J. at 181.

Cite pleadings according to **rule 21.5.1(f)** and court rules and acts according to **rule 21.5.1(g)**. If necessary, cite yearbooks and annual reports of the World Court according to **rules 21.7.8** and **21.15**.

(a) Case name. Give the case name as found on the first page of the report. Omit the word "Case." Omit articles, such as "the." Do not abbreviate the names of countries where they appear in case names:

▶ Continental Shelf

Not: Case Concerning the Continental Shelf

Note that an application may appear as the case name:

▶ Application of Convention on Prevention and Punishment of Crime of Genocide (Bosn. & Herz. v. Serb. & Montenegro), 1996 I.C.J. 595, ¶ 31 (July 11).

(b) Parties' names. Give the names of the parties involved in a parenthetical phrase immediately following the case name. Abbreviate the names of countries according to **table T10**. When a dispute is brought by a unilateral application of one country against another, the countries' names are separated by "v." If the case is brought on the basis of a special agreement between two countries, the names of the parties are separated by a slash:

▶ (Nicar. v. U.S.)

▶ (Indon./Malay.)

In advisory opinions, no parties are listed:

▶ Interpretation of Peace Treaties with Bulgaria, Hungary and Romania, Advisory Opinion, 1950 I.C.J. 65 (Mar. 30).

▶ Polish Postal Service in Danzig, Advisory Opinion, 1925 P.C.I.J. (ser. B) No. 11, at 6 (May 16).

(c) Volume number and name of publication. Identify the volume by the date, as required by **rule 3.1(a)**. The International Court of Justice publishes its opinions in *Reports of Judgments, Advisory Opinions and Orders* (I.C.J.):

▶ 1950 I.C.J. 65

Decisions and other documents of the P.C.I.J. were published in seven series (lettered A through F, including A/B). Indicate the series in citations to P.C.I.J. documents:

▶ 1925 P.C.I.J. (ser. B) No. 11

(d) Page or case number. Cite I.C.J. cases to the page on which they begin. Cite cases of the P.C.I.J. by number:

▶ 2006 I.C.J. 107

► 1937 P.C.I.J. (ser. A/B) No. 70

Use pincites to refer to specific paragraphs, if available, or pages:

► 1986 I.C.J. 14, ¶ 15

► 1933 P.C.I.J. (ser. C) No. 62, at 12

See **rule 3.3** for more information about paragraph numbers.

(e) Date. Provide the month and day:

► Nuclear Tests (N.Z. v. Fr.), Interim Protection Order, 1973 I.C.J. 135 (June 22).

(f) Separately published pleadings. Cite separately published pleadings by the designation given in the document itself, followed by the name of the case (**rule 21.5.1(a)**); the names of the parties in a parenthetical (**rule 21.5.1(b)**); the volume number and name of the publication (**rule 21.5.1(c)**); and the full date of the pleading. Separately published pleadings before the I.C.J. are published in *Pleadings, Oral Arguments, Documents* (I.C.J. Pleadings), while P.C.I.J. rules and acts were published in P.C.I.J.:

► Memorial of United Kingdom, Corfu Channel (U.K. v. Alb.), 1949 I.C.J. Pleadings 19 (Sept. 30, 1947).

► Memorial of Denmark, Legal Status of Eastern Greenland (Den. v. Nor.), 1933 P.C.I.J. (ser. C) No. 62, at 12 (Oct. 31, 1931).

(g) Court rules and acts. Cite court rules and acts by title, volume number and name of publication, and page or document number. I.C.J. rules and acts are published in *Acts and Documents Concerning the Organization of the Court* (abbreviated I.C.J. Acts & Docs.), while those adjudicated by the P.C.I.J. were published in P.C.I.J.:

► Travel and Subsistence Regulations of the International Court of Justice, 1947 I.C.J. Acts & Docs. 94.

► Revised Rules of the Court, 1926 P.C.I.J. (ser. D) No. 1, at 33.

(h) Online materials. I.C.J. materials that have not been published may be cited to International Legal Materials (I.L.M.) (**rule 21.4.5(c)**) or to the I.C.J. website (http://www.icj-cij.org) (**rule 18.1**):

► Maritime Delimitation in Black Sea (Rom. v. Ukr.), Judgment, ¶ 5 (Feb. 3, 2009), https://www.icj-cij.org/files/case-related/132/132 -20090203-JUD-01-00-BI.pdf.

For oral pleadings, the date parenthetical should include the specific date and session time:

► LaGrand Case (Ger. v. U.S.), Verbatim Record, ¶¶ 5.1–5.19 (Nov. 14, 2000, 3:00 p.m.), https://www.icj-cij.org/files/case-related/104/104 -20001114-ORA-02-00-BI.pdf.

21.5.2 European Union Courts

Cite a case before the Court of Justice of the European Union (formerly the Court of Justice of the European Communities) or the General Court (formerly the Court of First Instance) by case number; the names of the parties, abbreviated according to **rule 10.2** and **table T6**; and the official reports of the Court, including the year of decision (**rule 21.5.2(a)**). A parallel citation to a private service may be made, if necessary (**rule 21.5.2(b)**).

For cases lodged before the Court of Justice since 1989, the case number will contain the prefix "C"; older cases will not have a prefix. Cases lodged before the General Court, created in 1989, will carry the prefix "T," and the Civil Service Tribunal will carry the prefix "F." Where the Commission, Council, or Parliament of the European Union is one of the parties, give its name as "Commission," "Council," or "Parliament," respectively:

▶ Case T-198/98, Micro Leader Bus. v. Comm'n, 1999 E.C.R. II-3989.

▶ Case C-213/89, The Queen v. Sec'y of State for Transp. *ex parte* Factortame Ltd., 1990 E.C.R. I-2433.

▶ Case 58/69, Elz v. Comm'n, 1970 E.C.R. 507.

Cases on European Union law are often decided in the courts of member states. These cases should be cited to the reporters of the particular member state. If necessary, such cases may also be cited to one of the unofficial reporters collecting materials regarding the European Union (see **rule 21.5.8**). When citing such a case to European Union materials, indicate the court and jurisdiction if not clear from the context, as provided by **rule 20.1**.

(a) Official reports. For pre-1990 cases, cite the *Reports of Cases Before the Court of Justice of the European Communities* (E.C.R.). For cases between 1990 and 2011, cite the *Reports of Cases Before the Court of Justice and the Court of First Instance* (also abbreviated E.C.R.). Place the year designation before the reporter abbreviation. Starting in 1990, page numbers in the E.C.R. begin with a "I," "II," or "III":

▶ Case C-286/01, Comm'n v. France, 2002 E.C.R. I-5463.

▶ Case 30/79, Land Berlin v. Wigei, 1980 E.C.R. 151.

▶ Joined Cases 56 & 58/64, Établissements Consten, S.A.R.L. v. Comm'n, 1966 E.C.R. 299.

The E.C.R. was discontinued after 2011.

Starting in 2012, use the European Case-Law Identifier (ECLI) to cite to EU Court cases. All decided EU cases will have a generated ECLI. The format has four components, in addition to the prefix "ECLI":

- "EU" indicates a decision delivered by one of the Courts of the European Union.
- An abbreviation corresponding to the court or tribunal that delivered the decision: "C" indicates the Court of Justice, "T" indicates the General Court, and "F" indicates the Civil Service Tribunal.
- The year of the decision.

- An ordinal number indicating that the decision is the nth ECLI assigned that year.

Post-2011, EU Court citations should include: (1) the case number; (2) the parties' names; (3) the ECLI, if available; (4) a pincite (using paragraph numbers, if available, rather than page numbers); and (5) the date:

▶ Case C-434/16, Peter Nowak v. Data Prot. Comm'r, ECLI:EU:C:2017:994, ¶¶ 54–55 (Dec. 20, 2017).

For pre-2011 official reports not available in print, cite to Curia, the official website of the Court of Justice of the European Union (http://curia.europa.eu) (**rule 18.1**), an electronic database (**rule 18.3**, or a private service (**rule 21.5.2(b)**). Citations to Curia should include: (1) the case number; (2) the parties' names; (3) a pincite (using paragraph numbers, if available, rather than page numbers); (4) the date; and (5) the website URL:

▶ Case C-279/06, CEPSA Estaciones de Servicio SA v. LV Tobar e Hijos SL, ¶ 62 (Sept. 11, 2008), http://curia.europa.eu/juris/document /document.jsf?text=&docid=70502&pageIndex=0&doclang=en &mode=1st&dir=&occ=first&part=1&cid=8112799.

▶ Case C-8/96, Locamion SA v. Directeur des Services Fiscaux d'Indre-et-Loire, ¶ 2 (Dec. 11, 1997), http://curia.europa.eu/juris/showPdf.jsf ?docid=43541&doclang=EN.

(b) Private services. If necessary, provide a parallel citation to one of the private services providing selected reports of the court's opinions. *Common Market Law Reports* (C.M.L.R.) is preferred. When citing volumes through 1973, include the full volume number; when citing volumes 1974 and later, include the issue number to reflect cessation of continuous issue numbering. Otherwise, use *Common Market Reporter* (Common Mkt. Rep. (CCH)) (through 1988) or *European Community Cases* (CEC (CCH)). See **rule 19** for treatment of CCH looseleaf services:

▶ Case 148/78, Pubblico Ministero v. Ratti, 1979 E.C.R. 1629, 1 C.M.L.R. 96 (1980).

▶ Case 48/69, Imperial Chem. Indus. v. Comm'n, 18 E.C.R. 619, [1971–1973 Transfer Binder] Common Mkt. Rep. (CCH) ¶ 8161 (1972).

European Court of Human Rights 21.5.3

Cite cases before the European Court of Human Rights to *European Court of Human Rights, Reports of Judgments and Decisions* (Eur. Ct. H.R.). *Reports of Judgments and Decisions* were discontinued after 2015. For cases after 2015, cite the Court's official website, HUDOC (http://www.echr.coe.int) (**rule 18.1**). Citations of HUDOC should include: (1) the parties' names (abbreviated according to **rule 10.2**); (2) the application number for the case; (3) a pincite (using paragraph numbers, if available, rather than page numbers); (4) the date; and (5) the document URL:

▶ S.M. v. Croatia, App. No. 60561/14, ¶ 81 (July 19, 2018), http://hudoc .echr.coe.int/eng?i=001-184665.

Recent volumes are numbered by year of publication and do not require a separate reference to the year. Older decisions may also be cited to *Publications of the European Court of Human Rights*, which was issued in multiple series (e.g., Eur. Ct. H.R. (ser. A)) or *Yearbook of the European Convention on Human Rights* (Y.B. Eur. Conv. on H.R.):

> ► Papon v. France (No. 2), 2001-XII Eur. Ct. H.R. 235.

> ► Kampanis v. Greece, 318 Eur. Ct. H.R. 29, 35 (1995).

For cases before the court between 1999 and 2015, cite by case name (abbreviated according to **rule 10.2**); volume number; reporter; page number, where applicable; and year.

Recent volumes contain several cases, but some earlier volumes contain only one case. Where a volume contains only one case, citing a beginning page is unnecessary, and all page numbers may be indicated directly by "at":

> ► Ireland v. United Kingdom, 23 Eur. Ct. H.R. (ser. B) at 23 (1976).

Until 1999, cases were also heard before the now-defunct European Commission on Human Rights. These cases should be cited to *Collections of Decisions of the European Commission on Human Rights* (Eur. Comm'n H.R. Dec. & Rep.) or Y.B. Eur. Conv. on H.R., if therein. If not, cite *European Human Rights Reports* (Eur. H.R. Rep.). When citing Y.B. Eur. Conv. on H.R., indicate parenthetically whether the case was before the Commission or the Court. Indicate both the parties and the application number for the case:

> ► Y. v. Netherlands, App. No. 7245/32, 32 Eur. Comm'n H.R. Dec. & Rep. 345, 358 (1982).

> ► Smith v. Belgium, App. No. 3324/76, 8 Eur. H.R. Rep. 445, 478 (1982).

> ► Iversen v. Norway, App. No. 1468/62, 1963 Y.B. Eur. Conv. on H.R. 278 (Eur. Comm'n on H.R.).

If a case before the European Court is not available in print, you may cite an unofficial printed source or the Court's official website, HUDOC (http://www .echr.coe.int) (**rule 18.1**).

....

21.5.4 Inter-American Commission on Human Rights

Cite cases before the Inter-American Commission on Human Rights to the *Annual Report of the Inter-American Commission on Human Rights* (Inter-Am. Comm'n H.R.). The citation should include the case name; the case number; the volume name; the report number, which includes the year of the decision; the series and docket numbers; the paragraph number, if applicable; and the year of the reporter:

> ► Tortrino v. Argentina, Case 11.597, Inter-Am. Comm'n H.R., Report No. 7/98, OEA/Ser.L./V/II.98, doc. 7 rev. ¶ 15 (1997).

> ► Calderón v. Colombia, Case 10.454, Inter-Am. Comm'n H.R., Report No. 32/92, OEA/Ser.L./V/II.83, doc. 14 (1992–1993).

Cite the English version whenever possible. If an official report is not yet available, cite the Commission's official website (http://www.cidh.org) (**rule 18.1**).

Inter-American Court of Human Rights

For cases before the Inter-American Court of Human Rights, cite the *Inter-American Court of Human Rights, Decisions and Judgments* (Inter-Am. Ct. H.R.). The citation should include the case name; the volume number; the series; the case number; the page number, if needed; and the date. Cite the English version whenever possible.

(a) Advisory Opinions. Cite Advisory Opinions by the name of the opinion; "Advisory Opinion" and opinion code; the report and volume number; the pincite, if any; and the date. Cite to Series A:

► Restrictions to the Death Penalty (Arts. 4(2) and 4(4) American Convention on Human Rights), Advisory Opinion OC-3/83, Inter-Am. Ct. H.R. (ser. A) No. 3, ¶ 70 (Sept. 8, 1983).

(b) Contentious Cases. Cite Contentious Cases by the name of the case; the matter of decision; the type of opinion; the report and volume number; the pincite, if any; and the date. Cite to Series C:

► Baldeon-Garcia v. Peru, Merits, Reparations, and Costs, Judgment, Inter-Am. Ct. H.R. (ser. C) No. 147, ¶ 169 (Apr. 6, 2006).

(c) Provisional Measures. Cite Provisional Measures by the name of the case or matter; "Provisional Measures"; and the type of opinion. When citing the print reports, cite Series E with the volume number and the first page of the decision; the section name in quotes; the pincite, if any; and the date. When citing an online version, cite the section name in quotes; the pincite, if any; the court and the date; and the website URL (**rule 18.1**):

► Bámaca Velázquez v. Guatemala, Provisional Measures, Order of the Court, Inter-Am. Ct. H.R. (ser. E) No. 4, at 1, "Decides," ¶ 2 (Sept. 5, 2001).

► Mendoza Prisons Regarding Argentina, Provisional Measures, Order of the President of the Court, "Having Seen," ¶ 21 (Inter-Am. Ct. H.R. Aug. 22, 2007), www.corteidh.or.cr/docs/medidas/penitenciariamendoza _se_04_ing.pdf.

(d) Compliances with Judgment. Cite Compliances with Judgment by the name of the case; "Monitoring Compliance with Judgment"; and the type of opinion. When citing the print reports, cite the volume number, the report name, and the first page of the decision; the section name in quotes; the pincite, if any; and the date. When citing an online version, cite to the section name in quotes; the pincite, if any; the court and date; and the website URL (**rule 18.1**):

► Genie Lacayo v. Nicaragua, Monitoring Compliance with Judgment, Order of the Court, 1998 Rep. Inter-Am. Ct. H.R. 335, "Resolves," ¶ 1 (Aug. 29, 1998).

► 270 Workers v. Panama, Monitoring Compliance with Judgment, Order of the President of the Court, "Considering," ¶ 14 (Inter-Am. Ct. H.R. Feb. 11, 2008), www.corteidh.or.cr/docs/supervisiones/baena_11_02 _08_ing.pdf.

21.5.6 International Tribunal for the Law of the Sea

Cite cases of the International Tribunal for the Law of the Sea to the *International Tribunal for the Law of the Sea Reports of Judgments, Advisory Opinions and Orders* (ITLOS Rep.). Cite cases before the Tribunal by the case name and the names of the parties in a parenthetical, abbreviated according to **table T10**; the case number; the type of ruling and date; the volume number, the name of the publication, and the page number; and the pincite, if any, with preference for paragraph numbers where available:

> ▶ M/V Saiga (No. 2) (St. Vincent v. Guinea), Case No. 2, Order of Jan. 20, 1998, 2 ITLOS Rep. 4, 5.

When print reports are unavailable, cite to the Tribunal's official website (http://www.itlos.org) (**rule 18.1**):

> ▶ M/V Louisa (St. Vincent v. Spain), Case No. 18, Order 2011/1 of Jan. 12, 2011, http://www.itlos.org/fileadmin/itlos/documents/cases/case _no_18_merits/18_order_120111_en.pdf

21.5.7 International Criminal Court and Other Tribunals

Cite cases of international criminal tribunals (e.g., the International Criminal Court, the International Criminal Tribunal for the Former Yugoslavia, the International Criminal Tribunal for Rwanda, the Extraordinary Chambers in the Courts of Cambodia, the Special Court for Sierra Leone, and the Special Tribunal for Lebanon) as follows: (1) case name (include only one party on each side of the "v." and include only the last name of individuals); (2) case number; (3) type of ruling (include only the last name of judges); (4) paragraph number, if necessary; and (5) date. If the tribunal's name is not contained in the case number, add the tribunal's name before the date:

> ▶ Prosecutor v. Katanga, ICC-01/04-01/07-3436-AnxI, Minority Opinion of Judge Wyngaert, ¶ 320 (Mar. 7, 2014).

> ▶ Prosecutor v. Tadić, Case No. IT-94-1-I, Decision on Defence Motion for Interlocutory Appeal on Jurisdiction, ¶ 70 (Int'l Crim. Trib. for the Former Yugoslavia Oct. 2, 1995).

> ▶ Prosecutor v. Kayishema, Case No. ICTR 95-1-T, Judgment, ¶ 126 (May 21, 1999).

Many cases can be found on official websites and should be cited pursuant to **rule 18.1**:

> ▶ Prosecutor v. Gombo, Case No. ICC-01/05-01/08, Warrant of Arrest, ¶ 22 (May 23, 2008), http://www.icc-cpi.int/iccdocs/doc/doc535163 .pdf.

> ▶ Prosecutor v. Simba, Case No. ICTR-01-76-T, Judgement and Sentence, ¶ 23 (Dec. 13, 2005), http://www.unictr.org/sites/unictr.org/files/case -documents/ictr-01-76/trial-judgements/en/051213.pdf.

> ▶ Prosecutor v. Lukić, Case No. IT-98-32/1-T, Order to Disclose Portions of the Transcript (Int'l Crim. Trib. for the Former Yugoslavia Jan. 22,

2009), http://www.icty.org/x/cases/milan_lukic_sredoje_lukic/tord
/en/090122.pdf.

Other International Courts   21.5.8

When citing other international courts, analogize the citation format to the format used for citing the courts described above in **rule 21.5.7**. An international court citation will generally contain the following information: (1) the parties to the case, if adversarial; (2) the court-assigned case number, if any; (3) the official reporter in which the case is published, with pincites, if the reporter has numbered pages and/or paragraphs; (4) the type of decision; (5) the court name, if not obvious from other parts of the citation; (6) the date of the decision; and (7) a web link, if any:

▶ Dabalorivhuwa Patriotic Front v. South Africa, Communication 335/2006, African Commission on Human and Peoples' Rights [Afr. Comm'n H.P.R.], ¶ 15 (Apr. 23, 2013), http://www.achpr.org/public /Document/file/English/achpr53_335_06_eng.pdf.

▶ Ababou v. Morocco, No. 007/2011, Decision, African Court on Human and Peoples' Rights [Afr. Ct. H.P.R.], ¶ 6 (Sept. 2, 2011), http://en.african-court.org/images/Cases/Decision/Decision%20 -%20APPLICATION%20NO.%20007.2011.pdf.

If cases cannot be found in official reports, cite the *International Law Reports* (I.L.R.) (1950–present) or *Annual Digest and Reports of Public International Law Cases* (Ann. Dig.) (1919–49). Volume numbers, rather than years, should be used. Early volumes of the Annual Digest have been renumbered according to tables appearing in all volumes after volume 25. Include the name of the court and the year of the decision in a parenthetical:

▶ Loomba v. Food & Agric. Org. of the U.N., 47 I.L.R. 382 (Int'l Lab. Org. Admin. Trib. 1970).

▶ Mayras v. Sec'y-Gen. of the League of Nations, 13 Ann. Dig. 199 (Admin. Trib. of the League of Nations 1946).

International Cases in National Courts   21.5.9

If an international case is decided by a national court whose reporter is not indicated in **table T2**, cite I.L.R., Ann. Dig., C.M.L.R., Common Mkt. Rep. (CCH), a yearbook (**rule 21.15**), or an online source (**rule 18.1**). Indicate the country and court of origin parenthetically if not otherwise clear from the citation:

▶ Abdul Ghani v. Subedar Shoedar Khan, 38 I.L.R. 3 (W. Pak. High Ct. 1964).

▶ Ko Maung Tin v. U Gon Man, 14 Ann. Dig. 233 (High Ct. 1947) (Burma).

International Arbitrations and Claims Commissions   21.6

Cite arbitral decisions and claims commission decisions by analogy to **rule 21.5**, modified as follows. If adversarial parties are named, name as you would for a court case:

> ► Massaut v. Stupp

Otherwise, cite by the name of the first-party plaintiff or by the subject matter if no name is given. Indicate parenthetically the countries involved, when available, if not otherwise evident:

> ► N. Atl. Coast Fisheries (U.K. v. U.S.), 11 R.I.A.A. 167, 196 (Perm. Ct. Arb. 1910).

Cite arbitral awards to the official source, if possible, unless that source is a pamphlet containing only a single judgment. Consult **table T5** for frequently cited arbitral reporters and claims commissions. Indicate the court or tribunal unless it is identified in the name of the reporter:

> ► Amoco Int'l Fin. Corp. v. Iran, 15 Iran-U.S. Cl. Trib. Rep. 189 (1987).
> ► Massaut v. Stupp, 9 Trib. Arb. Mixtes 316 (Ger.-Belg. 1929).
> ► Savarkar (Fr. v. Gr. Brit.), Hague Ct. Rep. (Scott) 275 (Perm. Ct. Arb. 1911).
> ► Case No. 5428 of 1988, 14 Y.B. Comm. Arb. 146 (ICC Int'l Ct. Arb.).

For International Centre for Settlement of Investment Disputes (ICSID) awards, include the full diplomatic names for each country involved, where relevant. After the case number, include a description of the type of decision or ruling, when relevant:

> ► Société Générale de Surveillance S.A. v. Republic of the Phil., ICSID Case No. ARB/02/6, Objections to Jurisdiction, ¶ 154 (Jan. 29, 2004), 8 ICSID Rep. 518 (2005).

When decisions do not appear in a traditional printed source, an internet source may be used pursuant to **rule 18.1**:

> ► *In re* Account of Gafner, Case No. CV96-4849, Certified Award, at 2 (Claims Resolution Trib. 2006), http://www.crt-ii.org/_awards/_apdfs/Gafner_Elisabeth.pdf.

21.7 United Nations Sources

The Official Records are the preferred source for United Nations citations, but masthead documents and documents drawn from U.N. websites are acceptable. Press releases, sales documents, yearbooks, and periodicals should be cited only when preferred sources are unavailable.

Whenever possible, paragraph and article numbers, rather than page numbers of the Official Records, should be used for pincites. Some documents utilize both unnumbered and numbered paragraphs, referred to as preambular and operative paragraphs, respectively; cite language in preambular paragraphs by page number and language in operative paragraphs by paragraph number. For General Assembly and Security Council resolutions, cite the Official Records and provide a parallel citation for the individual resolution.

This section covers the principal organs of the United Nations and several subsidiaries of the General Assembly. Subsidiaries of organs or committees should be included in citations whenever appropriate. Other organs and committees not specifically covered by this section should be cited analogously to the examples in this rule. If a committee is known by an abbreviation, write out the committee's full name and include an abbreviation in brackets if useful for subsequent citations.

Verbatim and Summary Records   21.7.1

The General Assembly, the Security Council, and the Economic and Social Council have Official Records. All citations to verbatim and summary records should be to the Official Records whenever possible.

Include the Official Records title; the subdivision of the organ, if necessary; the session and meeting number; the pincite, if necessary; the U.N. document symbol; and the date:

> ▶ U.N. GAOR, 56th Sess., 1st plen. mtg. at 3, U.N. Doc. A/56/PV.1 (Sept. 12, 2001).

> ▶ U.N. SCOR, 59th Sess., 4893d mtg. at 2, U.N. Doc. S/PV.4893 (Jan. 15, 2004).

Resolutions and Decisions   21.7.2

Authorized versions of resolutions appear in the Official Records. It has become customary, however, to cite electronic versions or resolutions found in the Official Document System (ODS) of the United Nations using resolution symbols. For pincites to material within a resolution, use paragraph or article numbers.

(a) General Assembly. After 1976, General Assembly resolution symbols are designated as session number/resolution number. The first resolution adopted during the forty-seventh General Assembly would thus be G.A. Res. 47/1.

Prior to 1976, the resolution symbols continued increasing from year to year and the session number was indicated as a Roman numeral in parentheses after the resolution number.

(i) **General Assembly resolutions**. General Assembly resolutions are cited by resolution number and date.

> ▶ G.A. Res. 832 (IX), at 19 (Oct. 21, 1954).

> ▶ G.A. Res. 47/163, ¶ 5 (Dec. 18, 1992).

(ii) **General Assembly decisions**. General Assembly decisions are cited by resolution number and date.

> ▶ G.A. Dec. 62/557, U.N. Doc. A/63/49 (Vol. III), at 106 (Sept. 15, 2008).

(iii) **General Assembly resolutions known by a popular name**. For General Assembly resolutions known by a specific title (e.g., the Universal Declaration of Human Rights), or for resolutions whose title is important in the context cited, insert the title after the resolution number. Note that some documents or statements, such as the last of the three below, are included as annexes to resolutions and need to be identified as such:

> ▶ G.A. Res. 217 (III) A, Universal Declaration of Human Rights (Dec. 10, 1948).

► G.A. Res. 60/1, 2005 World Summit Outcome (Sept. 16, 2005).

► G.A. Res. 47/135, annex, Declaration on the Rights of Persons Belonging to National or Ethnic, Religious and Linguistic Minorities (Dec. 18, 1992).

(b) Security Council resolutions. Security Council resolutions and statements of the Security Council President are cited by resolution number and date.

► S.C. Res. 508, ¶ 3 (June 5, 1982).

► S.C. Res. 1325, ¶ 8 (Oct. 31, 2000).

► S.C. Pres. Statement 2008/48 (Dec. 22, 2008).

(c) Resolutions issued by other organs. Resolutions issued by other U.N. organs should be cited analogously to General Assembly and Security Council resolutions. List the title of the U.N. organ first.

► Economic and Social Council Res. 1990/26 (May 24, 1990).

► Trusteeship Council Res. 2014 (XXVI), at 2 (June 1, 1960).

(d) Resolutions by subsidiary bodies. Resolutions by subsidiary bodies of the principal U.N. organs should be cited by the name of the subsidiary body and resolution number; the U.N. document symbol; the pincite, if any; and the date:

► Human Rights Council Res. 5/1, U.N. Doc. A/62/53, at 48 (June 18, 2007).

(e) Short form. Resolutions can subsequently be cited in short form, with "*supra*" and a pincite:

► S.C. Res. 508, *supra* note 1, ¶ 2.

► H.R.C. Res. 5/1, *supra* note 2, ¶ 1.

21.7.3 U.N. Reports

(a) In general. Reports from U.N. organs, committees, or the Secretariat should include the name of the body and the subcommittee (both abbreviated according to **rule 15.1(d)**), if any; the title of the report; the pincite, if any; the document symbol; and the date. If a personal author is given, that person should be named as the author, with official role noted in parentheses if relevant (e.g., Maurice Kamto (Special Rapporteur)).

(b) Reports of subsidiary bodies to parent organs. Reports of subsidiary bodies to parent organs are usually part of the Official Records of the parent organ, as are the reports of the principal organs to the General Assembly. Include the title of the report; the name of the body; the session number; the dates of the session; the pincite, if any; the document symbol; the Official Record supplement number; and the date of publication:

► Rep. of the S.C., at 16–17, U.N. Doc. A/63/2 (2008).

▶ Comm. on the Peaceful Uses of Outer Space, Rep. of the Legal Subcomm. on Its Fifty-Third Session, U.N. Doc. A/AC.105/1067 (2014).

▶ Int'l L. Comm'n, Rep. on the Work of Its Sixty-Fourth Session, U.N. Doc. A/67/10, at 46–51 (2012).

▶ Rep. of the Group of Experts on Côte d'Ivoire (2006), transmitted by Letter dated 17 October 2007 from the Chairman of the Security Council Comm. Established Pursuant to Resolution 1572 (2004) Concerning Côte d'Ivoire Addressed to the President of the Security Council, ¶¶ 61–80, U.N. Doc. S/2007/611 (Oct. 18, 2007).

(c) Reports from the Secretary-General or other officials. When citing a report published by the Secretary-General, or anyone acting in an official capacity as a committee chair, representative, envoy, etc., include in the citation: the author of the report; the title of the report; the pincite, if any; the body to which the document is delivered, if needed; the document symbol; and the date. If a personal author is given, that person should be named as author, with his or her official role noted in parentheses if relevant:

▶ U.N. Secretary-General, *An Agenda for Peace: Preventive Diplomacy, Peacemaking and Peace-Keeping*, ¶ 14, U.N. Doc. A/47/277-S/24111 (June 17, 1992).

▶ Executive Chairman of the U.N. Monitoring, Verification and Inspection Comm'n (UNMOVIC), *8th Quarterly Rep. of the Executive Chairman*, U.N. Doc. S/2002/195, annex (Feb. 26, 2002).

▶ Maurice Kamto (Special Rapporteur on the Expulsion of Aliens), *Fourth Rep. on the Expulsion of Aliens*, U.N. Doc. A/CN.4/594 (Mar. 24, 2008).

(d) Reports from conferences. If a report is the product of a conference or a series of conferences, include in the citation: the conference name; the report title; the pincite, if any; the document symbol, if available; and the official document date. Do not include the location and dates of conferences if listed separately on the title page of the document. Do not include dates if they are integrated into the title of the document (e.g., "Report of High-Level Conference of May 2012 Concerning Rights of Indigenous Peoples."):

▶ World Conference on Human Rights, *Vienna Declaration and Programme of Action*, ¶ 37, U.N. Doc. A/CONF.157/23 (June 25, 1993).

▶ U.N. Conference on Environment and Development, *Rio Declaration on Environment and Development*, U.N. Doc. A/CONF.151/26/Rev.1 (Vol. I), annex I (Aug. 12, 1992).

(e) Short forms. For reports with long names, it is appropriate to list a short form in brackets at the end of the full citation (**rule 4.2(b)**).

Masthead Documents   21.7.4

Most U.N. documents are issued as masthead documents. Some documents originally published in masthead form, such as General Assembly and Security Council resolutions, are subsequently issued in the Official Records. Cite the Official Record when possible. Masthead documents should be cited by the name of the institutional author, if any (**rule 21.7.4(a)**); the title of the document (**rule 21.7.4(b)**); the pincite, if any; the document symbol (**rule 21.7.4(c)**); and the date of publication.

▶ U.N. Secretary-General, Letter dated Mar. 2, 2006 from the Secretary-General addressed to the President of the General Assembly, U.N. Doc. A/60/706 (Mar. 3, 2006).

▶ U.N. President of the S.C., Letter dated Dec. 9, 2008 from the President of the Security Council to the Secretary-General, U.N. Doc. S/2008/757 (Dec. 9, 2008).

▶ Prevention Through Education, Ministerial Declaration of the 1st Meeting of the Ministers of Health and Education to Stop HIV/AIDS and Sexually Transmitted Infections in Latin America and the Carib-bean, in letter dated Aug. 15, 2008 from the Chargé d'affaires a.i. of the Permanent Mission of Mexico to the United Nations addressed to the Secretary-General, U.N. Doc. A/63/307 (Aug. 19, 2008).

▶ Permanent Rep. of Somalia to the U.N., Letter dated May 12, 2008 from the Permanent Rep. of Somalia to the United Nations addressed to the President of the Security Council, U.N. Doc. S/2008/323 (May 14, 2008).

▶ U.N. Secretariat, Expulsion of Aliens, Memorandum by the Secretariat, ¶¶ 702–44, Int'l Law Comm'n, U.N. Doc. A/CN.4/565 (July 10, 2006).

(a) Author. Include the name of the author, as listed on the cover page of the document:

▶ U.N. Secretary-General, Letter dated Mar. 2, 2006 from the Secretary-General addressed to the President of the General Assembly, U.N. Doc. A/60/706 (Mar. 3, 2006).

▶ U.N., Econ. & Soc. Council, Comm. on Arrangements for Consultation with Non-Governmental Orgs., Dev. of Tourism on the African Conti-nent, Statement Submitted by the Int'l Union of Official Travel Orgs., U.N. Doc. E/C.2/562 (1960).

(b) Title. Capitalize the title in accordance with **rule 8**.

(c) United Nations document symbol. Include the U.N. document symbol (**rule 21.7.1**), if available.

. . . .

21.7.5   U.N. Press Releases and Memoranda

Cite U.N. press releases and memoranda according to **rule 17.2.3**, but also include the U.N. press release symbol:

▶ Press Release, Security Council, Security Council Takes Up Report on Diamonds, Arms in Sierra Leone; Expert Panel Says Council Sanctions Broken 'with Impunity,' U.N. Press Release SC/6997 (Jan. 25, 2001).

. . . .

21.7.6   Adjudicatory Bodies Established by the United Nations

The International Criminal Tribunals for the Former Yugoslavia and Rwanda, the Special Court for Sierra Leone, and other ad hoc and regional tribunals should be cited according to **rule 21.5.7**. The U.N. Administrative Tribunal should be cited to *Judgments of the U.N. Administrative Tribunal* (Judgments U.N. Admin. Trib.) by judgment number:

▶ Eldridge v. Secretary-General of the United Nations, Judgments U.N. Admin. Trib., No. 32, at 144, U.N. Doc. AT/DEC/32 (1953).

Sales Publications   21.7.7

Numerous U.N. agencies publish reports, studies, proceedings, and other documents for sale. Citation of sales publications should include the author and title (**rule 21.7.7(a)**); the page(s) or paragraph(s) (**rule 21.7.7(b)**); the U.N. document symbol, if available (**rule 21.7.7(c)**); the sales number (**rule 21.7.7(d)**); and the year (**rule 21.7.7(e)**).

(a) Author and title. Include the author and title according to **rules 15.1** and **15.3**. Include the name of the author if it is not apparent from the title of the document:

▶ U.N. Dep't of Int'l Econ. & Soc. Affairs, U.N. Model Double Taxation Convention Between Developed and Developing Countries, at 243, U.N. Doc. ST/ESA/102, U.N. Sales No. E.80.XVI.3 (1980).

▶ U.N. Dep't of Econ. & Soc. Affairs, Comm. for Dev. Policy, Handbook on the Least Developed Country Category: Inclusion, Graduation and Special Support Measures, U.N. Sales No. E.07. II.A.9 (2008).

(b) Pages or paragraphs. The volume and subdivision designations should be followed by the page(s) or paragraph(s) to which reference is made. Introduce page numbers with the word "at."

(c) United Nations document symbol. Include the U.N. document symbol (**rule 21.7.1**), if available.

(d) United Nations sales number. Include the U.N. sales number:

▶ U.N. Dep't of Int'l Econ. & Soc. Affairs, World Economic Survey 1977, at I-19, U.N. Doc. ST/ESA/82, U.N. Sales No. E.78.II.C.1 (1977).

(e) Year. Give the year of publication.

Yearbooks and Periodicals   21.7.8

United Nations yearbooks and periodicals collect summaries of the work of subsidiary organizations and related documents. Citations should include the author and/or title of the document or separately designated article (if any); the name of the yearbook or periodical (abbreviated according to **rule 16.4**); and the U.N. document symbol (**rule 21.7.1**) or, if none, the U.N. sales number (**rule 21.7.7(d)**):

▶ *Summary Records of the 1447th Meeting*, [1977] 1 Y.B. Int'l L. Comm'n 175, U.N. Doc. A/CN.4/SER.A/1977.
▶ *Human Rights in the Union of Burma in 1953*, 1953 Y.B. on H.R. 31, U.N. Sales No. 1955.XIV.1.
▶ 1981 U.N. Jurid. Y.B. 41, U.N. Doc. ST/LEG/SER.C/19.
▶ 1985 U.N.Y.B. 1391, U.N. Sales No. E.84.I.1.

Material reprinted in yearbooks from other U.N. documents should be cited to the original source or to the official records of a U.N. organ:

▶ *Report of the International Law Commission to the General Assembly*, 19 U.N. GAOR Supp. No. 9, at 1, U.N. Doc. A/5509 (1963), *reprinted in* [1963] 2 Y.B. Int'l L. Comm'n 187, U.N. Doc. A/CN.4/SER.A/1963/Add.1.

21.7.9 Regional Organization Documents

Resolutions, reports, and other similar documents produced by regional organizations, such as the Organization of American States or the African Union, should be cited analogously to U.N. materials with pincites, if the reporter has numbered pages and/or paragraphs.

21.7.10 U.N. Charter

See **rule 21.4**:

▶ U.N. Charter art. 43, ¶ 1.

21.7.11 U.N. Internet Materials

You may cite a website URL for materials without document or press release symbols. United Nations websites are preferable to all other websites. Cite materials in accordance with **rule 21.7.4** and format them pursuant to **rule 18.1**:

▶ U.N. Secretary-General, High-Level Event on the Millennium Development Goals 25 September 2008: Committing to Action: Achieving the Millennium Development Goals: Background Note by the Secretary-General (July 25, 2008), http://www.un.org/millenniumgoals /2008highlevel/pdf/commiting.pdf.

▶ Letter from the President of the G.A. to all Permanent Representatives and Permanent Observers to the U.N. (Dec. 4, 2008), http://www.un .org/ga/president/63/letters/udhrprogramme41208.pdf.

▶ U.N. President of the G.A., Remarks on the Work to Date of the Sixty-Third Session of the U.N. G.A. (Dec. 23, 2008), http://www.un.org/ga /president/63/statements/ga231208.shtml.

21.8 League of Nations

Cite the League of Nations Covenant as:

▶ League of Nations Covenant art. 16.

Cite conventions and treaties promulgated by the League of Nations according to **rule 21.4**.

Cite other League of Nations materials by issuing body (if not included in the title); title; document number; and year:

▶ *Reports Presented by the Comm. of Technical Experts on Double Taxation and Tax Evasion*, League of Nations Doc. C.216M.85 1927 II (1927).

European Union 21.9

(a) Acts of the Council and Commission.

(i) **Sources**. Cite publications of the Council and Commission published beginning February 1, 2003, to the *Official Journal of the European Union* (O.J.). Cite documents published between January 1, 1973, and January 31, 2003, to the *Official Journal of the European Communities* (also abbreviated O.J.). Cite documents published before January 1, 1973, to the Special Edition of the *Official Journal of the European Communities* (O.J. SPEC. ED.), if available; otherwise cite to the *Journal Officiel des Communautés Européennes* (J.O.). For pincites, use paragraph numbers, if available, rather than page numbers, unless only page numbers are available.

Beginning with the 1998 editions, the O.J. is available at the European Union's official website, http://eur-lex.europa.eu/en/index.htm. The online editions may be cited as official editions and should generally include the same information as citations to paper versions.

Cite volumes of O.J. and J.O. by year. J.O. volumes published prior to 1968 were numbered in a single series. Since 1968, O.J. and J.O. have been published in parallel series, paginated separately by issue. Legislative acts appear in the "L" series, while other documents appear in the "C" series. Citations to J.O. before 1968 must include the issue number, while citations to O.J. and J.O. since 1968 must include both the series and the issue number:

▶ 1971 J.O. (L 20) 1.

▶ 1975 O.J. (L 337) 7.

▶ 1964 J.O. (234) 5.

Citations to the O.J. SPEC. ED. must indicate the period covered by the issue:

▶ 1965–1966 O.J. SPEC. ED. 265.

(ii) **Legislative acts of the Council and Commission.** Cite Regulations, Directives, and Decisions of the Council and Commission by the issuing institution, type of legislation, number, and subdivision (if applicable). If it is unclear from the context that the source is a European Union (EU) or European Community (EC) act, indicate this with a parenthetical at the end of the citation (**rule 20.1**). If the act was not issued under the Treaty on the Functioning of the European Union, indicate the authority for the promulgation of the act:

▶ Council Directive 90/476, art. 5, 1990 O.J. (L 266) 1, 2 (EC).

▶ Council Directive 66/45, art. 15, 1965–1966 O.J. SPEC. ED. 265, 268 (Euratom).

▶ Commission Regulation 725/67, 1967 J.O. (253) 1.

The full name of the legislation may also be provided, with or without the date:

▶ Commission Regulation 2751/90 of Sept. 26, 1990, Fixing the Import Levies on Compound Feeding Stuffs, annex, 1990 O.J. (L 264) 37, 38.

▶ Directive 2001/18, of the European Parliament and of the Council of 12 March 2001 on the Deliberate Release into the Environment of Genetically Modified Organisms and Repealing Council Directive 20/220/EEC, 2001 O.J. (L 106) 1, 3.

(iii) **Other publications of the Council and Commission.** Cite proposed Regulations, Directives, Decisions, Conclusions, Resolutions, and other notices of the Council and Commission by issuing institution and title, as given at the beginning of the item.

For Common Positions, the complete date and the complete or short form title may be included:

▶ Council Common Position (EC) No. 57/2003 of 25 June 2003, art. 2, 2003 O.J. (C 277) 1, 2.

▶ Administrative Commission on Social Security for Migrant Workers, 2009 O.J. (C 213) 6, 8.

(iv) **COM and SEC documents.** "COM" documents are proposed legislation and other Commission communications to other European institutions, and the Commission's preparatory papers. "SEC" documents are internal documents of the Secretariat-General concerning the operations of Commission departments. Cite "COM" and "SEC" documents by the issuing body (unless clear from the title); the title; the pincite, if any; the "COM" or "SEC" number, which includes the year of publication in parentheses and the running number assigned to the document, if any; the word "final" (unless the version cited is not final); and the date:

▶ *Commission Proposal for a Directive of the European Parliament and of the Council to Establish a New Financial Services Committee Organisational Structure*, at 11, COM (2003) 659 final (Nov. 5, 2003).

▶ *Proposal for a Regulation of the European Parliament and of the Council Concerning the Registration, Evaluation, Authorisation and Registration of Chemicals (Reach)*, COM (2003) 644 final (Oct. 29, 2003).

(b) Documents of the European Parliament.

(i) **Debates.** Debates of the European Parliament are bound and published in the *European Parliamentary Debates* (EUR. PARL. DEB.). The debates are also published in the annex to the *Official Journal of the European Union*. It is acceptable to cite debates to the Official Journal (O.J.) before they are bound. Include in the citation the name of the speaker, the document number, the full date, and relevant information, including the name of the speaker, in parentheticals:

▶ EUR. PARL. DEB. (378) 4 (May 24, 1989) (remarks of Mr. Kuijpers).

▶ 1975 O.J. (Annex 193) 123 (July 9, 1975) (remarks of President Ortoli).

(ii) **Documents.** Cite documents to *European Parliament Session Documents* (EUR. PARL. DOC.) (entitled *European Parliament Working Documents* prior to 1988), if therein; otherwise cite *Parlement Européen Documents de Séance* (PARL. EUR. DOC.). Include the document number:

▶ EUR. PARL. DOC. (COM 258) 5 (1973).

▶ PARL. EUR. DOC. (SEC 64) 6 (1963).

The name may be included as well:

▶ Resolution on Action Required Internationally to Provide Effective Protection for Indigenous Peoples, EUR. PARL. DOC. PV 58(II) (1994).

(c) Founding treaties. Cite founding treaties according to **rule 21.4.5**:

▶ Treaty of Lisbon Amending the Treaty on European Union and the Treaty Establishing the European Community, Dec. 13, 2007, 2007 O.J. (C 306) 1 [hereinafter Treaty of Lisbon].

▶ Consolidated Version of the Treaty on the Functioning of the European Union art. 15, May 9, 2008, 2008 O.J. (C 115) 47 [hereinafter TFEU].

▶ Treaty of Amsterdam Amending the Treaty on European Union, the Treaties Establishing the European Communities and Certain Related Acts, Oct. 2, 1997, 1997 O.J. (C 340) 1.

Subsequent citations should use the appropriate short form:

▶ TFEU art. 177.

▶ Treaty of Lisbon arts. 4–5.

▶ Euratom Treaty art. 4.

The Treaty of Lisbon renamed the Treaty Establishing the European Community (EC Treaty) to the Treaty on the Functioning of the European Union (TFEU) and renumbered its articles. For current references to the founding treaty, cite the TFEU according to its renumbered articles. To cite previous versions of the EU's founding treaty, cite the name of the treaty, the article, the date (in parentheses), and the current number of the article as found in the TFEU (in parentheses), if still active:

▶ EC Treaty art. 49 (as in effect 2005) (now TFEU art. 56).

▶ EC Treaty art. 53 (as in effect 1994) (repealed by the Treaty of Amsterdam).

▶ EEC Treaty art. 30 (as in effect 1958) (now TFEU art. 34).

(d) Reports, Green Papers, and White Papers. Cite reports from institutions and working groups within the European Union or European Communities according to **rule 21.7.3**. Include in the citation of reports the issuing body and the committee, division, or group that produced the report, if applicable. If a report is not given a document number, provide enough information to locate the document:

▶ *Commission White Paper on European Governance*, at 17, COM (2001) 482 final (July 25, 2001).

▶ *Initial Report of the Committee of Wise Men on the Regulation of European Securities Markets*, at 4 (Nov. 9, 2000), http://ec.europa.eu /internal_market/securities/docs/lamfalussy/wisemen/initial-report -wise-men_en.pdf.

White Papers, Green Papers, comments, notices, opinions, and proposals should also be cited as reports:

▶ *Opinion of the Committee of the Regions on the "CoR Proposals for the Intergovernmental Conference,"* 2004 O.J. (C 32) 1, 2.

If a source takes a form analogous to other reports and is not given the type of document number that Commission and Council acts are given (e.g., Council Directive (EC) No. 2504/90), then it should be cited as a report.

(e) Press releases, Presidency Conclusions, and memoranda. European Union and European Community press releases and memoranda should be cited by source (with an indication of the status of the press release, including a number if applicable); the title; and the date in parentheses:

> ▶ European Commission Press Release IP/14/650, The Commission, the Council and the Parliament Debate the Future of the European Union with Religious Leaders (June 10, 2014).

Treat Presidency Conclusions of the Council like press releases and include the exact date as well as the meeting place of the Council:

> ▶ Presidency Conclusions, Brussels European Council (Dec. 12, 2003).

(f) European Court of Justice materials. Cite European Court of Justice materials according to **rule 21.5.2**.

21.10 Council of Europe

Cite debates of the Parliamentary Assembly, formerly the Consultative Assembly, to the official reports:

> ▶ EUR. CONSULT. ASS. DEB. 10th Sess. 639 (Oct. 16, 1958).

> ▶ EUR. PARL. ASS. DEB. 23d Sess. 499 (Sept. 30, 1980).

Cite documents as follows:

> ▶ Eur. Consult. Ass., *Reply of the Comm. of Ministers*, 12th Sess., Doc. No. 1126 (1960).

Recent Council of Europe materials can be found on the Council of Europe's official website (http://assembly.coe.int) (and should be cited according to **rule 18.2**).

21.11 World Trade Organization

If it is unclear from the context that a citation refers to a WTO or GATT document, explain the reference in a parenthetical following the citation.

(a) WTO panel and Appellate Body materials. Cite reports of WTO panels and the Appellate Body by their official document symbol:

> ▶ Panel Report, *United States—Sections 301–310 of the Trade Act of 1974*, WTO Doc. WT/DS152/R (adopted Jan. 25, 2000) [hereinafter Section 301 Panel Report].

> ▶ Appellate Body Report, *Brazil—Export Financing Programme for Aircraft*, ¶ 19, WTO Doc. WT/DS46/AB/R (adopted Aug. 20, 1999).

Cite communications of panels and the Appellate Body, as well as members' communications to panels and the Appellate Body, in a like format:

- Preliminary Ruling by the Panel, *Canada—Measures Relating to Exports of Wheat and Treatment of Imported Grain*, ¶ 23, WTO Doc. WT/DS276/12 (July 21, 2003).

- Request for Consultations by the United States, *European Communities—Measures Affecting the Approval and Marketing of Biotech Products*, WTO Doc. WT/DS291/1 (May 20, 2003).

- Request for the Establishment of a Panel by Brazil, *United States—Subsidies on Upland Cotton*, WTO Doc. WT/DS267/7 (Feb. 7, 2003).

A member's written submissions and oral statements to panels and the Appellate Body are made public at the discretion of the individual member. Because these documents are not normally publicly available, include precise information regarding their location:

- First Written Submission of the United States, *United States—Subsidies on Upland Cotton*, WT/DS267 (July 11, 2003), https://ustr.gov/sites/default/files/uploads/Countries%20Regions/africa/agreements/pdfs/dispute_settlement/ds267/asset_upload_file148_5598.pdf.

(b) General Agreement on Tariffs and Trade (GATT) panel decisions. Cite *Basic Instruments and Selected Documents* (B.I.S.D.), if therein. Include the title; case number, if listed; the document date; the ordinal number of the supplement (annual volume); the page; and the year of publication:

- Report of the Panel, *Japan—Restrictions on Imports of Certain Agricultural Products*, ¶ 5.2.2, L/6253 (Feb. 2, 1988), GATT B.I.S.D. (35th Supp.), at 163, 229 (1989).

- *Netherlands Measure of Suspension of Obligations to the United States* (Nov. 8, 1952), GATT B.I.S.D. (1st Supp.), at 32 (1953).

(c) Reports. Cite reports from the WTO Secretariat and other bodies as you would those from the United Nations (**rule 21.7.3**):

- Council for Trade-Related Aspects of Intellectual Prop. Rights, *Note by the Secretariat: Available Information on the Existence of Patents in Regard to the Diseases Referred to in the Declaration on the TRIPS Agreement and Public Health*, WTO Doc. IP/C/W/348 (June 11, 2002).

- Special Session of the Council for Trade in Servs., *Guidelines and Procedures for the Negotiations on Trade in Services*, WTO Doc. S/L/93 (Mar. 29, 2001).

- GATT Secretariat, *An Analysis of the Proposed Uruguay Round Agreement, with Particular Emphasis on Aspects of Interest to Developing Countries*, GATT Doc. MTN.TNC/W/122 (Nov. 29, 1993).

(d) Founding agreements. Cite founding agreements according to **rule 21.4.5**:

- Marrakesh Agreement Establishing the World Trade Organization, Apr. 15, 1994, 1867 U.N.T.S. 154 [hereinafter Marrakesh Agreement].

- General Agreement on Tariffs and Trade, Oct. 30, 1947, 61 Stat. A-11, 55 U.N.T.S. 194 [hereinafter GATT].

The Marrakesh Agreement concluded the Uruguay Round, which resulted in a set of agreements and appended annexes, some of which constitute agreements on separate trade issues. Indicate the part(s) of the agreement(s) they attach to, if any:

▶ Understanding on Rules and Procedures Governing the Settlement of Disputes art. 1, Apr. 15, 1994, Marrakesh Agreement Establishing the World Trade Organization, Annex 2, 1869 U.N.T.S. 401 [hereinafter DSU].

GATT-era side agreements should be cited to an unofficial treaty source, such as B.I.S.D.:

▶ Agreement Regarding International Trade in Textiles, Dec. 20, 1973, GATT B.I.S.D. (21st Supp.), at 4 (1975).

Subsequent citations should use the appropriate short form, citing only to articles or paragraphs:

▶ Marrakesh Agreement ¶ 5.

▶ DSU art. 3.7.

(e) Ministerial documents. Cite ministerial documents by name of issuing body and document number, and to an unofficial source, such as International Legal Materials, if therein:

▶ World Trade Organization, Ministerial Declaration of 14 November 2001, WTO Doc. WT/MIN(01)/DEC/1, 41 ILM 746 (2002) [hereinafter Doha Declaration].

(f) Other documents.

(i) **Arbitration documents.** Cite ICSID arbitration documents according to **rule 21.6.**

(ii) **Press releases.** Cite press releases according to **rule 17.2.3.**

(iii) **WTO website.** Some documents may be found on the WTO's website and should be cited in accordance with **rule 18.1.**

21.12   International Monetary Fund

(a) Reports. When citing IMF Annual Reports, Regional Economic Reports, World Economic Outlook Reports, Global Financial Stability Reports, Fiscal Monitors, or any other reports published by the IMF, cite them as you would those from the United Nations (according to **rule 21.7.3**):

▶ IMF, *Promoting a More Secure and Stable Global Economy*, Annual Report 2013 (Apr. 2013).

▶ IMF, *Building Momentum in a Multi-Speed World*, Regional Economic Outlook: Sub-Saharan Africa (May 2013).

▶ IMF, *Hopes, Realities, and Risks*, World Economic Outlook (Apr. 2013).

▶ IMF, *Transition Challenges to Stability*, Global Financial Stability Report (Oct. 2013).

(b) Executive Board documents. Executive Board documents are official papers for circulation to the Executive Board, the Executive Board's Committees, and the staff. The citation should include the name of the body (abbreviated according to **rule 15.1(d)**); the title of the report; the pincite, if available; the document symbol; and the date:

> ► Comm. on Rules for the Regular Election of Exec. Dirs., *Report of the Executive Directors to the Board of Governors on the Fifth Regular Election of Executive Directors*, EB/CREED/54/1 Supp. 1 (July 15, 1954).

> ► Comm. on the Budget, *Notice and Agenda of Meeting 95/3*, EB/CB/A/95/3 (June 26, 1995).

> ► Comm. of the Whole for the 2006 Annual Report, *2006 Annual Report, First Draft—Installment 1*, EB/CW/AR/06/1 (July 18, 2006).

(c) Institutional archives. Institutional archives are departmental archives and other collections. The holdings come in a range of formats including manuscripts, digital records, photographs, audio recordings, and multimedia. Cite these sources in accordance with the rule that governs the format of the document.

(d) Founding agreements. Cite sources as indicated in **rule 21.4.5**:

> ► Articles of Agreement of the IMF art. 8, § 3, 60 Stat. 1401, 2 U.N.T.S. 39.

Other Intergovernmental Organizations   21.13

Cite documents by other international organizations in the same manner as United Nations documents (**rule 21.7**) or the forms in **rules 21.8–21.12**. Citations should generally include: (1) the full name of the author or organization (including an abbreviation from **table T3** in brackets); (2) the title; (3) a pincite, if available; (4) a document number, if available; (5) the full date in parentheses; and (6) a web link or other information essential for locating the document:

> ► Int'l Atomic Energy Agency [IAEA], *Supply Agreement for a Research Reactor in Romania*, at 3, IAEA Doc. INFCIRC/206 (June 12, 1974).

> ► Int'l Civil Aviation Org. [ICAO], *Manual of All-Weather Operations*, at 2-2, ICAO Doc. 9365-AN/910 (3d ed. 2013), http://www.caa.md/files/2013_12/543.pdf.

> ► Org. of African Unity [OAU] Charter art. 3, ¶ 2.

> ► *Decision on the Report of the African Committee of Experts on the Rights and the Wellbeing of Infants*, Executive Council, Seventeenth Ordinary Session, EX.CL/Dec. 569(XVII) (July 19, 2010).

> ► *AMISOM in Action*, African Union Mission in Somalia Newsletter, Issue 1, Aug. 2008, at 10.

> ► Pact of the League of Arab States [LAS] art. 10.

> ► Ass'n of Se. Asian Nations [ASEAN] Charter art. 6, ¶ 2(a).

▶ *Agreement on the Use and Maintenance of the Premises of the ASEAN Secretariat*, art. 2, ¶ 3 (Nov. 25, 1981), http://agreement.asean.org/media/download/20140416152504.pdf.

▶ Moazzam Ali et al., *A Global Research Agenda for Family Planning*, 92 BULLETIN OF THE WORLD HEALTH ORGANIZATION [WHO] 93, 95 (2013), http://www.who.int/bulletin/volumes/92/2/13-122242.pdf.

▶ Christopher Dye et al., *The World Health Report 2013*, WORLD HEALTH ORGANIZATION [WHO] (2013), http://apps.who.int/iris/bitstream /10665/85761/2/9789240690837_eng.pdf.

Cite resolutions in similar fashion to U.N. General Assembly and Security Council resolutions (**rule 21.7.2**), listing the organization, the document number, and the date:

▶ Int'l Atomic Energy Agency [IAEA], General Conference Res. 434, at 2, IAEA Doc. GC (XXVIII)/RES/434 (Sept. 28, 1984).

▶ Int'l Atomic Energy Agency [IAEA], Assembly Res. A15-7 (1964) (no longer in force), *in* Assembly Resolutions in Force, at I-21, ICAO Doc. 9509 (1986).

If useful, provide the title of a resolution or regulation. As with U.N. resolutions, the title comes after the resolution or regulation number:

▶ Int'l Atomic Energy Agency [IAEA], Assembly Res. A15-7, *Condemnation of the Policies of Apartheid and Racial Discrimination of South Africa* (1964) (no longer in force), *in* Assembly Resolutions in Force, at I-21, ICAO Doc. 9509 (1986).

▶ Int'l Telecomm. Union [ITU], Reg. 4.2, *Geographical Distribution and Gender Distribution*, *in* General Secretariat of the International Telecommunication Union, Staff Regulations and Staff Rules, at 32 (2013).

A citation of a source that is difficult to find except online should include information indicating the online location, preferably citing to an official database of sources:

▶ Int'l Maritime Org. [IMO], A. 585 (14), *Provision of Facilities in Ports for the Reception of Oily Wastes from Ships* (Nov. 20, 1985), http://www .imo.org/KnowledgeCentre/IndexofIMOResolutions/Pages/Assembly -%28A%29.aspx.

21.14 International Non-Governmental Organizations (NGOs)

Cite materials from international NGOs analogously to United Nations materials in **rule 21.7**. Include the name of the organization, including the appropriate abbreviation according to **rule 21.13**; the title of the document; the document number, if any; and the date:

▶ Amnesty Int'l, *Sierra Leone: Ending Impunity an Opportunity Not to Be Missed*, AI Index AFR 51/60/2000 (July 26, 2000).

Yearbooks 21.15

Cite United Nations yearbooks according to **rule 21.7.8**. Cite other international yearbooks or annual reports as periodicals (**rule 16**). Italicize article titles, but do not italicize the names of materials not ordinarily italicized (such as case names in footnotes). Give the yearbook title in the original language (abbreviated according to **tables T3, T6, and T13, and rule 20.2.3**) and, if not obvious, the name of the issuing organization. For example:

▶ Ronald Graveson, *The Inequality of the Applicable Law*, 1980 Brit. Y.B. Int'l L. 231, 233.

▶ Revised Staff Regulations, 1922–1925 P.C.I.J. Ann. Rep. (ser. E) No. 1, at 81 (1925).

▶ X. v. Belgium, 1961 Y.B. Eur. Conv. on H.R. (Eur. Comm'n of H.R.) 224.

▶ Jean Boulouis, *Cour de Justice des Communautés Européennes*, 1965 Annuaire Français de Droit International (Centre National de la Recherche Scientifique) 333.

▶ *Recommendations of the Customs Co-Operation Council on the Customs Treatment of Products Imported for Testing*, 1972 Eur. Y.B. (Council of Eur.) 429.

Digests 21.16

Citations to digests should be avoided whenever a more official source is available.

(a) Annual digests. Since 1973, the United States Department of State has published an annual Digest of United States Practice in International Law. Provide the title for the subsection, the year, the title of digest, the chapter and subsection number, and a pincite if available:

▶ U.N. Plan for Namibian Independence, 1989–90 Digest of United States Practice in International Law, ch. 7, §A(1), at 198.

(b) Named digests. Early digests were multi-volume sets edited by a single editor and known by that editor's name. For these digests, provide the title of the section (including subtitles, if relevant, as under **rule 15.3**), the volume cited, the editor's name followed by the word Digest, and the chapter and section number as appropriate, if any:

▶ Access to Courts, 8 Whiteman Digest, ch. 23, §7, at 408.

(c) Foreign digests. When citing digests of another country, cite analogously to those published in the United States. If the digest is published as an annual series, cite according to **rule 21.16(a)**. If the digest is identified by its editor's name, cite according to **rule 21.16(b)**. The first time a foreign digest is cited, always provide the full title, followed by the abbreviation in brackets if useful for subsequent citations, similar to **rule 20.2.3**.

(d) Digests published as periodical sections. When a digest appears as an annual or periodical section of a journal, cite the digest as an article under

rule 16. Otherwise, cite the particular section in question as included in a larger work:

> ▶ John R. Crook, *Contemporary Practice of the United States Relating to International Law*, 104 AM. J. INT'L L. 489 (2010).

21.17 Short Citation Forms

(a) **Treaties and other international agreements.** Subsequent citations to treaties and other international agreements may use both "*id.*" and "*supra.*" Provide the name of the treaty, followed by "*supra*," and the page(s) on which the cited material appears:

> ▶ Convention for the Avoidance of Double Taxation, *supra* note 6, at 25.

> ▶ Treaty on the Non-Proliferation of Nuclear Weapons, *supra* note 1, 21 U.S.T. at 486, 729 U.N.T.S. at 167.

If the first citation contains a "hereinafter" short title, use that short title in subsequent "*supra*" cites.

(b) **International law cases and arbitrations.** Use short forms analogous to those provided in **rule 10.9**.

(c) **United Nations and other intergovernmental organization materials.** Subsequent citations to materials of intergovernmental organizations may use both "*id.*" and "*supra*":

> ▶ G.A. Res. 1962, *supra* note 4, at 22.

> ▶ *Permanent Missions to the United Nations: Report of the Secretary-General*, *supra* note 6, at 18.

If the first citation contains a "hereinafter" short title, use the short title in subsequent "*supra*" cites:

> ▶ Completing the Internal Market, *supra* note 12, at 9.

(d) **Yearbooks and digests.** Subsequent citations to articles in yearbooks and digests should follow the short forms for periodicals (**rule 16.9**). Subsequent citations may use both "*id.*" and "*supra.*"

T1   UNITED STATES JURISDICTIONS

The abbreviations and citation conventions listed in this table, except as noted, are primarily intended to serve a national audience. Practitioners should also adhere to local citation rules (see **Bluepages table BT2**). The preferred sources of citation are suggested when relevant. In the absence of such preference, the user may cite to any listed sources, as appropriate. In general, when citing to online sources, be sure to cite to stable URLs of the specific provision cited in accordance with the principles of **rule 18**.

T1.1   Federal Judicial and Legislative Materials

For more information about the federal court system, including a list of the district courts and the territorial jurisdiction of the courts of appeals, access http://www.uscourts.gov.

Supreme Court (U.S.): Cite to U.S., if therein; otherwise, cite to S. Ct., L. Ed., or U.S.L.W., in that order of preference.

- ▸ United States Reports
    - ▸ 91 U.S. to date   1875–date   U.S.
    - ▸ Wallace   1863–1874   e.g., 68 U.S. (1 Wall.)
    - ▸ Black   1861–1862   e.g., 66 U.S. (1 Black)
    - ▸ Howard   1843–1860   e.g., 42 U.S. (1 How.)
    - ▸ Peters   1828–1842   e.g., 26 U.S. (1 Pet.)
    - ▸ Wheaton   1816–1827   e.g., 14 U.S. (1 Wheat.)
    - ▸ Cranch   1801–1815   e.g., 5 U.S. (1 Cranch)
    - ▸ Dallas   1790–1800   e.g., 1 U.S. (1 Dall.)
- ▸ Supreme Court Reporter   1882–date   S. Ct.
- ▸ United States Supreme Court   1790–date   L. Ed., L. Ed. 2d
  Reports, Lawyers' Edition
- ▸ United States Law Week   1933–date   U.S.L.W.

Circuit Justices (e.g., Sotomayor, J., in chambers): Cite to U.S., if therein; otherwise, cite to S. Ct., Rapp, L. Ed., or U.S.L.W., if therein, in that order of preference.

- ▸ United States Reports   1893–date   U.S.
- ▸ Supreme Court Reporter   1893–date   S. Ct.
- ▸ Rapp's In Chambers Opinions   1925-date   Rapp
- ▸ United States Supreme Court   1790–date   L. Ed., L. Ed. 2d
  Reports, Lawyers' Edition
- ▸ United States Law Week   1933–date   U.S.L.W.

Some cases presided over by Circuit Justices are found in other reporters and should be cited as follows:

- ▶ Halperin v. Kissinger, 807 F.2d 180 (Scalia, Circuit Justice, D.C. Cir. 1986).
- ▶ United States v. Benson, 31 F. 896 (Field, Circuit Justice, C.C.D. Cal. 1887).

Courts of Appeals (e.g., 2d Cir., D.C. Cir.), previously Circuit Courts of Appeals (e.g., 2d Cir.), and **Court of Appeals of/for the District of Columbia** (D.C. Cir.): Cite to F., F.2d, or F.3d, if therein.

▸ Federal Reporter	1891–date	F., F.2d, F.3d
▸ Federal Appendix	2001–date	F. App'x

Circuit Courts (e.g., C.C.S.D.N.Y., C.C.D. Cal.) (abolished 1912): Cite to F. or F. Cas.

▸ Federal Reporter	1880–1912	F.
▸ Federal Cases	1789–1880	F. Cas.

Citations to F. Cas. should give the case number parenthetically.

▸ Oelrich v. Pittsburgh, 18 F. Cas. 598 (C.C.W.D. Pa. 1859) (No. 10,444).

Temporary Emergency Court of Appeals (Temp. Emer. Ct. App.) (created 1971, abolished 1993), **Emergency Court of Appeals** (Emer. Ct. App.) (created 1942, abolished 1961), and **Commerce Court** (Comm. Ct.) (created 1910, abolished 1913): Cite to F. or F.2d.

▸ Federal Reporter	1910–1993	F., F.2d

United States Court of Appeals for the Federal Circuit (Fed. Cir.) (created 1982), successor to the **United States Court of Customs and Patent Appeals** (C.C.P.A.) (previously the **Court of Customs Appeals** (Ct. Cust. App.)) and the appellate jurisdiction of the **Court of Claims** (Ct. Cl.): Cite to F., F.2d, or F.3d, if therein; otherwise, cite to the respective official reporter.

▸ Federal Reporter	1910–date	F., F.2d, F.3d
▸ Court of Claims Reports	1956–1982	Ct. Cl.
▸ Court of Customs and Patent Appeals Reports	1929–1982	C.C.P.A.
▸ Court of Customs Appeals Reports	1910–1929	Ct. Cust.

United States Court of Federal Claims (Fed. Cl.) (created 1992), formerly **United States Claims Court** (Cl. Ct.) (created 1982), and successor to the original jurisdiction of the **Court of Claims** (Ct. Cl.): Cite to one of the following reporters:

▸ Federal Claims Reporter	1992–date	Fed. Cl.
▸ United States Claims Court Reporter	1983–1992	Cl. Ct.
▸ Federal Reporter	1930–1932	F.2d
	1960–1982	F.2d
▸ Federal Supplement	1932–1960	F. Supp.
▸ Court of Claims Reports	1863–1982	Ct. Cl.

United States Court of International Trade (Ct. Int'l Trade) (created 1980), formerly **United States Customs Court** (Cust. Ct.) (created 1926): Cite to the official reporters, if possible; if unavailable, cite to F. Supp., F. Supp. 2d, or F. Supp. 3d, to Cust. B. & Dec. (an official publication), or to I.T.R.D. (BL), in that order of preference.

▸ Court of International Trade Reports	1980–date	Ct. Int'l Trade
▸ Customs Court Reports	1938–1980	Cust. Ct.
▸ Federal Supplement	1980–date	F. Supp., F. Supp. 2d, F. Supp. 3d
▸ Customs Bulletin and Decisions	1967–date	Cust. B. & Dec.
▸ International Trade Reporter Decisions	1980–date	I.T.R.D. (BL)

District Courts (e.g., D. Mass., S.D.N.Y.): For cases after 1932, cite to F. Supp., F. Supp. 2d, F. Supp. 3d, F.R.D., or B.R., if therein; otherwise, cite to Fed. R. Serv., Fed. R. Serv. 2d, or Fed. R. Serv. 3d. For prior cases, cite to F., F.2d, or F. Cas., if therein.

▸ Federal Supplement	1932–date	F. Supp., F. Supp. 2d, F. Supp. 3d
▸ Federal Rules Decisions	1938–date	F.R.D.
▸ West's Bankruptcy Reporter	1979–date	B.R.
▸ Federal Rules Service	1938–date	Fed. R. Serv. (Callaghan), Fed. R. Serv. 2d (Callaghan), Fed. R. Serv. 3d (West)
▸ Federal Reporter	1880–1932	F., F.2d
▸ Federal Cases	1789–1880	F. Cas.

Citations to F. Cas. should give the case number parenthetically.

▸ *Ex parte* McKean, 16 F. Cas. 186 (E.D. Va. 1878) (No. 8,848).

Bankruptcy Courts (e.g., Bankr. N.D. Cal.) and **Bankruptcy Appellate Panels** (e.g., B.A.P. 1st Cir.): Cite to B.R., if therein; otherwise, cite to a service (**rule 19**).

▸ Bankruptcy Reporter	1979–date	B.R.

Judicial Panel on Multidistrict Litigation (J.P.M.L.) (created 1968) and **Special Court, Regional Rail Reorganization Act** (Reg'l Rail Reorg. Ct.) (created 1973): Cite to F. Supp., F. Supp. 2d., or F. Supp. 3d.

▸ Federal Supplement	1968–date	F. Supp., F. Supp. 2d, F. Supp. 3d

Tax Court (T.C.) (created 1942), previously **Board of Tax Appeals** (B.T.A.): Cite to T.C. or B.T.A., if therein; otherwise, cite to T.C.M. (CCH), T.C.M. (P-H), T.C.M. (RIA), or B.T.A.M. (P-H).

▸ United States Tax Court Reports	1942–date	T.C.
▸ Reports of the United States Board of Tax Appeals	1924–1942	B.T.A.
▸ Tax Court Memorandum Decisions	1942–date	T.C.M. (CCH)
	1942–1991	T.C.M. (P-H)
	1991–date	T.C.M. (RIA)
▸ Board of Tax Appeals Memorandum Decisions	1928–1942	B.T.A.M. (P-H)

United States Court of Appeals for Veterans Claims (Vet. App.), previously **United States Court of Veterans Appeals** (Vet. App.) (created 1988): Cite to Vet. App., if therein.

▸ West's Veterans Appeals Reporter   1990–date   Vet. App.

United States Court of Appeals for the Armed Forces (C.A.A.F.), previously **United States Court of Military Appeals** (C.M.A.): Cite to C.M.A., if therein.

▸ Decisions of the United States Court 1951–1975   C.M.A.
   of Military Appeals
▸ West's Military Justice Reporter   1978–date   M.J.
▸ Court Martial Reports   1951–1975   C.M.R.

Military Service Courts of Criminal Appeals (A. Ct. Crim. App., A.F. Ct. Crim. App., C.G. Ct. Crim. App., N-M. Ct. Crim. App.), previously **Courts of Military Review** (e.g., A.C.M.R.), previously **Boards of Review** (e.g., A.B.R.): For cases after 1950, cite to M.J. or C.M.R. For earlier cases, cite to the official reporter.

▸ West's Military Justice Reporter   1975–date   M.J.
▸ Court Martial Reports   1951–1975   C.M.R.

Statutory compilations: Cite to U.S.C., if therein.

▸ United States Code (26 U.S.C. may be abbreviated as I.R.C.)	‹tit. no.› U.S.C. § x (‹year, if desired›)
▸ United States Code Annotated	‹tit. no.› U.S.C.A. § x (West ‹year, if desired›)
▸ United States Code Service	‹tit. no.› U.S.C.S. § x (LexisNexis ‹year, if desired›)
▸ Gould's United States Code Unannotated	‹tit. no.› U.S.C.U. § x (Gould ‹year, if desired›)
▸ Revised Statutes of the United States	‹tit. no.› Rev. Stat. § x (‹edition› ‹year, both edition and year optional›)

Session laws

▸ United States Statutes at Large	‹vol. no.› Stat. ‹page no.› (‹year›)

(Cite public laws before 1957 by chapter number; cite subsequent acts by public law number.)

T1.2   Federal Administrative and Executive Materials

The following is a non-exclusive table of administrative agency and executive materials, with an emphasis on citation forms that vary from **rule 14**. Where an agency entry only lists that agency's official publications, no unique citation format is used and agency materials can be cited following **rule 14**.

Armed Services Board of Contract Appeals (ASBCA)

Decisions: Cite decisions as: ‹case name›, ASBCA No. ‹decision number›, ‹citation to service›. Note that in citations to the *Board of Contract Appeals*

Decisions (BCA), published by Commerce Clearing House, the publisher is not indicated and the volume number serves to indicate the year of the decision.

▶ KAMP Sys., Inc., ASBCA No. 55317, 08-1 BCA ¶ 33,748.

Civilian Board of Contract Appeals (CBCA)

Decisions: Cite in the same manner as decisions of the Armed Services Board of Contract Appeals, but include the opposing agency in the case name. Cite decisions of its predecessors, the Board of Contract Appeals for the Departments of Agriculture, Energy, Housing and Urban Development, Interior, Labor, Transportation, Veterans Affairs, and the General Services Administration, in the same manner.

▶ Flathead Contractors, LLC v. Dep't of Agric., CBCA 118-R, 07-2 BCA ¶ 33,688.

Commodity Futures Trading Commission (CFTC)

Decisions: Cite as: ‹case name›, CFTC No. ‹docket number›, ‹citation to a secondary source if available› (‹date›).

▶ Conway Family Trust v. Dorman Trading, LLC, CFTC No. 12-R002, 2014 WL 2001047 (May 9, 2014).

▶ *In re* J.P. Morgan Sec. LLC, CFTC No. 14–19, 2014 WL 3817865 (July 29, 2014).

Interpretive Letters, No-Action Letters, and Exemptive Letters: Cite a service (**rule 19**) or an electronic database (**rule 18.3**), if therein. Include the full name of the correspondent, if available, the CFTC docket number, and the full date on which the letter became publically available.

▶ Kenneth M. Rosenzweig, CFTC No-Action Letter, CFTCLTR No. 13-54, 2013 WL 5488947 (Sept. 27, 2013).

▶ CFTC No-Action Letter, CFTCLTR No. 94-70, Comm. Fut. L. Rep. (CCH) ¶ 26,159 (May 23, 1994).

Consumer Financial Protection Bureau (CFPB)

Decisions: Cite decisions as: ‹case name›, CFPB No. ‹decision number›, ‹citation to secondary source if available› (‹date›).

▶ ACE Cash Express, Inc., CFPB No. 2014-CFPB-0008 (July 8, 2014).

Department of Agriculture (USDA)

Decisions: Cite to the Agriculture Decisions (Agric. Dec.).

▶ Western Cattle Co., 47 Agric. Dec. 992, 1052 (U.S.D.A. 1988).

Directives: Numerous organizations within the USDA issue directives. These should be cited as: ‹issuing agency abbreviated according to table below› Directive ‹directive number›, ‹directive title› (U.S.D.A. ‹year›).

▶ FSIS Directive 7160.3, Advanced Meat Recovery Using Beef Vertebral Raw Materials (U.S.D.A. 2002).

► Agricultural Marketing Service	AMS
► Agricultural Research Service	ARS
► Animal and Plant Health Inspection Service	APHIS

▸ Center for Nutrition Policy and Promotion	CNPP
▸ Cooperative State Research, Education, and Extension Service	CSREES
▸ Economic Research Service	ERS
▸ Farm Service Agency	FSA
▸ Food and Nutrition Service	FNS
▸ Food Safety and Inspection Service	FSIS
▸ Foreign Agricultural Service	FAS
▸ Forest Service	FS
▸ Grain Inspection, Packers and Stockyards Administration	GIPSA
▸ National Agricultural Library	NAL
▸ National Agricultural Statistics Service	NASS
▸ National Institute of Food and Agriculture	NIFA
▸ National Resources Conservation Service	NRCS
▸ Risk Management Agency	RMA
▸ Rural Business-Cooperative Service	RBS
▸ Rural Development	RD
▸ Rural Housing Service	RHS
▸ Rural Utilities Service	RUS

Department of Commerce, National Oceanic and Atmospheric Administration (NOAA)

Decisions in Consistency Appeals Under the Coastal Zone Management Act: Cite decisions of the Secretary of Commerce under the Coastal Zone Management Act as: Decision and Findings in the Consistency Appeal of ‹party name›, from an objection by ‹state or relevant state agency's name› (Sec'y of Com. ‹date›). To date these decisions are not published in an official reporter; indicate the source where the decision is located.

▶ Decision and Findings in the Consistency Appeal of the Va. Elec. and Power Co., from an objection by the N.C. Dep't of Env't, Health and Nat. Res. (Sec'y of Com. May 19, 1994), http://coast.noaa.gov/data /czm/ consistency/appeals/fcappealdecisions/mediadecisions /virginiaelectric.pdf.

Other NOAA Decisions: Cite decisions of administrative law judges in civil administrative law cases to the *Ocean Resources and Wildlife Reporter* (O.R.W.), if therein. Otherwise cite to an appropriate secondary source.

▶ J.H. Miles & Co., 4 O.R.W. 223 (NOAA 1985).
▶ Rio San Marcos, Inc., 2008 WL 642099 (NOAA Feb. 12, 2008).

Decisions of the Administrator for Appeals (NOAA App.) should so specify.

▶ Lars Vinjerud Fisheries, Inc., 6 O.R.W. 210 (NOAA App. 1990).

Department of Commerce, Patent and Trademark Office (USPTO)

Decisions: Cite decisions of the Commissioner of Patents to *Decisions of the Commissioner of Patents* (Dec. Comm'r Pat.) following **rule 14.3**, except that if the party name includes a procedural phrase, it should be included.

▶ *Ex parte* Latimer, 1889 Dec. Comm'r Pat. 123.

Cite decisions by the Patent Trial and Appeal Board (P.T.A.B.) as: ‹case name›, No. ‹docket number›, ‹citation to secondary source if available› (P.T.A.B. ‹date›). Cite decisions of its predecessor, the Board of Patent Appeals and Interferences (B.P.A.I.) as: ‹case name›, No. ‹docket number›, ‹citation to secondary source if available› (B.P.A.I. ‹date›).

▶ SAP Am., Inc. v. Versata Dev. Grp., Inc., No. CBM2012-00001 (P.T.A.B. June 11, 2013).

▶ *Ex parte* Baggett, No. 2007-2648 (B.P.A.I. Mar. 10, 2008).

▶ *Ex parte* Fallaux, No. 2008-2251, 2008 WL 2463014 (B.P.A.I. June 17, 2008).

Cite decisions of the Trademark Trial and Appeal Board (T.T.A.B.) as: ‹case name›, ‹citation to secondary source› (T.T.A.B. ‹year›).

▶ Bos. Red Sox Baseball Club, Ltd. v. Sherman, 88 U.S.P.Q.2d (BL) 1581 (T.T.A.B. 2008).

Patents: Cite the patent number. The date the patent was filed may be included if relevant.

▶ U.S. Patent No. 4,405,829 (filed Dec. 14, 1977).

The patent name and/or issuing date may be included if relevant.

▶ Cryptographic Commc'ns Sys. & Method, U.S. Patent No. 4,405,829 (filed Dec. 14, 1977) (issued Sept. 20, 1983).

To cite a specific field of the title page, include the field code in brackets.

▶ U.S. Patent No. 4,405,829, at [75] (filed Dec. 14, 1977).

Cite a specific portion of patent text, a patent figure, or an item within a figure according to the following examples:

▶ U.S. Patent No. 4,405,829 col. 2 l. 30 (filed Dec. 14, 1977).

▶ U.S. Patent No. 4,405,829 fig.3 (filed Dec. 14, 1977).

▶ U.S. Patent No. 4,405,829 fig.3, item 22 (filed Dec. 14, 1977).

The short form for a patent includes an apostrophe followed by the last three digits of the patent number.

▶ '829 Patent.

Trademarks: Cite registered trademarks as: ‹TRADEMARK NAME›, Registration No. ‹registration number›.

▶ INTERNATIONAL WALKIE TALKIE, Registration No. 3,016,449.

Where the trademark is unnamed, the description filed with the Trademark Office may be used.

▶ The mark consists of a stylized representation of a peacock, Registration No. 1,931,255.

Cite trademarks that have been filed, but not approved, as: U.S. Trademark Application Serial No. ‹Serial Number› (filed ‹date›).

▶ U.S. Trademark Application Serial No. 77/341,910 (filed Dec. 1, 2007).

Official Publications:

▸ Official Gazette of the United States Patent Office (1872–1971)	Off. Gaz. Pat. Office
▸ Official Gazette of the United States Patent and Trademark Office	Off. Gaz. Pat. & Trademark Office
▸ Trademark Manual of Examining Procedure	TMEP (5th ed. Sept. 2007)
▸ Manual of Patent Examining Procedure	MPEP (8th ed. Rev. 7, Sept. 2008)
▸ Trademark Trial and Appeal Board Manual of Procedure	TBMP (3d ed. Rev. 2, June 2013)

Department of Education

Reports: Cite reports of the *Institute of Education Sciences* as: Institute of Education Sciences, ‹title› ‹page› (‹date›).

▶ Institute of Education Sciences, Evaluation of the Personnel Development Program to Improve Services and Results for Children with Disabilities 12 (2014).

Proceedings: Cite federal student aid proceedings as: ‹case name›, U.S. Dep't of Educ., No. ‹docket number› (‹date›).

▶ Va. Polytechnic Inst. & State Univ., U.S. Dep't of Educ., No. 11-30-SF (Mar. 29, 2012).

Department of Homeland Security, Bureau of Customs and Border Protection

The Bureau of Customs and Border Protection and its predecessors have two official reporters: *Administrative Decisions Under Immigration and Nationality Laws* (I. & N. Dec.) and the *Customs Bulletin and Decisions* (Cust. B. & Dec.).

Department of Justice

Advisory Opinions: Cite published, formal advisory opinions in the same manner as adjudications under **rule 14.3**. Cite Attorney General opinions to *Opinions of the Attorneys General* (Op. Att'ys Gen.) and opinions from the Office of Legal Counsel to *Opinions of the Office of Legal Counsel of the Department of Justice* (Op. O.L.C.).

▶ Legality of Revised Phila. Plan, 42 Op. Att'ys Gen. 405 (1969).

▶ Applicability of Exec. Order No. 12,674 to Pers. of Reg'l Fishery Mgmt. Councils, 17 Op. O.L.C. 150, 154 (1993).

Justice Manual: Cite policies and guidance from the *Justice Manual* (formerly the *U.S. Attorneys' Manual*) as: U.S. Dep't of Just., ‹name of manual›, § ‹section› (‹year›).

▶ U.S. Dep't of Just., Just. Manual § 7-3.300 (2018).

▶ U.S. Dep't of Just., U.S. Att'ys' Manual § 1-1.600 (1988).

Department of Labor

Decisions in Petition for Modification Cases Under Section 101(c) of the Mine Act, 30 U.S.C. § 811(c): At the time of publication, these decisions were not reported in any official reporter or service. Cite as: ‹description of decision›, ‹case name›, Docket No. ‹docket number› (Dep't of Labor ‹date›).

▶ Administrator's Proposed Decision and Order, RAG Emerald Res., Docket No. 2002-MSA-3 (Dep't of Labor Aug. 6, 2002).

▶ ALJ's Decision and Order, RAG Emerald Res., Docket No. 2002-MSA-3 (Dep't of Labor May 16, 2003).

Decisions in Enforcement Actions Brought by the Office of Federal Contract Compliance Programs: At the time of publication, these decisions were not reported in any official reporter or service. Cite as: ‹case name›, ‹docket number›, ‹description of decision› (Dep't of Labor ‹date›).

▶ OFCCP v. Greenwood Mills, Inc., 89-OFC-039, Secretary's Decision and Order of Remand (Dep't of Labor Nov. 20, 1995).

▶ OFCCP v. S. Pac. Transp. Co., 79-OFC-10A, ALJ's Recommended Decision (Dep't of Labor Nov. 9, 1982).

Decisions by the Benefits Review Board: Cite to a service following **rule 19**.

▶ P.M.N. v. Bajkowski Coal Co., 33 Black Lung Rep. (Juris) 1-10 (Ben. Rev. Bd. 2009).

▶ T.M. v. Reinhalter Shipping Co., 44 Ben. Rev. Bd. Serv. (MB) 21, 23 (2009).

Department of the Interior

Cite agency decisions to *Interior Decisions* (Interior Dec.) or *Interior and General Land Office Cases Relating to Public Lands* (Pub. Lands Dec.), if published therein, as per **rule 14.3**.

Where a board within the agency issues the opinion, note the board in the same parenthetical as the date, using the abbreviations below:

▶ Fortune Oil Co., 90 Interior Dec. 84 (IBLA 1983).

▸ Interior Board of Land Appeals   IBLA
▸ Interior Board of Indian Appeals   IBIA

Department of State

Reports: The Department of State publishes reports of the Bureau of Democracy, Human Rights, and Labor. Cite as: U.S. Dep't of State, Bureau of Democracy, H.R. and Lab., ‹title› ‹page› (‹date›).

▶ U.S. Dep't of State, Bureau of Democracy, H.R. and Lab., International Religious Freedom Report 13 (2012).

Department of the Treasury

Regulations: Although Department of Treasury regulations are published under title 26 of the C.F.R., cite as: Treas. Reg. § ‹Treas. Reg. section number›. For unamended regulations, cite to the year of promulgation. If the regulation is a temporary regulation, indicate such:

▶ Treas. Reg. § 1.72-16(a) (1963).

▶ Temp. Treas. Reg. § 1.338-4T(k) (1985).

Citations to specific questions and answers should be cited as:

▶ Treas. Reg. § 1.72-16(a), Q&A (3)(a) (1963).

If any subsection of the cited section has been amended or for some other reason appears in substantially different versions, give the year of the last amendment. Follow this form even if the particular subsection cited has never been amended.

▶ Treas. Reg. § 1.61-2(c) (as amended in 1995).

When the source of the amendment is relevant, indicate it.

▶ Treas. Reg. § 1.61-2(c) (as amended by T.D. 8607, 1995-36 I.R.B. 8).

Cite proposed Treasury regulations to the *Federal Register*.

▶ Prop. Treas. Reg. § 1.704-1, 48 Fed. Reg. 9871, 9872 (Mar. 9, 1983).

Treasury Determinations: Cite Revenue Rulings, Revenue Procedures, and Treasury Decisions to the *Cumulative Bulletin* (C.B.) or its advance sheet, the *Internal Revenue Bulletin* (I.R.B.), or to *Treasury Decisions Under Internal Revenue Laws* (Treas. Dec. Int. Rev.), in that order of preference.

▶ Rev. Rul. 83-137, 1983-2 C.B. 41.

▶ Rev. Proc. 85-47, 1985-37 I.R.B. 10.

▶ T.D. 2747, 20 Treas. Dec. Int. Rev. 457 (1918).

The *Cumulative Bulletin* has been numbered in three series: by volume number from 1919 to 1921, by volume number and part number from 1921 to 1936, and by year and part number from 1937 to date.

▶ T.B.R. 29, 1 C.B. 230 (1919).

▶ I.T. 2624, 11-1 C.B. 122 (1932).

▶ T.D. 7522, 1978-1 C.B. 59.

The abbreviations used in the above examples and other abbreviations are explained in the introductory pages of each volume of the *Cumulative Bulletin*.

Private Letter Rulings: Cite by number and the date issued, if available.

▶ I.R.S. Priv. Ltr. Rul. 86-01-012 (Sept. 30, 1985).

Technical Advice Memoranda: Cite by number and the date issued, if available.

▶ I.R.S. Tech. Adv. Mem. 85-04-005 (Sept. 28, 1984).

General Counsel Memoranda: Cite by number and the date on which the memorandum was approved.

▶ I.R.S. Gen. Couns. Mem. 39,417 (Sept. 30, 1985).

Other Treasury Determinations: Cite all other Treasury materials, including Delegation Orders (Deleg. Order), Treasury Orders (Treas. Order), Treasury Directives (Treas. Dir.), Notices, Announcements, and News Releases to the

Cumulative Bulletin, *Internal Revenue Bulletin*, or *Internal Revenue Manual* (IRM), if therein. Otherwise cite by number and date issued.

▶ I.R.S. Deleg. Order 1-35 (Rev. 1), IRM 1.2.40.17 (June 19, 2008).

▶ I.R.S. Notice 84-9, 1984-1 C.B. 341.

▶ I.R.S. News Release IR-84-111 (Oct. 19, 1984).

Cases: Cite the names of Tax Court and Board of Tax Appeals decisions as those of a court (**rule 10.2**), not as those of an agency.

▶ Benson v. Comm'r, 80 T.C. 789 (1983).

▶ Kovens v. Comm'r, 46 T.C.M. (CCH) 657 (1983).

If the Commissioner of the Internal Revenue Service has published an acquiescence (*acq.*), acquiescence in result only (*acq. in result*), or nonacquiescence (*nonacq.*) in a decision of the Tax Court or Board of Tax Appeals, that fact may be indicated in the citation of the case.

▶ N.M. Bancorp. v. Comm'r, 74 T.C. 1342 (1980), *acq. in result*, 1983-2 C.B. 1.

Similarly, an action on decision (*action on dec.*) may be cited as subsequent history by appending its identifying number, if any, and its full date.

▶ Keller v. Comm'r, 79 T.C. 7 (1982), *action on dec.*, 1984-037 (Apr. 23, 1984).

See generally **rule 10.7** (prior and subsequent history of cases).

Environmental Protection Agency (EPA)

Decisions: Cite decisions to *Environmental Administrative Decisions* (E.A.D.), if therein. Indicate whether the Environmental Appeals Board (EAB) or an administrative law judge made the decision, if not obvious from the source.

▶ Solutia, Inc., 10 E.A.D. 193, 214 (EAB 2001).

▶ Geron Furniture, Inc., 1994 EPA ALJ LEXIS 53.

Equal Employment Opportunity Commission (EEOC)

Decisions: Most EEOC decisions do not have readily identifiable titles, and should therefore be cited using the decision number in place of the title, and otherwise per **rule 14.3**.

▶ EEOC Decision No. 71-444, 4 Fair Empl. Prac. Cas. (BL) 18 (1971).

EEOC Federal Sector decisions have party names and should therefore be cited in accordance with **rule 14.3**.

Executive Office of the President

Executive Orders, Presidential Proclamations, and Reorganization Plans: Cite by page number to 3 C.F.R. as per **rule 14.2** except that, because not all executive orders are reprinted in successive years of the C.F.R., cite to the year of the first edition of the C.F.R. where the executive order was reprinted, rather than that of the most recent edition of the C.F.R. Append a parallel citation to the U.S.C. if also therein.

▶ Exec. Order No. 11,609, 3 C.F.R. 586 (1971–1975), *reprinted as amended in* 3 U.S.C. § 301 app. at 404–07 (2006).

Cite to the *Federal Register* if the material is not in the C.F.R.

▶ Proclamation No. 5366, 50 Fed. Reg. 37365 (Sept. 14, 1985).

A parallel citation to the *Statutes at Large* may also be given.

▶ Reorganization Plan No. 1 of 1978, 3 C.F.R. § 321 (1978), *reprinted in* 5 U.S.C. app. at 1366 (2006), and in 92 Stat. 3781 (1978).

Other Presidential Papers: Cite to the *Public Papers of the Presidents* (PUB. PAPERS), if therein. For material not recorded in the Public Papers, cite the *Weekly Compilation of Presidential Documents* (WEEKLY COMP. PRES. DOC.), published from 1965 to January 29, 2009, the *Daily Compilation of Presidential Documents* (DAILY COMP. PRES. DOC.), published from January 29, 2009 to date, or the *U.S. Code Congressional and Administrative News* (U.S.C.C.A.N.) (**rule 12.6**).

▶ Memorandum on New Tools to Help Parents Balance Work and Family, 1 PUB. PAPERS 841 (May 24, 1999).

▶ Presidential Statement on Signing the Consolidated Appropriations Resolution, 2003, 39 WEEKLY COMP. PRES. DOC. 225 (Feb. 20, 2003).

▶ Remarks on the National Economy, 2009 DAILY COMP. PRES. DOC. 2 (Feb. 4, 2009).

Budgets: Cite governmental budgets as books (**rule 15**).

▶ [OFF.] OF MGMT. & BUDGET, EXEC. [OFF.] OF THE PRESIDENT, BUDGET OF THE UNITED STATES GOVERNMENT, FISCAL YEAR 2003 (2002).

Federal Aviation Administration (FAA)

Decisions: Cite decisions of administrative law judges in civil penalty enforcement matters adjudicated under 14 C.F.R. Part 13, Section 13.16 and subpart G, as slip opinions following **rule 14.3.2(b)**.

▶ Siddall, Docket No. CP05WP0016 (FAA Oct. 7, 2008).

Decisions of the Administrator or his delegate are cited using an order number rather than a docket number.

▶ Alaska Airlines, Inc., FAA Order No. 2004-8, 2004 WL 319820 (Oct. 4, 2004).

Decisions of the Office of Dispute Resolution for Acquisition (ODRA) adjudicated under 14 C.F.R. Part 17 should incorporate the type of dispute in the citation.

▶ Protest of the United Parcel Service, Docket No. 08-ODRA-0400 (Sept. 12, 1999).

Citations to other FAA decisions and orders should indicate the nature of the decision preceding the date.

▶ Paul D. Asmus & P.D. Aviation Consulting v. Haw. Dep't of Transp., Docket No. 16-05-11, Determination of the Director of Compliance and Field Operations (Apr. 12, 2006).

▶ Steere v. County of San Diego, FAA Docket No. 16-99-15, Final Agency Decision (Dec. 7, 2004).

Federal Communications Commission (FCC)
Cite to the *Federal Communications Commission Reports* (F.C.C., F.C.C.2d), published 1934–1986, or the *Federal Communications Commission Record* (FCC Rcd.), published since 1986.

Federal Energy Regulatory Commission (FERC)
Cite decisions to the *Federal Energy Guidelines: FERC Reports* (FERC).

Federal Labor Relations Authority (FLRA)
Cite decisions to the *Decisions of the Federal Labor Relations Authority* (F.L.R.A.).

Federal Mine Safety and Health Review Commission (FMSHRC)
Cite decisions to the *Federal Mine Safety and Health Review Commission Decisions* (FMSHRC).

Federal Reserve System
Enforcement Actions: Cite written agreements resulting from enforcement actions as: Written Agreement Between ‹private bank name› and ‹Federal Reserve Bank name›, Docket No. ‹docket number› (‹date›).

▶ Written Agreement Between Ridgedale State Bank and Federal Reserve Bank of Minneapolis, Docket No. 03-024-WA/RB-SM (July 29, 2003).

Federal Trade Commission (FTC)
Cite decisions to the *Federal Trade Commission* (F.T.C.).

Government Accountability Office (GAO)
Bid Protest Decisions: Cite to *Decisions of the Comptroller General of the United States* (Comp. Gen.), if therein.

▶ Astrophysics Research Corp., 66 Comp. Gen. 211 (1987).

Cite unpublished decisions to a readily accessible source, as follows: ‹protesting party›, ‹docket number›, ‹volume number or year› ‹source› ‹location within source volume or year› (Comp. Gen. ‹date›). Note that when citing these cases to the *Comptroller General's Procurement Decisions*, published by West, the publisher is not indicated:

▶ Def. Sys. Grp., B-240295, 1990 WL 293536 (Comp. Gen. Nov. 6, 1990).
▶ Info. Ventures, Inc., B-232094, 88-2 CPD ¶ 443 (Comp. Gen. Nov. 4, 1988).

Where a decision resolves multiple bid protests, each of which has its own docket number, indicate this by inserting "et al." after the docket number.

▶ Midland Supply, Inc., B-298720 et al., 2007 CPD ¶ 2 (Comp. Gen. Nov. 29, 2006).

International Trade Commission (USITC)
Publications: For investigations, cite as: ‹title or case name›, Inv. No. ‹number›, USITC Pub. ‹number› (‹date›) (‹status›). Where a single decision contains multiple investigation numbers, this should be indicated. For other publications, omit investigation number and status.

▶ Certain Tissue Paper Prods. from China, Inv. No. 731-TA-1070B, USITC Pub. 3758 (Mar. 25, 2005) (Final).

▶ Grain-Oriented Silicon Elec. Steel from It. & Japan, Inv. Nos. 701-TA-355, 731-TA-659-660, USITC Pub. 3396 (Feb. 7, 2001) (Preliminary).

Merit Systems Protection Board (MSPB)

Cite decisions to the *Decisions of the United States Merit Systems Protection Board* (M.S.P.B.).

National Labor Relations Board (NLRB)

Cite decisions and orders to the *Decisions and Orders of the National Labor Relations Board* (N.L.R.B.).

National Mediation Board (NMB)

Cite decisions to the *Decisions of the National Mediation Board* (N.M.B.).

National Transportation Safety Board (NTSB)

Cite decisions to the *National Transportation Safety Board Decisions* (N.T.S.B.), published from 1967–1977, if therein.

Nuclear Regulatory Commission (NRC)

Cite decisions of the Nuclear Regulatory Commission to the *Nuclear Regulatory Commission Issuances* (N.R.C.). Cite decisions of its predecessor, the Atomic Energy Commission (1956–1975), to the *Atomic Energy Commission Reports* (A.E.C.).

Occupational Safety and Health Review Commission (OSHRC)

Decisions: Cite commission decisions reported in a service as: ‹party name›, ‹service volume number› ‹publisher› ‹service, abbreviated as below› ‹page/paragraph number› (No. ‹docket number›, ‹year›).

▶ Burkes Mech., Inc., 21 BL OSHC 2136 (No. 04-0475, 2007).
  or: Burkes Mech., Inc., 2007 CCH OSHD ¶ 32,922 (No. 04-0475, 2007).

Where an administrative law judge, rather than the commission itself, issued the decision, indicate this parenthetically at the end of the citation.

▶ Pike Elec., Inc., 21 BL OSHC 2153 (No. 06-0166, 2007) (ALJ).

OSHRC uses abbreviations for services reporting its decisions that vary from **table T15**:

▶ Occupational Safety & Health Cases (BL)   OSHC
▶ Occupational Safety & Health Decisions   OSHD

Where a decision is not cited in any service or database, it may be cited as a slip opinion using **rule 14.3.2(b)**.

▶ Z & P Builders, No. 08-0930 (OSHRC Dec. 19, 2008).

Securities and Exchange Commission (SEC)

Interpretive Letters, No-Action Letters, and Exemptive Letters: Cite a service (**rule 19**) or an electronic database (**rule 18.3**). Include the full name of the correspondent and the full date on which the letter became publicly available.

▶ Union Carbide Corp., SEC Staff No-Action Letter, [1994–1995 Transfer Binder] Fed. Sec. L. Rep. (CCH) ¶ 76,911 (Apr. 15, 1994).

▶ Squadron, Ellenoff, Plesent & Lehrer, SEC Interpretive Letter, 1992 WL 55818 (Feb. 28, 1992).

Releases: Cite the *Federal Register*, SEC Docket, or a service (**rule 19**). If the release has a subject-matter title, it may be presented in a shortened form. Include the act under which the release was issued, the release number, and the full date.

▶ Customer Limit Orders, Exchange Act Release No. 34,753, [1994–1995 Transfer Binder] Fed. Sec. L. Rep. (CCH) ¶ 85,434 (Sept. 29, 1994).

▶ Regulation of Securityholder Communications, Exchange Act Release No. 29,315, 49 SEC Docket 147 (June 17, 1991).

If the release is an adjudication, abbreviate the parties' names according to **rule 14.3.1(a)**.

▶ Am. Kiosk Corp., Exchange Act Release No. 58504, 2008 WL 2574438 (June 27, 2008).

If the adjudication occurred before an administrative law judge, indicate this fact in the date parenthetical.

▶ Am. Kiosk Corp., Exchange Act Release No. 57866, 2008 WL 2229644 (ALJ May 30, 2008) (default order).

If a particular release is issued under the Securities Act, the Exchange Act, or the Investment Company Act, a parallel citation should be given in that order.

▶ Implementation of Standards of Professional Conduct for Attorneys, Securities Act Release No. 8150, Exchange Act Release No. 46,868, Investment Company Act Release No. 25,829, 67 Fed. Reg. 71670 (proposed Dec. 2, 2002).

Staff Interpretations: Cite SEC Staff Accounting Bulletins, Staff Legal Bulletins, and Telephone Interpretations as follows:

▶ SEC Staff Accounting Bulletin No. 56, 49 Fed. Reg. 4936 (May 23, 1984).

SEC Filings: For annual reports, proxy statements, and other company filings required under federal securities laws, provide the name of the company (abbreviated according to **rule 15.1(d)**), the title as given in the document, the form type in parentheses, the page number if applicable, and the full date of filing with the SEC.

▶ Coca-Cola Co., Annual Report (Form 10-K) (Feb. 27, 2004).

▶ Sony Music Entm't Inc., Statement of Changes in Beneficial Ownership (Form 4/A) (Jan. 23, 2004).

If citing annual reports, proxy statements, or other documents in a form other than that filed with the SEC, treat as books under **rule 15**.

▶ Coca-Cola Co., 2003 Summary Annual Report 7 (2004).

Small Business Administration (SBA)
Decisions: Cite decisions as: ‹party name›, SBA No. ‹docket number› (‹date›).

▶ Ace Tech., LLC, SBA No. SDBA-178 (Apr. 17, 2008).

The docket number indicates the type of decision:

- ▸ Economically Disadvantaged Women Owned   EDWOSB
  Small Business
- ▸ Business development program   BDP
- ▸ Service disabled veteran owned business   VET
- ▸ Size determination   SIZ
- ▸ Small disadvantaged business   SDBA
- ▸ North American Industry Classification   NAICS
  System
- ▸ Women Owned Small Business Program   WOSB

Social Security Administration (SSA)

Rulings and Acquiescence Rulings: Cite to the *Social Security Rulings, Cumulative Edition* (S.S.R. Cum. Ed.), if therein. If not located therein, cite to another official source, such as the *Code of Federal Regulations* or the *Federal Register*. Otherwise, cite a commercial database or other readily available source. Cite Social Security Rulings as SSR and Social Security Acquiescence Rulings as SSAR.

- ▶ SSAR 92-2(6), 57 Fed. Reg. 9262 (Mar. 17, 1992).
- ▶ SSR 00-4p, 2000 WL 1898704 (Dec. 4, 2000).

Surface Transportation Board (STB)

Cite materials from the Surface Transportation Board (STB) to the *Surface Transportation Board Reporter* (S.T.B.). Cite materials from its predecessor, the Interstate Commerce Commission (ICC), to the *Interstate Commerce Commission Reporter* (I.C.C., I.C.C.2d).

For unpublished decisions, the official date is the date on which the STB (or ICC) served the decision on the parties or otherwise filed it, not the date of the decision itself.

T1.3   States and the District of Columbia

....

Alabama (Ala.)

http://judicial.alabama.gov
http://alisondb.legislature.state.al.us/acas/ACASLoginMac.asp

Supreme Court (Ala.): Cite to So., So. 2d, or So. 3d, if therein.

▸ Southern Reporter	1886–date	So., So. 2d, So. 3d
▸ Alabama Reports	1840–1976	Ala.
▸ Porter	1834–1839	Port.
▸ Stewart and Porter	1831–1834	Stew. & P.
▸ Stewart	1827–1831	Stew.
▸ Minor	1820–1826	Minor

Court of Civil Appeals (Ala. Civ. App.) and **Court of Criminal Appeals** (Ala. Crim. App.), before 1969 **Court of Appeals** (Ala. Ct. App.): Cite to So., So. 2d, or So. 3d, if therein.

▸ Southern Reporter	1911–date	So., So. 2d, So. 3d
▸ Alabama Appellate Courts Reports	1911–1974	Ala. App.

Statutory compilations: Cite to ALA. CODE (published by West), if therein.

- Code of Alabama, 1975 (West)   ALA. CODE § x-x-x ‹year›
- Michie's Alabama Code, 1975 (LexisNexis)   ALA. CODE § x-x-x (LexisNexis ‹year›)

Session laws: Cite to Ala. Laws, if therein.

- Alabama Laws   ‹year› Ala. Laws ‹page no.›
- West's Alabama Legislative Service   ‹year› Ala. Legis. Serv. ‹page no.› (West)
- Michie's Alabama Code ‹year› Advance Legislative Service (LexisNexis)   ‹year›-‹pamph. no.› Ala. Adv. Legis. Serv. ‹page no.› (LexisNexis)

Administrative compilation

- Alabama Administrative Code   ALA. ADMIN. CODE r. x-x-x.x (‹year›)

Administrative register

- Alabama Administrative Monthly   ‹vol. no.› Ala. Admin. Monthly ‹page no.› (‹month day, year›)

....

Alaska (Alaska)

http://www.courts.alaska.gov
http://w3.legis.state.ak.us

Supreme Court (Alaska): Cite to P.2d or P.3d.

- Pacific Reporter   1960–date   P.2d, P.3d

Court of Appeals (Alaska Ct. App.): Cite to P.2d or P.3d.

- Pacific Reporter   1980–date   P.2d, P.3d

District Courts of Alaska (D. Alaska): These courts had local jurisdiction from 1884 to 1959. Cite to F. Supp., F., or F.2d, if therein; otherwise, cite to Alaska or Alaska Fed., in that order of preference.

- Federal Supplement   1946–1959   F. Supp.
- Federal Reporter   1886–1932   F., F.2d
- Alaska Reports   1887–1958   Alaska
- Alaska Federal Reports   1869–1937   Alaska Fed.

United States District Courts for California and Oregon, and **District Courts of Washington** (D. Cal., D. Or., D. Wash.): These courts had local jurisdiction in Alaska until 1884. Cite to F. or F. Cas.

- Federal Reporter   1880–1884   F.
- Federal Cases   1867–1880   F. Cas.

(Citations to F. Cas. should give the case number parenthetically, e.g., The Ocean Spray, 18 F. Cas. 558 (D. Or. 1876) (No. 10,412).)

- Alaska Federal Reports   1869–1937   Alaska Fed.

Statutory compilations: Cite to ALASKA STAT., if therein.

▶ Alaska Statutes (LexisNexis)	ALASKA STAT. § x.x.x (‹year›)
▶ West's Alaska Statutes Annotated	ALASKA STAT. ANN. § x.x.x (West ‹year›)

Session laws: Cite to Alaska Sess. Laws, if therein.

▶ Session Laws of Alaska	‹year› Alaska Sess. Laws ch. x, § x
▶ Alaska Statutes ‹year› Advance Legislative Service (LexisNexis)	‹year›-‹pamph. no.› Alaska Adv. Legis. Serv. ‹page no.› (LexisNexis)
▶ West's Alaska Legislative Service	‹year› Alaska Legis. Serv. ‹page no.› (West)

Administrative compilation

▶ Alaska Administrative Code (LexisNexis)	ALASKA ADMIN. CODE tit. x, § x.x (‹year›)

....

Arizona (Ariz.)

http://www.azcourts.gov
http://www.azleg.gov/ArizonaRevisedStatutes.asp

Supreme Court (Ariz.): Cite to P., P.2d, or P.3d, if therein.

▶ Pacific Reporter	1883–date	P., P.2d, P.3d
▶ Arizona Reports	1866–date	Ariz.

Court of Appeals (Ariz. Ct. App.): Cite to P.2d or P.3d, if therein.

▶ Pacific Reporter	1965–date	P.2d, P.3d
▶ Arizona Reports	1976–date	Ariz.
▶ Arizona Appeals Reports	1965–1977	Ariz. App.

Tax Court (Ariz. Tax Ct.): Cite to P.2d or P.3d, if therein.

▶ Pacific Reporter	1988–date	P.2d, P.3d

Statutory compilations: Cite to one of the following codes.

▶ Arizona Revised Statutes Annotated (West)	ARIZ. REV. STAT. ANN. § x-x (‹year›)
▶ Arizona Revised Statutes (LexisNexis)	ARIZ. REV. STAT. § x-x (LexisNexis ‹year›)

Session laws: Cite to Ariz. Sess. Laws, if therein.

▶ Session Laws, Arizona	‹year› Ariz. Sess. Laws ‹page no.›
▶ Arizona Legislative Service (West)	‹year› Ariz. Legis. Serv. ‹page no.› (West)

Administrative compilation

▶ Arizona Administrative Code	ARIZ. ADMIN. CODE § x-x-x (‹year›)

Administrative register

▸ Arizona Administrative Register ⟨vol. no.⟩ Ariz. Admin. Reg. ⟨page no.⟩ (⟨month day, year⟩)

. . . .

Arkansas (Ark.)

http://www.arcourts.gov
http://www.arkleg.state.ar.us

Public domain citation format: Arkansas has adopted a public domain citation format for cases after February 13, 2009. The format is:

▶ Smith v. Hickman, 2009 Ark. 12, at 1, 273 S.W.3d 340, 343.

▶ Doe v. State, 2009 Ark. App. 318, at 7, 2009 WL 240613, at *8.

For additional instruction, consult Arkansas Supreme Court Rule 5-2.

Supreme Court (Ark.): Cite to S.W., S.W.2d, or S.W.3d, if therein.

▸ South Western Reporter	1886–date	S.W., S.W.2d, or S.W.3d
▸ Arkansas Reports	1837–2009	Ark.

Court of Appeals (Ark. Ct. App.): Cite to S.W.2d OR S.W.3d, if therein.

▸ South Western Reporter	1979–date	S.W.2d, S.W.3d
▸ Arkansas Appellate Reports	1981–2009	Ark. App.
▸ Arkansas Reports	1979–1981	Ark.

Statutory compilations: Cite to ARK. CODE ANN. (published by LexisNexis), if therein.

▸ Arkansas Code of 1987 Annotated (LexisNexis)	ARK. CODE ANN. § x-x-x (⟨year⟩)
▸ West's Arkansas Code Annotated	ARK. CODE ANN. § x-x-x (West ⟨year⟩)

Session laws: Cite to Ark. Acts, if therein.

▸ Acts of Arkansas (West)	⟨year⟩ Ark. Acts ⟨page no.⟩
▸ Arkansas Code of 1987 Annotated ⟨year⟩ Advance Legislative Service (LexisNexis)	⟨year⟩-⟨pamph. no.⟩ Ark. Adv. Legis. Serv. ⟨page no.⟩ (LexisNexis)
▸ West's Arkansas Legislative Service	⟨year⟩ Ark. Legis. Serv. ⟨page no.⟩ (West)

Administrative compilation

▸ Code of Arkansas Rules (LexisNexis)	x-x-x ARK. CODE R. § x (LexisNexis ⟨year⟩)

Administrative registers: Cite to Ark. Reg., if therein.

▸ Arkansas Register	⟨vol. no.⟩ Ark. Reg. ⟨page no.⟩ (⟨month year⟩)
▸ Arkansas Government Register	⟨iss. no.⟩ Ark. Gov't Reg. ⟨page no.⟩ (LexisNexis ⟨month year⟩)

....

California (Cal.)

http://www.courts.ca.gov
http://leginfo.legislature.ca.gov

Supreme Court (Cal.): Cite to P., P.2d, or P.3d, if therein.

▸ Pacific Reporter	1883–date	P., P.2d, P.3d
▸ California Reports	1850–date	Cal., Cal. 2d, Cal. 3d, Cal. 4th
▸ West's California Reporter	1959–date	Cal. Rptr., Cal. Rptr. 2d, Cal. Rptr. 3d
▸ California Unreported Cases	1855–1910	Cal. Unrep.

Court of Appeal (Cal. Ct. App.), previously **District Court of Appeal** (Cal. Dist. Ct. App.): Cite to P. or P.2d (before 1960) or Cal. Rptr., Cal. Rptr. 2d (after 1959), or Cal. Rptr. 3d, if therein.

▸ West's California Reporter	1959–date	Cal. Rptr., Cal. Rptr. 2d, Cal. Rptr. 3d
▸ Pacific Reporter	1905–1959	P., P.2d
▸ California Appellate Reports	1905–date	Cal. App., Cal. App. 2d, Cal. App. 3d, Cal. App. 4th

Appellate Divisions of the Superior Court (Cal. App. Dep't Super. Ct.): Cite to P. or P.2d (before 1960) or to Cal. Rptr., Cal. Rptr. 2d (after 1959), or Cal. Rptr. 3d, if therein.

▸ West's California Reporter	1959–date	Cal. Rptr., Cal. Rptr. 2d, Cal. Rptr. 3d
▸ Pacific Reporter	1929–1959	P., P.2d
▸ California Appellate Reports Supplement (bound with Cal. App.)	1929–date	Cal. App. Supp., Cal. App. 2d Supp., Cal. App. 3d Supp., Cal. App. 4th Supp.

Statutory compilations: Cite to either the West or the Deering subject-matter code, if therein.

▸ West's Annotated California Codes	Cal. ⟨Subject⟩ Code § x (West ⟨year⟩)
▸ Deering's California Codes, Annotated (LexisNexis)	Cal. ⟨Subject⟩ Code § x (Deering ⟨year⟩)
▸ Agricultural (renamed "Food and Agricultural" in 1972)	Agric.
▸ Business and Professions	Bus. & Prof.
▸ Civil	Civ.
▸ Civil Procedure	Civ. Proc.
▸ Commercial	Com.
▸ Corporations	Corp.
▸ Education	Educ.
▸ Elections	Elec.
▸ Evidence	Evid.
▸ Family	Fam.
▸ Financial	Fin.
▸ Fish and Game	Fish & Game
▸ Food and Agricultural (formerly "Agricultural")	Food & Agric.
▸ Government	Gov't
▸ Harbors and Navigation	Harb. & Nav.
▸ Health and Safety	Health & Safety

▸ Insurance	INS.
▸ Labor	LAB.
▸ Military and Veterans	MIL. & VET.
▸ Penal	PENAL
▸ Probate	PROB.
▸ Public Contract	PUB. CONT.
▸ Public Resources	PUB. RES.
▸ Public Utilities	PUB. UTIL.
▸ Revenue and Taxation	REV. & TAX.
▸ Streets and Highways	STS. & HIGH.
▸ Unemployment Insurance	UNEMP. INS.
▸ Vehicle	VEH.
▸ Water	WATER
▸ Welfare and Institutions	WELF. & INST.

Session laws: Cite to Cal. Stat., if therein.

▸ Statutes of California	‹year› Cal. Stat. ‹page no.›
▸ West's California Legislative Service	‹year› Cal. Legis. Serv. ‹page no.› (West)
▸ Deering's California Advance Legislative Service (LexisNexis)	‹year›-‹pamph. no.› Cal. Adv. Legis. Serv. ‹page no.› (LexisNexis)

Administrative compilation

▸ California Code of Regulations (West)	CAL. CODE REGS. tit. x, § x (‹year›)

Administrative register

▸ California Regulatory Notice Register	‹iss. no.› Cal. Regulatory Notice Reg. ‹page no.› (‹month day, year›)

Colorado (Colo.)

http://www.courts.state.co.us
http://www.leg.colorado.gov

Public domain citation format: Colorado has adopted a public domain citation format for cases after January 1, 2012. The format is:

▶ Iannone v. Callahan, 2012 CO 22, ¶ 13.

▶ Callahan v. Iannone, 2015 COA 14, ¶¶ 8–12.

For additional information, consult Rules of the Supreme Court of Colorado, Chief Justice Directive 12-01.

Supreme Court (Colo.): Cite to P., P.2d, or P.3d, if therein; otherwise, cite to Colo., if therein, or to Colo. Law. or Brief Times Rptr.

▸ Pacific Reporter	1883–date	P., P.2d, P.3d
▸ Colorado Reports	1864–1980	Colo.
▸ Colorado Lawyer	1972–date	Colo. Law.
▸ Brief Times Reporter	1977–1996	Brief Times Rptr.
▸ Colorado Journal	1996–2002	Colo. J.
▸ Law Week Colorado	2002–date	L. Week Colo.

Court of Appeals (Colo. App.): Cite to P., P.2d, or P.3d, if therein; otherwise, cite to Colo. App., if therein, or else to one of the other reporters listed below.

► Pacific Reporter	1970–date	P.2d, P.3d
	1912–1915	P.
	1891–1905	P.
► Colorado Court of Appeals Reports	1891–1905	Colo. App.
	1912–1915	Colo. App.
	1970–1980	Colo. App.
► Colorado Lawyer	1972–date	Colo. Law.
► Brief Times Reporter	1977–1996	Brief Times Rptr.
► Colorado Journal	1996–2002	Colo. J.
► Law Week Colorado	2002–date	L. Week Colo.

Statutory compilations: Cite to COLO. REV. STAT., if therein.

► Colorado Revised Statutes (LexisNexis)	COLO. REV. STAT. § x-x-x (‹year›)
► West's Colorado Revised Statutes Annotated	COLO. REV. STAT. ANN. § x-x-x (West ‹year›)

Session laws: Cite to Colo. Sess. Laws, if therein.

► Session Laws of Colorado (LexisNexis)	‹year› Colo. Sess. Laws ‹page no.›
► Colorado Legislative Service (West)	‹year› Colo. Legis. Serv. ‹page no.› (West)

Administrative compilations: Cite to COLO. CODE REGS., if therein.

► Colorado Code of Regulations	COLO. CODE REGS. § x-x (‹year›)
► Code of Colorado Regulations (LexisNexis)	‹vol. no.› COLO. CODE REGS. § x-x (LexisNexis ‹year›)

Administrative register

► Colorado Register	‹iss. no.› Colo. Reg. ‹page no.› (‹month year›)

....

Connecticut (Conn.)

http://www.jud.ct.gov
http://www.cga.ct.gov/current/pub/titles.htm

Supreme Court (Conn.), previously **Supreme Court of Errors** (Conn.): Cite to A., A.2d, or A.3d, if therein.

► Atlantic Reporter	1885–date	A., A.2d, A.3d
► Connecticut Reports	1814–date	Conn.
► Day	1802–1813	Day
► Root	1789–1798	Root
► Kirby	1785–1789	Kirby

Appellate Court (Conn. App. Ct.): Cite to A.2d or A.3d, if therein.

► Atlantic Reporter	1983–date	A.2d, A.3d
► Connecticut Appellate Reports	1983–date	Conn. App.

Superior Court (Conn. Super. Ct.) and **Court of Common Pleas** (Conn. C.P.): Cite to A.2d or A.3d, if therein; otherwise, cite to Conn. Supp., if therein, or else to one of the other reporters listed below.

▸ Atlantic Reporter	1954–date	A.2d, A.3d
▸ Connecticut Supplement	1935–date	Conn. Supp.
▸ Connecticut Law Reporter	1990–date	Conn. L. Rptr.
▸ Connecticut Superior Court Reports	1986–1994	Conn. Super. Ct.

Circuit Court (Conn. Cir. Ct.): Cite to A.2d or A.3d, if therein.

▸ Atlantic Reporter	1961–1974	A.2d, A.3d
▸ Connecticut Circuit Court Reports	1961–1974	Conn. Cir. Ct.

Statutory compilations: Cite to CONN. GEN. STAT., if therein.

▸ General Statutes of Connecticut	CONN. GEN. STAT. § x-x (‹year›)
▸ Connecticut General Statutes Annotated (West)	CONN. GEN. STAT. ANN. § x-x (West ‹year›)

Session laws: Cite to Conn. Acts, Conn. Pub. Acts, or Conn. Spec. Acts, if therein.

▸ Connecticut Public & Special Acts	1972–date	‹year› Conn. Acts ‹page no.› ([Reg. or Spec.] Sess.)
▸ Connecticut Public Acts	1650–1971	‹year› Conn. Pub. Acts ‹page no.›
▸ Connecticut Special Acts	1789–1971	‹year› Conn. Spec. Acts ‹page no.›

(published under various titles—i.e., Resolves & Private Laws, Private & Special Laws, Special Laws, Resolves & Private Acts, Resolutions & Private Acts, Private Acts & Resolutions, and Special Acts & Resolutions—and with various volume designations—i.e., by year or volume number)

▸ Connecticut Legislative Service (West)	‹year› Conn. Legis. Serv. ‹page no.› (West)

Administrative compilation

▸ Regulations of Connecticut State Agencies	CONN. AGENCIES REGS. § x-x-x (‹year›)

Administrative registers: Cite to Conn. L.J., if therein.

▸ Connecticut Law Journal	‹vol. no.› Conn. L.J. ‹page no.› (‹month day, year›)
▸ Connecticut Government Register (LexisNexis)	‹iss. no.› Conn. Gov't Reg. ‹page no.› (LexisNexis ‹month year›)

Delaware (Del.)

http://www.courts.delaware.gov
http://www.delcode.delaware.gov

Supreme Court (Del.), previously **Court of Errors and Appeals** (Del.): Cite to A., A.2d, or A.3d, if therein.

- ► Atlantic Reporter   1886–date   A., A.2d, A.3d
- ► Delaware Reports
  - ► 31 Del. to 59 Del.   1919–1966   Del.
  - ► Boyce   1909–1920   e.g., 24 Del. (1 Boyce)
  - ► Pennewill   1897–1909   e.g., 17 Del. (1 Penne.)
  - ► Marvel   1893–1897   e.g., 15 Del. (1 Marv.)
  - ► Houston   1855–1893   e.g., 6 Del. (1 Houst.)
  - ► Harrington   1832–1855   e.g., 1 Del. (1 Harr.)
  - ► Delaware Cases   1792–1830   Del. Cas.

Court of Chancery (Del. Ch.): Cite to A., A.2d, or A.3d, if therein.

- ► Atlantic Reporter   1886–date   A., A.2d, A.3d
- ► Delaware Chancery Reports   1814–1968   Del. Ch.
- ► Delaware Cases   1792–1830   Del. Cas.

Superior Court (Del. Super. Ct.), previously **Superior Court and Orphans' Court** (Del. Super. Ct. & Orphans' Ct.): Cite to A.2d or A.3d, if therein; otherwise, cite to one of the official reporters listed under **Supreme Court** (Del.).

- ► Atlantic Reporter   1951–date   A.2d, A.3d

Family Court (Del. Fam. Ct.): Cite to A.2d or A.3d.

- ► Atlantic Reporter   1977–date   A.2d, A.3d

Statutory compilations: Cite to DEL. CODE ANN., if therein.

- ► Delaware Code Annotated   DEL. CODE ANN. tit. x, § x
  (LexisNexis)   (‹year›)
- ► West's Delaware Code Annotated   DEL. CODE ANN. tit. x, § x
                                            (West ‹year›)

Session laws: Cite to Del. Laws, if therein.

- ► Laws of Delaware   ‹vol. no.› Del. Laws ‹page no.›
                                            (‹year›)
- ► Delaware Code Annotated ‹year› Advance   ‹year›-‹pamph. no.›
  Legislative Service (LexisNexis)   Del. Code. Ann. Adv.
                                            Legis. Serv. ‹page no.›
                                            (LexisNexis)
- ► West's Delaware Legislative   ‹year› Del. Legis. Serv. ‹page
  Service   no.› (West)

Administrative compilations: Cite to DEL. ADMIN. CODE, if therein.

- ► Delaware Administrative Code   x-x-x DEL. ADMIN. CODE § x
                                            (‹year›)
- ► Code of Delaware Regulations (LexisNexis)   x-x-x DEL. CODE REGS. § x
                                            (LexisNexis ‹year›)

Administrative registers: Cite to Del. Reg. Regs., if therein.

- ► Delaware Register of Regulations   ‹vol. no.› Del. Reg. Regs.
                                            ‹page no.› (‹month day,
                                            year›)
- ► Delaware Government Register (LexisNexis)   ‹iss. no.› Del. Gov't Reg.
                                            ‹page no.› (LexisNexis
                                            ‹month year›)

District of Columbia (D.C.)

http://www.dccourts.gov
https://code.dccouncil.us/dc/council/code/

Court of Appeals (D.C.), previously **Municipal Court of Appeals** (D.C.): Cite
to A.2d or A.3d.

► Atlantic Reporter	1943–date	A.2d, A.3d

United States Court of Appeals for the District of Columbia Circuit (D.C.
Cir.), previously **Court of Appeals of/for the District of Columbia** (D.C. Cir.),
previously **Supreme Court of the District of Columbia** (D.C.): Cite to F., F.2d,
or F.3d, if therein.

► Federal Reporter	1919–date	F., F.2d, F.3d
► United States Court of Appeals Reports	1941–date	U.S. App. D.C.
► Appeal Cases, District of Columbia	1893–1941	App. D.C.
► District of Columbia Reports		
► Tucker and Clephane	1892–1893	21 D.C. (Tuck. & Cl.)
► Mackey	1880–1892	12–20 D.C. (Mackey 1–9) e.g., 12 D.C. (1 Mackey)
► MacArthur and Mackey	1879–1880	11 D.C. (MacArth. & M.)
► MacArthur	1873–1879	8–10 D.C. (MacArth. 1–3) e.g., 8 D.C. (1 MacArth.)
► District of Columbia Reports (reported by Mackey)	1863–1872	6–7 D.C. e.g., 6 D.C.
► Hayward & Hazleton, Circuit Court (Circuit Court Reports, vols. 6–7)	1840–1863	1–2 Hay. & Haz. e.g., 1 Hay. & Haz.
► Cranch, Circuit Court	1801–1840	1–5 D.C. (Cranch 1–5) e.g., 2 D.C. (2 Cranch)

Superior Court (D.C. Super. Ct.), previously **Municipal Court** (D.C. Mun. Ct.):
Cite to Daily Wash. L. Rptr.

► Daily Washington Law Reporter	1971–date	Daily Wash. L. Rptr.

Statutory compilations: Cite to D.C. CODE, if therein.

► District of Columbia Official Code (LexisNexis)	D.C. CODE § x-x (‹year›)
► West's District of Columbia Code Annotated (West)	D.C. CODE ANN. § x-x (West ‹year›)

Session laws: Cite to Stat., D.C. Reg., or D.C. Code Adv. Leg. Serv., if therein.

► United States Statutes at Large	‹vol. no.› Stat. ‹page no.› (‹year›)
► District of Columbia Register	‹vol. no.› D.C. Reg. ‹page no.› (‹month day, year›)
► District of Columbia Official Code Lexis Advance Legislative Service	‹year›-‹pamph. no.› D.C. Code Adv. Leg. Serv. ‹page no.›
► District of Columbia Session Law Service West	‹year› D.C. Sess. L. Serv. ‹page no.› (West)

Municipal regulations: Cite to D.C. Mun. Regs., if therein.

▸ Code of D.C. Municipal Regulations	D.C. Mun. Regs. tit. x, § x (‹year›)
▸ Code of District of Columbia Municipal Regulations (LexisNexis)	D.C. Code Mun. Regs. tit. x § x (LexisNexis ‹year›)

Administrative register

▸ District of Columbia Register	‹vol. no.› D.C. Reg. ‹page no.› (‹month day, year›)

....

Florida (Fla.)

http://www.flcourts.org
http://laws.flrules.org

Supreme Court (Fla.): Cite to So., So. 2d, or So. 3d, if therein.

▸ Southern Reporter	1886–date	So., So. 2d, So. 3d
▸ Florida Reports	1846–1948	Fla.
▸ Florida Law Weekly	1978–date	Fla. L. Weekly

District Court of Appeal (Fla. Dist. Ct. App.): Cite to So. 2d or So. 3d, if therein.

▸ Southern Reporter	1957–date	So. 2d, So. 3d
▸ Florida Law Weekly	1978–date	Fla. L. Weekly

Circuit Court (Fla. Cir. Ct.), **County Court** (e.g., Fla. Orange County Ct.), **Public Service Commission** (Fla. P.S.C.), and other lower courts of record: Cite to Fla. Supp. or Fla. Supp. 2d, if therein.

▸ Florida Supplement	1950–1991	Fla. Supp., Fla. Supp. 2d
▸ Florida Law Weekly Supplement	1992–date	Fla. L. Weekly Supp.

Statutory compilations: Cite to FLA. STAT., if therein.

▸ Florida Statutes	FLA. STAT. § x.x (‹year›)
▸ West's Florida Statutes Annotated	FLA. STAT. ANN. § x.x (West ‹year›)
▸ LexisNexis Florida Statutes Annotated	FLA. STAT. ANN. § x.x (LexisNexis ‹year›)

Session laws: Cite to Fla. Laws, if therein.

▸ Laws of Florida	‹year› Fla. Laws ‹page no.›
▸ West's Florida Session Law Service	‹year› Fla. Sess. Law Serv. ‹page no.› (West)

Administrative compilation

▸ Florida Administrative Code Annotated (LexisNexis)	FLA. ADMIN. CODE ANN. r. x-x.x (‹year›)

Administrative register: Cite to Fla. Admin. Reg., if therein.

▸ Florida Administrative Register	2012–date	‹vol. no.› Fla. Admin. Reg. ‹page no.› (‹month day, year›)

| ▶ Florida Administrative Weekly (LexisNexis) | 1996–2012 | ‹vol. no.› Fla. Admin. Weekly ‹page no.› (‹month day, year›) |

Georgia (Ga.)

https://www.georgiacourts.org
http://www.legis.ga.gov/Legislation/en-US/default.aspx

Supreme Court (Ga.): Cite to S.E. or S.E.2d, if therein.

| ▶ South Eastern Reporter | 1887–date | S.E., S.E.2d |
| ▶ Georgia Reports | 1846–date | Ga. |

Court of Appeals (Ga. Ct. App.): Cite to S.E. or S.E.2d, if therein.

| ▶ South Eastern Reporter | 1907–date | S.E., S.E.2d |
| ▶ Georgia Appeals Reports | 1907–date | Ga. App. |

Statutory compilations: Cite to GA. CODE ANN. (published by LexisNexis), if therein.

| ▶ Official Code of Georgia Annotated (LexisNexis) | GA. CODE ANN. § x-x-x (‹year›) |
| ▶ West's Code of Georgia Annotated | GA. CODE ANN. § x-x-x (West ‹year›) |

Session laws: Cite to Ga. Laws, if therein.

▶ Georgia Laws	‹year› Ga. Laws ‹page no.›
▶ Georgia ‹year› Advance Legislative Service (LexisNexis)	‹year›‹pamph. no.› Ga. Code Ann. Adv. Legis. Serv. ‹page no.› (LexisNexis)
▶ West's Georgia Legislative Service	‹year› Ga. Code Ann. Adv. Legis. Serv. ‹page no.› (West)

Administrative compilation

| ▶ Official Compilation Rules and Regulations of the State of Georgia | GA. COMP. R. & REGS. x-x-x.x (‹year›) |

Administrative register

| ▶ Georgia Government Register (LexisNexis) | ‹iss. no.› Ga. Gov't Reg. ‹page no.› (LexisNexis ‹month year›) |

Hawaii (Haw.)

http://www.courts.state.hi.us
http://www.capitol.hawaii.gov/docs/HRS.htm

Supreme Court (Haw.): Cite to P.2d or P.3d, if therein.

▶ Pacific Reporter	1959–date	P.2d, P.3d
▶ West's Hawaii Reports (begins with vol. 76)	1994–date	Haw.
▶ Hawaii Reports (ends with vol. 75)	1847–1994	Haw.

Intermediate Court of Appeals (Haw. Ct. App.): Cite to P.2d or P.3d, if therein.

- Pacific Reporter   1980–date   P.2d, P.3d
- West's Hawaii Reports (begins 1994–date   Haw.
  with vol. 76)
- Hawaii Appellate Reports   1980–1994   Haw. App.

Statutory compilations: Cite to Haw. Rev. Stat., if therein.

- Hawaii Revised Statutes   Haw. Rev. Stat. § x-x (‹year›)
- Michie's Hawaii Revised Statutes Annotated Haw. Rev. Stat. Ann. § x-x
  (LexisNexis)   (LexisNexis ‹year›)
- West's Hawai'i Revised Statutes Annotated   Haw. Rev. Stat. Ann. § x-x
                                              (West ‹year›)

Session laws: Cite to Haw. Sess. Laws, if therein.

- Session Laws of Hawaii   ‹year› Haw. Sess. Laws ‹page
                                              no.›
- Michie's Hawaii Revised Statutes Annotated ‹year›-‹pamph. no.› Haw. Rev.
  Advance Legislative Service (LexisNexis)   Stat. Ann. Adv. Legis. Serv.
                                              ‹page no.› (LexisNexis)
- West's Hawai'i Legislative Service   ‹year› Haw. Legis. Serv. ‹page
                                              no.› (West)

Administrative compilation

- Code of Hawaii Rules (LexisNexis)   Haw. Code R. § x-x-x
                                              (LexisNexis ‹year›)

Administrative register

- Hawaii Government Register   ‹iss. no.› Haw. Gov't Reg.
  (LexisNexis)   ‹page no.› (LexisNexis
                                              ‹month year›)

Idaho (Idaho)

http://www.isc.idaho.gov
https://legislature.idaho.gov/statutesrules/idstat/

Supreme Court (Idaho): Cite to P., P.2d, or P.3d, if therein.

- Pacific Reporter   1883–date   P., P.2d, P.3d
- Idaho Reports   1866–date   Idaho

Court of Appeals (Idaho Ct. App.): Cite to P.2d or P.3d, if therein.

- Pacific Reporter   1982–date   P.2d, P.3d
- Idaho Reports   1982–date   Idaho

Statutory compilations: Cite to Idaho Code (published by LexisNexis), if therein.

- Idaho Code (LexisNexis)   Idaho Code § x-x (‹year›)
- West's Idaho Code Annotated   Idaho Code Ann. § x-x (West
                                              ‹year›)

Session laws: Cite to Idaho Sess. Laws, if therein.

- Idaho Session Laws   ‹year› Idaho Sess. Laws
                                              ‹page no.›

▶ Idaho Code Annotated Advance Legislative Service (LexisNexis)   ⟨year⟩-⟨pamph. no.⟩ Idaho Code Ann. Adv. Legis. Serv. ⟨page no.⟩ (LexisNexis)

▶ West's Idaho Legislative Service   ⟨year⟩ Idaho Legis. Serv. ⟨page no.⟩ (West)

Administrative compilation: http://adminrules.idaho.gov/rules/current/

▶ Idaho Administrative Code   IDAHO ADMIN. CODE r. x.x.x.x (⟨year⟩)

Administrative register

▶ Idaho Administrative Bulletin   ⟨vol. no.⟩ Idaho Admin. Bull. ⟨page no.⟩ (⟨month day, year⟩)

....

Illinois (Ill.)

http://www.illinoiscourts.gov
http://www.ilga.gov/legislation/ilcs/ilcs.asp

Public domain format: Illinois has adopted a public domain citation format for cases filed after June 30, 2011. The format is:

▶ People v. Jolly, 2014 IL 117142, ¶ 32.

▶ People v. Jolly, 2016 IL App (4th) 150494-V, ¶¶ 7–11.

For additional instruction, consult Illinois Supreme Court Rule 6.

Supreme Court (Ill.): Cite to N.E., N.E.2d, or N.E.3d, if therein.

▶ North Eastern Reporter   1884–date   N.E., N.E.2d, N.E.3d
▶ Illinois Official Reports   2011–date   ⟨year⟩ IL ⟨docket no.⟩
▶ Illinois Reports
  ▶ 11 Ill. to date   1849–2011   Ill., Ill. 2d
  ▶ Gilman   1844–1849   e.g., 6 Ill. (1 Gilm.)
  ▶ Scammon   1832–1843   e.g., 2 Ill. (1 Scam.)
  ▶ Breese   1819–1831   1 Ill. (Breese)
▶ West's Illinois Decisions   1976–date   Ill. Dec.

Appellate Court (Ill. App. Ct.): Cite to N.E.2d or N.E.3d, if therein.

▶ North Eastern Reporter   1936–date   N.E.2d, N.E.3d
▶ Illinois Official Reports   2011–date   ⟨year⟩ IL ⟨docket no.⟩
▶ Illinois Appellate Court Reports   1877–2011   Ill. App., Ill. App. 2d, Ill. App. 3d
▶ West's Illinois Decisions   1976–date   Ill. Dec.

Illinois Circuit Court (Ill. Cir. Ct.), previously **Court of Claims** (Ill. Ct. Cl.): Cite to Ill. Ct. Cl., if therein.

▶ Illinois Court of Claims Reports   1889–date   Ill. Ct. Cl.

Statutory compilations: Cite to ILL. COMP. STAT., if therein.

▶ Illinois Compiled Statutes   ⟨ch. no.⟩ ILL. COMP. STAT. ⟨act no.⟩ / ⟨sec. no.⟩ (⟨year⟩)

▸ West's Smith-Hurd Illinois Compiled Statutes Annotated	‹ch. no.› ILL. COMP. STAT. ANN. ‹act no.› / ‹sec. no.› (West ‹year›)
▸ Illinois Compiled Statutes Annotated (LexisNexis)	‹ch. no.› ILL. COMP. STAT. ANN. ‹act no.› / ‹sec. no.› (LexisNexis ‹year›)

Session laws: Cite to Ill. Laws, if therein.

▸ Laws of Illinois	‹year› Ill. Laws ‹page no.›
▸ Illinois Legislative Service (West)	‹year› Ill. Legis. Serv. ‹page no.› (West)
▸ Illinois Compiled Statutes Annotated Advance Legislative Service (LexisNexis)	‹year›-‹pamph. no.› Ill. Comp. Stat. Ann. Adv. Legis. Serv. ‹page no.› (LexisNexis)

Administrative compilations: Cite to ILL. ADMIN. CODE, if therein.

▸ Illinois Administrative Code	ILL. ADMIN. CODE tit. x, § x (‹year›)
▸ Code of Illinois Rules (LexisNexis)	‹vol. no.› ILL. CODE R. ‹rule no.› (LexisNexis ‹year›)

Administrative register

▸ Illinois Register	‹vol. no.› Ill. Reg. ‹page no.› (‹month day, year›)

Indiana (Ind.)

https://www.in.gov/judiciary
http://iga.in.gov/legislative/laws/2019/ic/titles/001

Supreme Court (Ind.): Cite to N.E., N.E.2d, or N.E.3d, if therein.

▸ North Eastern Reporter	1885–date	N.E., N.E.2d, N.E.3d
▸ Indiana Reports	1848–1981	Ind.
▸ Blackford	1817–1847	Blackf.

Court of Appeals (Ind. Ct. App.), previously **Appellate Court** (Ind. App.): Cite to N.E., N.E.2d, or N.E.3d, if therein.

▸ North Eastern Reporter	1891–date	N.E., N.E.2d, N.E.3d
▸ Indiana Court of Appeals Reports (prior to 1972, Indiana Appellate Court Reports)	1890–1979	Ind. App.

Tax Court (Ind. T.C.): Cite to N.E.2d or N.E.3d, if therein.

▸ North Eastern Reporter	1986–date	N.E., N.E.2d, N.E.3d

Statutory compilations: Cite to IND. CODE, if therein.

▸ Indiana Code	IND. CODE § x-x-x-x (‹year›)
▸ West's Annotated Indiana Code	IND. CODE ANN. § x-x-x-x (West ‹year›)
▸ Burns Indiana Statutes Annotated (LexisNexis)	IND. CODE ANN. § x-x-x-x (LexisNexis ‹year›)

Session laws: Cite to Ind. Acts, if therein.

- Acts, Indiana — ⟨year⟩ Ind. Acts ⟨page no.⟩
- West's Indiana Legislative Service — ⟨year⟩ Ind. Legis. Serv. ⟨page no.⟩ (West)
- Burns Indiana Statutes Annotated Advance Legislative Service (LexisNexis) — ⟨year⟩-⟨pamph. no.⟩ Ind. Stat. Ann. Adv. Legis. Serv. ⟨page no.⟩ (LexisNexis)

Administrative compilations: Cite to IND. ADMIN. CODE, if therein.

- Indiana Administrative Code — ⟨tit. no.⟩ IND. ADMIN. CODE ⟨rule no.⟩ (⟨year⟩)
- West's Indiana Administrative Code — ⟨tit. no.⟩ IND. ADMIN. CODE ⟨rule no.⟩ (West ⟨year⟩)

Administrative register

- Indiana Register — ⟨vol. no.⟩ Ind. Reg. ⟨page no.⟩ (⟨month day, year⟩)

Iowa (Iowa)

https://www.iowacourts.gov
https://www.legis.iowa.gov/law/statutory

Supreme Court (Iowa): Cite to N.W. or N.W.2d, if therein.

North Western Reporter	1879–date	N.W., N.W.2d
Iowa Reports (Cite to edition published by Clarke for vols. 1–8.)	1855–1968	Iowa
Greene	1847–1854	Greene
Morris	1839–1846	Morris
Bradford	1838–1841	Bradf.

Court of Appeals (Iowa Ct. App.): Cite to N.W.2d.

North Western Reporter	1977–date	N.W.2d

Statutory compilations: Cite to IOWA CODE, if therein.

- Code of Iowa — IOWA CODE § x.x (⟨year⟩)
- West's Iowa Code Annotated — IOWA CODE ANN. § x.x (West ⟨year⟩)

Session laws: Cite to Iowa Acts, if therein.

- Acts of the State of Iowa — ⟨year⟩ Iowa Acts ⟨page no.⟩
- Iowa Legislative Service (West) — ⟨year⟩ Iowa Legis. Serv. ⟨page no.⟩ (West)

Administrative compilation

- Iowa Administrative Code — IOWA ADMIN. CODE r. x-x.x (⟨year⟩)

Administrative register

- Iowa Administrative Bulletin — ⟨vol. no.⟩ Iowa Admin. Bull. ⟨page no.⟩ (⟨month day, year⟩)

Kansas (Kan.)

https://www.kscourts.org
http://www.kslegislature.org

Supreme Court (Kan.): Cite to P., P.2d, or P.3d, if therein.

▸ Pacific Reporter	1883–date	P., P.2d, P.3d
▸ Kansas Reports	1862–date	Kan.
▸ McCahon	1858–1868	McCahon

Court of Appeals (Kan. Ct. App.): Cite to P., P.2d, or P.3d, if therein.

▸ Pacific Reporter	1895–1901	P.
	1977–date	P.2d, P.3d
▸ Kansas Court of Appeals Reports	1895–1901	Kan. App.
	1977–date	Kan. App. 2d

Statutory compilations: Cite to KAN. STAT. ANN., if therein.

▸ Kansas Statutes Annotated	KAN. STAT. ANN. § x-x (⟨year⟩)
▸ West's Kansas Statutes Annotated	KAN. STAT. ANN. § x-x (West ⟨year⟩)

Session laws: Cite to Kan. Sess. Laws, if therein.

▸ Session Laws of Kansas	⟨year⟩ Kan. Sess. Laws ⟨page no.⟩
▸ West's Kansas Legislative Service	⟨year⟩ Kan. Legis. Serv. ⟨page no.⟩ (West)

Administrative compilation

▸ Kansas Administrative Regulations (updated by supplements)	KAN. ADMIN. REGS. § x-x-x (⟨year⟩)

Administrative register

▸ Kansas Register	⟨vol. no.⟩ Kan. Reg. ⟨page no.⟩ (⟨month day, year⟩)

Kentucky (Ky.)

https://www.courts.ky.gov
https://legislature.ky.gov/Law/Statutes/Pages/default.aspx

Supreme Court (Ky.): before 1976 the **Court of Appeals** (Ky.) was the highest state court. Cite to S.W., S.W.2d, or S.W.3d, if therein.

▸ South Western Reporter	1886–date	S.W., S.W.2d, S.W.3d
▸ Kentucky Reports		
▸ 78 Ky. to 314 Ky.	1879–1951	Ky.
▸ Bush	1866–1879	e.g., 64 Ky. (1 Bush)
▸ Duvall	1863–1866	e.g., 62 Ky. (1 Duv.)
▸ Metcalf	1858–1863	e.g., 58 Ky. (1 Met.)
▸ Monroe, Ben	1840–1857	e.g., 40 Ky. (1 B. Mon.)
▸ Dana	1833–1840	e.g., 31 Ky. (1 Dana)
▸ Marshall, J.J.	1829–1832	e.g., 24 Ky. (1 J.J. Marsh.)
▸ Monroe, T.B.	1824–1828	e.g., 17 Ky. (1 T.B. Mon.)
▸ Littell	1822–1824	e.g., 11 Ky. (1 Litt.)
▸ Littell's Selected Cases	1795–1821	e.g., 16 Ky. (1 Litt. Sel. Cas.)

▸ Marshall, A.K.	1817–1821	e.g., 8 Ky. (1 A.K. Marsh.)
▸ Bibb	1808–1817	e.g., 4 Ky. (1 Bibb)
▸ Hardin	1805–1808	3 Ky. (Hard.)
▸ Sneed	1801–1805	2 Ky. (Sneed)
▸ Hughes	1785–1801	1 Ky. (Hughes)
▸ Kentucky Opinions	1864–1886	Ky. Op.
▸ Kentucky Law Reporter	1880–1908	Ky. L. Rptr.
▸ Kentucky Appellate Reporter	1994–2000	Ky. App.
▸ Kentucky Attorneys Memo	2001–2007	Ky. Att'y Memo
▸ Kentucky Law Summary	1966–date	Ky. L. Summ.

Court of Appeals (Ky. Ct. App.) (for decisions before 1976, see **Kentucky Supreme Court**): Cite to S.W.2d or S.W.3d, if therein.

▸ South Western Reporter	1976–date	S.W.2d, S.W.3d
▸ Kentucky Appellate Reporter	1994–2000	Ky. App.
▸ Kentucky Attorneys Memo	2001–2007	Ky. Att'y Memo
▸ Kentucky Law Summary	1966–date	Ky. L. Summ.

Statutory compilations: Cite to one of the following codes:

▸ Baldwin's Kentucky Revised Statutes Annotated (West)	KY. REV. STAT. ANN. § x.x (West ⟨year⟩)
▸ Michie's Kentucky Revised Statutes Annotated (LexisNexis)	KY. REV. STAT. ANN. § x.x (LexisNexis ⟨year⟩)

Session laws: Cite to Ky. Acts, if therein.

▸ Acts of Kentucky	⟨year⟩ Ky. Acts ⟨page no.⟩
▸ Kentucky Revised Statutes and Rules Service (West)	⟨year⟩ Ky. Rev. Stat. & R. Serv. ⟨page no.⟩ (West)
▸ Michie's Kentucky Revised Statutes Advance Legislative Service (LexisNexis)	⟨year⟩-⟨pamph. no.⟩ Ky. Rev. Stat. Adv. Legis. Serv. ⟨page no.⟩ (LexisNexis)

Administrative compilation

▸ Kentucky Administrative Regulations Service	⟨tit. no.⟩ KY. ADMIN. REGS. ⟨rule no.⟩ (⟨year⟩)

Administrative register

▸ Administrative Register of Kentucky	⟨vol. no.⟩ Ky. Admin. Reg. ⟨page no.⟩ (⟨month year⟩)

....

Louisiana (La.)

http://www.lasc.org
http://www.legis.la.gov/legis/LawSearch.aspx

Public domain citation format: Louisiana has adopted a public domain citation format for cases after December 31, 1993. The format is:

▶ State v. Ray, 97-1093 (La. App. 3 Cir. 2/4/98), 705 So. 2d 1295.

▶ State v. Ray, 97-1093, p. 2 (La. App. 3 Cir. 2/4/98), 705 So. 2d 1295, 1296.

▶ State v. Fleury, 2001-0871, p. 5 (La. 10/16/01), 799 So. 2d 468, 472.

For additional information, consult Rules of the Supreme Court of Louisiana, part G, section 8.

Supreme Court (La.), before 1813 the **Superior Court of Louisiana** (La.) and the **Superior Court of the Territory of Orleans** (Orleans): Cite to So., So. 2d, or So. 3d, if therein.

▸ Southern Reporter	1886–date	So., So. 2d, So. 3d
▸ Louisiana Reports	1901–1972	La.
▸ Louisiana Annual Reports	1846–1900	La. Ann.
▸ Robinson	1841–1846	Rob.
▸ Louisiana Reports	1830–1841	La.
▸ Martin (Louisiana Term Reports)	1809–1830	Mart. (o.s.), Mart. (n.s.)

Court of Appeal (La. Ct. App.): Cite to So., So. 2d, or So. 3d, if therein.

▸ Southern Reporter	1928–date	So., So. 2d, So. 3d
▸ Louisiana Court of Appeals Reports	1924–1932	La. App.
▸ Peltier's Decisions, Parish at Orleans	1917–1924	Pelt.
▸ Teissier, Orleans Court of Appeals	1903–1917	Teiss.
▸ Gunby's Reports	1885	Gunby
▸ McGloin	1881–1884	McGl.

Statutory compilations: Cite to one of the following codes:

▸ West's Louisiana Statutes Annotated	LA. STAT. ANN. § x:x (⟨year⟩)
▸ West's Louisiana Children's Code Annotated	LA. CHILD. CODE ANN. art. x (⟨year⟩)
▸ West's Louisiana Civil Code Annotated	LA. CIV. CODE ANN. art. x (⟨year⟩)
▸ West's Louisiana Code of Civil Procedure Annotated	LA. CODE CIV. PROC. ANN. art. x (⟨year⟩)
▸ West's Louisiana Code of Criminal Procedure Annotated	LA. CODE CRIM. PROC. ANN. art. x (⟨year⟩)
▸ West's Louisiana Code of Evidence Annotated	LA. CODE EVID. ANN. art. x (⟨year⟩)
▸ West's Louisiana Constitution Annotated	LA. CONST. ANN. art. x (⟨year⟩)

Session laws: Cite to La. Acts, if therein.

▸ State of Louisiana: Acts of the Legislature	⟨year⟩ La. Acts ⟨page no.⟩
▸ West's Louisiana Session Law Service	⟨year⟩ La. Sess. Law Serv. ⟨page no.⟩ (West)

Administrative compilation

▸ Louisiana Administrative Code	LA. ADMIN. CODE tit. x, pt. x, § x (⟨year⟩)

Administrative register

▸ Louisiana Register	⟨vol. no.⟩ La. Reg. ⟨page no.⟩ (⟨month day, year⟩)

Maine (Me.)

https://www.courts.maine.gov
http://www.legislature.maine.gov/legis/statutes

Public domain citation format: Maine has adopted a public domain citation format for cases after December 31, 1996. The format is:

▶ Bangor Publ'g Co. v. Union St. Mkt., 1998 ME 37, 706 A.2d 595.

▶ Bangor Publ'g Co. v. Union St. Mkt., 1998 ME 37, ¶ 3, 706 A.2d 595, 595.

Supreme Judicial Court (Me.): Cite to A., A.2d, or A.3d, if therein.

▶ Atlantic Reporter	1885–date	A., A.2d, A.3d
▶ Maine Reports	1820–1965	Me.

Statutory compilations: Cite to ME. STAT., if therein.

▶ West's Maine Statutes	ME. STAT. tit. x, § x (⟨year⟩)
▶ Maine Revised Statutes Annotated (West)	ME. REV. STAT. ANN. tit. x, § x (West ⟨year⟩)

Session laws: Cite to Me. Laws, if therein.

▶ Laws of the State of Maine	⟨year⟩ Me. Laws ⟨page no.⟩
▶ Maine Legislative Service (West)	⟨year⟩ Me. Legis. Serv. ⟨page no.⟩ (West)

Administrative compilation

▶ Code of Maine Rules (LexisNexis)	x-x-x ME. CODE R. § x (LexisNexis ⟨year⟩)

Administrative register

▶ Maine Government Register (LexisNexis)	⟨iss. no.⟩ Me. Gov't Reg. ⟨page no.⟩ (LexisNexis ⟨month year⟩)

Maryland (Md.)

https://www.courts.state.md.us
http://mgaleg.maryland.gov/mgawebsite/laws/statutes

Court of Appeals (Md.): Cite to A., A.2d, or A.3d, if therein.

▶ Atlantic Reporter	1885–date	A., A.2d, A.3d
▶ Maryland Reports	1851–date	Md.
▶ Gill	1843–1851	Gill
▶ Gill and Johnson	1829–1842	G. & J.
▶ Harris and Gill	1826–1829	H. & G.
▶ Harris and Johnson	1800–1826	H. & J.
▶ Harris and McHenry	1770–1774 1780–1799	H. & McH.

Court of Special Appeals (Md. Ct. Spec. App.): Cite to A.2d or A.3d, if therein.

▶ Atlantic Reporter	1967–date	A.2d, A.3d
▶ Maryland Appellate Reports	1967–date	Md. App.

Statutory compilations: Cite by subject to either Michie's MD. CODE ANN. or West's MD. CODE ANN., if therein.

▸ Michie's Annotated Code of Maryland
  (LexisNexis)

MD. CODE ANN., ‹subject› §
x-x (LexisNexis ‹year›)

▸ West's Annotated Code of Maryland

MD. CODE ANN., ‹subject› §
x-x (West ‹year›)

▸ Agriculture	AGRIC.
▸ Alcoholic Beverages	AL. BEV.
▸ Business Occupations and Professions	BUS. OCC. & PROF.
▸ Business Regulation	BUS. REG.
▸ Commercial Law	COM. LAW
▸ Constitutions	CONST.
▸ Corporations and Associations	CORPS. & ASS'NS
▸ Correctional Services	CORR. SERVS.
▸ Courts and Judicial Proceedings	CTS. & JUD. PROC.
▸ Criminal Law	CRIM. LAW
▸ Criminal Procedure	CRIM. PROC.
▸ Economic Development	ECON. DEV.
▸ Education	EDUC.
▸ Election Law	ELEC. LAW
▸ Environment	ENV'T
▸ Estates and Trusts	EST. & TRUSTS
▸ Family Law	FAM. LAW
▸ Financial Institutions	FIN. INST.
▸ General Provisions	GEN. PROVIS.
▸ Health–General	HEALTH–GEN.
▸ Health Occupations	HEALTH OCC.
▸ Housing and Community Development	HOUS. & CMTY. DEV.
▸ Human Services	HUM. SERVS.
▸ Insurance	INS.
▸ Labor and Employment	LAB. & EMPL.
▸ Land Use	LAND USE
▸ Local Government	LOCAL GOV'T
▸ Natural Resources	NAT. RES.
▸ Public Safety	PUB. SAFETY
▸ Public Utility	PUB. UTIL.
▸ Real Property	REAL PROP.
▸ State Finance and Procurement	STATE FIN. & PROC.
▸ State Government	STATE GOV'T
▸ State Personnel and Pensions	STATE PERS. & PENS.
▸ Tax–General	TAX–GEN.
▸ Tax–Property	TAX–PROP.
▸ Transportation	TRANSP.

Session laws: Cite to Md. Laws, if therein.

▸ Laws of Maryland — ‹year› Md. Laws ‹page no.›
▸ Michie's Annotated Code of Maryland Advance Legislative Service (LexisNexis) — ‹year›-‹pamph. no.› Md. Code Ann. Adv. Legis. Serv. ‹page no.› (LexisNexis)
▸ West's Maryland Legislative Service — ‹year› Md. Legis. Serv. ‹page no.› (West)

Administrative compilation

▸ Code of Maryland Regulations — MD. CODE REGS. ‹reg. no.› (‹year›)

Administrative register

▸ Maryland Register ⟨vol. no.⟩ **Md. Reg.** ⟨page no.⟩
⟨month day, year⟩

....

Massachusetts (Mass.)

https://www.mass.gov/orgs/massachusetts-court-system
https://malegislature.gov/Laws/GeneralLaws

Supreme Judicial Court (Mass.): Cite to N.E., N.E.2d, or N.E.3d, if therein.

▸ North Eastern Reporter	1885–date	N.E., N.E.2d, N.E.3d
▸ Massachusetts Reports		
▸ 97 Mass. to date	1867–date	Mass.
▸ Allen	1861–1867	e.g., 83 Mass. (1 Allen)
▸ Gray	1854–1860	e.g., 67 Mass. (1 Gray)
▸ Cushing	1848–1853	e.g., 55 Mass. (1 Cush.)
▸ Metcalf	1840–1847	e.g., 42 Mass. (1 Met.)
▸ Pickering	1822–1839	e.g., 18 Mass. (1 Pick.)
▸ Tyng	1805–1822	e.g., 2 Mass. (1 Tyng)
▸ Williams	1804–1805	1 Mass. (1 Will.)

Appeals Court (Mass. App. Ct.): Cite to N.E.2d or N.E.3d, if therein.

▸ North Eastern Reporter	1972–date	N.E.2d, N.E.3d
▸ Massachusetts Appeals Court Reports	1972–date	Mass. App. Ct.

Lower Courts (Mass. Dist. Ct., Bos. Mun. Ct.): Cite to Mass. App. Div., if therein; otherwise cite to Mass. Supp. or Mass. App. Dec., if therein.

▸ Reports of Massachusetts Appellate Division	1936–1950 1980–date	Mass. App. Div.
▸ Massachusetts Reports Supplement	1980–1983	Mass. Supp.
▸ Massachusetts Appellate Decisions	1941–1977	Mass. App. Dec.
▸ Appellate Division Advance Sheets	1975–1979	⟨year⟩ Mass. App. Div. Adv. Sh. ⟨page no.⟩

Statutory compilations: Cite to MASS. GEN. LAWS, if therein.

▸ General Laws of Massachusetts (Mass. Bar Ass'n/West)	MASS. GEN. LAWS ch. x, § x ⟨year⟩
▸ Massachusetts General Laws Annotated (West)	MASS. GEN. LAWS ANN. ch. x, § x (West ⟨year⟩)
▸ Annotated Laws of Massachusetts (LexisNexis)	MASS. ANN. LAWS ch. x, § x (LexisNexis ⟨year⟩)

Session laws: Cite to Mass. Acts, if therein.

▸ Acts and Resolves of Massachusetts	⟨year⟩ Mass. Acts ⟨page no.⟩
▸ Massachusetts Legislative Service (West)	⟨year⟩ Mass. Legis. Serv. ⟨page no.⟩ (West)
▸ Massachusetts Advance Legislative Service (LexisNexis)	⟨year⟩-⟨pamph. no.⟩ Mass. Adv. Legis. Serv. ⟨page no.⟩ (LexisNexis)

Administrative compilations: Cite to official MASS. CODE REGS., if therein.

▸ Code of Massachusetts Regulations
⟨tit. no.⟩ MASS. CODE REGS. ⟨sec. no.⟩ (⟨year⟩)

▸ Code of Massachusetts Regulations (LexisNexis)
⟨tit. no.⟩ MASS. CODE REGS. ⟨sec. no.⟩ (LexisNexis ⟨year⟩)

Administrative register

▸ Massachusetts Register
⟨iss. no.⟩ Mass. Reg. ⟨page no.⟩ (⟨month day, year⟩)

....

Michigan (Mich.)

http://www.courts.michigan.gov
http://www.legislature.mi.gov

Supreme Court (Mich.): Cite to N.W. or N.W.2d, if therein.

▸ North Western Reporter	1879–date	N.W., N.W.2d
▸ Michigan Reports	1847–date	Mich.
▸ Douglass	1843–1847	Doug.
▸ Blume, Unreported Opinions	1836–1843	Blume Unrep. Op.
▸ Blume, Supreme Court Transactions	1805–1836	Blume Sup. Ct. Trans.

Court of Appeals (Mich. Ct. App.): Cite to N.W.2d, if therein.

▸ North Western Reporter	1965–date	N.W.2d
▸ Michigan Appeals Reports	1965–date	Mich. App.

Court of Claims (Mich. Ct. Cl.): Cite to Mich. Ct. Cl.

▸ Michigan Court of Claims Reports	1939–1942	Mich. Ct. Cl.

Statutory compilations: Cite to MICH. COMP. LAWS, if therein.

▸ Michigan Compiled Laws
MICH. COMP. LAWS § x.x (⟨year⟩)

▸ Michigan Compiled Laws Annotated (West)
MICH. COMP. LAWS ANN. § x.x (West ⟨year⟩)

▸ Michigan Compiled Laws Service (LexisNexis)
MICH. COMP. LAWS SERV. § x.x (LexisNexis ⟨year⟩)

Session laws: Cite to Mich. Pub. Acts, if therein.

▸ Public and Local Acts of the Legislature of the State of Michigan
⟨year⟩ Mich. Pub. Acts ⟨page no.⟩

▸ Michigan Legislative Service (West)
⟨year⟩ Mich. Legis. Serv. ⟨page no.⟩ (West)

▸ Michigan Advance Legislative Service (LexisNexis)
⟨year⟩-⟨pamph. no.⟩ Mich. Adv. Legis. Serv. ⟨page no.⟩ (LexisNexis)

Administrative compilation

▸ Michigan Administrative Code
MICH. ADMIN. CODE r. x.x (⟨year⟩)

Administrative register

▸ Michigan Register   ⟨iss. no.⟩ Mich. Reg. ⟨page
                                              no.⟩ (⟨month day, year⟩)

Minnesota (Minn.)

http://www.mncourts.gov
https://www.revisor.mn.gov/pubs

Supreme Court (Minn.): Cite to N.W. or N.W.2d, if therein.

▸ North Western Reporter	1879–date	N.W., N.W.2d
▸ Minnesota Reports	1851–1977	Minn.

Court of Appeals (Minn. Ct. App.): Cite to N.W.2d.

▸ North Western Reporter	1983–date	N.W.2d

Statutory compilations: Cite to MINN. STAT., if therein.

▸ Minnesota Statutes	MINN. STAT. § x.x (⟨year⟩)
▸ Minnesota Statutes Annotated (West)	MINN. STAT. ANN. § x.x (West ⟨year⟩)

Session laws: Cite to Minn. Laws, if therein.

▸ Laws of Minnesota	⟨year⟩ Minn. Laws ⟨page no.⟩
▸ Minnesota Session Law Service (West)	⟨year⟩ Minn. Sess. Law Serv. ⟨page no.⟩ (West)

Administrative compilation

▸ Minnesota Rules   MINN. R. ⟨rule no.⟩ (⟨year⟩)

Administrative register

▸ Minnesota State Register   ⟨vol. no.⟩ Minn. Reg. ⟨page
                                              no.⟩ (⟨month day, year⟩)

Mississippi (Miss.)

https://courts.ms.gov
https://www.sos.ms.gov/Education-Publications/Pages/Mississippi-Code.aspx

Public domain citation format: Mississippi has adopted a public domain
citation format for cases after July 1, 1997. The format is:

▶ Pro-Choice Miss. v. Fordice, 95-CA-00960-SCT (Miss. 1998).

▶ Pro-Choice Miss. v. Fordice, 95-CA-00960-SCT (¶ 1) (Miss. 1998).

For additional information, consult Mississippi Rules of Appellate Procedure,
Rule 28(f).

Supreme Court (Miss.): Cite to So., So. 2d, or So. 3d, if therein.

▸ Southern Reporter	1886–date	So., So. 2d, So. 3d
▸ Mississippi Reports		
▸ 23 Miss. to 254 Miss.	1851–1966	Miss.
▸ Smedes and Marshall	1843–1850	e.g., 9 Miss. (1 S. & M.)
▸ Howard	1834–1843	e.g., 2 Miss. (1 Howard)

▸ Walker	1818–1832	1 Miss. (1 Walker)
▸ Mississippi Decisions	1820–1885	Miss. Dec.

Court of Appeals (Miss. Ct. App.): Cite to So. 2d or So. 3d.

▸ Southern Reporter	1995–date	So. 2d, So. 3d

Statutory compilations: Cite to Miss. Code Ann. (published by LexisNexis), if therein.

▸ Mississippi Code 1972 Annotated (LexisNexis)	Miss. Code Ann. § x-x-x (‹year›)
▸ West's Annotated Mississippi Code	Miss. Code Ann. § x-x-x (West ‹year›)

Session laws: Cite to Miss. Laws, if therein.

▸ General Laws of Mississippi	‹year› Miss. Laws ‹page no.›
▸ Mississippi General Laws Advance Sheets (LexisNexis)	‹year›-‹pamph. no.› Miss. Laws Adv. Sh. ‹page no.› (LexisNexis)
▸ West's Mississippi Legislative Service	‹year› Miss. Legis. Serv. ‹page no.› (West)

Administrative compilation

▸ Code of Mississippi Rules (LexisNexis)	‹tit. no.›-‹ch. no.› Miss. Code R. § x (LexisNexis ‹year›)

Administrative register

▸ Mississippi Government Register (LexisNexis)	‹iss. no.› Miss. Gov't Reg. ‹page no.› (LexisNexis ‹month year›)

Missouri (Mo.)

http://www.courts.mo.gov
https://revisor.mo.gov/main/Home.aspx

Supreme Court (Mo.): Cite to S.W., S.W.2d, or S.W.3d, if therein.

▸ South Western Reporter	1886–date	S.W., S.W.2d, S.W.3d
▸ Missouri Reports	1821–1956	Mo.

Court of Appeals (Mo. Ct. App.): Cite to S.W., S.W.2d, or S.W.3d, if therein.

▸ South Western Reporter	1902–date	S.W., S.W.2d, S.W.3d
▸ Missouri Appeals Reports	1876–1954	Mo. App.

Statutory compilations: Cite to Mo. Rev. Stat., if therein.

▸ Missouri Revised Statutes	Mo. Rev. Stat. § x.x (‹year›)
▸ Vernon's Annotated Missouri Statutes (West)	Mo. Ann. Stat. § x.x (West ‹year›)

Session laws: Cite to Mo. Laws, if therein.

▸ Session Laws of Missouri	‹year› Mo. Laws ‹page no.›
▸ Missouri Legislative Service (West)	‹year› Mo. Legis. Serv. ‹page no.› (West)

Administrative compilation

▶ Missouri Code of State Regulations Annotated Mo. Code Regs. Ann. tit. x, § x-x.x (‹year›)

Administrative register

▶ Missouri Register   ‹vol. no.› Mo. Reg. ‹page no.› (‹month day, year›)

....

Montana (Mont.)

http://www.montanacourts.org
https://www.leg.mt.gov/bills/mca/index.htm

Public domain citation format: Montana has adopted a public domain citation format for cases after January 1, 1998. The format is:

▶ Mont. Env't Info. Ctr. v. Dep't of Env't Quality, 1999 MT 248, 296 Mont. 207, 988 P.2d 1236.

▶ Mont. Env't Info. Ctr. v. Dep't of Env't Quality, 1999 MT 248, ¶ 21, 296 Mont. 207, 988 P.2d 1236.

For additional instruction, consult Order *In re*: Opinion Forms and Citation Standards of the Supreme Court of Montana, and the Adoption of Public Domain and Neutral-Format Citation (Dec. 16, 1997), and Order in the Matter of Amending Citation Standards for the Montana Supreme Court (Jan. 22, 2009).

Supreme Court (Mont.): Cite to P., P.2d, or P.3d, if therein.

▶ Pacific Reporter	1883–date	P., P.2d, P.3d
▶ Montana Reports	1868–date	Mont.
▶ State Reporter	1945–date	State Rptr.

Statutory compilations: Cite to Mont. Code Ann., if therein.

▶ Montana Code Annotated   Mont. Code Ann. § x-x-x (‹year›)

▶ West's Montana Code Annotated   Mont. Code Ann. § x-x-x (West ‹year›)

Session laws

▶ Laws of Montana   ‹year› Mont. Laws ‹page no.›

Administrative compilation

▶ Administrative Rules of Montana   Mont. Admin. R. ‹rule no.› (‹year›)

Administrative register

▶ Montana Administrative Register   ‹iss. no.› Mont. Admin. Reg. ‹page no.› (‹month day, year›)

Nebraska (Neb.)

https://www.supremecourt.nebraska.gov/
http://www.nebraskalegislature.gov/laws/browse-statutes.php

Supreme Court (Neb.): Cite to N.W. or N.W.2d, if therein.

► North Western Reporter	1879–date	N.W., N.W.2d
► Nebraska Reports	1860–date	Neb.

Court of Appeals (Neb. Ct. App.): Cite to N.W.2d, if therein.

► North Western Reporter	1992–date	N.W.2d
► Nebraska Appellate Reports	1992–date	Neb. App.

Statutory compilations: Cite to NEB. REV. STAT., if therein.

► Revised Statutes of Nebraska	NEB. REV. STAT. § x-x (‹year›)
► Revised Statutes of Nebraska Annotated (LexisNexis)	NEB. REV. STAT. ANN. § x-x (LexisNexis ‹year›)
► West's Revised Statutes of Nebraska Annotated	NEB. REV. STAT. ANN. § x-x (West ‹year›)

Session laws: Cite to Neb. Laws, if therein.

► Laws of Nebraska	‹year› Neb. Laws ‹page no.›
► West's Nebraska Legislative Service	‹year› Neb. Legis. Serv. ‹page no.› (West)

Administrative compilation

► Nebraska Administrative Code	‹tit. no.› NEB. ADMIN. CODE § x-x (‹year›)

Nevada (Nev.)

http://www.nvcourts.gov
http://www.leg.state.nv.us/law1.cfm

Supreme Court (Nev.): Cite to P., P.2d, or P.3d, if therein.

► Pacific Reporter	1883–date	P., P.2d, P.3d
► Nevada Reports	1865–date	Nev.

Statutory compilations: Cite to NEV. REV. STAT., if therein.

► Nevada Revised Statutes	NEV. REV. STAT. § x.x (‹year›)
► Michie's Nevada Revised Statutes Annotated (LexisNexis)	NEV. REV. STAT. ANN. § x.x (LexisNexis ‹year›)
► West's Nevada Revised Statutes Annotated	NEV. REV. STAT. ANN. § x.x (West ‹year›)

Session laws: Cite to Nev. Stat., if therein.

► Statutes of Nevada	‹year› Nev. Stat. ‹page no.›
► West's Nevada Legislative Service	‹year› Nev. Legis. Serv. ‹page no.› (West)

Administrative compilation

► Nevada Administrative Code	NEV. ADMIN. CODE § x.x (‹year›)

Administrative register

▶ Nevada Register of Administrative Regulations
⟨vol. no.⟩ Nev. Reg. Admin. Regs. ⟨reg. no.⟩ (⟨month day, year⟩)

New Hampshire (N.H.)

http://www.courts.state.nh.us
http://www.gencourt.state.nh.us/rsa/html/indexes/default.html

Supreme Court (N.H.): Cite to A., A.2d, or A.3d, if therein.

▶ Atlantic Reporter	1885–date	A., A.2d, A.3d
▶ New Hampshire Reports	1816–date	N.H.

Statutory compilations: Cite to N.H. Rev. Stat. Ann. (published by West), if therein.

▶ New Hampshire Revised Statutes Annotated (West)
N.H. REV. STAT. ANN. § x:x (⟨year⟩)

▶ LexisNexis New Hampshire Revised Statutes Annotated
N.H. REV. STAT. ANN. § x:x (LexisNexis ⟨year⟩)

Session laws: Cite to N.H. Laws or N.H. Legis. Serv., if therein.

▶ Laws of the State of New Hampshire (West)
⟨year⟩ N.H. Laws ⟨page no.⟩

▶ New Hampshire Legislative Service (West)
⟨year⟩ N.H. Legis. Serv. ⟨page no.⟩

▶ LexisNexis New Hampshire Revised Statutes Annotated Advance Legislative Service (LexisNexis)
⟨year⟩ ⟨pamph. no.⟩ N.H. Rev. Stat. Ann. Adv. Legis. Serv. ⟨page no.⟩ (LexisNexis)

Administrative compilations: Cite to N.H. CODE ADMIN. R. ANN., if therein.

▶ New Hampshire Code of Administrative Rules Annotated (LexisNexis)
N.H. CODE ADMIN. R. ANN. ⟨dep't name as abbreviated in Rules⟩ ⟨rule no.⟩ (⟨year⟩)

▶ Code of New Hampshire Rules (LexisNexis)
N.H. CODE R. ⟨dep't name as abbreviated in Rules⟩ ⟨rule no.⟩ (LexisNexis ⟨year⟩)

Administrative registers: Cite to N.H. Rulemaking Reg., if therein.

▶ New Hampshire Rulemaking Register
⟨vol. no.⟩ N.H. Rulemaking Reg. ⟨page no.⟩ (⟨month day, year⟩)

▶ New Hampshire Government Register (LexisNexis)
⟨iss. no.⟩ N.H. Gov't Reg. ⟨page no.⟩ (LexisNexis ⟨month year⟩)

New Jersey (N.J.)

http://www.njcourts.gov
http://www.njleg.state.nj.us

Supreme Court (N.J.), previously **Court of Errors and Appeals** (N.J.): Cite to A., A.2d, or A.3d, if therein.

▶ Atlantic Reporter	1885–date	A., A.2d, A.3d
▶ New Jersey Reports	1948–date	N.J.

▸ New Jersey Law Reports	1790–1948	N.J.L.
▸ New Jersey Equity Reports	1845–1948	N.J. Eq.
▸ New Jersey Miscellaneous Reports	1923–1948	N.J. Misc.

Superior Court (N.J. Super. Ct. App. Div., N.J. Super. Ct. Ch. Div., N.J. Super. Ct. Law Div.), previously **Court of Chancery** (N.J. Ch.), and **Prerogative Court** (N.J. Prerog. Ct.): Cite to A., A.2d, or A.3d, if therein.

▸ Atlantic Reporter	1885–date	A., A.2d, A.3d
▸ New Jersey Superior Court Reports	1948–date	N.J. Super.
▸ New Jersey Law Reports	1790–1948	N.J.L.
▸ New Jersey Equity Reports	1830–1948	N.J. Eq.
▸ New Jersey Miscellaneous Reports	1923–1948	N.J. Misc.

County Court (e.g., Essex County Ct.) and other lower courts: Cite to A.2d, if therein.

Tax Court (N.J. Tax Ct.): Cite to N.J. Tax.

| ▸ New Jersey Tax Court Reports | 1979–date | N.J. Tax |

Statutory compilations: Cite to N.J. STAT. ANN., if therein.

| ▸ New Jersey Statutes Annotated (West) | N.J. STAT. ANN. § x:x (West ⟨year⟩) |
| ▸ New Jersey Revised Statutes | N.J. REV. STAT. § x:x (⟨year⟩) |

Session laws: Cite to N.J. Laws, if therein.

| ▸ Laws of New Jersey | ⟨year⟩ N.J. Laws ⟨page no.⟩ |
| ▸ New Jersey Session Law Service (West) | ⟨year⟩ N.J. Sess. Law Serv. ⟨page no.⟩ (West) |

Administrative compilation

| ▸ New Jersey Administrative Code (LexisNexis) | N.J. ADMIN. CODE § x:x-x.x (⟨year⟩) |

Administrative register

| ▸ New Jersey Register (LexisNexis) | ⟨vol. no.⟩ N.J. Reg. ⟨page no.⟩ (⟨month day, year⟩) |

Administrative report

| ▸ New Jersey Administrative Reports | 1979–1997 | N.J. Admin., N.J. Admin. 2d |

··

New Mexico (N.M.)

http://www.nmcourts.gov
http://www.nmonesource.com

Public domain citation format: New Mexico has adopted a public domain citation format for cases effective July 1, 2013. The format is:

▸ Atlixco Coal. v. Maggiore, 1998-NMCA-134, 125 N.M. 786, 965 P.2d 370.

▸ Atlixco Coal. v. Maggiore, 1998-NMCA-134, ¶ 14, 125 N.M. 786, 965 P.2d 370.

For additional information, consult New Mexico Supreme Court Rule 23-112 (effective June 4, 2004) and New Mexico Supreme Court Order No. 13-8300-013 (effective July 1, 2013).

Supreme Court (N.M.): Cite to P., P.2d, or P.3d, if therein.

▶ Pacific Reporter	1883–date	P., P.2d, P.3d
▶ New Mexico Reports	1852–2012	N.M.

Court of Appeals (N.M. Ct. App.): Cite to P.2d or P.3d, if therein.

▶ Pacific Reporter	1967–date	P.2d, P.3d
▶ New Mexico Reports	1967–2012	N.M.

Statutory compilations: Cite to N.M. STAT. ANN., if therein.

▶ New Mexico Statutes Annotated 1978 (Conway Greene)	N.M. STAT. ANN. § x-x-x ⟨year⟩
▶ West's New Mexico Statutes Annotated	N.M. STAT. ANN. § x-x-x (West ⟨year⟩
▶ Michie's Annotated Statutes of New Mexico (LexisNexis)	N.M. STAT. ANN. § x-x-x (LexisNexis ⟨year⟩

Session laws: Cite to N.M. Laws, if therein.

▶ Laws of the State of New Mexico	⟨year⟩ N.M. Laws ⟨page no.⟩
▶ New Mexico Advance Legislative Service (Conway Greene)	⟨year⟩ N.M. Adv. Legis. Serv. ⟨page no.⟩
▶ West's New Mexico Legislative Service	⟨year⟩ N.M. Legis. Serv. ⟨page no.⟩ (West)

Administrative compilation

▶ Code of New Mexico Rules (LexisNexis)	N.M. CODE R. § x.x.x.x (LexisNexis ⟨year⟩

Administrative register

▶ New Mexico Register	⟨vol. no.⟩ N.M. Reg. ⟨page no.⟩ (⟨month day, year⟩)

New York (N.Y.)

http://www.nycourts.gov
http://nyassembly.gov/leg/

Court of Appeals (N.Y.) after 1847: Cite to N.E., N.E.2d, or N.E.3d, if therein.

▶ North Eastern Reporter	1885–date	N.E., N.E.2d, N.E.3d
▶ New York Reports	1847–date	N.Y., N.Y.2d, N.Y.3d
▶ West's New York Supplement	1956–date	N.Y.S.2d, N.Y.S.3d

(The first series of N.Y. is reprinted in N.Y.S. and N.Y.S.2d without separate pagination. Do not include a parallel cite to N.Y.S. or N.Y.S.2d in citations to the first series of N.Y.)

Court for the Correction of Errors (N.Y.) and **Supreme Court of Judicature** (N.Y. Sup. Ct.) (highest state court of law before 1846): Cite to one of the following reporters.

▶ Lockwood's Reversed Cases	1799–1847	Lock. Rev. Cas.

▶ Denio's Reports	1845–1848	Denio
▶ Hill and Denio Supplement (Lalor)	1842–1844	Hill & Den.
▶ Hill's Reports	1841–1844	Hill
▶ Edmond's Select Cases	1834–1853	Edm. Sel. Cas.
▶ Yates' Select Cases	1809	Yates Sel. Cas.
▶ Anthon's Nisi Prius Cases	1807–1851	Ant. N.P. Cas.
▶ Wendell's Reports	1828–1841	Wend.
▶ Cowen's Reports	1823–1829	Cow.
▶ Johnson's Reports	1806–1823	Johns.
▶ Caines' Reports	1803–1805	Cai.
▶ Caines' Cases	1796–1805	Cai. Cas.
▶ Coleman & Caines' Cases	1794–1805	Cole. & Cai. Cas.
▶ Johnson's Cases	1799–1803	Johns. Cas.
▶ Coleman's Cases	1791–1800	Cole. Cas.

Court of Chancery (N.Y. Ch.) (highest state court of equity before 1848): Cite to one of the following reporters.

▶ Edwards' Chancery Reports	1831–1850	Edw. Ch.
▶ Barbour's Chancery Reports	1845–1848	Barb. Ch.
▶ Sandford's Chancery Reports	1843–1847	Sand. Ch.
▶ Saratoga Chancery Sentinel	1841–1847	Sarat. Ch. Sent.
▶ Paige's Chancery Reports	1828–1845	Paige Ch.
▶ Clarke's Chancery Reports	1839–1841	Cl. Ch.
▶ Hoffman's Chancery Reports	1839–1840	Hoff. Ch.
▶ Hopkins' Chancery Reports	1823–1826	Hopk. Ch.
▶ Lansing's Chancery Reports	1824–1826	Lans. Ch.
▶ Johnson's Chancery Reports	1814–1823	Johns. Ch.
▶ New York Chancery Reports Annotated	1814–1847	N.Y. Ch. Ann.

Supreme Court, Appellate Division (N.Y. App. Div.), previously **Supreme Court, General Term** (N.Y. Gen. Term): Cite to N.Y.S., N.Y.S.2d, or N.Y.S.3d, if therein.

▶ West's New York Supplement	1888–date	N.Y.S., N.Y.S.2d, N.Y.S.3d
▶ Appellate Division Reports	1896–date	A.D., A.D.2d, A.D.3d
▶ Supreme Court Reports	1874–1896	N.Y. Sup. Ct.
▶ Lansing's Reports	1869–1873	Lans.
▶ Barbour's Supreme Court Reports	1847–1877	Barb.

Other lower courts (e.g., N.Y. App. Term, N.Y. Sup. Ct., N.Y. Ct. Cl., N.Y. Civ. Ct., N.Y. Crim. Ct., N.Y. Fam. Ct.): Cite to N.Y.S., N.Y.S.2d, or N.Y.S.3d, if therein.

| ▶ West's New York Supplement | 1888–date | N.Y.S., N.Y.S.2d, N.Y.S.3d |
| ▶ New York Miscellaneous Reports | 1892–date | Misc., Misc. 2d |

Other lower courts before 1888: Cite to one of the following reporters.

▸ Abbott's New Cases	1876–1894	Abb. N. Cas.
▸ Abbott's Practice Reports	1854–1875	Abb. Pr., Abb. Pr. (n.s.)
▸ Howard's Practice Reports	1844–1886	How. Pr., How. Pr. (n.s.)

Statutory compilations: Cite to one of the following sources, if therein.

▸ McKinney's Consolidated Laws of New York Annotated (West)	N.Y. ‹SUBJECT› LAW § x (McKinney ‹year›)
▸ New York Consolidated Laws Service (LexisNexis)	N.Y. ‹SUBJECT› LAW § x (Consol. ‹year›)
▸ New York Consolidated Laws Unannotated (LexisNexis)	N.Y. ‹SUBJECT› LAW § x (LexisNexis ‹year›)
▸ Abandoned Property	ABAND. PROP.
▸ Agricultural Conservation	AGRIC. CONSERV.
▸ Agriculture and Markets	AGRIC. & MKTS.
▸ Alcoholic Beverage Control	ALCO. BEV. CONT.
▸ Alternative County Government	ALT. COUNTY GOV'T
▸ Arts and Cultural Affairs	ARTS & CULT. AFF.
▸ Banking	BANKING
▸ Benevolent Orders	BEN. ORD.
▸ Business Corporation	BUS. CORP.
▸ Canal	CANAL
▸ Civil Practice Law and Rules	N.Y. C.P.L.R. ‹rule no.› (McKinney ‹year›) or: N.Y. C.P.L.R. ‹rule no.› (Consol. ‹year›)
▸ Civil Rights	CIV. RIGHTS
▸ Civil Service	CIV. SERV.
▸ Commerce	COM.
▸ Cooperative Corporations	COOP. CORP.
▸ Correction	CORRECT.
▸ County	COUNTY
▸ Criminal Procedure	CRIM. PROC.
▸ Debtor and Creditor	DEBT. & CRED.
▸ Domestic Relations	DOM. REL.
▸ Economic Development	ECON. DEV.
▸ Education	EDUC.
▸ Elder	ELDER
▸ Election	ELEC.
▸ Eminent Domain Procedure	EM. DOM. PROC.
▸ Employers' Liability	EMPL'RS LIAB.
▸ Energy	ENERGY
▸ Environmental Conservation	ENV'T CONSERV.
▸ Estates, Powers and Trusts	EST. POWERS & TRUSTS
▸ Executive	EXEC.
▸ Financial Services	FIN. SERV.
▸ General Associations	GEN. ASS'NS

▸ General Business	GEN. BUS.
▸ General City	GEN. CITY
▸ General Construction	GEN. CONSTR.
▸ General Municipal	GEN. MUN.
▸ General Obligations	GEN. OBLIG.
▸ Highway	HIGH.
▸ Indian	INDIAN
▸ Insurance	INS.
▸ Judiciary	JUD.
▸ Judiciary Court Acts	JUD. CT. ACTS
▸ Labor	LAB.
▸ Legislative	LEGIS.
▸ Lien	LIEN
▸ Limited Liability Company	LTD. LIAB. CO.
▸ Local Finance	LOCAL FIN.
▸ Mental Hygiene	MENTAL HYG.
▸ Military	MIL.
▸ Multiple Dwelling	MULT. DWELL.
▸ Multiple Residence	MULT. RESID.
▸ Municipal Home Rule and Statute of Local Governments	MUN. HOME RULE
▸ Navigation	NAV.
▸ Not-for-Profit Corporation	NOT-FOR-PROFIT CORP.
▸ Optional County Government	OPT. CNTY. GOV'T
▸ Parks, Recreation and Historic Preservation	PARKS REC. & HIST. PRESERV.
▸ Partnership	P'SHIP
▸ Penal	PENAL
▸ Personal Property	PERS. PROP.
▸ Private Housing Finance	PRIV. HOUS. FIN.
▸ Public Authorities	PUB. AUTH.
▸ Public Buildings	PUB. BLDGS.
▸ Public Health	PUB. HEALTH
▸ Public Housing	PUB. HOUS.
▸ Public Lands	PUB. LANDS
▸ Public Officers	PUB. OFF.
▸ Public Service	PUB. SERV.
▸ Racing, Pari-Mutuel Wagering and Breeding	RAC. PARI-MUT. WAG. & BREED.
▸ Railroad	R.R.
▸ Rapid Transit	RAPID TRANS.
▸ Real Property	REAL PROP.
▸ Real Property Actions and Proceedings	REAL PROP. ACTS.
▸ Real Property Tax	REAL PROP. TAX
▸ Religious Corporations	RELIG. CORP.
▸ Retirement and Social Security	RETIRE. & SOC. SEC.
▸ Rural Electric Cooperative	RURAL ELEC. COOP.
▸ Second Class Cities	SECOND CLASS CITIES

▸ Social Services	Soc. Serv.
▸ Soil and Water Conservation Districts	Soil & Water Conserv. Dist.
▸ State	State
▸ State Administrative Procedure Act	A.P.A.
▸ State Finance	State Fin.
▸ State Printing and Public Documents	State Print. & Pub. Docs.
▸ State Technology	State Tech.
▸ Statutes	Stat.
▸ Surrogate's Court Procedure Act	Surr. Ct. Proc. Act
▸ Tax	Tax
▸ Town	Town
▸ Transportation	Transp.
▸ Transportation Corporations	Transp. Corp.
▸ Unconsolidated	Unconsol.
▸ Uniform Commercial Code	U.C.C.
▸ Vehicle and Traffic	Veh. & Traf.
▸ Village	Village
▸ Volunteer Ambulance Workers' Benefit	Vol. Ambul. Workers' Ben.
▸ Volunteer Firefighters' Benefit	Vol. Fire. Ben.
▸ Workers' Compensation	Workers' Comp.

Uncompiled laws: Cite to one of the following sources, if therein. For the user's convenience, the McKinney's volume in which the law appears is indicated parenthetically below.

▸ McKinney's Consolidated Laws	N.Y. ‹LAW› § x (McKinney ‹year›)
▸ Consolidated Laws Service	N.Y. ‹LAW› § x (Consol. ‹year›)
▸ New York Consolidated Laws Unannotated	N.Y. ‹LAW› § x (LexisNexis ‹year›)
▸ New York City Civil Court Act (29A)	City Civ. Ct. Act
▸ New York City Criminal Court Act (29A)	City Crim. Ct. Act
▸ Code of Criminal Procedure (11A)	Code Crim. Proc.
▸ Court of Claims Act (29A)	Ct. Cl. Act
▸ Family Court Act (29A)	Fam. Ct. Act
▸ Uniform City Court Act (29A)	Uniform City Ct. Act
▸ Uniform District Court Act (29A)	Uniform Dist. Ct. Act
▸ Uniform Justice Court Act (29A)	Uniform Just. Ct. Act

Session laws: Cite to official N.Y. Laws, if therein; otherwise, cite to N.Y. Sess. Laws, if therein.

▸ Laws of New York	‹year› N.Y. Laws ‹page no.›
▸ McKinney's Session Laws of New York (West)	‹year› N.Y. Sess. Laws ‹page no.› (McKinney)
▸ New York Consolidated Laws Service Advance Legislative Service (LexisNexis)	‹year›-‹pamph. no.› N.Y. Consol. Laws Adv. Legis. Serv. ‹page no.› (LexisNexis)

Administrative compilation

▶ Official Compilation of Codes, Rules & Regu- N.Y. COMP. CODES R. & REGS.
lations of the State of New York (West)   tit. x, § x ‹year›

Administrative register

▶ New York State Register   ‹vol. no.› N.Y. Reg. ‹page no.›
‹month day, year›

···

North Carolina (N.C.)

https://www.nccourts.gov
https://www.ncleg.gov/laws/generalstatutes

Supreme Court (N.C.): Cite to S.E. or S.E.2d, if therein.

▶ South Eastern Reporter	1887–date	S.E., S.E.2d
▶ North Carolina Reports		
▶ 63 N.C. to date	1868–date	N.C.
▶ Phillips' Equity	1866–1868	62 N.C. (Phil. Eq.)
▶ Phillips' Law	1866–1868	61 N.C. (Phil.)
▶ Winston	1863–1864	60 N.C. (Win.)
▶ Jones' Equity (54–59)	1853–1863	e.g., 54 N.C. (1 Jones Eq.)
▶ Jones' Law (46–53)	1853–1862	e.g., 46 N.C. (1 Jones)
▶ Busbee's Equity	1852–1853	45 N.C. (Busb. Eq.)
▶ Busbee's Law	1852–1853	44 N.C. (Busb.)
▶ Iredell's Equity (36–43)	1840–1852	e.g., 36 N.C. (1 Ired. Eq.)
▶ Iredell's Law (23–35)	1840–1852	e.g., 23 N.C. (1 Ired.)
▶ Devereux & Battle's Equity (21–22)	1834–1839	e.g., 21 N.C. (1 Dev. & Bat. Eq.)
▶ Devereux & Battle's Law (18–20)	1834–1839	e.g., 20 N.C. (3 & 4 Dev. & Bat.)
▶ Devereux's Equity (16–17)	1826–1834	e.g., 16 N.C. (1 Dev. Eq.)
▶ Devereux's Law (12–15)	1826–1834	e.g., 12 N.C. (1 Dev.)
▶ Hawks (8–11)	1820–1826	e.g., 8 N.C. (1 Hawks)
▶ Murphey (5–7)	1804–1813 1818–1819	e.g., 5 N.C. (1 Mur.)
▶ Taylor's North Carolina Term Reports	1816–1818	4 N.C. (Taylor)
▶ Carolina Law Repository	1813–1816	4 N.C. (Car. L. Rep.)
▶ Haywood (2–3)	1789–1806	e.g., 2 N.C. (1 Hayw.)
▶ Conference by Cameron & Norwood	1800–1804	1 N.C. (Cam. & Nor.)
▶ Taylor	1798–1802	1 N.C. (Tay.)
▶ Martin	1778–1797	1 N.C. (Mart.)

Court of Appeals (N.C. Ct. App.): Cite to S.E.2d, if therein.

▶ South Eastern Reporter	1968–date	S.E.2d
▶ North Carolina Court of Appeals Reports	1968–date	N.C. App.

Statutory compilations: Cite to N.C. GEN. STAT. (published by LexisNexis), if therein.

▸ General Statutes of North Carolina (LexisNexis)	N.C. GEN. STAT. § x-x ⟨year⟩
▸ West's North Carolina General Statutes Annotated	N.C. GEN. STAT. ANN. § x-x (West ⟨year⟩)

Session laws: Cite to N.C. Sess. Laws, if therein.

▸ Session Laws of North Carolina	⟨year⟩ N.C. Sess. Laws ⟨page no.⟩
▸ North Carolina ⟨year⟩ Advance Legislative Service (LexisNexis)	⟨year⟩-⟨pamph. no.⟩ N.C. Adv. Legis. Serv. ⟨page no.⟩ (LexisNexis)
▸ North Carolina Legislative Service (West)	⟨year⟩ N.C. Legis. Serv. ⟨page no.⟩ (West)

Administrative compilation

▸ North Carolina Administrative Code (West)	⟨tit. no.⟩ N.C. ADMIN. CODE ⟨rule no.⟩ (⟨year⟩)

Administrative register

▸ North Carolina Register (LexisNexis)	⟨vol. no.⟩ N.C. Reg. ⟨page no.⟩ (⟨month day, year⟩)

....

North Dakota (N.D.)

https://www.ndcourts.gov
https://www.legis.nd.gov

Public domain citation format: North Dakota has adopted a public domain citation format for cases after December 31, 1996. The format is:

▸ Kautzman v. Kautzman, 2003 ND 140, 668 N.W.2d 59.

▸ Kautzman v. Kautzman, 2003 ND 140, ¶ 9, 668 N.W.2d 59, 63.

For additional information, consult North Dakota Rules of Court, Rule 11.6.

Supreme Court (N.D.): Cite to N.W. or N.W.2d, if therein.

▸ North Western Reporter	1890–date	N.W., N.W.2d
▸ North Dakota Reports	1890–1953	N.D.

Supreme Court of Dakota (Dakota): Cite to N.W., if therein.

▸ North Western Reporter	1879–1889	N.W.
▸ Dakota Reports	1867–1889	Dakota

Court of Appeals of North Dakota (N.D. Ct. App.): Cite to N.W.2d.

▸ North Western Reporter	1987–date	N.W.2d

Statutory compilations: Cite to N.D. CENT. CODE, if therein.

▸ North Dakota Century Code (LexisNexis)	N.D. CENT. CODE § x-x-x (⟨year⟩)
▸ West's North Dakota Century Code Annotated	N.D. CENT. CODE ANN. § x-x-x (West ⟨year⟩)

Session laws: Cite to N.D. Laws, if therein.

▸ Laws of North Dakota		⟨year⟩ N.D. Laws ⟨page no.⟩
▸ North Dakota Century Code ⟨year⟩ Advance Legislative Service (LexisNexis)		⟨year⟩-⟨pamph. no.⟩ N.D. Cent. Code Adv. Legis. Serv. ⟨page no.⟩ (LexisNexis)
▸ West's North Dakota Legislative Service		⟨year⟩ N.D. Legis. Serv. ⟨page no.⟩ (West)

Administrative compilation

▸ North Dakota Administrative Code	N.D. ADMIN. CODE ⟨rule no.⟩ (⟨year⟩)

Ohio (Ohio)

https://www.sconet.state.oh.us
https://codes.ohio.gov/orc

Public domain citation format: Ohio has adopted a public domain citation format for cases decided after April 30, 2002. The format is:

▶ State v. Lynch, 98 Ohio St. 3d 514, 2003-Ohio-2284, 787 N.E.2d 1185.

▶ State v. Lynch, 98 Ohio St. 3d 514, 2003-Ohio-2284, 787 N.E.2d 1185, at ¶ 3.

For additional information, consult the SUPREME COURT OF OHIO WRITING MANUAL (2d ed. 2013).

Supreme Court (Ohio): Cite to N.E., N.E.2d, or N.E.3d, if therein.

▸ North Eastern Reporter	1885–date	N.E., N.E.2d, N.E.3d
▸ Ohio State Reports	1852–date	Ohio St., Ohio St. 2d, Ohio St. 3d
▸ Ohio Reports	1821–1851	Ohio
▸ Wilcox's Condensed Reports	1821–1831	Wilc. Cond. Rep.
▸ Wright	1831–1834	Wright
▸ Ohio Unreported Cases	1809–1899	Ohio Unrep. Cas.

Court of Appeals (Ohio Ct. App.): Cite to N.E., N.E.2d, or N.E.3d, if therein.

▸ North Eastern Reporter	1926–date	N.E., N.E.2d, N.E.3d
▸ Ohio Appellate Reports	1913–date	Ohio App., Ohio App. 2d, Ohio App. 3d
▸ Ohio Circuit Court Reports	1914–1917	Ohio C.C.
▸ Ohio Courts of Appeals Reports	1916–1922	Ohio Ct. App.

Other law courts: Cite to N.E., N.E.2d, or N.E.3d, if therein; otherwise, cite to another reporter in the following order of preference.

▸ North Eastern Reporter	1926–date	N.E., N.E.2d, N.E.3d
▸ Ohio Miscellaneous Reports	1962–2012	Ohio Misc., Ohio Misc. 2d
▸ Ohio Bar Reports	1982–1987	Ohio B.
▸ Ohio Opinions	1934–1982	Ohio Op., Ohio Op. 2d, Ohio Op. 3d
▸ Ohio Law Abstract	1922–1964	Ohio Law Abs.
▸ Ohio Nisi Prius Reports	1903–1934	Ohio N.P., Ohio N.P. (n.s.)
▸ Ohio Decisions	1894–1921	Ohio Dec.

▸ Ohio Decisions, Reprint	1840–1893	Ohio Dec. Reprint
▸ Ohio Circuit Decisions	1885–1923	Ohio Cir. Dec.
▸ Ohio Circuit Court Decisions	1901–1923	e.g., 13-23 Ohio C.C. Dec.
▸ Ohio Circuit Court Reports	1885–1901	Ohio C.C.
▸ Ohio Law Bulletin	1876–1921	Ohio L. Bull.
▸ Ohio Circuit Court Reports, New Series	1903–1917	Ohio C.C. (n.s.)
▸ Ohio Law Reporter	1903–1934	Ohio L.R.
▸ Tappen's Reports	1816–1819	Tapp. Rep.
▸ Anderson's Unreported Ohio Appellate Cases	1990	Ohio App. Unrep.

Statutory compilations: Cite to one of the following codes.

▸ Page's Ohio Revised Code Annotated (LexisNexis)	OHIO REV. CODE ANN. § x.x (LexisNexis ⟨year⟩)
▸ Baldwin's Ohio Revised Code Annotated (West)	OHIO REV. CODE ANN. § x.x (West ⟨year⟩)

Session laws: Cite to Ohio Laws, if therein.

▸ State of Ohio: Legislative Acts Passed and Joint Resolutions Adopted	⟨year⟩ Ohio Laws ⟨page no.⟩
▸ Page's Ohio Legislative Bulletin (LexisNexis)	⟨year⟩ Ohio Legis. Bull. ⟨page no.⟩ (LexisNexis)
▸ Baldwin's Ohio Legislative Service Annotated (West)	⟨year⟩ Ohio Legis. Serv. Ann. ⟨page no.⟩ (West)

Administrative compilation

▸ Baldwin's Ohio Administrative Code (West)	OHIO ADMIN. CODE ⟨rule no.⟩ (⟨year⟩)

Administrative and executive registers: Cite to one of the following registers.

▸ Baldwin's Ohio Monthly Record	1977–date	Ohio Monthly Rec. ⟨page no.⟩ (⟨month year⟩)
▸ Ohio Government Reports	1965–1976	Ohio Gov't ⟨page no.⟩ (⟨month day, year⟩)
▸ Ohio Department Reports	1914–1964	Ohio Dep't ⟨page no.⟩ (⟨month day, year⟩)

Oklahoma (Okla.)

https://www.oscn.net
http://www.oklegislature.gov/osstatuestitle.html

Public domain citation format: Oklahoma has adopted a public domain citation format for cases after May 1, 1997. The format is:

▸ Herbert v. Okla. Christian Coal., 1999 OK 90, 992 P.2d 322.

▸ Herbert v. Okla. Christian Coal., 1999 OK 90, ¶ 2, 992 P.2d 322, 325.

For additional information, consult Oklahoma Supreme Court Rule 1.200(e) and Oklahoma Criminal Appeals Rule 3.5(c).

Supreme Court (Okla.): Cite to P., P.2d, or P.3d, if therein.

▸ Pacific Reporter	1890–date	P., P.2d, P.3d

▸ Oklahoma Reports   1890–1953   Okla.

Court of Appeals of Indian Territory (Indian Terr.): Cite to S.W., if therein.

▸ South Western Reporter   1896–1907   S.W.
▸ Indian Territory Reports   1896–1907   Indian Terr.

Court of Criminal Appeals (Okla. Crim. App.), previously **Criminal Court of Appeals** (Okla. Crim. App.): Cite to P., P.2d, or P.3d, if therein.

▸ Pacific Reporter   1908–date   P., P.2d, P.3d
▸ Oklahoma Criminal Reports   1908–1953   Okla. Crim.

Court of Civil Appeals (Okla. Civ. App.): Cite to P.2d or P.3d.

▸ Pacific Reporter   1971–date   P.2d, P.3d

Statutory compilations: Cite to OKLA. STAT., if therein.

▸ Oklahoma Statutes (West)   OKLA. STAT. tit. x, § x (‹year›)
▸ Oklahoma Statutes Annotated (West)   OKLA. STAT. ANN. tit. x, § x
                                              (West ‹year›)

Session laws: Cite to Okla. Sess. Laws, if therein.

▸ Oklahoma Session Laws (West)   ‹year› Okla. Sess. Laws ‹page
                                              no.›
▸ Oklahoma Session Law Service (West)   ‹year› Okla. Sess. Law Serv.
                                              ‹page no.› (West)

Administrative compilation

▸ Oklahoma Administrative Code   OKLA. ADMIN. CODE § x:x-x-x
                                              (‹year›)

Administrative registers: Cite to one of the following sources.

▸ Oklahoma Register   1983–date   ‹vol. no.› Okla. Reg. ‹page
                                                     no.› (‹month day, year›)
▸ Oklahoma Gazette   1962–1983   ‹vol. no.› Okla. Gaz. ‹page
                                                     no.› (‹month day, year›)

Oregon (Or.)

https://www.courts.oregon.gov/pages/default.aspx
https://www.oregonlegislature.gov/bills_laws

Supreme Court (Or.): Cite to P., P.2d, or P.3d, if therein.

▸ Pacific Reporter   1883–date   P., P.2d, P.3d
▸ Oregon Reports   1853–date   Or.

Court of Appeals (Or. Ct. App.): Cite to P.2d or P.3d, if therein.

▸ Pacific Reporter   1969–date   P.2d, P.3d
▸ Oregon Reports, Court of   1969–date   Or. App.
  Appeals

Tax Court (Or. T.C.): Cite to Or. Tax.

▸ Oregon Tax Reports   1962–date   Or. Tax

Statutory compilations: Cite to Or. Rev. Stat., if therein.

▸Oregon Revised Statutes	Or. Rev. Stat. § x.x ⟨year⟩
▸West's Oregon Revised Statutes Annotated	Or. Rev. Stat. Ann. § x.x (West ⟨year⟩)

Session laws: Cite to Or. Laws, if therein. When citing statutes repealed during or after 1953, indicate parenthetically the former Or. Rev. Stat. sections.

▸Oregon Laws and Resolutions	⟨year⟩ Or. Laws ⟨page no.⟩ ⟨year⟩ Or. Laws Spec. Sess. ⟨page no.⟩ ⟨year⟩ Or. Laws Adv. Sh. No. x, ⟨page no.⟩
▸West's Oregon Legislative Service	⟨year⟩ Or. Legis. Serv. ⟨page no.⟩ (West)

Administrative compilation

▸Oregon Administrative Rules	Or. Admin. R. ⟨rule no.⟩ (⟨year⟩)

Administrative register

▸Oregon Bulletin	⟨vol. no.⟩ Or. Bull. ⟨page no.⟩ (⟨month day, year⟩)

Pennsylvania (Pa.)

https://ujsportal.pacourts.us
https://www.legis.state.pa.us/cfdocs/legis/li/public

Supreme Court (Pa.): Cite to A., A.2d, or A.3d, if therein.

▸Atlantic Reporter	1885–date	A., A.2d, A.3d
▸Pennsylvania State Reports	1845–date	Pa.
▸Monaghan	1888–1890	Monag.
▸Sadler	1885–1889	Sadler
▸Walker	1855–1885	Walk.
▸Pennypacker	1881–1884	Pennyp.
▸Grant	1814–1863	Grant
▸Watts and Sergeant	1841–1845	Watts & Serg.
▸Wharton	1835–1841	Whart.
▸Watts	1832–1840	Watts
▸Rawle	1828–1835	Rawle
▸Penrose and Watts	1829–1832	Pen. & W.
▸Sergeant and Rawle	1814–1828	Serg. & Rawle
▸Binney	1799–1814	Binn.
▸Yeates	1791–1808	Yeates
▸Addison	1791–1799	Add.
▸Dallas	1754–1806	Dall.
▸Alden	1754–1814	Ald.

Superior Court (Pa. Super. Ct.): Cite to A., A.2d, or A.3d, if therein. For cases decided after December 31, 1998, use the following public domain citation format:

▸ Rapagnani v. Judas Co., 1999 PA Super 203, ¶ 3.

▸Atlantic Reporter	1931–date	A., A.2d, A.3d

▸ Pennsylvania Superior Court Reports   1895–1997   Pa. Super.

Commonwealth Court (Pa. Commw. Ct.): Cite to A.2d or A.3d, if therein.

▸ Atlantic Reporter	1970–date	A.2d, A.3d
▸ Pennsylvania Commonwealth Court Reports	1970–1994	Pa. Commw.

Other lower courts: Cite to Pa. D. & C., Pa. D. & C.2d, Pa. D. & C.3d, Pa. D. & C.4th, or Pa. D. & C.5th, if therein. Not all lower court decisions are reproduced in the reporters listed below, and it may be necessary, on occasion, to cite to the legal reporter for an individual county, if available. For a comprehensive list of Pennsylvania county court reports, consult chapter seven, appendix four, FRANK Y. LIU ET AL., PENNSYLVANIA LEGAL RESEARCH HANDBOOK (2008).

▸ Pennsylvania District and County Reports	1918–date	Pa. D. & C., Pa. D. & C.2d, Pa. D. & C.3d, Pa. D. & C.4th, Pa. D. & C.5th
▸ Pennsylvania District Reports	1892–1921	Pa. D.
▸ Pennsylvania County Court Reports	1870–1921	Pa. C.

Statutory compilations: Cite to PA. CONS. STAT. (79 titles), if therein. These publications should not be confused with PA. CODE, which is a code of regulations, not of legislation.

▸ Pennsylvania Consolidated Statutes	‹tit. no.› PA. CONS. STAT. § x (‹year›)
▸ Purdon's Pennsylvania Statutes and Consolidated Statutes Annotated (West)	‹tit. no.› PA. STAT. AND CONS. STAT. ANN. § x (West ‹year›)
▸ Purdon's Pennsylvania Statutes and Consolidated Statutes (West)	‹tit. no.› PA. STAT. AND CONS. STAT. § x (West ‹year›)

Session laws: Cite to Pa. Laws, if therein.

▸ Laws of Pennsylvania	‹year› Pa. Laws ‹page no.›
▸ Purdon's Pennsylvania Legislative Service (West)	‹year› Pa. Legis. Serv. ‹page no.› (West)

Administrative compilation

▸ Pennsylvania Code (Fry Communications)	‹tit. no.› PA. CODE § x.x (‹year›)

Administrative register

▸ Pennsylvania Bulletin (Fry Communications)	‹vol. no.› Pa. Bull. ‹page no.› (‹month day, year›)

Rhode Island (R.I.)

https://www.courts.ri.gov/pages/default.aspx
http://webserver.rilin.state.ri.us/Statutes

Supreme Court (R.I.): Cite to A., A.2d, or A.3d, if therein.

▸ Atlantic Reporter	1885–date	A., A.2d, A.3d
▸ Rhode Island Reports	1828–1980	R.I.

Statutory compilations: Cite to R.I. GEN. LAWS, if therein.

▸ General Laws of Rhode Island (LexisNexis) ⟨tit. no.⟩ R.I. GEN. LAWS § x-x-x ⟨year⟩
▸ West's General Laws of Rhode Island Annotated ⟨tit. no.⟩ R.I. GEN. LAWS ANN. § x-x-x (West ⟨year⟩)

Session laws: Cite to R.I. Pub. Laws, if therein.

▸ Public Laws of Rhode Island and Providence Plantations ⟨year⟩ R.I. Pub. Laws ⟨page no.⟩
▸ Acts and Resolves of Rhode Island and Providence Plantations ⟨year⟩ R.I. Acts & Resolves ⟨page no.⟩
▸ Rhode Island Advance Legislative Service (LexisNexis) ⟨year⟩-⟨pamph. no.⟩ R.I. Adv. Legis. Serv. ⟨page no.⟩ (LexisNexis)
▸ West's Rhode Island Advance Legislative Service ⟨year⟩ R.I. Adv. Legis. Serv. ⟨page no.⟩ (West)

Administrative compilation

▸ Code of Rhode Island Rules (LexisNexis) ⟨tit. no.⟩-⟨ch. no.⟩ R.I. CODE R. § x (LexisNexis ⟨year⟩)

Administrative register

▸ Rhode Island Government Register (LexisNexis) ⟨iss. no.⟩ R.I. Gov't Reg. ⟨page no.⟩ (LexisNexis ⟨month year⟩)

South Carolina (S.C.)

https://www.sccourts.org
https://www.scstatehouse.gov/code/statmast.php

Supreme Court after 1868 (S.C.): Cite to S.E. or S.E.2d, if therein.

▸ South Eastern Reporter	1887–date	S.E., S.E.2d
▸ South Carolina Reports	1868–date	S.C.

Court of Appeals (S.C. Ct. App.): Cite to S.E.2d, if therein.

▸ South Eastern Reporter	1983–date	S.E.2d
▸ South Carolina Reports	1983–date	S.C.

Courts of law before 1868: Cite to S.C.L.

▸ South Carolina Law Reports

▸ Richardson (37–49)	1850–1868	e.g., 37 S.C.L. (3 Rich.)
▸ Strobhart (32–36)	1846–1850	e.g., 32 S.C.L. (1 Strob.)
▸ Richardson (30–31)	1844–1846	e.g., 30 S.C.L. (1 Rich.)
▸ Speers (28–29)	1842–1844	e.g., 28 S.C.L. (1 Speers)
▸ McMullan (26–27)	1840–1842	e.g., 26 S.C.L. (1 McMul.)
▸ Cheves	1839–1840	25 S.C.L. (Chev.)
▸ Rice	1838–1839	24 S.C.L. (Rice)
▸ Dudley	1837–1838	23 S.C.L. (Dud.)
▸ Riley	1836–1837	22 S.C.L. (Ril.)
▸ Hill (19–21)	1833–1837	e.g., 19 S.C.L. (1 Hill)
▸ Bailey (17–18)	1828–1832	e.g., 17 S.C.L. (1 Bail.)
▸ Harper	1823–1824	16 S.C.L. (Harp.)

▸ McCord (12–15)	1821–1828	e.g., 12 S.C.L. (1 McCord)
▸ Nott and McCord (10–11)	1817–1820	e.g., 10 S.C.L. (1 Nott & McC.)
▸ Mill (Constitutional) (8–9)	1817–1818	e.g., 8 S.C.L. (1 Mill)
▸ Treadway (6–7)	1812–1816	e.g., 6 S.C.L. (1 Tread.)
▸ Brevard (3–5)	1793–1816	e.g., 3 S.C.L. (1 Brev.)
▸ Bay (1–2)	1783–1804	e.g., 1 S.C.L. (1 Bay)

Courts of equity before 1868: Cite to S.C. Eq.

▸ South Carolina Equity Reports		
▸ Richardson's Equity (24–35)	1850–1868	e.g., 24 S.C. Eq. (3 Rich. Eq.)
▸ Strobhart's Equity (20–23)	1846–1850	e.g., 20 S.C. Eq. (1 Strob. Eq.)
▸ Richardson's Equity (18–19)	1844–1846	e.g., 18 S.C. Eq. (1 Rich. Eq.)
▸ Speers' Equity	1842–1844	17 S.C. Eq. (Speers Eq.)
▸ McMullan's Equity	1840–1842	16 S.C. Eq. (McMul. Eq.)
▸ Cheves' Equity	1839–1840	15 S.C. Eq. (Chev. Eq.)
▸ Rice's Equity	1838–1839	14 S.C. Eq. (Rice Eq.)
▸ Dudley's Equity	1837–1838	13 S.C. Eq. (Dud. Eq.)
▸ Riley's Chancery	1836–1837	12 S.C. Eq. (Ril. Eq.)
▸ Hill's Chancery (10–11)	1833–1837	e.g., 10 S.C. Eq. (1 Hill Eq.)
▸ Richardson's Cases	1831–1832	9 S.C. Eq. (Rich. Cas.)
▸ Bailey's Equity	1830–1831	8 S.C. Eq. (Bail. Eq.)
▸ McCord's Chancery (6–7)	1825–1827	e.g., 6 S.C. Eq. (1 McCord Eq.)
▸ Harper's Equity	1824	5 S.C. Eq. (Harp. Eq.)
▸ Desaussure's Equity (1–4)	1784–1817	e.g., 1 S.C. Eq. (1 Des. Eq.)

Statutory compilation

▸ Code of Laws of South Carolina 1976 Annotated	S.C. CODE ANN. § x-x-x (‹year›)

Session laws

▸ Acts and Joint Resolutions, South Carolina	‹year› S.C. Acts ‹page no.›

Administrative compilation: Administrative regulations appear in volumes 1–10 of S.C. CODE ANN. This publication should not be confused with the statutory compilation of the same name, which also contains volumes 1–10.

▸ Code of Laws of South Carolina 1976 Annotated: Code of Regulations (West)	S.C. CODE ANN. REGS. ‹reg no.› (‹year›)

Administrative register

▸ South Carolina State Register	‹vol. no.› S.C. Reg. ‹page no.› (‹month day, year›)

....

South Dakota (S.D.)

https://ujs.sd.gov
http://sdlegislature.gov/statutes/codified_laws/default.aspx

Public domain citation format: South Dakota has adopted a public domain citation format for cases after December 31, 1996. The format is:

▸ Wulf v. Senst, 2003 SD 105, 669 N.W.2d 135.

▸ Wulf v. Senst, 2003 SD 105, ¶ 14, 669 N.W.2d 135, 141.

For additional information, consult South Dakota Rules of Civil Procedure § 15-26A-69.1.

Supreme Court (S.D.): Cite to N.W. or N.W.2d, if therein.

▶ North Western Reporter 1890–date N.W., N.W.2d
▶ South Dakota Reports 1890–1976 S.D.

Supreme Court of Dakota (Dakota): Cite to N.W., if therein.

▶ North Western Reporter 1879–1889 N.W.
▶ Dakota Reports 1867–1889 Dakota

Statutory compilation

▶ South Dakota Codified Laws (West) S.D. CODIFIED LAWS § x-x-x ‹year›

Session laws: Cite to S.D. Sess. Laws, if therein.

▶ Session Laws of South Dakota ‹year› S.D. Sess. Laws ‹ch. x § x› ‹page no.›

Administrative compilation

▶ Administrative Rules of South Dakota S.D. ADMIN. R. ‹rule no.› (‹year›)

Administrative register

▶ South Dakota Register ‹vol. no.› S.D. Reg. ‹page no.› (‹month day, year›)

Tennessee (Tenn.)

http://www.tncourts.gov
http://www.lexisnexis.com/hottopics/tncode

Supreme Court (Tenn.): Cite to S.W., S.W.2d, or S.W.3d, if therein.

▶ South Western Reporter 1886–date S.W., S.W.2d, S.W.3d
▶ Tennessee Reports
  ▶ 60 Tenn. to 225 Tenn. 1872–1972 Tenn.
  ▶ Heiskell 1870–1874 e.g., 48 Tenn. (1 Heisk.)
  ▶ Coldwell 1860–1870 e.g., 41 Tenn. (1 Cold.)
  ▶ Head 1858–1860 e.g., 38 Tenn. (1 Head)
  ▶ Sneed 1853–1858 e.g., 33 Tenn. (1 Sneed)
  ▶ Swan 1851–1853 e.g., 31 Tenn. (1 Swan)
  ▶ Humphreys 1839–1851 e.g., 20 Tenn. (1 Hum.)
  ▶ Meigs 1838–1839 19 Tenn. (Meigs)
  ▶ Yerger 1818–1837 e.g., 9 Tenn. (1 Yer.)
  ▶ Martin & Yerger 1825–1828 8 Tenn. (Mart. & Yer.)
  ▶ Peck 1821–1824 7 Tenn. (Peck)
  ▶ Haywood 1816–1818 e.g., 4 Tenn. (1 Hayw.)
  ▶ Cooke 1811–1814 3 Tenn. (Cooke)
  ▶ Overton 1791–1815 e.g., 1 Tenn. (1 Overt.)

Court of Appeals (Tenn. Ct. App.): Cite to S.W.2d or S.W.3d, if therein.

▶ South Western Reporter 1932–date S.W.2d, S.W.3d
▶ Tennessee Appeals Reports 1925–1971 Tenn. App.

Court of Criminal Appeals (Tenn. Crim. App.): Cite to S.W.2d or S.W.3d, if therein.

▸ South Western Reporter	1967–date	S.W.2d, S.W.3d
▸ Tennessee Criminal Appeals Reports	1967–1971	Tenn. Crim. App.

Statutory compilations: Cite to TENN. CODE ANN. (published by LexisNexis), if therein.

▸ Tennessee Code Annotated (LexisNexis)	TENN. CODE ANN. § x-x-x ⟨year⟩
▸ West's Tennessee Code Annotated	TENN. CODE ANN. § x-x-x (West ⟨year⟩)

Session laws: Cite to Tenn. Pub. Acts or Tenn. Priv. Acts, if therein.

▸ Public Acts of the State of Tennessee	⟨year⟩ Tenn. Pub. Acts ⟨page no.⟩
▸ Private Acts of the State of Tennessee	⟨year⟩ Tenn. Priv. Acts ⟨page no.⟩
▸ Tennessee Code Annotated Advance Legislative Service (LexisNexis)	⟨year⟩-⟨pamph. no.⟩ Tenn. Code Ann. Adv. Legis. Serv. ⟨page no.⟩ (LexisNexis)
▸ West's Tennessee Legislative Service	⟨year⟩ Tenn. Legis. Serv. ⟨page no.⟩ (West)

Administrative compilation

▸ Official Compilation Rules & Regulations of the State of Tennessee	TENN. COMP. R. & REGS. ⟨rule no.⟩ (⟨year⟩)

Administrative register

▸ Tennessee Administrative Register	⟨vol. no.⟩ Tenn. Admin. Reg. ⟨page no.⟩ (⟨month year⟩)

....

Texas (Tex.)

http://www.txcourts.gov
http://www.statutes.legis.state.tx.us

Supreme Court (Tex.): Cite to S.W., S.W.2d, or S.W.3d, if therein.

▸ South Western Reporter	1886–date	S.W., S.W.2d, S.W.3d
▸ Texas Reports	1846–1962	Tex.
▸ Synopses of the Decisions of the Supreme Court of Texas Arising from Restraints by Conscript and Other Military Authorities (Robards)	1862–1865	Robards (no vol. number)
▸ Texas Law Review (containing previously unpublished cases from the 1845 term)	1845–1846	65 TEX. L. REV. [e.g., Lamar v. Houston (Tex. 1845), 65 Tex. L. Rev. 382 (Paulsen rep. 1986)]
▸ Digest of the Laws of Texas (Dallam's Opinions)	1840–1844	Dallam (no vol. number)
▸ Texas Supreme Court Journal	1957–date	TEX. SUP. CT. J.

Court of Criminal Appeals (Tex. Crim. App.), previously **Court of Appeals** (Tex. Ct. App.): Cite to S.W., S.W.2d, or S.W.3d, if therein.

► South Western Reporter	1892–date	S.W., S.W.2d, S.W.3d
► Texas Criminal Reports	1892–1962	Tex. Crim.
► Texas Court of Appeals Reports	1876–1892	Tex. Ct. App.
► Condensed Reports of Decisions in Civil Causes in the Court of Appeals (White & Willson vol. 1) (Willson vols. 2–4)	1876–1883 1883–1892	White & W. Willson

Commission of Appeals (Tex. Comm'n App.): Cite to S.W. or S.W.2d, if therein.

► South Western Reporter	1886–1892 1918–1945	S.W. S.W.2d
► Texas Reports	1879–1892 1918–1945	Tex.
► Texas Unreported Cases (Posey)	1879–1884	Posey
► Condensed Reports of Decisions in Civil Causes in the Court of Appeals (White & Willson)	1879–1883	White & W.

Officially published opinions of the Commission of Appeals from 1879 to 1892 were adopted by the Supreme Court and should be cited as opinions of the Supreme Court. Opinions of the Commission of Appeals from 1918 to 1945 have a notation from the Supreme Court that usually appears in the final paragraph of the opinion, e.g., "opinion adopted," "holding approved," or "judgment adopted." Commission opinions that were adopted by the Supreme Court should be cited as opinions of the Supreme Court. "Holding approved" and "judgment adopted" opinions are cited by using "holding approved" or "judgm't adopted," e.g., Savage v. Cowen, 33 S.W.2d 433 (Tex. Comm'n App. 1930, judgm't adopted).

Courts of Appeals (Tex. App.), previously **Courts of Civil Appeals** (Tex. Civ. App.): Cite to S.W., S.W.2d, or S.W.3d, if therein.

► South Western Reporter	1892–date	S.W., S.W.2d, S.W.3d
► Texas Civil Appeals Reports	1892–1911	Tex. Civ. App.

For additional information on the history and structure of Texas courts and on local citation rules, the following sources are suggested: Texas Law Review Ass'n, The Greenbook: Texas Rules of Form (14th ed. 2018); Lydia M. V. Brandt, Texas Legal Research (1995); and A Reference Guide to Texas Law and Legal History (Karl T. Gruben & James E. Hambleton eds., 2d ed. 1987).

Statutory compilations: Texas is nearing the completion of a recodification of its laws. Cite to the new subject-matter Tex. Code Ann., if therein; otherwise, cite to Tex. Rev. Civ. Stat. Ann. or to one of the independent codes contained in the series *Vernon's Texas Civil Statutes* or *Vernon's Texas Statutes Annotated*. Note that the independent codes are not part of the new subject-matter Tex. Code Ann.

► Vernon's Texas Codes Annotated (West)	TEX. ⟨SUBJECT⟩ CODE ANN. § x (West ⟨year⟩)
► Vernon's Texas Revised Civil Statutes Annotated (West)	TEX. REV. CIV. STAT. ANN. art. x, § x (West ⟨year⟩)
► Vernon's Texas Business Corporation Act Annotated (West)	TEX. BUS. CORP. ACT ANN. art. x (West ⟨year⟩)
► Vernon's Texas Code of Criminal Procedure Annotated (West)	TEX. CODE CRIM. PROC. ANN. art. x (West ⟨year⟩)
► Vernon's Texas Insurance Code Annotated (West)	TEX. INS. CODE ANN. art. x (West ⟨year⟩)
► Vernon's Texas Probate Code Annotated (West)	TEX. PROB. CODE ANN. § x (West ⟨year⟩)
► Agriculture	AGRIC.
► Alcoholic Beverage	ALCO. BEV.
► Business and Commerce	BUS. & COM.
► Business Organizations (effective Jan. 1, 2006)	BUS. ORGS.
► Civil Practice and Remedies	CIV. PRAC. & REM.
► Education	EDUC.
► Election	ELEC.
► Estates	EST.
► Family	FAM.
► Finance	FIN.
► Government	GOV'T
► Health and Safety	HEALTH & SAFETY
► Human Resources	HUM. RES.
► Insurance	INS.
► Labor	LAB.
► Local Government	LOC. GOV'T
► Natural Resources	NAT. RES.
► Occupations	OCC.
► Parks and Wildlife	PARKS & WILD.
► Penal	PENAL
► Property	PROP.
► Special District Local Laws	SPEC. DISTS.
► Tax	TAX
► Transportation	TRANSP.
► Utilities	UTIL.
► Water	WATER

Session laws: Cite to Tex. Gen. Laws, if therein.

► General and Special Laws of the State of Texas	⟨year⟩ Tex. Gen. Laws ⟨page no.⟩
► Vernon's Texas Session Law Service (West)	⟨year⟩ Tex. Sess. Law Serv. ⟨page no.⟩ (West)
► Laws of the Republic of Texas	⟨year⟩ Repub. Tex. Laws ⟨page no.⟩

Session laws passed before 1941 must be cited according to the exact title, e.g., Tex. Loc. & Spec. Laws, Tex. Gen. & Spec. Laws, and Tex. Gen. Laws. The Revised Statutes were enacted and published separately in 1879, 1895, 1911, and 1925 and should be cited as ⟨year⟩ Tex. Rev. Civ. Stat. xxx. The Code of Criminal

Procedure and Penal Code were enacted and published separately in 1856, 1879, 1895, 1911, and 1925 and should be cited as ‹year› Tex. Crim. Stat. xxx.

Administrative compilation

▸ Texas Administrative Code (West) ‹tit. no.› TEX. ADMIN. CODE § x.x (‹year›)

Administrative register

▸ Texas Register (LexisNexis) ‹vol. no.› Tex. Reg. ‹page no.› (‹month day, year›)

....

Utah (Utah)

http://www.utcourts.gov
http://le.utah.gov/documents/code_const.htm

Public domain citation format: Utah has adopted a public domain citation format for cases after December 31, 1998. The format is:

▸ Wickham v. Galetka, 2002 UT 72, 61 P.3d 978.

▸ Gilley v. Blackstock, 2002 UT App 414, ¶ 10, 61 P.3d 305.

For additional information, consult Utah Supreme Court Standing Order No. 4 (effective Jan. 18, 2000).

Supreme Court (Utah): Cite to P., P.2d, or P.3d, if therein.

▸ Pacific Reporter	1881–date	P., P.2d, P.3d
▸ Utah Reports	1873–1974	Utah, Utah 2d

Court of Appeals (Utah Ct. App.): Cite to P.2d or P.3d, if therein.

▸ Pacific Reporter	1987–date	P.2d, P.3d

Statutory compilations: Cite to one of the following codes, if therein.

▸ Utah Code Annotated (LexisNexis) UTAH CODE ANN. § x-x-x (LexisNexis ‹year›)
▸ West's Utah Code Annotated UTAH CODE ANN. § x-x-x (West ‹year›)

Session laws: Cite to Utah Laws, if therein.

▸ Laws of Utah ‹year› Utah Laws ‹page no.›
▸ Utah Code ‹year› Advance Legislative Service (LexisNexis) ‹year›-‹pamph. no.› Utah Adv. Legis. Serv. ‹page no.› (LexisNexis)
▸ Utah Legislative Service (West) ‹year› Utah. Legis. Serv. ‹page no.› (West)

Administrative compilation

▸ Utah Administrative Code (LexisNexis) UTAH ADMIN. CODE r. x-x-x (LexisNexis ‹year›)

Administrative register

▸ Utah State Bulletin ‹iss. no.› Utah Bull. ‹page no.› (‹month day, year›)

....

Vermont (Vt.)

http://www.vermontjudiciary.org
http://legislature.vermont.gov/statutes

Public domain citation format: Vermont has adopted a public domain citation format for cases after December 31, 2002. The format is:

▶ Charbonneau v. Gorczyk, 2003 VT 105, ¶ 3, 176 Vt. 140, 838 A.2d 117.

For additional information, consult Vt. R. App. P. 28.2.

Supreme Court (Vt.): Cite to A., A.2d, or A.3d, if therein.

▶ Atlantic Reporter	1885–date	A., A.2d, A.3d
▶ Vermont Reports	1826–date	Vt.
▶ Aikens	1825–1828	Aik.
▶ Chipman, D.	1789–1824	D. Chip.
▶ Brayton	1815–1819	Brayt.
▶ Tyler	1800–1803	Tyl.
▶ Chipman, N.	1789–1791	N. Chip.

Statutory compilations: Cite to VT. STAT. ANN. (published by LexisNexis), if therein.

▶ Vermont Statutes Annotated (LexisNexis)	VT. STAT. ANN. tit. x, § x ‹year›
▶ West's Vermont Statutes Annotated	VT. STAT. ANN. tit. x, § x (West ‹year›)

Session laws: Cite to Vt. Acts & Resolves, if therein.

▶ Acts and Resolves of Vermont	‹year› Vt. Acts & Resolves ‹page no.›
▶ Vermont ‹year› Advance Legislative Service (LexisNexis)	‹year›-‹pamph. no.› Vt. Adv. Legis. Serv. ‹page no.› (LexisNexis)
▶ West's Vermont Legislative Service	‹year› Vt. Legis. Serv. ‹page no.› (West)

Administrative compilation

▶ Code of Vermont Rules (LexisNexis)	‹tit. no.›-‹ch. no.› VT. CODE R. § x (‹year›)

Administrative and executive register

▶ Vermont Government Register (LexisNexis)	‹iss. no.› Vt. Gov't Reg. ‹page no.› (LexisNexis ‹month year›)

Virginia (Va.)

http://www.courts.state.va.us
http://lis.virginia.gov/000/src.htm

Supreme Court (Va.), previously **Supreme Court of Appeals** (Va.): Cite to
S.E. or S.E.2d, if therein.

▸ South Eastern Reporter	1887–date	S.E., S.E.2d
▸ Virginia Reports		
▸ 75 Va. to date	1880–date	Va.
▸ Grattan	1844–1880	e.g., 42 Va. (1 Gratt.)
▸ Robinson	1842–1844	e.g., 40 Va. (1 Rob.)
▸ Leigh	1829–1842	e.g., 28 Va. (1 Leigh)
▸ Randolph	1821–1828	e.g., 22 Va. (1 Rand.)
▸ Gilmer	1820–1821	21 Va. (Gilmer)
▸ Munford	1810–1820	e.g., 15 Va. (1 Munf.)
▸ Hening & Munford	1806–1810	e.g., 11 Va. (1 Hen. & M.)
▸ Call	1779–1825	e.g., 5 Va. (1 Call)
▸ Virginia Cases, Criminal	1789–1826	e.g., 3 Va. (1 Va. Cas.)
▸ Washington	1790–1796	e.g., 1 Va. (1 Wash.)

Court of Appeals (Va. Ct. App.): Cite to S.E.2d, if therein.

▸ South Eastern Reporter	1985–date	S.E.2d
▸ Virginia Court of Appeals Reports	1985–date	Va. App.

Circuit Court (Va. Cir. Ct.): Cite to Va. Cir.

▸ Virginia Circuit Court Opinions	1957–date	Va. Cir.

Statutory compilations: Cite to VA. CODE ANN. (published by LexisNexis),
if therein.

▸ Code of Virginia 1950 Annotated (LexisNexis)	VA. CODE ANN. § x-x ⟨year⟩
▸ West's Annotated Code of Virginia	VA. CODE ANN. § x-x (West ⟨year⟩)

Session laws: Cite to Va. Acts, if therein.

▸ Acts of the General Assembly of the Commonwealth of Virginia	⟨year⟩ Va. Acts ⟨page no.⟩
▸ Virginia ⟨year⟩ Advance Legislative Service (LexisNexis)	⟨year⟩-⟨pamph. no.⟩ Va. Adv. Legis. Serv. ⟨page no.⟩ (LexisNexis)
▸ West's Virginia Legislative Service	⟨year⟩ Va. Legis. Serv. ⟨page no.⟩ (West)

Administrative compilation

▸ Virginia Administrative Code (West)	⟨tit. no.⟩ VA. ADMIN. CODE § x-x-x (⟨year⟩)

Administrative register

▸ Virginia Register of Regulations (LexisNexis)	⟨vol. no.⟩ Va. Reg. Regs. ⟨page no.⟩ (⟨month day, year⟩)

Washington (Wash.)

http://www.courts.wa.gov
http://app.leg.wa.gov/rcw

Supreme Court (Wash.): Cite to P., P.2d, or P.3d, if therein.

► Pacific Reporter	1880–date	P., P.2d, P.3d
► Washington Reports	1889–date	Wash., Wash. 2d
► Washington Territory Reports	1854–1888	Wash. Terr.

Court of Appeals (Wash. Ct. App.): Cite to P.2d or P.3d, if therein.

► Pacific Reporter	1969–date	P.2d, P.3d
► Washington Appellate Reports	1969–date	Wash. App.

Statutory compilations: Cite to WASH. REV. CODE, if therein.

► Revised Code of Washington	WASH. REV. CODE § x.x.x (‹year›)
► West's Revised Code of Washington Annotated	WASH. REV. CODE ANN. § x.x.x (West ‹year›)
► Annotated Revised Code of Washington (LexisNexis)	WASH. REV. CODE ANN. § x.x.x (LexisNexis ‹year›)

Session laws: Cite to Wash. Sess. Laws, if therein.

► Session Laws of Washington	‹year› Wash. Sess. Laws ‹page no.›
► West's Washington Legislative Service	‹year› Wash. Legis. Serv. ‹page no.› (West)

Administrative compilation

► Washington Administrative Code	WASH. ADMIN. CODE § x-x-x (‹year›)

Administrative register

► Washington State Register	‹iss. no.› Wash. Reg. ‹page no.› (‹month day, year›)

West Virginia (W. Va.)

http://www.courtswv.gov
https://www.wvlegislature.gov/wvcode/code.cfm

Supreme Court of Appeals (W. Va.): Cite to S.E. or S.E.2d, if therein.

► South Eastern Reporter	1886–date	S.E., S.E.2d
► West Virginia Reports	1864–date	W. Va.

Statutory compilations: Cite to W. VA. CODE, if therein.

► West Virginia Code	W. VA. CODE § x-x-x (‹year›)
► Michie's West Virginia Code Annotated (LexisNexis)	W. VA. CODE ANN. § x-x-x (LexisNexis ‹year›)
► West's Annotated Code of West Virginia	W. VA. CODE ANN. § x-x-x (West ‹year›)

Session laws: Cite to W. Va. Acts, if therein.

▶ Acts of the Legislature of West Virginia ⟨year⟩ W. Va. Acts ⟨page no.⟩
▶ West Virginia ⟨year⟩ Advance Legislative ⟨year⟩-⟨pamph. no.⟩ W. Va.
   Service (LexisNexis)   Adv. Legis. Serv. ⟨page no.⟩
   (LexisNexis)
▶ West's West Virginia Legislative Service ⟨year⟩ W. Va. Legis. Serv.
   ⟨page no.⟩

Administrative compilation

▶ West Virginia Code of State Rules   W. VA. CODE R. § x-x-x (⟨year⟩)

Administrative register

▶ West Virginia Register   ⟨vol. no.⟩ W. Va. Reg. ⟨page
   no.⟩ (⟨month day, year⟩)

Wisconsin (Wis.)

http://www.wicourts.gov
http://docs.legis.wisconsin.gov/statutes

Public domain citation format: Wisconsin has adopted a public domain citation format for cases decided after December 31, 1999. The format is:

▶ Glaeske v. Shaw, 2003 WI App 71, 261 Wis. 2d 549, 661 N.W.2d 72.
▶ Glaeske v. Shaw, 2003 WI App 71, ¶ 9, 261 Wis. 2d 549, 661 N.W.2d 72.

For additional information, consult Wisconsin Supreme Court Rule 80.

Supreme Court (Wis.): Cite to N.W. or N.W.2d, if therein.

▶ North Western Reporter	1879–date	N.W., N.W.2d
▶ Wisconsin Reports	1853–date	Wis., Wis. 2d
▶ Pinney	1839–1852	Pin.
▶ Chandler	1849–1852	Chand.
▶ Burnett	1842–1843	Bur.
▶ Burnett (bound with session laws for Dec. 1841)	1841	Bur.

Court of Appeals (Wis. Ct. App.): Cite to N.W.2d, if therein.

▶ North Western Reporter	1978–date	N.W.2d
▶ Wisconsin Reports	1978–date	Wis. 2d

Statutory compilations: Cite to WIS. STAT., if therein.

▶ Wisconsin Statutes   WIS. STAT. § x.x (⟨year⟩)
▶ West's Wisconsin Statutes Annotated   WIS. STAT. ANN. § x.x (West
   ⟨year⟩)

Session laws: Cite to Wis. Sess. Laws, if therein.

▶ Wisconsin Session Laws   ⟨year⟩ Wis. Sess. Laws ⟨page
   no.⟩
▶ West's Wisconsin Legislative Service   ⟨year⟩ Wis. Legis. Serv. ⟨page
   no.⟩ (West)

Administrative compilation

▶ Wisconsin Administrative Code
Wis. Admin. Code ⟨agency abbreviation⟩ § x-x (⟨year⟩)

Administrative register

▶ Wisconsin Administrative Register
⟨iss. no.⟩ Wis. Admin. Reg. ⟨page no.⟩ (⟨month day, year⟩)

. . . .

Wyoming (Wyo.)

http://www.courts.state.wy.us
http://www.wyoleg.gov/statestatutes/statutesconstitution

Public domain citation format: Wyoming has adopted a public domain citation format for cases decided after December 31, 2003. The format is:

▶ CLC v. Wyoming, 2004 WY 2, 82 P.3d 1235 (Wyo. 2004).

▶ CLC v. Wyoming, 2004 WY 2, ¶ 4, 82 P.3d 1235, 1236 (Wyo. 2004).

For additional information, consult Order Amending Citation Format (Aug. 19, 2005).

Supreme Court (Wyo.): Cite to P., P.2d, or P.3d, if therein.

▶ Pacific Reporter	1883–date	P., P.2d, P.3d
▶ Wyoming Reports	1870–1959	Wyo.

Statutory compilations: Cite to Wyo. Stat. Ann. (published by LexisNexis), if therein.

▶ Wyoming Statutes Annotated (LexisNexis)
Wyo. Stat. Ann. § x-x-x (⟨year⟩)

▶ West's Wyoming Statutes Annotated
Wyo. Stat. Ann. § x-x-x (West ⟨year⟩)

Session laws: Cite to Wyo. Sess. Laws, if therein.

▶ Session Laws of Wyoming
⟨year⟩ Wyo. Sess. Laws ⟨page no.⟩

▶ West's Wyoming Legislative Service
⟨year⟩ Wyo. Legis. Serv. ⟨page no.⟩ (West)

Administrative compilation

▶ Code of Wyoming Rules (LexisNexis)
⟨tit. no.⟩-⟨ch. no.⟩ Wyo. Code R. § x (LexisNexis ⟨year⟩)

Administrative register

▶ Wyoming Government Register (LexisNexis)
⟨iss. no.⟩ Wyo. Gov't Reg. ⟨page no.⟩ (LexisNexis ⟨month year⟩)

T1.4   Other United States Jurisdictions

American Samoa

https://new.asbar.org

High Court of American Samoa (Am. Samoa): Cite to Am. Samoa, Am. Samoa 2d, or Am. Samoa 3d.

▸ American Samoa Reports   1900–date   Am. Samoa, Am. Samoa 2d, Am. Samoa 3d

Statutory compilation

▸ American Samoa Code Annotated   AM. SAMOA CODE ANN. § x (‹year›)

Administrative compilation

▸ American Samoa Administrative Code   AM. SAMOA ADMIN. CODE § x (‹year›)

Canal Zone (C.Z.)

(now part of Panama)

United States District Court for the Eastern District of Louisiana (E.D. La.): This court has jurisdiction over litigation pending as of April 1, 1982, in the United States District Court for the District of the Canal Zone. Cite to F. Supp.

▸ Federal Supplement   1982–1983   F. Supp.

United States District Court for the District of the Canal Zone (D.C.Z.): This court ceased to exist on March 31, 1982. Cite to F. Supp.

▸ Federal Supplement   1946–1982   F. Supp.

Statutory compilation

▸ Panama Canal Code   C.Z. CODE tit. x, § x (‹year›)

(enacted as Canal Zone Code, Pub. L. No. 87-845, 76A Stat. 1 (1962), and redesignated and continued partially in force by the Panama Canal Act of 1979, Pub. L. No. 96-70, § 3303(b), 93 Stat. 452, 499).

Guam (Guam)

http://guamsupremecourt.com

Guam cases that cannot be located in paper form may be available at the following location:

▶ http://www.guamsupremecourt.com/supreme-court-opinions/supreme-court-opinions.asp

Supreme Court of Guam (Guam): Cite using the following public domain format:

▶ Adams v. Duenas, 1998 Guam 15.

▶ Adams v. Duenas, 1998 Guam 15 ¶ 2.

District Court of Guam (D. Guam): Cite to F. Supp., F. Supp. 2d, or F. Supp. 3d, if therein.

▸ Federal Supplement	1951–date	F. Supp., F. Supp. 2d, F. Supp. 3d
▸ Guam Reports	1955–1980	Guam

Statutory compilation

▸ Guam Code Annotated	‹tit. no.› GUAM CODE ANN. § x (‹year›)

Session laws

▸ Guam Session Laws	Guam Pub. L. ‹law no.› (‹year›)

Administrative compilation

▸ Administrative Rules & Regulations of the Government of Guam	‹tit. no.› GUAM ADMIN. R. & REGS. § x (‹year›)

....

Navajo Nation

http://www.navajocourts.org

Supreme Court (Navajo), previously **Court of Appeals** (Navajo): Cite to Navajo Rptr.

▸ Navajo Reporter	1969–date	Navajo Rptr.

District Court (Navajo D. Ct.): Cite to Navajo Rptr.

▸ Navajo Reporter	1969–date	Navajo Rptr.

Statutory compilation

▸ Navajo Nation Code Annotated (West)	NAVAJO NATION CODE ANN. tit. x, § x (‹year›)

....

Northern Mariana Islands (N. Mar. I.)

http://www.cnmilaw.org

Public domain citation format: The Commonwealth of the Northern Mariana Islands has adopted a public domain citation format for cases after June 15, 1996. The format is:

▸ Lifoifoi v. Lifoifoi-Aldan, 1996 MP 14.

Supreme Court (N. Mar. I.): Cite to N. Mar. I.

▸ Northern Mariana Islands Reporter	1989–date	N. Mar. I.

District Court for the Northern Mariana Islands, Trial and Appellate Divisions (D. N. Mar. I. and D. N. Mar. I. App. Div.), and **Commonwealth Superior Court** (N. Mar. I. Commw. Super. Ct.), previously **Commonwealth Trial Court** (N. Mar. I. Commw. Trial Ct.): Cite to F. Supp., F. Supp. 2d, or F. Supp. 3d, if therein.

| ► Federal Supplement | 1979–date | F. Supp., F. Supp. 2d, F. Supp. 3d |
| ► Northern Mariana Islands Commonwealth Reporter | 1979–date | N. Mar. I. Commw. |

Statutory compilation

| ► Northern Mariana Islands Commonwealth Code (LexisNexis) | ‹tit. no.› N. Mar. I. Code § x (‹year›) |

Session laws

| ► Northern Mariana Islands Session Laws | ‹year› N. Mar. I. Pub. L. ‹law no.› |

Administrative compilation

| ► Northern Mariana Islands Administrative Code | ‹tit. no.› N. Mar. I. Admin. Code § x (‹year›) |

Administrative register

| ► Northern Mariana Islands Commonwealth Register | ‹vol. no.› N. Mar. I. Reg. ‹page no.› (‹month day, year›) |

Oklahoma Native Americans

Tribal Courts, Courts of Indian Offenses (Appellate Division), Courts of Indian Appeals, and **Courts of Indian Offenses**: Cite to Okla. Trib.

| ► Oklahoma Tribal Court Reports | 1979–date | Okla. Trib. |

Puerto Rico (P.R.)

http://www.ramajudicial.pr (in Spanish)

Public domain citation format: Puerto Rico has adopted a public domain citation format for cases decided after December 31, 1997. The format is:

► Spanish: Guzman Rosario v. Departamento de Hacienda, 98 TSPR 148.

► English: Guzman Rosario v. Departamento de Hacienda, 98 PRSC 148.

Supreme Court (P.R.): Cite to P.R. or P.R. Offic. Trans., if therein; otherwise, cite to P.R. Dec. or P.R. Sent., in that order of preference.

► Puerto Rico Reports	1899–1978	P.R.
► Official Translations of the Opinions of the Supreme Court of Puerto Rico	1978–date	P.R. Offic. Trans.
► Decisiones de Puerto Rico	1899–date	P.R. Dec.
► Sentencias del Tribunal Supremo de Puerto Rico	1899–1902	P.R. Sent.

Circuit Court of Appeals (P.R. Cir.): Cite to T.C.A.

| ► Decisiones del Tribunal de Circuito de Apelaciones de Puerto Rico | 1995–date | T.C.A. |

Statutory compilation

▶ Laws of Puerto Rico Annotated (LexisNexis)   P.R. LAWS ANN. tit. x, § x ⟨year⟩

▶ Leyes de Puerto Rico Anotadas (LexisNexis)   P.R. LEYES AN. tit. x, § x ⟨year⟩

Session laws

▶ Laws of Puerto Rico   ⟨year⟩ P.R. Laws ⟨page no.⟩
▶ Leyes de Puerto Rico (LexisNexis)   ⟨year⟩ P.R. Leyes ⟨page no.⟩

....

Virgin Islands (V.I.)

http://www.visupremecourt.org

All courts: Cite to V.I.

▶ Virgin Islands Reports   1917–date   V.I.

Statutory compilation

▶ Virgin Islands Code Anno-   1962–date   V.I. CODE ANN. tit. x,
tated (LexisNexis)   § x-x ⟨year⟩

Session laws: Cite to V.I. Sess. Laws, if therein.

▶ Session Laws of the Virgin Islands   ⟨year⟩ V.I. Sess. Laws ⟨page no.⟩

▶ Virgin Islands Code Annotated Advance   ⟨year⟩-⟨pamph. no.⟩ V.I. Code
Legislative Service (LexisNexis)   Ann. Adv. Legis. Serv. ⟨page no.⟩ (LexisNexis)

Administrative compilation

▶ Code of U.S. Virgin Islands Rules   ⟨tit. no.⟩-⟨ch. no.⟩ V.I. CODE R.
(LexisNexis)   § x-x (LexisNexis ⟨year⟩)

Administrative register

▶ Virgin Islands Government Register   ⟨iss. no.⟩ V.I. Gov't Reg. ⟨page
(LexisNexis)   no.⟩ (LexisNexis ⟨month year⟩)

T2   FOREIGN JURISDICTIONS

Table 2 has moved online. Please visit http://www.legalbluebook.com for free access to T2.

T3   INTERGOVERNMENTAL ORGANIZATIONS

T3.1   United Nations

United Nations Documents: cite to U.N. Docs.

▸ United Nations Documents   U.N. Docs.

United Nations Principal Organs: In citations to official records, abbreviate the records of the principal organs of the United Nations as follows:

▸ General Assembly   GAOR
▸ Security Council   SCOR
▸ Economic and Social Council   ESCOR
▸ Trusteeship Council   TCOR

Courts: International Court of Justice (I.C.J.): Cite decisions to I.C.J.; cite pleadings to I.C.J. Pleadings; cite acts and documents to I.C.J. Acts & Docs.

▸ Judgments, Advisory Opinions, and Orders   1946–date   ⟨year⟩ I.C.J. xx
▸ Pleadings, Oral Arguments, and Documents   1946–date   ⟨year⟩ I.C.J. Pleadings xx
▸ Acts and Documents   1946–date   ⟨year⟩ I.C.J. Acts & Docs. xx

Treaties and international agreements: Cite to U.N.T.S.

▸ United Nations Treaty Series   1946–date   ⟨volume⟩ U.N.T.S. xxx

T3.2   League of Nations

Courts: Permanent Court of International Justice (P.C.I.J.): Cite decisions, pleadings, rules, and acts to P.C.I.J., indicating the series and the case or document number.

▸ Judgments, Advisory Opinions, and Orders   1920–1945   ⟨year⟩ P.C.I.J. (ser. x) No. x

Treaties and international agreements: Cite to L.N.T.S.

▸ League of Nations Treaty Series   1920–1945   ⟨volume⟩ L.N.T.S. xxx (⟨year⟩)

T3.3   European Union

Courts: Cite cases before the **Court of Justice of the European Union** (E.C.J.) and the **General Court** (Ct. of First Instance) to E.C.R., if therein. If not, cite to C.M.L.R., Common Mkt. Rep. (CCH), or CEC (CCH), if therein, in that order. If not, cite to official online sources.

► Reports of Cases Before the Court of Justice	1973–date	‹year› E.C.R. xxx
► Common Market Law Reports	1962–date	‹year› C.M.L.R. xxx
► Common Market Reports	1962–1988	‹year› Common Mkt. Rep. (CCH) xxx
► European Community Cases	1989–2007	‹year› CEC (CCH) xxx

Legislative acts: Cite acts of the European Council and the European Commission to O.J. (the Official Journal of the European Union, formerly the Official Journal of the European Communities), if therein. If not, cite to O.J. SPEC. ED., if therein. If not, cite to J.O., if therein. For issues of J.O. before 1967, indicate the issue number. For issues of O.J. and J.O. dating from 1967 and later, indicate the series and issue number.

► Official Journal of the European Union	1973–date	‹year› O.J. (L ‹act number›) xxx
► Official Journal of the European Community, Special Edition	1952–1972	‹year› O.J. SPEC. ED. xxx
► Journal Officiel des Communautés Européennes	1958–date	‹year› J.O. (L ‹act number›) xxx

Parliamentary documents: Cite as follows:

► European Parliamentary Debates	EUR. PARL. DEB. (‹debate number› x
► European Parliament Working Session or Session Documents	EUR. PARL. DOC. (COM ‹document number› x
► Parlement Européen Documents de Séance	PARL. EUR. DOC. (SEC ‹document number› x

---

T3.4   European Commission of Human Rights

Cite to Eur. Comm'n H.R. Dec. & Rep., Y.B. Eur. Conv. on H.R., or Eur. H.R. Rep., in that order.

► European Commission of Human Rights Collections of Decisions	‹volume› Eur. Comm'n H.R. Dec. & Rep. xxx
► European Human Rights Reports	‹volume› Eur. H.R. Rep. xxx
► Yearbook of the European Convention on Human Rights	Y.B. Eur. Conv. on H.R.

T3.5   European Court of Human Rights

Cite to Eur. Ct. H.R. or to Y.B. Eur. Conv. on H.R.

▸ European Court of Human Rights Reports of   xx Eur. Ct. H.R. (‹year›)
  Judgments and Decisions
▸ Yearbook of the European Convention on   Y.B. Eur. Conv. on H.R.
  Human Rights

T3.6   Inter-American Commission on Human Rights

Cite to Inter-Am. Comm'n H.R.

▸ Inter-American Commission on Human   Inter-Am. Comm'n H.R.
  Rights Annual Reports

T3.7   Inter-American Court of Human Rights

Cite to Series, to Rep. Inter-Am. Ct. H.R., or to official online sources.

Series:

▸ A - Judgments and Opinions   Inter-Am. Ct. H.R. (ser. A) No. xx
▸ B - Pleadings, Oral Arguments and   Inter-Am. Ct. H.R. (ser. B) No. xx, xxx
  Documents (Relative to Series A)
▸ C - Decisions and Judgments   Inter-Am. Ct. H.R. (ser. C) No. xx
▸ D - Pleadings, Oral Arguments and   Inter-Am. Ct. H.R. (ser. D) No. xx, xxx
  Documents (Relative to Series C)
▸ E - Provisional Measures   Inter-Am. Ct. H.R. (ser. E) No. xx, xxx
▸ F - Procedural Decisions   Inter-Am. Ct. H.R. (ser. F) No. xx, xxx

Annual Reports of the Inter-American Court of Human Rights:

▸ Complete Opinions   1970–date   Rep. Inter-Am. Ct. H.R. xxx

T3.8   International Tribunal for the Law of the Sea

Cite to ITLOS Rep.

▸ International Tribunal for the Law of the Sea   1956–date   ITLOS Rep.
  Reports of Judgments, Advisory Opinions
  and Orders

T3.9   Intergovernmental Organizations

▸ Comprehensive Nuclear-Test-Ban Treaty Organization   CTBTO
▸ Food and Agriculture Organization   FAO
▸ Global Environment Facility   GEF
▸ Intergovernmental Panel on Climate Change   IPCC
▸ International Atomic Energy Agency   IAEA
▸ International Bank for Reconstruction and Development   IBRD
▸ International Centre for Settlement of Investment Disputes   ICSID
▸ International Civil Aviation Organization   ICAO
▸ International Criminal Police Organization   INTERPOL
▸ International Development Association   IDA
▸ International Finance Corporation   IFC

▶ International Fund for Agricultural Development	IFAD
▶ International Labour Organization	ILO
▶ International Maritime Organization	IMO
▶ International Monetary Fund	IMF
▶ International Refugee Organization	IRO
▶ International Telecommunication Union	ITU
▶ International Union for Conservation of Nature	IUCN
▶ Multilateral Investment Guarantee Agency	MIGA
▶ Organisation for Economic Co-operation and Development	OECD
▶ Organisation for the Prohibition of Chemical Weapons	OPCW
▶ United Nations	U.N.
▶ United Nations Children's Fund	UNICEF
▶ United Nations Development Programme	UNDP
▶ United Nations Educational, Scientific and Cultural Organization	UNESCO
▶ United Nations Environment Programme	UNEP
▶ United Nations Industrial Development Organization	UNIDO
▶ Universal Postal Union	UPU
▶ World Bank Group	WBG
▶ World Customs Organization	WCO
▶ World Health Organization	WHO
▶ World Intellectual Property Organization	WIPO
▶ World Meteorological Organization	WMO
▶ World Tourism Organization	UNWTO
▶ World Trade Organization	WTO

You may abbreviate other intergovernmental organizations as well. On first mention, provide the full name of the organization, while indicating the abbreviation you will use in brackets.

T4   TREATY SOURCES

The dates in the center column refer to the years of the treaties contained in the source, not the years in which the source was published.

T4.1   Official U.S. Sources

▶ United States Treaties and Other International Agreements	1950–date	‹volume› U.S.T. xxx
▶ Statutes at Large (indexed at 64 Stat. B1107)	1778–1949	‹volume› Stat. xxx
▶ Treaties and Other International Acts Series	1945–date	T.I.A.S. No. x
▶ Treaty Series	1778–1945	T.S. No. x
▶ Executive Agreement Series	1922–1945	E.A.S. No. x
▶ Senate Treaty Documents	1981–date	S. TREATY DOC. No. x
▶ Senate Executive Documents	1778–1980	S. EXEC. DOC. No. x

T4.2   Intergovernmental Treaty Sources

▸ United Nations Treaty Series	1946–date	‹volume› U.N.T.S. xxx
▸ League of Nations Treaty Series	1920–1945	‹volume› L.N.T.S. xxx
▸ Pan-American Treaty Series	1949–date	‹volume› Pan-Am. T.S. xxx
▸ European Treaty Series	1948–2003	E.T.S. No. xxx
▸ Organization of American States Treaty Series	1970–date	O.A.S.T.S. No. xxx
▸ Council of Europe Treaty Series	2004–date	C.E.T.S. No. xxx

T4.3   Unofficial Treaty Sources

▸ U.S. Treaties on LEXIS	1776–date	Lexis xxx
▸ International Legal Materials	1962–date	‹volume› I.L.M. xxx
▸ Parry's Consolidated Treaty Series	1648–1919	‹volume› Consol. T.S. xxx
▸ Hein's United States Treaties and Other International Agreements	1984–date	Hein's No. KAV xxxx
▸ Bevans	1776–1949	‹volume› Bevans xxx

T5   ARBITRAL REPORTERS

This list provides abbreviations for arbitration reporters. See **rule 21.6** for guidance on citing international arbitrations.

▸ Arbitration Materials	Arb. Mat'l
▸ Hague Court Reports, First Series	Hague Ct. Rep. (Scott)
▸ Hague Court Reports, Second Series	Hague Ct. Rep. 2d (Scott)
▸ International Centre for Settlement of Investment Disputes (ICSID) Reports	ICSID Rep.
▸ International Centre for Settlement of Investment Disputes (ICSID) Review	ICSID Rev.
▸ International Chamber of Commerce Arbitration	Int'l Comm. Arb.
▸ International Tribunal for the Law of the Sea Reports of Judgments, Advisory Opinions and Orders	ITLOS Rep.
▸ Investment Treaty Arbitration Investment Treaty Cases	ITA Inv. Treaty Cases
▸ Permanent Court of Arbitration Case Repository	PCA Case Repository
▸ United Nations Reports of International Arbitral Awards	R.I.A.A.
▸ World Arbitration Reporter	World Arb. Rep. (‹issue number›)

T6 COMMON WORDS IN CASE NAMES, INSTITUTIONAL AUTHOR NAMES, AND PERIODICAL TITLES

Abbreviate case names, institutional author names, and periodical titles in citations by abbreviating any word listed below (**rules 10.2.2 and 16**). It is permissible to abbreviate other words of eight letters or more if substantial space is thereby saved and the result is unambiguous in context. (Thus, it would be permissible to abbreviate "Encyclopaedia Britannica" to "Encyc. Britannica" or "Petroleum" to "Petrol.") Unless otherwise indicated, plurals are formed by adding the letter "s." Abbreviate any word in the possessive form by adding an apostrophe if the word is plural and an apostrophe with the letter "s" if the word is singular (Thus, abbreviate "Employees'" to "Emps.'" and "Employee's" to "Emp.'s").

For periodical titles only, the rules in this paragraph apply. Abbreviate "University" as "U." ("U. Chi. L. Rev."). Also, omit the words "a," "at," "in," "of," and "the" (but retain the word "on"). Furthermore, if the title consists of only one word after the words "a," "at," "in," "of," and "the" have been omitted, do not abbreviate the remaining word. **Rule 6.1(a)** explains the spacing of abbreviations.

► Academ[ic, y]	Acad.	► Board	Bd.
► Account[ant, ing, ancy]	Acct.	► British	Brit.
		► Broadcast[er, ing]	Broad.
► Administrat[ive, ion]	Admin.	► Brothers	Bros.
► Administrat[or, rix]	Adm'[r, x]	► Brotherhood	Bhd.
► Advertising	Advert.	► Building	Bldg.
► Advoca[te, cy]	Advoc.	► Bulletin	Bull.
► Affair	Aff.	► Business[es]	Bus.
► Africa[n]	Afr.	► Capital	Cap.
► Agricultur[e, al]	Agric.	► Casualt[y, ies]	Cas.
► Alliance	All.	► Catholic	Cath.
► Alternative	Alt.	► Cent[er, re]	Ctr.
► Amendment	Amend.	► Central	Cent.
► America[n]	Am.	► Chemical	Chem.
► Ancestry	Anc.	► Children	Child.
► and	&	► Chronicle	Chron.
► Annual	Ann.	► Circuit	Cir.
► Appellate	App.	► Civil	Civ.
► Arbitrat[ion, or]	Arb.	► Civil Libert[y, ies]	C.L.
► Artificial Intelligence	A.I.	► Civil Rights	C.R.
► Associate	Assoc.	► Coalition	Coal.
► Association	Ass'n	► College	Coll.
► Atlantic	Atl.	► Commentary	Comment.
► Attorney	Att'y	► Commerc[e, ial]	Com.
► Authority	Auth.	► Commission	Comm'n
► Automo[bile, tive]	Auto.	► Commissioner	Comm'r
► Avenue	Ave.	► Committee	Comm.
► Bankruptcy	Bankr.	► Communication	Commc'n
► Behavior[al]	Behav.	► Community	Cmty.

► Company	Co.	► Engineering	Eng'g
► Comparative	Compar.	► English	Eng.
► Compensation	Comp.	► Enterprise	Enter.
► Computer	Comput.	► Entertainment	Ent.
► Condominium	Condo.	► Environment[al]	Env't
► Conference	Conf.	► Equality	Equal.
► Congress[ional]	Cong.	► Equipment	Equip.
► Consolidated	Consol.	► Estate	Est.
► Constitution[al]	Const.	► Europe[an]	Eur.
► Construction	Constr.	► Examiner	Exam'r
► Contemporary	Contemp.	► Exchange	Exch.
► Continental	Cont'l	► Executive	Exec.
► Contract	Cont.	► Execut[or, rix]	Ex'[r, x]
► Conveyance[r]	Conv.	► Explorat[ion, ory]	Expl.
► Cooperat[ion, ive]	Coop.	► Export[er, ation]	Exp.
► Corporat[e, ion]	Corp.	► Faculty	Fac.
► Correction[s, al]	Corr.	► Family	Fam.
► Cosmetic	Cosm.	► Federal	Fed.
► Counsel[or, ors, or's]	Couns.	► Federation	Fed'n
► County	Cnty.	► Fidelity	Fid.
► Court	Ct.	► Financ[e, ial, ing]	Fin.
► Criminal	Crim.	► Fortnightly	Fort.
► Defen[d, der, se]	Def.	► Forum	F.
► Delinquen[t, cy]	Delinq.	► Foundation	Found.
► Department	Dep't	► General	Gen.
► Detention	Det.	► Global	Glob.
► Develop[er, ment]	Dev.	► Government	Gov't
► Digest	Dig.	► Group	Grp.
► Digital	Digit.	► Guarant[y, or]	Guar.
► Diplomacy	Dipl.	► Hispanic	Hisp.
► Director	Dir.	► Histor[ical, y]	Hist.
► Discount	Disc.	► Hospital[ity]	Hosp.
► Dispute	Disp.	► Housing	Hous.
► Distribut[or, ing, ion]	Distrib.	► Human	Hum.
► District	Dist.	► Humanity	Human.
► Division	Div.	► Immigration	Immigr.
► Doctor	Dr.	► Import[er, ation]	Imp.
► East[ern]	E.	► Incorporated	Inc.
► Econom[ic, ical, ics, y]	Econ.	► Indemnity	Indem.
► Editor[ial]	Ed.	► Independen[ce, t]	Indep.
► Education[al]	Educ.	► Industr[y, ial, ies]	Indus.
► Electr[ic, ical, icity, onic]	Elec.	► Inequality	Ineq.
		► Information	Info.
► Employ[ee, er, ment]	Emp.	► Injury	Inj.
► Enforcement	Enf't	► Institut[e, ion]	Inst.
► Engineer	Eng'r	► Insurance	Ins.

► Intellectual	Intell.	► Nationality	Nat'y
► Intelligence	Intel.	► Natural	Nat.
► Interdisciplinary	Interdisc.	► Negligence	Negl.
► Interest	Int.	► Negotiat[ion, or]	Negot.
► International	Int'l	► Newsletter	Newsl.
► Invest[ment, or]	Inv.	► North[ern]	N.
► Journal[s]	J.	► Northeast[ern]	Ne.
► Judicial	Jud.	► Northwest[ern]	Nw.
► Juridical	Jurid.	► Number	No.
► Jurisprudence	Juris.	► Offic[e, ial]	Off.
► Justice	Just.	► Opinion	Op.
► Juvenile	Juv.	► Order	Ord.
► Labor	Lab.	► Organiz[ation, ing]	Org.
► Laboratory	Lab'y	► Pacific	Pac.
► Law[s]	L.	► Parish	Par.
► Law (first word)	Law	► Partnership	P'ship
► Lawyer	Law.	► Patent	Pat.
► Legislat[ion, ive]	Legis.	► Person[al, nel]	Pers.
► Liability	Liab.	► Perspective	Persp.
► Librar[y, ian]	Libr.	► Pharmaceutic[al]	Pharm.
► Limited	Ltd.	► Philosoph[ical, y]	Phil.
► Litigation	Litig.	► Planning	Plan.
► Local	Loc.	► Policy	Pol'y
► Machine[ry]	Mach.	► Politic[al, s]	Pol.
► Magazine	Mag.	► Practi[cal, ce, tioner]	Prac.
► Maintenance	Maint.	► Preserv[e, ation]	Pres.
► Management	Mgmt.	► Priva[cy, te]	Priv.
► Manufacturer	Mfr.	► Probat[e, ion]	Prob.
► Manufacturing	Mfg.	► Problems	Probs.
► Maritime	Mar.	► Proce[edings, dure]	Proc.
► Market	Mkt.	► Product[ion]	Prod.
► Marketing	Mktg.	► Profession[al]	Pro.
► Matrimonial	Matrim.	► Property	Prop.
► Mechanic[al]	Mech.	► Protection	Prot.
► Medic[al, inal, ine]	Med.	► Psycholog[ical, ist, y]	Psych.
► Memorial	Mem'l	► Public	Pub.
► Merchan[t, dise, dising]	Merch.	► Publication	Publ'n
		► Publishing	Publ'g
► Metropolitan	Metro.	► Quarterly	Q.
► Military	Mil.	► Railroad	R.R.
► Mineral	Min.	► Railway	Ry.
► Modern	Mod.	► Record	Rec.
► Mortgage	Mortg.	► Referee	Ref.
► Municipal[ity]	Mun.	► Refin[ing, ement]	Refin.
► Mutual	Mut.	► Regional	Reg'l
► National	Nat'l		

► Register	Reg.	► Statistic[s, al]	Stat.
► Regulat[ion, or, ory]	Regul.	► Steamship[s]	S.S.
► Rehabilitat[ion, ive]	Rehab.	► Street	St.
► Relation	Rel.	► Studies	Stud.
► Report[er]	Rep.	► Subcommittee	Subcomm.
► Reproduct[ion, ive]	Reprod.	► Supreme Court	Sup. Ct.
► Research	Rsch.	► Surety	Sur.
► Reserv[ation, e]	Rsrv.	► Survey	Surv.
► Resolution	Resol.	► Symposium	Symp.
► Resource[s]	Res.	► System[s]	Sys.
► Responsibility	Resp.	► Taxation	Tax'n
► Restaurant	Rest.	► Teacher	Tchr.
► Retirement	Ret.	► Techn[ical, ique, ology, ological]	Tech.
► Review, Revista	Rev.	► Telecommunication	Telecomm.
► Rights	Rts.	► Tele[phone, graph]	Tel.
► Road	Rd.	► Temporary	Temp.
► Savings	Sav.	► Township	Twp.
► School	Sch.	► Transcontinental	Transcon.
► Scien[ce, tific]	Sci.	► Transnational	Transnat'l
► Scottish	Scot.	► Transport[ation]	Transp.
► Secretary	Sec'y	► Tribune	Trib.
► Securit[y, ies]	Sec.	► Trust[ee]	Tr.
► Sentencing	Sent'g	► Turnpike	Tpk.
► Service	Serv.	► Uniform	Unif.
► Shareholder, Stockholder	S'holder	► United States	U.S.
► Social	Soc.	► University	Univ.
► Society	Soc'y	► Urban	Urb.
► Sociolog[ical, ist, y]	Socio.	► Utility	Util.
► Solicitor	Solic.	► Village	Vill.
► Solution	Sol.	► Week	Wk.
► South[ern]	S.	► Weekly	Wkly.
► Southeast[ern]	Se.	► West[ern]	W.
► Southwest[ern]	Sw.	► Yearbook (or Year Book)	Y.B.

T7   COURT NAMES

The following alphabetical list provides abbreviations for court names to be used in citing cases according to **rule 10.4**. If the abbreviation for the full name of the court is not listed below, a composite abbreviation may be assembled using the words listed in this table.

► Administrative Court	Admin. Ct.
► Admiralty [Court, Division]	Adm.
► Aldermen's Court	Alder. Ct.
► Appeals Court	App. Ct.
► Appellate Court	App. Ct.

► Appellate Department	App. Dep't
► Appellate Division	App. Div.
► Armed Services Board of Contract Appeals	ASBCA
► Bankruptcy Appellate Panel	B.A.P.
► Bankruptcy [Court, Judge]	Bankr.
► Board of Contract Appeals	B.C.A.
► Board of Immigration Appeals	B.I.A.
► Board of Patent Appeals and Interferences	B.P.A.I.
► Board of Tax Appeals	B.T.A.
► Borough Court	‹Name› Bor. Ct.
► Central District	C.D.
► Chancery [Court, Division]	Ch.
► Children's Court	Child. Ct.
► Circuit Court (old federal)	C.C.
► Circuit Court (state)	Cir. Ct.
► Circuit Court of Appeals (federal)	Cir.
► Circuit Court of Appeals (state)	Cir. Ct. App.
► City Court	‹Name› City Ct.
► Civil Appeals	Civ. App.
► Civil Court of Record	Civ. Ct. Rec.
► Civil District Court	Civ. Dist. Ct.
► Claims Court	Cl. Ct.
► Commerce Court	Comm. Ct.
► Commission	Comm'n
► Common Pleas	C.P. ‹when appropriate, name county or similar subdivision›
► Commonwealth Court	Commw. Ct.
► Conciliation Court	Concil. Ct.
► County Court	‹Name› Cnty. Ct.
► County Judge's Court	Cnty. J. Ct.
► Court	Ct.
► Court of Appeal (English)	C.A.
► Court of Appeals (federal)	Cir.
► Court of Appeal[s] (state)	Ct. App.
► Court of Appeals for the Armed Forces	C.A.A.F.
► Court of Appeals for Veterans Claims	Vet. App.
► Court of Civil Appeals	Civ. App.
► Court of Claims	Ct. Cl.
► Court of Common Pleas	Ct. Com. Pl.
► Court of Criminal Appeals	Crim. App.
► Court of Customs and Patent Appeals	C.C.P.A.
► Court of Customs Appeals	Ct. Cust. App.
► Court of Errors	Ct. Err.
► Court of Errors and Appeals	Ct. Err. & App.
► Court of Federal Claims	Fed. Cl.

▸ Court of [General, Special] Sessions	Ct. ‹Gen. or Spec.› Sess.
▸ Court of International Trade	Ct. Int'l Trade
▸ Court of Military Appeals	C.M.A.
▸ Court of Military Review	C.M.R.
▸ Court of Special Appeals	Ct. Spec. App.
▸ Criminal Appeals	Crim. App.
▸ Criminal District Court	Crim. Dist. Ct.
▸ Customs Court	Cust. Ct.
▸ District Court (federal)	D.
▸ District Court (state)	Dist. Ct.
▸ District Court of Appeal[s]	Dist. Ct. App.
▸ Division	Div.
▸ Domestic Relations Court	Dom. Rel. Ct.
▸ Eastern District	E.D.
▸ Emergency Court of Appeals	Emer. Ct. App.
▸ Equity [Court, Division]	Eq.
▸ Family Court	Fam. Ct.
▸ High Court	High Ct.
▸ Judicial District	Jud. Dist.
▸ Judicial Division	Jud. Div.
▸ Judicial Panel on Multidistrict Litigation	J.P.M.L.
▸ Justice of the Peace's Court	J.P. Ct.
▸ Juvenile Court	Juv. Ct.
▸ Land Court	Land Ct.
▸ Law Court	Law Ct.
▸ Law Division	Law Div.
▸ Magistrate Division	Magis. Div.
▸ Magistrate's Court	Magis. Ct.
▸ Middle District	M.D.
▸ Municipal Court	‹Name› Mun. Ct.
▸ Northern District	N.D.
▸ Orphans' Court	Orphans' Ct.
▸ Parish Court	‹Name› Parish Ct.
▸ Police Justice's Court	Police J. Ct.
▸ Prerogative Court	Prerog. Ct.
▸ Probate Court	Prob. Ct.
▸ Public Utilities Commission	P.U.C.
▸ Real Estate Commission	Real Est. Comm'n
▸ Recorder's Court	Rec's Ct.
▸ Southern District	S.D.
▸ Special Court Regional Rail Reorganization Act	Reg'l Rail Reorg. Ct.
▸ Superior Court	Super. Ct.
▸ Supreme Court (federal)	U.S.
▸ Supreme Court (other)	Sup. Ct.
▸ Supreme Court, Appellate Division	App. Div.

▸ Supreme Court, Appellate Term	App. Term
▸ Supreme Court of Errors	Sup. Ct. Err.
▸ Supreme Judicial Court	Sup. Jud. Ct.
▸ Surrogate's Court	Surr. Ct.
▸ Tax Appeal Court	Tax App. Ct.
▸ Tax Court	T.C.
▸ Teen Court	Teen Ct.
▸ Temporary Emergency Court of Appeals	Temp. Emer. Ct. App.
▸ Territor[ial, y]	Terr.
▸ Trademark Trial and Appeal Board	T.T.A.B.
▸ Traffic Court	Traffic Ct.
▸ Tribal Court	‹Name› Tribal Ct.
▸ Tribunal	Trib.
▸ Water Court	Water Ct.
▸ Western District	W.D.
▸ Workmen's Compensation Division	Workmen's Comp. Div.
▸ Youth Court	Youth Ct.

T8   EXPLANATORY PHRASES

The following table lists a number of explanatory phrases (some of which contain abbreviations) commonly used to indicate prior or subsequent history and weight of authority of judicial decisions. As indicated below, phrases that are followed by a case citation as their direct object (such as "*aff'g*" or "*overruled by*") are *not* followed by commas. Phrases introducing a case citation for the action indicated by the explanatory phrase (such as "*cert. denied,*") are followed by commas, which are *not* italicized (see **rule 2.1(f)**). See **rule 10.7** for guidance in using explanatory phrases.

▸ *acq.*	▸ *dismissing appeal from*
▸ *acq. in result*	▸ *enforced,*
▸ *aff'd,*	▸ *enforcing*
▸ *aff'd by an equally divided court,*	▸ *invalidated by*
▸ *aff'd mem.,*	▸ *mandamus denied,*
▸ *aff'd on other grounds,*	▸ *modified,*
▸ *aff'd on reh'g,*	▸ *modifying*
▸ *aff'g*	▸ *nonacq.*
▸ *amended by*	▸ *overruled by*
▸ *appeal denied,*	▸ *perm. app. denied,*
▸ *appeal dismissed,*	▸ *perm. app. granted,*
▸ *appeal docketed,*	▸ *petition for cert. filed,*
▸ *appeal filed,*	▸ *prob. juris. noted,*
▸ *argued,*	▸ *reh'g granted [denied],*
▸ *cert. denied,*	▸ *rev'd,*
▸ *cert. dismissed,*	▸ *rev'd on other grounds,*
▸ *cert. dismissed as improvidently granted,*	▸ *rev'd per curiam,*
▸ *cert. granted,*	▸ *rev'g*
▸ *certifying questions to*	▸ *vacated,*
▸ *denying cert. to*	▸ *vacating as moot*
	▸ *withdrawn,*

T9   LEGISLATIVE DOCUMENTS

This table gives suggested abbreviations for citation of the words most commonly found in legislative documents. In some cases, it indicates that a word should not be abbreviated. Words of more than six letters not appearing on the list may also be abbreviated if the abbreviation selected is unambiguous. Omit all articles and prepositions from any abbreviated title if the document can be identified unambiguously without them.

► Annals	Annals
► Annual	Ann.
► Assembly[man, woman, member]	Assemb.
► Bill	B.
► Committee	Comm.
► Concurrent	Con.
► Conference	Conf.
► Congress[ional]	Cong.
► Debate	Deb.
► Delegate	Del.
► Document[s]	Doc.
► Executive	Exec.
► Federal	Fed.
► House	H.
► House of Delegates	H.D.
► House of Representatives	H.R.
► Joint	J.
► Law	L.
► Legislat[ion, ive]	Legis.
► Legislature	Leg.
► Miscellaneous	Misc.
► Number	No.
► Order	Order
► Public	Pub.
► Record	Rec.
► Register	Reg.
► Regular	Reg.
► Report	Rep.
► Representative	Rep.
► Resolution	Res.
► Senate	S.
► Senator	Sen.
► Service	Serv.
► Session	Sess.
► Special	Spec.
► Subcommittee	Subcomm.

T10   GEOGRAPHICAL TERMS

The following list provides abbreviations for geographical locations for use in case citations (**rules 10.2.2 and 10.4**), names of institutional authors (**rule 15.1(c)**), periodical abbreviations (**rule 16** and **table T13**), foreign materials (**rule 20.1**), and treaty citations (**rule 21.4.2**).

T10.1   U.S. States, Cities, and Territories

States

▸ Alabama	Ala.	▸ Montana	Mont.
▸ Alaska	Alaska	▸ Nebraska	Neb.
▸ Arizona	Ariz.	▸ Nevada	Nev.
▸ Arkansas	Ark.	▸ New Hampshire	N.H.
▸ California	Cal.	▸ New Jersey	N.J.
▸ Colorado	Colo.	▸ New Mexico	N.M.
▸ Connecticut	Conn.	▸ New York	N.Y.
▸ Delaware	Del.	▸ North Carolina	N.C.
▸ Florida	Fla.	▸ North Dakota	N.D.
▸ Georgia	Ga.	▸ Ohio	Ohio
▸ Hawaii	Haw.	▸ Oklahoma	Okla.
▸ Idaho	Idaho	▸ Oregon	Or.
▸ Illinois	Ill.	▸ Pennsylvania	Pa.
▸ Indiana	Ind.	▸ Rhode Island	R.I.
▸ Iowa	Iowa	▸ South Carolina	S.C.
▸ Kansas	Kan.	▸ South Dakota	S.D.
▸ Kentucky	Ky.	▸ Tennessee	Tenn.
▸ Louisiana	La.	▸ Texas	Tex.
▸ Maine	Me.	▸ Utah	Utah
▸ Maryland	Md.	▸ Vermont	Vt.
▸ Massachusetts	Mass.	▸ Virginia	Va.
▸ Michigan	Mich.	▸ Washington	Wash.
▸ Minnesota	Minn.	▸ West Virginia	W. Va.
▸ Mississippi	Miss.	▸ Wisconsin	Wis.
▸ Missouri	Mo.	▸ Wyoming	Wyo.

Cities

Abbreviations for city names may also be composed from state name abbreviations above. For example, "Oklahoma City" should be shortened to "Okla. City."

▸ Baltimore	Balt.
▸ Boston	Bos.
▸ Chicago	Chi.
▸ Dallas	Dall.
▸ District of Columbia	D.C.
▸ Houston	Hous.
▸ Los Angeles	L.A.
▸ Miami	Mia.
▸ New York	N.Y.C.
▸ Philadelphia	Phila.
▸ Phoenix	Phx.
▸ San Francisco	S.F.

Territories

▸ American Samoa	Am. Sam.
▸ Guam	Guam
▸ Northern Mariana Islands	N. Mar. I.
▸ Puerto Rico	P.R.
▸ Virgin Islands	V.I.

T10.2 Australian States and Canadian Provinces and Territories

Australia

▸ Australian Capital Territory	Austl. Cap. Terr.
▸ New South Wales	N.S.W.
▸ Northern Territory	N. Terr.
▸ Queensland	Queensl.
▸ South Australia	S. Austl.
▸ Tasmania	Tas.
▸ Victoria	Vict.
▸ Western Australia	W. Austl.

Canada

▸ Alberta	Alta.
▸ British Columbia	B.C.
▸ Manitoba	Man.
▸ New Brunswick	N.B.
▸ Newfoundland & Labrador	Nfld.
▸ Northwest Territories	N.W.T.
▸ Nova Scotia	N.S.
▸ Nunavut	Nun.
▸ Ontario	Ont.
▸ Prince Edward Island	P.E.I.
▸ Québec	Que.
▸ Saskatchewan	Sask.
▸ Yukon	Yukon

T10.3 Countries and Regions

▸ Afghanistan	Afg.
▸ Africa	Afr.
▸ Albania	Alb.
▸ Algeria	Alg.
▸ Andorra	Andorra
▸ Angola	Angl.
▸ Anguilla	Anguilla
▸ Antarctica	Antarctica

► Antigua & Barbuda	Ant. & Barb.
► Argentina	Arg.
► Armenia	Arm.
► Asia	Asia
► Australia	Austl.
► Austria	Austria
► Azerbaijan	Azer.
► Bahamas	Bah.
► Bahrain	Bahr.
► Bangladesh	Bangl.
► Barbados	Barb.
► Belarus	Belr.
► Belgium	Belg.
► Belize	Belize
► Benin	Benin
► Bermuda	Berm.
► Bhutan	Bhutan
► Bolivia	Bol.
► Bosnia & Herzegovina	Bosn. & Herz.
► Botswana	Bots.
► Brazil	Braz.
► Brunei	Brunei
► Bulgaria	Bulg.
► Burkina Faso	Burk. Faso
► Burundi	Burundi
► Cambodia	Cambodia
► Cameroon	Cameroon
► Canada	Can.
► Cape Verde	Cape Verde
► Cayman Islands	Cayman Is.
► Central African Republic	Cent. Afr. Rep.
► Chad	Chad
► Chile	Chile
► China, People's Republic of	China
► Colombia	Colom.
► Comoros	Comoros
► Congo, Democratic Republic of the	Dem. Rep. Congo
► Congo, Republic of the	Congo
► Costa Rica	Costa Rica
► Côte d'Ivoire	Côte d'Ivoire
► Croatia	Croat.
► Cuba	Cuba
► Cyprus	Cyprus
► Czech Republic	Czech
► Denmark	Den.
► Djibouti	Djib.
► Dominica	Dominica

▶ Dominican Republic	Dom. Rep.
▶ Ecuador	Ecuador
▶ Egypt	Egypt
▶ El Salvador	El Sal.
▶ England	Eng.
▶ Equatorial Guinea	Eq. Guinea
▶ Eritrea	Eri.
▶ Estonia	Est.
▶ Ethiopia	Eth.
▶ Europe	Eur.
▶ Falkland Islands	Falkland Is.
▶ Fiji	Fiji
▶ Finland	Fin.
▶ France	Fr.
▶ Gabon	Gabon
▶ Gambia	Gam.
▶ Georgia	Geor.
▶ Germany	Ger.
▶ Ghana	Ghana
▶ Gibraltar	Gib.
▶ Great Britain	Gr. Brit.
▶ Greece	Greece
▶ Greenland	Green.
▶ Grenada	Gren.
▶ Guadeloupe	Guad.
▶ Guatemala	Guat.
▶ Guinea	Guinea
▶ Guinea-Bissau	Guinea-Bissau
▶ Guyana	Guy.
▶ Haiti	Haiti
▶ Honduras	Hond.
▶ Hong Kong	H.K.
▶ Hungary	Hung.
▶ Iceland	Ice.
▶ India	India
▶ Indonesia	Indon.
▶ Iran	Iran
▶ Iraq	Iraq
▶ Ireland	Ir.
▶ Israel	Isr.
▶ Italy	It.
▶ Jamaica	Jam.
▶ Japan	Japan
▶ Jordan	Jordan
▶ Kazakhstan	Kaz.
▶ Kenya	Kenya
▶ Kiribati	Kiribati

▶ Korea, North	N. Kor.
▶ Korea, South	S. Kor.
▶ Kosovo	Kos.
▶ Kuwait	Kuwait
▶ Kyrgyzstan	Kyrg.
▶ Laos	Laos
▶ Latin America	Lat. Am.
▶ Latvia	Lat.
▶ Lebanon	Leb.
▶ Lesotho	Lesotho
▶ Liberia	Liber.
▶ Libya	Libya
▶ Liechtenstein	Liech.
▶ Lithuania	Lith.
▶ Luxembourg	Lux.
▶ Macau	Mac.
▶ Macedonia	Maced.
▶ Madagascar	Madag.
▶ Malawi	Malawi
▶ Malaysia	Malay.
▶ Maldives	Maldives
▶ Mali	Mali
▶ Malta	Malta
▶ Marshall Islands	Marsh. Is.
▶ Martinique	Mart.
▶ Mauritania	Mauritania
▶ Mauritius	Mauritius
▶ Mexico	Mex.
▶ Micronesia	Micr.
▶ Moldova	Mold.
▶ Monaco	Monaco
▶ Mongolia	Mong.
▶ Montenegro	Montenegro
▶ Montserrat	Montserrat
▶ Morocco	Morocco
▶ Mozambique	Mozam.
▶ Myanmar	Myan.
▶ Namibia	Namib.
▶ Nauru	Nauru
▶ Nepal	Nepal
▶ Netherlands	Neth.
▶ New Zealand	N.Z.
▶ Nicaragua	Nicar.
▶ Niger	Niger
▶ Nigeria	Nigeria
▶ North America	N. Am.
▶ Northern Ireland	N. Ir.

► Norway	Nor.
► Oman	Oman
► Pakistan	Pak.
► Palau	Palau
► Panama	Pan.
► Papua New Guinea	Papua N.G.
► Paraguay	Para.
► Peru	Peru
► Philippines	Phil.
► Pitcairn Island	Pitcairn Is.
► Poland	Pol.
► Portugal	Port.
► Qatar	Qatar
► Réunion	Réunion
► Romania	Rom.
► Russia	Russ.
► Rwanda	Rwanda
► Saint Helena	St. Helena
► Saint Kitts & Nevis	St. Kitts & Nevis
► Saint Lucia	St. Lucia
► Saint Vincent & the Grenadines	St. Vincent
► Samoa	Samoa
► San Marino	San Marino
► São Tomé and Príncipe	São Tomé & Príncipe
► Saudi Arabia	Saudi Arabia
► Scotland	Scot.
► Senegal	Sen.
► Serbia	Serb.
► Seychelles	Sey.
► Sierra Leone	Sierra Leone
► Singapore	Sing.
► Slovakia	Slovk.
► Slovenia	Slovn.
► Solomon Islands	Solom. Is.
► Somalia	Som.
► South Africa	S. Afr.
► South America	S. Am.
► Spain	Spain
► Sri Lanka	Sri Lanka
► Sudan	Sudan
► Suriname	Surin.
► Swaziland	Swaz.
► Sweden	Swed.
► Switzerland	Switz.
► Syria	Syria
► Taiwan	Taiwan
► Tajikistan	Taj.

▸ Tanzania	Tanz.
▸ Thailand	Thai.
▸ Timor-Leste (East Timor)	Timor-Leste
▸ Togo	Togo
▸ Tonga	Tonga
▸ Trinidad & Tobago	Trin. & Tobago
▸ Tunisia	Tunis.
▸ Turkey	Turk.
▸ Turkmenistan	Turkm.
▸ Turks & Caicos Islands	Turks & Caicos Is.
▸ Tuvalu	Tuvalu
▸ Uganda	Uganda
▸ Ukraine	Ukr.
▸ United Arab Emirates	U.A.E.
▸ United Kingdom	U.K.
▸ United States of America	U.S.
▸ Uruguay	Uru.
▸ Uzbekistan	Uzb.
▸ Vanuatu	Vanuatu
▸ Vatican City	Vatican
▸ Venezuela	Venez.
▸ Vietnam	Viet.
▸ Virgin Islands, British	Virgin Is.
▸ Wales	Wales
▸ Yemen	Yemen
▸ Zambia	Zam.
▸ Zimbabwe	Zim.

T11   JUDGES AND OFFICIALS

Abbreviate titles of judges and other officials according to the following table. See **rule 9** for further guidance in using abbreviated titles.

▸ Administrative Law Judge	A.L.J.
▸ Arbitrator	Arb.
▸ Assembly[man, woman, member]	Assemb.
▸ Attorney General	Att'y Gen.
▸ Baron	B.
▸ Chancellor	C.
▸ Chief Baron	C.B.
▸ Chief Judge, Chief Justice	C.J.
▸ Commissioner	Comm'r
▸ Delegate	Del.
▸ Honorable	Hon.
▸ Judge, Justice	J.
▸ Judges, Justices	JJ.
▸ Lord Justice	L.J.
▸ Magistrate	Mag.
▸ Master of the Rolls	M.R.
▸ Mediator	Med.
▸ Referee	Ref.
▸ Representative	Rep.
▸ Senator	Sen.
▸ Vice Chancellor	V.C.

T12   MONTHS

In citations, abbreviate the names of months as follows:

▸ January	Jan.
▸ February	Feb.
▸ March	Mar.
▸ April	Apr.
▸ May	May
▸ June	June
▸ July	July
▸ August	Aug.
▸ September	Sept.
▸ October	Oct.
▸ November	Nov.
▸ December	Dec.

T13 INSTITUTIONAL NAMES IN PERIODICAL TITLES

Always use the title of the periodical that appears on the title page of the issue you are citing, even if the title of the periodical has changed over time.

Note that preferred abbreviation conventions for individual journals may differ from those listed in this table. The abbreviation conventions listed here are primarily intended to serve a national audience and to clearly indicate the cited source.

To abbreviate English language periodical titles, use **tables T13, T6,** and **T10.** Common institutional names (e.g., law schools, professional organizations, and geographic units commonly found in institutional names) are listed in **table T13.** If an institutional name is not listed in **table T13,** individual words should be abbreviated using **tables T6** and **T10.** If a word in an institutional name is not listed in these tables, use the full word in the abbreviated periodical title. Other words in the periodical title should be abbreviated using **tables T6** and **T10.** If a word is not listed in either **table T6** or **T10,** use the full word in the abbreviated title.

Omit the words "a," "at," "in," "of," and "the" (but retain the word "on"). Also, if the title consists of only one word after the words "a," "at," "in," "of," and "the" have been omitted, do not abbreviate the remaining word. **Rule 6.1(a)** explains the spacing of abbreviations:

▶ Maggie Blackhawk, *Federal Indian Law as Paradigm Within Public Law*, 132 Harv. L. Rev. 1787 (2019).

If a periodical title itself contains an abbreviation, use that abbreviation in the abbreviated title:

▶ IMF Surv.

Omit commas from periodical title abbreviations but retain other punctuation:

▶ Peter H. Huang & Ho-Mou Wu, *More Order Without More Law: A Theory of Social Norms and Organizational Cultures*, 10 J.L. Econ. & Org. 390 (1994).

▶ *Nineteen States Adopt Code of Judicial Conduct*, Oyez! Oyez!, Feb. 1974, at 11.

▶ Amy Hackney Blackwell & Christopher William Blackwell, *Hijacking Shared Heritage: Cultural Artifacts and Intellectual Property Rights,* 13 Chi.-Kent J. Intell. Prop. 137 (2013).

For periodical titles containing colons, omit words following the colon from the abbreviation:

▶ Darren J. Mills, *Personal Goodwill, a Corporate Asset, or No Asset at All*, 91 Taxes 47 (2013).

   Not: Darren J. Mills, *Personal Goodwill, a Corporate Asset, or No Asset at All*, 91 Taxes: The Tax Magazine 47 (2013).

If a periodical has been renumbered in a new series, indicate that fact:

▶ Jill Martin, *The Statutory Sub-Tenancy: A Right Against the World?*, 41 Conv. & Prop. Law. (n.s.) 96 (1977).

For periodical abbreviations in languages other than English, see **rules 20.2.3** and **20.6**.

For online supplements to the print publication, use the citation for the print publication, followed by the online supplement name:

▶ Colum. L. Rev. Sidebar

▶ Harv. L. Rev. F.

▸ Adelaide	Adel.
▸ Air Force	A.F.
▸ Albany	Alb.
▸ American Bar Association (ABA)	A.B.A.
▸ American Intellectual Property Law Association	AIPLA
▸ American Law Institute	A.L.I.
▸ [Journal of the] American Medical Association	[J]AMA
▸ American Society of Composers, Authors & Publishers	ASCAP
▸ American University	Am. U.
▸ Boston College	B.C.
▸ Boston University	B.U.
▸ Brigham Young University	BYU
▸ Brooklyn	Brook.
▸ Buffalo	Buff.
▸ California (California Law Review only)	Calif.
▸ Capital	Cap.
▸ Chapman	Chap.
▸ Chartered Life Underwriters	C.L.U.
▸ Cincinnati	Cin.
▸ City University of New York	CUNY
▸ Cleveland	Clev.
▸ Columbia	Colum.
▸ Cumberland	Cumb.
▸ Denver	Denv.
▸ Detroit	Det.
▸ Dickinson	Dick.
▸ Duquesne	Duq.
▸ East[ern]	E.
▸ Florida International University	FIU
▸ Foreign Broadcast Information Service	F.B.I.S.
▸ George Mason	Geo. Mason
▸ George Washington	Geo. Wash.
▸ Georgetown	Geo.
▸ Gonzaga	Gonz.
▸ Harvard	Harv.
▸ Howard	How.

▸ John Marshall	J. MARSHALL
▸ Judge Advocate General['s]	JAG
▸ Las Vegas	L.V.
▸ Lawyers Reports Annotated	L.R.A.
▸ Loyola	LOY.
▸ Marquette	MARQ.
▸ Melbourne	MELB.
▸ Memphis	MEM.
▸ New England	NEW ENG.
▸ New York University [School of Law]	N.Y.U.
▸ North[ern]	N.
▸ Northeast[ern]	NE.
▸ Northwest[ern]	NW.
▸ Pepperdine	PEPP.
▸ Pittsburgh	PITT.
▸ Richmond	RICH.
▸ Rocky Mountain Mineral Law Institute	ROCKY MTN. MIN. L. INST.
▸ Saint Louis	ST. LOUIS
▸ San Fernando Valley	SAN FERN. V.
▸ South[ern]	S.
▸ Southeast[ern]	SE.
▸ Southern Methodist University	SMU
▸ Southwest[ern]	SW.
▸ Stanford	STAN.
▸ State	ST.
▸ Temple	TEMP.
▸ Thomas Jefferson	T. JEFFERSON
▸ Thomas M. Cooley	T.M. COOLEY
▸ Thurgood Marshall	T. MARSHALL
▸ Toledo	TOL.
▸ Tulane	TUL.
▸ Universidad de Puerto Rico	U. P.R.
▸ University of California	U.C.
▸ University of California - Los Angeles	UCLA
▸ University of Missouri Kansas City	UMKC
▸ University of the District of Columbia, David A. Clarke School of Law	UDC/DCSL
▸ University of West Los Angeles	UWLA
▸ Valparaiso	VAL.
▸ Vanderbilt	VAND.
▸ Villanova	VILL.
▸ Washington & Lee	WASH. & LEE
▸ West[ern]	W.
▸ William & Mary	WM. & MARY
▸ William Mitchell	WM. MITCHELL

T14 PUBLISHING TERMS

Abbreviate publishing terms in citations according to **rule 15.4** and the following table:

▸ abridge[d, ment]	abr.
▸ annotated	ann.
▸ anonymous	anon.
▸ circa	c.
▸ compil[ation, ed]	comp.
▸ copyright	copy.
▸ draft	drft.
▸ edit[ion, or]	ed.
▸ manuscript	ms.
▸ mimeograph	mimeo.
▸ new series	n.s.
▸ no date	n.d.
▸ no place	n.p.
▸ no publisher	n. pub.
▸ offprint	offprt.
▸ old series	o.s.
▸ permanent	perm.
▸ photoduplicated reprint	photo. reprt.
▸ printing	prtg.
▸ replacement	repl.
▸ reprint	reprt.
▸ revis[ed, ion]	rev.
▸ special	spec.
▸ temporary	temp.
▸ tentative	tent.
▸ translat[ion, or]	trans.
▸ unabridged	unabr.
▸ volume	vol.

T15 SERVICES

Abbreviations commonly used in referring to service publishers include the following:

▸ Bloomberg Law	BL
▸ Commerce Clearing House	CCH
▸ Matthew Bender	MB
▸ Research Institute of America	RIA

Abbreviations for some of the most frequently cited services are listed below. Following each looseleaf service title, the list indicates the appropriate abbreviation of the service, the publisher, and corresponding bound services. Names of bound services that differ markedly from their looseleaf forms are printed in italics and cross-referenced to the looseleaf forms. See **rule 19** for further guidance on citation to services.

► Administrative Law Third Series	Admin. L.3d (BL)
► Affirmative Action Compliance Manual for Federal Contractors	Aff. Action Compl. Man. (BL)
► AIDS Law & Litigation Reporter	AIDS L. & Litig. Rep. (Univ. Pub. Group)
► All States Tax Guide	All St. Tax Guide (RIA)
► American Federal Tax Reports, Second Series	A.F.T.R.2d (RIA)
► American Stock Exchange Guide	Am. Stock Ex. Guide (CCH)
► Antitrust & Trade Regulation Report	Antitrust & Trade Reg. Rep. (BL)
► Aviation Law Reporter	Av. L. Rep. (CCH)
bound as Aviation Cases	Av. Cas. (CCH)
► BL's Banking Report	Banking Rep. (BL)
► Bankruptcy Court Decisions	Bankr. Ct. Dec. (LRP)
► Bankruptcy Law Reports	Bankr. L. Rep. (CCH)
► Benefits Review Board Service	Ben. Rev. Bd. Serv. (MB)
► BioLaw	BioLaw (LexisNexis)
► Blue Sky Law Reporter	Blue Sky L. Rep. (CCH)
► *Board of Contract Appeals Decisions*—see Contract Appeals Decisions	
► Business Franchise Guide	Bus. Franchise Guide (CCH)
► Canadian Commercial Law Guide	Can. Com. L. Guide (CCH)
► Canadian Tax Reporter	Can. Tax Rep. (CCH)
► Chemical Regulation Reporter	Chem. Reg. Rep. (BL)
► Chicago Board Options Exchange Guide	Chicago Bd. Options Ex. Guide (CCH)
► Collective Bargaining Negotiations & Contracts	Collective Bargaining Negot. & Cont. (BL)
► Collier Bankruptcy Cases, Second Series	Collier Bankr. Cas. 2d (MB)
► Commodity Futures Law Reporter	Comm. Fut. L. Rep. (CCH)
► Communications Regulation	Commc'ns Reg. (BL)
► Congressional Index	Cong. Index (CCH)
► Consumer Credit Guide	Consumer Cred. Guide (CCH)
► Consumer Product Safety Guide	Consumer Prod. Safety Guide (CCH)
► Contract Appeals Decisions	Cont. App. Dec. (CCH)
bound as Board of Contract Appeals Decisions	B.C.A. (CCH)
► *Contracts Cases, Federal*—see Government Contracts Reporter	
► Copyright Law Decisions	Copyright L. Dec. (CCH)
► Copyright Law Reporter	Copyright L. Rep. (CCH)
► Cost Accounting Standards Guide	Cost Accounting Stand. Guide (CCH)
► The Criminal Law Reporter	Crim. L. Rep. (BL)
► Daily Labor Report	Daily Lab. Rep. (BL)
► Dominion Tax Cases	Dominion Tax Cas. (CCH)
► EEOC Compliance Manual	EEOC Compl. Man. (BL)
► EEOC Compliance Manual	EEOC Compl. Man. (CCH)
► Employee Benefits Cases	Empl. Benefits Cas. (BL)
► Employee Benefits Compliance Coordinator	Empl. Coordinator (RIA)

► Employment Practices Guide
   bound as Employment Practices Decisions—
   see also Labor Law Reporter
	Empl. Prac. Dec. (CCH)

► Employment Safety and Health Guide
   bound as Occupational Safety and Health
   Decisions
	Empl. Safety & Health
	   Guide (CCH)
	   O.S.H. Dec. (CCH)

► Employment Testing: Law & Policy Reporter	Empl. Testing (Univ. Pub. Am.)
► Energy Management & Federal Energy Guidelines	Energy Mgmt. (CCH)

► Environment Reporter
   bound as Environment Reporter Cases
	Env't Rep. (BL)
	   Env't Rep. Cas. (BL)

► Environmental Law Reporter	Env't L. Rep. (Env't Law Inst.)
► Exempt Organizations Reports	Exempt Org. Rep. (CCH)
► *Fair Employment Practice Cases*—see Labor Relations Reporter	
► The Family Law Reporter	Fam. L. Rep. (BL)
► Family Law Tax Guide	Fam. L. Tax Guide (CCH)
► Federal Audit Guides	Fed. Audit Guide (CCH)
► Federal Banking Law Reporter	Fed. Banking L. Rep. (CCH)

► Federal Carriers Reports
   bound as Federal Carriers Cases
	Fed. Carr. Rep. (CCH)
	   Fed. Carr. Cas. (CCH)

► Federal Contracts Report	Fed. Cont. Rep. (BL)
► Federal Election Campaign Financing Guide	Fed. Election Camp. Fin. Guide (CCH)

► Federal Energy Regulatory Commission
   Reporter
	Fed. Energy Reg. Comm'n
	   Rep. (CCH)

► Federal Estate and Gift Tax Reporter
   bound as Standard Federal Tax Reporter
	Fed. Est. & Gift Tax Rep.
	   (CCH)
	   Stand. Fed. Tax Rep.
	   (CCH)

► Federal Excise Tax Reporter	Fed. Ex. Tax Rep. (CCH)
► Federal Income, Gift and Estate Taxation	Fed. Inc. Gift & Est. Tax'n (MB)
► Federal Rules Service, Second Series	Fed. R. Serv. 2d (West)
► Federal Securities Law Reporter	Fed. Sec. L. Rep. (CCH)
► Federal Tax Coordinator Second	Fed. Tax Coordinator 2d (RIA)
► Federal Tax Guide Reports	Fed. Tax Guide Rep. (CCH)
► *Fire & Casualty Cases*—see Insurance Law Reports	
► Food Drug Cosmetic Law Reporter	Food Drug Cosm. L. Rep. (CCH)

► Government Contracts Reporter
   bound as Contracts Cases, Federal
	Gov't Cont. Rep. (CCH)
	   Cont. Cas. Fed. (CCH)

► Government Employee Relations Report	Gov't Empl. Rel. Rep. (BL)
► Housing & Development Reporter	Hous. & Dev. Rep. (RIA)
► Human Resources Management OSHA Compliance Guide	OSHA Comp. Guide (CCH)
► Immigration Law Service	Immigr. L. Serv. (West)
► Insurance Law Reports bound as:	Ins. L. Rep. (CCH)

► Personal and Commercial Liability	Personal and Comm. Liab. (CCH)
► Life, Health & Accident Insurance Cases Second	Life Health & Accid. Ins. Cas. 2d (CCH)
► International Environment Reporter	Int'l Env't Rep. (BL)
► International Trade Reporter	Int'l Trade Rep. (BL)
► IRS Positions	IRS Pos. (CCH)
► Labor Arbitration Awards	Lab. Arb. Awards (CCH)
► Labor Arbitration and Grievance Guide	Lab. Arb. & Grievance Guide (BL)
► Labor Law Reporter bound as:	Lab. L. Rep. (CCH)
► Labor Cases	Lab. Cas. (CCH)
► NLRB Decisions—see also Employment Practices Guide	NLRB Dec. (CCH)
► Labor Relations Guide	Lab. Rel. Guide (BL)
► Labor Relations Reporter bound as:	Lab. Rel. Rep. (BL)
► Fair Employment Practice Cases	Fair Empl. Prac. Cas. (BL)
► Labor Arbitration Reports	Lab. Arb. Rep. (BL)
► Labor Relations Reference Manual	L.R.R.M. (BL)
► Wage and Hour Cases	Wage & Hour Cas. (BL)
► ABA/Bloomberg Law Lawyers' Manual on Professional Conduct	ABA/BLAW Law. Man. on Prof. Conduct (ABA/BLAW)
► ABA/BNA Lawyers' Manual on Professional Conduct	Laws. Man. on Prof. Conduct (ABA/BLAW)
► *Life, Health & Accident Insurance Cases*—see Insurance Law Reports	
► Liquor Control Law Reporter	Liquor Cont. L. Rep. (CCH)
► Media Law Reporter	Media L. Rep. (BL)
► Medical Devices Reporter	Med. Devices Rep. (CCH)
► Medicare and Medicaid Guide	Medicare & Medicaid Guide (CCH)
► Mutual Funds Guide	Mut. Funds Guide (CCH)
► National Reporter on Legal Ethics & Professional Responsibility	Nat'l Rep. Legal Ethics (Univ. Pub. Am.)
► New York Stock Exchange Guide	N.Y.S.E. Guide (CCH)
► *NLRB Decisions*—see Labor Law Reporter	
► Nuclear Regulation Reporter	Nuclear Reg. Rep. (CCH)
► Occupational Safety & Health Reporter bound as Occupational Safety & Health Cases	O.S.H. Rep. (BL) O.S.H. Cas. (BL)
► OFCCP Federal Contract Compliance Manual	OFCCP Fed. Cont. Compl. Man. (CCH)
► Patent, Trademark & Copyright Journal	Pat. Trademark & Copyright J. (BL)
► Pension & Benefits Reporter	Pens. & Ben. Rep. (BL)
► Pension Plan Guide	Pens. Plan Guide (CCH)
► Pension & Profit Sharing Second	Pens. & Profit Sharing 2d (RIA)

▸ Product Safety & Liability Reporter	Prod. Safety & Liab. Rep. (BL)
▸ Products Liability Reporter	Prod. Liab. Rep. (CCH)
▸ Public Utilities Reports	Pub. Util. Rep. (PUR)
▸ School Law Reporter	School L. Rep. (Educ. Law Ass'n.)
▸ Search & Seizure Bulletin	Search & Seizure Bull. (Quinlan)
▸ SEC Accounting Rules	SEC Accounting R. (CCH)
▸ Secured Transactions Guide	Secured Transactions Guide (CCH)
▸ Securities and Federal Corporate Law Report	Sec. & Fed. Corp. L. Rep. (West)
▸ Securities Regulation & Law Report	Sec. Reg. & L. Rep. (BL)
▸ Shipping Regulation	Shipping Reg. (BL)
▸ Social Security Reporter	Soc. Sec. Rep. (CCH)
▸ Standard Federal Tax Reporter bound as U.S. Tax Cases	Stand. Fed. Tax Rep. (CCH) U.S. Tax Cas. (CCH)
▸ State and Local Tax Service	St. & Loc. Tax Serv. (RIA)
▸ *State and Local Taxes*—see All States Tax Guide	
▸ State Inheritance, Estate, and Gift Tax Reporter	St. Inher., Est. & Gift Tax Rep. (CCH)
▸ State Tax Guide	St. Tax Guide (CCH)
▸ State Tax Reporter	St. Tax Rep. (CCH)
▸ Tax Court Memorandum Decisions bound in Tax Court Reporter	T.C.M. (RIA) T.C.M. (CCH) [or (RIA)]
▸ Tax Court Reported Decisions	Tax Ct. Rep. Dec. (RIA)
▸ Tax Court Reports	Tax Ct. Rep. (CCH)
▸ Trade Regulation Reporter bound as Trade Cases	Trade Reg. Rep. (CCH) Trade Cas. (CCH)
▸ Unemployment Insurance Reporter	Unempl. Ins. Rep. (CCH)
▸ Uniform Commercial Code Reporting Service Second	UCC Rep. Serv. (West)
▸ Union Labor Report Newsletter	Union Lab. Rep. Newsl. (BL)
▸ The United States Law Week	U.S.L.W. (BL—publisher need not be indicated)
▸ The United States Patents Quarterly bound in same name	U.S.P.Q. (BL), U.S.P.Q.2d (BL)
▸ *U.S. Tax Cases* —see Federal Estate and Gift Tax Reporter; Standard Federal Tax Reporter	
▸ U.S. Tax Reporter	U.S. Tax Rep. (RIA)
▸ U.S. Tax Treaties Reporter	U.S. Tax Treaties Rep. (CCH)
▸ Utilities Law Reports	Util. L. Rep. (CCH)

T16   SUBDIVISIONS

The following list provides abbreviations for names of document subdivisions frequently used in legal citations. See **rule 3** for further guidance in using these abbreviations. For those abbreviations shown in blue ink, no space appears between the subdivision abbreviation and the number/letter:

► ch. 3

► tbl.3

► addendum	add.
► amendment	amend.
► annotation	annot.
► appendi[x, ces]	app., apps.
► article	art.
► attachment	attach.
► bibliography	bibliog.
► book	bk.
► chapter	ch.
► clause	cl.
► column	col.
► comment[ary]	cmt.
► decision	dec.
► department	dept.
► division	div.
► example	ex.
► figure	fig.
► folio	fol.
► footnote[s]	
in cross-references	note, notes
in other references	n., nn.
► historical note[s]	hist. n., hist. nn.
► hypothetical	hypo.
► illustration[s]	illus.
► introduction	intro.
► line[s]	l., ll.
► number	no.
► page[s]	
in cross-references	p., pp.
in other references	[at]
► paragraph[s]	
if symbol appears in source	¶, ¶¶
if otherwise	para., paras.
► part[s]	pt., pts.
► preamble	pmbl.
► principle	princ.
► publication	pub.
► rule	r.
► schedule	sched.
► section[s]	
in amending act	sec., secs.
in all other contexts	§, §§
► series, serial	ser.
► subdivision	subdiv.
► subsection	subsec.
► supplement	supp.
► table	tbl.
► title	tit.
► volume	vol.

Index

Abbreviations
adjacent spacing of, 88
administrative reporters, 89, 112,
  145–46, 230–42
administrative reports, 145
agencies, 89
American Bar Association, 133
American reporters, 104–05, 227–98
"and," in case names, 99
arbitral reporters, 196, 209–10, 303
authors, 148–49
bound services, 323–27
business firms, 99, 101
case history, 109–12
case names, 96–103
case names, in citations, 102–03
case names, international, 201–10
citations, repeating, 79–82
closing up of, 88
codes, statutory, 123–25
commonly abbreviated names, 9, 89,
  99, 101–02, 304–07
congressional reports and documents,
  135–42, 311
corporate authors, 148–49
countries, (see foreign countries)
court documents, 29–30
court of decision, 105–07, 307–10
dollar symbol, 90
editions of books, 150–51, 323
English-language periodicals, 87–89,
  304–07, 320–22
English *Law Report* series, 299
English monarchs, 299
European Court and Commission of
  Human Rights materials, 205–06,
  300–01
European Union materials, 204–05,
  217–20, 300
explanatory phrases, 70, 80–81,
  110–11, 310
foreign countries, 313–18
foreign courts, 188–89 (see also name
  of jurisdiction)
foreign materials, 188–90, 299
foreign periodicals, 193–94
generally, 87–89
"hereinafter," use of, 81–82, 198, 200,
  219, 220–22, 226
history of cases, 110–11
initials, commonly recognized, 11–12,
  89, 99, 101
institutional authors, 148–49
Inter-American Commission on Human
  Rights materials, 195, 206, 301

intergovernmental organizations,
  210–24, 299–303
international and world organization
  materials, 195–226, 299–303
international arbitrations and claims
  commissions, 209–10
judges, titles, 94, 319
law journals and reviews, 304–07,
  320–22
League of Nations materials, 216, 299
looseleaf services, 186–87, 323–27
model codes, 131–33
months, 319
multiple citations of same work, 79–82
multiple editions and printings, 150–51
municipal ordinances, 130
names, commonly abbreviated, 9, 89,
  99–102, 304–07
new series, 320
newsletters, 167
newspapers, 161–62
no date, 161
officials, titles, 94, 319
ordinances, 130
paragraph symbols, 76–77, 90, 328
parties to treaties, 198
percent symbols, 89–90
periodicals, 88, 157–68, 193–94,
  320–22
periodicals, English-language,
  304–07, 320–22
periodicals, foreign-language, 193–94
pluralization of, 304
prepositions in periodical names, 304
prior case history, 110–12, 310
publishers of services, 323–27
publishing terms, 323
punctuation of, 87–89
repeating citations, 79–82
reporters, foreign, 189–90 (see also
  name of jurisdiction)
reporters, United States, 103–06,
  227–98
restatements, 77–78, 131–33
section symbols, 76–77, 90
services, 323–27
session laws, 125–27 (see also name of
  jurisdiction)
spacing of, 87–89
standards, 131–33
statutes, 120–34 (see also name of
  jurisdiction)
subdivisions (e.g., section, article,
  chapter), 72–78, 90, 119, 199,
  327–28

Index

Abbreviations, continued
subsequent case history, 110–12, 310
taxation materials, 20, 235–37
titles of books, reports, and other nonperiodic materials, 150
titles of individuals, 94, 319
treaty series, 302–03
unions, 101
United Nations materials, 210–16, 299
"United States," 89, 100, 149
use of abbreviations not listed in this book, 88
"Abrogated by," **in case history,** 111
Abstracts, in law reviews, 163
"Accord," **as signal,** 62
"Acquiescence," **in tax cases,** 237, 310
"Act," capitalization of, 92
Action on decision, 237
Acts (see Codes, Session laws, Statutes)
Addenda, 77–78
Addresses (speeches), 70, 152, 171–72
Administrative agencies
abbreviation of, 89, 142, 230–42
adjudications, 144–46
arbitrations, 144–46
reporters, 89, 145–46, 230–42
reports, 142–46
Administrative cases
citation of, 144–46, 230–42
exact date, when required, 145–46
number of case, when required, 145–46
omission of procedural phrases, 145
parallel citation, 145–46
recent, 145–46
services, when cited, 146
"sub nom.," use on appeal, 111–12
Administrative law judges, 94, 319
Administrative materials
adjudications, 144–46, 230–42
agency publications, 142–44, 230–42
basic citation forms, 142
cases, 144–46
Code of Federal Regulations, 142–44, 146–47
compilations of regulations, 142–44, 146–47
court administrative orders, 116
executive orders, 237–38
Federal Register, 142–44, 146–47
federal rules and regulations, 142–44
foreign (see name of country)
generally, 142–47, 230–42
Internal Revenue Service, 20, 235–37
Internet sources, 146
names of rules and regulations, 142–44
notices, 143–44
official releases, 142–44
opinions, formal advisory, 234
order within signal, 65
popular names of rules and regulations, 143
presidential orders, 237–38
presidential papers, 237–38
presidential proclamations, 237-38
proposed rules and regulations, 143–44
regulations, 142–44
revenue materials, 20, 235–37
revenue rulings, 20, 235–37
rules, 142–44
slip opinions, 145–46
state, 142, 242–94
tax materials, 20, 235–37
Treasury decisions, 20, 235–37
Treasury materials, 20, 235–37
Treasury regulations, 20, 235–37
U.N. Administrative Tribunal, 214–15
United Kingdom, 299
varieties of, 142
Administrative Procedure Act, 18–19, 134, 140
Advisory committee notes, 77–78
Affidavits, 25–26, 29
"Affirmed" **and** *"affirming,"* **in case history,** 11, 15–16, 96, 109–10, 310
Agencies, administrative (see Administrative agencies)
Agreements, international, 195, 197–201, 226
Alabama
citation rules and style guides, 46
sources of law, 242–43
Alaska
citation rules and style guides, 46
sources of law, 243–44
All England Law Reports, 299
Alphabets, foreign, 190–91, 299
Alterations in quotations, 84–86
Alternative holding, indication of, 108
"Amended by"
in constitution citation, 119
in statute citation, 122, 126–27, 129
Amended constitution, 119
Amended statutes, 122, 126–27, 129
Amendments
constitutional, 119
model codes, 132–33
restatements, 132–33
session laws, 126
standards, 132–33
statutes, 122, 126–27, 129
Treasury regulations, 236
uniform acts, 131–32
"Amendment(s)," **abbreviation of,** 304, 327–28
American Bar Association
abbreviation as ABA, 133

publications, 133, 166–67
section reports, 166–67
American Jurisprudence (Am. Jur.), 23, 153
American Law Institute
generally, 131–33
proceedings, 166–67
publications, 131–33, 166–67
American Law Reports (A.L.R.), 166
American Samoa
sources of law, 295
Ampersand
authors' names, 22–23, 148
books titles and other nonperiodic
materials, 22–23
case names, 12, 99
editors' names, 149
footnote citation, 75–76
URL, 181
volumes, parts, and supplements, 73
Annals of Congress, 140
Annexes
European Union materials, 218
generally, 77–78
U.N. records, 211–12
World Trade Organization materials,
222
Annotations
A.L.R., L.R.A., 166
generally, 77–78
*Annual Digest and Reports of Public
International Law Cases,* 209
Annual reports
government agencies, 144
Inter-American Commission on Human
Rights, 206
International Court of Justice, 202
"Appeal dismissed," in case history, 110
Appeal docketed, 96, 107
Appeals, 96, 107, 109–10
Appendices
codes, 124
generally, 77–78
statutes reprinted in codes, 124
U.S. Sentencing Guidelines Manual,
132–33
"Appendi[x, ces]," abbreviation of, 328
Arabic numerals
monarchs, 299
volumes, 7, 72
Arbitrations
administrative, 142, 144–45
international, 196, 209–10, 222, 226
"Arbitrator," abbreviation of, 319
Arbitrators, indicated parenthetically, 145
Argentine Republic
sources of national law, 299
Arizona
citation rules and style guides, 46–47
sources of law, 244–45

Arkansas
citation rules and style guides, 47
sources of law, 245
Armed Services Board of Contract
Appeals, 230–31
Article (part of speech)
capitalization of, 91
omission of, 29, 150, 159, 169, 202, 311
Articles
appearing in two or more parts,
167–68
basic citation forms, 157–58
collected essays, printed in, 152
essays in collection, 152
foreign periodicals, 193–94
forthcoming publications, 172
law reviews and journals, 157–61
magazines, 157, 160–61
multipart, 165–66
newspapers, 157, 161–62
page citation, 73–74
periodicals, 157–69
typeface in law review citations, 69–70
typeface in law review text, 70–72
typeface in non-journal legal writing,
6–7
"Article(s)," abbreviation of, 327–28
"Ass'n," in case names, 12, 99, 101, 304
"At," used in citation of pages or sections,
7, 8, 16, 17, 23, 25, 73, 78–82
"At," used in electronic databases and
other media, 14, 176, 179, 185–86
"Attorney General," abbreviation of, 319
Attorney General, opinions, 234
Audio recordings, 115, 184
Auditing standards, 132
Australia
sources of national law, 299
Australian states and territories, 299
Austria
sources of national law, 299
Authentic or official online documents,
174, 176
Authorities in text, identification of, 61
Authorities previously cited, 79–82
Authors
annotations, 166
articles in periodicals, 159
book reviews, 164
books, reports, and other nonperiodic
materials, 148–49
collected essays, 151–52
colloquy, names not given, 165
congressional documents and reports,
139
direct internet citations, 178
essays in collection, 151–52
forewords, 153
institutional, 148–49

Index

Authors, continued
    law reviews and journals, 160, 163–64
    model codes, 133
    multiple, books, reports, and other
        nonperiodic materials, 148–49
    multivolume works, 148
    news reports and articles, 159
    newspapers, 159
    no author, 81, 161–62, 163–64,
        167–69, 173–74, 178, 185, 201
    periodical materials, 159
    periodicals, surveys and symposia
        in, 165
    prefaces, 153
    restatements, 131–33
    reviewer of book, 164
    standards, 131–33
    student, 159, 163–64
    symposium, names not given, 165
    U.N. material, 210–16
Author's mistakes in quoted material, 84
Ballentine's Law Dictionary, 153
Bankruptcy
    appellate panels, 98, 106, 229, 308
    cases, 98, 186, 188
    courts, 98, 229
    pending or unreported cases, 113
Bankruptcy Reporter, 229
Bar publications, 166–67
"Baron," abbreviation of, 319
Basic charters, international and world
    organizations, 195–96, 197–98, 216,
    223–24
Bible, 154
Bills
    bills and resolutions, 136–37
    congressional, 136–37
    state, 137
Black's Law Dictionary, 23, 153
Blackstone's *Commentaries,* 74, 153–54
Block quotations, 8–9, 83–84, 86
Blogs, 174, 175, 177–79
The Bluebook, 149, 154
Bloomberg Law services, 323
Board of Tax Appeals
    citation of cases, 20, 229, 237, 308
Book notes, 158, 159, 164
Book reviews
    periodicals, 163–64
"Book(s)," abbreviation of, 328
Books, reports, and other nonperiodic
    materials
    ABA publications, 133, 166–67
    abbreviation of title, 150
    administrative agency records and
        reports, 142–46
    A.L.I. publications, 131–33
    author, 148–49
    basic form of citation, 147
    book reviews, 164

capitalization, 91, 150
citation, components of, 147
citation analyzed, 147
collected documents, 152
collected essays, 151–52
congressional materials, 135–42
corporate author, 148–49
date, 150–51
date in title, 150
date not given by source, 151
Declaration of Independence, 76
dictionaries, legal, 153
edition, 150–51
editor, when indicated, 149
electronic media and online sources,
    154–55.
encyclopedias, legal, 147
The Federalist, 154
footnote typefaces, 68
forewords, 153
forthcoming publications, 172
generally, 147–56
given names of authors, 148–49
government agencies as authors,
    148–49
government agency reports, 144
institutional authors, 148–49
internet sources, 154–55
italicization, when referred to in text,
    70–72
law reviews and journals, 23–24, 69,
    160–61, 193–94, 304–07, 320–22
legal dictionaries and encyclopedias,
    23, 152
letters, 152, 170–71
manuscripts, typed, 169–70
multiple authors, 148
multiple editions, 150–51
multiple printings, 150–51
multivolume works, 22–23, 148, 150
name of author, 148–49
names and titles, capitalization,
    91–92, 150, 159
number, serial, 153
order within signal, 5, 65
page citation, 73–76, 147
paragraph citation, 76–77
periodicals, 304–07, 320–22
photoduplicated reprints, 151, 323
place of publication not given by
    source, 151
place of publication, when required,
    151
pocket parts, 151
pre-1900 works, 151
prefaces, 153
printings, 150–51
publication number, 150–51
repeated citation of, 79–82

reprints, 150–51
restatements, 18–19, 131–33
sections, 76–77
serial number, 153
series of, 153
short citation forms, 155–56
shorter works in collection, 151–52, 155–56
special citation forms, 153–54
star pages, 74, 153–54
subdivisions of, 72, 78–79
subtitles, omitted, 150
supplements, 151
theses, unpublished, 170
titles, 150
translator, when given, 149
typeface, 6–7, 69, 70–72, 147
typeface, authors, 7, 69, 70–72, 148–49
typeface in court documents and legal memoranda, 6–7
typeface in law review citations, 68–70
typeface in law review text, 70–72
unpublished works, 169–73
volume designations, 72–73
well-known works, 23, 153–54
writer of, 148–49
year, 150–51
Bound services
abbreviations, 323–27
generally, 186–88
typeface, 186
Brackets
alterations in quotations, 84–86
establishing short citation or translation, used in, 82, 188–94
quotations, used in, 84–86
volume designations, 72–73, 186–87
years, 186–87
Brazil
sources of national law, 299
treaty source, 299
Briefs and legal memoranda (see Court documents and legal memoranda)
Briefs and records, citation of
generally, 114–16
British Columbia
sources of law, 299
British materials (see England)
Broadcasts, 175, 183, 185–86
Business firms, in case names, 99, 101
"But cf.," as signal, 63
"But see," as signal, 63
Byline, newspaper articles, 161–62
California
sources of law, 246–47
Canada
sources of national law, 299
treaty source, 299

Canadian Guide to Uniform Legal Citation, 299
Canal Zone
sources of law, 299
Canon Law, 299
Canons of Professional Responsibility, 133
Cantons, Swiss, 299
Capitalization
change in quotation, indication of, 84–86
court documents and legal memoranda, 10
courts, 93
generally, 91–94
headings, 91
Internet main page titles and URLs, 92
party designations, 10
people or groups, nouns referring to, 92–94
titles of books and articles, 91, 150, 159
titles of foreign documents, 189
Case comments in law reviews, 163–64
Case history (see History of cases)
Case names
abbreviations, 96–103, 304–07
abbreviations, in citations, 102–03, 304–07
abbreviations, in textual sentences, 96–102
administrative actions, 142–47, 230–42
"administrator," omission of, 99
ampersand, use of in text, 99
appeal, when different on, 111–12
"appellee," omission of, 99
arbitrations, 145
arbitrations, international, 209–10
"Ass'n," abbreviation in text, 99
bankruptcy, 98
"Bros.," abbreviation in text, 99
business firms, 101
citations, abbreviations in, 102–03, 304–07
cite first listed party only, 97–98
"Co.," abbreviation in text, 99, 101
Commissioner of Internal Revenue, as party, 101
Common Market cases, 205
common names, when different from name in reporter, 101–02, 117
consolidated actions, 97–98
"Corp.," abbreviation in text, 99, 101
court documents and legal memoranda, 11–12
"d/b/a," omission of, 97
descriptive terms, 99
different on appeal, 111–12
"estate of," 98

Index

Case names, continued

"et al.," 97
European Court of Justice, 204–05, 220
"executor," omission of, 99
"*ex parte*," 98
"*ex rel.*," 98
first word, retention in full, 97
foreign cases, 191–92
generally, 96–103
geographical terms, 99–101
given names and initials of parties, 100
"*id.*," use of, 116–18
"*In re*," 98
in rem actions, 98
"Inc.," abbreviation in text, 99
"Inc.," when omitted, 101
Internal Revenue Commissioner, as party, 101
international arbitrations, 196, 209–10
International Court of Justice, 195, 201–203
"Judgment of," 97
Latin words italicized, 90–91
"licensee," omission of, 99
"Ltd.," abbreviation in text, 99
"Ltd.," when omitted, 101
mandamus actions, 102
multiple dispositions, when indicated, 102
"No.," abbreviation in text, 99
omissions in, 97–102
parenthetical indication of alternate name, 98, 101
parties, only first–listed named, 97
partnerships, 97
Permanent Court of International Justice, 201–03
popular names, 97, 99, 101
procedural phrases, 98
real property, as party, 98
running heads, words omitted in, 97
short citation form, to entire decision, 117
short forms, 116–18
short names, 101–02
state as party in state court decision, 99
surnames, 100
textual references, 12, 68, 70–72, 96–97
"The," omission of, 99
transcripts, 114–16
"trustee," omission of, 99
typeface used in court documents, 6–7, 68
typeface used in law review citations, 68–70
typeface used in law review text, 68, 70–72

unions as parties, 101
"Will of," 98
Case notes in law reviews, 163–64
Case number
administrative cases, 145–46
appeal or petition for certiorari, 95–96, 114–16
court documents, 114–16
Federal Cases, 227–30
pending cases, 96, 112–14
unreported cases, 96, 112–14
Case writeups
citation of, 163–64
cited with case, 67–68
Cases (see also individual jurisdiction or court)
administrative actions, 142, 144–46
appeal, disposition on, 96
appeal docketed, 96, 107
arbitrations, 142, 144–45, 196, 209–10, 222, 226
bankruptcy, 98, 106, 113
basic citation forms, 95–96
before decision, 14–15, 96, 107, 112–14
Bloomberg, 182
briefs, citation of, 24–26, 96, 114–16
British, 299
certiorari, citation of petition for, 114–16
citation, basic forms of, 95–96
citation, components of, 11, 95–96
citation order, 65
citation to particular page, 7, 13, 72–76
civil law (foreign), 192–94
commentary on, cited with case, 67–68
common law (foreign), 192–94
components of citations, 11, 95–96
computerized research services, 14-15, 112–14, 173, 176–77, 182
concurring opinion, 15, 108
country, indication of, 188
court of decision, 14–15, 105–07
court of decision, abbreviations, 307–10
court of decision, American, 13–14, 105–07
court of decision, other jurisdictions, 191–92
court, when indicated, 105–07
dates, 13, 95, 107, 112–14
denial of rehearing, 109, 111–12
dictum, 108
different name on appeal, 111–12
dissenting opinion, 15, 108
docket number, 14–15, 89–90, 96, 112–16
dual citation of sources, 14, 103, 145–46

Index

electronic databases, 14–15, 112–14, 173, 176–77, 182
England, 299
European Union, 217–20, 299
explanatory phrases, 5–6, 65–66, 110–11
federal court, 227–30
filed, 96
foreign, 191–92
history on remand, 109–10
history, prior and subsequent, 16, 109–10
in-chambers opinions, 108–09
in rem, 11, 98
interim orders, 96
international and world organization, 195–96, 201–09, 223–24
international arbitrations, 209–10, 303
International Court of Justice, 201–03, 299
Internet sources, 26–27, 112–14, 173–82
italicization of names in court documents, 6
italicization of names in text, 70–72
italicization of procedural phrases in citations, 70
italicized words in history of, 110, 310
Judge or Justice writing opinion, 108
LEXIS, cited to, 14–15, 112–14, 176–77, 182, 185
medium-neutral citation, 103–05
memoranda, citations to, 170–71
memorandum decision, 108
motions, citation to, 114–16
name cited as in official report, 97
named in text, initial and subsequent citation, 12, 79–81, 96–97, 118
names, 11–12, 96–103
newspapers, cited in, 103, 161–62
no name, citation of, 97
non-common-law, 192
number of case, 95–96, 112–14
official reporters, when cited, 13–14, 103–04
online, 112–14
order within signal, 5, 65
page citations, 73–74
parallel citation of sources, 14, 103
parenthetical information, 108
pending, 14–15, 107, 112–14
per curiam decisions, 108
periodicals, when cited, 23–24, 113, 120, 127–28, 157–58
Permanent Court of International Justice, 201–03, 299
plurality opinion, 108
prior history, 110
procedural phrases, 98

public domain format, 104–05
published decision, 96
recent, 96, 107
records, citation of, 24–26, 96, 114–16
releases of administrative agencies, cited to, 142–47
repeating citations of, 8, 16–18, 79–81, 116–18
reporters, 104
reporters, defined, 104
reporters, reprinted, 104
services, appearing in, 96–97
services, when cited, 103
short citation form, 8, 16–18, 116–18
slip opinions, reported in, 96, 107, 113, 117–18
sources, 103–04
state courts, 106–07, 242–98
statutory material, cited with, 67–68
subsequent history, 96, 109–10
transcript of record, citations to, 24–26, 96, 114–16
typeface used in court documents, 6–7
typeface used in law review citations, 68–70
typeface used in law review text, 70–72
unofficial reporter, when cited, 103–04, 145–46
unreported, 14–15, 112–14
weight of authority, 15, 108, 110
Westlaw, cited to, 14–15, 112–13
year of decision, 13–14, 107
Catholic Church, codes, 299
CD-ROM, 182, 185
Certiorari
    applied for, granted, denied, 16, 96, 110
    indication in case history, 16, 110
    petition, citation of, 114–16
    "sub nom." not used, 111–12
"Cf.," as signal, 5, 63
C.F.R., 22, 142–44, 146–47
"Chancellor," abbreviation of, 319
Chapters
    codes, statutory, 76–77
    number, when given for federal statute, 123
"Chapter(s)," abbreviation of, 328
Charters, international organizations, 197–98
"Chief Baron," "Justice," "Judge," abbreviation of, 319
Chile, Republic of
    sources of national law, 299
China, People's Republic of
    sources of national law, 299
"Circuit," capitalization of, 93
Circuit courts of appeals (see Courts)

Index

Circuit courts, old federal, 106, 28
Circuit Justices, 227
Citation of commentary with case or book, 67–68
Citation order, 64–65
Citation sentences and clauses, 3–4, 61–62
Citations (see also specific types of material)
  abbreviations of case names, 304–07
  analogous authority, 63
  authentic or official online documents, 174–76
  authoritativeness, order within citation, 5, 65
  authorities, 5, 65
  background authority, 64
  citations analyzed, 61–62
  comparing authorities, 63
  contradictory proposition, 63
  court documents and legal memoranda, 29–60
  direct contradiction, 63
  direct support, 62
  footnotes, 7, 13, 61
  law review text and footnotes, 13, 61–62, 83–84
  material cited more than once, 8, 16–18, 79–82, 116–18, 167–69, 173–74, 185–186, 188, 198, 198, 226
  numerous authorities, 8, 79–82
  omission from quotation, indication of, 86–87
  opposing proposition, 63
  order of, 5, 65
  pages, 73–74
  parenthetical explanations, 65–66
  placement, 5, 65
  placement after quotation, 83–84
  punctuation of, 61–70, 76–77
  quotations, 83–86
  related authority, 67–68
  repeating citations, 8, 16–18, 79–81, 116–18
  sampling of authorities, 61–62
  signals in, 4–5, 62–64
  string citations, 61–62
  subdivisions, 72–76
  supplementary material, 64
  supporting proposition, 62–63
  typeface used, 6–7, 69–70
  weight of, 108
Citations analyzed
  books, 147
  cases, 11, 95, 108
  constitutions, 119–20
  periodical materials, 157
  regulations, 142–44
  rules, 142–44

  statutes, 120
  treaties, 197–98
  United Nations materials, 210–16
"Cited in," use of, 67
"Citing," in case parentheticals, 70, 109
City and county ordinances, 130
"City of," when omitted in case names, 99
Civil law jurisdictions (see also name of jurisdiction)
  cases, 192, 194
  codes, 193
  constitutions, 192, 194
  statutes, 193
Civil Rights Act of 1964, 140
"Clause(s)," abbreviation of, 328
Clean Air Act, 140
Closing up of abbreviations, 87–89
C.M.L.R. *(Common Market Law Reports),* 204–05, 300
"Co.," in case names, 12, 99, 101, 304
"Code," capitalization of, 93
Code, Internal Revenue (see Internal Revenue Code)
Code of Federal Regulations (C.F.R.), 22, 142–44, 146–47
Code of Justinian, 299
Code of Theodosius, 299
Codes (see also Statutes)
  abbreviations, 123
  administrative compilations, 142–45
  American, 121–23
  appendices, 124
  appendix with reprinted statute, 124
  basic citation forms, 120–21
  chapters, 123–24
  compilations of, 124
  components of citation, 121–25
  date, 125
  editors, 124
  electronic databases, 127
  ethics, 133
  federal, 121–23
  foreign, 192–93 (see also name of jurisdiction)
  future location of statutes, 128
  historical fact of enactment, 122
  Internal Revenue, 20, 130
  legislative materials, 18–19, 123–28
  LEXIS, 182
  materially different from statute, 122–23
  official and unofficial, 123–24
  ordinances, city, 130
  ordinances, county, 130
  ordinances, municipal, 130
  parallel citation to, 125–27
  pocket parts, 124–25
  positive law, enacted into, 122
  publishers of, 124

Roman law, 299
scattered sections, 122
secondary sources cited to, 121, 127–28
sections cited, 122
state, 123–24, 242–294 (see also name of individual state)
statutes, when cited to, 120–22
subject-matter, 123
supplements, 122, 124
tax materials, 20, 130
titles, 123
Treasury materials, 20, 235–37
typeface used, 18, 120–21
uncodified laws, 124
uniform acts, 19–20, 131–33
unofficial, differently numbered, 128
volumes, 123
Westlaw, 127
which to cite, 121–22
year, 125
Codification
session laws, parenthetical indication of, 125–26
Collected works
citation of works in, 151–52
editor, 150–52
"*id.*" short form, 155–56
"*in*," used to introduce collection, 67
parallel citation to, using "*reprinted in*," 67
"*supra*" short form, 155–56
Colloquia, in periodicals, 165
Colorado
citation rules and style guides, 46
sources of law, 247–48
"Column(s)," abbreviation of, 328
Comma
citing commentary with case or statute, 67–68
citing multiple sections of code, 76–77
"compare . . . with" signal, 63
italicization, 62, 70–72, 310
periodical names, 320–22
titles ending in dates, 74, 150
Command number, English, 299
Command Papers, English, 299
"Comment," abbreviation of, 328
"Comment," designating student work, 163–64
Commentary
citation of, 67–68
Commentaries & special article designations, 165–66
Comments
model codes, 131–33
periodicals, 163–64
restatements, 131–33
rules of ethics, 133

sentencing guidelines, 131–33
standards, 131–33
Commerce Clearing House (CCH) services, 186–87, 323 (see also Services and topical reporters)
Commerce Court, 228–308
Commercial electronic databases (see Electronic databases)
"Commissioner," abbreviation of, 319
Commissioner of Internal Revenue, in case names, 101
Committee materials, U.N., 210–12
Committee prints, 135, 138–39
Common law jurisdictions (see also name of jurisdiction)
cases, 191–92
codes, 192–93
constitutions, 192
statutes, 192–93
Common Market Law Reports (C.M.L.R.), 204–05, 300
Common Market materials, 204–05, 300
Common Market Reporter, 204–05, 300
"Commonwealth of"
capitalization, 93
when omitted in case names, 99
"*Compare . . . with . . . ,*" as signal, 5, 63
Compilations
administrative regulations, 142–45
treaties, 197–201, 302–03
Compilations of statutes (see also Codes, Statutes)
federal, 123
foreign, 192–93, (see also name of jurisdiction)
state, 123–24, 242–98
Compiler of codes, 124
Computerized research services (see Electronic databases)
Concurrent resolutions, 136–37
Concurring opinions, 15, 108
"Congress," capitalization of, 92
Congressional debates, 135, 140
Congressional Globe, 140
Congressional materials
bills and resolutions, 21–22, 135, 136–37
committee prints, 135, 138–39
concurrent resolutions, 136–37
debates, 135, 140
documents, 135, 138–39
hearings, 21, 137–38
joint resolutions, 136–37
parallel citations, 137–38, 140
reports, 21, 135, 138–39
resolutions, 135, 136–37
secondary authority, 135–36, 140
unnumbered documents, 139

Index

Congressional Record
  daily edition, 135, 140
  debates, 140
  permanent edition, 138, 140
  resolutions cited to, 136–37
Conjunctions, capitalization of, 91
Connecticut
  citation rule and style guide, 47
  sources of law, 248–49
Consecutive pages or footnotes, citation of, 73–74
Consecutive sections of codes, 76–77
Consolidated actions, case names, 96–97
Constitutions
  amended provisions, 119
  capitalization of parts of, 93
  citation order, 65
  electronic databases and online sources, 119
  federal and state, 119–20
  foreign, 192 (see also name of jurisdiction)
  generally, 17, 119–20
  order within signal, 5, 65
  repealed provisions, 119
  short form, 120
  subdivision, 119
  superseded, 119
  typeface in footnotes, 119
"Construed in," use of, 67
"Construing," use of, 67
"Contra," as signal, 63
Conventions, international, 195, 197–99, 226
"Corp.," in case names, 99, 101
Corporations
  abbreviations, 99, 101, 149
  authors, 149
  case names, 99, 101
Corpus Juris Secundum (C.J.S.), 153
Council of Europe materials, 220
Countries (see also name of jurisdiction)
  abbreviated in case names, 102
  abbreviated in international law cases, 202
  abbreviated in international arbitrations, 209–10
  abbreviated in treaty citations, 198
  abbreviations of, 313–18
County and city ordinances, 130
"Court," capitalization of, 93–94
Court administrative orders, 116
Court documents and legal memoranda
  abbreviations of documents in, 29–30
  audio recordings of court proceedings, 115
  block quotations in, 8–9
  books, citations to, 22–23
  cases, citations to, 10–17

  capitalization in, 9–10
  constitutions, citations to, 17
  Electronic Case Filings, 26, 114–16
  explanatory parentheticals in, 5–6
  federal taxation materials, citations to, 20
  Internal Revenue Code, citations to, 20
  legislative materials, citations to, 21–22
  parallel citations in, 14, 16–17, 27
  periodical materials, citations to, 23–24
  signals in, 4–5
  short forms in, 16–17, 20–21, 23–24, 26–27
  statutes, citations to, 18–21
  typeface of citations in, 6–7
Court filings, 114–16
Court of Claims, 228
Court of Customs and Patent Appeals, 228
Court of decision
  abbreviations, 105–07, 307–10
  American, 13–14, 105–07
  civil law jurisdictions, 192
  common law jurisdictions, 192
  international arbitrations, 209–10
  international courts and tribunals, 201–09
  International Court of Justice cases, 201–03
  state, 13–14, 106–07
  when indicated, 95, 105–07, 113, 192
  when omitted, 106–07
Court of International Trade, 228–29
Court of Justice of the European Union, 195, 204–05, 300
Court of Military Appeals, 228
Courts (see also name of court or jurisdiction)
  abbreviations, 105–07, 307–310
  administrative orders, 116
  Appeals, District of Columbia Circuit, Court of, 105–06, 228
  Appeals, District of Columbia Municipal Court of, 251–52
  Appeals for the Armed Forces, Court of, 230
  appeals, United States courts of, 105–06, 228
  Arbitration, Permanent Court of, 303
  bankruptcy, 106, 113, 229
  bankruptcy appellate panels, 106, 229
  Board of Tax Appeals, 229
  circuit courts, old federal, 105, 228
  Circuit Justices, 227
  civil law countries, 192 (see also name of jurisdiction)
  Claims Court, 228
  Commerce Court, 228

common law countries, 192 (see also name of jurisdiction)

Court of Appeals for the Armed Forces, Court of, 228

Court of First Instance, 204, 300

Court of Justice of the European Union, 201, 204, 300

Customs and Patent Appeals, Court of, 64, 228

district, federal, 106, 229

Emergency Court of Appeals, 65, 228

English, 299

European Court of Human Rights, 195, 205–06, 300–01

federal, 30–45, 227–300

foreign countries, 192 (see also name of jurisdiction)

Foreign Intelligence Surveillance Court, 106

Foreign Intelligence Surveillance Court of Review, 106

foreign, language used in citation of, 189–91

General Court, 204–05, 300

Inter-American Commission on Human Rights, 195, 206, 301

Inter-American Court of Human Rights, 195, 207, 301

international, 201–10

International Criminal Tribunals, 196, 208–09

International Criminal Court, 196, 208–09

International Court of Justice, 195, 201–03, 299

International Trade, Court of, 228–29

International Tribunal for the Law of the Sea, 195, 208

Judicial Panel on Multidistrict Litigation, 106, 229

Military Appeals, Court of, 230

Military Review, Courts of, 230

Military Service Courts of Criminal Appeals, 230

old circuit, federal, 106, 228

Pennsylvania, early federal and state, 104

Permanent Court of Arbitration, 196, 209–10

Permanent Court of International Justice, 201–03, 299

Rail Reorganization Court, 229

rules of evidence and procedure, 130–31

state, 46–59, 106-07, 242–94

Tax Court, 229, 237

Temporary Emergency Court of Appeals, 228

terms, 95

territories, 59–60, 295–98

U.S. Supreme (see United States Supreme Court)

Courts of Military Review, 230

Cross-references

court documents and legal memoranda, 6

generally, 78–79

groups of authorities previously cited, 78–79

order of authorities, 65

previous footnotes, 78–79

textual material in same work, 78–79

Cumulative Bulletin, 20, 237

Customs Court, 228–29

Cyclopedia of the Law of Private Corporations, 150

Czech Republic

sources of national law, 299

Daily Compilation of Presidential Documents, 238

Dash

graphical material, used in citing, 76

page range, used in citing, 13, 74

sections of code, used in citing, 77

Databases (see Electronic databases)

Dates

administrative compilations, 142–44

amended constitutional provisions, 119

amended statutes, 129

bilateral and multilateral treaties, 199–201

books, reports, and other nonperiodic materials, 147, 150–51

case history, 107, 109–10

cases, 95–96, 107

cases, cited to U.S.L.W., 96, 107

cases, in electronic databases, 96, 103, 107, 175

cases, in looseleaf services, 107, 187

cases, in newspapers, 96, 103, 107

cases, in slip opinions, 96, 103, 107, 113

cases, international, 195–96

cases, International Court of Justice, 195, 203

cases, pending, 107, 112–14

cases, unreported, 96, 112–14

Code of Federal Regulations, 122, 142–43

codifications of statutes, 121, 125

constitutions, when used, 119

enactment, session laws, 126–27

ethical opinions, 133

ethical rules, 133

exact date, administrative cases, 145

exact date, cases, 96, 107, 112–13, 187

exact date, Congressional debates, 135

exact date, international agreements, 197–99

Index

Dates, continued

exact date, International Court of
Justice cases, 195, 203
exact date, letters, speeches, and
interviews, 170–72
exact date, ordinances, 130
exact date, periodicals, 157–58,
160–62
exact date, services, 187
exact date, statutes, 126–27
exact date, treaties, 197–99
exact date, unpublished works,
169–72
exact date, unreported cases, 14–15,
112–13
exchange of notes, 199
filing of appeal, 96
filing of cases, 96, 114
forewords, 153
Internal Revenue Code, 20, 130
international agreements, 197–99
Internet sources, 180
legislative materials, 21–22, 135–42
looseleaf statutory codifications, 125
model codes, 131–33
multilateral treaties, 195, 199
multiple decisions in one year, 107
multivolume works, 148
newspapers, 24, 157, 161–62
ordinances, municipal, 130
periodicals, 23–24, 157
pocket parts, books, 151
prefaces, 153
prior to 1900, books, 151
regnal years, in English statutes, 299
repealed constitutional provisions, 119
repealed statutes, 128–29
restatements, 131–33
rules of court, 131
rules of procedure, 20, 130–31
services, 187
session laws, 19, 126–27
standards, 131–33
statutes, 18–19, 125
statutes, amended, 129
statutes, cited to session laws, 125–27
statutes, foreign, 192–93
statutes, in current code, 121, 125
statutes, in supplements to code, 125
statutes, not in current code, 122, 125
statutes, repealed, 128–29
statutes, uniform acts, 131–33
supplements, books, 73, 151
supplements, codes, 73, 124
titles ending in, 73, 150
treaties, 195, 199
U.N. materials, 210–16
undated journals, 160–61
uniform acts, 20, 131–33
unreported cases, 95, 112–14

U.S. Supreme Court cases, 95, 105–06
year of decision of case, 105–06
"d/b/a," omission in case names, 97
Debates
congressional, 135, 140
European Parliamentary Assembly,
218, 300
legislative, 135, 140
Republic of Ireland, 299
United Kingdom, 299
Decimal point, 89
"Decision(s)," abbreviation of, 328
Declaration of Independence, 76
Delaware
citation rule and style guide, 47–48
sources of law, 249–50
Deletions from quotations, 83–87
Denial of certiorari, 16, 70, 110, 310
Denial of rehearing, when given, 109–10
Department of Agriculture, 231–32
Department of Commerce
National Oceanic and Atmospheric
Administration, 232
Patent and Trademark Office, 233–34
Department of Education, 234
Department of Energy, Nuclear Regulatory
Commission, 240
Department of Homeland Security, 234
Department of Justice, 234
Department of Labor, 235
Department of State publications,
199–200, 225–26, 235
Department of the Interior, 235
Department of the Treasury, 235–37
Department, state court, 14, 106–07
Depublished cases, 114
Descriptive terms, omitted in case
names, 99
"Developments in the Law," 164
Dictionaries, 23, 153
Dictum, indication of, 91, 108
Digest of Justinian, 299
Digest of United States Practice in
International Law, 225
Digests, international, 225
Disciplinary rules, 133
Discussion drafts, 133
Dismissal of appeal, 107, 111, 310
Dismissal without opinion, 107
Dissenting opinions, 15, 74, 97, 108
Dissertations and Theses, 170
District court, federal
cases in, 106
rules of, 130–31
District of Columbia
Circuit Court of Appeals for the, 31,
105–06
citation rule and style guide, 48–49
sources of law, 251–52

Index

Divided court, parenthetical indication
of, 108, 112
Division, federal courts, 105–06
Docket number
appeal or petition for certiorari, 96
briefs, court filings, transcripts, 114–16
pending cases, 112–14
renumbering, 113
unreported cases, 96, 112–14
Document number
intergovernmental organizations'
materials, 223–24
U.N. publications, 210–16
Documents
intergovernmental organizations,
210–24
legislative, 135–36, 138–39
published, collected, 152
U.N., 210–16
unpublished, collected, 152
Dollar amounts
numerals used, 89–90
Dual citation, when required, 14, 16, 103
DVDs, 183
Economic and Social Council, official
records, U.N., 211, 299
E.C.R. *(European Community Reports),*
205, 300
Editions
abbreviation of, 147, 323
books, reports, and other nonperiodic
materials, 150–51
Code of Federal Regulations, 142–43
Congressional Record, 140
The Federalist, 154
first edition, when cited, 151
names of, 150–51
when indicated, books, reports, and
other nonperiodic materials, 150–51
year, 150–51
Editors
books, reports, and other, 149, 151
codes, 124
collected works, 152
reporters, 104
shorter works in collection, 151
"E.g.," as signal, 4–5, 62
Egypt, Arab Republic of
sources of national law, 299
Electronic Case Filings (ECF), 26, 115
Electronic databases
Bloomberg, 112, 182, 323, 326
books, reports, and other nonperiodic
materials, 154–55, 182
cases, 14–15, 117, 182
codes, 121, 127, 182
Dialog, 162, 167, 182
generally, 182
legislative materials, 140–41, 182

LEXIS, 14–15, 112–13, 127, 140–41, 182
Loislaw.com, 113, 117, 127, 182
news reports, 162, 182
periodicals, 167, 182
secondary materials, 182
short citation forms, 117, 185
statutes, 121, 127, 182
unpublished sources, 173
VersusLaw, 113, 127
Westlaw, 14–15, 112, 127, 134, 141–42,
154–55, 182
Eleventh Circuit (see Fifth Circuit Split)
Ellipsis, 83–87
E-Mail, 169–71
Emergency Court of Appeals, 228, 309
Emphasis in quotations, 84–85
Emphasis, italics for, 70, 90
"En banc," parenthetical indication of, 66,
70, 108, 110
Encyclopedias, legal, 23, 147, 152
Endnotes, 7, 75
"Enforced," in case history, 112, 310
"Enforcing," in case history, 310
England and Wales
sources of national law, 299
English Reports—Full Reprint, 299
Enslaved, 111
Environmental Protection Agency, 237
Epilogues, 153
Equal Employment Opportunity Act, 140
Equal Employment Opportunity
Commission, 237
Essays in collection (see also Shorter
works in collection)
citation of material in, 151–52
editor, 152
parallel citation to, 67
"supra" short form, 156
typeface, 152
"Estate of," in case names, 11, 98
"Et al."
authors' names, 22–23, 148
case names, omitted, 11, 97
editors' names, 147, 149
"Et seq.," prohibition on use, 76
Ethical considerations, 133
Ethics, codes of, 133
European Commission of Human Rights,
300
European Court of Human Rights, 195,
205–06, 300–01
European Court of Justice (see Court of
Justice of the European Communities)
European Parliament Working Document,
218–19, 300
European Parliamentary Assembly, 220,
300
European Union materials, 204–05,
217–20, 300

Index

Evidence, rules of, 20, 130–31
"*Ex rel.*," in case names, 11, 69–70, 91, 97–98
Executive Agreement Series (E.A.S.), 199, 302
Executive Office of the President, 237–38
Executive orders, 237–38
Explanation of cited authorities, use of parentheticals (see Explanatory parentheticals)
Explanatory parentheticals
    cases, 15–16, 108–09
    European Parliament debates, 218
    generally, 5–6, 62–64, 65–66, 71
    internet sources, 177, 183–84
    order within citation, 66
    statutes, 129
Explanatory phrases
    abbreviations used in case citation, 310
    amended statutes, 129
    constitutions, amended or repealed, 119
    italicization of, 110, 310
    repealed statutes, 128–29
    typeface used in court documents and legal memoranda, 6
    typeface used in law review citations, 7, 70
    weight of authority, 110–11
    weight of authority in court documents and legal memoranda, 15–16
Expressions, mathematical, 91
Federal Appendix, 107, 228
Federal Aviation Administration, 238
Federal Communications Commission, 239
Federal courts (see also individual court name)
    citation rules and style guides, 30–46
    courts of appeals, 228
    courts of decision, 105–07
    district courts, 229
    generally, 227–30
    Supreme Court, official cite only, 227
Federal Energy Regulatory Commission, 239
Federal government (see United States)
Federal Judicial Center
    Manual for Complex Litigation, 154
Federal Labor Relations Authority, 239
Federal Mine Safety and Health Review Commission, 239
Federal Practice and Procedure, 23, 148, 154
Federal Register, 5, 22, 129, 142, 143–44, 147, 236, 238, 241, 242
Federal Regulations, Code of, 22, 142–44, 147, 242
Federal Reporter, 13, 228–29, 243, 251
Federal Reserve, 239

Federal Rules Decisions, 229
Federal Rules of Appellate Procedure, 131
Federal Rules of Civil Procedure, 20, 78, 130–31
Federal Rules of Criminal Procedure, 131
Federal Rules of Evidence, 20, 131
Federal Rules Service, 186, 229, 325
Federal statutes (see Statutes, *Statutes at Large*)
Federal Supplement, 14, 228–29, 243, 295–97
Federal taxation materials (see Tax materials)
The Federalist, 154, 156
Fifth Circuit Split, 114
"Figure," 75–76, 328
Films, 175, 183, 185–86
First editions, when cited, 151, 153
First listed relator, not omitted in case names, 97
First names and initials
    authors of articles, 159, 167–68
    authors of books, reports, and other nonperiodic materials, 148–49, 155–56
    case names, 100
Florida
    citation rules and style guides, 49
    sources of law, 252–53
"Folio(s)," abbreviation of, 328
Footnotes
    abbreviation of, 13, 74–75, 328
    citation of, 74–75
    consecutive and nonconsecutive, 75
    cross-reference to, 78–79
    material previously cited in, 78–82
    multipage, 74–75
    multiple, 75
    numbers in, 89–90
    omission from quotation, indication of, 84–85, 87
    spanning several pages, 74
    textual material, typeface used in, 70–71
    typeface used for citations in, 69–70
"Footnote(s)," abbreviation of, 13, 74–75, 328
"For the use of," abbreviated to "*ex rel.*," 98
Foreign alphabets, 190–91, 299
Foreign countries (see also name of individual country)
    abbreviation of, 313–18
    International Court of Justice cases, 195, 201–203, 299
Foreign derivation, italicization of words of, 6, 90–91
Foreign Intelligence Surveillance Court, 106

Foreign Intelligence Surveillance Court of Review, 106
Foreign language
  abbreviation of words, 189–90
  constitutions, 192
  court name and location, give English version, 192
  English versions and translations, 189–91, 198, 201, 207
  names, 100
  words italicized, 6, 90–91
Foreign materials (see also name of individual country)
  abbreviations, 189–90
  alphabet, 190–91
  cases, generally, 191–92
  civil law, 192 (see also name of jurisdiction)
  codes, statutory, 192–93
  common law, 191–92 (see also name of jurisdiction)
  constitutions, 192
  English used in naming courts, 192
  establishing abbreviations in initial citation, 189–90
  international (see International agreements, International organization materials)
  international agreements, 195, 197–201
  jurisdiction, 188–89
  official treaty sources, 302–03
  periodicals, 193–94
  short citation forms, 302–03
  statutes, 192–93
  treaties, 195, 197–201
  treaty sources, 302–03
Forewords, 73, 153, 159–60
Formal opinions on professional responsibility, 133
Forthcoming publications, 169, 172
France
  sources of national law, 299
Frequently cited authorities, short forms for, 79–82
"F.S.B.," in case names, 101
Gaius, Institutes of, 299
General Agreement on Tariffs and Trade (GATT), 220–22
General Assembly, official records, U.N., 196, 210–13, 216
Generally Accepted Accounting Principles, 132
Generally Accepted Auditing Standards, 132
Geographical terms
  abbreviations, 312–18
  case names, 99–100
Georgia
  citation rules and style guides, 49

sources of law, 253
Germany
  Länder (see Länder, Germany)
  sources of national law, 299
Given names
  authors, 148–49
  corporation, partnership, and business names, 97–98, 101, 148–49
  individuals, 100
Government Accountability Office, 139, 239
Government agencies
  annual and regular reports, 138–39
  authors, as, 139, 148–49
  books and numbered publications, 153
  capitalization of, 92
Government Publishing Office Style Manual, 92
Government publications, U.S., 142–44, 230–42
Graphical materials, 75–76
Greece
  sources of national law, 299
Groups of authorities previously cited, reference to, 78–79
Guam
  citation rules and style guides, 59
  sources of law, 295–96
Hague Court Reports, 196, 210, 303
Hawaii
  citation rules and style guides, 49
  sources of law, 253–54
Headings, capitalization in, 91
Hearings
  congressional, 21, 65, 81–82, 135, 137–38
  titles of, printed in italic type, 21, 137–38
  typeface used in court documents, 6–7
"Hereinafter," used for shortened citation forms, 8, 82
History of cases
  both prior and subsequent, 16, 108
  dates of decisions, 13–14, 107
  different case name on appeal, 16, 111–12
  explanatory words, abbreviations, 310
  explanatory words italicized or underscored, 6–7, 16, 70, 110–11, 310
  "mem.," opinions designated as, 108
  multiple decisions within single year, 107
  multiple dispositions, 102, 111
  overruled cases, 111
  "per curiam," opinions designated as, 108
  position of parentheticals, 66, 108
  prior and subsequent, 16, 109–12

Index

History of cases, *continued*
    prior history indicated for
      memorandum decision, 110
    prior history, when given, 110
    remand, when given, 109–10
    separate decisions of other issues,
      when cited, 110
    significance of disposition, 110
    subsequent history, 16, 66, 96, 109–12
    subsequent history, appeal filed,
      docketed, 96, 310
    subsequent history, certiorari applied
      for, granted, denied, 96, 109–10, 310
    subsequent history, names of parties,
      when different on appeal, 111–12
    subsequent history, reason for
      subsequent disposition, 110
    typeface, 7, 110, 310
    weight of authority, 110–11
History of statutes
    amended statutes, 120–21, 126, 129
    parenthetically indicated, 129
Holdings
    alternative, indication of, 108
    concurring opinion, 15, 74, 85, 108, 118
    contrary to citations, 63
    dictum, 108
    dissenting opinion, 15, 74, 85, 108,
      109, 118
    implied, indication of, 108
    plurality opinion, 108
    unclear, indication of, 108
Hong Kong
    sources of law, 299
House of Commons
    debates and Journal, 299
House of Lords
    court, 299
    debates and Journal, 299
House of Representatives (see
    Congressional materials)
Human Rights
    European Commission of, 300
    European Court of, 195, 205–06, 220,
      300–01
    Inter-American Commission on, 195,
      206, 301
    Inter-American Court of, 195, 207, 301
Hungary, Republic of
    sources of national law, 299
"*Id.*," use of, 8, 79–81
    cases, 118
Idaho
    citation rules and style guides, 35, 50
    sources of law, 254–55
Illinois
    citation rules and style guides, 35, 50
    sources of law, 255–56
Implied holdings, indication of, 108
"*In re*," in case names, 11–12, 98

In rem jurisdiction, 12, 98–99
"In the matter of," abbreviated to "*In re*,"
    11, 98
"*In*," use of, 67, 152
"Inc.," in case names, 12, 99, 101
Inclusive numbers, 73–77
Income tax materials (see Tax materials)
India
    sources of national law, 299
Indiana
    citation rules and style guides, 35, 50
    sources of law, 256–57
Indian Nations (see Navajo Nation and
    Oklahoma Native Americans)
Informal opinions on professional
    responsibility, 133
"*Infra*," use of, 78–79
Initials
    authors of books, reports, and other
      nonperiodic materials, 148
    authors of periodicals, 160, 167
    closing up of, 88
    commonly abbreviated names, 89
    editors, 149
    parties in case names, 97–98
    punctuation of, 88–89
    translators, 149
Insertions in quotations, 84–86
Institutes of Gaius, 299
Institutes of Justinian, 299
Institutes, regular publications by,
    166–67
Institutional authors, 148–49
Inter-American Commission on Human
    Rights, 195, 206, 301
Inter-American Court of Human Rights,
    195, 207, 301
Intergovernmental organization materials
    (see also U.N. materials)
    abbreviated names, 299
    arbitrations, 196, 209–10
    basic citation forms, 195–96
    cases, 201–09
    Common Market, 205, 300
    Council of Europe, 220
    Court of Justice of the European
      Communities, 195, 204–05, 300
    courts, 195–96, 201–09
    debates, European Parliamentary
      Assembly, 218, 300
    document number of League of Nations
      materials, 216, 299
    document number of U.N. materials,
      196, 210–16
    European Commission of Human
      Rights, 206, 300
    European Union, 195, 204–05, 217–20,
      300

European Court of Human Rights, 195, 205–06, 300–01

founding documents, U.N., 28, 196–97

General Agreement on Tariffs and Trade, 221

generally, 195–226, 299–302

Inter-American Commission on Human Rights, 195, 206, 301

Inter-American Court of Human Rights, 195, 207, 301

International Court of Justice, 195, 201–03, 299

League of Nations, 216, 299

League of Nations covenant, 216

League of Nations Treaty Series (L.N.T.S.), 199–201, 299, 303

number, League of Nations documents, 216

number, U.N. document, 196, 210–16

number, U.N. sales, 215

official records, U.N., 211

Permanent Court of International Justice, 201–03

Reports of International Arbitral Awards, United Nations, 303

sales number of U.N. materials, 215

sources, 299–302

treaty sources, 302–03

United Nations Treaty Series (U.N.T.S.), 299

yearbooks, international, 225

yearbooks, U.N., 215–16

Interim orders, 96

Internal Revenue Code

citation to other than current code, 130

court documents and legal memoranda, citations in, 20

generally, 20, 130

legislative history, 140

supplements, 130

unofficial codes, 130

year, 130

Internal Revenue Commissioner, in case names, 101

"Internal Revenue," omitted in case names, 101

Internal revenue regulations and rulings, 20, 236–37

International agreements

American treaties, 195, 197–201

basic citation forms, 195, 197–201

bilateral, 195, 197–201

citation, basic form of, 195, 197–201

compilations of agreements, 302–03

components of citation, 197

country names, 198

date, 199

entry into force, 199

Executive Agreement Series (E.A.S.), 302

foreign language, titles in, 189–91

foreign sources (see name of jurisdiction)

intergovernmental organization materials, 210–24, 299–302

language of source, 189–91

League of Nations Treaty Series (L.N.T.S.), 199–201, 299, 303

multilateral, 195, 197–201

name, 198

official sources, 302–03

opening for signature, 199

parallel citation, 200

parties to, 198

popular name, 198

short citation forms, 226

sources, intergovernmental, 303

sources, official, foreign (see name of jurisdiction)

sources, official, U.S., 302

sources, unofficial, 303

State Department sources, 235

Statutes at Large (Stat.), 302

subdivisions, 199

subject matter, 198

title, 198

Treaties and Other International Acts Series (T.I.A.S.), 199–200, 302

Treaty Series (T.S.), 199–200, 302

United Nations Treaty Series (U.N.T.S.), 199, 197–201, 299, 303

United States

U.S. a party, 195, 199–200

U.S. not a party, 195, 200–01

U.S. Treaties and Other International Agreements (U.S.T.), 195, 302

year, 199

International Court of Justice, 195, 201–03, 299

International law

arbitrations, 196, 209–10

cases, 195–96, 201–09

Common Market, 204–06, 300

Council of Europe, 220

courts, 201–09

digests, 225–26

European Union, 195, 204–05, 217–20, 300

generally, 195–226

intergovernmental organizations, 210–24, 299–302

international agreements, 195, 197–201

League of Nations, 216

short citation forms, 226

treaties, 195, 197–201

U.N., 210–16

Index

International law, continued
    yearbooks, international, 225
    yearbooks, U.N., 215–16
International Law Reports (I.L.R.), 209
International Legal Materials (I.L.M.), 195, 196, 200, 303
International materials
    arbitrations, 209–10
    basic citation forms, 195–97
    cases, 195–96, 201–09
    Common Market, 204–06, 300
    Council of Europe, 220
    digests, 225–26
    European Union, 195, 204–05, 217–20, 299–300
    generally, 195–226
    international agreements, 195, 197–201
    jurisdiction, 197
    League of Nations, 216
    non-English language documents, 189–91, 198
    short citation forms, 226
    treaties,195, 197–201
    treaty series, 195, 197–201, 302–03
    U.N., 210–216
    yearbooks, international, 225
    yearbooks, U.N., 215–16
International organization materials (see Intergovernmental organization materials)
International Trade Commission, 239–40
Internet, electronic media, and other nonprint resources
    archival, 177, 180
    authentic or official, 174, 176
    authors, Internet citations, 178
    basic citation principles, 174–83
    blogs, 174, 177–82
    cases, 112–13, 117, 174, 175, 182
    code, 124, 127, 134, 182
    constitutions, 119, 182
    date, 180
    document format, 181
    e-mail, 169, 171
    explanatory parentheticals, 177
    generally, 174–182
    online postings, 176–182
    pagination, 181
    parenthetical information, 177
    PDF files, 174, 176, 181
    periodicals, 167, 182
    pinpoint citation, 112–13, 174–75, 181–82
    photographs and illustrations, 184–85
    preservation of information, 177, 180
    official or authenticated, 174, 176
    short forms, 185–86
    statutes, 121, 127, 134, 182
    title, Internet citations, 178–80
    URL, 174, 176–77, 181
Interviews, citation of, 171
Introductions, citation of, 153
Introductory signals (see Signals)
Invalidated statutes, 128
"Invalidated by"
    in statute citation, 128
Invalidation, citation of, 128
Iowa
    citation rules and style guides, 50
    sources of law, 257
"I.R.C." replacing "26 U.S.C.," 20, 130, 230
Iran, Islamic Republic of
    sources of national law, 299
Iraq, Republic of
    sources of national law, 299
Ireland, Northern, 299
Ireland, Republic of
    sources of national law, 299
Israel
    sources of national law, 299
Italicization (see also Typeface)
    in court documents, 6–7
    emphasis, 90
    equations, 91
    foreign words, 90–91
    hypothetical parties, 91
    mathematical expressions, 91
    stylistic purposes, 90
Italy, Republic of
    sources of national law, 299
Japan
    sources of national law, 299
Joining citations
    order of citations, 66
    punctuation, 61
Joint resolutions, 136–37
Journal
    European Communities, Official, 217
    federal legislative, 139
    House of Commons, 299
    House of Lords, 299
"Journal," abbreviation of, 306
Judge
    indication of, in citation, 94, 102, 319
    used as title, 94, 319
"Judge," capitalization of, 94
"Judge(s)," abbreviation of, 94, 319
Judges and Justices
    order of listing, 94
    titles, use of, 94
"Judgment of," use in citation, 97
Judgments of the U.N. Administrative Tribunal, 214–15
Judicial history of cases (see History of cases)
Judicial Panel on Multidistrict Litigation, 106, 229

Index

Jump cites (see Pinpoint citations)
Jurisdiction, indication of
    American cases, 105–07
    American statutes, 123–24, 125–27
    foreign materials, 188–89
    international materials, 197
    municipal ordinances, 130
    session laws, 125–27
Justice
    indication of, in citation, 94, 319
"Justice," capitalization of, 94
"Justice(s)," abbreviation of, 94, 319
Justinian, Institutes, Digest, and Code
    of, 299
Kansas
    citations rules and style guides, 50
    sources of law, 90, 117, 258
Kentucky
    citations rules and style guides, 50–51
    sources of law, 258–59
Kenya
    sources of national law, 299
"L" italicized as letter in subdivision, 91
Labor unions, in case names, 101
Länder, Austrian, 299
Länder, German, 299
Large and small capitals (see Typeface)
Latin words
    case names, italicization in, 69, 97–98
    citation forms, italicization in, 90–91
    italicization of, 90–91
    procedural phrases in case names,
        69, 97–98
    short citation forms, italicization in,
        69, 79–82
Law Journal Reports, 299
Law journals and reviews
    abbreviations, English-language,
        304–07, 320–22
    abbreviations, spacing of, 88
    authors' names, 23–24, 159
    basic citation forms, 157–58
    book reviews, 164
    citation analyzed, 157
    colloquia, 165
    commentaries and special article
        designations, 165
    commentary cited with case, 67–68
    comments, 163–64
    components of citation, 23–24, 157–58
    consecutively paginated, 23–24, 160
    electronic databases, 167, 173, 182,
        185
    foreign, 193–94
    generally, 157–61, 163–69
    new series (n.s.), 323
    nonconsecutively paginated, 24,
        160–61
    notes, 24, 163–64

projects, 163–64
short citation forms, 24, 167–69
short commentary, 163
student material, 24, 163–66
special issues, 160
surveys, 165
symposia, 165
typeface in court documents and legal
    memoranda, 3, 6–7
typeface in law review citations, 69–70
typeface in law review text, 70–72
Law Times Reports, 299
Lawyer's Reports Annotated (L.R.A.),
    annotations in, 166
Leaflets, 153
League of Nations materials (see
    Intergovernmental organization
    materials)
League of Nations Treaty Series (L.N.T.S.),
    299, 303
Lebanon, Republic of
    sources of national law, 299
Legal dictionaries, 23, 153
Legal encyclopedias, 23, 153
Legal newspapers (see Newspapers)
Legal services, looseleaf (see Services
    and topical reporters)
Legislation (see Codes, Session laws,
    Statutes)
Legislative histories, 136–40
Legislative materials
    basic citation forms, 135–36
    bills and resolutions, 21–22, 136–37
    committee prints, 138–39
    components of citation, 135–36
    Congressional Research Service
        reports, 139
    debates, 140
    documents, 138–39
    electronic media and online sources,
        140–41
    English, 299
    Government Accountability Office
        reports, 139
    hearings, 21, 92, 135, 137–38
    Internet sources, 140–42
    legislative histories, 136–40
    online sources, 140–42
    parallel citations, 136–38, 140
    presidential messages, 243–44
    reports, 21, 138–39
    secondary authorities, 140
    short citation forms, 141–42
    state, 21, 135, 137–39
    typeface used in court documents and
        legal memoranda, 6–7
    United Kingdom, 299
    unnumbered documents, 139

Index

Letters and memoranda, 151–53, 156, 161–62, 170–71, 173–74, 177, 236, 240–41
Letters of the alphabet, altered in quotations, 84
LEXIS, 96, 103, 112–13, 117, 127, 141, 146, 174, 182, 185
Local court rules, 3, 30–60, 103, 227
Location, phrases of
    letters, speeches, and interviews, 170–72
    omitted from case names, 99–101
    unpublished works, 169–72
Loislaw, 113, 117, 127
Long case names, 87–88
    "hereinafter" form, when used, 81–82
Looseleaf services (see Services and topical reporters)
Looseleaf statutory codifications, 125
"Lord Justice," abbreviation of, 319
Louisiana
    citation rules and style guides, 51
    sources of law, 81, 105, 116, 119, 126, 259–60
"Ltd.," in case names, 12, 99, 101, 149
Magazines
    abbreviations, 304–07
    citation analyzed, 157
    consecutively paginated, 160
    generally, 157–61
    Internet sources, 167
    nonconsecutively paginated, 160–61
"Magistrate," abbreviation of, 319
Maine
    citation rules and style guides, 51
    sources of law, 98, 118, 261
Mandamus actions, 102
Manual for Complex Litigation, 154
Manuscripts,
    published as part of a collection, 151–52
    unpublished, 169–70
Maryland
    citation rules and style guides, 51
    sources of law, 14, 21, 137–38, 261–62
Massachusetts
    citation rules and style guides, 51
    sources of law, 13, 88, 96, 103, 106, 124, 263–64
"Master of the Rolls," abbreviation of, 319
Materially different language in code and statute, 122–23
Mathematical expressions, 91
Matthew Bender services (MB), 323 (see also Services and topical reporters)
"Mediator," abbreviation of, 319
Medium neutral citation (see Public domain citation)
Memorand[um, a], 24–26, 29, 170–71

Memorandum decision
    indication of, 108
    prior history must be given, 110
Merit Systems Protection Board, 240
Mexico
    sources of national law, 299
Michigan
    citation rules and style guides, 52
    sources of law, 14, 106, 113, 144, 264–65
Microfiche (see Microform)
Microform, 182–83, 185
Military courts, 230
    Military Service Courts of Criminal Appeals, 230
Military Justice Reporter, 230
Minnesota
    citation rules and style guides, 52
    sources of law, 14, 98, 103, 121, 126, 265
Mississippi
    citation rules and style guides, 52
    sources of law, 105, 265–66
Missouri
    citation rules and style guides, 52
    sources of law, 62, 266–67
Mistakes in quotations, indicated by "[sic]," 84
Model Code of Professional Responsibility, 133
Model codes, 131–33
Model Penal Code, 132
Model Rules of Professional Conduct, 133
"*Modified*" and "*modifying*," in case history, 102, 310 (see also Explanatory phrases)
Monarchs, English, 299
Montana
    citation rules and style guides, 52
    sources of law, 62, 77, 267
Month used to indicate volume, 160–61
Months, abbreviation of, 319
Moore's Federal Practice, 76, 150
Motions, 24–26
Multinational materials (see International materials)
Multipart articles, 165–66
Multiple authors, 22–23, 148
Multiple decisions within a single year, 107
Multiple dispositions of a case, 110–112
Multiple editions and printings of book, 150–51
Multiple pages, footnotes, and endnotes, 72–75
Multiple parties, words indicating, omitted in case names, 11, 96–97
Municipal ordinances, 127, 130
Music (see Audio recordings)

"N.A.," in case names, 101
Name of state, when omitted in case name, 99
Names
    authors, articles, 157, 159
    authors, books, reports, and other nonperiodic materials, 148–49
    book reviews, 157–58, 163–64
    bound services, abbreviated, 323–27
    commonly abbreviated, 87–89, 99, 102–03, 312–18
    editions of books, reports, and other nonperiodic materials, 150–56
    editors, 151
    looseleaf services, abbreviated, 323–27
    newspaper sections, 161–62
    newspapers, abbreviated, 320–22
    parties, when different on appeal, 111–12
    periodicals, abbreviated, English language, 320–22
    periodicals, abbreviation and typeface, 157–58
    prepositions in periodical names, 320
    rules and regulations, 142–44
    services, 186–87
    services, abbreviated, 323–27
    session laws, 125–27
    state, when omitted, 99, 106
    statutes, 121–25
    translators, 149
    treaties, 196–98
Names of cases (see Case names)
National Labor Relations Act, 140
National Labor Relations Board, 240
National Mediation Board, 240
National Oceanic and Atmosphereic Administration, 232
National Reporter System (see Unofficial reporters)
National Transportation Safety Board, 240
Navajo Nation
    sources of law, 296
Nebraska
    citation rules and style guides, 52–53
    sources of law, 98, 125, 268
Netherlands, Kingdom of the
    sources of national law, 299
Nevada
    citation rules and style guides, 53
    sources of law, 62, 123, 127, 268–69
New Brunswick
    sources of law, 299, 313
New Hampshire
    citation rules and style guides, 53
    sources of law, 269
New Jersey
    citation rules and style guides, 53

    sources of law, 269–70
New Mexico
    citation rules and style guides, 54
    sources of law, 69, 76, 105, 270–71
New series (n.s.) of periodical, 320, 323
New York
    citation rules and style guides, 54
    sources of law, 12, 14–16, 19, 78, 106–07, 124, 271–76
New Zealand
    sources of national law, 299
    treaty source, 299
Newfoundland
    sources of law, 299, 313
Newsletters, 167
Newspapers
    abbreviated names, 320–22
    articles, 24, 161–62
    authors, 161
    bylines of articles, 161
    cases cited to, 96, 103
    citation analyzed, 157
    citation of, 157, 161–62
    columns, not indicated, 161
    consecutively paginated, 162
    dates, 161–62
    editions, 161–62
    editorials, 161
    electronic databases, 162, 167
    foreign, 197
    generally, 161–62
    letters to the editor, 161
    online, 162
    op-ed. articles, 161
    pages, 157, 161
    pinpoint citations, 161
    sections, 161
    statutes cited to, 120, 127–28
    titles of articles, 161
    titles of, printed in italic type, 68–72
    typeface, 3, 6–7, 68–72, 157, 161–62
    typeface in court documents and legal memoranda, 6–7
    typeface in law reviews, 68–72
    when cited, 103, 121
Nicaragua
    sources of national law, 299
Nigeria
    sources of national law, 299
"No.," in case names, 99
"[No signal]" as signal, 4, 62
No-action letters, SEC, 240–41
Nonconsecutive pages, citation of, 74
Nonconsecutive sections, citation of, 76–77
Nonperiodic materials (see Books, reports, and other nonperiodic materials)

Index

North Carolina
citation rules and style guides, 54
sources of law, 123, 276–77
North Dakota
citation rules and style guides, 55
sources of law, 277–78
Northern Ireland
sources of national law, 299
Northern Mariana Islands
citation rules and style guides, 60
sources of law, 296–97, 313
Northwest Territories
sources of law, 299, 313
"Note," designating student work,
157–58, 163–64
"Noted in," use of, 67
Notes (see also Footnotes)
appended material, 77–78
statutory notes, 124
student-written, 163–64
Nouns, capitalization of, 92–94
Nova Scotia
sources of law, 299, 313
Novels (Roman Law), 299
Nuclear Regulatory Commission, 240
Number and series
European Community materials,
217–20
League of Nations materials, 216
Permanent Court of International
Justice, 201–03
U.N. materials, 196, 210–16
Number of case
administrative cases, 145–47
appeal or petition for certiorari, 96,
114–16
court documents, 114–16
federal cases, 227–30
medium-neutral citation, 103
pending cases, 14–15, 96, 107, 112–14
public domain citation, 104–05
renumbered, 113
service citations, 186–87
unreported cases, 14–15, 96, 112–14
Numbers
Arabic numerals designating
monarchs, 299
Arabic numerals designating volumes,
7, 72–73
beginning sentence, 89
Circuit number, capitalization, 93
commas in, 89
Congress and session, 135–36
designating subdivision, numerals
used, 89
docket (see Number of case)
dollar amounts, numerals used, 89
English monarchs, 299
ethical opinion, 133

four or more digits, 89
generally, 89
inclusive pages, 74
inclusive paragraphs, 77
inclusive sections of codes, 76–77
legislature, 135–36
ordinal, 90
ordinance, 130
patent number, 233
percentages, numerals used, 89
round numbers spelled out, 89
Roman numerals, 73
serial, of books, reports, and other
nonperiodic materials, 144
serial, of publications, 153
series, consistency in, 89
spacing of, in abbreviations, 88
volumes designated by Arabic
numerals, 7, 72
"Number(s)," abbreviation of, 306
Occupational Safety and Health Act, 140,
240
"Of America," omitted in case names, 100
Office of Legal Counsel, opinions, 234
Official reporters
generally, 104
U.S. Supreme Court, 227
Official codes
American, 123
foreign, 192 (see also name of
jurisdiction)
online, 121, 127
*Official Journal of the European
Communities,* 217–18, 300
Official Journal of the European Unions,
217–18, 300
Official names of statutes, 123
Official or authenticated online
documents, 174, 176
Official public domain citation, 104
Official records (see Records)
Official records, U.N., 210–16
Official releases of administrative
agencies, 144–45, 230–42
Official reporters (see also name of
individual jurisdiction)
abbreviations used, 227–98
administrative cases, 145, 230–42
foreign cases, 191–92 (see also name
of jurisdiction)
state cases, 13–14, 104, 106–07,
242–94
U.S. Supreme Court cases, 227
when to cite, 13, 104
Official sources
international agreements, 299,
302–03
international arbitrations, 303
public domain citation, 104–05

statutes, foreign (see name of jurisdiction)
treaties, 299, 302–03
Offprints (see Photoduplicated reprints)
Ohio
citation rules and style guides, 55
sources of law, 278–79
Oklahoma
citation rules and style guides, 55
sources of law, 279–80
Oklahoma Native Americans
sources of law, 297
Omissions
book and pamphlet titles, 150
case names, 97–101
quotations, 86–87
"On the relation of," abbreviated to "*ex rel.*," 11, 98
Online recordings, 175, 184
Online sources, official or authenticated, 174
"*Opened for signature*," use of, 199
Opinions
administrative, 144–46
concurring and dissenting, 15, 74, 108
ethics, 133
formal advisory, 144, 234
seriatim, 108
Opinions of Attorney General, 234
Opposing citations, introductory signals to, 63
Order of citation, 5, 64–65
Order of parentheticals, 66, 109
parallel Internet citations, 177
Orders, regulations, and rulings of administrative agencies, 142–47, 230–42
Ordinal numbers, 90
Ordinances, municipal and county, 130
Oregon
citation rules and style guides, 55–56
sources of law, 280–81
Original edition of books, citation to star pages, 74, 153–54
Original source
identified after a quotation, 66
"Overruled by," in case history, 111, 310
PACER, 24–26, 115
Pages
administrative compilations, 142–44
annotations, 166
"at," used in citations to particular pages, 16–17, 23, 24, 25, 72–73, 76, 161–62, 185, 206, 215
books, reports, and other nonperiodic materials, 73–76, 150
bound services, 104, 186–87
Code of Federal Regulations, 22, 142–44, 242

collected works, 152
Common Market cases, 205
consecutive and nonconsecutive, 13, 74
Federal Register, 142–43, 236, 238, 241, 242
first page of authority, citation to, 74
generally, 73–76
graphical materials, 75–76
inclusive, 74
institutes, publications by, 166–67
International Court of Justice cases, 201–03
law journals and reviews, 157–58, 160–61
legislative reports and documents, 136–40
looseleaf services, 120, 125, 186–87, 205
multipart articles, 165–66
multiple, citation of, 13, 74
newspapers, 161–62
online sources, 174–75, 181–82
particular, reference to, 73–74, 77–78,
"*passim*," use of, 13, 74
periodicals, 157–58, 160–61
Permanent Court of International Justice cases, 201–03
reporters, 103–05
reprinted reporters with different pagination, 104
services, 186–87
session laws, 126
shorter works in collection, 151–52
slip opinions, 113
star, in books, reports, and other nonperiodic materials, 74, 153–54
statutes, 123–24
statutes, secondary sources, 127–28
U.N. materials, 210–16
unpublished opinion, 112–14
World Court cases, 201–03
"Page(s)," abbreviation of, 73, 78, 328
Pakistan, Islamic Republic of
sources of national law, 299
Pamphlets (see books, reports, and other nonperiodic materials)
Panama (see Canal Zone)
Paragraph number, 76–77, 187
Paragraphed reporters (see Services and topical reporters)
Paragraphs
ABA section reports, 166–67
A.L.I. proceedings, 166
books, reports, and other nonperiodic materials, 76–77, 147
citations to, 76–77, 90
consecutive and nonconsecutive, 77
indented but unmarked, 76

Index

Paragraphs, continued
    institutes, publications by, 166–67
    international agreements, 197–201
    multiple, 77
    omission of, in quotations, 83–84
    proceedings, 166–67
    public domain citations, 104–05
    services, 186–88
    treaties, 197–201
    U.N. materials, 210–16
    unnumbered, citation of, 76
"Paragraph(s)," abbreviation of, 76, 90,
    328
Parallel citations
    articles and collected essays, 67
    briefs and court filings, 115–16
    cases, administrative, 145–46
    cases, American, 103–05
    cases, federal, 103–05
    cases, in id. form, 16–17, 118
    cases, international, 210–11
    cases, reprinted reporters, 104
    cases, state, 103
    European Union materials, 204–05
    international agreements, 199–200
    medium neutral citation, 103–05
    order of citations, parallel and official,
        103–05
    public domain citation, 103–05
    repeating citations, 103–05
    services, 186–87
    statutes, American, 136–37
    statutes, foreign (see name of
        individual country)
    Treasury regulations, 235–37
    treaties, 200
    treaty collections, 200
Parenthetical explanations of authorities
    (see Explanatory Parentheticals)
Parenthetical indications
    administrative adjudications, 145
    alterations and omissions in
        quotations, 84–87
    alternative holding, 108
    amended statutes, 129
    arbitration, international, 210
    arbitrator, 145
    author of opinion, 15, 108
    broadcasts, 183
    Bible version, 154
    "by implication," 108
    "citing," 70, 109
    codification of session laws, 126–27
    commentary, 65–66
    common names of cases, 101–102
    concurring opinions, 108
    court of decision, 105–07
    dates of cases, 107
    depublished status, 114
    dictum, 108

    dissenting opinions, 108
    divided court, 108
    docket numbers, renumbered, 113
    editors of books, 149
    editors of reporters, 104
    date of statute, 125–27
    en banc decisions, 108
    ethical opinions, 133
    explanatory phrases, 15, 110–11
    films, 183
    forthcoming publications, 172
    id. identifying different opinions, 118
    identifier of cases, 101–02
    implied holding, 108
    International Court of Justice, 201–03
    judge writing opinion, 15, 108
    jurisdiction, American cases, 105–07
    jurisdiction, international materials,
        188–89, 197
    Justice writing opinion, 15, 108
    letters, 170–71
    location of email correspondence and
        listserv postings, 171
    location of letters, speeches, and
        interviews, 170–72
    location of unpublished works, 169–72
    mandamus, judge target of, 102
    memorandum decisions, 108
    microform, 182–83
    model codes, 131–33
    multipart articles, 165–66
    new series (n.s.), 320, 323
    number and series of books, reports,
        and other nonperiodic materials, 153
    order, 66, 109
    order of, in internet citations, 177
    per curiam decision, 108
    Permanent Court of International
        Justice, 201–03
    primary authority commentary, 67–68
    plurality opinions, 108
    popular name of statute, 123, 125
    prior history of statute, 129
    proposed or amended drafts of
        statutes, 132–33
    "quoting," 70, 109
    quoting an authority, 65–66
    repealed statutes, 121–22, 128–29, 131
    restatements, 131–33
    sentencing guidelines, 131–33
    separate opinions, 108, 201–02
    serial number, books, reports, and
        other nonperiodic materials, 153
    seriatim, 108
    series and number in series
        publications, 153
    services, later bound form, 186
    session laws, 122, 125–27, 129
    split decisions, 108

Index

standards, 131–33
statutes, 120
statutes, amended, 129
statutes, history of, 129
statutes, prior history, 129
statutes, repealed, 128–29
tentative draft of statute, 132
translators of books, 149, 151
"translating," 70
unclear holdings, 108
weight of authority, 108
when nested, 109
year, English cases, 299
Parlement Européen Documents de Séance, 218–19, 300
Parliamentary materials, British, 299
Parties
appeal, under different names, 111–12
citation in case names, 96–103
hypothetical, 91
international agreements, 198
international arbitrations, 209–10
International Court of Justice, 202
omitted in case names, 96–101
Permanent Court of International Justice, 202
treaties, 198
Partnership names in cases, 97
"Part(s)," abbreviation of, 328
"Passim," use of, 13, 74
Patent and Trademark Office, 233–34
Patents, 233
PDF files, 27, 175, 176–77, 181–82
Pending cases, 96, 107, 111–13
Pennsylvania
citation rules and style guides, 56
early federal and state cases, 104
sources of law, 281–82
"People of," omitted in case names, 99
"Per curiam"
in case history, 108
parenthetical indication of, 15, 66, 108
Percentages, numerals used, 89
Periodicals
ABA section reports, 166–67
abbreviations, English-language, 320–22
abstracts in, 163
A.L.I. proceedings, 166
annotations, 166
articles, 157–58
authors, 159
basic citation forms, 157–58
book notes, 164
book reviews, 164
case comments, 163–64
case notes, 163–64
cases, when cited to, 103–04
citation order, 65
colloquia, 165
comments, law review, 163–64
components of citation, 23, 157–58
consecutively paginated, 23–24, 160
date, 157–58, 160–61
electronic media and online sources, 167
foreign, 193–94
forthcoming materials, 172
"Developments in the Law," 164
generally, 157–69
institutes, regular publications by, 166–67
internet journals, 167, 174–82
multipart articles, 165–66
names, abbreviation of, 189–90, 193–94, 320–22
names, typeface used, 158
new series (n.s.), 320, 323
newsletters, 167
newspapers, 161–62
noncommercial, 167
nonconsecutively paginated, 24, 160–61
notes, law review, 163–64
online, 162, 174–82
order within signal, 65
page citation, 73–74
pages, 160–61
pinpoint citations, 23–24, 160–61
proceedings, 166–67
punctuation in titles, when omitted, 320–21
recent cases, 163–64
recent developments, 163–64
recent statutes, 163–64
short citation forms, 167–69
special projects, law review, 163–64
statutes cited to, 127–28
student-written material, 163–64
Supreme Court note, 163–64
surveys of law, 165
symposia, 165
titles, 159
typeface, in court documents, 6–7, 23–24
typeface, in law reviews, 68–72
undated, 161
volume, 72
year, 160
Periods, to indicate omissions in quotations, 86–87
Permanent Court of Arbitration, 196, 209–10, 303
Permanent Court of International Justice, 195, 201–03, 299
Philippines
sources of national law, 299
Photoduplicated reprints, 151, 323

Index

Phrases of location
    letters, speeches, and interviews, 170–72
    omitted from case names, 99–100
    unpublished works, 169–73
Pinpoint citations
    books, other nonperiodic materials, 22–23, 72–76, 147
    court and litigation documents, 25, 112–14
    European Union materials, 217–20
    Federal Register, 143, 147
    forthcoming publications, 172
    generally, 13, 73–75
    id., 16–18, 79–81
    intergovernmental organization materials, other, 223–24
    International Court of Justice cases, 201–03
    Internet sources, 181–82
    manuscripts, 169–70
    medium-neutral citation, 104–05
    multipart articles, 165–66
    newspapers, 161–62
    parallel citations in state court documents, 14
    pending, unreported cases, 14–15, 112–14
    periodicals, 23–24, 160–61
    public domain citation, 104–05
    session laws, 18–19, 125–27
    short form citations, in 16–17, 26, 79–81, 116–18
    speeches, 171–72
    statutes, 123–27
    treaties, 197, 199–201
    U.N. materials, 210–16
Pleadings
    generally, 24–26, 114–16
    International Court of Justice cases, 202–03, 299
    League of Nations, 299
Pleadings, Oral Arguments, Documents, 203
Plenary materials, U.N., 210–16
Plurality opinion, indication of, 66, 108
Pluralization
    of abbreviations, 76, 304
    symbols representing, 18, 29, 74, 75, 76–77
Pocket parts (see also entries under Supplements)
    books, reports, and other nonperiodic materials, 151
    codes, 73, 124, 125
Podcasts, 175, 184
Popular names
    cases, 99, 101–02
    international agreements, 198

session laws, 125–6
statutes, 18–19, 123
treaties, 198
Positive law, codes enacted into, 122–23
Pre-1900 works, 151
Preamble, constitutional, 119
Prefaces, 153
Prepositions
    capitalization, 91
    in case names, 98–100
    in court document titles, 29–30
    in legislative document titles, 311
    in periodical names, 320–22
Presidential papers and executive orders, 237–38
Press releases
    European Union, 220
    generally, 170
    short form for, 173–74
    United Nations, 214
    World Trade Organization, 222
Previously cited authorities (see also entry under Authorities previously cited; Short citation forms)
    cross-reference to, 78–82
Prince Edward Island
    sources of law, 299
Printing, when indicated, 150
Prior history (see History of cases; History of statutes)
Private laws, 122
Private letter rulings, 20, 236
Privy Council
    Australian cases, 299
    Canadian cases, 299
    Hong Kong cases, 299
    Indian cases, 299
    Kenyan cases, 299
    New Zealand cases, 299
    Nigerian cases, 299
    South African cases, 299
    United Kingdom cases, 299
"*Probable jurisdiction noted*," in case history, 310
Procedural phrases
    in administrative adjudications, 145
    in case names, 11–12, 69, 70, 91, 98
    in international cases, 201
    in short form citations, 116
    in subsequent history of cases, 111–12
Procedure, rules of, 20, 130–131
Proceedings
    audio recordings of court, 115
    institutional, 166–70
    United Nations, 215
Professional Responsibility, Code of, 133
Projects, in law reviews, 163–64
Proposed administrative rules and regulations, 143–44

Proposed drafts, restatements and model codes, 132
Provinces, Canadian, 299
Public domain citation, 104–05
Public International Law Cases, Annual Digest and Reports of, 209
Public law number, when given for federal statutes, 19, 125–26
Public Papers of the Presidents, 238
Publication number
  administrative opinions, 145
  European Union materials, 217–20
  intergovernmental organizations' materials, 223–24
  International Court of Justice rules and acts, 201–03
  League of Nations publications, 216, 299
  series publications, 153
  U.N. publications, 210–16, 299
  WTO materials, 220–22
Publication, place of
  books, pre–1900, 151
  newspapers, 162
Publications
  ABA section reports, 166–67
  A.L.I. proceedings, 166
  considered periodicals or reporters, 104
  forthcoming, 169, 172
  institutes, regular publications, 166–67
  proceedings, 166
  typeface in court documents and legal memoranda, 6–7
  typeface in law review citations, 69
  typeface in law review text, 69–72
  typeface used for case names, 69
Publisher
  books, 150–51
  CD-ROM, 182
  codes, 123–24
  foreign codes, 193–94
  microform collections, 182–83
  services, 187
  session laws, 125–27
  statutes, 124
Puerto Rico
  citation rules and style guides, 60
  sources of law, 297–98
Punctuation
  between case and commentary, 67–68
  between statute and case construing it, 67–68
  citations, separated by semicolons, 5, 64
  initials, 89
  italicization of, 70
  periodical titles, 320

quotations, 83–87
subdivisions, 76–77
subsequent history of cases, 110
with introductory signals, 62–64
Quasi-statutory material, 135–44
Queen's Bench, 299
"Questioned in," use of, 67
Quotation marks, 83–86
Quotations
  alteration of, 84–87
  generally, 83–87
  identification of original source, 84–86
  long and short, 83–84
  mistakes in, indicated by "[sic]," 84
  omissions in, 86–87
"Quoted in," use of, 67
"Quoting," use of, 65–66
  in case parentheticals, 84–86, 109
Radio broadcasts, 175, 183
Recent cases, citation of, 97–98, 103, 112–13
Recent cases, in law reviews, 163–64
Recent decisions, in law reviews, 163–64
Recent developments, in law reviews, 163–64
Recent statutes, 121–22, 125
Recent statutes, in law reviews, 163–64
Recordings, audio, 115, 184
Records
  cases, 24–26, 114–16
  U.N., 211
"Referee," abbreviation of, 306, 319
References to previously cited authorities, 79–82
Regional Rail Reorganization Court, 229, 309
Regional reporters, 13, 103–04
Regnal years, in English statutes, 299
Regulations of administrative agencies
  generally, 22, 142–44
  Internal Revenue, 20, 130, 236–37
  short citation forms, 146–47
  Treasury, 20, 235–37
Rehearing
  denial, when indicated, 110, 111–12
  "sub nom." not used, 112
"Rehearing granted [denied]," in case history, 310
Related authority, 67–68
"Relation of," abbreviated to *"ex rel.,"* 11, 97
Relator, first listed, not omitted, 97
Releases, SEC, 241
Remand, history of case on, 109–10
Renumbered and reprinted reporters, 104
Reorganization plans, 237–38
Repagination
  books, reports, and other nonperiodic materials, 150–51

Index

Repagination, *continued*
    case reporters, 104
"Repealed by"
    in constitution citation, 119
    in statute citation, 128–29
Repealed constitutions, 119
Repealed statutes, 128–29
Repeating citations, 79–82
Reports of Judgments, Advisory Opinions and Orders, 202, 299
Reporter editor, when given, 104
Reporters of cases (see also Services and topical reporters)
    abbreviations, 104
    administrative, 145–46, 230–42
    American, 227–98
    annotations of cases, 166, 192
    Common Market cases, 205, 300
    computer services, 117, 175, 182
    court administrative orders, 116
    dual citations, 14, 103, 104, 115, 118
    early American, 104
    editor named, 104
    electronic databases, 107, 112–13, 127–28
    federal, 227–30
    foreign, 191–92 (see also name of jurisdiction)
    generally, 13, 95–96, 104
    international arbitrations, 196, 210, 303
    jurisdiction named, 105–06
    medium-neutral citation, 103, 104–05
    official and West, when cited, 13, 103
    page citation, 104
    parallel citation, 14, 103, 104–05, 115, 118
    public domain citation, 104–05
    publications considered as, 104
    renumbered and reprinted, 104
    requiring dual citation, 14, 103, 104–05
    services, permanently bound, 186–87
    state, 13, 103, 106–07
    unofficial, when cited, 103
    volume citation, 104
    International Court of Justice, 195, 201–03
Reports (see also Reporters of cases)
    administrative and executive, 144, 230–42
    Congressional Research Service, 139
    Government Accountability Office, 139
    legislative, 135, 138–39
"Representative," abbreviation of, 319
Reprinted case reporters, 104
"Reprinted in," use of, 67, 78, 124, 138–39, 140
"Reprinted in," with multiple sources, 136, 237–38

Reprints, photoduplicated, 151
Research Institute of America (RIA)
    services, 323 (see also Services and topical reporters)
Resolutions
    congressional, 135, 136–37
    European Union, 218–19
    intergovernmental organizations, 224
    state, 22, 135, 137
    statutory, 136–37
    U.N. organs, 194, 211–12
Restatements, 20, 131–33
    comments, 20, 132
Revenue Acts, 20, 130
Revenue Rulings, 20, 236–37
Revenue Procedures, 236–37
Reversals, in subsequent case history, 110
"Reversed," in case history, 16, 110, 310
Reversed names of parties, citation of on appeal, 111–12
"Reversing," in case history, 310
Review, cited with book reviewed, 67, 164
"Reviewed by," use of, 67
Reviewer of book, 164
"Reviewing," use of in book review citation, 164
Revised Reports, 299
Revision (Canadian statutes), 299
Rhode Island
    sources of law, 282–83
Roman Catholic Church (see Catholic Church)
Roman law references, 299
Roman numerals, when not used, 7, 72, 299
Roman type (see Typeface)
"R.R.," in case names, 101, 102
Rules
    administrative, 142–44
    court, 130–31
    ethics, 133
    evidence, 20, 130–31
    procedure, 20, 142–44
Rules and regulations, proposed, 143–44
Russian Federation
    sources of national law, 299
    treaty sources, 299
Sales number, U.N., 215
Saskatchewan
    sources of law, 299
Scattered sections of code, 77, 122
"Schedule(s)," abbreviation of, 328
Scotland
    sources of law, 299
SEC materials
    releases, 241
    no-action letters, 240–41
Secondary authorities
    administrative reporters, 22, 145–46

Index

books, reports, and other nonperiodic
  materials, 22–23, 147–56
citation order, 5, 65
congressional materials, 135–42
law journals and reviews, 23–24,
  157–69
legislative histories, 140
letters, speeches, interviews, 170–72
newsletters, 167
newspapers, 24, 161–62
magazines, 24, 160–61, 304–07,
  312–18, 320–23
order within signal, 5, 65
periodicals, 157–69
periodicals, English-language,
  304–07, 312–18, 320–23
periodicals, foreign-language, 193–94
services, 186–87, 323–27
statutes cited to, 18–19, 121–24,
  128–29
Treasury regulations, 20, 143, 235–36
unpublished works, 169–72
Section number
  generally, 76–77, 90, 328
  services, 187
Sections
  ABA section reports, 166–67
  administrative compilations, 142–44
  A.L.I. proceedings, 166–67
  amending act, 76
  books, reports, and other nonperiodic
    materials, 22–23, 76, 147
  citation to, 18, 126
  Code of Federal Regulations, 142–44,
    147
  codes, consecutive, 18–19, 76–77
  codes, statutory, 18–19, 123
  generally, 76–77, 90
  institutes, publications by, 166–67
  international agreements, 199
  model codes, 131–33
  newspapers, 161–62
  ordinances, municipal, 130
  proceedings, 166–67
  restatements, 19–20, 131–33
  scattered, 77, 122
  sentencing guidelines, 20, 131–33
  services, 187
  session laws, 18–19, 126
  standards, 131–33
  statutes, 123–24
  treaties, 199
"Section(s)," abbreviation of, 76–77, 90,
328
  scattered, 77
  sentencing guidelines, 131–33
  services, 187
  session laws, 126
  standards, 131–33

statutes, 123
treaties, 199
Securities Exchange Act of 1934, 140
Security Council official records, U.N.,
210–11
"See also," as signal, 5, 63
"See," as signal, 4, 62
"See, e.g.," as signal, 4–5, 62
"See generally," as signal, 5, 64
**Senate materials (see Congressional
materials)**
"Senator," abbreviation of, 311, 319
Sentencing guidelines, 131–33
**Separate decisions of other issues, in
case history,** 110
Separate opinions
  indication of, 74, 97, 108
  slip opinions, 113
Serial numbers
  books, reports, and other nonperiodic
    materials, 153
  European Union materials, 217–20
  executive orders, 237–38
  intergovernmental organizations'
    materials, 223–24
  International Court of Justice cases,
    201–03
  leaflets, 153
  League of Nations documents, 216
  monographs, 153
  proclamations, 237–38
  publications in series, 153
  reorganization plans, 237–38
  U.N. documents, 210–16
**"Series" and "Serial(s)," abbreviation
of,** 328
**Series, books, reports, and other
nonperiodic materials in,** 153
Series, renumbered, 104, 320
Services and topical reporters
  abbreviations, 323–27
  abbreviations of publishers, 323
  administrative rules and
    announcements, 144
  basic citation form, 186–87
  cases, 95
  citation of cases, 104
  Common Market materials, 205, 300
  components of citation, 186–87
  dates, 187
  dates of materials in, 187
  European Community materials, 205,
    300
  generally, 186–87
  looseleaf, citations of, 186–87
  name, 186
  pages, 187
  paragraphs, 187

Index

Services and topical reporters, *continued*

    parallel citations, for administrative cases, 146

    parenthetical indications of later bound form, 186

    publishers, 187, 323

    sections, 187

    short citation forms, 188

    statutes, 121, 127–28

    subdivisions, 187

    title of service, 186, 323–27

    transfer binders, 187

    typeface, 186

    U.S. Law Week, 96, 327

    volumes and editions, 72–73, 186–87

    years, 187

Session laws (see also Codes, Statutes)

    abbreviations, 126

    "Act of _____," 125–26

    amendments cited to, 122–23, 126

    chapter numbers, 125–26, 230

    citation, basic forms, 121

    cited by page, 126

    codification, future, 127

    dates, 126–27

    effective date of statutes, 126–27

    enactment, year or date, 126–27

    federal, 125–27

    foreign countries, 192–3

    former version of statute, 122

    historical fact, statutes cited as, 122

    jurisdiction, abbreviated name of, 125–27

    municipal ordinances, 130

    name, 125–26

    official and privately published, 121–22

    omission of words in title, 125

    ordinances, uncodified, 130

    pages, when cited to, 126

    parallel citation of, 125, 126–27, 137

    pinpoint citations, 126

    printed in roman type, 126

    public law number, 125

    recent statutes, 128

    scattered sections of code, 122

    sections and subsections, 76–77, 126

    short title of statute, 125

    signature by executive, year of, 128

    statute cited as historical fact, 122

    statute, name of, 125–26

    statute not in current code but in force, 121

    statute not in force, 122

    Statutes at Large, 19, 126, 138, 230, 238, 251

    statutes, when cited to, 121

    subsections and sections, 76–77, 126

    typeface, 126

U.S. Code Congressional and Administrative News, cited to, 127–28

    volume, 125–26

    year as volume number, 126

Shakespeare, 154

Short citation forms

    administrative materials, 146–47

    audio recordings, 115, 185–86

    books, reports, and other nonperiodic materials, 155–56

    broadcasts, 185–86

    cases, 116–18

    CD-ROM, 185

    constitutions, 120

    court documents and legal memoranda, 26

    electronic media, 185

    films, 185–86

    foreign materials, 194

    forthcoming sources, 173–74

    generally, 79–82

    international materials, 226

    Internet sources, 185

    legislative materials, 141–42

    nonprint resources, 185–86

    periodicals, 167–69

    regulations, 146–47

    repeating citations, 79–82

    services, 188

    statutes, 133–34

    treaties, 226

    unpublished sources, 173–74

    works in collection, 155–56

Shorter works in collection

    citation form, 151–52

    editor, 152

    "*in*," 152

    parallel citation, 67

    "*supra*" short form, 81–82

"[Sic]," use of, 84

Signals

    analogous support, 63

    authority from different jurisdiction, 62

    authority stating proposition, 62

    background material, 64

    comparison, 63

    contradiction, 63

    direct contradiction, 63

    direct support, 62

    generally, 4–5, 62–64

    identification, 62

    order of authorities within signal, 65

    order of citation, 64

    sampling of authorities, 62

    source of quotation, 62

    string citations, 61–62, 64

    support, 62–63

Index

table of signals, 4–5, 62–64
typeface used in court documents and legal memoranda, 6–7
typeface used in law review citations, 69–70
Slave cases, 111
Slip opinions, 96, 107, 113, 117–18, 145–46
Small Business Administration, 241–42
Social Security Administration, 242
Social media, 175, 178, 180
Songs, 184
Sound recordings, 115, 175, 184–86
South Africa
sources of national law, 299
South Carolina
citation rules and style guides, 56–57
sources of law, 56–57, 283–84
South Dakota
citation rules and style guides, 57
sources of law, 57, 284–85
South Korea
sources of national law, 299
Spacing of abbreviations and initials, 88
Spain
sources of national law, 299
Special issues in law journals and reviews, 160
Special projects in periodicals, 163–67
Special reports of government agencies, 144
Speeches, 171–72
Split decision
indication of, 110–11
SSRN, 172–73, 176–77
Standards, 131–33
Star pages in books, reports, and other nonperiodic materials, 74, 153–54
State administrative agencies
generally, 242–98
reports, 145–46
State cases
court of decision, abbreviations, 106–07, 242–98
court of decision, indication of, 106–07
department or division of court, 106–07
official and unofficial reporters, 12–13, 103–04
parallel citations, 14, 103, 242–98
reporters (see name of individual state)
State courts
citation to cases of, 105–07
generally, 242–98
rules of court, 130–31
State Department publications, 200–01, 235
"State of," omitted in case names, 99
States (see also name of individual jurisdiction)

abbreviated in case names, 102
abbreviation of, 312
omitted in case names, 99
reporters, 242–98
session laws, 125–27, 242–98
statutes, 120–34, 242–98
statutory codes, 242–98
Statutes (see also Codes, Session laws)
administrative rules and regulations, 142–44, 146–47
amended, 129
amended, uniform acts, 131–33
amendments, 129
appendices to codes, appearing in, 124
basic forms of citation, 120–121
bills and resolutions, 136–37
case construing statute, cited with, 67–68
citation analyzed, 120
citation order, 65
cited by page, 126
city ordinances, 130
code appendices, appearing in, 124
commentary on, cited with, 67–68
compilations, 124
components of citation, 120–35
concurrent resolutions, 136–37
county ordinances, 130
current code, 123
date, Internal Revenue Code, 130
dates, 125
dates of amendment, 129
effective date, 125, 129
electronic databases and online sources, 127
ethics, rules of, 133
explanatory parenthetical phrases, 129
federal and state, 121–24
foreign jurisdictions, 197
future codification, 127
generally, 120–134
historical fact, cited as, 122
history of, as amended, 122, 128–29
Internal Revenue Code, 20, 130
Internet sources, 121, 127, 177–82
invalidated, 128
joint resolutions, 135, 136–37
legislative history, 135–42
legislative materials, 135–42
materially different from code, 122–23
miscellaneous citation forms, 130–133
multiple sections and subsections, 76–77
municipal ordinances, 130
name of, in session laws, 125–26
names, 123
newspapers, cited to, 120, 161–62
no longer in force, 122
not in current code, 121, 128

Index

Statutes, continued
  online, authenticated or official, 121, 174–77
  order within signal, 65
  ordinances, municipal and county, 130
  original enactment, indication of, 129
  pages, when cited to, 126
  parenthetical indications, 129
  parenthetical indications of amendment, 129
  periodicals, cited to, 120
  prior history, 129
  private editor or compiler, 124
  private laws, 122
  privately published, Internal Revenue Code, 130
  publication of, 120–21
  publisher, 124
  recent, 128
  related authority, 67–68
  repealed, 122, 128–29
  reprinted in appendix of code, 124
  resolutions, 136–37
  scattered sections of code, 77, 122
  secondary sources, 120–21, 127–28
  sections, citation to, 76–77
  services and topical reporters, 120–21, 127–28
  short citation forms, 133–34
  source to cite, 120–23
  special citation forms, 130–33
  state, 242–98
  state, uniform acts, 131–33
  subsequent history, 128–29
  substance, parenthetical indication of, 129
  superseded, 132
  supplements, 124
  Treasury regulations, 20, 235–36
  uncodified, 124, 127, 130
  uniform acts, 131–33
  United States Code (U.S.C.), 123–24, 230
  United States Code Annotated (U.S.C.A.), 123–24, 230
  United States Code Service (U.S.C.S.), 123–24, 230
  withdrawn, uniform acts, 132
Statutes at Large, 19, 126–28, 137, 230, 238, 251, 302
  (see also Session laws)
Statutes of Canada, 299
String citations, 61–62
Structure of the *Bluebook*, 1, 3
Student work, in periodicals, 163–64
  order within citations, 65
Style
  abbreviations, 9, 87–89, 304–28
  capitalization, 10, 91–94
  Chicago Manual of Style, 92

  quotations, 83–87
  titles of officials, 94, 319
  typeface, 6–7, 68–72
  U.S. Government Publishing Office Style Manual, 92
"*Sub nom.*," in case history, 16, 111–12
Subdivisions in cited material
  ABA section reports, 166–67
  abbreviations, 327–28
  administrative compilations, 142–43
  A.L.I. proceedings, 166–67
  appended material, 77–78
  "at," used to indicate page citations, 73–74
  Code of Federal Regulations, 142–43
  codes, statutory, 123–24
  constitutions, 119–20
  cross-references, internal, 78–79
  endnotes, 75
  English statutes, 299
  footnotes, 74–75
  flush language, 77
  generally, 72–78
  graphical materials, 75–76
  "*in,*" used to indicate location in an entire work, 67–68, 152
  institutes, publications by, 166–67
  international agreements, 199
  model codes, 131–33
  multipart articles, 165–66
  multiple pages, 73–74
  multiple paragraphs, 76–77
  multiple sections, 76–77
  newspapers, 161–62
  ordinances, municipal, 130
  pages, generally, 73–74
  pages or sections, in books, 73–77
  pages or sections, in codes, 73–77, 123–24
  pages or sections, in session laws, 126
  paragraphs, 76–77
  parts, 73
  "*passim,*" use of, 13, 74
  proceedings, 166–67
  restatements, 131–32
  sections and subsections, 76–77
  separately paginated, 73
  services, 187
  session laws, 76, 126
  standards, 131
  statutes, 76–77, 126
  supplements, 73
  treaties, 199
  U.N. materials, 210–13
  volumes, 72
Subject-matter titles of codes, 124
Subsections
  multiple, in statutes, 76–77
  session laws, 126

Index

Subsequent citations, short forms, 79–82
Subsequent history (see History of cases, History of statutes)
Substitutions in quotations, 84–85
Subtitles of books, 150
Successive citations, short forms, 79–81
"Superseded by statute," in case history, 111
Supplementing citations
   introductory signals to, 62–64
Supplements
   books, reports, and other nonperiodic materials, 73
   codes, 124
   Internal Revenue Code, 130
   separately paginated, 73
   statutory, 124
Supporting citation
   introductory signals to, 62–64
"Supra"
   groups of authorities in work, 78–79, 81
   order of authorities, 65
   previously cited authority, 81–82, 155–56
   textual material in work, 78–79
Supreme Court Justice sitting as Circuit Justice, 105
Supreme Court note, 163–64
Supreme Court Foreword, 165
Supreme Court Reporter, 13, 105, 227
Supreme Court Review, 164
Supreme Court, U.S. (see United States Supreme Court)
Surface Transportation Board, 242
Surnames, composed of two words, 100
Surveys, in periodicals, 165
Sweden
   sources of national law, 299
Switzerland
   Cantons (see Cantons, Swiss)
   sources of national law, 299
Symbols, 90
Symposia, in periodicals, 165
"Table," 75
Taiwan, Republic of China
   sources of law, 299
Tax Court, citation of cases, 46, 237, 244
Tax materials
   cases, 46, 237, 244
   codes, 20, 130
   Cumulative Bulletin, 20, 236–37
   general counsel memoranda, 20, 236
   generally, 235–37
   Internal Revenue Bulletin, 236–37
   Internal Revenue Code, 20, 130
   practitioners' citation forms, 20
   private letter rulings, 20, 236
   revenue procedures, 236

revenue rulings, 236
technical advice memoranda, 236
Treasury decisions, 236
Treasury regulations, 20, 236
Telephone interviews, 171
Television broadcasts, 183
Temporary Emergency Court of Appeals, 228, 310
Tennessee
   citation rules and style guides, 57
   sources of law, 289–90
Tentative drafts, restatements, and model codes, 132
"Term," capitalization of, 95
Term of court, 95
Territories, U.S.
   abbreviation of, 295–98
   citation rules and style guides, 59–60
   souces of law, 295–98
Texas
   citation rules and style guides, 57
   sources of law, 286–89
Text
   abbreviation of case names in, 97–103
   court documents and legal memoranda, typeface in, 6–7
   law reviews, typeface in, 70–72
   numbers in, 89–90
Textual footnote materials
   typeface used in, 70–71
Textual material in same work, cross reference to, 78–79
Textual reference to statutes, 133–134
"The," in case name, 99
Theses, unpublished, 170
Times Law Reports, 299
Titles
   abbreviations, 150
   articles in periodicals, 159
   book reviews, 163–64
   books, reports, and other nonperiodic materials, 150
   capitalization of, 91, 150
   codes, statutory, 123–24
   collected documents, 152–53
   congressional documents and reports, 139–42
   direct Internet citations, 178–80
   ending with date, 150
   foreign, 189
   hearings, 137–38
   international agreements, 199–201
   multivolume works, 150
   newspaper articles, 161–62
   personal titles, 94, 304–06
   services, 186
   student-written materials, 163–64
   subtitles of books, 150
   Supreme Court Justices, 94, 306

Index

Titles, continued
surveys and symposia, 165
treaties, 199–201
typeface, 3, 6–7, 68–70, 150, 152–53, 169
U.N. materials, 196, 210–16
unpublished works, 169–73
"Title(s)," **abbreviation of,** 304–07
"To," **used in place of hyphen,** 74, 77
"To be codified at," 121, 127, 128, 142, 143, 147
Topical reporters (see Services and topical reporters)
Trademarks, 233–34
Transcript of record, 25, 115
Transcripts, 114–16
audio recordings of court proceedings, 115
Transfer binders, services, 186–87
Translations of titles, 189
"Translating," 70
Translators of books, 149
Treasury decisions, 235–37
Treasury Decisions Under Internal Revenue Laws, 236
Treasury regulations, 20, 235–36
Treaties (see also International agreements)
citation analyzed, 195, 197–98
generally, 28, 197–201
Treaties and Other International Acts Series (T.I.A.S.), 199, 302
Treatises, 22–23, 147–51 **(see also Books, reports, and other nonperiodic materials)**
Treaty collections, 299, 302–03
Treaty Series (T.S.), 302
Trusteeship Council Official Records, U.N., 299
Typed manuscripts, 169–70
Typeface
articles, authors of, 159
articles, titles of, 159
authors, articles, 159
authors, books, 148–49
authors, works in collection, 152
bills and resolutions, 136–37
books, authors of, 148–49
books, cited in court documents and legal memoranda, 6–7
books, cited in law reviews, 147–51
books, titles of, 150
bound services, 186–87
case history terms, 16, 109–11
case names, in court documents and legal memoranda, 6–7
case names, in explanatory parentheticals, 71
case names, in law review citations, 69
case names, in law review text, 70–71

citations in court documents and legal memoranda, 6–7
codes, 123–27
collected works, 151–52
commentary, indication of, 67–68
constitutions, 119–20
court documents and legal memoranda, 6–7
documents, legislative, 138–39
explanatory parentheticals, 71
explanatory phrases in court documents and legal memoranda, 6–7
explanatory phrases in law review footnotes, 70
footnotes, citations in, 61–62, 70
footnotes, text in, 70
generally, 6–7, 68–72
hearings, 137–38
international agreements, 197–201
interviews, 171
italics, 6–7
italics, in footnote citations, 68–70
italics, in law review text, 70–72
italics represented by underscoring, 6–7
italics showing style, 90
large and small capitals, 68–69, 123–24, 130, 131, 138–39, 148–49, 150–51, 152, 158, 179, 183
large and small capitals, in footnote citations, 68–69
law review citations, 68–70
law review text, 70–72
letters, memoranda, and press releases, 170–71
looseleaf services, 186–87
manuscripts, 169–70
model codes, 131–33
newspapers, 161–62
ordinances, municipal, 130
ordinary roman type, 6–7, 68–72
periodicals, names of, 160–61
publications, cited in court documents and legal memoranda, 6–7
publications, cited in law review text, 70
punctuation, 71–72
related authority, indication of, 67–68
reporters, 103–05
reports, legislative, 138–39
restatements, 131–33
roman type, in footnote citations, 68–70
roman type, in text, 70–72
rules of court procedure, 130–31
services, 186–88
session laws, 125–27
shortened citation form, 79–82

signals, 6–7, 69–70
speeches, citations to, 171–72
standards, 131–33
student-written materials, 163–64
subsequent and prior history of cases,
    109–12, 310
textual footnote material, 70–72
textual material in law reviews, 70–72
theses, 170
titles, 69, 70
treaties and other international
    agreements, 197
underscoring, use of to represent
    italics, 6
uniform acts, 131–33
Unclear holdings, indication of, 108
Uncodified laws, 124
Understandings, international, 195, 198
Uniform acts, 131–33
Uniform Adoption Act, 132
Uniform Commercial Code (U.C.C.), 131
Uniform Laws Annotated (U.L.A.), 131
Unions, in case names, 101
United Kingdom
    sources of national law, 299
United Nations materials
    Charter, 196
    citation analyzed, 196
    generally, 210–16
    official records, 210–13
    periodicals, 215–16
    sales documents, 215
    yearbook, 215–16
*United Nations Reports of International
    Arbitral Awards,* 303
United Nations Treaty Series (U.N.T.S.),
    28, 195, 197–201, 221, 223, 226, 299,
    303
United States
    administrative publications, 22,
        142–44, 230–42
    bankruptcy appellate panels, 106, 229
    bankruptcy courts, 97, 106, 113, 229
    Board of Tax Appeals, 20, 229, 237
    circuit courts, old federal, 106, 228
    Circuit Justices, 227
    Claims Court, 228
    Commerce Court, 228
    Court of Appeals for the Armed
        Forces, 230
    Court of Appeals for the Federal
        Circuit, 228
    Court of Appeals for Veterans
        Claims, 230
    Court of Claims, 228
    Court of Customs and Patent
        Appeals, 228
    Court of Customs Appeals, 228
    Court of Federal Claims, 228

Court of International Trade, 228–29
Court of Military Appeals, 230
Court of Military Review, 230
Court of Veterans Appeals, 230
courts of appeals, 13, 105–06, 228
Customs Court, 228–29
district courts, 14, 105, 229
Emergency Court of Appeals, 228
international agreements, 195,
    197–201
Judicial Panel on Multidistrict
    Litigation, 106, 229
Military Service Courts of Criminal
    Appeals, 230
Regional Rail Reorganization Act, 229
session laws, 18–19, 120–21, 125–27,
    134, 230
statutory compilations, 18–19, 123–25,
    230
Supreme Court (see U.S. Supreme
    Court)
Tax Court, 20, 229, 237
Temporary Emergency Court of
    Appeals, 228
treaties, 28, 195, 197–201
"United States," abbreviation of, 89,
    102–03
United States Code (U.S.C.)
    appendix, 124
    generally, 18–19, 120, 123–25
    supplement, 124
United States Code Annotated (U.S.C.A.),
    18–19, 121, 124, 230
*United States Code Congressional &
    Administrative News* (U.S.C.C.A.N.),
    128, 135–36, 138–39, 238
United States Code Service (U.S.C.S.),
    123–24, 230
United States Department of State
    official treaty sources, 199–200
United States Law Week (U.S.L.W.), 105,
    227, 327
United States Reports, 105, 227
United States Supreme Court
    abbreviation of, 105, 227
    administrative orders, 116
    capitalization of, 9, 93
    Circuit Justices, 105, 227
    citation, 95, 227
    citation in subsequent history, 96, 110
    cite only to official reporter, 227
    date of decision, 107
    docket numbers, 96, 112–14
    Justice, sitting as Circuit Justice, 105,
        227
    Lawyers' Edition, 227
    recent decisions, 95–96, 227
    renumbered and reprinted reporters,
        104, 227

Index

United States Supreme Court, continued
   rules, 130–31
   seriatim opinions of, 108
   subsequent history, 109–11
   Supreme Court Reporter, 105, 227
   U.S. Law Week, 105, 227
   U.S. Reports, 105, 227
United States Treasury, decisions and regulations, 235–37
United States Treaties and Other International Agreements (U.S.T.), 197–201, 226, 302–03
Unofficial codes, differently numbered, 123–24
Unofficial reporters (see also name of individual jurisdiction)
   administrative cases, 144–46
   federal courts, 227–30
   state courts, 14–15, 103
Unofficial sources
   international arbitration awards, 303
   statutes, American, 121–22
   statutes, foreign, generally, 192–93
Unpublished materials, 169–73
Unreported cases, 14–15, 96, 112–14
"Use of," changed to "*ex rel.*" in case names, 98
Utah
   citation rules and style guides, 57
   sources of law, 289
"*Vacated,*" in case history, 109, 310
"*Vacated as moot,*" in case history, 110
"*Vacating as moot,*" in case history, 96, 310
Vermont
   citation rules and style guides, 57–58
   sources of law, 290
VersusLaw, 113, 127
"Vice Chancellor," abbreviation of, 319
Videotapes, noncommercial, 183
Virgin Islands
   citations rules and style guides, 60
   sources of law, 298
Virginia
   citation rules and style guides, 58
   sources of law, 291
Volume number
   administrative reports, 142–44
   A.L.I. proceedings, 166
   Arabic numerals, 72
   books, reports, and other nonperiodic materials, 72, 147, 149
   case reports, 104
   codes, statutory, 72, 123–24
   Common Market cases, 205
   Federal Register, 143
   generally, 72
   International Court of Justice cases, 201–02
   law journals and reviews, 160–61

   location in citation, 72
   looseleaf services, 186–87
   newspaper, 161–62
   periodicals, 72, 157, 160–61, 165–67
   services, 186
   session laws, 125–26
   year used to indicate, 160, 186–87
"Volume(s)," abbreviation of, 323
Wales (see England)
Washington
   citation rules and style guides, 58
   sources of law, 292
Weekly Compilation of Presidential Documents, 238
Weight of authority (see Parenthetical indications)
West reporters (see also Unofficial reporters)
   generally, 12–13, 121, 124
West Virginia
   citation rules and style guides, 59
   sources of law, 292–93
Westlaw, 14, 112, 119, 121, 127, 134, 140–41, 155, 174–75, 182
"Will of," in case name, 98
Wisconsin
   citation rules and style guides, 59
   sources of law, 293–94
Working papers, 169, 172–73
World Trade Organization, 196, 220–22, 302
World Wide Web, 174–82, 184–86 (see also Internet sources)
Writers (see Authors)
Wyoming
   citation rules and style guides, 59
   sources of law, 294
Years (see also Dates)
   administrative agency reports, 142–44
   books, reports, and other nonperiodic materials, 150–51
   Code of Federal Regulations, 142–43
   codes, 125
   Common Market cases, 205
   enactment, session laws, 126–27
   ethical opinions, 133
   ethical rules, 133
   Federal Register, 142–43
   forewords, 153
   Internal Revenue Code, 20, 130
   Internet, 180
   League of Nations materials, 216
   legislative materials, 135–40
   model codes, 131–33
   ordinances, municipal, 130
   periodicals, 157, 160–62, 164
   pocket parts, 125, 151
   prefaces, 153
   regnal, in English statutes, 299

restatements, 131–33
rules of court, 130–31
rules of procedure, 130–31
services, 187
session laws, 126–27
standards, 131–33
statutes, uniform acts, 131–33
supplements, 73, 121, 124, 151
Treasury regulations, 235–36
treaties, 199–201
U.N. materials, 210–16
uniform acts, 131–33
Yearbooks
basic citation forms, 225
generally, 225
International Court of Justice, 202
sales number, cited to, 215
U.N., 215–16
Zambia, Republic of
sources of national law, 299

Notes

Notes

Notes

Notes

Notes

Notes

Quick Reference: Court Documents and Legal Memoranda

This table gives examples of commonly used citation forms printed in the typefaces used in briefs and legal memoranda (as explained in the **Bluepages**). The inside front cover and first page present examples in the typefaces used in law review footnotes (as explained in **rule 2**). Although underlining is used in these examples, italicization would also be appropriate.

CASES rule 10 (Bluepages B10)	
reporter rule 10.3	<u>Jackson v. Metro. Edison Co.</u>, 348 F. Supp. 954, 956–58 (M.D. Pa. 1972), <u>aff'd</u>, 483 F.2d 754 (3d Cir. 1973), <u>aff'd</u>, 419 U.S. 345 (1974). <u>Herrick v. Lindley</u>, 391 N.E.2d 729, 731 (Ohio 1979).
service rule 19	<u>In re Looney</u>, [1987–1989 Transfer Binder] Bankr. L. Rep. (CCH) ¶ 72,447, at 93,590 (Bankr. W.D. Va. Sept. 9, 1988).
pending and unreported cases rule 10.8.1	<u>Albrecht v. Stanczek</u>, No. 87-C9535, 1991 U.S. Dist. LEXIS 5088, at *1 n.1 (N.D. Ill. Apr. 18, 1991). <u>Jackson v. Virginia</u>, No. 77-1205, slip op. at 3 (4th Cir. Aug. 3, 1978) (per curiam), <u>aff'd</u>, 443 U.S. 307 (1979). <u>Ross v. Weissman</u>, No. 90-345 (D. Mass. filed Sept. 18, 1990) <u>Cleary v. Rizkalla</u>, 925 F. 2d 314 (1st Cir. 1991), <u>petition for cert. filed</u>, 60 U.S.L.W. 3422 (U.S. Jan. 14, 1992) (No. 92-212).
CONSTITUTIONS rule 11 (Bluepages B11)	N.M. Const. art. IV, § 7.
STATUTES rule 12 (Bluepages B12)	
code rule 12.3	Administrative Procedure Act § 6, 5 U.S.C. § 555. 22 U.S.C. § 2567 (Supp. I 1983).
session laws rule 12.4	Department of Transportation Act, Pub. L. No. 89-670, § 9, 80 Stat. 931, 944–47 (1996).
rules of evidence and procedure: restatements; uniform acts rule 12.9	Fed. R. Civ. P. 12(b)(6). Restatement (Second) of Torts § 90 cmt. a (Am. Law Inst. 1965). U.C.C. § 2-202 (Am. Law Inst. & Unif. Law Comm'n 1977). U.S. Sent'g Guidelines Manual § 2D1.1(c) (U.S. Sent'g Comm'n 2004).
LEGISLATIVE MATERIALS rule 13 (Bluepages B13)	
unenacted bill rule 13.2	S. 516, 106th Cong. § 2 (1997).
report rule 13.4	S. Rep. No. 95-797, at 4 (1978), <u>as reprinted in</u> 1978 U.S.C.C.A.N. 9260, 9263.
LETTERS rule 17.2.3	Letter from Graham Sternberg, Bluebook Ed. & Strategy Chair, Harvard L. Rev., to author (Feb. 13, 2020) (on file with author).
INTERVIEWS rule 17.2.5	Telephone Interviews with Michael Leiter, President, Harvard Law Review (Oct. 22, 1999).
TREATIES rule 21.4 (Bluepages B21)	Treaty of Friendship, Commerce and Navigation, Japan-U.S., art. X, Apr. 2, 1953, 4 U.S.T. 2063.